The Savage Storm

www.penguin.co.uk

THE SAVAGE STORM

The Battle for Italy 1943

James Holland

bantam

TRANSWORLD PUBLISHERS
Penguin Random House, One Embassy Gardens,
8 Viaduct Gardens, London SW11 7BW
www.penguin.co.uk

Transworld is part of the Penguin Random House group of companies
whose addresses can be found at global.penguinrandomhouse.com

Penguin
Random House
UK

First published in Great Britain in 2023 by Bantam
an imprint of Transworld Publishers

A CIP catalogue record for this book
is available from the British Library.

ISBNs 9781787636682 (hb)
9781787636699 (tpb)

Typeset in 11.25/14pt Minion Pro by Jouve (UK), Milton Keynes
Printed and bound in Great Britain by Clays Ltd, Elcograf S.p.A.

Maps drawn by Lovell Johns Ltd

The authorized representative in the EEA is Penguin Random House Ireland,
Morrison Chambers, 32 Nassau Street, Dublin D02 YH68.

Penguin Random House is committed to a sustainable future
for our business, our readers and our planet. This book is made
from Forest Stewardship Council® certified paper.

For David Walsh

Contents

List of Maps   ix
Principal Personalities   xli
Note on the Text   xlix
Glossary   li

Prologue   1

Part I: Summer

1   The Burning Blue   9
2   Conundrums   24
3   At General Clark's HQ   46
4   BAYTOWN   56
5   Uncertainty   72
6   Mistrust   86
7   Bluffing   98

Part II: Autumn

8   AVALANCHE   111
9   Toehold   127
10   Italy's Collapse   144
11   Build-up and Containment   161
12   Fritz X   178
13   Crisis   191
14   Turn of Fortune   200
15   Breakout   214
16   Naples   231
17   Termoli   243
18   Desolation   258
19   The Volturno   267

Part III: Winter

20	Despair	287
21	Questions of Morale	301
22	A World Turned Upside Down	310
23	Continuous Pressure	320
24	The Winter Line	330
25	Slow Death	344
26	The Sangro	357
27	The Good Cause	370
28	RAINCOAT	383
29	Valley of Death	398
30	The Tyranny of OVERLORD	409
31	Death of a Village	427
32	Try and Try Again	442
33	Merry Christmas and a Happy New Year	455

Postscript   469

APPENDIX I: Timeline of Events   477
APPENDIX II: Order of Battle: Allied and German
    Armies at the Beginning of December 1943   493
Notes   497
Selected Sources   515
Acknowledgements   537
Picture Acknowledgements   543
Index   551

List of Maps

Italy Terrain Map   xi

Eighth Army's Invasion of Southern Italy   xii–xiii

Operation AVALANCHE   xiv–xv

German Counter-attack at Salerno   xvi–xvii

Advance to Foggia and Naples   xviii–xix

Termoli   xx

Progress of the Hasty Ps and the Faughs   xxii–xxiii

Fifth Army's Advance to the Volturno   xxviii–xxix

The Volturno   xxx–xxxi

Fifth Army's Advance to the Bernhard Line   xxxii–xxxiii

Eighth Army's Advance to the Sangro   xxxiv–xxxv

Fifth Army's Assault of the Bernhard Line   xxxvi–xxxvii

Ortona Battleground   xxxviii–xxxix

Map Key

ALLIED UNITS ▢ **AXIS UNITS** ▨

STANDARD MILITARY SYMBOLS

I	= Company	X	= Brigade
II	= Battalion	XX	= Division
III	= Regiment	XXX	= Corps
		XXXX	= Army
		XXXXX	= Army Group

OTHER ABBREVIATIONS

Armd = Armoured

Bde = Brigade

Bn = Battalion

Br. = British

Can. = Canadian

Div. = Division

Ger. = German

HG = Hermann Göring

Inf. = Infantry

NZ = New Zealand

PG = Panzergrenadier

Pi. Bn = Pionier-Bataillon

PIR = Parachute Infantry Regiment

PPCLI = Princess Patricia's Canadian Light Infantry

RCT = Regimental Combat Team

SRS = Special Raiding Squadron

SSF = Special Service Force

US = United States

WNSR = West Nova Scotia Regiment

ITALY TERRAIN MAP

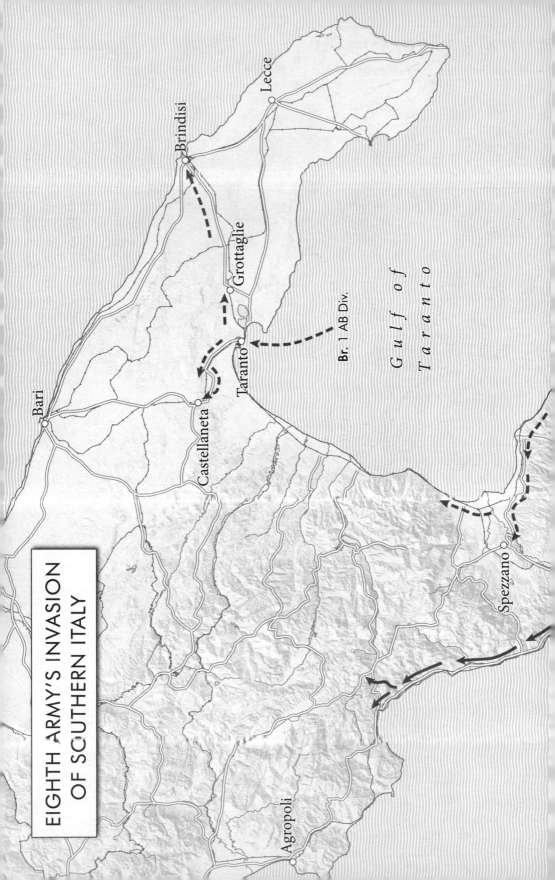

EIGHTH ARMY'S INVASION
OF SOUTHERN ITALY

Lecce

Brindisi

Grottaglie

Br. 1 AB Div.

Gulf of
Taranto

Taranto

Bari

Castellaneta

Spezzano

Agropoli

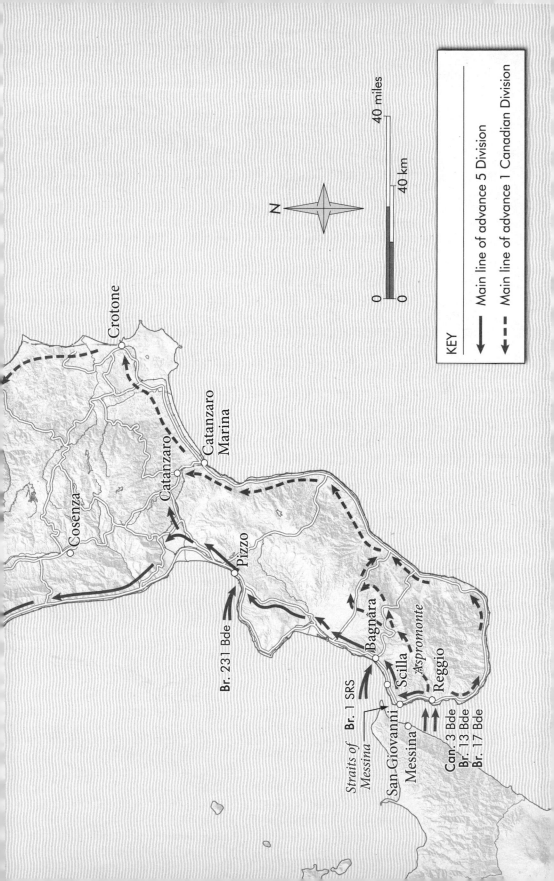

KEY

Main line of advance 5 Division

Main line of advance 1 Canadian Division

N

40 miles

40 km

Crotone

Cosenza

Catanzaro

Catanzaro
Marina

Pizzo

Bagnâra

Scilla

Aspromonte

Reggio

Br. 231 Bde

Straits of   Br. 1 SRS
Messina

San Giovanni

Messina

Can. 3 Bde
Br. 13 Bde
Br. 17 Bde

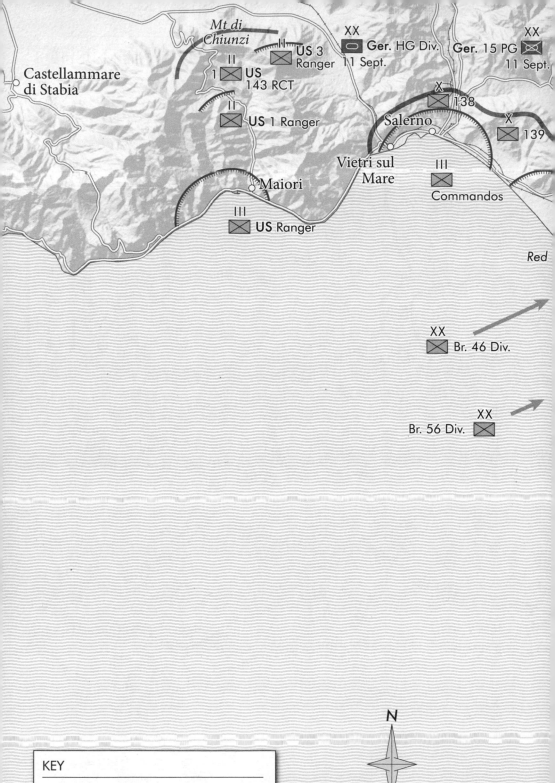

Castellammare di Stabia

Mt di Chiunzi

II | US 3 Ranger

XX | Ger. HG Div. 11 Sept.

XX | Ger. 15 PG 11 Sept.

1 | II US 143 RCT

II | US 1 Ranger

X | 138

X | 139

Salerno

Vietri sul Mare

III | Commandos

Maiori

III | US Ranger

Red

XX | Br. 46 Div.

Br. 56 Div. | XX

N

KEY

▨▨▨▨	The Beachead, 9 Sept.
——	Allied advance, 1600 13 Sept.
▰	Enemy position

0   5 miles

0   5 km

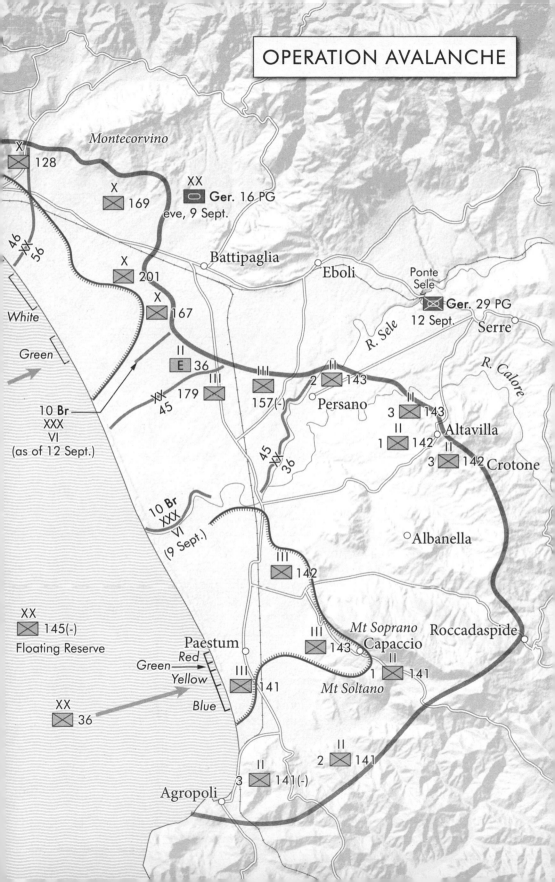

OPERATION AVALANCHE

Montecorvino

X 128

X 169

XX ▭ Ger. 16 PG
eve, 9 Sept.

46 XX 56

White

Green →

X 201

X 167

Battipaglia

Eboli

Ponte Sele

Ger. 29 PG
12 Sept.

R. Sele

Serre

R. Calore

10 Br
XXX
VI
(as of 12 Sept.)

II E 36

XX 45 III 179

157 (-)

2 143

Persano

3 143

1 142

3 142 Crotone

Altavilla

10 Br
XXX
VI
(9 Sept.)

45 XX 36

Albanella

III 142

XX 145(-)
Floating Reserve

XX 36

Paestum

Red
Green
Yellow

Blue →

III 141

III 143

Mt Soprano

Capaccio

1 141

Mt Soltano

Roccadaspide

2 141

Agropoli

3 141(-)

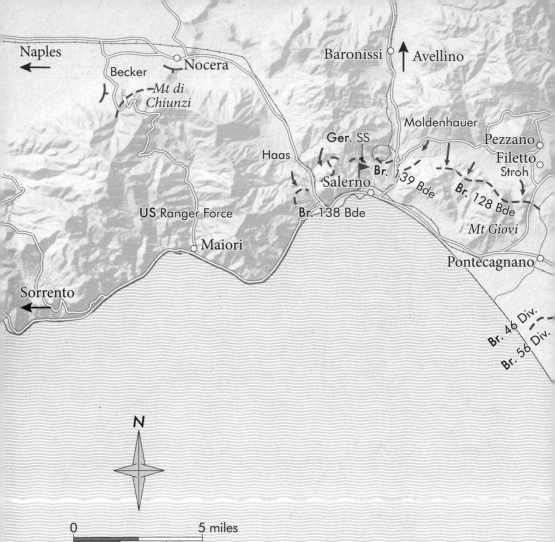

Naples

Becker

Nocera

Mt di Chiunzi

Baronissi

↑ Avellino

Moldenhauer

Pezzano
Filetto
Stroh

Haas

Ger. SS

Br.

Salerno

Br. 139 Bde

Br. 128 Bde

US Ranger Force

Br. 138 Bde

Mt Giovi

Maiori

Pontecagnano

Sorrento

Br. 46 Div.

Br. 56 Div.

N

| 0 | 5 miles |
| 0 | 5 km |

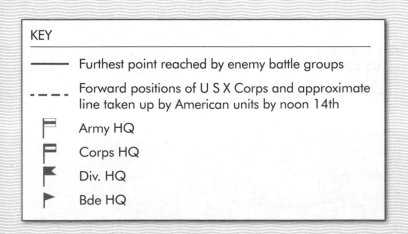

KEY

——— Furthest point reached by enemy battle groups

– – – Forward positions of U S X Corps and approximate line taken up by American units by noon 14th

⊢ Army HQ

⊩ Corps HQ

◀ Div. HQ

▶ Bde HQ

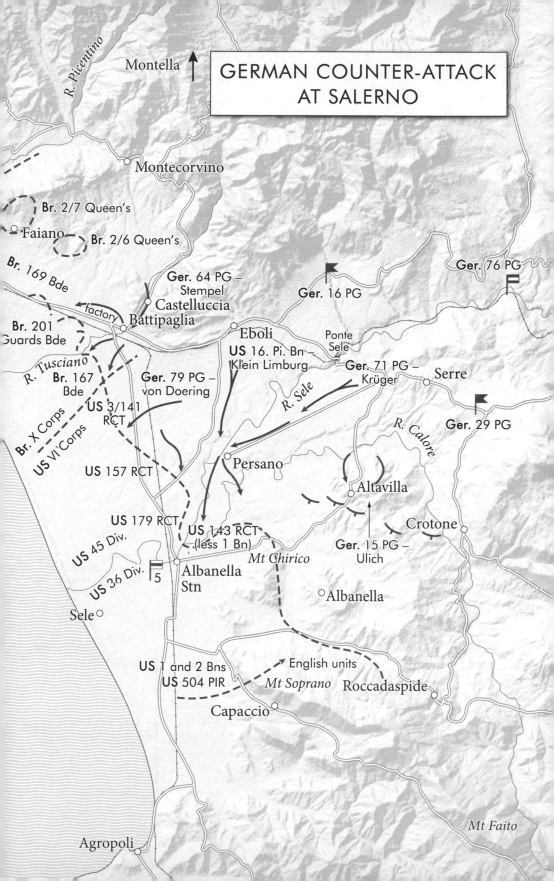

GERMAN COUNTER-ATTACK AT SALERNO

R. Picentino

Montella ↑

Montecorvino

Br. 2/7 Queen's

Faiano

Br. 2/6 Queen's

Br. 169 Bde

Ger. 64 PG –
Stempel
Castelluccia

factory

Battipaglia

**Br. 201
Guards Bde**

Eboli

US 16. Pi. Bn –
Klein Limburg

Ponte
Sele

Ger. 16 PG

Ger. 76 PG

R. Tusciano

**Br. 167
Bde**

Ger. 79 PG –
von Doering

**US 3/141
RCT**

**Ger. 71 PG –
Krüger**

Serre

R. Sele

Ger. 29 PG

Br. X Corps

US VI Corps

US 157 RCT

Persano

R. Calore

Altavilla

US 179 RCT

US 143 RCT
(less 1 Bn)

Crotone

**Ger. 15 PG –
Ulich**

US 45 Div.

Mt Chirico

US 36 Div. 5

Albanella
Stn

Albanella

Sele

US 1 and 2 Bns
US 504 PIR

→ English units

Mt Soprano

Roccadaspide

Capaccio

Mt Faito

Agropoli

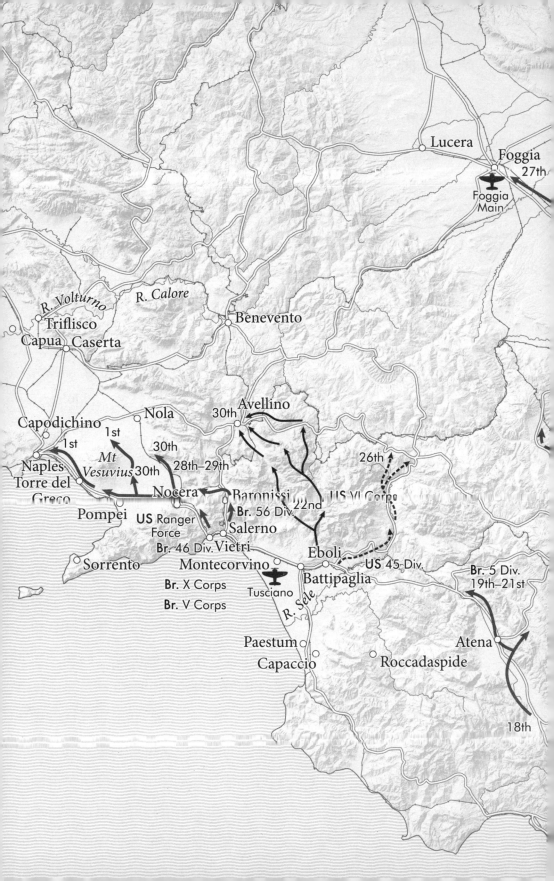

Lucera

Foggia
27th

Foggia
Main

R. Volturno   R. Calore

Triflisco   Benevento

Capua   Caserta

Capodichino   Nola   Avellino
                                30th
             1st
      1st   30th
Naples   *Mt*   28th–29th   26th
Torre del   *Vesuvius* 30th
Greco   Nocera   Baronissi   US VI Corps
                                            22nd
        Pompei   Br. 56 Div.
             US Ranger   Salerno
             Force
                    Br. 46 Div. Vietri
    Sorrento   Montecorvino   Eboli   US 45 Div.
                                                Br. 5 Div.
             Br. X Corps   19th–21st
             Br. V Corps   Tusciano   Battipaglia
                                                Atena
                    Paestum
             R. Sele
                    Capaccio   Roccadaspide
                                                18th

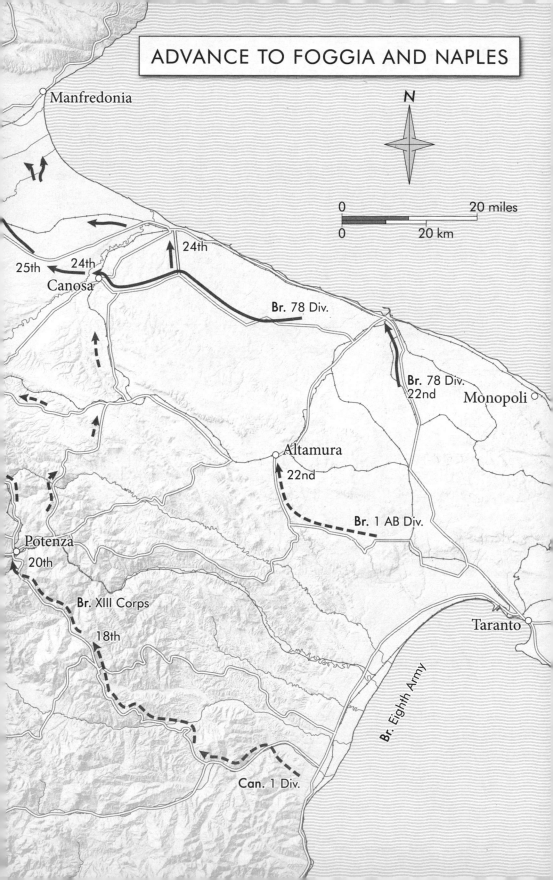

ADVANCE TO FOGGIA AND NAPLES

N

0 _____ 20 miles
0 _____ 20 km

Manfredonia

24th

Canosa

25th   24th

Br. 78 Div.

Br. 78 Div.
22nd

Monopoli

Altamura

22nd

Br. 1 AB Div.

Potenza

20th

Br. XIII Corps

18th

Taranto

Br. Eighth Army

Can. 1 Div.

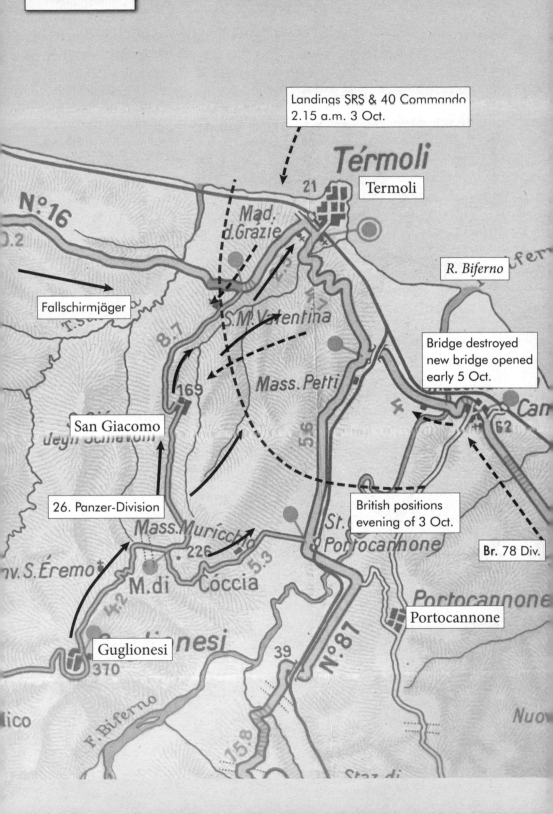

TERMOLI

Landings SRS & 40 Commando 2.15 a.m. 3 Oct.

Térmoli

Termoli

21

R. Biferno

Mad. d.Grazie

Fallschirmjäger

S.M.Valentina

Bridge destroyed new bridge opened early 5 Oct.

Mass. Petti

N°16

.0.2

8.7

4.7

2.5

5.6

4

169

San Giacomo

Cam

62

26. Panzer-Division

British positions evening of 3 Oct.

Mass.Muriccio

226

5.3

St.

Portocannone

Br. 78 Div.

Guglionesi

M. di Cóccia

v. S.Éremo

4.2

nesi

39

N°87

Portocannone

Portocannone

370

F. Biferno

ico

15.8

Nuo

Staz di

A 56th Division Bren gunner, spare barrel on the wall to his left, and his sergeant, beside him with binoculars, keep an eye on the enemy from the old *castello* of Calvi Vecchia. The date is 24 October 1943.

PROGRESS OF THE HASTY PS AND THE FAUGHS

Faughs

Hasty Ps

Salerno

Paestum

Volturno

Upper Volturno

Monte Camino

Monte Corno

The Mignano Gap

Monte Trocchio and the Monte Cassino Massif

Capua

XX
Br. 56 Div.

Caserta

XX
US 3 Div.

XX
Br. 7 Div.

R. Volturno

Maddaloni

Cancello

Aversa

XX
US 82 AB

II
US Ranger
Force

Naples

Mt Vesuvius

Pompei

Torre Annunziata

XX
US 82 AB

Ischia

Castellammare di Stabia

II
US Ranger Force

X
Br. 23 Armd Bde

Sorrento

N

Capri

0   10 miles

0   10 km

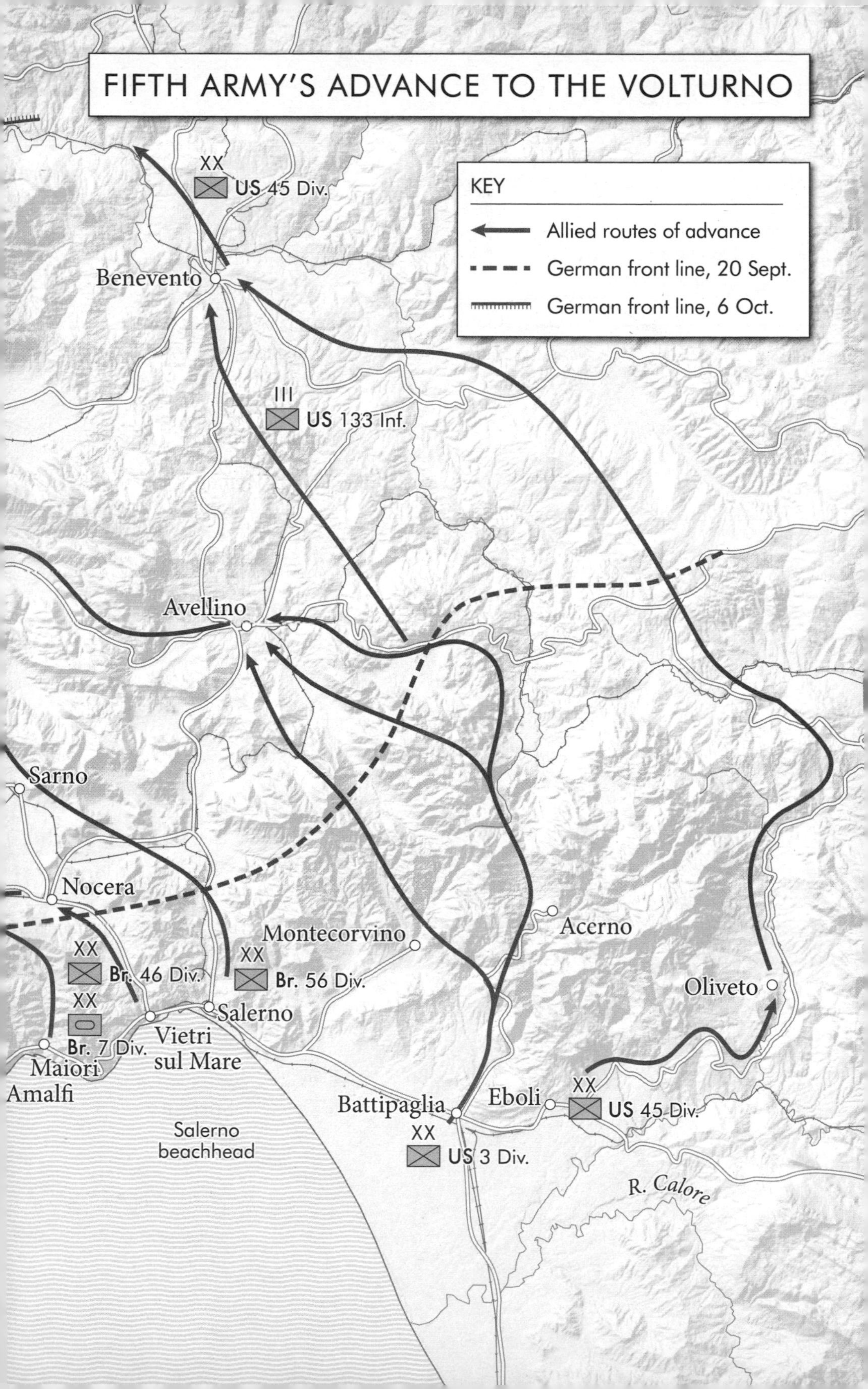

FIFTH ARMY'S ADVANCE TO THE VOLTURNO

KEY

→ Allied routes of advance

----- German front line, 20 Sept.

⊥⊥⊥⊥ German front line, 6 Oct.

XX US 45 Div.

Benevento

III US 133 Inf.

Avellino

Sarno

Nocera

Montecorvino

Acerno

XX Br. 46 Div.

XX Br. 56 Div.

Oliveto

XX Br. 7 Div.

Salerno

Maiori
Amalfi

Vietri
sul Mare

Salerno
beachhead

Battipaglia

Eboli

XX US 45 Div.

XX US 3 Div.

R. Calore

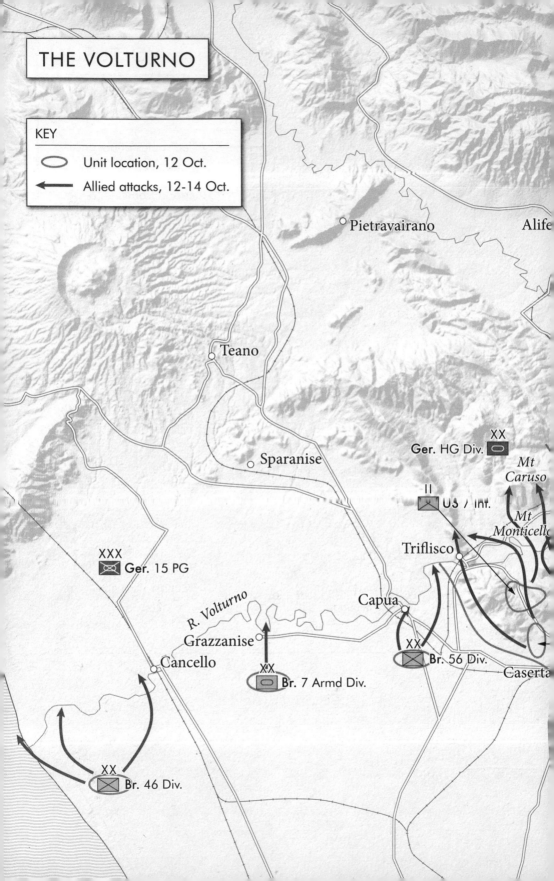

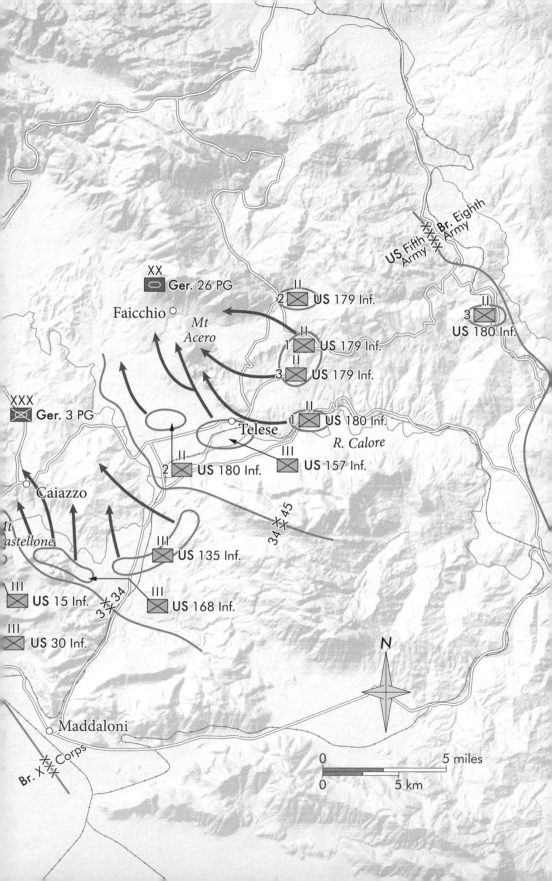

US Fifth Army
Br. Eighth Army

XX
Ger. 26 PG

Faicchio ○

Mt Acero

II
2 | US 179 Inf.

II
1 | US 179 Inf.

II
3 | US 179 Inf.

II
3 | US 180 Inf.

XXX
Ger. 3 PG

○ Telese

II
1 | US 180 Inf.

R. Calore

II
2 | US 180 Inf.

III
US 157 Inf.

○ Caiazzo

It astellone

34 ✕ 45

III
US 135 Inf.

III
US 15 Inf.

3 ✕ 34

III
US 168 Inf.

III
US 30 Inf.

N

○ Maddaloni

Br. ✕✕ Corps

0 — 5 miles

0 — 5 km

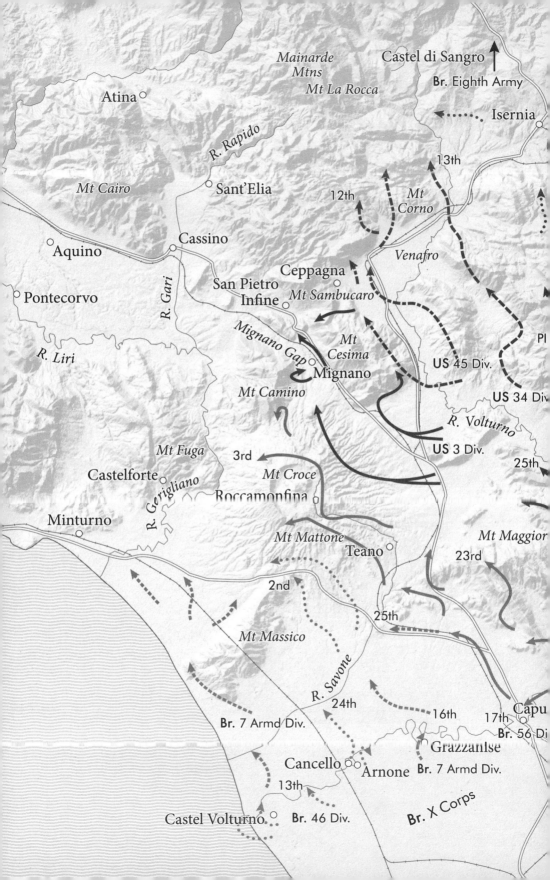

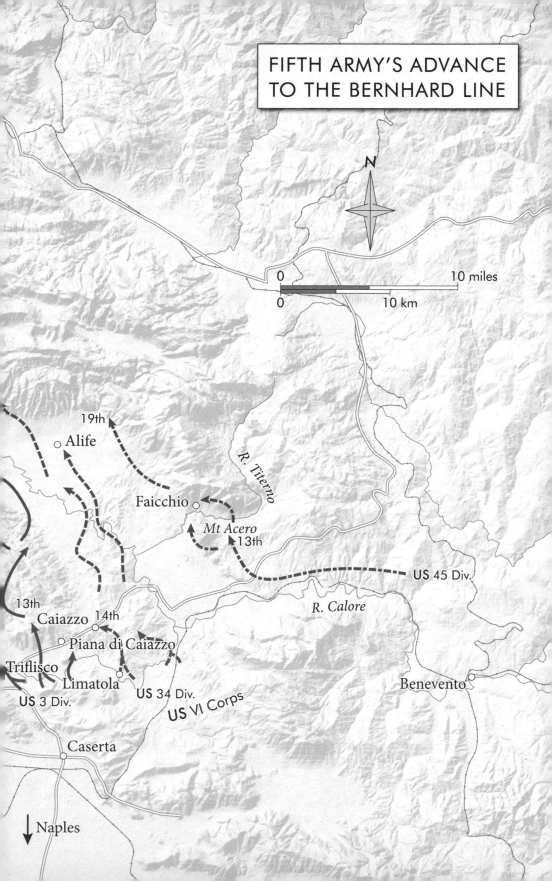

FIFTH ARMY'S ADVANCE
TO THE BERNHARD LINE

N

0   10 miles
0   10 km

19th

Alife

R. Titerno

Faicchio

Mt Acero

13th

US 45 Div.

R. Calore

13th

Caiazzo   14th

Piana di Caiazzo

Triflisco

Limatola

US 3 Div.   US 34 Div.

US VI Corps

Benevento

Caserta

Naples

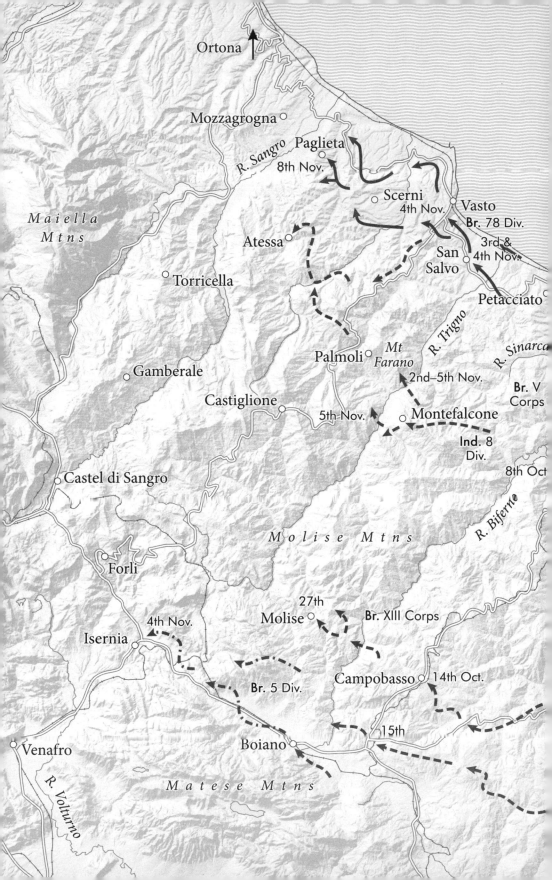

Ortona

Mozzagrogna

Paglieta
8th Nov.

R. Sangro

Scerni
4th Nov.

Vasto
Br. 78 Div.

3rd &
4th Nov.

Atessa

San
Salvo

*Maiella
Mtns*

Petacciato

Torricella

R. Trigno

R. Sinarca

Palmoli

*Mt
Farano*
2nd–5th Nov.

**Br. V
Corps**

Gamberale

Castiglione
5th Nov.

Montefalcone

**Ind. 8
Div.**

Castel di Sangro

8th Oct

Molise   Mtns

R. Biferno

Forli

27th

Molise

Br. XIII Corps

Isernia
4th Nov.

Br. 5 Div.

Campobasso   14th Oct.

Venafro

Boiano

15th

R. Volturno

Matese   Mtns

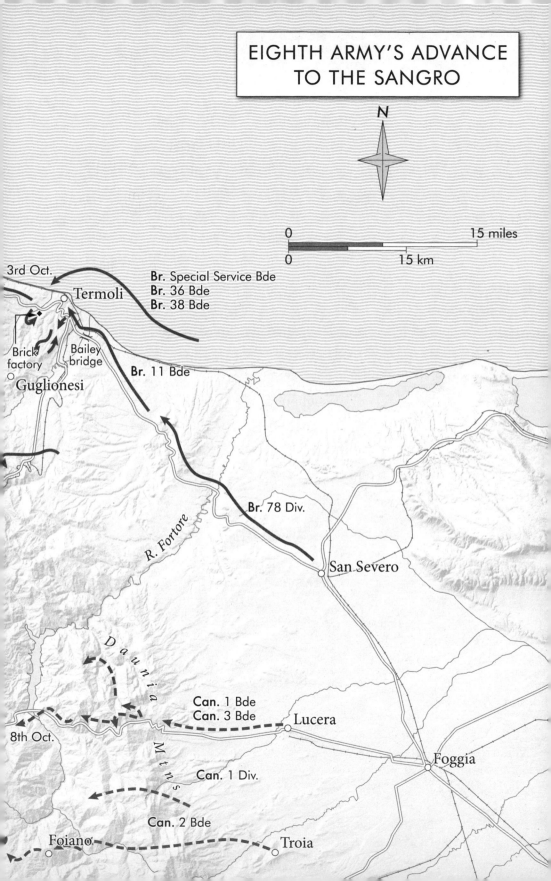

EIGHTH ARMY'S ADVANCE
TO THE SANGRO

N

0   15 miles

0   15 km

3rd Oct.

Termoli

Br. Special Service Bde
Br. 36 Bde
Br. 38 Bde

Brick
factory

Bailey
bridge

Br. 11 Bde

Guglionesi

Br. 78 Div.

R. Fortore

San Severo

D a u n i a

Can. 1 Bde
Can. 3 Bde

Lucera

M t n s

Foggia

8th Oct.

Can. 1 Div.

Can. 2 Bde

Foiano

Troia

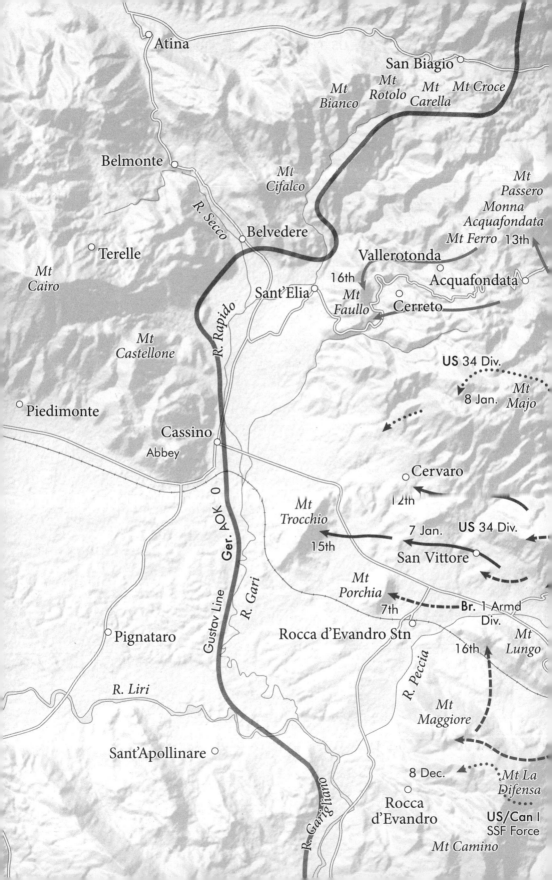

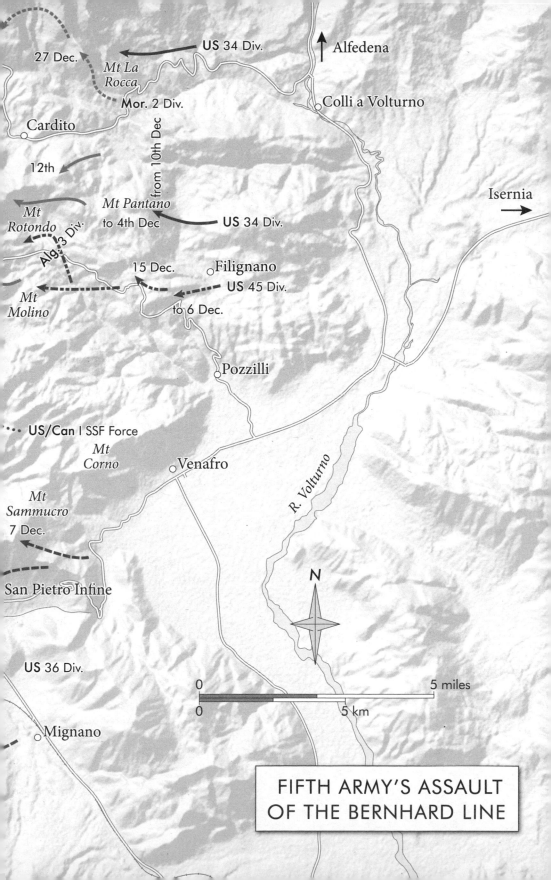

US 34 Div.

27 Dec.

Mt La Rocca

↑ Alfedena

Mor. 2 Div.

○ **Colli a Volturno**

Cardito
○

from 10th Dec

12th

Isernia →

Mt Rotondo

Alg. 3 Div.

Mt Pantano
to 4th Dec

US 34 Div.

15 Dec.

○ **Filignano**

Mt Molino

US 45 Div.

to 6 Dec.

○ **Pozzilli**

R. Volturno

US/Can I SSF Force

Mt Corno

Venafro
○

Mt Sammucro
7 Dec.

N

San Pietro Infine

US 36 Div.

0   5 miles

0   5 km

○ **Mignano**

FIFTH ARMY'S ASSAULT OF THE BERNHARD LINE

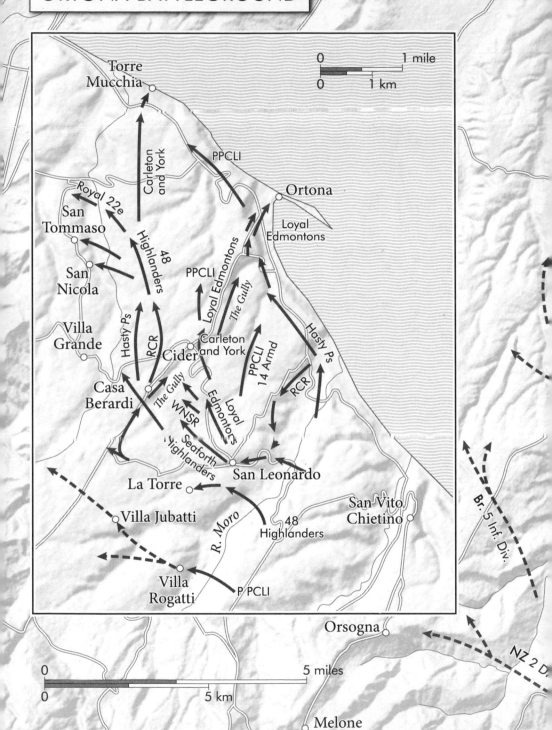

ORTONA BATTLEGROUND

Torre Mucchia

Royal 22e

San Tommaso

San Nicola

Villa Grande

Carleton and York

48 Highlanders

PPCLI

Ortona

Loyal Edmontons

PPCLI

Loyal Edmontons

The Gully

Hasty Ps

RCR

Cider

Carleton and York

PPCLI 14 Armd

Hasty Ps

Casa Berardi

The Gully

WNSR

Loyal Edmontons

RCR

Seaforth Highlanders

La Torre

San Leonardo

San Vito Chietino

Villa Jubatti

R. Moro

48 Highlanders

Villa Rogatti

P PCLI

Br. 5 Inf. Div.

Orsogna

NZ 2 D.

Melone

0   1 mile
0   1 km

0   5 miles
0   5 km

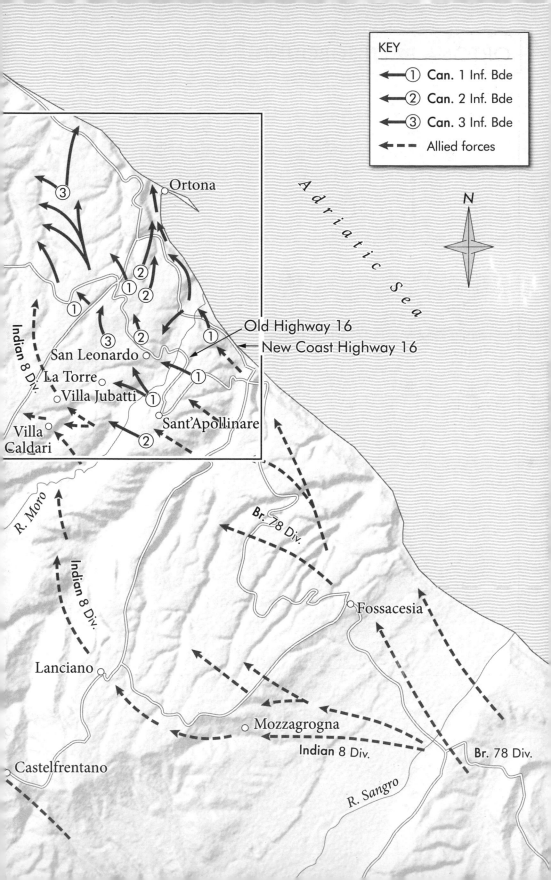

KEY

← ① **Can.** 1 Inf. Bde
← ② **Can.** 2 Inf. Bde
← ③ **Can.** 3 Inf. Bde
←--- Allied forces

A d r i a t i c   s e a

N

Ortona

Old Highway 16
New Coast Highway 16

San Leonardo
La Torre
Villa Jubatti
Sant'Apollinare
Villa Caldari

Indian 8 Div.

R. Moro

Indian 8 Div.

Br. 78 Div.

Fossacesia

Lanciano

Mozzagrogna

Indian 8 Div.

Br. 78 Div.

Castelfrentano

R. Sangro

Principal Personalities

American

Sergeant Isaac Akinaka
A Company, 100th 'Nisei' Battalion, 133rd Infantry Regiment, 34th Division

General Mark Clark
Commander, US Fifth Army

Colonel William O. Darby
Commander, Army Ranger Force

Lieutenant Charles Dills
Fighter pilot with 522nd Squadron, 27th Fighter-Bomber Group

Captain Roswell K. Doughty
Intelligence officer, S-2, and commanding officer of Intelligence and Reconnaissance Platoon, 141st Infantry Regiment, 36th 'Texas' Division

Lieutenant-General John Lucas
Commander, VI Corps, Fifth Army

Corporal Audie Murphy
B Company, 1st Battalion, 15th Infantry Regiment, 3rd Infantry Division

Private Frank Pearce
C Company, 111th Engineer Battalion, attached to 143rd Infantry Regiment, 36th Infantry Division

Ernie Pyle
Reporter for Scripps-Howard Newspapers

Lieutenant James E. Reed
59th Fighter Squadron, 33rd Fighter Group

Quent Reynolds
Reporter for *Colllier's Weekly*

General Carl 'Tooey' Spaatz
Commander, Mediterranean Strategic Air Forces, later commander, US Fifteenth Air Force

Lieutenant T. Michael Sullivan
Bombardier, 429th Bomb Squadron, 2nd Bomb Group, Fifteenth Air Force

Lieutenant Robert A. 'Smoky' Vrilakas
P-38 Lightning pilot, 94th Fighter Squadron, 1st Fighter Group

Corporal Bud Wagner
2nd Battalion, 151st Field Artillery, 34th Infantry Division

Australian

Major Lawrence Franklyn-Vaile
Royal Irish Fusiliers, 38th Irish
Brigade, 78th Division

Alan Moorehead
War correspondent for the *Daily Express*

British

General Sir Harold Alexander
Commander, 15th Army Group

Lieutenant Peter Bull, RNVR
Commander, HM Landing Craft
Flak 16

Lieutenant Christopher Bulteel
No. 3 Company, 3rd Coldstream
Guards, 201st Guards Brigade, 56th
Division

Lieutenant David Cole
Battalion Signals Officer, 2nd Royal
Inniskilling Fusiliers, 13th Infantry
Brigade, 5th Division

Lieutenant Peter Davis
Special Raiding Squadron

Wing Commander Hugh 'Cocky' Dundas
Deputy commander, 324 Wing

Sergeant Norman Lewis
British intelligence officer with 312th
Field Security Service

Harold Macmillan
Minister of State

Lieutenant Peter Moore
Platoon commander with 2/5th
Battalion, Leicestershire Regiment,
139th Infantry Brigade, 46th
Division

Captain Bertie Packer, RN
Commander, HMS *Warspite*, Force
H, Mediterranean Fleet

Sergeant-Major Jack Ward
RSM 56th Heavy Regiment, Royal
Artillery, X Corps

Corporal Harry Wilson
Cipher clerk with 8th Indian
Division HQ and later 17th Indian
Brigade

Canadian

Major Alex Campbell
Commander, A Company, Hastings
and Prince Edward Regiment, 1st
Infantry Brigade

Major the Reverend Roy Durnford
Padre, Seaforth Highlanders of
Canada, 1st Canadian Division

Captain Farley Mowat
Intelligence officer, Hastings and
Prince Edward Regiment, 1st
Infantry Brigade

German

Obergefreiter Siegfried Bähr
5. Kompanie, 2. Bataillon,
3. Fallschirmjäger-Regiment,
1. Fallschirmjäger-Division

Generalleutnant Hermann Balck
Acting commander, XIV
Panzerkorps

Oberleutnant Hans Golda
Commander, 8. Batterie, Werfer-
Regiment 71

Feldwebel Robert Gugelberger
Fighter pilot, 4. 2/Jagdgeschwader 53

Feldmarschall Albert Kesselring
German Oberbefehlshaber Süd

Unteroffizier Jupp Klein
2. Kompanie, Fallschirm-Pionier-
Bataillon 1, 1. Fallschirmjäger-Division

Oberstarzt Wilhelm Mauss
Senior Medical Officer, XIV
Panzerkorps headquarters

Gefreiter Werner Mork
12. Kompanie, 2. Bataillon, 200.
Panzergrenadier-Regiment, 90.
Panzergrenadier-Division

Leutnant Martin Pöppel
1. Kompanie, Maschinengewehr-
Bataillon, 1.
Fallschirmjäger-Division

Oberst Wilhelm Schmalz
Commander, Brigade Schmalz,
Panzerdivision-Hermann Göring

**Generalleutnant Fridolin von
Senger und Etterlin**
Commander, XIV Panzerkorps

Feldwebel Gerhard Waag
Fighter pilot with 6. 2/
Jagdgeschwader 53

Major Georg Zellner
Commander, 3. Bataillon, 44.
Reichsgrenadier-Regiment, 44.
'Hoch- und
Deutschmeister'-Division

Italian

Carla Capponi
Member of Rome-based partisan
movement Gruppi di Azione
Patriottica

Count Filippo Caracciolo
Member of the Partito d'Azione
based in Naples

Generale Giacomo Carboni
Head of SIM and commander of
Corpo d'Armata Motocorazzato

Pasqualina Caruso
Civilian living in Naples

Tenente Eugenio Corti
2a Batteria, 61 Raggruppamento di
Artiglieria, Corpo d'Armata

Dom Eusebio Grossetti
Benedictine monk at the Abbey of
Monte Cassino

Pierinio Di Mascio
Civilian living in Vallerotonda

Benedetto Pagano
Civilian living in San Pietro Infine

Serafino Masalla
Civilian living in San Pietro Infine

Enrichetta Pagano
Civilian living in San Pietro Infine

New Zealander

Private Roger Smith
A Company, 24th Battalion, New
Zealand Expeditionary Force

Isaac Akinaka

General Sir Harold Alexander

Siegfried Bähr

Hermann Balck

Peter Bull

Christopher Bulteel

Alex Campbell

Carla Capponi

Filippo Caracciolo

General Mark Clark

David Cole

Admiral Andrew
Browne Cunningham

William O. Darby

Peter Davis

Roswell Doughty

Hugh 'Cocky' Dundas

Lawrie Franklyn-Vaile

Feldmarschall Albert
Kesselring

Jupp Klein

General John Lucas

Harold Macmillan

Willhelm Mauss

Peter Moore

Alan Moorehead

Werner Mork

Farley Mowat

Audie Murphy

Bertie Packer

Benedetto and Enrichetta Pagano

Martin Pöppel

Quent Reynolds

Wilhelm Schmalz

General Fridolin von
Senger und Etterlin

Robert 'Smoky' Vrilakas

Harry Wilson

Note on the Text

Writing a campaign history such as this is a complicated undertaking, but although dealing with American, British, Canadian, German and Italian units across the armed services, I've tried to keep the numbers of unit names as low as possible. To help distinguish one side from another, I have used a form of vernacular – styling German units more or less as they would be written in German, and likewise with the Italian units. This really is not to be pretentious in any way, but just to help with the reading and cut down on any confusion.

For those who are not familiar with the scale and size of wartime units, the basic fighting formation on which the size of armies was judged was the division. Germans had panzer divisions, which were an all-arms formation of motorized infantry, artillery and tanks; they also had panzer grenadier divisions, which had fewer panzers – tanks – and more motorized infantry – a grenadier was simply an infantryman who was provided with motor transport to get from A to B. German infantry divisions tended to have much less motorization by 1943.

As a rule of thumb, a division was around 15,000 men, although some divisions could have as many as 20,000. Two divisions or more made up a corps, usually denoted in Roman numerals to distinguish them. Two corps or more constituted an army, and two armies or more an army group. Going back down the scales, American, German and Italian divisions were divided into regiments, while British, Canadian and New Zealand divisions were divided into brigades. Regiments and brigades were much the same, consisting of three core components, which, in the case of an infantry regiment/brigade, were three battalions. An infantry battalion was around 850 men, divided into companies of some 120 men, which in turn broke down into three platoons and finally to the smallest formation, the ten-man squad, Gruppe, or section, depending on the nationality. I hope that this and the Glossary that follows help.

Glossary

AF	air force
AFHQ	Allied Forces HQ
AMGOT	Allied Military Government of the Occupied Territories
AOK	Armeeoberkommando, German Army Command
Aufklärungs-Abteilung	reconnaissance battalion
AWOL	absent without leave
BAR	Browning automatic rifle, a light machine gun
batman	British officer's soldier-servant
Bn	battalion
Bren	British light machine gun
C-in-C	commander-in-chief
CEF	Corps Expéditionnaire Français, French Expeditionary Corps
CIGS	Chief of the Imperial General Staff
CLN	Comitato di Liberazione Nazionale, National Liberation Committee
CO	commanding officer
CP	command post
CSM	company sergeant-major
DUKE	Dominion, UK and Empire forces
Fallschirmjäger	paratroopers
FDL	forward defence line
Feldmarschall (Generalfeldmarschall)	field marshal (US five-star General of the Army)
Feldwebel	sergeant
Fliegerkorps	air corps
FOO	forward observation officer
FS	field security
GAP	Gruppi di Azione Patriottica, partisans operating in Rome under command of CLN Military Council
Gefreiter	lance corporal
Generalleutnant	lieutenant-general
Generalmajor	major-general
Generaloberst	general
GNR	Guardia Nazionale Repubblicana, National Republican Guard, a Fascist militia force of the RSI

GOC	general officer commanding
Grenadier	private in a grenadier unit
Hauptmann	captain
Heeresgruppe	army group
HG	Hermann Göring
HKL	Hauptkampflinie, main defence line
I & R	intelligence and reconnaissance
Jabo	Jagdbomber, German slang for a fighter-bomber or any low-flying Allied aircraft
Jerry	British slang for a German
JG	Jagdgeschwader, fighter group
Kraut	American slang for a German
LCF	landing craft, flak
LCI	landing craft, infantry
LCR	landing craft, rocket
LCT	landing craft, tank
Leutnant	second lieutenant
LOB	left out of battle
LSI	landing ship, infantry
MG42	Maschinengewehr 42, German rapid-firing light machine gun
MO	medical officer
NASAF	Northwest African Strategic Air Forces
NATAF	Northwest African Tactical Air Forces
NCO	non-commissioned officer
NZEF	New Zealand Expeditionary Force
OB	Oberbefehlshaber, commander-in-chief
Oberfeldwebel	staff sergeant
Obergefreiter	corporal
Oberleutnant	lieutenant
Oberst	colonel
Oberstarzt	chief medical officer
Oberstleutnant	lieutenant-colonel
OKH	Oberkommando des Heeres, German Army Staff
OKW	Oberkommando der Wehrmacht, German General Staff
OP	observation post
Pak	Panzerabwehrkanone, anti-tank gun
PBI	'Poor Bloody Infantry'
Pfc	private first class
PG	Panzergrenadier, motorized armoured infantry
PIR	parachute infantry regiment
POW	prisoner of war
PPCLI	Princess Patricia's Canadian Light Infantry
RAF	Royal Air Force

RAP	regimental aid post
RCT	regimental combat team
Regio Esercito	Italian Royal Army
RSHA	Reichssicherheitshauptamt, Reich Security Main Office, run by the SS and incorporating all police, secret police and Nazi intelligence services
RSI	Repubblica Sociale Italiana, the Italian Socialist Republic, the new puppet Fascist state set up under Mussolini by the Germans
RSM	regimental sergeant-major
SIM	Servizio Informazioni Militare
SRS	Special Raiding Squadron, formally SAS
StuG	Sturmgeschütz, assault gun
Ted	from *Tedeschi*, Italian for Germans
Tenente	lieutenant
Tommy	German slang for DUKE forces
Unteroffizier	non-commissioned officer
USAAF	United States Army Air Force
Waldlager	forest camp
Wehrmacht	German armed forces
XO	executive officer (second-in-command)
Zambuk	slang for a medic – from the Zam-Buk 'miracle balm'

Prologue

MID-AUGUST, 1943. A DAY crossing of the Straits of Messina, the slight sea breeze offering some relief from the relentless heat of the broiling sun. Leutnant Hans Golda stood on the ferry gazing back at Sicily. He was a sentimental fellow on occasion, and he couldn't help feeling wistful about the island that had become so dear to him. The mountains rose up almost from the shore, looming magnificent and immutable against the deep-azure sky, and beyond, Etna, that still-smouldering volcano that so dominated the north-east of the island – the part over which they had been fighting these past seven weeks. And because he was prone to sentimentality but also optimism, Golda had rather filtered out the more disagreeable aspects of Sicily: the relentless burning rays of the sun, or the surly Sicilians with whom they'd associated so little. Italians who were still, on paper at any rate, allies. People who, for the most part, had struck him at earlier moments during his time there as dirty and distant. Weeks before, he'd been shocked by the squalor, by the garbage and filth left near the front door of almost every house. He had cursed the clouds of flies that swarmed around anything edible. And also the bitterness of battle. The blackened corpses. The destruction. The defeat. The knowledge that they had fought so hard and yet had been pushed back, leaving the dead and captured behind. The enemy had crushing material superiority, but Golda had put such considerations to the back of his mind, so that now, as he crossed those narrow waters, where Odysseus had skirted past the six-headed Scylla and survived being swallowed by Charybdis, he did not feel despondent or beaten up, but rather a sense of pride at how his men had performed and something close to affection for the magnificence of the island. The Battle of Sicily was over, but, as he was well aware, the Battle of Italy was surely soon to begin.

Not quite 40,000 German troops had managed to get away from Sicily, of whom only 26,000 were from the four fighting divisions – divisions that should have had around 15,000 men each. Golda and his men were part of the badly mauled 15. Panzergrenadier-Division. How that division had been dragged through the mill over the past few years! Sent to Africa in April 1941, it had been part of the spearheading Deutsches Afrika-korps; but then it had been savaged at Alamein eighteen months later and utterly destroyed in Tunisia six months after that. From a skeleton, and then from odds and ends – men recovering from wounds, an artil-lery company here, a panzer battalion there, office clerks and back-room boys – Division Sizilien had been formed, to which Golda's Werfer-Regiment 71 had been attached; they were equipped with 210mm five-barrelled rocket launchers firing high-explosive warheads known as Nebelwerfers – literally, 'fog throwers'. They gave a high-pitched moan as they sped through the air.

In July, Division Sizilien had grown enough to become 15. Panzergrenadier-Division – a motorized, all-arms unit of infantry, armour, artillery, engineers and reconnaissance troops, but also a reflection that the Wehrmacht had fewer tanks to spare than it once had. Golda still liked to call it 'Sizilien', but those days were over, and in any case most of its number had remained forever on the island. No one was under any illusion that the division now needed rebuilding yet again. It was like a phoenix, repeatedly reborn. It was also indicative of Germany's parlous situation: it was losing the war.

None the less, they would fight on. And if 15. Panzergrenadier-Division were to emerge from the fire again, it would need a little time and space, and that meant heading north, more or less out of harm's way. There, replacement troops would arrive, more equipment, more vehicles – if they were lucky – and then they would turn and face the enemy once more. How long did they have? That was anyone's guess, but Golda was just glad to be alive, to still have his vehicles, at least some of his Nebel-werfers, and for the time being, at any rate, a break from the fighting.

Their orders were to head first to Palmi, a little over twenty miles away, where the remains of the regiment were due to reassemble. First, though, they needed to safely reach the other side. Earlier, as they'd waited to board, an enemy reconnaissance plane had buzzed over, but immediately more than 300 guns had opened fire either side of the Straits. Golda had watched the tracer, fingers of death reaching up into the sky, and the plane hurriedly scuttled off.

Relief. Soon enough everyone was across safely; no further Allied planes had dared to disrupt the evacuation. Slowly, carefully, Golda rolled his Volkswagen off the ferry at Villa San Giovanni in the toe of the Italian boot, mountains gazing down at them in almost a mirror of those the far side of the Straits. Golda was at the wheel, the compact car packed with boxes and with his trusted Franz sitting on top trying to keep these precious treasures together. Behind them, the Werfers of his 7. Batterie, these six-barrelled rocket mortars, towed by trucks and half-tracks. Gingerly they trundled their way along the coast road, the Tyrrhenian Sea wine-dark on their left, wheezing up switchbacks behind the coast towns of Bagnara and Sant'Elia until, crossing a valley thick with olive and citrus groves, they reached the little coastal town.

Golda's heart ached to see what this once-charming little port had become since last he'd passed through. Dead and abandoned. Houses smashed, streets torn open by bombs. He was glad to push on through, away from the desolation, to Division Sizilien's assembly area beyond. They rolled in, marching group after marching group threaded into a movement order marshalled by large numbers of field gendarmerie. Golda was happy to follow, no longer needing to look at a map or think about where to go. There was only one coast road, and he could always follow the vehicle in front. Where there were detours, posts had been erected to show them the right way. The sun bore down, dust swirled. Throats became parched, but they were used to that. Then night again. On they drove. Rosario was badly smashed, and an excited lone bomber dropped some fragmentation bombs as they passed through. But no one was hit; just a factory shed set on fire, the flames vividly bright against the night sky.

One day they reached Sapri, a quiet fishing town in a horseshoe bay, mountains once again rising behind. The mountains – they were never far away in Italy. The coast road wound its way through the little town, kissing the coast, and here they paused in the shade of an orange grove for a rest and a swim in the twinkling sea. Just a little way out a white hospital ship was at anchor, the red crosses shining in the sun. Small boats were ferrying out the wounded, and Golda found himself wishing for a light wound, just so that he could sail on this magnificent ship.

Precious hours. A little garden gift from God, he thought.

And then on again. At dawn they were climbing along another stretch of mountain road: steep sides to their right, a sheer drop to their left. Suddenly, a low-flying aircraft thundered over them. They were sitting ducks! One long sheaf of fire and the road would have been closed for a day, but inexplicably the pilot never opened fire; perhaps his ammunition was already out. Perhaps he felt merciful that day.

They reached the Bay of Salerno and a brief, narrow strip of coastline with the mountains pushed back a little way inland. Golda marvelled at the ruins of Paestum, for a brief moment a tourist, not a warrior, as he gazed at those ancient Greek temples, city walls and amphitheatre, thousands of years old and less touched than some of the shattered towns they'd passed through. On they rumbled, through Salerno itself, just as the bombers began circling for home. Following a hastily cleared path around bomb craters, dodging freshly collapsed buildings, through air still thick with smoke and dust. Up ahead, several vehicles had been struck. Anti-aircraft – flak – guns boomed, shells pumping the sky. Golda saw several of these deadly giants hit; one even broke up in the sky, its debris crashing down into the town below. A second bomber plunged into the mountains overlooking the port, while from a third, thick black smoke trailed across the sky in the distance. It was Thursday, 19 August 1943. Three days after Axis forces had abandoned Sicily forever.

Whatever gloom Golda and his men may have momentarily felt, he was cheered by the magnificence of Vesuvius and the glow of lava spilling from its summit, vividly blood-red against the night sky. Naples, that great city port, they bypassed and pushed on, then rumbled by Caserta with its vast, dominating palace that so dwarfed the rest of the town. On, further still, until they reached Capua, where suddenly, unexpectedly, as they crossed over the railway bridge – the road bridge had been smashed – they were drenched by a thunderstorm. Once across, they finally reached Cascano, the division's primary destination.

A pause. And while they paused, Golda watched yet more Allied aircraft – bombers heading north. He and his men counted the machines. If only they had such air power, they thought. But then their mood lightened as three Luftwaffe fighter planes roared in to attack, cannons and machine guns blazing. Shouts of jubilation, then cheers as first one, then a second and third bomber fell. One trundled slowly earthwards, another fell like a stone, a mighty trail of smoke following in its wake.

An Italian farmer suddenly appeared accompanied by some German officers. Italians were still allies. The farmer was irate. More than a dozen of his chickens stolen! The officers wondered whether Golda's men were guilty of this misdemeanour. Golda was incensed. No, his men had not stolen any chickens. What a suggestion! The rules were strict: no pilfering. A German soldier was allowed to barter for goods but not steal; commanders were authorized to shoot those who broke these rules. It didn't mean such draconian measures were often enforced, but Golda, for one, was prepared to back his men. They were innocent. What an outrageous slur! Frustrated, the farmer and the officers moved on, continuing their search for the culprits.

Later, though, suspicious wafts of roasting chicken drifted across their hastily constructed encampment. Shortly after, one of his men offered him a portion of *Hendl Haxen* – a chicken drumstick – which he ate both with considerable pleasure and with little research into its origin.

A day at Cascano, and then they were ordered to their final destination for the time being: the village of Roccamonfina, nestling high along the edge of an ancient volcano crater. A serpentine climb up a dusty *strada bianca* and into a beautiful chestnut grove at the village's edge. Below them was Sessa, with its ancient Roman amphitheatre, and an enchanting view to the dark Tyrrhenian Sea and the Bay of Gaeta beyond. Immediately all around them, a belt of still-dense woods of chestnuts, oaks, sycamores and olive groves, distant villages peeking through the verdant haze. Vehicles and Werfers parked up, tents erected. What a country! What a view! Golda was determined to enjoy himself: a brief chance to take things a little easy. Some bathing in that warm, inviting, sparkling sea just a few miles away, and a chance to unwind. Really, their new surroundings could hardly be more perfect.

A few days of calm, then, but it was not going to last long. This bitter war was not over, not by a long chalk, despite the turning of the Axis tide. The momentary lull was just a pause and nothing more. The clouds of war were rolling in again and Golda and his men would soon be caught up in the typhoon. So too would countless hundreds of thousands, millions, even.

Winter was coming.

PART I

Summer

CHAPTER 1

The Burning Blue

MORNING, FRIDAY, 20 AUGUST 1943. At Cancello airfield, thirty miles or so north-west of Naples, the fighter pilots of 2/Jagdgeschwader – JG – 53 were waiting at their squadron dispersal. This crew base for the pilots was not a building, not a hut, not even a tent. Rather, just an awning: a mottled brown camouflage canvas, pegged to the ground at the back and propped up by square posts and guy ropes. Under the shade of the awning were a few camp beds and some woollen rugs laid on the hard-baked clay. Ahead, thin bleached grass, and across the flat expanse of the airfield in the distance, hazy blue hills rising gently. The early morning sun was already casting a warm glow over the airfield.

Immediately in front of them were freshly dug slit trenches, the piles of dark-brown spoil offering a little extra protection. Not far away, within easy running distance, stood their Messerschmitt 109s, 'Gustavs' – painted in a similar mottled pattern to that of their awning, but grey rather than khaki. A few other features singled out these fighter planes: the black and white spiral spinner and the single *Pik A* painted on to each of the engine cowlings – for JG53 were known as the 'Ace of Spades'.

A little distance away, a wooden trailer that looked rather like a short railroad carriage. This was 6. Staffel – or squadron – command post. Each of the three Staffeln had their own command post, own dispersal, and own areas for their personal tents. There were makeshift wooden tables, benches and an assortment of chairs where meals were eaten, but this was as much a campsite as it was an airfield. The 2./JG53 were camping out here at Cancello, and had been since they'd arrived from Sicily three weeks earlier. It was rough and ready, to say the least.

Much was asked of these young men – both the pilots, who were expected to get into their machines and take on a superior enemy, and the ground crews, who had to keep these fighter planes in the air with limited supplies and insufficient facilities. Flying combat aircraft was exhausting, physically and mentally. It was tougher when the surroundings were so basic, with the sun blazing down, with mosquitoes a constant menace, when you were very rarely able to get all twelve of the Staffel's machines in the air. When senior commanders far away in Rastenburg or Berlin were constantly berating your efforts. When you were losing.

It was hot already. Not a breath of wind. The pilots only wore sand-coloured khaki shorts and short-sleeved shirts, something not encouraged in the Allied air forces no matter how hot it was on the ground: if an aircraft caught fire, clothing was an extra barrier between flame and skin. But Luftwaffe pilots were willing to take that chance. At dispersal, on this already bright August morning, most of the pilots tried to use the time for extra sleep, and so lay on the rugs on the hard ground. Some slept, others dozed. Feldwebel Eugen Kurz, on the other hand, was wide awake, perched on a camp bed, staring out at the airfield. Waiting. The Allies would be over at some point. Big four-engine bombers, twin-engine medium bombers and their escorts of P-38 Lightnings. Every day, pounding airfields and railway yards, and because there were comparatively few Luftwaffe to defend these Allied targets – and even fewer Italians of the Regia Aeronautica, the air force – more was expected of those who did still have machines, who could still fly.

And so here they were, another day, another morning, sitting, lying, sleeping at their dispersal, waiting for the call that would inevitably come.

It came a little after midday. *Alarm!* Pilots up immediately, whether sleeping or not. Running across the baked dusty soil, brittle grass prickling at their bare legs. Ground crew starting up the engines, puffs of flame and smoke from the exhaust stubs. Parachutes and flying helmets snatched from the wing, foot into the groove on the fuselage, up on to the wing and clamber into the cockpit. That familiar smell: oil, rubber, metal and fuel. Radio leads in, oxygen leads in, signal to the ground crew, open the throttle, rumble forward, jolting across the earthen field, port rudder because of the immense torque from the Daimler-Benz engine. Speed rising. Clouds of dust. Visibility poor if you were last to get airborne. Then the shaking stopped and the shadows on the ground parted company with the machine as the Messerschmitts rose from the ground.

Clear again. Their corner of Italy spread before them, the sea just a short distance on their port side. The crackle of static in the headphones and a voice announcing an enemy formation approaching Capua – a small town on the River Volturno just below them.

Both 4. and 6. Staffeln had been scrambled. The 4./JG53 were based across the airfield from 6./JG53, and among those now climbing was Feldwebel Robert Gugelberger, still one of the new boys in his Staffel – he'd joined them in Sicily on 17 July straight from training and flown his first combat mission the following day, and, fortunately for him and his comrades, had lived to tell the tale. The quality of fresh pilots had taken a huge dip since the start of the war: back in September 1939, when Germany had invaded Poland, the Luftwaffe had had four years to build up strength, gain combat experience in the Spanish Civil War and create a cadre of highly experienced pilots who would help spearhead the Blitz-krieg years of victory and territorial gains. Now, though, almost four years on, Germany was running short of just about everything, from manpower to essential resources. This had a huge effect on the Luftwaffe because there was simply not enough fuel to train pilots sufficiently. Furthermore, training had to be done over the skies of Europe, where the weather was unreliable and where large parts were threatened by enemy air activity. Demand for pilots was also rising because of the terrible toll being taken: since November the previous year, the Luftwaffe had lost nearly 6,000 aircraft in the Mediterranean theatre alone. It was a stagger-ing number. Lack of fuel, crippling losses and demand all conspired to ensure that pilots like Robert Gugelberger were reaching the front and being flung into the fray with perhaps 120 hours in their logbooks – in total – if they were lucky, and often less. This was not nearly enough. Allied fighter pilots, by contrast, were trained in North America and Africa, where the skies were wide and clear and where decent weather could be guaranteed. They were reaching squadrons with as much as 350 hours in their logbooks and were then nurtured for a week or so before being allowed to fly operationally. The mismatch in pilot skill on the opposing sides was becoming significant.

So too, in the Mediterranean, were the numbers. Those losses had been replaced in part but not in total. Most of II. Fliegerkorps was now in north-ern Italy, protecting the passes in and out of Italy and the Reich's southern borders. Only a few fighter groups could be spared to defend the south.

Nor were young pilots like Gugelberger helped by the aircraft they were flying, which, in the case of the men of JG53, was the Messerschmitt 109G.

It had a quick rate of climb, could dive very fast and was highly manoeuvrable but had small wings, which gave it a high wing-loading and meant it could be a cruel mistress in which to take off and land, the big engine a bit too powerful for the size of the airframe. It was not an issue in the hands of an experienced pilot, but was for those new to it with insufficient flying training. The trouble was, because there were no two-seater varieties, a young pilot's first flight was always a considerable leap of faith in a 109.

If they made it through this first introduction, and the second and third, then chances of survival began to improve. They then had to confront their first combat mission, for which none were sufficiently prepared, but again, if they survived that and the next few, the odds began to lengthen. So a month on from joining 4./JG53, Gugelberger was an old hand, having flown combat sorties just about every single day and having repeatedly found himself tussling with superior numbers of enemy aircraft. A sink-or-swim kind of scenario. So far Gugelberger had managed to swim, although he was yet to shoot down an enemy aircraft. Accurate gunnery was incredibly difficult to master, which is why the majority of aircraft shot down were targeted by a small minority of superior marksmen. Poor marksmanship, however, was also another inevitable by-product of insufficient training and exacerbated by the vastly superior numbers of enemy aircraft every time they were airborne.

Gugelberger and his fellows climbed to some 18,000 feet until, away to their right, perhaps 1,000 metres below, he could see two formations of enemy bombers with escorts of P-38 Lightnings. Out to sea, just a short distance away, more aircraft. Then bombs were exploding below, ripples of orange flashes and smoke. Suddenly, a huge explosion rising high into the sky as a munitions dump was hit. Lightnings directly below them, and now Gugelberger peeled over and dived, the sun behind him. But his target had already spotted him and begun banking around, so that as Gugelberger approached, the American pilot was now turning towards him and opening fire, stabs of tracer fizzing across the sky. Gugelberger veered away, pulling up and turning towards the sea and clear out of the fray.

A chance to get his bearings and try to calmly spot another target. Beneath him, several more flights of Lightnings, one trailing the white smoke of coolant. It crashed on land in a ball of flame. A little way below, a wild dogfight. One plane hit the water in flames. No parachute. Five Lightnings turned back towards land, maybe 500 metres below. Gugelberger dived again, aiming to open fire on the last. Thumb on the fire buttons, the airframe juddering, machine-gun bullets and cannon shells streaking across the sky. But he had fired too soon, and from an angle, and the Lightning had seen him, and once again Gugelberger found his enemy turning towards him with scarcely believable speed. Unable to break away, he continued diving, the engine screaming, his airspeed indicator flickering at more than 750 kph. Air pressure intense. He pulled the stick, worried he'd never make it out of the dive, but then at last felt his machine begin to level. Ahead, three 109s on the tail of a Lightning. Feldwebel Steinmüller was scoring strikes, but with little obvious effect. Then suddenly the American pilot bailed, his parachute opening just as he hit the sea, and a little way away his Lightning plunged into the water.

Above, the sky had begun to clear and so Gugelberger turned for home, landing at 11.35 a.m. It had been another combat sortie in which he'd done very little other than survive. Outclassed and outnumbered, these Luftwaffe fighter pilots were in a constant state of reaction, rarely able to take any initiative.

And it was no wonder. At this moment in late August 1943, the Allied air forces operating in and around the Mediterranean amounted to a staggering 4,570 aircraft, which were divided into a number of different commands and forces, from the Northwest African Air Forces – which was home to the bulk, some 3,500 aircraft – to the Malta Air Command and the Middle East Air Command. All came under the overall control of Mediterranean Air Command.

Both the British and the Americans were equally wedded to the conviction that air power was key to Allied victory. Strategic air power – using air forces on their own to attack enemy targets – was at the very heart of both nations' war planning in the 1930s and remained a vital component of Allied strategy. From Britain, RAF Bomber Command had been attacking German targets since the night of 17 May 1940 and, from early March 1943, had launched its all-out Strategic Air Campaign against Germany, initially targeting the Ruhr industrial heartland in western Germany and then largely destroying Germany's largest city, Hamburg, at the end of July and beginning of August in what had been grimly called Operation GOMORRAH. There had also been devastating one-off raids such as that of 16/17 May 1943, when just nineteen specially adapted Lancaster bombers had destroyed two of Germany's largest dams and badly damaged a third in a daring low-level raid. For the most part, the RAF believed in bombing by night, when the risks from enemy aircraft were considered to be less.

By contrast, the United States Army Air Force (USAAF) entered the war championing daylight bombing using massed formations of heavily armed four-engine bombers. At the Casablanca Conference in January 1943, the Americans had suggested a strategic air campaign that focused on making its primary task destroying the Luftwaffe – targeting factories but also trying to lure aircraft into the air. This was formally adopted as Operation POINTBLANK in June. The theory was that once the Luftwaffe was destroyed the Allies would have much greater freedom to accurately attack other targets, because for all the enemy's anti-aircraft defences, it was their aircraft which unquestionably posed the greatest threat to Allied bombers.

In the Mediterranean a similar rule of thumb had taken hold, with RAF bomber forces operating mostly by night and the US bombers by day. The division of labour ensured that RAF and USAAF bombers could largely operate under their own steam, but also enabled the Allies to relentlessly target the enemy in Italy by day and night. Strategic air forces operating from both North Africa and Britain were now pounding targets in Italy daily. RAF Bomber Command hammered Milan as well as Genoa and Turin over four nights in mid-August, for example. In Milan, some 1,500 buildings were completely destroyed and a further 1,700 badly damaged. On the raid of the night of 12/13 August, more than 500 RAF heavies hit Milan, killing over 1,000 Italians. The main railway station was hit, so too was La Scala opera house, and a number of churches were also caught in the blast, including the Church of Santa Maria delle Grazie. As the day dawned, just one wall of the Refectory remained still standing; fortunately, this was the wall on which Leonardo da Vinci's *The Last Supper* was painted. Miraculously, it was untouched, but overall there was a devastating cultural cost to bombing as well as the tragic human one. The Allies were on the side of democracy but also of freedom. They viewed themselves as liberators. Increasingly, though, now the war had spread away from the vast open spaces of the desert to populous Europe, that liberty was being bought at a terrible price.

While bombers from England were hitting the cities of northern Italy, heavies from North Africa were also playing their part in the wider POINTBLANK plan, underlining the huge importance which long-range strategic targets held for the Allies; there might have been an invasion of Italy to prepare for, but Mediterranean Air Command bombers were still expected to operate further afield. The Ploesti oilfields in Romania had been hit by North African-based heavies on 1 August, for example, while the Messerschmitt Wiener-Neustadt plant had been bombed two days later. This was the first target within the Reich itself struck from bases in the Mediterranean.

Commanding this enormous air effort were a number of highly charismatic and enlightened men, pioneers of a dynamic and rapid evolution that had long since overtaken anything the Axis could bring to bear. In many ways, it had begun a couple of years earlier, under the then Air Chief Marshal Arthur Tedder, the C-in-C of RAF Middle East, and Air Marshal Arthur Coningham, commander of the Desert Air Force. Both championed air power in the round: bombers to hit strategic targets further afield, coastal air power to assault enemy shipping, and then tactical air forces to provide close air support for the armies on the ground. Britain had begun the war with no tactical air force as such, which was why, in the autumn of 1941, Tedder and Coningham began to pioneer how close air support might work. Key was maintaining the decisions over what targets to hit rather than allowing the army to call the shots. This was because army commanders had less understanding and appreciation of how air power worked, and also because they could rarely see beyond the immediate battlefield. The doctrine that Tedder and Coningham developed, and which had been subsequently sanctioned by Churchill, was that army commanders could request specific air support and the air commanders would do their best to comply, but the decision as to what they provided and when remained theirs and theirs alone. It was an approach that had paid off handsomely the previous summer of 1942, when the Desert Air Force had saved Eighth Army from annihilation after the fall of Tobruk. It was also air power, working in tandem with a rejuvenated Eighth Army, that helped the DUKE forces – Dominions, UK and Empire – smash the Panzerarmee at Alamein and surge westwards all across Egypt and Libya and into Tunisia.

By the end of the war in North Africa, in Tunisia in May 1943, Coningham was commander of the North African Tactical Air Force, and Tedder now the overall Allied air commander. They were, however, also working hand-in-glove with equally enlightened American air commanders, all of whom were every bit as excited by the possibilities of air power. Driving them were the opportunities aviation offered to reduce the risk on the ground. If air power could save the lives of the young men in the infantry and tanks leading the attacks below, then so much the better.

It was a principle to which men like Major-General Jimmy Doolittle and Lieutenant-General Carl 'Tooey' Spaatz – pronounced 'Spots' – were wedded. Doolittle was one of the most famous men in America: a pioneering aviator, winner of numerous air speed records – including the Schneider Trophy Air Race of 1925 – a sparkling character and, following his leadership of a daring carrier-borne raid on Tokyo in April 1942, also recipient of the Medal of Honor, the United States' highest award for valour. His surname could hardly have been less appropriate: Doolittle had crammed a huge amount into his forty-six years.

He was now in command of the Northwest African Strategic Air Forces, so was responsible for the relentless attacks on Axis lines of communication in Italy, but his immediate superior was General Spaatz. Fifty-one, with resolute jaw, trim silver moustache and ever-twinkling eyes, Spaatz exuded self-assured charisma and authority. With combat experience from the First World War, Spaatz had been a mainstay of the fledgling US Army Air Corps between the wars, believed absolutely in the primacy of air power, and had been at the forefront of modernizing the United States' air forces. Forward-thinking, visionary and extremely energetic, he oozed competence and good sense from every pore.

Sent to Britain in 1940 to observe the unfolding Battle of Britain, Spaatz had swiftly and correctly realized that the Luftwaffe could not win. Rather, the experience helped convince him that immense weight of numbers and ever-improving technology was what was needed for strategic air power to be decisive. In 1942, he had been posted back to England as the first commander of Eighth Air Force, but had then been summoned to North Africa to take over the Twelfth.

He quickly recognized that the Allied air forces out there were far too disjointed to be properly effective. Spaatz had urged greater cooperation and had been listened to. In February 1943, all Allied air forces, whether American or British, came under the single Mediterranean Air Command, with Tedder as its C-in-C. By far the largest component was the Northwest African Air Forces, command of which was given to Spaatz. So it was that by early 1943, British and American air commanders were operating cheek-by-jowl in the Mediterranean, bonded by a pioneering spirit of what they might achieve and working together, for the most part, very effectively too. Complacency was not allowed to creep in; men like Tedder, Spaatz, Doolittle, Coningham and others were always striving to further hone what assets they had and to make air power more effective.

New techniques had emerged during the Sicilian campaign. Pinpointing ground targets was often difficult, especially when flying at high speed and when something on the ground might look like a pinprick even from comparatively low altitudes. 'Rover Davids' had been developed to help counteract this. An RAF officer would team up with an army forward observer and together, in an armoured car, would liaise with both ground and air forces using VHF radio sets, directing aircraft on to the target. Such fighter control techniques still had problems. VHF radios could easily overheat; there were also gaps in the mobile radar network, and even with radio contact it was not always easy to effectively direct aircraft on to a small target. But this was still a brave new world and air power remained an evolving science. The key was to learn and move forward, which the Allied air forces were unquestionably doing; much experience had been gained, particularly during these first eight months of 1943 – knowledge that was now being effectively absorbed. 'The training here,' wrote General Hap Arnold, C-in-C of the USAAF, to Spaatz on 20 August, 'is rapidly catching up with your war experience.' Certainly, Allied senior commanders were agreed that air power remained absolutely key to bringing the war to a swift end.

With this in mind, the opportunities for establishing a strategic air force in Italy began to emerge. Spaatz, for one, was above all a bomber man, and now wedded to the POINTBLANK concept of destroying the Luftwaffe as soon as possible. 'If we can establish ourselves in Italy,' he wrote in a letter to Arnold in June, well before Sicily had even been invaded or a detailed plan for Italy been made, 'much of Germany can be reached from there with better weather conditions at our airdromes than prevail normally in England. This would immediately, when applied, force a dispersion of the German fighter and anti-aircraft defenses.' Arnold was not convinced at that point, but Spaatz did not drop the matter. Three weeks later in July, and with Sicily successfully invaded, Spaatz urged Arnold to back his plans for operating strategic air forces from Italy. 'I am confident we will progress up the Italian Peninsula,' he wrote to his chief, 'and before too many weeks have passed, will be in a position to bomb the fighter production plants in the vicinity of Vienna and other places now beyond the effort out of UK.' He reckoned that from Italy bombers would be able to strike at up to 97 per cent of German fighter production plants.

Arnold was still not entirely persuaded, but Air Chief Marshal Sir Charles Portal, the British Chief of the Air Staff, was thinking very much the same way as Spaatz and eager to have heavy bombers in Italy, within closer range of crucial German aircraft industry targets. As far as Portal was concerned, the Allies should not only invade Italy but move as many strategic air forces there as logistics would allow. Portal's views carried even more weight than those of Spaatz because he was a member of the Combined Chiefs of Staff.

In the meantime, however, those strategic bombers would continue operating from North Africa. The distance was a lot further, but, in tandem with bombers based in Britain, they could further tighten the noose around both the Luftwaffe and the Nazi war effort as a whole.

Meanwhile, Spaatz's Northwest African Air Forces was doggedly carrying out its other roles, and, in this second half of August, that meant primarily blasting enemy lines of communication. Rail marshalling yards and airfields, especially, found themselves relentlessly bombed. So it was that the Allied bombers returned to the Capua area on 26 August, this time hammering Cancello. The pilots of 2./JG53 had already been airborne once that morning and had barely touched back down again at around 11.15 a.m. when they were scrambled once more. It was too late, however, for them to get airborne. Instead, Robert Gugelberger and his fellows in 4. Staffel made a dash for their slit trenches. Across the airfield, Feldwebel Gerhard Waag and the pilots of 6. Staffel were in the same boat. 'This has become standard practice for the Allies,' Waag later jotted in his diary, 'who somehow always know if we have landed.' He could see the bombers coming so, like Gugelberger, dashed for a slit trench. 'Then a frightful crash,' he noted. 'The ground shook and rumbled, clods of dirt fell on us – we were half buried.' When the raiders had passed, he and his comrades crawled out, his legs trembling with fear. Then they saw that a bomb had blasted out a crater that almost reached their slit trench. Another half-metre and they could all have been killed. They'd been lucky. 'Everywhere piles of wreckage,' wrote Waag, 'fuel trucks and aircraft burning, ammunition from the aircraft flying through the air.'

Despite the devastation, none of the pilots or ground crew were even injured, although a number of local Italians had been killed. The following day, Waag looked on as a donkey cart trundled by. He watched an Italian man clamber down and start scooping up the various body parts. Waag was quite shocked. 'It was,' he noted, 'horrible to watch.'

One of those who had been regularly flying against the men of 2./JG53 was Lieutenant Robert 'Smoky' Vrilakas, a fighter pilot in the 94th Fighter Squadron, part of 1st Fighter Group. The son of a Cretan father and an

American mother, Vrilakas had been brought up on a farm in northern California and had initially joined the Army Ground Forces back in early 1941, before the US was even at war. Much to his frustration, however, he had ended up as a typist at 7th Infantry Division HQ. With no interest at all in sitting out the war as a pen-pusher, he began thinking about transferring to the Air Corps. He'd applied without much expectation, but by that time had two years of college education to his name, was bright, fit and ticked all the boxes required by the Air Corps and so, much to his delight and astonishment, he was accepted. A year later he was on his way to the Mediterranean, and flew his first combat mission on 15 July, around the same time as Robert Gugelberger had reached the theatre. Unlike Gugelberger, however, Vrilakas had almost 400 hours' flying time in his logbook, including ninety-eight in the P-38 Lightning.

The Lightning was the only viable fighter escort the Allies could use over targets as high up the Italian leg as Naples, Caserta and Capua. This was because as a twin-boom, twin-engine aircraft it could carry considerably more fuel than a smaller, single-engine fighter. Nor was the Lightning purely a fighter, but rather a multi-role aircraft; it could carry 2 tons of bombs, as much as a German Heinkel 111, for example. It was also bristling with weaponry, with one 20mm cannon and four .50 calibre machine guns, and was used as a day fighter, night fighter, fighter-bomber and ground-attack aircraft, and adapted versions were also used for photo-reconnaissance. And it was fast, as Robert Gugelberger had repeatedly discovered, with speeds well over 400 mph, a terrific rate of climb and a robust airframe. As a twin-engine aircraft it wasn't as manoeuvrable as a single-engine fighter, and its Allison V-1710 engine became less effective the higher the altitude at which it operated, but despite these flaws it remained a formidable aircraft; more to the point, it was the only fighter currently in the Allied arsenal that had the range to escort the bombers as far as Naples and beyond.

On Friday, 30 August 1940 Vrilakas was scheduled to fly his nineteenth combat mission. At Mateur, some twenty miles south-west of Bizerte in northern Tunisia, the pilots of 1st Fighter Group gathered in the briefing tent at 7 a.m. Much of Tunisia was mountainous and hilly, but here, just south of Lake Ichkeul, it was flat, wheat-growing farmland that had once been a lake itself, ideal for a makeshift grass airfield. For a young American, used to the highest living standards of any population in the world, life at Mateur had initially been something of a shock to the system. Vrilakas was not used to existing under canvas, but the airfield was a sea of tents: mess tents, briefing tents, medical tents, maintenance tents, crew tents and tents in which to sleep. Vrilakas found himself sharing a four-man tent with folding cots for beds and a mosquito net – which was needed also to keep out scorpions, beetles and a mass of other bugs. Latrines and showers – fashioned from 50 gallon steel drums – were also primitive and surrounded by canvas. Food was eaten from a mess tin, which every man had to clean himself, but there was only minimal water and never enough soap. As a result, everyone got diarrhoea at some point. In many ways it was not so different from Cancello, just considerably more remote. It had also been home to JG53 earlier in the year; there was still a Messerschmitt there, abandoned when they had moved out. Vrilakas had wasted no time in having himself photographed beside it.

The sun bore down on them relentlessly; it had been blisteringly hot ever since he'd arrived in July, and this Monday morning looked like it was going to be no different: outside, the vast burning blue above them, cloudless and infinite. There was some shade in the briefing tent. Men sat on rough wooden benches, smoking, wearing light summer khaki shirts and chinos, notebooks and pencils in hand to take down the details of call signs, start-engine time and take-off time and any other key pieces of information. Today the target was the marshalling yards at Aversa, north of Naples and south-west of Caserta – close by Cancello. Their task: to escort and protect the twin-engine B-26 bombers of the 319th and 320th Bombardment Groups. Briefing over, they then had to wait. An hour passed, then two.

They finally took off around 10 a.m. amid clouds of swirling dust and the roar of forty-eight P-38 Lightnings, sixteen from each of the group's three squadrons. In no time the coast of North Africa disappeared behind them, then a stretch across the dark Mediterranean until Sicily loomed up ahead, and here they met the formations of B-26 Martin Marauders. Bombing altitude for medium bombers was lower than it was for heavies – generally 10,000–12,000 feet – and so Vrilakas and the rest of the fighter group flew a little above, some 1,000 feet higher. As they neared Italy Vrilakas could hear a humming in his headphones, the sound rising and falling; it was the whirr of the enemy's radar system, scanning the skies for intruders.

Cancello, 11.39 a.m. Scramble! Robert Gugelberger and the pilots of 6./ JG53 run to their machines. Parachute on, climb on to the wing root and clamber into the cockpit. Leads, engine spluttering into life. Throttle open, brakes off. Go. Dust, grit, visibility terrible. Up off the ground.

Begin climbing into the blue. An enemy formation with strong fighter escort approaching. Level off at 4,000 metres – 12,000 feet. Get higher than the enemy escorts. The group had been equipped with rockets slung under the wings – used for the first time the day before and not very effectively. No time had been allowed or fuel spared for practising with these new weapons.

Below, the enemy. Gugelberger could see them: the bombers attacking Aversa, the fighters circling behind them. He and his Staffel dived steeply, reversed course, and then hurtled towards the bombers from dead ahead. A target filled his gunsight. Gugelberger fired his rockets and saw them streak across the sky, straight through the middle of the enemy formation and then explode behind them. Another miss. Gugelberger dived beneath the bombers and then pulled up. There was Steinmüller. They closed up and attacked the P-38 Lightnings, Gugelberger diving and firing a burst of bullets and cannons. No obvious strikes.

Smoky Vrilakas had reached the target amid a few puffs of flak. Bombers completed their run. Bombs away. Ripples of flame and smoke below. Bombers already turning for home, and now it was their turn too. At that moment someone called out, 'Bogies high!' Vrilakas turned his head and saw a mass of enemy fighters – a whole gaggle – diving down towards them. Urgent manoeuvring. Formation flights broken up as Lightnings turned to evade the attackers. Hurtling around the sky, Vrilakas saw Messerschmitt 109s, Italian Macchi 202s and P-38 Lightnings all mixing it up in a swirling melee. An aircraft diving, trailing smoke, others blowing up and plummeting earthwards. Tracer criss-crossing the blue. Suddenly a P-38 and a 109 collided head-on, exploding in a vivid and shocking ball of fire and angry, swirling black smoke. And there, heading out to sea – Harry Rigney's aircraft, on fire. A 94th Fighter Squadron man. A parachute swinging down.

Moments later the aircraft bellied into the water.

In the same part of the sky, Robert Gugelberger, with Feldwebel Steinmüller still flying alongside him, managed to get on the tail of two Lightnings. Positioning himself behind the second, he pressed down on the gun button and fired. Bursts on target. But now tracer and bullets fizzing and whistling past him in turn. Pulling back hard on the stick, his machine climbing vertically. Relief to have got away. Still alive. Glancing down, he saw his target disappearing in flames, shot down by one of his fellow pilots.

A quick look at the fuel gauge. Running low. Time to turn home.

Smoky Vrilakas was wondering whether he'd ever make it home. Everywhere he looked P-38 Lightnings seemed to be plunging out of the sky. They'd been bounced for once, and no mistake. A glance at his fuel gauge. Dogfighting used up juice. Time to turn for home, and he heard his squadron leader, Lieutenant Jimmy Dibble, give the order to head around the Bay of Naples and try and reform. Suddenly, a 27th Squadron P-38 sped past him, a 109 on his tail, firing. Vrilakas broke into him, opened fire, cannon and .50 calibre machine guns raking the enemy aircraft. Moments later it broke off, diving in a spiralling, uncontrolled spin.

A victory, but there was danger ahead as the manoeuvre had taken him out over the Bay of Naples and towards more enemy fighters. The rest of the squadron was now out of sight. Vrilakas was on his own. And badly outnumbered.

Only one thing for it. Vrilakas pushed forward the control column and dived for the sea. Tracer whipping past him. Glance in the mirror and behind. The black and white spinner of a Messerschmitt 109 just 100 yards behind. Bullets rattling his airframe with a rippling metallic clang, then an occasional louder burst as a cannon shell exploded. Kick left rudder to yaw the ship – make it a harder target. Tracer veering too far, then another clatter as the German pilot corrected his aim once more. Vrilakas hugged the sea, as close as he dared. Spumes of water ahead of him where his enemy's bullets were hitting the water.

At any moment his engine could explode or his P-38 plunge into the water. Why hadn't it? But now he saw he was overtaking another Messerschmitt directly ahead and 100 feet above him. Thoughts racing through his mind. If he climbed up and opened fire, he would expose himself to the 109 behind him. On the other hand, he was travelling so fast he would soon overtake it and then he'd have two enemy on his tail, not one. *If I'm going*, thought Vrilakas, *I'm taking him with me.*

Pulling up, he opened fire with all four machine guns and his cannon. Smoke from the 109, but also a crash on his own airframe as his pursuer opened fire again. One bullet creased the canopy, knocking out the rear plexiglas, which shattered all around the cockpit. Some even went into his mouth. Dive for the deck again. Right engine oil temperature rising – but mercifully no more bullets. Shut down starboard engine; a glance at the left. Despite cannon and bullet holes, his P-38 was still flying. No rapid fuel loss either. Behind him, his pursuer had gone. Low on fuel, no doubt, and the P-38 looking good to soon hit the water.

Vrilakas called up Dibble on the radio. His squadron leader and two others agreed to turn round, find him and nurse him home – not to Mateur, but to Sicily, which thank God was now in Allied hands. Then there they were, on his wings, flying over the sea, Sicily taking an interminably long time to appear. Would his ship make it? His airframe was riddled with bullet and cannon holes. One blackened engine was out.

At last he spotted Sicily. An airfield under construction, but with enough pierced-steel planking for him to attempt a landing. Carefully, Vrilakas lined up and came in to land. Relief. But now a truck was crossing the end of the runway ahead of him, and so at the last moment he pulled up and went around again, heart in his mouth. Runway lining up a second time. This occasion clear. Speed dropping, height dropping. Touch down. Taxi clear and shut down – only for his second engine to now burst into flames. A waiting fireman rushed forward, spraying the flames with an extinguisher.

'I sat quietly in the cock for a moment,' noted Vrilakas, 'considering how fortunate I had just been to survive.' He tried to let the adrenaline subside. Physically and emotionally, he was exhausted. Silently he offered thanks to God. When he did finally clamber down, his P-38 looked like a sieve. Between sixty and eighty holes had perforated his machine. Even the props had several holes in them.

The 94th alone lost five planes that day, including two pilots killed, while the 71st lost three and the 27th one. Those were high figures for one fighter group – losses they were not used to suffering. For once, it seemed, the Axis fighter pilots had come out on top, although not by much: six German planes had also been shot down, including Unteroffizier Leo Niesen from 4./JG53. The Italians had not lost any on this occasion.

The air battle over Italy would continue in the days and weeks to come, but soon was to be joined by the battle on the ground. The following day, Tuesday, 31 August, Italian Generale Giuseppe Castellano arrived at General Sir Harold Alexander's 15th Army Group HQ at Cassibile in Sicily to talk terms. The next day, the fourth anniversary of Germany's invasion of Poland, those terms would be accepted. Italy was about to get out of the war, yet the war was coming to Italy.

The typhoon of steel was approaching.

CHAPTER 2

Conundrums

SATURDAY, 4 SEPTEMBER 1943 was the nineteenth birthday of Pasqualina Caruso, a young Neapolitan girl whose world, like those of most of the 40 million Italians, had been turned upside down by the war. The daughter of the Chief Secretary of the State Railways in Naples, she had grown up in a comfortable middle-class existence, and one that had supported Mussolini and Fascism. Back in June 1940, as a sixteen-year-old, she had thought *Il Duce* a great man and had been excited, as had so many, at the prospect of war and military victories. Yet, my, how those promises had been ground into the dust! Just over three years on, Italy lay ruined, many of its cities bombed and crushed, just as the British had warned they would be in the days before Mussolini's declaration of war.

Pasqualina – or 'Lina' as she was known to her family and friends – could not imagine a worse birthday. It was, she thought, the saddest day of her life. Every day came reports of more air raids, of more people killed and of beautiful buildings crushed. She had heard and seen the bombers thundering over, waves of them, often filling the sky. 'What most scares me in this war,' she confided to her diary, 'are the bombs.' She was living in Eboli, a town some fifty miles south-east of Naples, with her mother, aunt and sisters; they had evacuated her home city earlier in the year after the first air raids and now lived in a modest house next to the old *castello* at the top of the town. Her father was still in Naples, however. She worried about him constantly. She worried about all of them, about Italy, about the future.

That evening, Eboli was deserted. Everyone in the town was demoralized. How could they not be? Food was short, yet, as her father reminded them, they were better off there than in Naples, where there was now no gas for cooking, no coal, no running water. The only water to be had was from trucks passing through distributing it to the population. Of course, there was never enough and so the crowds fought to get just a litre. Even out in Eboli there were no medicines, no disinfectants, no quinine, no cotton wool, no bandages.

'Lord, Lord,' she implored, 'help us save ourselves.'

That evening, Lina Caruso felt absolutely wretched. 'By now,' she scribbled, 'Italy is a land of the dead: we no longer laugh, we no longer sing, we no longer play, we no longer enjoy, we only cry and die.'

She was not alone in feeling the blackest despair. Countless Italians felt the same way. They had had enough of war, and frankly who could blame them? Since the glory days of victory against poorly armed Ethiopians in Abyssinia more than seven years earlier, the strutting militarism and grandiose plans for a new Italian empire had been shown up for the total sham they always had been. Parades, cockerel feathers in helmets and march-pasts were one thing; the harsh reality of a brutal war for which Italy was never remotely prepared was quite another. Stuck in the Mediterranean, the Italians had no real access to the world's oceans, not much of a merchant fleet, few natural resources of their own, and a military that was cumbersome, top-heavy, corrupt and shamefully out of date compared with nations like Britain, with whom, from June 1940, they had become embroiled. War was declared on Britain and France on the assumption that both would soon exit the war with Germany. Only France had signed an armistice, however. The gamble had been a disastrous one because from the outset Italian strategy had faltered badly.

The trouble was, the vision for Italy's war had been driven not by the King, Vittorio Emanuele III, nor his ministers, but by Benito Mussolini, the autocratic leader of the Fascist Party. Since 1922, Italy had been a one-party dictatorship under this unquestionably charismatic but fatally flawed man. As dictator, Mussolini had tended to listen to what he wanted to hear. When ministers cautioned him, he ignored them. When his senior military commanders warned him that baiting the British in Egypt was not a good idea, he ordered them to press ahead anyway. He believed in the edifice that he had created despite its palpable fragility: that his Italy would be a new Rome, and that it was his destiny to rule most of the Mediterranean, as well as vast swathes of North and East Africa. The King, a rather insipid figure at the best of times, had not been willing to blunt *Il Duce.* Nor had the senior military figures in Italy. Nor even

Mussolini's son-in-law, Count Galeazzo Ciano, Italy's Foreign Minister, who had tried hard to avert war but not so hard that he was prepared to stand up to the dictator.

How horribly mistaken all those who had marched to the Fascist drum had proved to be. Humiliated by the Greeks in 1940, they then lost two armies in Egypt and Libya and all the territory they had gained in East Africa. At sea, their navy – the most modern part of their armed forces – was humbled at Taranto and sent to the seabed at Cape Matapan. As if that wasn't bad enough, a further army was lost in the snow and misery of the Eastern Front, while Italian troops struggled to control the ever-fractious Balkans and Greeks once the Germans had come to their rescue. In both places, Italian troops were responsible for razing villages and massacring locals, just as they had in Abyssinia.

Along with their German allies, a further quarter of a million troops subsequently surrendered in Tunisia, including most of the best trained and experienced, and then, in thirty-eight days in July and August 1943, Sicily was overrun.

This was not at all what Mussolini had promised. Italy had never had much in the first place, but by mid-July 1943 it was broken. There was almost no fuel, either for vehicles or for heating; most private vehicles had been requisitioned in any case. Electricity was frequently cut. Food was not just short but scarce: Italians in cities were lucky to eke out 1,000 calories a day through rationing and, more often than not, there was not even enough to keep to the ration scales. Shops were bare of goods. An entire generation of young men were now dead, in prisoner-of-war camps in Britain and North America, or dotted across territory Italy could no longer effectively control.

The Allies had begun bombing Italy the previous year, but this had intensified since the spring and was now rising to a crescendo. Few in Italy endured the bombings with the weary stoicism shown by German civilians. Suffering terror bombing had not been part of Mussolini's pledge either. Half the population of Milan had left, while the southern cities – Naples and Taranto especially – were increasingly visited by huge formations of Allied heavy bombers. Sicily's cities, which had borne the brunt since the end in North Africa in May, now lay crushed. Millions in Italy were destitute and starving. Infrastructure lay wrecked, nothing worked and normal existence was impossible. If there was worthwhile motivation for facing these appalling challenges, the situation might have been different, but most in Italy felt motivation for one thing only: an end to the war in very quick order.

The Fascist Grand Council had forced Mussolini out on 25 July 1943, and Ciano had played a key part in his defenestration, at last standing up to his father-in-law. Even the King had finally found the necessary steel to endorse the deposition. And while a number of diehards refused to believe that Mussolini could be to blame for the catastrophe confronting Italy and had insisted that culpability lay with his craven ministers, these were comparatively few. For the most part, the news of Mussolini's fall prompted scenes of widespread jubilation. Mussolini had gone! Fascism was over! And, as if to prove the point, photographs of the King and Maresciallo Pietro Badoglio, who had taken over as Prime Minister, now showed only their heads and shoulders, so no one could see the Fascist symbols on the uniforms they had worn until a day earlier.

Maresciallo Badoglio had been called by the King to take over as head of the government shortly after Mussolini had been arrested on 26 July. He was white-haired, with a trim but full white moustache and rather large, sad, deep-brown eyes. Badoglio was also a couple of months short of his seventy-second birthday, so was an old man. It was Badoglio who had led Italian troops into Abyssinia and who had also authorized the use of mustard gas on the native Ethiopians; much blame could be directed Mussolini's way, but not this. It had been Badoglio's idea.

He had also been Chief of Staff of the Armed Forces, the Comando Supremo, from 1925 until December 1940, and so was in large part responsible for the hapless state of the Italian military when it went to war in June 1940. In fairness, he'd been pessimistic about Italy's chances, recognizing that victories against native East Africans with the help of chemical weapons were probably the limit of its capabilities. On the other hand, when Mussolini pressed for war he did nothing to stop him. Since resigning after the woeful invasion of Greece, Badoglio had been sitting out an easy retirement, suffering very little compared with so many Italians. Summoned by the King on that fateful July afternoon to take over as Prime Minister, he felt unable to refuse his offer. 'I knew that the King trusted me, that His Majesty would be embarrassed if I refused,' he noted, 'and that my refusal would still further complicate a situation which called for immediate reaction.' And so, taking a deep breath, he decided to do the decent thing and accept. It was a brute of a job, but someone had to do it.

Badoglio might have looked like an aged basset hound, but there was arrogance and even hubris in his acceptance of the singular honour the King was handing him. It was reminiscent of how Pétain had taken control as

France collapsed, except that the Maréchal had been a genuine hero to many and a highly competent commander.

Now, in Italy's hour of need, someone younger, fitter, less tarnished by the despicable regime that had just been overthrown, with a bit less blood on his hands, might have been a better choice, but then again the King had sat back and first watched Fascism take hold in Italy and then allowed Mussolini to bring the country into war, so hoping that Vittorio Emanuele III might make a half-decent decision was probably expecting too much.

In truth, the King had not chosen Badoglio because he was trusted by the people. He had called upon him because he was a conservative, a royalist, and he knew that he could rely on him to be true to his monarch. In an age when Western monarchs increasingly believed their role was to serve the people, Vittorio Emanuele firmly belonged to an earlier era in which it was the people's duty to serve the King; following Mussolini's fall, he decided his first task was to save the monarchy rather than his subjects' misery, and he reckoned Badoglio was the man most likely to safeguard his future. As if to press the point, the King had laid down some rules for his new Prime Minister. Aware of growing republican sentiments among those who blamed him as well as Mussolini for Italy's predicament, there were to be no political parties. Fascism was dead, but a dictatorship was not. At least Fascism had been a political party; now there was nothing – just Old Man Badoglio and a strange void.

In fairness to Badoglio, he was aware of the poisoned chalice he'd been given. Italy was in a truly terrible situation, between the devil and the deep blue sea. Clearly, almost no one in the country had any stomach left to continue the fight. Italy was on its knees, broken, physically, materially and spiritually. Yet the country was now swarming with German troops. If the Italians suddenly announced they were done with fighting, they could not expect the Germans to acquiesce and sue for peace too. Rather, the German response would be immediate and extremely violent. And who could be trusted? Certainly not the Germans; their entire alliance had been built around mutual mistrust. What about the Allies? Could they be trusted, should the Italians sue for an armistice? No, they could not. And whom could he trust within the military and political elites in Italy itself, who had all been plotting behind each other's backs for months? A rock and a hard place, without doubt.

So, what to do? How on earth were they going to get out of this mess? For several days Badoglio, the King, Generale Vittorio Ambrosio – the current head of the Comando Supremo – and the new military ministers frantically assessed their options. As if to help them, the Allies also eased up on the bombing of Italian targets. By 31 July, the Italians had decided to make contact with the Allies and seek an armistice – the marginally better of two evils. It was vital, though, that the Germans should not find out. So, outwardly Badoglio reassured the Germans that Italy was still very much in the fight. 'The war continues,' he announced, dismaying Italian civilians, who stopped their street parties immediately, but convincing absolutely no one else. The words had barely left his lips when the Allied bombers returned, hitting Rome on 1 August. A thousand people were killed and a further 2,000 wounded.

A few days later, the Italians made clandestine contact with the Allies, and it was arranged that Generale Giuseppe Castellano would travel to Madrid and then Lisbon under the pretence of meeting the Italian ambassador to Chile, who was visiting. Castellano, a Sicilian, had become the youngest general in the Italian Army, was considered one of its brightest stars, and at fifty was still darkly good-looking and also a close friend of Count Ciano. At any rate, Castellano was well connected and smooth as glass, and currently working on Ambrosio's staff. In other words, he was smart and dependable, vehemently anti-German, but not an especially big fish – ideally placed to open surrender negotiations under the German radar.

Castellano had travelled by train using a false passport made out for 'Raimond Imas' and in Madrid met Sir Samuel Hoare, the British ambassador to Spain, on 15 August, two days before the fall of the Axis powers in Sicily. It was a strange reversal of the situation in 1940, when Britain had been staring down the barrel and the Italians had offered to be the go-between for any peace feelers to Germany. Italy's position, Castellano admitted to Hoare, was terrible. German troops were pouring down the Brenner Pass, the old boundary between Italy and Austria, and via Trieste, and there was nothing the Italians could do about it; their army, although large, was badly equipped, especially when compared with the Germans. Morale was terrible. The Regia Aeronautica was now almost non-existent. Feelings in Italy against the Germans were intense. But the Italians were powerless unless supported by strong Allied landings along the boot of Italy. If that happened, the million Italian troops in Italy would then be prepared to immediately switch sides and fight alongside the Allies against the Germans. Badoglio, Castellano reported, regarded every passing hour as critical because of the never-ending arrival of more

German troops. The Italians had demanded that this cease and had even manned defences up near the Brenner Pass, but the Germans had largely ignored such requests. There were no less than thirteen German divisions already in Italy.

This was immediately fed back to General Dwight D. Eisenhower – or 'Ike' as he was widely known, the American Supreme Allied Commander in the Mediterranean – at his HQ which was still, in the blazing heat of mid-August, in Algiers, 700 miles as the crow flies from the toe of the boot of Italy.

Yet if Italy was staring at total collapse and brutal German vengeance, the Allies' position was also problematic, to say the least, despite the victory in Sicily. The Allies were becoming badly stretched with the demands of this global war. They were currently very committed to the Mediterranean, while the Americans and Australians were fighting the Japanese in the Pacific and the British and Indian Army in Burma. The Americans, especially, were also pouring huge amounts of supplies into China to support the Nationalists, which meant getting these first to Assam, a remote corner of north-east India, and then flying them over the Himalayas. Then there was the Allies' strategic air campaign against Germany, which involved first building and establishing ever more air bases in England, and then flying increasing numbers of heavy bombers to target the Reich. Both the Americans, particularly, and Britain were also shipping immense quantities of supplies to the Soviet Union. The US was additionally sending war materiel to Britain, while Britain was providing no small amount of war materiel to the Americans to help their build-up of forces in the UK. As if those commitments weren't enough, the ongoing shipping war in the Atlantic, which, admittedly, had abated since May, still required a considerable naval effort. Every part of this global war effort absorbed gargantuan levels of shipping – shipping that was still in short supply because of miscalculations made the previous autumn as to how long the Tunisian campaign would last. A backlog had been caused which was still being felt, but which was also understandable when the turnaround time from the US to the Mediterranean could be more than seventy-five days and to the south-west Pacific more than 115 days, and when the British and Americans had different approaches to calculating and operating merchant shipping.

They also had different approaches to strategy, even though a broad approach had been agreed by the United States and Britain back in

December 1941, following the American entry into the war. This was to pursue a Germany-first policy, but there had been a considerable shift this current year, 1943. In December 1941, the US had been a fledgling military power whose factories were just beginning to realize their enormous potential. In January 1943, the United States' war leaders were still feeling their way, and at the Casablanca Conference had been completely outmanoeuvred by the better-prepared British.

The next major conference had been Trident, held in Washington in May 1943 – so a home advantage for the Americans, but also begun with a far clearer notion on their part of what their strategic priorities were. Although the invasion of Sicily had been locked in at the Casablanca Conference in January, nothing had been agreed beyond that, so there was a lot to resolve. The British began the talks believing a cross-Channel invasion might not even be possible in 1944, while the Americans absolutely wanted to ring-fence it for the first half of that year. They also substantially accelerated commitment to the war against Japan, with operations in Burma, increased support for the Chinese, and a greater effort in the Pacific. The Mediterranean didn't feature at all in American aims; but it was the centrepiece of British plans for the future war against the Axis in Europe.

There was unquestionably mutual respect between the Americans and the British and, for the most part, the senior commanders and political leaders got on very well. President Franklin D. Roosevelt and Prime Minister Winston Churchill had a strong working relationship, while the leading commanders – the Combined Chiefs of Staff – also mostly liked and respected one another. There were, though, inevitably differences of approach and priority, and there were also suspicions and elements of mistrust on both sides. And while they were known collectively as the 'Allies', there had never been any formal alliance signed by the United States and Britain. Rather, they were coalition partners. They were still cooperating to achieve a common aim, but not bound as formally as an alliance.

The British way, ever since France had collapsed in June 1940, tended to approach strategy opportunistically, responding to various crises and trying to exploit their enemy's weaknesses. North Africa had been a case in point. Germany's strength had lain primarily in its land power and, to an extent, air power. What it lacked was shipping, especially of the freighter variety. Militarily, Britain's focus had been its dominant maritime power and burgeoning air power, so it had made sense to fight in far-off places which were much harder for the Axis forces to supply. The British also firmly believed that a Germany-first strategy meant that winning the war in Europe was the top priority, and that the Japanese could be held at bay until the Nazis were no more and then dealt with.

By contrast, the Americans wanted to go all-out with a different strategic approach, which was, in essence, to draw a straight line to Berlin, attack along the shortest route and work out what they needed to make that happen. Obviously, this meant launching an assault from Britain across the English Channel and into occupied northern France. There was very sound good sense to this. Britain could become an enormous base camp from which to launch – and then maintain – such an operation. The Mediterranean, on the other hand, was quite a long way from Britain, even further from the United States, and if the Allies now invaded Italy the logistical challenges would be suddenly switched; supplying Italy overland from the Reich was obviously more straightforward than sailing literally every bullet and box of bully beef through the Mediterranean or from the Middle East. What's more, dealing with Japan as quickly as possible was the highest priority for Admiral Ernest King, the C-in-C of the US Navy, for the President and for the US Chiefs of Staff.

So from the American perspective there were some very obvious stumbling blocks in continuing an ongoing strategy in the Mediterranean. Churchill had grandiose plans to secure the entire Aegean and eastern Mediterranean, bring in Turkey and support the partisans, although, as he made clear, an invasion of Italy was the centrepiece of these intentions; and, in fairness, there were some logical reasons for that. Italy was only an inch away from Sicily across the Straits of Messina, and then Allied forces would be on mainland Europe. If Italy could be forced out of the war, that would mean German troops would have to either retreat – which seemed unlikely, because Hitler had proved time and again his reluctance to ever do so – or replace the Italian troops now garrisoning Italy itself, the Balkans and much of Greece and the Aegean with German troops. These forces would have to come from somewhere – probably the Eastern or Western Fronts, or both. There were currently thirty-two Italian divisions in the Balkans, for example, no small number. In addition there were some 1,400 aircraft of the Regia Aeronautica in the region; without them, the already overstretched Luftwaffe would be even more overcommitted. Drawing the Germans to much greater involvement in the Mediterranean was clearly good news for the Allies: it would relieve some pressure for the Soviets, but also make the task of crossing the English Channel the following summer that little bit easier. Tying down German troops in the south was unquestionably a good thing for the Allies to do.

The Americans accepted the validity of these arguments, but future strategy was really about prioritizing. Naturally, it would be good to bring greater pressure on Germany – and Japan – from all angles and multiple fronts, but even the American arsenals would only stretch so far. All Allied operations involved gargantuan amounts of shipping, and so this was the prime limiting factor. The Trident Conference was of enormous importance because it set the pattern for future US and British global strategy, but also demonstrated the growing weight of American opinion compared with that of the British. Commitment was given by the British to a cross-Channel invasion in 1944. They wanted to launch in June, the Americans April; they settled for 1 May. There was also a commitment to POINTBLANK, the strategic air campaign to destroy the Luftwaffe ahead of the cross-Channel invasion, which had been first proposed at Casablanca; this was formally launched the following month, June 1943. In addition, Britain accepted that the Americans would substantially accelerate the Pacific campaign; the overall strategy might still be Germany first, but it was Japan only fractionally second, and first in terms of the US Navy. On the other hand, the US chiefs did accept a less ambitious approach to South East Asia and China. Furthermore, they agreed to continue operations in the Mediterranean, but with some very strict caveats: crucially, that three bomb groups, plus all assault shipping and seven Allied divisions currently in theatre, would leave for Britain by 1 November 1943. Any amphibious operations in the Mediterranean were to be complete by then.

Trident had taken place before the Allies had launched HUSKY, the invasion of Sicily; but by 25 July, when Mussolini was overthrown and by which time the outcome of the Sicilian campaign was no longer in doubt, thoughts were sharpening over the shape of future operations in the Mediterranean. Two major concerns remained in the minds of the American chiefs with regard to the British. The first was a suspicion that British hearts were not really in OVERLORD, as the cross-Channel invasion had now become. At Trident, it had prompted pessimistic assessments from the British chiefs; the Americans were very aware that the shadow of the Western Front and the defeat of 1940 still clouded British thinking, a fact openly admitted by Churchill. 'The fearful price we had to pay in human life and blood for the great offensives of the First World War,' noted Churchill, 'was graven in my mind.' This did not mean the British were against it, however; they perked up considerably and many of the concerns of the cross-Channel operation melted away when transposed on to an invasion of Italy. 'The wish,' General George C. Marshall, the US Chief of Staff, gently wondered, 'might have been father to the thought.'

And this was the nub of the second concern – that the Mediterranean campaign would suck in ever more resources. As Marshall had pointed out during the Trident talks, offensives, once launched, always generated demands for yet greater resources. 'The only limit to TORCH,' he had said of the invasion of North-west Africa in November 1942, 'was the availability of shipping. The Tunisian campaign continued to draw in more and more troops. Operations invariably create a vacuum in which it is essential to pour in more and more means. Once undertaken the operation must be backed to the limit.' What worried him, then, was that any future Mediterranean campaign would inevitably increase in scale and commitment, and very possibly at the expense of OVERLORD.

Meanwhile, Eisenhower, while also overseeing the campaign in Sicily, had got his planners working on the limited future operations in the Mediterranean that would follow the battle there. Eisenhower had been appointed Supreme Allied Commander back at the Casablanca Conference at the start of the year. So far he had handled the multinational coalition air, land and naval forces very well, with tact, deft diplomacy and even-handedness; but as far as he was concerned the heavy caveat imposed by the Americans limited what could be reasonably expected, and in this he was absolutely right. Plans were drawn up for attacks on Sardinia, Corsica and also the toe of Italy, but by this time General Marshall had had something of a change of heart. In June he had visited Allied Forces HQ in Algiers with Churchill, and although he had stood up pretty well to the Prime Minister's all-out charm offensive he had started to wonder whether there might be some advantages to an operation on the Italian mainland after all. The subsequent successful landings in Sicily had also allowed Churchill to give full voice to much more ambitious plans for Italy. 'Why should we crawl up the leg like a harvest-bug from the ankle upwards?' the Prime Minister put to the Combined Chiefs. 'Let us rather strike at the knee.' That way, he argued, they could capture Rome, which would undoubtedly prove a huge psychological and political victory. Furthermore, they could then secure the airfield complex around Foggia.

The town of Foggia lay at the heart of an area of flat plain in central southern Italy, which was ideal for air operations. If the Foggia area could be captured, then the Allies could send a heavy bomber force there. These bombers could further tighten the noose around Nazi Germany, but would also be closer to the German aircraft plants in southern Germany and Austria, the destruction of which lay at the heart of POINTBLANK. Even better, they would be far closer to Ploesti in Romania, the only source of real – rather than synthetic – oil for Germany.

Marshall had begun to accept that by exploiting the imminent collapse of Italy there were clear advantages for OVERLORD. On 16 July, he persuaded the Combined Chiefs to instruct Eisenhower to explore the possibilities of an amphibious operation in the Naples area. He also stressed the importance of 'boldness and taking justifiable risks'. This was music to the ears of Churchill, who was without doubt the greatest advocate of a substantial and ongoing Mediterranean strategy. However, it was the airfields at Foggia that were uppermost in Marshall's mind. They were too for General Hap Arnold, who had swiftly come round to Spaatz's way of thinking that strategic air bases in Italy would be a huge benefit for POINTBLANK and so also OVERLORD. Since Spaatz had first argued for the build-up of strategic air forces in Italy, British intelligence had learned of German plans to disperse aircraft assembly plants even further into Austria and elsewhere, beyond bomber range from England. This meant they could only be effectively reached from Italy. But while for the Americans and the air chiefs the airfields around Foggia and even further north, in the Po Valley, were key, for Churchill a further glittering prize existed. 'All being said and done,' he wrote to General Alexander, 'no objective can compete with the capture of Rome.'

Plans got under way to prepare for a host of different options, which would allow that flexible, opportunistic strategy the British so favoured; what course they eventually took depended on how events panned out in Sicily. With the battle there going well, Churchill was chomping at the bit for a resolution; psychologically, he'd crossed a point where there was to be no turning back from the goal of taking Rome. 'The moment is now approaching when this choice must be made,' Churchill wrote to his old friend, the South African General Jan Smuts, on 16 July, 'and I need not tell you I shall make it a capital issue . . . I will in no circumstances allow the powerful British and British-controlled armies in the Mediterranean to stand idle.' Smuts was a sympathetic ear. Rome had to be taken, Churchill wrote, and their armies should then march as far north in Italy as possible. 'I am confident of a good result,' he added, 'and I shall go to all lengths to procure the agreement of our Allies. If not, we have ample forces to act by ourselves.'

The truth, however, was that the British did not have enough to go it alone in Italy. If they were honest, they didn't really have enough even with the buy-in of the Americans, who were now on board with the Italian venture, despite misgivings.

This was the awful conundrum the Allies now found themselves in on that Tuesday, 17 August 1943, when giant events all seemed to be converging. They had too many troops in the Mediterranean to do nothing, and very many good strategic reasons to invade Italy, but they did not have enough to win these prizes easily or even with anything like a guarantee of success.

Yet the stone had already begun to roll down the hill. Strategic momentum had taken root. By 17 August, the modest plans to attempt a grab of just Sardinia, Corsica and a foothold in the toe of the boot had already been kicked into the long grass – but at the direction of the Combined Chiefs of Staff and, specifically, by General George C. Marshall. Churchill and his grandiose plans could be kept in check, but Marshall's intervention in July had made all the difference now that the Americans held the ascendency in terms of future strategy.

What was now being planned was altogether more ambitious: the Corps Expéditionnaire Français – the French Expeditionary Corps, or CEF – was going to be given the task of clearing out Sardinia and Corsica, while in addition Eighth Army was to cross the Straits of Messina and get into the toe of Italy. But then, a few days later, the US Fifth Army would land much further up the peninsula in the Naples area: this last point had been insisted upon by the Combined Chiefs on 27 July, following Eisenhower's recommendation to invade the mainland. Naples was 300 miles by winding road, much of it through mountains, from the Straits. Quite a significant distance would be separating the two forces. The idea was that Eighth Army would clear the toe and southern part of the boot, Fifth Army would make its landing a short time later, and then, soon after, the two forces would meet, clear the rest of southern Italy and the Foggia airfields and advance on Rome. There were other plans too: possible further landings at Crotone, at the base of the boot, where there was a large airfield, and Taranto, in the western heel, which was a major naval base and port. Suddenly the plans for Italy had ballooned.

These plans – albeit still imprecise ones – were none the less largely ironed out by Eisenhower at Algiers on 16 August, and rubber-stamped with his senior commanders the following day. Operation BAYTOWN would see Eighth Army, under General Sir Bernard Montgomery, cross the Straits of Messina sometime between 1 and 4 September. Shipping available for this would be limited, which was why there was no further thought of landing Eighth Army a little bit further up the boot; it was one thing beetling back and forth across the few miles of the Straits of Messina, but quite another to land a force of similar size further afield. So BAYTOWN was to be in the toe.

Then, on 9 September, General Mark Clark's Fifth Army would launch Operation AVALANCHE, landing not at Naples but at Salerno, around thirty miles to the south. There might then also be a limited landing north of the toe by part of Eighth Army, code-named Operation BUT-TRESS. Eisenhower hoped this would not be needed, however. These plans still had to be confirmed by the Combined Chiefs, now converging in Quebec for the Quadrant Conference.

The Supreme Allied Commander had barely concluded the com-manders' conference about the plans for invading Italy when, after lunch, news reached his HQ at Algiers from Madrid that Generale Castellano wanted to hold talks in Lisbon. Ike immediately called Brigadier Kenneth Strong, the British head of his intelligence staff, and also the British Resi-dent Minister of State in the Mediterranean, Harold Macmillan. The latter had only just returned from a week in London. Churchill and the Chiefs of Staff were about to start the Quadrant Conference that very same day, but Macmillan had had an opportunity to gauge the British mood back home and also receive instructions. On the former, he reported that weariness was creeping in after nearly four years of war. On the latter, and somewhat paradoxically, the British were insisting on the terms laid out at Casablanca in January: only unconditional surrender from the Axis would do, whether they be German or Italian.

After consultation, Eisenhower, Strong and Macmillan agreed that one or more staff officers should be sent to Lisbon. Approval for this was then granted by the President, Prime Minister and Combined Chiefs in Wash-ington. So it was that on Thursday, 19 August 1943 Brigadier Strong and Eisenhower's Chief of Staff, General Walter Bedell-Smith, found themselves at the British Embassy in Lisbon talking with 'Raimond Imas' – Generale Giuseppe Castellano. It was all very cloak-and-dagger in a city that had become a hotbed of spies, but Castellano's paranoia about being caught by the Germans was considerable and, frankly, understandable.

Castellano confessed to loathing the Germans. Rolling out a map, he pointed to where all the German divisions in Italy were now based, which was sobering and dwarfed the number of German forces there had been on Sicily. Neither party had the authority to conclude an armistice, but Bedell-Smith made it clear that only unconditional surrender would cut it. Castellano, on the other hand, made it equally clear that the Italians wanted to switch sides and fight alongside the Allies. 'Where is Mussolini?' Bedell-Smith asked him.

'Hitler would like to know too,' Castellano replied cryptically, without elaborating.

Castellano was sent on his way, both with the gist of Allied demands – which were immediately named the 'Short Terms' and which had been largely drawn up by Macmillan – and also a small transmitter and appropriate cipher to allow for a secure radio channel between Rome and Algiers.

Yet no sooner had Castellano departed Lisbon than a second Italian general arrived, Generale Giacomo Zanussi. He had been sent not by Ambrosio but by the tough former head of the Italian 2a Armata in Yugoslavia, Generale Mario Roatta, now the Italian Chief of Staff. This made him number two to Ambrosio. Roatta had been concerned that they'd heard nothing at all from Castellano since 12 August. Fearing he had been arrested by the Allies, Roatta had accordingly dispatched Zanussi, although it soon became clear he'd done so without much, if any, consultation with either Badoglio or Ambrosio. At any rate, Zanussi presented himself to the Allies on 27 August, but with the British General Adrian Carton de Wiart in tow as a sign of good faith. Carton de Wiart was a one-eyed Victoria Cross winner who had amputated his own hand during the Battle of Passchendaele back in 1917. He was one of the most senior prisoners in Italian hands, having been captured during a clandestine mission to Yugoslavia in 1941.

Bedell-Smith promptly handed Zanussi a copy of the Allies' 'Long Terms' – in other words the small print of a proposed armistice, which outlined the economic, financial and political obligations that were to be assumed by the Italians. The arrival of first Castellano and then Zanussi seemed to the Allies either rather fishy or hapless; it was not clear which. Neither Castellano nor Zanussi appeared to be part of any Italian joined up thinking, which was largely because they were not. Badoglio had sent Castellano; Roatta had sent Zanussi. In truth, the Italians were panicking. German troops were flooding in, the Allies were playing hardball, and disaster loomed.

However, from the Allied perspective it did now seem likely that one of the reasons for invading Italy was about to be met. An armistice had not been agreed yet, but it was looking odds-on to happen imminently. What form that would take and how events would play out, however, was still very much up for grabs; and without as many amphibious assault vessels as the Allies would like, which in turn would severely limit the number of troops that could be landed at Salerno, the position of the Italian military was now taking an altogether more significant turn.

In the meantime, Allied plans for the invasion continued, with the clock ticking inexorably and the day of judgement fast approaching. Caution and minimizing risk had been the watchwords for HUSKY. Little more than seven weeks later, those appeared to have been thrown out with the dishwater. The Allies had got themselves into a bit of a pickle, because no matter how Eisenhower and his senior commanders and planners looked at it, BAYTOWN appeared too half-hearted and AVALANCHE seemed increasingly like an appallingly high-risk undertaking. Nor were the two operations sufficiently mutually supportive; even with Eighth Army landing ahead of Fifth Army at Salerno, 300 miles over mountains and rivers across which all bridges could be expected to have been destroyed was a very big distance. Clark's troops at Salerno would need Monty's men to join them in quick order, but that was a very big ask.

What to do? Without adequate assault shipping, there was not much they could do about it. The Combined Chiefs had instructed them to plan for an amphibious assault near Naples, and that was exactly what they had done. The plans for AVALANCHE were the best that could be achieved in the time and with the hamstrung resources available. Yet there was no doubting that political and strategic pressure had suddenly put operational and tactical plans into a very tight corner.

It was a conundrum with no obvious solution, and one made worse by the lack of concrete intelligence about German intentions. By 20 August, decrypts of German radio traffic, known as 'Ultra', confirmed what Generale Castellano had warned about Germany reinforcing Italy. The Allies now knew that sixteen German divisions were in Italy, including the four badly mauled in Sicily; there had been just two on that island when the Allies had landed back in July. They also knew that Feldmarschall Erwin Rommel was commanding the newly formed Heeresgruppe – army group – B and that Feldmarschall Albert Kesselring, a Luftwaffe field marshal, had been commander-in-chief, South of all German troops since the end of 1941. That meant two Heeresgruppen. That was a lot.

What's more, Ultra decrypts confirmed all that Castellano had told them. The list of German divisions he'd given them tallied.

Castellano also offered more information, which was passed on to the Combined Chiefs in Quebec: that there were several thousand SS troops in Rome as well as the 3. Panzergrenadier and 2. Fallschirmjäger (para chute) divisions close by. Castellano also maintained that in the event of an Allied invasion, the Germans eventually planned to make the Pisa–Rimini Line across the peninsula their main line of defence; however there was absolutely no Ultra intelligence to support this claim.

Despite this increasingly worrying picture, the Combined Chiefs confirmed Eisenhower's plans on Tuesday, 24 August 1943. The first phase of the Allied assault was to hasten the elimination of Italy from the war – something that appeared to be imminent. The second was to seize Sardinia and Corsica, while the third phase was the 'maintenance of unremitting pressure on German forces in north Italy', which would help create favourable conditions for OVERLORD and for a potential invasion of southern France.

Had the Combined Chiefs forgotten General Marshall's warnings in May at the Trident talks about operations always sucking in more resources than planned? Enforcing 'unremitting pressure' sounded like a pretty full commitment, and yet as things stood those bomb groups, those seven divisions and all that assault shipping were still due to leave the theatre on 1 November – by which time there would only be nineteen Allied divisions in Italy and Sicily. Both AVALANCHE and BAYTOWN were being given the green light without an obvious Plan B. What happened if Hitler decided to massively reinforce Italy, as he had Tunisia? And what if the Germans didn't pull back north of Rome as expected? What if, as had occurred in Tunisia, the winter weather seriously hampered the Allies' ability to manoeuvre and their vastly superior air power? It was all very well planning these operations in the relentless heat of a Mediterranean summer, but so far in this war the winters in Europe had been brutal. So what would be the consequences if the Allied ground forces became bogged down and, worse, faced a possible reversal? It seemed that only the potential benefits – admittedly considerable – were being considered by the Combined Chiefs rather than factoring in any kind of contingency. In the minds of these Allied war leaders, Italy was to be a short, sharp campaign – a useful time-filler before OVERLORD – but it was dependent on a set of assumptions for which there was absolutely no guarantee whatsoever. In fact, the entire enterprise was fraught with the very risks Marshall had highlighted in May.

What's more, the optimistic notion that the Germans would withdraw north of Rome was based on pretty woolly intelligence, information that had been passed on by Castellano but which was otherwise entirely unsubstantiated. In fact, the intelligence brief from Allied Forces HQ in Algiers was careful to stress how little they really knew about German intentions. Rather, the best they could offer the Combined Chiefs was to suggest that 'it looks as if they intend to withdraw their divisions in southern Italy to the north', although they were careful to add that they were not at all confident this was the case. On the contrary, they had serious concerns that new divisions in the north might well be sent south to reinforce those opposing AVALANCHE at Salerno. In other words, Eisenhower's team were in no way brushing over the considerable risks posed by mounting AVALANCHE. Quite the opposite – they were making it very clear that AVALANCHE was going against the Allied strategy of meticulous materiel build-up and caution.

At the daily noon conference at the Wolf's Lair a few weeks earlier on Monday, 26 July, the mood had been agitated, to say the least. Hitler's bunker complex headquarters at Rastenburg in East Prussia might have been a long way from the Mediterranean, but events in the south were causing him and his senior commanders at the Oberkommando der Wehrmacht – the OKW, the German General Staff – as much consternation as were events in the east. The alliance with Italy, drawn up in May 1939, had always been one of convenience: Hitler had wanted his southern flank secure and to cause him no trouble, while Mussolini had desired to be left alone to his own expansionist devices across the Mediterranean and into Africa.

But then Italy had needed rescuing almost from the outset, drawing precious troops and resources southwards. Once the Balkans had been cleared and Greece and the rest of the Aegean secured, Hitler had been happy to hand over garrisoning duties largely to the Italians. The exception had been North Africa, which Hitler had insisted should be heavily reinforced, and then Sicily, where German troops were, at the end of July, fighting a losing battle almost entirely on their own.

Hitler was obsessed with his southern flank and always had been, which is why he had insisted on committing so many resources there to ensure its security. It was why he had risked much of his air transport fleet and some of his very best troops to capture Crete back in May 1941, just a few weeks before the invasion of the Soviet Union. It was why he had insisted on pounding Malta, the tiny British island midway along the Mediterranean. And it was why he had poured so many troops, aircraft, guns and even precious Tiger tanks into Tunisia. All had been lost, along with 6,000 aircraft since the previous November. A fraction of that number had been lost on the Eastern Front in that time. Additionally, around 600 Axis vessels had been sunk in the theatre; these were irretrievable. There was no shipbuilding capacity left.

Of course, Hitler and his acolytes had known the Italians were wavering, which was why, just a week earlier, he had taken his train to Feltre in Italy to visit Mussolini and put a bit of backbone into his old friend. Plans had already been drawn up by the OKW to move troops into Italy – Operation ALARIC – and into the Balkans and Greece – KONSTANTIN. The idea was to disarm the Italians immediately should they renege on the alliance and take over these territories themselves. Finding the troops to do this was not easy, but Hitler insisted. They had to be found. Protecting the Southern Front was vital.

At the daily conference, Reichsmarschall Hermann Göring, the head of the Luftwaffe, but also still – just – the second most powerful Nazi in the Reich, suggested they disarm the Italians in Greece right away. 'Otherwise,' he said, 'they'll sell their weapons.'

'C-in-C South-East,' interjected General Walter Warlimont, the OKW's Chief of Plans, 'has given general instructions that all weapons are to be removed from Italian troops the moment they show signs of wavering.'

'They'll sell them!' Hitler agreed with Göring. He knew a thing or two about his feckless allies. They were absolutely hopeless. Couldn't be trusted as far as you could see them.

'They'll sell the buttons off their pants for English pounds,' added Göring. Warlimont then tried to steer them away from such talk. Hitler wanted Feldmarschall Erwin Rommel, who was present, to be overall commander.

'Kesselring hasn't got the reputation,' Hitler opined. 'We'll publish that the moment we move in – Generalfeldmarschall Rommel!'

It was a major crisis they were facing, but even Hitler, not known for calm and rational thought, eventually agreed that for the time being they should not immediately start disarming any Italians but rather tread carefully: take the Italians at their word, assume their ally would continue the fight, but at the same time feed troops into Italy and the Balkans. Hitler was also anxious to find Mussolini, who had been imprisoned in some remote location unknown to the Germans, spring him from his incarceration and put him back into power as head of a puppet Fascist state. This particular challenge was referred to within the OKW as 'a game of cops and robbers'. Rommel, who was to be in charge of the newly formed Heeresgruppe B, was to remain in the shadows for the time being so as not to arouse the Italians' suspicions.

That was the situation at the end of July, but events since had been moving quickly. Throughout the first half of August, the Germans suspected – but had no proof at all – that the Italians had made contact with the Allies and were actively plotting their exit strategy. Meetings were held with the Italian Chiefs of Staff, first at Tarvisio up in the Alps close to the Austrian border on 6 August, and then at Bologna nine days later. General Warlimont attended the first with Feldmarschall Wilhelm Keitel, the head of the OKW. Warlimont, still only forty-nine and a career staff officer after a brief period in the artillery during the last war, had been a key member of the planning team at the OKW since before the start of this current conflict. It had never been an easy task: the OKW could advise Hitler, make preparations and plan for certain eventualities, but invariably they were operating merely as the Führer's mouthpiece, and with it his whims, assertions and flights of fancy.

At Tarvisio there was nothing to suggest the meeting was between allied nations. Warlimont was surrounded by SS guards for the entire journey and throughout the meeting. Hitler had warned them not to eat any food until the Italians had sampled it first; in the event they had ignored this advice, survived despite the Führer's fears, and ended the meeting by pledging to continue to fight side by side until victory was secured. None the less, mutual mistrust had hung heavy in the air.

No sooner had Warlimont and Keitel returned to the Wolf's Lair than news arrived that two Italian Alpini divisions had been posted to the Brenner area. This valley was the primary Alpine route between Austria and northern Italy, with a main road and railway running through it. The Italian Comando Supremo, the high command, also demanded the withdrawal of German troops. At the same time, Italian naval forces were actively operating against the Allies, so the messages from Italy were somewhat mixed. Then the Italians announced they were withdrawing their Fourth Army from south-east France and bringing it back into Italy, along with some divisions in the Balkans. This did not auger well.

The next meeting in Bologna was led by General Alfred Jodl, the Chief of the Operations Staff at the OKW and effectively Keitel's number two, and also Rommel. This time Jodl did not beat about the bush. Was the moving of Fourth Army, he asked, for use against the English or against German troops at the Brenner? The Italians deftly batted these remarks aside. Trust cut both ways; they wanted more information as to why Germany was sending so many troops without consultation. They were committed allies still, but German activities were making them uneasy. And in any case, the Allies might be invading Italy soon. It was their sovereign right to defend themselves. 'Italian intentions,' Jodl cabled afterwards, 'are no clearer than before. Our reasons for suspicion are still as valid as ever.'

Hitler was always willing to veer towards suspicion and paranoia over trust – it was ever thus with autocrats – and so the very next day, 16 August, Rommel moved his headquarters to Lake Garda in northern Italy, the cloak-and-dagger days over. Rommel was to be in charge of the north, Kesselring was to command forces south of the line until such time that they pulled back to the Pisa-Rimini position. The difference between Hitler's view and what Castellano claimed was that when this withdrawal to the Pisa–Rimini Line would take place had not been remotely decided.

The OKW also regarded the Naples Salerno area as a likely place for an Allied amphibious assault and fully intended to contest such landings. As a consequence, Kesselring was ordered to reinforce the area with the bulk of his armoured formations, which included 16. Panzer, now reformed after Stalingrad; it was another German phoenix division, but one with a mostly very proud history. Generaloberst Heinrich von Vietinghoff, who had successfully commanded a Panzerkorps during the invasion of the Soviet Union in 1941, was swiftly moved from France, where he'd been commanding 15. Armee, and a new 10. Armee was hastily formed to be part of Kesselring's Heeresgruppe C. Von Vietinghoff arrived in the last week of August to take the reins.

ALARIC and KONSTANTIN were also now to be combined into one coordinated operation: ACHSE, or AXIS, an ironic joke if ever there was one. Instructions to this effect were issued by the OKW on Hitler's orders on Monday, 30 August 1943 with detailed instructions for the occupation of all territories under Italian rule including Italy itself, as well as the execution of 'destruction measures' of infrastructure vital to the Italians and Allies, the control of all mountain passes and crossings, and the hasty movement south of Rommel's forces in the north of Italy to link up with those currently under Kesselring's command. The moment the Italians threw in the towel, German troops would descend on all Italian barracks, camps and formation headquarters and disarm the lot.

This was a nightmare situation for the Germans, however, and especially so following catastrophic reversals at Stalingrad earlier in the year and more recently, in July, at Kursk. German forces on the Eastern Front were no longer heading eastwards but backwards, towards Germany. It was also clear from the build-up of forces in Britain that a cross-Channel assault would be mounted by the Allies in the not-too-distant future. So the last thing the Germans needed was to find some fifty divisions with which to occupy their southern front. For men like Warlimont, desperately trying to plug holes in a listing ship, such demands were impossible to square. Even so, the Führer had insisted. He would brook no dissent. And, by the last week of August 1943, those troops had largely been found. Italy was now teeming with Germans.

Sicily had been defended by a raggle-taggle of German forces. The Germans would not make the same mistake again. If the Italians betrayed them, they could expect the full wrath of a vengeful partner, determined to ensure no Italians fought against them. And if the Allies dared to invade Italy, they too would be made to pay.

CHAPTER 3

At General Clark's HQ

THE PAST FEW DAYS had been a bit of a whirlwind for the Supreme Allied Commander as the Allied forces in the Mediterranean prepared to invade Italy and with the Italians so very close to surrender. On Sunday, 29 August, General Eisenhower had flown over from Allied Forces HQ in Algiers to Catania in Sicily. It was the nature of the command that he spent much of his time travelling between Algiers, Tunis, Malta and now Sicily, hopping from one place to another by plane. This in itself was not without risk; yet the chance of mechanical failure or some accident en route or while landing and taking off had to be offset against the necessities of the post, and Eisenhower was not so arrogant as to assume that nobody else could fill his shoes should the worst happen. They were in the middle of a war, for goodness sake. War was a risky business.

Fine weather and cerulean skies certainly made the flight across the Mediterranean less hazardous, and having left Maison Blanche in Algeria at 6.40 a.m. in his specially adapted B-17, they touched down safely some hours later at Cassibile, south of Syracuse, then transferred to a C-47 transport and, escorted by Spitfires, made a short flight up the east coast to Catania. Here he was met by General Sir Bernard Montgomery, commander of the British Eighth Army. The Brits were shortly due to cross the Straits of Messina and invade the toe of Italy, and after a tour to visit some of the troops Monty took Eisenhower and his two aides to his tented HQ south of Messina. Had the Supreme Commander come a few days earlier, he would have been entertained at the luxurious Villa Florida in the clifftop resort of Taormina. Montgomery, however, with the invasion of Italy looming, had decided that such rarefied surroundings were not conducive to proper military planning and so had shifted to his more familiar personal caravan and tented encampment.

They enjoyed a small dinner that night with Monty on good, confident form and joshing with his aides, cicadas ticking and clicking in the surrounding trees. In early 1942, when he had first met Eisenhower, Montgomery had reprimanded the American for smoking in his presence. Yet even though Monty was still both a non-smoker and teetotal, cigarettes and wine were on offer that night. Monty was a tonic at such times. While others wore the stress, anxiety and misgivings of the eve of battle all too obviously, he exuded nothing but confidence and self-assurance. It was reassuring.

The following day, Monday 30 August, Eisenhower headed south again to visit General Sir Harold Alexander at his tented command post near Cassibile, where the Allied Army Group commander was expecting to conduct the surrender negotiations with the Italians. General Bedell-Smith, Eisenhower's Chief of Staff, was going to join Alexander to lead the negotiations. Surrounded by olive trees, the camp was none the less hot, dusty and with too many flies. Alexander and Eisenhower got on extremely well; all the American commanders warmed to Alex, as he was known. His vast experience, his innate good sense, imperturbability and effortless charm made him not only easy to like but easy to trust too. He'd fought and commanded troops on the Western Front in the last war, Germans in the Baltic Landwehr in Poland's war against Russia; he'd commanded a brigade in the Indian Army on the North-West Frontier in the 1930s, been the last British soldier – let alone officer – to leave Dunkirk back in 1940, had successfully overseen the retreat of British forces from Burma into north-east India and had then helped orchestrate the British victory at Alamein. In February, in Tunisia, Alexander had become the first Allied Army Group commander, had transformed Allied operations on the ground within little more than a fortnight, and had since then been overall land commander for the invasion and capture of Sicily.

In a black canvas tent, Eisenhower and Alexander talked through plans – and the not inconsiderable risks they faced – all the while with the heat beating down upon them from another cloudless deep-blue sky. It was hard to imagine it ever raining again, so relentless was the sun, and yet it was almost September 1943, and in a few days' time the next phase of the war would begin.

An offer to stay for lunch was declined and then they were off again, the Supreme Commander, his aides in tow, flying back to Algiers. A bite to eat on the flight back and then Eisenhower was straight into his office to catch up on the never-ending stream of messages which needed answering.

The next day, Tuesday, 31 August, Eisenhower, accompanied by Air Chief Marshal Sir Arthur Tedder, flew early to see General Mark Clark, commander of the US Fifth Army, whose HQ was now at the coastal town of Mostaganem, in the Bay of Arzew in Algeria. This was for a final run-through of the plans for Operation AVALANCHE, Fifth Army's landings at Salerno.

The conference began at 10 a.m., with Clark addressing the gathered commanders at some length. Planning had been difficult – partly because for a large part of the time the Sicilian battle was still being fought, but also because the various headquarters involved were widely separated. Now, for once, air, naval and army commanders were all in one place together; it was a chance for them to iron out any controversial points.

Clark was keenly aware that AVALANCHE promised to be a major test, although one he had eagerly sought and in which he was determined to succeed. Mark Clark – or 'Wayne' as friends knew him from his middle name – was only forty-seven, tall at 6 foot 3 inches, lean and muscular, his hair still dark and despite a prominent, hawkish nose he was a youthful-looking and striking three-star general who towered over most of his subordinates and superiors alike. He had an imposing, energetic presence and natural authority, and although he most definitely had a sense of humour, he was deadly serious about command and the business of war. Clark was prepared to argue vociferously for what he believed was right and to stand up to anyone; an eyeballing from him was an unnerving experience.

A man, then, who had the courage of his convictions, but who also had proven physical courage – he was one of the few American commanders who had seen action in the last war, having led a battalion in France in 1917, until wounded when a shell exploded nearby. At the war's end he was a captain, a rank at which he remained for the next sixteen years. Those were frustrating times for many in the US Army; men like him needed determination and self-belief that one day the frustrations of languishing in the military doldrums would be worth it. Long years of low pay and low rank were deeply demoralizing for ambitious men like Clark.

Yet his patience won out because finally, in 1933, his fortunes began to change, with promotion followed by time spent at both the US Command and General Staff College and the Army War College, marking him out for an elevated future. By the summer of 1937 he had joined 3rd Division, where he renewed his friendship with his old friend, Dwight D. Eisenhower – the two had been together at the US Army's officer school, West Point. By 1940 Clark had been promoted again, to lieutenant-colonel, and was appointed Chief of Staff to General Lesley McNair, the man commanded to expand, train and completely reorganize the then tiny US Army to be ready for war. Clark wasted no time in showing his exceptional aptitude for planning and organization, demonstrating great resources of energy, intelligence, enthusiasm and an impressive ability to cut through the cloth and get things done fast.

Catching the eye of General George C. Marshall, the US Chief of Staff, Clark, by then a two-star major-general, was sent to Britain in June 1942, along with Eisenhower, to arrange for the reception and training of US troops and to begin preparations for Operation SLEDGEHAMMER, the planned invasion of Continental Europe. When, in July, immediate Allied plans were directed towards an invasion of North-west Africa, Eisenhower was made C-in-C with Clark as his deputy. As head of planning for TORCH, Clark deservedly won a great deal of credit for pulling off what at the time was the largest seaborne invasion the world had ever known, and in which three separate amphibious forces, one from the US and two from Britain, had all landed at pretty much the right place and pretty much on time and then swiftly fulfilled their objectives. Not only that, Clark had personally risked his life by clandestinely landing in Algeria by submarine and canoe ahead of the invasion for secret talks with the Vichy French command. TORCH had done much to heighten Clark's reputation and standing.

Yet no matter how much he had proved himself as a planner and diplomat, he desperately wanted the chance for operational command. As Eisenhower's deputy, however, he knew he was at risk of sitting out the war as a pen-pusher. At heart Clark was a soldier, not an administrator, and he craved the chance to command men in battle.

So, while the Tunisian campaign was playing out, he began to badger his chief for his own command until Eisenhower eventually relented and gave him the newly created Fifth Army, the first American Army HQ ever to be created outside the United States. Activated on 5 January 1943, it was initially little more than a training organization, and although

Seventh Army, under General George S. Patton, was subsequently the first into action on Sicily, Clark had spent the past eight months aware that it was merely a question of time before the Fifth was tested in battle. At long last, that moment was now just around the corner.

AVALANCHE was on and due to launch in the early hours of 9 September, and would be the main event as far as the Allied invasion of Italy was concerned, although Clark had spent an anxious few weeks waiting for this to be confirmed as Eisenhower and his senior commanders and planners wrestled with the multiple and differing options for the invasion of the Italian mainland. The nub of the matter was this: should AVALANCHE be launched without a firm foothold in the toe of Italy? Gaining the toe of the boot would not only draw German troops south away from the Naples area but would also open up the shipping channels through the Straits of Messina, vital for swift amphibious deployment further up the leg.

On the other hand, no one was quite sure how many troops would be needed to achieve this control of the toe, and so three further and separate operations had been planned. BAYTOWN was pretty much locked in from the outset, but there were also good grounds for carrying out BUTTRESS too, the assault on the north of the toe, because that would secure the shipping channels to the north, so vital for the success of AVALANCHE.

Clark found this deeply frustrating. It brought out both an impatient side to his nature and also his paranoia that somehow his thunder would be stolen by the British. Clark was not Anglophobic; he had enjoyed his experience in England the previous year, had a good relationship with Churchill and made numerous friends along the way. He also liked and got on very well with Alexander especially. But he did have a chip on his shoulder about his relative lack of command experience, especially when compared with many British generals. Neither he nor his fellow compatriots could help that; men like Alexander and Montgomery simply did have more experience: they had fought longer in the last war, been more active between the wars and had filled their boots with combat command since the outbreak of this current war, which was more than two years ahead of the US entry into the conflict. It meant that men like Clark had some catching up to do and a very steep learning curve in the art of high command.

Clark knew he was ready for such a challenge, but he worried that others might not share his self-belief and that at the last moment this wonderful opportunity to lead a major Allied invasion force would be denied him. In early August he had become really agitated, not helped by his move to Mostaganem. His villa, a nineteenth-century house and rather 'old fashioned', was comfortable enough but the hubbub from the street outside, chicken yards each side and the shouting of local children who never seemed to go to bed, combined to make sleep difficult at night. It was no wonder he was a little ratty.

What had really worried him was that the plans for southern Italy would take the lion's share of shipping and so make AVALANCHE impossible. 'It is obvious,' Clark railed in his diary, 'that Alexander and Montgomery are pulling for this.' In fact, it was no such thing. Nor was he entirely confident that his friend and boss would stand his ground. 'The question remains,' he added, 'as to whether General Eisenhower will insist on AVALANCHE or allow himself to be again persuaded by the British to follow their wishes and make use of BUTTRESS and GOBLET.' The latter was yet another plan to land troops in the boot, this time to take the airfield at Crotone.

In truth, Clark was working himself into a lather unnecessarily. Alexander and Montgomery were, at the time, focused primarily on the Sicilian campaign and both had experienced enough setbacks in this war to favour a bold but circumspect approach. 'There shall be no more retreats,' was a line Alexander had insisted upon the moment he became C-in-C Middle East in early August 1942; it was a mantra to which Montgomery was equally wedded. Whichever way one looked at it, launching an invasion further up the leg with insufficient shipping was a high-risk strategy. It was understandable that they should pause and question whether it really was the right option, particularly at a time when they were still battling hard in Sicily.

However, the idea for a landing around Naples had originally been Churchill's, first mooted on 13 July, and he remained as fixated on this as he had ever been. He did have a point, despite the inherent risks, because if the Allies were forced to slog their way up the entire peninsula they would likely soon lose the initiative. The narrowness of Italy and its mountainous terrain meant it would be an easy place to defend. If the Allies wanted to get to Rome swiftly, then the closer to the city they landed the better. They needed to make the most of their superiority in terms of naval and air forces, not least because Italy's geography favoured amphibious outflanking manoeuvres but worked against land operations with lengthy supply lines.

Eisenhower and Tedder were both agreed that four groups of heavy bombers from England, loaned on a temporary basis from Eighth Air

Force, would make a massive difference to AVALANCHE, but the request was refused; the Eighth was stretched enough as it was. And so BUTTRESS had remained an option. Alexander might have been erring on the side of caution, but ultimately the buck stopped with Eisenhower, and before he committed wholly to AVALANCHE he wanted to know that shipping could safely pass through the Straits of Messina and that German troops would be drawn away from the Naples area into the boot of Italy. That could only be achieved by some form of assault across the Straits ahead of AVALANCHE. 'I feel very strongly, as you know,' he had written to Alexander on 7 August, 'that we must maintain as much flexibility as possible.'

At any rate, no one was trying to scupper Clark's plans for Fifth Army; they were simply trying to make the best decisions in very difficult circumstances. Certainly, the idea that Eisenhower was being leaned on by the British was absurd. He was perfectly capable of seeing the risks of AVALANCHE with vivid clarity for himself. What's more, the debate was not being run on Anglo-US lines. Tedder was for AVALANCHE, and so was Lieutenant-General Brian Horrocks, the commander of British X Corps, due to be assigned to either BUTTRESS or AVALANCHE. Alexander wasn't against the Salerno operation; he just wanted to minimize risk, as did Eisenhower.

Some days later, on 11 August, Clark was further whipped up by Général Henri Giraud, the head of the Free French in North Africa. Time was of the essence, Giraud told him. 'It would be better to start against the Italian mainland tomorrow than the day after.' Naples, he suggested, should be the first objective, then Rome, then Florence and the flat land of the Po Valley in the north. He made it all sound so easy. Yet the battle in Sicily was still being fought and still using Allied shipping, which therefore could not be deployed in an amphibious assault on Italy.

Eisenhower, Alexander and the Combined Chiefs were all very aware that more German troops were arriving in Italy with every passing day. Of course, it would be best to attack right away, but any Allied army was totally and utterly dependent on the navy and air forces, and despite their strength these were limiting factors. Ships could not be in two places at once. Nor could aircraft, and these planes could only go as far as the fuel tanks in them allowed. This was why AVALANCHE had been planned for Salerno; Clark had wanted to land north of Naples – close to Cancello airfield, in fact – where the beaches were good and where there were no immediate mountains from which German observers could watch their every move. But that was more than 200 miles from the north Sicilian coast, about 40 to 50 more than the Salerno area. That meant 80 to 100 miles further, because it was a question not just of getting there but also making it home again. The difference in distance ensured that single-engine fighters would barely be over the beachhead before they had to turn round and head for home again. P-38 Lightnings could comfortably reach north of Naples, but there were not enough of them to secure total control of the air. An amphibious landing without air superiority was a non-starter – that was a universal truth even Hitler had recognized in 1940, when he had abandoned his planned invasion of Britain once it was clear the Luftwaffe had failed to destroy the RAF. There were enough risks to AVALANCHE as it was and it needed the very best air support possible.

Such were the debates in the first half of August, but with Sicily falling on the 17th and signs of few German troops in the toe, BUTTRESS was at last thrown out and AVALANCHE given primacy, just as Clark had hoped. He'd been agitated for nothing. BAYTOWN, Eighth Army's crossing of the Straits of Messina, was now scheduled for 3 September. Once the toe was secured and shipping freed up, AVALANCHE would take place six days later, on 9 September.

And so on 31 August Clark was holding forth at his HQ in Mostaganem, briefing all the senior commanders for the operation ahead – an operation now set in stone. British X Corps, as planned, had been attached to Fifth Army because, following the Sicily campaign, there weren't enough American divisions ready for immediate deployment. Two British divisions would land at Salerno itself and to the south of the town. One, the 46th, had some experience of fighting in Tunisia, the other, the 56th, had very little. The American component, the 36th 'Texas' Division, would land fifteen miles further south around the ancient Greek ruins of Paestum. The Texans were entirely untried in battle. The 45th 'Thunderbird' Division, Sicily combat veterans, would be held in reserve since there weren't enough landing craft to get them to shore as well. X Corps was no longer commanded by Horrocks because he'd been wounded in Sicily. Dick McCreery, Alexander's former Chief of Staff and whom Clark barely knew, was now the British corps commander. Standing before them all, Clark spoke of his pride that his army was a truly Allied one, with American, British and French elements. Together, he promised them, they would achieve great things.

*

On Monday, 30 August, the day before Clark held this conference, he had penned a memo for all his troop commanders. 'Great opportunities lie ahead of our Fifth Army,' he had written, 'opportunities which will lead to the complete liberation of Europe from its present rule of tyranny.' It was, he added, a great privilege for Fifth Army to be associated with such a noble enterprise. 'Our cause,' he concluded, 'is a righteous one, and God will direct us in our undertaking.'

By the time he was writing this, most of Sicily's cities had been pounded into rubble, and large numbers of towns had similarly been reduced to dust. Many hundreds of thousands of Italians, both in Sicily and further afield in Italy, were discovering that modern war was brutally destructive in a way that had been unimaginable to most people in the decade or so before the war had begun, and despite the warnings of prophets such as Giulio Douhet of the supremacy of air power in future wars.

Yet Clark was not alone in believing the Allied cause was just and noble. Neither Nazism nor Fascism could be allowed to prevail. For those commanding the Allied armies they were cancers, evils that had to be stopped as quickly as possible with the minimum loss of life. That was no easy task, but Clark, along with his fellow senior commanders in the Mediterranean, understood that victory could not be achieved without young men under their command getting killed. To keep the casualties down meant using bombers and immense firepower, mechanization and modernity to do a lot of the hard yards. And if that involved destroying cities, towns and villages which barred the Allies' path, then it was the price that had to be paid. Better a building than young Allied lives. Better Italian civilians than young Allied lives. After all, the Allies never asked the Italians to enter the war. Yet there was the paradox, for if the Allies were liberators, was it right that they should be killing the people they were supposed to be liberating? And also destroying the homes and lives of those they were pledging to help? The war had been a simpler under-taking in the desert, where the population had been so very sparse. Italy was home to 44 million people, most of whom lived in towns and villages along the coast and in the valleys – precisely where the Allies would be fighting.

Unless, of course, the Germans chose not to fight and swiftly retreated north, but Eisenhower's words of caution on this matter had been wafted aside. The path on which they were to embark had been agreed. The course set. There could be no turning back now. On 31 August, Allied Forces HQ decided to spell out the risk in greater detail. It was now estimated that facing the Salerno landings would be one panzer division and possibly two or three parachute battalions. By D plus 5 – five days after the landing – enemy opposition was likely to be two and a half panzer divisions, of which one and a half might be weak and understrength, plus one and a half Panzergrenadier divisions and one Fallschirmjäger division. They spelled out these types of enemy formation very specifically because panzer divisions were generally of a high standard, Panzergrenadier divisions were well armed and mostly motorized – in contrast to ordinary infantry divisions – and parachute divisions were known and respected for being of fierce and determined fighting quality. In other words, the opposition at Salerno could be expected to be strong. By D plus 10, they could reckon on facing a further panzer and one weak Panzergrenadier division in the bridgehead. In Sicily they had faced just two German divisions, and later four. To oppose these, the Allies had had two entire armies. For Italy, they also had two armies, but most of their component parts would be stuck in Sicily and North Africa even ten days into the invasion.

The contrast between the enemy strength they had confronted in Sicily and what they could expect to face at Salerno was enormous. What's more, these warnings were based on a pretty accurate intelligence picture about the newly formed German 10. Armee in southern Italy. Even worse, Ultra decrypts had revealed more enemy units arriving in Italy, raising the number of German divisions there to eighteen. How Germany planned to use these growing forces, however, was not clear, as no incoming decrypts offered either concrete information or even clues. But as for the planned retreat north to the so-called Pisa–Rimini Line, they only had two rather uncertain pieces of evidence. The first was via Japan's ambassador in Berne, Switzerland. In a decrypted message he stated that he believed Germany would hold a line in the north if the Italians collapsed. This, however, had been dated 29 May, so three months earlier. A lot had happened since. The second was Castellano's supporting claim that this remained Hitler's intention. Both of these meagre pieces of intelligence were far from being bulletproof.

As August 1943 gave way to September, there was no doubt that Allied political pressures and high strategy had trumped operational limitations and tactical good sense.

There had always been a considerable level of risk to AVALANCHE. As it drew closer those risks, far from diminishing, were starting to look even greater.

CHAPTER 4

BAYTOWN

'T ODAY IS SUNDAY,' WROTE Captain David Cole in a letter home to his parents on 29 August. 'As usual, it is a bright sunny morning and, as usual, the sky is dark with Allied aircraft streaming over our heads in endless procession from dawn to sunset.' He remembered being back home in England in the summer of 1940 when he'd seen a lone Spitfire hurtle towards a dense formation of German bombers. How the tables had turned! 'Now at last,' Cole added, 'vengeance is ours.'

Cole was twenty-three years old and had landed in Sicily as a young, green lieutenant just seven weeks earlier. From Newmarket in Suffolk in the east of England, he had interrupted his history degree at Cambridge to join the war effort and, like so many now fighting, had never thought a few years earlier that he would end up a soldier. Yet he'd survived his first test in Sicily, won a promotion, and become an old hand in a battalion now brought back up to strength with a number of replacements. Cole was also aware that he and his fellows in the 2nd Inniskillings would soon be heading across the Straits of Messina and into the toe of Italy, but had none of the fears that had plagued him before the Sicilian invasion. Rather, he reckoned it seemed unlikely the Germans would risk leaving large portions of their army to be cut off in the toe, so was confident the Allies would have an easy ride. Sicily had been a tough fight – his battalion had had a particularly hard time in the Catania Plain – but they were still feeling flush with victory and had spent the past couple of weeks swimming in the sea, drinking far too much wine, watching Fred Astaire movies and rejoicing in still being alive and part of a winning team.

Two days earlier, Montgomery himself had paid a visit. Monty's car had stopped just a few yards from Cole – and there he was with his famous black beret on his head, clutching a fly swat. Eagerly, the men gathered round while the general stood up. 'These Italians are a rotten crowd,' he told them. 'They just lie among their grapes and lemons and breed. Far too many of them. That's the trouble. Far too many of them.' He was then very complimentary about 5th Division, of which the 2nd Inniskillings were a part, and reassured them they would have no difficulty at all in the forthcoming crossing into Italy. The men loved it, Cole included.

Feeling considerably less relaxed was Lieutenant Farley Mowat, now intelligence officer with the Hastings and Prince Edward Regiment of the Canadian 1st Infantry Brigade. Following nearly four weeks of brutal and costly fighting in Sicily, Mowat and the rest of the battalion had been promised a chance to 'enjoy a period of relaxation and the rewards for a job well done'. The reality had not lived up to the billing, for the rest camp at Militello was set among parched, bleached ground and thin olive trees inland and nowhere near the sea. Rather than relax, they were subject to numerous inspections, tedious visits by VIPs and asinine training exercises. Officers like Mowat also faced demands for endless reports none of them felt remotely interested in writing. And all the while the August sun bore down, relentlessly, inescapably, while mosquitoes and other insects buzzed and whined and bit them.

To make matters worse the mail bags were slow to arrive, and when they did finally come, at the very end of August and after a month of hearing nothing from home, a number of 'Dear John' letters informed brave soldier husbands and boyfriends that their partners had found someone new. News from home was also grim: anti-conscription riots, strikes by war-workers demanding more pay, and anger among the civilian population because of sugar rationing. Mowat, for one, found it all hugely dispiriting. In fact, for much of the time in the purgatory of Militello he was seething with barely controlled anger. He felt as though he was being treated like an inmate at a reform school. 'It seemed to us,' he noted, 'that instead of being rewarded for our victories, we were being forced to do penance.' He'd not seen good friends die for this.

'You should see all the boys busy writing,' Major Alex Campbell wrote to his sister, Mary. 'It makes me shudder to think of all the letters I have to censor.' Officers had to censor all letters by the rank and file, although they self-censored their own, which meant they were often considerably more open and frank about what they had been experiencing. Campbell was thirty-three, a genial square-jawed bear of a man and much loved by the men of A Company, whom he commanded. His father had been killed in 1917 during the last war, leaving his mother, Sarah, to raise him and his two sisters alone. The family was extremely close and Campbell wrote regularly to his mother and sisters, but in this latest batch there had been nothing from his mother, about which he was very disappointed. Generally, mail was proving slow to reach Eighth Army. It was not at all good for morale; despite being surrounded by mates and like-minded fellows, these young men had been sent a long, long way from home. News from families and that tactile link to a better, more peaceful world were vital, especially so after long years away – the Hasty Ps had arrived in Britain on 1 January 1940 – and having been through such a baptism of fire in Sicily.

On 1 September, their 'holiday' came to an end at long last as they left Militello for good. 'Reveille sounded at 0300 hrs,' recorded the war diary, and an hour later the battalion were clambering into trucks and moving off. They wound their way in a long column along the dusty, sun-blasted roads of Sicily northwards to Messina, the trucks jouncing and jolting all the way. 'Just a short line,' Campbell wrote to his mother, 'to say that we are on the way again. By the time this reaches you, the news will be in all the papers.'

They reached Messina and could see across the narrow straits to the hazy purple mountains of Calabria on the far side. Farley Mowat didn't sense any of the excited anticipation he'd felt before heading to Sicily; that was what combat experience had done for him. As he had left Campbell's A Company and was now intelligence officer, several of his old friends asked him for news. 'Will Tedeschi be laying for us on the beaches? What d'you think?' Paddy Ryan asked him. The 'Tedeschi' were Germans – a new nickname from Sicily, picked up from the Italian word.

Mowat had no idea, and didn't want to think about it too hard either. 'Who can tell?' he replied. 'Those assholes at Corps Intelligence don't seem to have a clue . . . How would *I* know?'

While the men of XIII Corps, both 5th Division and the Canadian 1st Division, had been moving up to Messina in readiness for Operation BAYTOWN, the Italian surrender negotiations had been continuing. With London and Washington faffing and unable to agree a stance for the Italians, Harold Macmillan had quietly drawn up the Short Terms and handed them to Eisenhower, who had in turn proposed them to his political chiefs. Macmillan had then been flown to London to smooth things over, so that by the time Castellano met with Bedell-Smith in Lisbon the Short Terms had been agreed. That in turn gave Eisenhower – and Bedell-Smith – the authority to negotiate.

Macmillan was forty-nine years old and had the look of a school-master about him: bespectacled, with a slightly full moustache that partly hid truly terrible buck teeth. He favoured bow ties and suits which, although well tailored, somehow gave off the appearance of being rather ill-fitting. A Grenadier Guardsman in the last war, he had been wounded first at Loos in 1915 and again at the Somme the following year while leading his men near Delville Wood. Hit first in the knee, he had kept going but then was struck by a bullet in the thigh. Managing to crawl into a shell-hole, he discovered that his water bottle was empty, having been hit by a fur-ther bullet. Feigning death when he heard German voices, he was then twice partially covered by earth as further shells crashed in close by. He managed to keep alive by alternately sleeping and reading a tome of Aeschylus in the original Greek, before finally being rescued more than twelve hours later.

Two long years of hospital and rehabilitation followed; twenty-seven years on from that terrible day in France, he still suffered pain in his leg. Yet Macmillan had survived and, after a brief stint in the family publish-ing firm, he began a career in politics. Well connected – he had married the daughter of the Duke of Devonshire – and clever, imperturbable and blessed with a warm sense of humour, he had none the less only started to rise up the political ranks in 1940, when he was appointed Parliamen-tary Secretary to the Minister of Supply after Churchill had become Prime Minister. Two years later, he was sent to Algiers as British Resident Minister at Allied Forces HQ. Reporting directly to Churchill, he now had a place in the Cabinet and was finally able to demonstrate his abun-dance of calm, cool-headed wisdom which he seemed able to combine with easy affability and charm. He soon made friends with his American counterpart, Robert Murphy, and with Eisenhower, and during the Casa-blanca Conference had proved he had a deft diplomatic hand. Since then his influence and authority had increased considerably.

Macmillan had nearly died again in late February 1943 when an air-craft he was in crashed on take-off, an event which underlined the inherent risks of air transport. Although quite badly burned, he had managed to get out of the stricken plane then turn back to rescue a Frenchman who had been one of the passengers. Only his glasses had saved his eyesight. Recovery had thankfully been swift and he returned to Allied Forces HQ, where he continued to play an increasingly trusted and important role. It was why he was able both to draft the Short Terms and have them so readily accepted by Eisenhower.

Now, though, Macmillan was about to take part in the final surrender negotiations with the Italians, although getting to this point had caused him endless frustration, largely because of the weight of interfering and contradictory missives reaching him from London. This concerned the insistence by the Combined Chiefs that the Italians adhere immediately to the demand for unconditional surrender, as had been agreed at Casablanca, which was outlined in the Long Terms but not the Short. Macmillan very strongly believed it was vital to simply get the armistice signed right away; the insistence on unconditional surrender could be hidden in the Long Terms and dealt with later; after all, by that time the Italians would be out of the war and, frankly, the Allies could then insist on whatever they wanted. It would mean hoodwinking the Italians, but this was realpolitik. There was a war to be won. And before that, there was a successful invasion of Italy to be undertaken.

Nor had his normal good humour been helped by repeatedly being woken each night with the arrival of ever more 'Most Immediate' telegrams, which had to be dealt with right away. 'The confusion and folly which is going on from London, Washington and Quebec,' he railed, 'is really very distressing.'

Eisenhower was similarly feeling caught between a rock and a hard place, although as Supreme Commander the pressures on him were far greater than those facing Macmillan. Having now committed to AVALANCHE, it really was essential that the Italians were out of the war before the landings took place at Salerno on 9 September; the dangers were bad enough as it was without having to factor in the Italians as well, with their huge army, coastal batteries, air force and still sizeable navy. His Chief of Staff, General Bedell-Smith, had arrived back from Lisbon on 28 August, but with Generale Zanussi in tow. Both Bedell-Smith and Ike had sensed that Zanussi was from a different faction in Rome. The Italian had also been given the Long Terms, at which he'd rather blanched; so it seemed safer, for the moment at any rate, to keep him in Algiers along with the copy he'd been given of the full terms. After all, if the Italians were prevaricating over the Short Terms, it was hard to see how they would accept the Long Terms, which included not only the demand for unconditional surrender but also ruthless economic and political conditions.

None the less, Bedell-Smith did take Zanussi with him for the planned armistice negotiations on Sicily; there, in olive groves not far from General Alexander's HQ, the Supreme Commander's advance HQ had also been established with a number of tents and caravans. It had been named Fairfield Camp. Already there was Generale Giuseppe Castellano, armed with instructions from Badoglio. And certainly, by the time Macmillan and Robert Murphy reached Fairfield for the talks on the morning of Tuesday, 31 August, there was a palpable air of expectation.

But hopes were swiftly dashed, for it was soon clear that the Italian position had changed somewhat. Castellano, despite being Badoglio's emissary, claimed he still had no authority to sign the armistice, even though the deadline for agreeing the Short Terms had now expired.

The Short Terms per se were not the issue, but rather the question of timing. The Allies had made it clear they wanted to announce the armistice just before the invasion, but that was putting the fear of God into Badoglio and his government. Rome was already effectively surrounded by German troops, and they worried that the royal family and government would be captured and then very likely swiftly executed. Badoglio, Castellano told them, wanted to know what the Allied plans were and with what strength they might invade Italy. The Italians were hedging their bets; they desperately wanted out, but by the same token they didn't then want to find themselves at the mercy of a vengeful former ally. They were prepared to fight the Germans, especially around Rome, but supplies of just about everything were very short and it would take them some time to get their forces ready. If the Allies could only tell them more about their strength and plans, then they would be better placed to make the right call.

This, though, was precisely why Bedell-Smith and the Allied delegation couldn't possibly reveal their hand; after all, what if the Italians reneged? Or told Germany, still their ally? Badoglio, Castellano now told them, felt unable to accept an armistice until the Allies had landed at least fifteen divisions, with the bulk of them north of Rome. Well, that wasn't going to happen – in fact, it was so wildly off the mark it was risible. No one, though, was laughing.

Castellano also suggested that the Italians would switch sides, but that was contrary to the unconditional surrender the Combined Chiefs were still insisting upon. As those in Cassibile could readily see, they were now in danger of failing to get a deal at all. And that would be a disaster at this stage in the planning, because it was one thing taking on an undesirably strong German force at Salerno, but quite another to have to contend with Italian forces as well, even poorly armed and trained. It was unthinkable to even contemplate. Rather, AVALANCHE had been planned on the assumption that the Italians would, in fact, turn on their former ally. Not only were missives from Washington and London threatening to scupper this part of the plan, so too were the ridiculous expectations of the Italians as to the strength the Allies could bring to bear. It was patently clear that the Italians had not thought much about how large-scale amphibious operations were mounted. Where on earth did they think the Allies would find shipping for fifteen divisions landing near Rome? Had it not occurred to them that air power was a vital component of such enterprises? It was incomprehensible they could be this obtuse. Because of this, the Allies had not expected there could be such a gulf between what they could practically undertake and Italian hopes.

That night, Castellano returned to Rome to try to persuade Badoglio and his government to accept the Short Terms as presented by Eisenhower's team – which still made no mention of unconditional surrender – while a conference was held in Alexander's caravan to see if they could suggest any military action that might stiffen Italian resolve. A solution was to drop the US 82nd Airborne Division near Rome. This was secretly communicated to the Italians and appeared to do the trick, for the following evening at around 10 p.m., after a long and anxious wait on the part of the Allied negotiating team, word arrived from the Italians that 'the answer is in the affirmative'.

A sigh of relief all round at Cassibile. An Italian delegation would arrive the following day, Thursday, 2 September 1943.

In this increasingly bizarre drama that was being acted out there were, inevitably, still more twists and turns. The first occurred the moment Castellano arrived that morning for further talks and told the Allied team he still had no authority to sign the armistice. Rather, he reported that the Italian government liked the sound of dropping the 82nd Airborne near Rome and was eager to continue with military talks. The Allied delegation were dismayed by this, but Macmillan now sent an urgent message to General Alexander, suggesting the moment had arrived when some tough talk was needed.

Alexander had intended to remain at his own encampment, a couple of miles from Fairfield Camp, but in cahoots with Murphy and Macmillan he had earlier agreed to be on hand should he be needed. A little performance was now required. Putting on his finest uniform, his peaked cap that had been specially designed for him by his hatters in St James's in London, and with his Army Group commander's flag fluttering, General Alexander drove over, pulling up outside the negotiations tent.

Clambering out with a great display of grandeur, he turned to Macmillan and Murphy.

'Good morning,' he said with as much pomposity as he could muster. 'I have come to be introduced to the General. I understand he has signed the instrument of surrender.'

As rehearsed, Macmillan stepped forward. 'I am sorry to say, sir, but General Castellano has not signed the instrument and says that he hasn't the authority from his government to sign such a document.'

Alexander then pretended to fly into a rage – something that had not been witnessed before by any who knew him. 'Why, there must be some mistake!' he exclaimed. 'Only this morning I have seen the telegram from Marshal Badoglio stating that he was to sign the armistice agreement! In that case, this man must be a spy! We must arrest him!' He then suggested that the only thing that could save Castellano was for the Italian to send a telegram to Badoglio demanding authority to sign. A flustered Castellano promptly did so.

The authorization came the following day, and at 4.30 p.m. the military armistice – the Short Terms – were at last signed by Castellano and Bedell-Smith, with Macmillan and Murphy as two of the witnesses. Signing this, however, also committed them to accept the Long Terms, just as Macmillan had planned, which were now immediately handed over to Castellano. Whether the Italians liked them or not, it was too late: rather unwittingly, they had agreed to surrender unconditionally after all. It was Friday, 3 September 1943, four years to the day that Britain and France had entered the war.

By the time of the signing, Allied troops were already on mainland Europe. Since they were men of Montgomery's Eighth Army very little had been left to chance, and so at 3.45 a.m., with the shroud of night still over them, some 630 guns had opened up from the Messina side of the Straits, pummelling the far shores. Watching this fireworks display was the Australian war correspondent Alan Moorehead. He and other journalists sat in the Sicilian hills above the town and could see the yellow stabs of flame emerging from a mass of olive groves where the guns were awkwardly dug in. The thunder of the guns, the scream of the shells travelling a few miles over the sea, and then the crash on the far side. The local

Sicilians had been warned beforehand to leave their homes because the blasts might well shatter the glass in their windows. However, they'd not budged until the barrage began. 'Then,' noted Moorehead, 'they ran screaming into the open.'

Moorehead was a good-looking, dark-haired thirty-three-year-old from Melbourne. A naturally gifted writer and keen observer, he was the son of a journalist and had followed in his father's footsteps, securing a job at the Melbourne *Herald*. For an ambitious young man wanting to see something of the world, Melbourne had soon seemed frustratingly insular and so, having saved up some money, in 1936 he set sail for England to find his fame and fortune.

He soon won a job with Lord Beaverbrook's *Daily Express,* the most popular daily in Britain at the time, and was posted to Gibraltar. Although this might have seemed like a backwater, the Spanish Civil War broke out in July that year, while with the rise of Mussolini's international ambitions there was plenty going on in the Mediterranean about which he could report.

By the outbreak of war he was one of Beaverbrook's rising stars and was posted to the Middle East in the second half of 1940, covering the Italian invasion of Greece and then the desert war that followed in North Africa. Since then he had seen a lot of the war and, like the very best correspondents, was always willing to get close to the front but also managed to speak to the generals and senior commanders. So although he was no soldier, he had followed the highs and lows of Allied fortunes and was by now reasonably well qualified to pass judgement on what he was witnessing.

And it seemed to him that the barrage was perhaps a little heavy-handed; certainly, no enemy gun was firing back at the British. Out on the water, Royal Navy destroyers and gun monitors swept back and forth along the Calabrian coast, firing and further pulverizing the towns of Reggio and Villa San Giovanni on the far side. Then, just before dawn, specially adapted landing ships armed with short-range rockets unleashed tearing broadsides that streaked and screamed through the air to crash on to the invasion beaches. Moorehead thought the rockets an extraordinary sight. 'A kind of upward-flowing yellow waterfall,' he wrote, 'and the noise was monstrous, even worse than the barrage.'

One of the reasons why Montgomery had wanted such fire support was because he lacked the number of landing craft he felt he needed. The Allies' biggest challenge was that every assault they made had to be backed up with ample air power, enough naval warships and, of course, enough landing craft. These vessels were a new phenomenon – Britain, for example, had had just sixteen on order but not yet completed in September 1939, while the first US Higgins Boats were only trialled in May 1941. Despite these trials and early orders, the war leaders of both Britain and the US had failed to foresee the vital importance they were likely to have until America was in the war, US troops were arriving in Britain, and the goal was to try and get across the Channel and into France as soon as possible. No troops would be setting foot on French soil without landing craft, however, and so suddenly, in April 1942, and with the US also realizing it had a war to fight in the Pacific, a crash landing craft production programme got under way. Between May 1942 and April 1943, 8,719 landing craft were built in the US alone, and while Britain was also manufacturing considerable numbers – albeit not on that scale – most of the marine engines for British craft were also being made in the States. The onus for these vessels really did lie with American shipyards.

The trouble was, this crash production programme interfered with the US Navy's requirement for freighters and naval warships, and so in April 1943 it was wound down in favour of other shipping. At the time the decision was made the only planned amphibious operation had been the invasion of Sicily, although the Americans did agree to underwrite the landing craft needs for an amphibious operation in Burma too. No one, however, had drawn up a possible future schedule of requirements because in early 1943 nothing else had been agreed; at the time, the cross-Channel invasion, for example, hadn't yet been given an operation code-name or date. A good number of landing craft were available for ongoing operations, but no thought had been given to exactly how many would be needed and where; and while the Americans wanted to allocate plenty for the Pacific and enough for the cross-Channel invasion, they had given no consideration to future operations in the Mediterranean beyond Sicily. The British, meanwhile, were in favour of going all-out to defeat Germany first and then properly dealing with the Japanese afterwards. And part of their plan for prioritizing Germany was to continue operations in the Mediterranean, where Allied armies and thousands of aircraft were already based. The consequence of all this was a dramatic shortage of landing craft for an invasion the Combined Chiefs had signed up for, which they were expecting their ground forces to undertake with insufficient assault craft for the scale of their plans.

Nor had anyone, back in the spring when the landing craft programme was curtailed, properly considered the effect of shipping these assault craft halfway around the world, or the number of combat losses, or general operational wear and tear. Again, not enough contingency had been factored in. The truth was, the global demands of shipping were so enormous that even in the United States the differing demands of ship construction were overwhelming.

Since the start of the Sicilian campaign on 10 July, those landing craft involved in the assault phase had continued to be used voraciously for the ongoing build-up of men and materiel, for other logistical tasks and for lesser operations on the north Sicilian coast right up until the end of the battle, and by this time they were suffering a widespread deterioration in serviceability. Generally speaking, the time needed to overhaul, refit and load in ports in Sicily for a new task was twenty-five days. Most were withdrawn from Sicilian operations by 19 August, but that left only twelve days for BAYTOWN and just thirteen for AVALANCHE, which, although planned for six days after the crossing of the Messina Straits, was located further away and required a longer time at sea for the invasion force. From a shipping point of view, it would have been far better to have postponed both operations, but a moon was needed for the Salerno landings and after 8/9 September the next opportunity was 21 September. That was simply too late – largely because of German build-up, but also because of the Allies' own timetable of operations. Assault shipping, rather than any shortage of manpower, was the limiting factor for the invasion.

From Messina the toe of Italy looked – and was – tantalizingly close, but it was not simply a case of ferrying troops across and then moving on to the next operation because there was then the build-up of material – supplies, vehicles, ammunition, fuel and so on – which had to follow. For example, a single infantry battalion of 845 men was issued with seventy-five vehicles. This was reduced to just twenty-nine for an amphibious assault phase, which was more manageable, but that number was only deemed sufficient to get the troops off the beaches and not much more. A 'light scale' was forty-nine vehicles, which gave a battalion a reach of thirty miles. That, though, wasn't going to cut it when Salerno was over 300 miles away. What's more, an entire division of three brigades, each with three battalions, required 3,000 vehicles, and even a light scale amounted to 2,000 vehicles. So if Eighth Army was to get across and get moving quickly and join the planned AVALANCHE assault with speed, then clearly more shipping was required.

But more shipping was not available. Montgomery's planners had demanded 344 landing craft of all kinds, which they reckoned would be enough for the transport of three divisions. However, they were flatly told they would have to make do with only 268 landing craft in all, almost 20 per cent fewer than they had asked for, which in turn was considerably less than were needed for a larger army-scale crossing. This meant Eighth Army would have to make do with just two divisions taking part in the initial assault rather than the seven it had on paper. It was not a lot.

The meagre intelligence gathered suggested that it would be enough, however. Landing parties had secretly crossed the Straits ahead of BAY-TOWN and a captured Italian had revealed that most civilians had already fled to the hills, as had the majority of the defenders, most of whom had abandoned their uniforms in the process. But despite this Montgomery was not prepared to take any risks, which as a rule of thumb was a very sensible approach. He did consider cancelling BAYTOWN altogether and landing further along the toe, but that would have been impossible because it would have entailed a longer and more time-consuming journey for each individual trip made by a landing craft. Any benefit of being further up the leg would have been swiftly lost by the greater time it would have taken to build up sufficient strength. Again, the lack of landing craft meant Monty's hands were tied, and clearly the most efficient way to use the few that he had was to cross at the shortest points.

Captain David Cole was among the first wave, the 2nd Inniskillings being one of the three 845-men-strong battalions of 13th Infantry Brigade – which in turn was one of three such brigades that made up the fighting heart of 5th 'Yorkshire' Division. Messina harbour had been largely wrecked and the air was pungent with the stench of decomposing corpses and detritus; the stink and abundant scenes of destruction had helped him swiftly acclimatize once again to the business of war. Then, at dusk on the 2nd, they had been shuffled on to the 50-yard-long LCI, packed like sardines. Tea and cold stew had been handed round. A fly had immediately begun swimming in Cole's mug. Darkness fell, and then they slipped their mooring and moved out into the water to form up. Later he found an empty bunk and went straight to sleep, waking only to the grind and thrum of the engines. It was 3.30 a.m. and they were on their way. His mouth was dry and his head felt heavy as he groped his way to the main body of the craft. A blast of cool air to clear the weariness away. Cole peered into the darkness, only faintly sensing the land mass ahead of them, then suddenly the Sicilian coast behind erupted in a flash of light. The barrage Alan Moorehead watched from the Sicilian hills had begun. Above Cole the air was heavy with the rushing, sucking whoosh of shells, followed by the shoreline ahead prickled with orange flashes as they detonated. Fires burned along the Calabrian coast. Searchlights now swivelled into the air to aid the landing craft towards the right beaches. Italy loomed, big, dark and imposing, the mountains rising from the shore. The noise was immense, the air suddenly dense with smoke and the sharp smell of fumes. Then rockets began fizzing and ripping through the air from the specially adapted landing craft, trails of yellow and orange curling in towards the coast. Very lights crackled and star-shells burst with twinkling light. A few enemy shells whooshed into the sea nearby as their own smoke shells burst to give the assault force cover as they neared the coast. A final crescendo, pulses of which could be felt through each of the men, and then silence but for the thrum of the land-ing craft. Thick, smoky fog now hid the coast. Occasionally, faint shapes and a sense of a looming land mass.

A bump and the landing craft stopped. Down went the ramp. Behind, Bren light machine guns at the stern of the craft covering them as they ran ahead. Cole wondered where the 2nd Cameronians were, who were also part of 13th Brigade and had been supposed to land before them. There was no sign of them. The beach almost invisible. Then there was the sea wall. Glimpses of the beach through gaps in the smoke. They clambered up the wall, then scurried forward through a blasted orchard. Any moment, Cole expected a machine gun to open fire or someone to detonate a mine. But there was nothing – just a cat that slunk past them. His heart, which had been thundering in his chest, quietened with relief. On they went, through the orchard until they reached the coast road. They were in the wrong place – of course they were – so a wireless set was swiftly produced to try and make contact with other companies. The road was pockmarked with craters, buildings had collapsed, smoke swirled thickly and Italian civilians began emerging from the ruins, fran-tically shouting 'Viva Inglesi' even though the Inglesi had decimated their homes. Now Italian soldiers emerged too, weapons abandoned, wander-ing in bewilderment with their hands in the air.

At around 9 a.m., Alan Moorehead drove down to Montgomery's HQ at Messina for a press briefing. The general, in an affable mood and stabbing at a map with a pencil, proceeded to show them where his troops had landed and where they were heading. Moorehead and his select few fellows were then invited to accompany Monty on to one of the 190 DUKWs – pronounced 'ducks' – that had been lent to Eighth Army by the Americans. These ingenious vehicles could swim then drive off the beach carrying twenty-five men or over 2 tons of supplies. For the short dash across the Straits, they were ideal.

Montgomery sat up front as they motored across the water. The far side was shrouded in smoke still. All around were landing craft, some big, some small, freighters and other vessels, so that Moorehead thought it seemed a little like a yachting regatta. Halfway across, biscuits and coffee were offered, Montgomery's cue to hold forth.

'You must never let the enemy choose the ground on which you fight,' he told them, echoing the thoughts of the Duke of Wellington, an earlier British general. 'You must never fight the battle *his* way. You must choose the ground. He must be made to fight the battle according to your plan. Never his plan. Never.' That was all very well, but the terrain and limited infrastructure of Italy would inevitably inhibit Monty's freedom of manoeuvre – and consequently choice of ground.

They neared the coast just north of Reggio. Suddenly, a gaggle of German aircraft dived out of the sun. Bombs whistled down, exploding with huge spumes of water, but otherwise hit nothing. When they came around for a second time, all on the DUKW, Montgomery included, hit the deck. The cannons on the DUKW opened up along with a host of others, shattering the otherwise calm and peaceful crossing. The German planes disappeared. Calm returned.

Soon after, they landed on the beach and drove off. Moorehead was impressed by the immense activity, with half a dozen large landing ships at the shore's edge, their bows open and trucks and tanks rumbling off directly on to the beach. Italian prisoners were already working alongside Tommies to lay down mesh to help vehicles off the beach. Other groups of men were making tea, relief etched into their faces that the invasion had been so very easy. 'One had the impression,' noted Moorehead, 'that all this had been going on here for months instead of just five hours.'

On seeing Montgomery, men cheered and whistled, and the general was handed large numbers of cigarette packets, which he distributed before moving on, stopping at each brigade HQ, where more men gathered around and more cigarettes from the stash of 10,000 in the DUKW were handed out. In Reggio itself even Italian troops, now prisoners, cheered him.

*

It was the Canadian 3rd Infantry Brigade that had landed first, on the northern edge of Reggio, while 5th Division landed a little to the north near Villa San Giovanni. Then follow-up brigades were to be shuttled over just as quickly as the available landing craft could get them. So it was that the Hasty Ps, part of the Canadian 1st Infantry Brigade, didn't land until around 3 p.m. Some Italian Fiat dive-bombers had half-heartedly appeared, but all their bombs had been wide; it was another indication that the Italians' hearts were no longer in the fight.

Having unloaded and got themselves reorganized, the battalion was ordered up into the mountains to secure the high ground. Farley Mowat thought they looked rather like an extended khaki snake as they wound their way up a track on the Aspromonte massif, looming imperiously some 6,000 feet above them. Then, tramping down towards them was a large column of Italians, singing and laughing and only too happy to submit themselves to the conquering Allies. As intelligence officer, it was Mowat's task to corral them and find out which units they were from and whether there were any others up in the mountains more determined than this lot to carry on the fight.

Meanwhile, the British 13th Brigade was also ordered up into the mountains. The 2nd Inniskillings were told to climb Monte San Nicolò and secure a mountain village called Ortì. Captain David Cole was a little worried that it had all been too easy thus far, and noticed from his map that while their approach from the coast meant a climb up a dusty mule track, on the far side of Ortì the approach looked to be by a half-decent road. In other words, the village could be held by the enemy with a clear line of retreat behind them.

With no vehicles available at this stage, they were forced to use their own two feet. It was still a hot day as they trudged their way up the winding track, past vineyards on the lower slopes, then endless cactus bushes, around a plunging gorge and slopes rich with baby oaks and chestnuts. 'Toiling up the mountain under a burning sun,' noted Cole, 'and weighed down by a barrow-load of personal military hardware, I felt less like a mountain goat than a kebab on a grill.'

Whatever troops had been on the summit had slipped away by the time they reached the top. There they found a monastery ahead of the village and paused to catch their breath. The view was stunning: Sicily, its mountains blue and Homeric, mighty Etna in the distance. The Straits were filled with shipping – both warships and landing craft scuttling back and forth, while the sun burnished the water. Really, the Straits did look little more than a river crossing from up there. The Allies were now on mainland Europe, which was no small feat after three long years.

But never had the word 'toehold' been more appropriately applied. Rome, the capital of Italy, was more than 430 miles away, and although, as the saying went, all roads led there, they did so through one of the most mountainous countries in Europe.

CHAPTER 5

Uncertainty

F LYING OVER THE NAPLES region was continuing to be a challenging and largely fruitless exercise for Feldwebel Robert Gugelberger. As if just surviving when so horribly outnumbered wasn't hard enough, the powers that be had now equipped 2./JG53 with rockets. One day, men had appeared to fit the firing mechanisms, then a stash of rockets themselves had arrived, and after loading one each on to the undersides of their wings the pilots had been scrambled and sent off to use these new wonder weapons. Of course, there had not been enough fuel for any practice sessions or training, and so on 29 August Gugelberger found himself high over Caserta lining up against some American P-38 Lightnings and fired both rockets for the first time, possibly more in hope than much expectation. 'A brief flash and both things blasted off,' he scribbled later. 'They shot towards the enemy formation at great speed but unfortunately exploded short of the target in clouds of black smoke.'

The next day he was tussling with the Lightnings yet again, but once more failed to hit anything. In fact, he'd fired his rockets and then found himself being pounced on. He reckoned he'd been lucky to get away. Unteroffizier Niesen had been reported missing on 30 August, but two days later, on 1 September, his remains were discovered. 'A hole three metres deep,' noted Gugelberger. 'A few shreds of our yellow neckerchief and a piece of scalp with blond hair, bent pieces of metal everywhere. That was all they found of him.'

On 3 September, as the armistice was being signed, Gugelberger was unable to fire his rockets at all, which was frustrating as he'd lined up a target nicely. It turned out the ignition wires had become loose in the slipstream. He saw some enemy planes going down, including a heavy – a four-engine bomber – that struck the ground and exploded. The next day, 4 September, they flew to intercept another formation of heavies. Gugelberger was flying wingman to Hauptmann Kraus, the Staffel commander, but Kraus reported oxygen problems and so turned back. That left Gugelberger alone, so he climbed to 33,000 feet, where he hoped to spot some prey and dive down on them, only to discover three Lightnings circling out of the sun and lining up on him instead. He frantically pushed his stick forward, both hands on the control column, and dived, down and down and down, right through subsequent swarms of Lightnings until he reached 12,000 feet, at which point he levelled out and ducked into a large thunder cloud. There he began to breathe a little more easily. 'I had far exceeded the prescribed maximum speed while diving,' he scribbled later, 'and was happy that my machine had stood up to it.'

Again, Gugelberger lived to fight another day, but although others were scoring a few victories against the Americans, German casualties were mounting and included some of their most revered and experienced aces – men like Oberleutnant Franz Schiess, the Staffel commander of 8./JG53, who was lost on 2 September, and Oberleutnant Martin Laube, who simply vanished in the same thunderstorm that had saved Gugelberger. Schiess had been a notable ace with sixty-seven victories to his name; these losses were catastrophic because their knowledge and experience were invaluable and because there was no one with similar skill to replace them. By 5 September, all three Staffeln in 2./JG53 were struggling; yet as if the intensity of the air combat was not enough, that day 150 Allied bombers plastered Cancello. Fortunately for Gugelberger and his fellows, they'd been scrambled to intercept the approaching raiders so had not been on the ground when the bombs started whistling down.

There was little Gugelberger or any of them could do about it; frantically scanning the sky, he saw Lightnings below him and above him, while down on the ground Cancello had disappeared amid spurts of orange and clouds of rolling, angry smoke and dust. 'Unable to land at our base,' he wrote later, 'as it was totally destroyed.' Instead, they'd turned north and touched down safely at Frosinone, twenty miles north of Cassino. The pilots referred to such hammerings ironically as 'Reich Party Days'. That night, camped at Frosinone, they reckoned the raid at

Cancello had been the twelfth such party day they'd experienced. It was hard not to wonder how many more they might survive.

Briefly back at Malta for rearming and refuelling was the British battle-ship HMS *Warspite*, the former flagship of Admiral Sir Andrew Browne Cunningham in the days when he'd been C-in-C of the Mediterranean Fleet and doing his best to keep the tiny British island afloat despite the very best efforts of the Luftwaffe and Regia Aeronautica operating from Sicily. *Warspite* had helped escort convoys, taken on the Italian Fleet at Calabria and Cape Matapan, supported the naval air assault on Taranto, overseen the evacuations of Greece and Crete, bombarded Axis ports in North Africa and supported the invasion of Sicily and, on 3 September, Eighth Army's crossing of the Straits of Messina. In between, it had even undertaken a stint in the Indian Ocean in the Eastern Fleet.

It was a fine ship, launched way back in 1913, and was known as the 'Grand Old Lady'. Even so, *Warspite* had undergone several refits and was a modern, powerful battleship with four twin 15-inch main guns, four-teen 6-inch guns, two 3-inch anti-aircraft guns and also four torpedo tubes. Her armour was a whopping 330mm thick in places, yet she could still manage 24 knots at full steam. Battleships like *Warspite* were marvels of engineering, ingenuity and immense firepower. Those big 15-inch guns, for example, could hurl their shells, each weighing not much less than a ton, some twenty miles. Admittedly, battleships were no longer the pre-eminent warship – fleet aircraft carriers were – but they still had a very important role to play, not least in the current operations in Italy; those guns offered the assaulting forces a huge amount of very powerful fire support. Furthermore, while the US Navy had overtaken the Royal Navy in size, Britain had begun the war with the world's largest navy, and, with the bulk of the US Navy in operations in the Pacific, had taken on the lion's share of the Allied Navy's role in the Mediterranean.

Commanding *Warspite* was a man who had seen almost as much action as the ship he had the honour to command. Captain Bertie Packer was forty-eight, and despite having a doctor for a father and a musician for a mother had entered the Royal Naval College at Dartmouth in south-west England at the age of fourteen. After several junior postings he had then joined *Warspite* as a twenty-year-old sub-lieutenant in February 1915, and as a gunnery officer had been on the battleship at the Battle of Jutland. Over nearly thirty years in the navy, he'd served all around the world, slowly but surely rising up the ranks. Since the outbreak of war he'd seen action in Norway and in the Mediterranean, as well as taking a posting at the navy's Gunnery School. A fine sportsman – he played one first-class cricket match for the navy against Cambridge University in 1920 – and an aggressive, highly combative sailor in the best Nelsonian tradition, Packer had experience, deep knowledge, imperturbability and easy affability. These were very useful characteristics for the commander of one of the Royal Navy's most illustrious battleships.

Earlier in the morning of 3 September, *Warspite* had been bombarding the Calabrian coast in support of BAYTOWN, but later that evening, after reaching Malta, Packer paused to write up his diary. He'd had a lot of experience fighting the Italians and had always thought their hearts had not really been in it, so it hadn't surprised him to learn that both the Canadians and 5th Division were ashore in the toe and meeting little or no opposition. He reckoned progress might well be pretty swift from here on. 'As a foolish prophecy,' he added, 'I'll give Italy south of Naples a fortnight and Rome a month!!' It was, he knew, a guess based on insufficient knowledge, but after the domino successes in the Mediterranean so far this year, Packer reckoned the wind was now sufficiently in the Allies' sails.

General Montgomery and the other senior Allied commanders would love to have felt as confident as Packer, but the Eighth Army commander did not like to be too openly optimistic. That way one was always setting oneself up for a fall, and anyone looking at a map of Italy would be foolish to think progress would be plain sailing. He was all too aware they had a ferociously challenging task on their hands, which was why he'd not entirely abandoned the notion of landing a force on the northern part of the toe – anything that might make their progress easier was a good idea as far as he was concerned. The much larger BUTTRESS plan was a non-starter – there simply weren't the landing craft – but he had managed to find the shipping for a much more modest assault to be made by the Special Raiding Squadron, who were to land at the tiny fishing port of Bagnara. The village nestled right next to the sea at the base of low mountains which rose to a cultivated plateau before, a couple of miles further inland, rising again to a further and much higher mountain chain. But weaving its way around the spurs that directly overlooked the sea was the coast road, with steep scrub and tree-covered rock above and equally sharp drops below. In other words, if the road was blown, there was no real means of getting around it and continuing with the journey.

While this road hugged the mountainside directly above Bagnara, it also gradually climbed, via a raft of tight turns and hairpin bends, to a lower plateau. From there it continued to weave its way along the top of the toe and then, eventually, northwards, with quite a lot more room to manoeuvre between the mountains and the sea.

Monty's planners saw the coast road at Bagnara as a potential pinch point. If the Germans carried out a series of demolitions here, 5th Division's march towards Salerno could easily get very badly held up. So the idea was that the Special Raiding Squadron would get there before any retreating Germans could do their worst and keep the road and bridge open.

The Special Raiding Squadron had formerly been 1 SAS, those wild desert marauders who had wreaked havoc behind enemy lines in Egypt and Libya, hurtling through the desert and emerging at night to blow up Axis aircraft and columns of supplies. And very effective they had been too; but with its founder, David Stirling, captured in Tunisia in February and North African shores in Allied hands, there had been less scope for them to continue with their rogue hit-and-run tactics. Instead they had been turned into the SRS and were treated as a very fit, very disciplined and very well-trained special operations strike force. In Sicily, they had brilliantly executed a seaborne attack on a large Italian coastal battery and then helped capture the port of Augusta. Since then they'd been twiddling their thumbs waiting for another mission. Bagnara was their next opportunity to show their mettle.

The plan was simple, devised by the SRS's imperturbable and charismatic commander, the Ulsterman Lieutenant-Colonel Blair 'Paddy' Mayne, one of the SAS 'Originals' and already something of a legend. His band of warriors were less than 300-strong, split into three troops, each of which was further divided into three sections and again into half-sections and three-man teams.

This small strike force was due to land in two LCIs to the south of Bagnara at around 1.30 a.m. on Saturday, 4 September, clear the town of any enemy troops and then climb up to the road, hold the stretch directly above and secure the bridge a mile further on over the gully. Around 2 a.m., however, the men were getting restless, not least Lieutenant Peter Davis, a twenty-one-year-old section leader in 2 Troop. Davis had joined 1 SAS almost straight from officer training in England a year earlier. Finding himself stuck in the base depot and eager to do something interesting and exciting, he had volunteered – and been accepted – for the 1st

Special Service Regiment, which had been originally set up to develop guerrilla warfare on the Syrian border with Turkey. It had never actually been put into action and so in March had been merged into 1 SAS, which had then become the Special Raiding Squadron. No matter its name, it was very much Paddy Mayne's force, moulded as he thought best, and among its number were plenty of other SAS Originals too, but also young adventurers like Peter Davis who had more than proved themselves during operations in Sicily.

Now, though, at around 3 a.m. it was clear something was amiss as they'd already gone past the river bed that was their landing point – even in the light of the thin moon, they had clearly recognized it. Then Captain Harry Poat, his 2 Troop commander, was beside him.

'Tell your section,' he told Davis, 'that in all probability we are being landed in the wrong place, and that we have not a minute to waste as it will be light in less than an hour.'

With a crash and a violent jolt they touched the shore a little while later. A rattle of chains and the ramp lowered, loud enough, Davis thought, to wake the entire town. No firing greeted them, and as Davis disembarked on to the beach he saw Mayne standing at the end of the ramp, watching his men off the craft. As Davis passed him, Mayne told him where he could find Harry Poat and the rest of the troop.

Sure enough, he and his section found Poat immediately. Having studied aerial photographs in great detail beforehand, they all knew they were in completely the wrong place. In fact, they'd landed two miles further north, beside a rocky outcrop that jutted over the northern edge of the little town. Paddy, Poat told them, had already completely changed the plan. They were no longer going to bother clearing the town but simply push through, scale the heights above and get on to the coast road; 2 Troop's task was to press ahead to the gully and secure the bridge on the hairpin there. 'Now get cracking,' Poat finished, 'but for heaven's sake, don't delay.'

Davis and his men hurried through the town in street fighting formation, a subsection either side of the road, but it appeared to be deserted. In no time, they had reached the inland edge of the town and were looking up at the cliffs rising above them. Following a snaking ravine, they then began climbing as the gully ended, taking the less precipitous slope to their left. Before long they reached a track. Here they paused, with the mountains above them and the sea to their backs.

Already, to the east, the first streaks of dawn began to light the sky so they could see quite clearly.

'Is that Number 3 Troop on the road behind us, sir?' Davis's runner, Johnny Hair, asked casually. Davis followed his gaze back south-westwards and saw a number of troops coming up the coast road. Squinting through his binoculars he said, 'Yes, they're ours,' then suddenly realized there was something unfamiliar about the peaked caps they were wearing.

'Watch out, lads!' he cried suddenly. 'They're Jerries!'

Before they could react, a Bren from another section opened fire. Davis cursed. Some Germans fell, others made for the scrub and disappeared, but firing was now ringing out all around them until suddenly it stopped as quickly as it had begun and a number of the startled enemy troops were meekly surrendering. Shortly after, a runner from Harry Poat appeared and Davis realized that the track led, via a tight hairpin, up to the coast road 100 feet above them. It was where Poat had set up Troop HQ. Hurrying up, on reaching Poat Davis learned that the captured Germans were engineers from 15. Panzergrenadier-Division, left behind to carry out demolitions. It seemed the SRS men had arrived not a moment too soon.

With his back to the sea and the town below them, Davis gazed up at the terraced slope rising sharply above. They were now on a sharp ninety-degree bend in the road as it turned round a jutting spur. A little further on, perhaps 200 yards away, was another right-hand bend, which, Poat told him, was being held by Derrick Harrison, like Davis a section commander in 2 Troop. As they knew from their maps and the aerial photographs they had studied, around 400 yards further on from the bend where Harrison was positioned was a dog-leg that ran over a steep but narrow gully before the road headed back towards the sea again. Securing that bridge over the gully was 2 Troop's objective. Poat now told Davis to get going and head beyond Harrison, secure the next stretch of the road and wait for him to follow with the rest of the troop.

Davis hurried forward and around the next bend found Harrison, crouching down behind a wall. His friend now frantically signalled to him to get down. They were being sniped at, Harrison told him. 'I honestly do not recommend you go beyond this point,' he said.

Davis brushed aside such concerns; he'd not seen or heard any sniping and he had his orders, so he and his men pushed on. Round the bend he realized there was almost no cover at all along the entire stretch to the hairpin and the bridge. Below were narrow, steep terraces, each about 4 feet wide and 4 deep, while above them the rock rose almost vertically.

About halfway along was a small single-storey house clinging to the side of the cliff, behind which there was some cover, but otherwise there was nothing at all, not a single place to hide. It was, Davis realized, a nasty position in which to get caught if the enemy did start firing, but as they scampered along the road all seemed quiet.

Then a crack and the fizz of a bullet just above his head. He and his men immediately hit the ground, only to hear the swish-swoosh of incoming mortars, a loud crash and showers of debris clattering around them. Now a machine gun opened fire, a sharp buzz of more than twenty bullets per second, the retort echoing around the tight ravine over which they looked.

'Come on!' Davis yelled, 'Make for that house!' Clambering to his feet, he sprinted as fast as he could, his men following him, bullets pinging and zipping around them but miraculously not hitting a single man. Just 15 yards from safety they realized there was a wire fence around the house. Hitting the ground again, and with only a large cactus plant offering any protection, Davis grabbed some wire cutters from one of his men, snapped a way through and they made a dash to the safety of the roadside wall. Looking around, Davis realized all his men were with him except Corporal Mitchell's subsection. They had been behind, but there was now no sign of them; he prayed they had fallen back to Harrison's position.

Davis cursed. Pinned down and unable to move, they were safe from bullets but a single mortar could easily wipe them all out if it landed over them and between the house and edge of the cliffs. After the hairpin the road doubled back, so the far side of the ravine, as it climbed up towards the next spur, was no more than 300 yards or so away and was clearly where the enemy were, hidden in the scrub, watching Davis and his men move down the road, only opening fire once it was too late for them to fall back. These German rearguards at Bagnara were the first the British had met in Italy, but Peter Davis and his men now found that their own advance had come to a perilous halt. *The cunning devils*, Davis thought. But what to do? They were in a tight spot with no obvious means of extricating themselves – at least not until some heavy firepower of their own joined them. Firepower the lightly armed SRS did not have.

In Rome that same Saturday was Filippo Caracciolo, a member of one of the most prominent families ever to have lived in Naples. He had been Duke of Melito since the age of three, and in 1938 had become the eighth

Prince of Castagneto; with it he held the hereditary post of Patrician of Naples. Just forty years old, Prince Filippo was tall, lean, good-looking and exuded elegant urbanity from every pore. A multi-linguist, he also had a doctorate in economics and had, throughout the 1930s, held a series of diplomatic posts. This, however, had not made him a Fascist; far from it. Rather, he was an ardent believer in democracy and had been working in the shadows to help several political parties keep going. Since January that year, for example, Caracciolo had been in regular contact with the British Special Operations Executive and the American Office of Strategic Services in Switzerland. The SOE was a clandestine organization set up in 1940 to help fan the flames of resistance in occupied Europe, while the OSS was the American overseas secret intelligence service. With his connections and flawless English, Caracciolo had been the ideal person to forge links between the Allies and democratic Italian parties such as the Partito d'Azione – the Action Party.

This was one of six main clandestine political parties in Italy, most of which had been bubbling under the surface for some years and even since the advent of Fascism. Although after the fall of Mussolini the King had insisted that political parties should continue to be banned, these had increasingly emerged from hiding. Key political figures, exiled since 1922, began making broadcasts and writing pamphlets, and those far from Italian shores, such as Count Carlo Sforza, who had been abroad since Mussolini had taken power over twenty years earlier, more recently in the United States, made it clear they wanted to return. A palpable atmosphere of change and anticipation was in the air – one that was defiantly anti-war, anti-German and, for the most part, anti-monarchy too. For men like Sforza and other political thinkers and anti-Fascists such as Benedetto Croce, the time had come to start speaking their minds, to begin laying the building blocks of a new Italy, one that was emerging from both absolutism and war.

It was not, then, perhaps so surprising that five of Italy's political parties had called for a brace of conferences, the first in Florence, due to be held on 5 September, and the second the following day in Milan. Caracciolo was not attending, however – instead he was heading north to catch up with the Americans in Switzerland; there was vital work to be done at this time. None the less, at Rome's Termini Station he bumped into a number of friends from the Action Party all heading to Florence. 'Everyone,' he noted in his diary, 'seems cheerful and talking animatedly.' Ideas were bursting from their mouths as they excitedly discussed the way forward and how Italy might walk a new path. It was thrilling but nerve-wracking too, and listening to his friends Caracciolo could easily imagine the discussions and verbal clashes that would take place the following day. When he left them to go and find his cabin, he did so with a bit of envy.

On the coast road above Bagnara that Saturday, Peter Davis and his men had remained stuck at the house for eight very long hours. One of them, Charlie Tobin, had been killed trying to make a dash for it. Two more, Ted Tunstall and Bill McNinch, had eventually made a move with a Bren, which had prompted an immediate burst of fire. Tunstall had caught a splinter in the face. Gurgling and with blood pouring from his mouth, they got him safely behind the wall and did their best to patch him up. Mitchell's subsection, caught by mortars at the start of the day, had also suffered casualties. Lying behind the house, the hours passing inexorably, with one of his best men dead beside him, Davis felt both impotent and utterly wretched.

Only at dusk were they finally able to move and make contact again with the rest of the troop. It turned out that Harry Poat had led some men up on to the cliffs above them but had been unable to clear the enemy from the far side. Poat had had a lucky escape when a bullet passed through his trouser pocket, killing the man, a signaller, behind him. Both the cotton trousers and the maps in the thigh pocket had caught fire, but he'd been able to put out the flames before getting badly burned himself.

The rest of the town had been swiftly cleared, however, and a number of caves were discovered where they found much of the town's population sheltering. By evening, the lead elements of 5th Division arrived and overnight the German rearguards slipped away – and without destroying the road or the bridge on the hairpin. Amazingly, only four SRS men had been killed and their objectives were all taken, so it was another success. It didn't seem that way to Peter Davis, though. Before moving out, he and his men buried Charlie Tobin, marking the grave with a roughly made cross, then marched back down the hill.

'You know, sir,' Sergeant McNinch said to him, 'it's funny that it is always the best that catch it. Charlie Tobin was the kindest-hearted man in the section – he would never say a hard word about anyone – and they have to go and kill him.'

In truth, the SRS's capture of Bagnara had been a minor engagement in the big scheme of things, but even there, in the toe of Italy, the enemy rearguards had laid down a troubling marker. Italy, it was all too clear, was a defender's dream. And an attacker's nightmare.

A little over 100 miles away to the north, but still in Calabria, stood the town of Cosenza, stretched lozenge-shaped in a narrow valley sur-rounded by ever more mountains. Here, currently, reorganizing and training after their heroics in Sicily, were the core of 1. Fallschirmjäger-Division. Part of the Luftwaffe, they were integrated into the army and, as with all German troops, after several long years fighting in the Mediter-ranean and along the Eastern Front they were well used to their units being savagely mauled and had become masters of tactical flexibility. Rigid discipline helped, and this, combined with growing experience, ensured that no matter how badly bashed about individual units had become they could very swiftly morph themselves into a functioning for-mation ready to face the next onslaught. The Germans called these units Kampfgruppen, or battle groups. So the survivors from Sicily had become Kampfgruppe Cosenza while they waited for reinforcements to arrive – a mixture of new recruits and those now recovered from earlier wounds and illnesses.

One of those surviving old hands was Leutnant Martin Pöppel, a vet-eran of Norway, the Balkans, Crete, Russia and Sicily, even though he was still only twenty-three and looked younger. His 1. Kompanie of the Maschinengewehr-Bataillon – machine-gun battalion – in which he'd been a platoon commander, had been merged with 4. Kompanie, and also a platoon of anti-tank soldiers and a further platoon of Pioniere – combat engineers – and placed under the command of an Oberleutnant, a mere first lieutenant. That was the battle group.

Pöppel couldn't understand why they were loitering in Calabria. 'Whatever we do,' he noted in his diary, 'Tommy will be successful in the south, where the Italians will put up little resistance. And then he'll prob-ably attack around Naples so as to isolate the boot of Italy.' Surely, he thought, the logical and most sensible approach was to create a really strong defensive line further north where they would have better pros-pects of successfully holding the enemy back. After all, the point had to be to protect the southern flanks of the Reich. Italy was narrow and with the help of the mountains might well be defended indefinitely if they chose the right stretch at which to make a stand. Soldiers like Pöppel had been taught that concentration of force was key. Spreading themselves too thinly, like it seemed to him they were doing, didn't make a lot of sense as far as he was concerned. Pöppel, though, was not aware of Operation ACHSE. Even so, he had a point.

He'd made that diary entry on 23 August. In the intervening fortnight they'd watched countless Allied bombers and fighter aircraft thundering over. Cosenza itself had earned two visits. They'd also gone on transport-hunting missions, requisitioning any lorries they could find from the local Italians, still, at that time, their allies. Now it was 4 September and the rumours of a move to the Taranto area that had been circulating were confirmed. The Allies had landed in the toe, just as he'd predicted, and, as he'd also known, the Italians had shown no appetite to fight. Well, that was no surprise, but it meant the paratroopers were now in the firing line again.

The first units of the battle group got going at 6.30 a.m. and Pöppel and his platoon were not far behind. They headed south, to the coast road of the sole of the boot. The sun was high and warm, the countryside varied, mountainous and beautiful. It felt like a holiday jaunt. 'A real Strength Through Joy outing,' Pöppel noted. Then they reached the coast. Most roads in Italy were of compressed clay and grit – *strade bianche* – and he could no longer see much beyond a permanent haze of dust caused by the trucks ahead of them. Occasionally, they passed a 'Zona Militare'. 'But these Italian coastal defences,' he wrote, 'are a mixture of joke and bluff.' He thought their trenches and machine-gun nests were pathetic.

They reached their camp a little after 4 p.m. that afternoon. It was near Altamura, in Apulia, on the south-eastern side of the boot. Taranto, that vital Italian naval base, lay on the western side of the heel, some fifty miles to the south-east in a flat plain; this corner was one of the few low-lying areas in the country. Less than thirty miles away, to the east on the Adriatic Coast, stood another key port, Bari. So, then. This was the area they were to defend.

Some way to the north, around Naples, Generalleutnant Hermann Balck was making a tour of inspection of his new corps. A deep thinker about war, he had also realized the enormous defensive opportunities Italy offered; generally, he felt his new fellows at XIV Panzerkorps appeared to rather overestimate the Allies and underestimate themselves. Really, the defensive advantages were enormous.

A couple of days earlier, on 2 September, Balck had landed in Rome via a flight over the old battleground across which he'd fought on the Italian Front in 1917; and here he was again in Italy after all those years. What a different time – and war – it was. He'd been fighting the Italians then; perhaps he would be fighting them again any day soon. Balck was forty-nine, a career soldier and a very competent one at that. In that last war, he'd been recommended for the Pour le Mérite – the so-called Blue Max, Imperial Germany's highest medal for valour; the war had ended before it could be processed, but he'd still collected an Iron Cross First Class and seven wounds.

In this latest war, he'd commanded the 1. Schützen-Regiment in 1940 and led the first men across the River Meuse – part of General Heinz Guderian's Panzerkorps. Promotion had followed, along with combat experience in Greece and then the Eastern Front, where he'd commanded 11. Panzer-Division and destroyed an entire Red Army tank corps and much of the Fifth Tank Army. He was justifiably considered one of the brightest panzer commanders in the army, with the Knight's Cross with Oak Leaves, Swords and Diamonds around his neck to prove it – a collection of medals that put him in extremely rare company.

Now forty-nine, and with a trim, clean-shaven face and still-youthful features, Balck was in Italy to take up temporary reins of XIV Panzer-korps while General Hans-Valentin Hube, who had commanded the corps in Sicily, was away on leave. He had immediately travelled to Feld-marschall Kesselring's headquarters near Frascati, outside Rome, for briefing. The Heeresgruppe C commander swiftly put him in the picture. An Allied invasion was expected between Gaeta, north of Naples, and Paestum to the south. The 16. Panzer-Division was already in the area with the Hermann Göring Division near Naples. In all, the German 10. Armee had eight divisions and XIV Panzerkorps three; they could not place all their units along this coastal strip largely because, should the Italians sur-render, troops would be needed across the country to rapidly disarm the Italian armed forces.

Briefing over, he hurried south, Hube formally handing over com-mand on a country road, then headed to Corps HQ, which was in a chestnut grove just to the south of Cassino, about forty miles north-west of Naples. Now, on 4 September, Balck was making an inspection tour of his divisions, his heart sinking somewhat as he realized how many new recruits there were. The Hermann Göring and 15. Panzergrenadier had taken a pasting in Sicily while 16. Panzer had been completely rebuilt since Stalingrad. Above, Allied aircraft seemed to swarm over the skies. Enemy air superiority was not something he had had to contend with in Russia; over here in Italy, he realized, it would determine all their actions.

Early the next morning, Balck determined to visit 16. Panzer a second time, as he was pretty convinced that their area, between Salerno and Paestum, was where the Allies would land. Unfortunately, his pilot was unable to lift the Fieseler Storch from the short airfield in time and crashed. Both pilot and general were very lucky to survive, but Balck broke multiple ribs. He was injured enough to abandon his planned visit to 16. Panzer, but not his new command. Despite the cracked ribs, Balck was determined to stick it out. When the Allies arrived, he would be waiting for them.

That same morning, the night train pulled into Milan and Filippo Caracciolo alighted to find a dense crowd on the platform and pullulating through the station in an atmosphere of excitement, near-panic; hysteria almost. It was Sunday, 5 September. He went in search of the Como train, only to discover another surge of people trying to cram themselves on to the next one due to leave, jostling and crying out as though boarding it was a matter of life and death. He eventually managed to get on and find a seat, and after a long and interminable journey finally reached Chiasso in Switzerland that night. 'As always in these times,' he wrote, 'a sense of order, cleanliness, solidity, and a physical sense of security touches me in contact with the Swiss soil.' Switzerland, after all, was not at war, was not in the throes of catastrophe.

The next day, refreshed and invigorated by the cool Alpine air, he met with Allen Dulles and John McCaffrey, both from the Office of Strategic Services. Dulles was head of the OSS in Berne, and they were meeting at the house of Rino De Nobili, a fellow Italian diplomat and anti-Fascist now based in Switzerland and working with Allied intelligence services. In lengthy conversations, Caracciolo learned of the armistice and its imminent announcement. They all agreed the situation was currently deteriorating fast because of the time that had been lost; German troops were continuing to flood into Italy. There were the uncertainties of just what unconditional surrender would mean. And what were the political possibilities in the immediate future? So much uncertainty. 'Cordial farewell to the two friends,' he jotted in his diary. 'When will we meet again?'

CHAPTER 6

Mistrust

IF ANYONE IN THE Allied command in the Mediterranean had thought
the signing of the armistice was the end of the Anglo-Italian negotiations, they were very much mistaken. Military talks resumed at Fairfield
Camp that afternoon of 3 September as soon as the ink was dry and had
continued through the night. It had been agreed with the Italians that
Castellano should head the Military Mission, while Alexander, as Army
Group commander, took the lead for the Allies. Alexander thought the
planned 82nd Airborne drop was a 'ticklish business'. Success depended
on what the Italians would do. If they fought hard on the Allied side, then
the American paratroopers might well be all right. Similarly, Castellano
and his team were desperately trying to find out the strength with which
the Allies were going to land. 'But, of course,' said Alexander, 'we wouldn't
tell them.' Of course not. The Allies were never going to trust the Italians;
after all, until they told the entire world they had surrendered they were
still the enemy.

Nor, for the very same reason, would they tell them when the invasion
was going to take place. Because the armistice announcement was tied in
with plans for AVALANCHE, in the days following the signing the Italians had no idea when the Allies were planning to broadcast it to the
world. They had agreed, however, that Badoglio should make an
announcement as soon as Eisenhower had done so. Intelligence suggested that the Germans still had no clear idea of what Allied plans were,
but as the next couple of days passed, anxiety about the proposed 82nd
Airborne drop at the mouth of the Tiber continued to rise. The paratroopers of the 'All American' – as the division was known – were

volunteers, highly trained, now combat-experienced and among the best troops in the US Army. However, there was only so much that such troops could achieve, because they could only fight with what they could carry with them – and that wasn't a huge amount. They were shock troops, designed for specific *coup de main* operations. If the Italians folded and the Germans concentrated considerable force on Rome, there was a high danger the 82nd Airborne could be wiped out. On the other hand, the prize of swiftly capturing Rome was an intoxicating one.

Maresciallo Badoglio and the senior Italian leadership, however, had been in a state of mounting panic since the signing of the armistice. It remained riven by factions, mutual distrust and differing views, and Badoglio was certainly not the man to rally his immediate subordinates effectively. They had no idea how long they had to ready themselves for the Allied invasion, but they were aware the country was teeming with Germans, their own fuel and ammunition stocks were low, and hovering over them was not only the risk of the surrender announcement going badly wrong but their own personal fates. This latter fear appeared to be trumping broader concerns. They had received the Long Terms on 5 September and had been shocked by their severity, especially the demand of 'unconditional surrender'. There was no reason, however, for them to be surprised because Generale Zanussi had been given these in Algiers; perhaps he never passed this key phrase on to his boss, Generale Roatta.

Then there was the vital question of timing. Castellano had failed to get even a hint from the Allies, although Bedell-Smith had conceded it would be within a fortnight. For no reason at all, Castellano had interpreted this as being more than in a week's time. 'From confidential information,' he wrote to Ambrosio, 'I presume that the landing will take place between 10th and 15th September, possibly the 12th.' The 12th then became the date on which the Italians fixed their planning.

That, though, was going to be cutting things fine. The Germans now dominated the road and rail network. Vehicles were being requisitioned, train lines prioritized and roads dominated. It meant a general paralysis of Italian military supply lines, which was exactly what the Germans intended. Roatta, for one, was nothing like as optimistic as Castellano had been during the negotiations about the Italian Army's ability to militarily support the Allies. Only by the 12th at the very earliest would the airfields in Rome and troops in and around the city be ready for the arrival of the 82nd Airborne. And only by then would the Italian 4a Armata, moving from southern France, be in position to fight, and the Balkan forces under Generale Gastone Gambara, and the remaining units scattered through Italy, be sufficiently reorientated to fight their former ally. With such dire shortages of motor transport and fuel, equipping over a million troops for action was not something that could happen overnight.

Nor were the Italians agreed on the signals that were being issued by the Allies. Roatta interpreted Bedell-Smith's instructions to have the Italian merchant fleet sail to ports south of Livorno – some 150 miles north of Rome – as confirmation that the Allies planned to land that far north. He was simply not thinking clearly and his interpretation was based on hope rather than any logical military appreciation. After all, if the Germans were fairly certain the Allies would be landing south of Naples, why hadn't the Italians worked that out? And what about the limitations of Allied air power? That alone restricted the scope of Allied operations. Roatta was C-in-C of the Italian Army. He should have known that.

Defending Rome, however, was the point about which the Italian leadership appeared to be most exercised. Defending the Eternal City was the Corpo d'Armata Motocorazzato – the armoured motor corps – commanded since the Fascist overthrow by Generale Giacomo Carboni. Aged fifty-four, with dark, lively eyes and a pencil-thin film-star moustache, Carboni was both very smart and a realist; as head of the Servizio Informazioni Militare – or SIM, the Italian secret intelligence service – before the war he had repeatedly warned Mussolini against entering the conflict. The SIM had been the one part of Italy's military to function effectively throughout the war. He had been given command of SIM once again and was certainly a good man to have in charge of the defence of Rome. He was also able to see the situation clearly, without panic or thoughts of how to save his own skin at the forefront of his mind. Carboni absolutely intended to fight it out with the Germans. It was a tragedy for all concerned that he had not been the man sent to negotiate the surrender. Castellano's shortcomings – his arrogance, slipperiness and lack of military judgement – were, in these crisis days, now all too clear.

On 4 September, Carboni had warned Badoglio and Ambrosio to urgently prepare a memorandum for all senior commanders in Italy, Greece and the Balkans with clear instructions about how they should both swiftly ready themselves for the armistice announcement and how they should immediately respond once it was made public. Foremost in his mind was to avoid the Italian armed forces being forcibly disarmed by the Germans. These secret instructions, he suggested, should be hand-delivered and the recipients ordered to burn them once read. If this was done right away, Italy's chances of emerging with some honour and ability to wrest the initiative from the Germans would be greatly enhanced. Both Ambrosio and Badoglio agreed, and the memo, known as 'OP 44', was promptly drafted.

Carboni, meanwhile, was keenly aware that his motor corps was not ready to take on two German divisions. Stocks of ammunition for his Piave and Ariete Divisions were sufficient for just twenty minutes of sustained fire, while he only had fuel for them to cover 100 kilometres – sixty miles. These concerns he reported to Roatta, who, as head of the army, was his immediate superior. Roatta was every bit as concerned, and even more so when he then learned that the 82nd Airborne intended to land over four consecutive nights. That was far too drawn out. In fact, the more Roatta looked at the plans, the more he was convinced the army could not possibly be ready to turn on the Germans by the 12th. Rather, he wanted the armistice announcement to be postponed until at least 15 September. At any rate, on the evening of 6 September Roatta sent a signal to Castellano, now in Carthage in Tunisia, via the secret radio, warning him to expect a courier to fly over the following day with a message of the utmost importance for the Allies. This was to urge them to hold off any invasion until that date, 15 September.

The same evening, Ambrosio informed Roatta that reconnaissance planes had spotted an invasion force approaching north-west Sicily. For Roatta there was only one interpretation: that the Allies were planning an invasion before the 12th. After all, from the Palermo area an invasion force would be in place to land in a matter of days. When he pointed this out, Ambrosio, the head of the Comando Supremo, shrugged it off and told him flatly that as far as he was concerned, the Allies would not land before the 12th. And regarding the shortage of fuel and ammunition, Ambrosio told him not to worry. Ambrosio was sixty-four – not as old as Badoglio, but certainly getting on in years. His ambivalence was hard to fathom, yet he was certainly not acting with any kind of urgency at all. He'd done nothing with Carboni's OP 44 instructions and was now shrugging off Roatta's deep concerns. That evening he departed Rome for Turin, his home city, to attend some unspecified family business.

Roatta, on the other hand, was most certainly deeply concerned. He was a tough individual, and with blood on his hands too, having ordered numerous executions, the taking of hostages and burning of villages in his war against the partisans while 2a Armata commander in Yugoslavia.

Ruthless and quite willing to be duplicitous if necessary, he was not, however, keen to simply roll over and hand the Italian Army to Germany, which was why he was prepared to urgently send an emissary to Castellano in North Africa. It was, of course, absurd that Roatta was taking such an action rather than Badoglio or Ambrosio, both his senior.

Roatta sent Maggiore Alberto Briatore, one of his staff officers from Army HQ. Flying a plane to Tunisia under the noses of the Germans came with risk, but Briatore safely reached Carthage the following evening, 7 September, and now just twenty-four hours before Eisenhower planned to announce the Italian armistice to the world. Although Castellano met Briatore at the airfield, he made it clear he was not anxious to hear his urgent message. First, Castellano insisted, they should have dinner. Throughout the meal, Castellano simply refused to talk shop. 'I know you wish to talk to me,' Castellano eventually told him once they had finally finished eating, 'but I haven't the time. I have important things to do and must go to a meeting at Allied headquarters.' He would, he told Briatore, see him in the morning.

Clearly, Castellano, who by this time knew exactly what the Allied plans were, was not prepared to be personally compromised at this moment. The die was cast. There could be no delays and he did not want to hear any orders from his superiors back in Rome to the contrary.

Sunday, 5 September. Oran harbour in Algeria was packed with ships and landing craft which were, in turn, packed with men. It had been hot work loading so many troops and so much equipment, with the sun beating down relentlessly, but all of the US 141st Infantry Regiment's staff and some of their fighting units were now aboard the attack transport ship, USS *James O'Hara*, one of the US Navy's purpose-built and lightly armed ocean-going troopships.

The 141st, along with the 142nd and 143rd, was an infantry regiment of the 36th 'Texas' Division. Attached to Regimental HQ was the Intelligence and Reconnaissance – I & R – Platoon, eighteen men whose task was to be the intelligence agency for the regimental commander. They were to scout ahead, sometimes behind enemy lines; they were to interrogate prisoners; they were to gather any useful information by any means. They were not expected to fight but they were certainly trained and equipped to do so.

Commanding the I & R was an officer known as the S-2 – 2 for Intelligence – and in the case of the 141st it was Captain Roswell K. Doughty, not a Texan at all but a New Englander from Boston, thirty-three years old, sharp as a tack, and a married man with two children at home, one of whom was a baby. Along with the rest of the 36th Texans, Doughty was yet to taste combat.

He had never seen a vessel quite so packed to the gunwales but had found a spot on which to perch in the wardroom, and was chatting with some of the other regimental staff officers when over the tannoy he heard, 'Captain Doughty report to the bridge.' There he was told that a small boat was waiting at the end of the ship's ladder to take him to the division's command ship, where he was to report to Colonel A. B. Crowther, the G-2 of 36th Texans – the division's chief intelligence officer.

It was by now after 8 p.m. and quite dark. As he was being taken across the water anti-aircraft guns started hammering away, and moments later bombs began to drop. The Luftwaffe, which had taken plenty of reconnaissance photos of the invasion fleet at harbour the previous day, had arrived in some strength – 180 aircraft in all. The response was swift: immense anti-aircraft fire and a hastily and very effectively laid smoke-screen. Fortunately, no bombs fell near Doughty and he reached the command ship without mishap, clambering on board just as the firing died down; in fact, not a single vessel had been hit, a poor return for so many enemy bombers.

Doughty might have escaped the Luftwaffe, but other dangers lurked. The ship was in blackout still because of the raid, so when he opened what he thought was the wardroom door he was not surprised to find it in darkness. Stepping over the threshold, he then discovered he was walking into thin air and a moment later hit the deck below; unlike the *James O'Hara*, this ship had a ladder rather than steps. Nothing appeared to be broken but he'd hurt his shoulder and chin and cut his nose. Never had he imagined that his first wounds would be caused by falling between decks on a blacked-out command ship.

Gingerly he clambered back up the ladder, found the wardroom, and despite bleeding all over his shirt was eventually taken to see Colonel Crowther.

'Doughty,' said Crowther, 'there's hell to pay!' He passed over some photographs which clearly showed tank tracks near Eboli, just a short distance from Salerno. The photos had been taken earlier that day. Allied intelligence already knew that 16. Panzer was in the area, but this showed they had armour almost within spitting distance of the beaches. It was hard not to draw the obvious conclusion: that the Germans knew where they would be landing. 'As a result,' Crowther told him, 'we're going up against far stiffer opposition than we had originally thought to be the case.' Even worse, Crowther added, Eisenhower was planning to broadcast the news of the armistice the evening before they landed. He reckoned that would make the men think it was going to be easy, that the battle was already over before they'd started. Crowther didn't want them to think that. He wanted them to be ready. And as if that wasn't enough, they were going to land without any naval or air bombardment first. It was General Fred Walker, the Texan Division commander's idea; he thought a heavy bombardment might confuse his troops in their first action.

Doughty could barely believe his ears and it was clear Crowther was far from happy either. 'But your job,' Crowther told him, 'is to convince your regimental officers of the fact that the fight will be the toughest one yet, since we shall now be up against odds that no one foresaw.'

Soon after, Doughty was heading back across the harbour to his own ship, nursing his bruised arm and shoulder and gently rubbing his jaw. Above, the sky was clear and dark but twinkling with stars. It all seemed very peaceful, but in a few days' time, when they landed, he realized they would be heading into a storm of fire.

The invasion fleet was being assembled from a number of different ports along the North African coast. The Texans were sailing from Oran, but at 6.30 a.m. on Monday, 6 September, Admiral H. Kent Hewitt's flagship, the USS *Ancon*, set sail for Salerno from Algiers. The *Ancon* was a former liner converted to a command ship and had been Hewitt's flagship for the invasion of Sicily as well. Hewitt, the Western Task Force commander, had taken General George S. Patton to Sicily; now General Mark Clark, the Commanding Officer of the US Fifth Army, was his guest. Once out at sea they were doing a modest 12 knots, a speed that ensured their entire convoy of some seventy vessels, including a number of landing ships, could all keep pace.

At 9 a.m. Clark held a conference with his staff, while he sent off one of Hewitt's naval planners and his own G-2 – intelligence – officer to brief a number of press men who were also aboard. This was a media age in which news was broadcast almost instantly, via radio and in print. Not only words would bring the war to the people back home, but images too; along with the war correspondents were photographers and film cameramen, there to record the historic landings in mainland Europe that would soon take place.

Among those assembled in Hewitt's operations room was forty-one-year-old Quent Reynolds, a big-shouldered and square-jawed New Yorker from the Bronx. A talented college sportsman at Brown University, he had played a season for the Brooklyn Lions in the National Football League before turning full-time to journalism, first as a sports reporter then writing more general pieces; for the past eight years he'd been an associate editor at *Collier's*, one of the best-selling magazines in America. Bright, quick-witted and never one to take life too seriously, Reynolds had won fans for his easy-going, bluff approach. He smoked, he drank, he played poker, but since the start of the war he had also taken himself to danger spots, whether it be crossing the Atlantic in a convoy or reporting from London at the height of the Blitz.

Now he was heading to Italy, and feeling pretty chipper about it too. The ship was big and comfortable and served decent coffee, and was re-assuringly so full of modern communications equipment he'd worried about sitting down in case he was electrocuted. Yet as the briefing began, his spirits started to sag. They were, he heard, going to land on the coast south of Salerno, and there was very little doubt the Germans knew they were on their way. The infantry would hit the beaches at precisely 3.30 a.m. on Thursday, 9 September. This was not an ideal landing place – not with mountains surrounding that stretch of the coast – but it was the highest part up the leg of Italy they could go with the constraints of air cover. Part of the covering force was to be provided by the Royal Navy's Force H, which included the fleet carriers *Illustrious* and *Formidable*, and Force V, which had the light fleet carrier *Unicorn* and four smaller escort carriers. There were also four battleships, sixteen cruisers, forty-four fleet destroyers, twenty-nine hunt destroyers and a number of minesweepers, gunboats and lesser craft. This was a fraction of the force with which the Allies had assaulted Sicily; the total number of vessels for AVALANCHE was 594, of which 90 were small motor launches, 359 were landing vessels and 24 were combat loaders and Liberty ship supply vessels; HUSKY, the invasion of Sicily, had included 472 warships, 237 freighters and 1,734 landing craft. HUSKY had also been supported by some 3,500 aircraft.

The carriers, however, did mean the landings would have the support of 670 aircraft in all and 58 over the beaches at all times during the daylight hours of D-Day; Allied commanders had hoped for more, but supplies of P-38 Lightnings had been halted in favour of the build-up of Eighth Air Force in England, and three groups of heavy bombers, which Spaatz and Eisenhower had pleaded for, had also been denied by the

Combined Chiefs. As a result, the Allies had just 206 P-38s, 322 single-engine Spitfires and P-40 Kittyhawks, 110 carrier-based Seafires and other fighters, and 32 night fighters. Lightnings could hang about for perhaps an hour, but Spitfires only for fifteen to twenty minutes. They hoped it would be enough but had to pray the Luftwaffe wouldn't try to contest the air too heavily.

AVALANCHE was a smaller operation in every way than HUSKY, but the opposition was larger, better trained and equipped, and the terrain tougher for the attackers. Quent Reynolds felt his heart sinking as he heard all this. All the while the *Ancon's* engines thrummed and the ship continued scything its way towards Italy. Outside, gorgeous weather: clear blue skies, the sun beating down, the ship's steel warming in the morning sun. Briefing over, the press men were then invited to see General Clark, and so trooped off to his cabin near the bridge. He greeted them cheerily enough and urged them to each find a seat. If Mark Clark was worried, he was not showing it. He had every reason to be, however. The latest intelligence picture of German strength was getting worse, not better. 'By D + 7,' was the signal from the Chiefs of Staff on 2 September, 'we estimate German build-up equals ours and overtakes ours after that until about D + 17 they have margin of one and a third divisions at least.' That was not good; a conservative rule of thumb was never to attack unless with a three-to-one advantage in manpower. 'Result of our examination,' the Chiefs concluded, 'indicates overwhelming importance of straining every nerve to increase our own rate of build-up.' That was all very well, but the only nerves being strained were those of the men about to launch an amphibious assault with insufficient landing vessels.

'How do you like our plan?' Clark asked once they'd all assembled.

'My God,' Reynolds blurted, 'it's daring!'

'My God, it *is* daring,' Clark smiled. 'Sure, we're spitting right into the lion's mouth. We know it. But we have to do that.' He explained that they'd explored other plans but this was the only feasible one.

'Do you expect either strategic or tactical surprise?' Reynolds asked.

'Certainly not strategic surprise,' Clark replied. He stretched out his legs. 'And I doubt if we'll get any tactical surprise. German G-2 is good.' He talked about the beaches and about the importance of Naples. The Germans knew its value and understood the limitations of air power too. 'We may get hurt,' he added, 'but you can't play with fire without the risk of burning your fingers.'

Reynolds couldn't help admiring the general's composure. This was the prime strike on mainland Europe and he could see, as they all could, that Clark's force was horribly undercooked for the task. Clark himself had never commanded anything more than a company of 120 men in battle before, over twenty-five years earlier. He was totally untried as an army commander and yet was about to land an insufficiently sized force straight on to defended beaches with little of the fire support the Allies had brought to earlier amphibious operations. Reynolds now asked him whether he was apprehensive about the enemy's air power.

'Apprehensive?' Clark answered. 'I'm scared stiff of what their air will do, but we hope to have two of their airfields by D plus 2, and then our fighters won't have that long pull from Sicily.' With a bit of luck, he told them, he'd have his HQ ashore by then too. If all went to plan – but, of course, he added, it never did.

On the convoy surged, across the Mediterranean towards Italy.

Back in Tunisia, both General Matthew Ridgway, the commander of 82nd Airborne Division, and his XO – second-in-command – Brigadier-General Maxwell Taylor were increasingly sceptical about the planned operation in Rome, code-named GIANT II. And well they might have been. Rome was 165 miles north of Salerno, which was a long way. As the Allies were well aware, there was now an entire German army south of Rome. The only way the 82nd Airborne drop would work was if the Italians could be sufficiently galvanized to fight in a way they had singularly failed to do at pretty much any point of the war thus far, and if the Germans also decided to hurriedly and dramatically retreat well north of the capital. There was very little evidence, except perhaps Allied wishful thinking, to suggest this was a likely scenario. Ridgway thought the whole idea was hare-brained. He wasn't wrong.

With this in mind, both Ridgway and Taylor agreed that before potentially sacrificing one of the best divisions in the US Army, someone should go to Rome first and get the lay of the land, a decision approved by Eisenhower and Alexander. A clandestine mission such as this was obviously a high-risk undertaking, but not as risky as sending an entire division blind into a city surrounded by German troops. Taylor agreed to go but took with him the divisional air intelligence officer, Colonel William Gardiner. With Castellano's help, arrangements were made and they set off for Rome, first by a British motor torpedo boat to the Italian island of Ustica, north of Sicily, and from there they transferred to an Italian corvette. They reached Gaeta on the afternoon of 7 September and, pretending to be prisoners of war, were roughly pushed on to the quay-side and transferred to a car, then to an ambulance, and driven to Rome, reaching the Palazzo Caprara, the headquarters of the Italian Army, at around 10 p.m. without, it seemed, raising any suspicions.

An hour later, Generale Carboni appeared and they began to talk. Immediately, it was clear there was a huge misunderstanding on both sides. Carboni was shocked to learn that the Allied invasion was now just a little over twenty-four hours away. Nor had he expected it to be so small. Taylor and Gardiner were equally horrified by Carboni's response. The Italian insisted the invasion must be postponed, then took them to meet Badoglio at his villa. Off they went again, shuffled into Carboni's limousine, and sped out through the blacked-out city, air raid sirens droning as they hurried through the streets. Even Carboni, however, had to stop at the many roadblocks along the way. Tense moments every time.

They reached Badoglio's sumptuous villa on the Via Bruxelles without mishap, however. The marshal had already gone to bed but, at Carboni's urging, managed to cast off his pyjamas and put on a dark-grey civilian suit, agreeing to talk to the Americans in his study. The room was filled with mementos from his long career, including a number of treasures looted from Emperor Haile Selassie of Ethiopia. Badoglio even had the Emperor's throne.

Badoglio sat down at his desk, looking tired and diminished. Carboni couldn't help feeling demoralized seeing the marshal sitting there, with his bald head, wrinkled neck and glassy hangdog eyes. By contrast, Taylor was tall, dark-haired, handsome and muscular, a physical superman in comparison. The American told Badoglio he could try asking for a post-ponement but that it was unlikely at this very late stage. By now, it was the early hours of 8 September – the planned day of the armistice announcement.

'If I announce the armistice,' Badoglio told them, 'and the Americans don't send sufficient reinforcements and don't land near Rome, the Germans will seize the city and put in a puppet Fascist government. Just suppose you Allies were to land at Salerno,' he continued. By this time it seems likely Castellano must have informed him of the plan. 'You'd run into serious trouble.' The old marshal then ran a hand across his neck. 'It is my throat which the Germans will cut.'

'You seem to fear the Germans more than you do the Allies,' Taylor told him. 'Don't forget that we could raze your cities, including Rome.'

Tears now appeared in Badoglio's eyes. 'But why would you want to do that? We are your friends.'

Taylor was appalled, but agreed to send a message to Eisenhower conveying Badoglio's urgent desire for a postponement. Then, with Carboni once again at the wheel, the two Americans drove with him back to the Palazzo Caprara.

'Let's hope,' Taylor told Carboni as they sped through the city, 'you find Eisenhower in a good mood, or Italy is done for, and our campaign in Italy will become extremely difficult.'

CHAPTER 7

Bluffing

ONLY FIFTEEN MILES AWAY from Badoglio's villa in the Via Bruxelles, Generalfeldmarschall Albert Kesselring was at his headquarters complex on the edge of the small hilltop town of Frascati. Kesselring liked to think of himself as a trusting kind of fellow and had been almost alone among his peers in rather warming to the Italians. He'd been in the Mediterranean a long time, first arriving at the end of 1941 and both orchestrating and overseeing the Blitz on the British island of Malta from Sicily, then becoming OB Süd – commander-in-chief South – of all German forces. He'd worked alongside the Italians during the campaign in North Africa and, even though he had known Italian morale had broken, had still tried to be as cooperative and collaborative as possible during the recent battle for Sicily. Even after Mussolini had been deposed he had remained comradely with his Italian allies, taking the King's and Badoglio's pledges of continued partnership at their word. 'I was,' admitted Kesselring, 'considered an Italophile.' His optimism and generous regard for Germany's ally had been reflected in his reports to the OKW. Even as late as 19 August, he had told them he confidently expected the Italians to continue fighting on Germany's side should the Allies attack the mainland. Hitler, however, ever mistrustful, did not believe it, and, knowing that Rommel was in the north of Italy and was soon due to take over in the country, Kesselring had offered his resignation on 14 August. The Führer had refused to accept it; he wanted Kesselring there, near Rome, to continue oiling the wheels with the Italians.

Kesselring, a Bavarian, was fifty-seven, and although he had begun his military life in the artillery he had, in 1933, joined first the Reich

Commissariat for Aviation as a colonel, and then, on its birth in 1935, the Luftwaffe. He'd even briefly been its Chief of Staff and had overseen the huge expansion of the force; both the Messerschmitt 109 and Junkers Ju87 'Stuka' dive-bomber had been brought into the Luftwaffe on his watch. Between such enormous duties he'd also found time to learn to fly, winning his licence at the age of forty-eight. By the start of the war he'd moved from the General Staff to operational command, and for his performance in Poland and then the campaign in the west he was promoted to Generalfeldmarschall. He continued to command an air fleet, Luftflotte 2, throughout the Battle of Britain. There was no doubting his abilities; strategically, he was astute. Operationally, he had always had a very clear and pragmatic appreciation of whatever situation he found himself in; the cancelling of the heavy bomber programme in the late 1930s, for example, which Germany later rued, had been very much against his wishes and advice. Tactically, as an air commander, he had also shown a deft hand; his handling of the earlier Blitzkrieg campaigns was testimony to that. The failure to win the Battle of Britain and subdue Malta had been largely because of decisions made over and above his head and, again, also against his advice.

The son of a schoolteacher, Kesselring had risen extraordinarily high for one from such a comparatively humble background; Hitler may have railed against the elites, but the Prussian aristocracy had still dominated the armed forces between the wars and continued to do so in this current war. Kesselring, ever the optimist, always quick to laugh, was known as 'Smiling Albert'; a genial team player, then, who could get on with anyone, even Italians. Even so, General Balck, on arriving in Italy, had quickly detected a strong antipathy towards him from his corps staff and divisional commanders. Perhaps it was snobbery on the part of Oberst Bogislaw von Bonin, Balck's Chief of Staff at XIV Panzerkorps, or mistrust that their chief was a Luftwaffe man. Certainly, Balck couldn't really understand why; he found it hard to level any criticism at Kesselring at all. Maybe Smiling Albert simply appeared to be too affable, too smiling. If so, it would have been to underestimate him, for behind this cheery exterior lurked a character of iron determination and single-minded ruthlessness. Kesselring was perfectly prepared to act the friend with his Italian colleagues, but in the past couple of weeks he had been less fooled by their unctuousness. Rather, he had become increasingly convinced that the Italians would throw in the towel and had been making preparations for such a moment.

First, he'd cajoled and charmed the Italians into agreeing to him sending divisions down into the southern half of the country. He also made sure he held regular meetings and conferences with them, always maintained a friendly, deferential tone, was unfailingly courteous and openly treated them as equals, even as his men were blocking roads and railway lines and cutting off the Italians' fuel supplies. He'd ask them for advice, make sure he fed them well, gave them the best wine. He was their friend. Their colleague. Yet all the while, however, plans were being put in place for the swift disarmament of Italian troops and the capture of key equipment such as coastal guns and essential infrastructure. As soon as he issued the code-word 'ACHSE' the immediate dismantling of Italy's armed forces would be set in motion.

So Kesselring had a very strong sense of what was coming, but still, on the morning of that Wednesday, 8 September, he had no idea that the announcement of the armistice was mere hours away. His troops in the very south of the country were thin on the ground, and so with the British crossing the Straits of Messina he ordered 29. Panzergrenadier-Division to carry out demolitions and hold the Allies up as much as possible but not to contest this part of the boot. In fact, in agreement with von Vietinghoff, his 10. Armee commander, he planned to pull back troops in the south to Rome once the Italian Army had been disarmed, but rather naively had expected the Italians to fight alongside his forces if the Allies attacked before a surrender was announced. What neither man had considered was a surrender announcement and an Allied landing almost concurrently. In the meantime, cooperation between the still-allies was to continue, at a superficial level at any rate.

In fact, conferences to discuss how German and Italian troops would cooperate in the event of an Allied landing were booked with Roatta and with Ammiraglio Raffaele de Courten, the C-in-C of the Regia Marina, the Italian Navy, that very day. At Kesselring's headquarters, the air raid sirens had begun wailing around midday while he was in a conference discussing defensive measures for the Allied invasion, which he was expecting that day; reconnaissance aircraft had taken very detailed photographs of troopships and landings ships crammed with materiel at Oran and Bizerte on 4 September. The Naples area seemed the likely target, but he couldn't be sure; it was why he and von Vietinghoff had kept troops in the south, in Calabria and Apulia. The following day, they'd picked up the convoys heading across the Mediterranean; they had then been discovered north of Sicily on the afternoon of the 7th, heading on a course that led them to the Salerno coast. Interpreting these aerial photographs had not been difficult, and immediately von Vietinghoff ordered

General Traugott Herr, the commander of LXXVI Panzerkorps, to hurriedly withdraw troops that were still in Calabria. In any case, because of the limitations of air cover it should have been perfectly obvious to Kesselring, with his vast experience of fighting the Allies in the Mediterranean, and even von Vietinghoff, that the twenty-mile stretch of beaches south of Salerno were very likely the Allies' target. Despite this, Kesselring still had a flicker of apprehension that the target might be the Rome area. He should have trusted his experience and military logic more.

At any rate, as he was leaving his office to visit de Courten and Roatta the first bombs began falling. Above, 130 B-17 Flying Fortresses were pasting Frascati in an effort to hammer his headquarters – its whereabouts having been passed on to the Allies by the treacherous Italians. Kesselring was lucky to get away in time, because bombs crashed close to his glass verandah and around his air raid shelter. A number of his staff were killed or injured, and it was estimated that the headquarters would be out of action for a few days at the very least. Hurrying away by car to his first meeting, he noticed the fire and air defence units from Rome already at the edge of Frascati; it convinced him that the Italians must have known about the attack beforehand.

Other intelligence had been arriving that morning, and as Kesselring sped his way to see de Courten he realized with increasing certainty that the Italians must have signed an armistice already; and the intelligence picture suggested an Allied invasion that night. All troops south of Rome were now at half an hour's notice.

Meanwhile, in Rome, the message from Taylor to Eisenhower, which had been written in Badoglio's own hand, had been finally coded and transmitted from a secret radio in an attic room in the SIM HQ. An acknowledgement arrived at 8 a.m., although nothing was said about either a postponement of the invasion or of GIANT II. Still holed up at the Army HQ at the Palazzo Caprara, Taylor had then asked Carboni if he could send a second message. He now had a very clear picture of the situation. The 3. Panzergrenadier-Division was based around Monterosi, nearly thirty miles north of Rome, while 2. Fallschirmjäger-Division was just to the south. In effect, the capital was surrounded. Kesselring's headquarters were just outside the city. There were plenty of Luftwaffe airfields round about too. There were Germans everywhere. Taylor wanted to send a personal message stressing the strength of the Germans around Rome and the obvious weakness of the Italians. Carboni agreed, then quizzed Taylor and Gardiner further about Allied plans. Only now did he learn that the main landings would be at Salerno. Gardiner explained the limitations of the Allied air umbrella. And what about a subsequent landing near Rome, Carboni asked them? Taylor admitted he was not privy to all Allied plans, but as far as he was aware none was planned. For Carboni, this was shocking news.

A little before noon, Taylor asked to send a third message, this time including the phrase 'situation innocuous', which was the code to cancel the planned airborne drop. At the very moment it was received and decoded, men of the 504th Parachute Infantry Regiment, the first due to be landed in Rome, were already loaded on to the transports. Several had even already taken off, although fortunately they were swiftly recalled. It was incredible that despite Taylor's earlier messages GIANT II had even got to this stage of readiness and was, perhaps, a reflection of the somewhat cumbersome nature of the Allied command with headquarters spread far and wide between Algeria, Tunisia, Malta and Sicily.

Even Carboni thought the airborne plan was a terrible idea. What could they possibly achieve, except to aggravate the Germans? No, the only chance, he believed, was to postpone the invasion. Ambrosio had arrived back in Rome from Turin that afternoon but refused to see Taylor and Gardiner. When he later talked with Carboni and Roatta, he again told them he believed the invasion would be some days later. He was either being extraordinarily obtuse or lying through his teeth. Either way, the current Italian leadership, at this moment of deep crisis, was lacking any kind of coordination or, to use a British term, grip.

At 4.30 p.m., after a half-hour delay, Taylor and Gardiner were driven out in another ambulance to Centocelle airfield, where they boarded an Italian bomber and flew back to North Africa, their cloak-and-dagger escapade over.

With Taylor gone, Carboni was summoned to see Badoglio. There he found the old man in a state of shock. Eisenhower had replied. 'I see by your behaviour,' the Supreme Allied Commander had signalled to Badoglio, 'you do not wish to comply with agreements. I have decided to announce the armistice tonight at 6.30. Follow me. Eisenhower.'

'We're ruined,' Badoglio kept mumbling. He appeared to be genuinely shocked by the revelation that this Thursday was indeed the day of the announcement. But it was, to a large extent, a problem of his own making. The Germans had been preparing for weeks for such an eventuality. Why hadn't the Italians? The armistice announcement might have been coming earlier than they would have liked, but Badoglio and Ambrosio had done nothing since it had been signed five days earlier except dither and succumb to visions of impending doom.

Really, their complacency and woeful lack of leadership were totally inexcusable. They had known they would be getting out of the war for over a month. Why hadn't they made plans even before negotiations had begun? It was as though they had been in a stupor, from which only the Allies, arriving in a force far larger than could ever have been reality, could rouse them. But even with limited fuel and ammunition, the Italian Army alone still had a million men at arms. They could have resisted any plans the Germans had for disarming them. It might cost some lives – even many lives – but not as many as were now threatened by their pathetic inaction.

Moments later, a message arrived from the King: both were urgently required at a hastily called meeting of the Crown Council. Carboni hurried to find the marshal's nephew, who was also his aide, and told him to fix Badoglio a drink. 'Or he won't make it to the royal palace.'

A postponement of the invasion, of course, was never going to happen. Back in Algiers, Resident Minister Harold Macmillan had spent the intervening days since the signing of the armistice attending a mass of meetings and fielding an endless stream of telegrams, most of which were contradictory or quickly became out of date with the pace of developments. 'We do our best,' he noted resignedly in his diary. An air of fevered but nervous excitement pervaded Allied Forces HQ. The heat was oppressive. 'This is the day!' Macmillan had noted at 7.30 a.m. that Thursday.

Then had come the news that Badoglio was wavering. Eisenhower had not replied immediately because he had wanted to consult with the Combined Chiefs and with his three service chiefs, Tedder, Cunningham and Alexander, whom he was with that day in Bizerte in Tunisia. Needless to say, all agreed there should be no postponement. By 5 p.m., Churchill and Roosevelt had also approved Eisenhower's course of action. Eisenhower was to record his announcement, which would be broadcast at 6.30 p.m. as planned, and the Information Services in Algiers would make a recording of the Italian armistice text, which would follow. Pressure would be applied to Badoglio to comply.

At 6 p.m., Macmillan headed over to the HQ of the Information Services in Algiers to listen to the broadcast and to find out whether it was picked up in Rome. When he got there, he learned that Rome had been off air since six. At 6.30 p.m., on the dot, Eisenhower made his broadcast. The Italians were out of the war. And Clark's Fifth Army would begin landing at Salerno in the early hours. There could now be no turning back. 'It only remained to be seen,' noted Macmillan, 'whether Marshal Badoglio would at any later time speak his own part himself.'

At the Quirinale, the royal palace in Rome, the Crown Council met as summoned. Badoglio was there, so too were Ambrosio and Roatta, as well as the King's ministers, his aide and the Chief of the Cabinet. Also Generale Giacomo Carboni. It was a hot, late afternoon. Almost soporific.

'As you gentlemen know,' the diminutive monarch began, 'the Anglo-Americans have decided to anticipate by four days the date of the armistice.' Most around the table knew nothing of this, and said so. Nor had the Allies ever said they were landing on the 12th; that had only ever been an educated guess by Castellano. The King looked annoyed at the reaction and turned to Badoglio, but he was still in such a state of shock that he stuttered and mumbled and Ambrosio stood instead. He explained that the armistice had been signed five days earlier but told them the Allies had insisted on announcing it this very evening, four days early, before Italy was ready.

Urgent discussions followed. Carboni pleaded with them all to stick with the armistice but to wait for General Taylor to reach Eisenhower. The American would explain the situation; the landings might yet be postponed. In the meantime, they could pretend to the Germans they were refusing the armistice. It would just be a bit of bluff. Playing for time. Time that was essential if they were to have any chance of repelling the Germans. They could explain this tactic to the Allies via the secret radio. At any rate, it had to be worth holding out until Taylor had arrived back in Tunis and met with Eisenhower.

Shortly after Carboni's plea, a message was brought in that had just arrived from Eisenhower, reiterating his intention to broadcast the announcement at 6.30 p.m. 'Failure on your part to carry out the full obligations to the signed agreement will have the most serious consequences for your country,' he told them. 'No future action of yours could then restore any confidence whatever in your good faith.' And that would, without doubt, unleash the vengeful Germans.

Badoglio looked crushed. Carboni tried to speak again but the King silenced him. 'There is no doubt now,' he said quietly, 'what must be done.'

At 7.45 p.m., Badoglio, his voice sombre, broadcast that Italy had accepted the armistice.

*

On board the USS *James O'Hara*, Captain Roswell Doughty sat with his fellow officers in the wardroom to listen to Eisenhower's broadcast. He'd passed on Colonel Crowther's warning, and now they all listened in silence. Once it was over, no one said a word for a moment, until one man said, 'Shiiiittt,' in a strong, drawn-out Texan drawl. Despite the warnings all the officers had passed on to the men, around the ship they heard cheers and whoops of excitement.

There were also cheers and yells of delight among the press men on board the USS *Ancon*. It didn't matter that Clark, personally, had warned them that they faced a tough fight. For Quent Reynolds and his fellows the announcement was a huge tonic. 'We all assured ourselves that it would be a walk-in now,' noted Reynolds. 'We knew that two Eyetie divisions were in the vicinity of Paestum, where our 36th Division was to land. If they were out of it our boys would have things easy.' Sure, the British contingent landing closer to Salerno would have 16. Panzer-Division to deal with, but the Texans could quickly mop up the Italians then strike north and help the Brits. A piece of cake.

Despite the earlier bombing, Feldmarschall Kesselring's headquarters had managed to establish some radio and phone links, but at 7 p.m. had not yet heard about the armistice announcement. Plans still needed to be coordinated with the Italians for the imminent Allied landings and so he sent his Chief of Staff, General Siegfried Westphal, to see Roatta at the Italian Army's new headquarters at Monterotondo, fifteen miles northwest of Rome, where they'd moved to avoid Allied bombing. During the meeting, Westphal was called to the telephone and told of Badoglio's announcement. He immediately confronted Roatta, who denied any knowledge and insisted it must be a lie. Generale Zanussi was rung next, now back at Army HQ. Had Zanussi heard this extraordinary news, Roatta asked him? No, Zanussi replied, his poker face never flinching. Incredibly, they then continued the conference about troop movements. Only when Westphal made to leave and report back to Kesselring did Roatta mutter to Zanussi, in French, 'We are fucked, abominably so.'

Kesselring, meanwhile, heard the news not on any radio but from General Jodl at the OKW. He was incensed. The Italians had committed what he considered the basest treachery; even though he'd known it was likely, he'd simply not expected it hand-in-glove with an Allied landing. He felt duped. 'Italian troops will be asked to continue the fight on our side by appeals to their honour,' he signalled to von Vietinghoff. 'Those who refuse are to be ruthlessly disarmed. No mercy must be shown to the traitors. Long live the Führer.' 'No mercy' was a barely disguised euphemism for shooting on the spot.

In Rome, meanwhile, Generale Giacomo Carboni had left the King's meeting and hurried back to his headquarters at the Palazzo Caprara. There he told his staff about the armistice and warned them all to be prepared to fight the Germans. He also issued a general alarm to his divisions in the Corpo d'Armata Motocorazzato.

'If we act resolutely,' he told his son, a young cavalry officer, over a hastily eaten dinner, 'and the Allies help us with an air strike and a small landing near Rome, we may still be able to make it.'

Carboni had also already been in touch with the leading anti-Fascist parties and had agreed that he would help distribute arms to young members who were prepared to fight the Germans. He now arranged for these weapons to be immediately handed out, then headed to his office at the SIM to see if he could pick up any intelligence about German moves. Curiously, there was none. An aide was sent to the German Embassy to try and pick up their reaction, and Carboni ordered his Montebello Regiment and a mobile group from the Ariete Division to support troops on the southern edge of the city who were facing 2. Fallschirmjäger-Division.

Outside, in the streets of Rome, crowds had quickly gathered and were shouting with joy. The war was over! Peace had returned! In Eboli, Lina Caruso and her mother had been praying in church and were heading back to their house near the castle when they heard the news from a refugee from Naples. 'They say that Radio London reported the armistice,' she told Lina and her mother. 'Let us pray, let us thank the Virgin.' Lina Caruso almost cried with joy but hardly dared believe it. Hurrying back to their house at the top of the town, they heard cheering, but Lina still didn't believe the news until she heard it with her own ears. Just as they turned into their street, they saw an army motorcycle dispatch rider pulling out of the castle and waved him down. He confirmed that the armistice had been signed. Hostilities would cease, and with them the bombings. 'Joy overflowed from our hearts,' Lina scribbled in her diary. 'We hugged and kissed and cried.'

Filippo Caracciolo was about to leave Lugano, taking the night train south. First, though, he had arranged to see Rino de Nobili, in whose house he had met the Americans. Caracciolo was walking along the lakefront heading to see his friend when he spotted him. As he neared, he could see that de Nobili looked pale and in shock. 'His voice trembles,' noted Caracciolo. 'He had heard the news of the armistice on the radio.' They walked together to the station then said their farewells. The train was crowded but at Chiasso, on the border, it emptied, with only Caracciolo remaining in his carriage. A soldier entered his compartment, demanding to look at his papers. All in order. Caracciolo was left alone. The train remained stationary. He got up, wandered the corridor, looked out of the window, then headed back to his compartment, wondering whether they would ever leave. 'I finally feel it starting slowly,' he noted, 'without shock, without sound.' Just after midnight, he reached Milan. It was now Thursday, 9 September 1943.

And so it was done. The Italians were out of the war, and the endless pretence, lying, duplicity and double dealing was finally at an end. The cat was out of the bag and General Mark Clark's Fifth Army was poised to land on the beaches of Salerno. Late that night, and with no real knowledge yet of the response in Italy, Harold Macmillan jotted in his diary. 'I can only say,' he scribbled, 'that it has been the most absurdly improbable detective story that has ever been written.' The armistice, he added, had been 'the biggest bluff in history!'.

The truth was, it had been a fiasco. Everyone involved had been bluffing, but the Italians were also guilty of bluffing among themselves. Impotent, with morale and confidence shattered, they had led their country to the precipice. Catastrophe beckoned. The King knew it, Badoglio knew it and Ambrosio knew it too. They were morally bankrupt and simply incapable of offering the resolute and determined leadership that was needed.

The Allies, meanwhile, had also been hoping the Italians might help compensate for the paucity of the initial invasion force for AVALANCHE. Earlier that day, Eisenhower had signalled the Combined Chiefs of Staff. 'Initial operations in Italy will be against greatly superior German Forces,' he cabled. 'The surrender of the Italian Government, if successfully exploited, can materially reduce the hazards of the operation by preventing effective German concentrations against our forces.' In other words, he was praying that the Italians might show some fight and distract the Germans. It was a rather reckless hope, but, through the political pressures created thousands of miles away, the invasion forces now found themselves in a ridiculously high-risk operation in which the chances of success looked very far from certain.

On that September night, with the moon shining down benignly on the invasion fleet as it neared the Salerno coastline, the Allies were about to take an almighty and totally out-of-character gamble. And it was the lives of the young men waiting to storm the beaches that were now at stake.

PART II

Autumn

CHAPTER 8

AVALANCHE

IT WAS STILL LIGHT, just, on the evening of Wednesday, 8 September when Leutnant Herbert Rocholl, a young platoon officer in Panzer Aufklärungs-Abteilung 16 – reconnaissance battalion – reached the observation post he had earlier chosen on a ridge just to the south-east of Salerno. From where he stood, he had a wonderful view. Directly in front of him was the sea, no more than a mile as the crow flies, while perhaps three miles away was Salerno, nestling in the hinge of the coastline as it jutted westwards and surrounded by dramatic mountains. Away to his left, extending for more than twenty miles, was the long, narrow beach that went all the way to the town of Agropoli as the coast protruded westwards again. Occasional lines of umbrella pines marked the edge of the beach, while in between the crescent of mountains was the coastal plain, running as much as five miles inland at its deepest and scored with farmsteads, vineyards and the odd industrial plant. But, like almost every part of Italy, it seemed, the mountains were never far away, and nestling at their base or higher up were a number of towns like Eboli, Battipaglia and Faiano. Salerno, and its plain, were completely enclosed by mountains. It was as though this whole little area of Italy was its own fiefdom, cut off from the rest. From a defender's point of view that was good news.

Even better: Rocholl saw also that on this saddle a heavy machine-gun section of 3. Kompanie had taken up position, which meant that together they formed a small combat force. Having made contact with the sergeant of the Maschinengewehr section, Rocholl then wondered where to place his three armoured cars. Currently, they were on the road which ran along the forward slope; when the enemy came they would be in full view, which wouldn't do at all. On the other hand, he also needed to make sure he had a good reception for the radio. After a bit of careful thought, he decided to place the radio car facing back along the road, just round a bend beneath the OP – observation post – and the other two even further back, so not exposed to direct enemy fire. 'In this spot,' he noted, 'the radio car, even if it meant a high aerial and 80 kw, would have good reception.'

There had been mounting urgency all day. The 16. Panzer-Division had been on alert since the day before but then, at 2 p.m., the call came through from battalion headquarters, 'Attention – Operation: FEUERS-BRUNST.' This was Alarm No. 1: stand by. It had made little impression, however, as such alarms had not been uncommon in recent days; Rocholl, for one, had not interrupted his afternoon siesta. Then suddenly, at 4.30 p.m., another message had come through: 'Attention – Operation ORKAN.' This was Alarm No. 2: get ready. It meant an enemy convoy was in sight. Feverish activity followed, but Rocholl had got his men well honed and within a short while his patrol was ready to move. When he reached company headquarters to receive his battle instructions and radio ciphers, he learned that Italy had unconditionally surrendered. 'At first,' he noted, 'the news came as a shock to me, but afterwards I realized that I had foreseen all this, and, in fact, had expected it.'

At last, everything was ready. He shook hands with the company commander and other company reconnaissance patrols and headed down to his three armoured cars, leather map case under his arm. He called the crews together, explained what was happening and ordered them to get going. Clambering into the radio car, he made sure to take out his pistol first – after all, one could never tell how the Italians might react. At high speed, they headed off down the road and into Salerno. Everywhere were Italians, standing in groups, clearly deep in excited discussions. They sped on through the town without a hitch and out the far side, until climbing up on to the ridge to the south-east where he carefully chose his OP.

Dusk fell, and then darkness. Ahead, the unknown mass of the sea. Somewhere out there, he knew, were the enemy. Away to his right, Salerno, now in blackout. He ordered his lads to fry some potatoes on the Esbit cooker, but scarcely had they begun peeling them than a dispatch rider arrived with orders to immediately take over the neighbouring Italian position. As an officer, Rocholl was expected to confront the Italians. Quickly, he made arrangements. One half of his platoon were to give him cover while the other would accompany him.

He found the Italian machine-gun nest positioned on the same ridge of high ground and, approaching them calmly, told them their country had capitulated and that he was there to disarm them. They could then go home. 'They threw their weapons away,' scribbled Rocholl, 'and showed their joy that the war was now over for them.'

But that was not all. There was also an entire artillery battery to disarm. Rocholl was appalled to discover the first Italian officer he met so obviously fearful, but the battery commander had a little more dignity; he'd not heard about the armistice and wanted to speak to his superior. Rocholl told him firmly that he could not allow that, and unless he surrendered immediately his men would open fire. That did the trick. In less than forty-five minutes from the arrival of the dispatch rider, he had disarmed and taken possession of a heavy machine-gun post and a battery of coastal guns. Not a shot had been fired. It had all been so very easy.

The dismantling of the Italian Army had begun.

The invasion fleet had sailed in several different convoys and had been periodically harried all the way. One landing ship had been hit by a torpedo bomber at Termini, on the north coast of Sicily, while waiting to refuel; another LCI – landing craft, infantry – was damaged by a lone Focke-Wulf 190 fighter-bomber. The destroyer HMS *Blankney* had been straddled by bombs. Force H, one of two naval covering forces, had left Malta at 4 p.m. on the 7th, and included four big battleships and two fleet carriers. On board *Warspite*, Captain Bertie Packer had heard the announcement of the Italian surrender and had hastily scribbled some thoughts in his diary. 'So what now?' he wondered. 'Will Italy become our ally?' And what, he wondered, would happen to the Italian fleet?

Such conjecturing was hastily brought to an end with the arrival of the first of several waves of enemy aircraft. Torpedo bombers were the biggest threat and Force H kept their anti-aircraft guns low. 'Our low barrages,' Packer added after the first attack, 'have so far kept them from damage.' Then, at around 9 p.m., by which time they were some sixty miles south-west of the island of Capri, they were again attacked by around thirty torpedo-carrying aircraft. Three aircraft were seen crashing into the sea and three more disappeared trailing smoke, but a number of white torpedo tracks had been seen speeding towards them. 'One sod dropped his torpedo 500 yards on our port bow,' noted Packer with no small amount of indignation. 'Fortunately, we heard him – I saw the splash, went hard a-port and it missed our stern by a few yards.' For a moment, Packer had felt convinced the torpedo would hit; it seemed to take an age for the quartermaster to get his helm over. The carrier *Formidable* had also had a close shave. None, however, had been struck. So far, the Luftwaffe had had poor returns for their efforts.

On board the *Ancon,* correspondent Quent Reynolds had been out on deck watching the milky moon a little later, sometime approaching midnight, when he heard the doleful sound of a bugle over the ship's tannoy followed by the boatswain saying, in flat, unemotional tones, 'General Quarters. General Quarters. Report to battle stations. Report to battle stations.' Then nothing happened. The convoy was moving slowly, engines throttled back. Almost silently. Reynolds had experienced such alarms before and the wait was always torturous. Then suddenly, in the darkness, a flare blossomed like a chandelier. A beacon laid by a Focke-Wulf for the bombers to follow. Another flare, then another, fireworks across the sky, Reynolds reckoned about five miles away. Then a low rumble of aircraft and flak pouring up into the sky furiously, but always looking so lazy, somehow, as the phosphorescence stabbed into the air. Distant thunder, a constant low rumble.

On his ridge south-east of Salerno, Leutnant Rocholl heard the planes going over and realized they were German bombers flying out to sea. The moon shone a weak crescent, low now, on the horizon. He strained his eyes but could not make out anything – no invasion fleet looming in the darkness. Then suddenly a terrific curtain of anti-aircraft fire lit up the horizon and there it was. 'We could see quite clearly,' he noted, 'that the entire convoy had advanced far into the Bay of Salerno.'

General Clark had listened to the armistice announcement in Admiral Kent Hewitt's cabin. He was well aware that in the terms of the armistice the Italians had agreed to offer passive resistance to the Germans and would not allow them to take over any coastal defences. They were due to help the Allies, not hinder them. Clark, though, doubted the terms would be effectively enforced. Well, they would soon find out.

What neither he nor any of those Allied armistice negotiators had appreciated, however, was that Hitler had planned to issue an ultimatum to the Italians on the very day of the landings, 9 September, and, perhaps unsurprisingly, he intended it to be uncompromising, to say the least. He wanted effective carte blanche for German troops in Italy, control of the Alpine border region, and German supremacy of decision-making in

Italy. These were not new demands, but in the previous meetings in August the Italians had been evasive. The Führer was sick of the uncertainty, deeply mistrustful, and wanted to show who was boss in this fragile alliance. Crucially, though, he also wanted the Italians to garrison the south so he could withdraw German forces north of Rome, where they could make a more effective and better-supplied defensive line. Between Pisa and Rimini was where he had in mind, where it was almost entirely mountainous with few decent roads. This move would also then free up several divisions for the Balkans. Castellano, who had assured the Allies this was the plan, had been right all along.

Such an ultimatum, of course, was blown out of the water with the Italian armistice, but the really significant consequence was that German troops remained south of Rome, both to disarm the Italians and to defend the Allied invasion, rather than pulling back swiftly to a defensive line to the north as Rommel – and Hitler – had planned. The terrible irony was that, had the Allies done what Ambrosio, Badoglio, Roatta and Carboni et al. had wanted and postponed the announcement – and the invasion – until 15 September, southern Italy would have been theirs for the taking. The outcome would have been the very opposite of what they had feared. What an incredible missed opportunity for the Allies! And for Italy, for that matter. But they had not known that. And so, already, the Italian campaign was starting to play out in a very different way to how all parties had envisioned.

Before sundown, Clark had stood out on deck watching the convoys manoeuvre into their three lines for the different assaults and saw the minesweepers move forward to begin the task of clearing channels to the designated landing places. The plan, he believed, was the best available in the circumstances; it had been a relief to him that the 82nd Airborne operation in Rome had been cancelled; that, to his mind, had been a non-starter and doomed to failure. He had suggested the division instead be used to secure crossings over the River Volturno, but even that was thirty to forty miles away. Now, he had the 82nd on standby to be dropped wherever and whenever he might need them.

Otherwise, the plan was as had been agreed a week earlier. Planning time had been painfully short and bedevilled by haggling over just how many landing craft were available. That was the frustrating aspect of this invasion. Back at Allied bases and camps in North Africa there was no shortage of troops, guns, tanks and all he needed to blast the Germans out of southern Italy. They just couldn't get them there for want of enough ships. And so only three divisions would be landing, plus a handful of special forces. Salerno stood on the hinge of the coastline as it turned sharply west to the mountainous Amalfi and Sorrento peninsula, and although these steep, rugged peaks plunged straight down to the sea and were hardly conducive to fighting, there were two passes that ran through them, cutting off the peninsula and leading directly to the key city of Naples and due north to the towns of San Severino and Avellino. So British Commandos were to land at the tiny fishing port of Vietri, just to the west of Salerno, while the US Army Rangers were going to assault on their left at a second fishing village, Maiori. The plan was for them to then secure the roads and passes.

Meanwhile, the British 46th Division would land around Salerno itself, on beaches code-named 'Uncle' Sector, and 56th Division would land further to the south but north of the River Sele, in 'Sugar' and 'Roger' Sectors. Because of the shipping shortage, only one US division would be landed initially, the 36th Texans, but some fifteen miles to the south around Paestum. This was the other side of the River Sele – a potentially problematic barrier between the two forces – and the Brits and Americans were landing dangerously far apart and barely able to offer mutual support. The trouble was, mountains and hills overlooked the northern half – Leutnant Rocholl was on one such – but also the lower half as the coastline jutted out west again. In between was the alluvial plain, but because the Germans had both guns and OPs on the hills and mountains, the key was to get off the beach and take the high ground as quickly as possible. The objectives for the Texans were ambitious – Monte Soprano, rising 3,000 feet and more than five miles inland, Monte Soltano at 1,800 feet, and the mountain village of Albanella, eight miles from their landing beaches. Geography – and, of course, a shortage of landing craft – was dictating where they landed. The gap between the Brits and the Americans was far from ideal, but couldn't be helped. As with every aspect of AVALANCHE, they were having to do the best with what was available. Clark hoped the Texans would secure their objectives swiftly; in a best-case scenario, the Germans would barely contest the landings at all and he might even land the 45th Thunderbirds, waiting in troopships offshore, directly into Naples. Far more realistic, however, was to land the Thunderbirds in between, either side of the River Sele. Had it not been for the goddamned shortage of landing craft, they would be hitting the shore in the early hours, alongside the Texans.

At ten minutes to midnight, Clark joined Hewitt out on the bridge as the *Ancon's* engines stopped, just a few miles offshore. The mountains of the Amalfi coast loomed away to the north and to the south around Agropoli. He had not realized just how helpless he would feel. There was absolutely nothing he could now do but wait.

Clark could have called upon the full weight of an aerial and naval bombardment, but accurate bombing and shelling still required visual help, so the best that could be achieved would be a general pummelling rather than the pinpointing of gun batteries and OPs. The alternative was to wait until first light, but that would mean the assaulting infantry landing in daylight; visual accuracy cut both ways. On the other hand, by landing at night the enemy might know they were coming and enemy flares would certainly give some visibility, but there would be the confusion of darkness and accurate enemy targeting would be harder. Aerial reconnaissance had shown that, other than mines and wire entanglements, there were no beach defences. If the assaulting infantry could get on to the beaches with comparative ease, once daylight dawned they could then push on and capture their key objectives. That was the thinking, at any rate, and although Admiral Hewitt had urged Clark to make the most of the naval forces' guns ahead of the assault, the Fifth Army commander had opted for arriving into the Bay of Salerno with stealth and without any softening-up bombardment ahead of the assault phase.

For a general commanding his first amphibious operation these were very tough and thorny decisions to make, but ones that were demanded by senior command. One had to weigh up the pros and cons of such options, make a call, stick to it and hope for the best. The truth, of course, was that Clark had been dealt a very tough hand because of the shortage of shipping. Needless to say, if the assault was a success, such debates would slide into the background.

As it happened, the Germans opened fire first, at 1.21 a.m., on the northern assault force of the British and US Army Rangers; one landing ship, USS *LST-357*, was hit, with fifty casualties, but otherwise the German guns were entirely inaccurate, which rather underlined the difficulties of firing at night. The seaplane tender, USS *Biscayne*, hastily made smoke, covering the landing craft very effectively with the fog of war as the LCAs – British assault craft – were lowered from their derricks on the troopships into the water below.

One of those now on the water in an LSI – landing ship, infantry – was Colonel William O. Darby, just thirty-two years old but the founder and commander of the Army Rangers. From Arkansas, Darby was a career soldier who had graduated from West Point in 1933. Blue-eyed and good-looking, with ambition, energy and charm in equal measures, he'd reached Britain in January 1942 with the 34th Red Bulls, the first US troops to be shipped over. An aide to the then division commander, Major-General Russell P. Hartle, Darby had soon become restless at the lack of activity. Unbeknown to him at the time, however, salvation was at hand, because General Marshall, the US Chief of Staff, had been anxious for a Commando-style force and so sent Colonel Lucian Truscott to join the British Combined Operations HQ, from which the Commandos had emerged. These troops had been formed to operate alongside the Royal Navy and carry out raids and sabotage operations. Truscott had liked what he'd seen, reported favourably, and Marshall agreed to form a similar American force but suggested the name 'Rangers' after the pre-Revolutionary force, Rogers' Rangers. Since the Red Bulls were the only complete division in Britain at the time they had been the source of the first recruitment drive, and Darby was given the challenge of getting this new force up and running. What he was after was bright, physically fit young men able to use their initiative and think on their feet – men who were prepared to go the extra yard. Men who wanted to be part of a special and elite unit. A recruitment circular was sent round, Darby then began interviewing volunteers and, once happy he had got the men he needed, they all headed to Scotland for intensive training alongside the Commandos. The 1st Ranger Battalion had been activated on 19 June with 471 men.

Since then, the Rangers, under Darby's leadership, had repeatedly proved their worth – in Tunisia and again in Sicily – and had expanded from one to four battalions. Darby was now a young colonel, Truscott a general and commanding 3rd Infantry Division. The American Army was developing so rapidly in this war that individuals who proved themselves were just as swiftly moving up the command ladder.

From the USS *Ancon*, Clark sent his first signal to General Alexander at 2.25 a.m., assuring him that they had arrived on schedule, that although two of the convoys had been attacked by enemy air action en route, casualties were believed to have been light, and that five enemy planes had been shot down. 'At writing this, 0200,' he signalled, 'boats have been lowered and are in position. Sea is calm. Indications are that beaches will be reached on time.' So far, then, so good.

To the south, more than fifteen miles from where the Rangers were now, the 36th Texans were getting ready for the assault. From USS *James O'Hara* Captain Roswell Doughty had seen flashes to the north and assumed it was artillery, but they were too far away for him to hear anything. Out on deck, the wind was warm on his face and the gentle, slow movement of the ship soothing. He didn't want to leave. The ship then came to a halt, anchors splashing into the water with ominous finality. It was almost time to go. Activity on the boat, men scampering through the metal corridors and companionways, lit by a dim blue light, imperceptible from outside. The now familiar smell of oil, metal, rubber, sweat. Heavy nets were flung over, whamming against the side, down which the men would soon climb into landing craft. Doughty was aware that the British Coppists – Combined Operations Assault Pilotage Parties, part of Combined Operations – had been carrying out beach surveys and reconnaissance from the submarine HMS *Shakespeare* for two weeks beforehand, and two of these Commandos now came aboard to brief him on the intelligence picture. There was considerable enemy armour, they reported, in and around Eboli, as well as a 280mm railway gun. There were also numerous German and Italian supply dumps in and around Agropoli. With grease pencils they then marked up the overlays on their maps with the locations of the many artillery positions 16. Panzer-Division had established. Having gorged themselves on American naval rations – which had a deservedly high reputation – the two Commandos then left the ship, and Doughty to share the information now marked up on his map.

Doughty felt on edge. A little earlier, he'd been talking to Captain Hersel Adams, a friend in one of the infantry companies. Adams had been acting strange, which Doughty assumed had been pre-battle nerves. Before parting company, his friend then turned to him and told him he knew, with absolute certainty, that he would die at Salerno. Doughty tried to reassure him, but his words had been unconvincing. It had been an unsettling conversation.

While Clark and his Fifth Army staff worked out the broad plan, the order and manner in which units assaulted was down to the corps and divisional commanders. In this case, the 36th Texans were part of VI Corps under General Ernest 'Mike' Dawley, while the division itself was commanded by Major-General Fred L. Walker, a month short of his fifty-sixth birthday and a decorated veteran of the Second Battle of the Marne in the last war, in which he'd commanded an infantry battalion. Between the wars he'd been an instructor at the Army Infantry School at Fort Benning in Georgia and later took command of the Shattuck School in Minnesota, where among others he'd taught Clark and Omar Bradley. Bradley was a rising star who had done well in Tunisia and Sicily, while Clark was now Walker's superior and army commander. To be overtaken by a man almost ten years his junior could have created awkwardness, but Walker and Clark had always got on well and there was unquestionably mutual respect. Certainly, Clark was happy to let Walker impose his own stamp on the Texans' assault. Broadly, the plan was for two of 36th Division's regiments, 141st and 142nd Infantry, to lead the assault along four beaches, code-named from the north Red, Green, Yellow and Blue, opposite the remains of the ancient Greek city of Paestum. With a bit of luck, they would stay that way; destroying superbly preserved temples, theatres and city walls would not be a good start to the Allies' quest for the liberation of oppressed peoples.

Walker had also decided to attack without any barrage at all; although Clark had eschewed a pre-invasion bombardment, Lieutenant-General Dick McCreery, commander of X Corps, to which the two British assaulting divisions were attached, had asked for naval fire support during the approach and landings. General Fred Walker, however, had decided to do without, worrying that it would cause confusion for his green troops and reasoning that a silent assault, with a degree of tactical surprise, would be better. In this, Dawley, his corps commander, was happy to concur, as was Clark.

The moon had slipped below the horizon at around 1 a.m. An hour later, all those in the initial assault were in their landing craft, and at 2.15 a.m. the naval barrage of the Northern Attack Force opened fire. Both Force K, which included *Warspite,* and Force V, with the escort carriers, had remained offshore to cover the invasion force and from a safer distance to launch carrier aircraft, so it was left to the destroyers with their heavy guns and cannons to carry out most of the bombardment. It was quickly clear that no matter how accurate or inaccurate their firing, whenever their guns were thundering, those of the enemy were quiet, so that the combination of smoke and naval fire gave the assaulting craft in the British section considerable cover.

Colonel Bill Darby was as confident as always and knew his men were up to the challenge, no matter what it was. But in their LSIs and LCIs, his biggest worry was actually landing in the right place. Towering mountains climbed up behind Maiori and the beach itself was tiny. 'The finest compass in the world,' he noted, 'swings back and forth when thirty-five steel-helmeted soldiers carrying rifles are aboard.' As he was well aware, troops could never be expected to sit still and that constant movement caused the compass to deflect.

Darby planned for 4th Battalion to land first and then secure and hold the bridgehead while the 1st and 3rd Rangers and 83rd Chemical Mortar Battalion followed up and pushed on straight up to the mountains and the Chiunzi Pass. The Chemical Mortar Battalion was equipped with gas shells should the Germans ever decide to use it first, but expected to be deployed in a more normal mortar-firing role. Rangers, like paratroopers, were lightly armed, so Darby wanted to make sure he had as much firepower as could be managed and reckoned the mortar teams were going to be invaluable up in the mountains.

Guiding them to the beach was a destroyer whose compass was impervious to interference from restless troops, and once formed up they headed towards the shore, the mountains of the Amalfi coast looming into the darkness of the night. Darby thought they looked a little like ducklings following their mother. No enemy fired at them, and although they only spotted the tiny beach on which they were to land about 200 yards from the shore, the leading craft touched down almost on the dot of 3.30 a.m., exactly as planned, and still to no opposition at all. Towering above them on their right was the vast mass of the 3,000-foot-high Monte dell'Avvocata, and a smaller, 1,500-foot peak of the Tramonti Mountains. Between them ran a narrow valley leading to the villages of Pucara and Campinola, and the road, the Chiunzi Pass, that cut through the mountains to the Plain of Naples beyond. Allied intelligence was aware that the Hermann Göring Division was based around Naples, with further divisions to the north, between Naples and Rome. There were two passes through the mountains to Naples: the Chiunzi Pass and the second, through which the main road ran through Cava and Nocera, five miles further east and almost directly north of Salerno. This was to be secured by the Commandos. Darby moved up out of Maiori with the 1st and 3rd Battalions, climbing the steep road that led up towards the pass. Scouts were ahead, the rest of the men marching either side of the road. It was pitch-dark and the only sounds Darby heard were the shuffle of rubber-soled combat boots, the gentle chink of equipment and the singing of crickets and cicadas in the night air.

While the Commandos were also meeting almost no opposition at

Vietri, just west of Salerno on the hinge of the Amalfi peninsula, the main British infantry assaults were landing to the south-east of the town. On his hilltop near Salerno, Leutnant Rocholl was watching this part of the invasion unfold, his radio man delivering near-constant updates; he worried the Allies might pick up such rapid signals, especially using an 80kw set and high aerial. 'But fortunately,' he noted, 'the Allies were too busy with their landings to intercept my station.' He was certainly impressed by the Allied firepower near Salerno. He estimated the offshore gunfire must be from cruisers – in fact they were smaller destroyers – but then he was shocked by the onslaught from rapid rocket mortars. These were the LCRs designed to smother enemy positions near the beach just before the landings. 'One could hear the whistling and whining shots,' he wrote, 'and the reverberations of the explosions.' Then he heard their own machine guns open fire. German MGs – Maschinengewehre – were rapid-firing – the MG42 model could fire at a rate of twenty-three bullets per second, so spat out bullets with a rapid *brrrppp* that made them very easy to identify. 'Tommy with his landing barges must be very close in now,' Rocholl hurriedly added in his notebook.

Considering the short time in which divisional and corps staff had to plan, and especially taking into account the ever-fluctuating situation as to precisely how many landing craft would, or would not, be available, the assault forces had done remarkably well. Lessons had been learned from Sicily, where too much emphasis had been laid on attacking infantry and not enough on support troops. So it was that the 36th Texans were assaulting their beaches with two regiments bolstered with a number of extra troops, and, more importantly, extra equipment. The 141st and 142nd Infantry were landing first, two battalions up front, one following. The first infantry to land had engineer obstacle-removing teams attached. The second wave, due to land just seven minutes later, had further rifle companies but also mine detector teams, recce parties and shore engineers. A further eight minutes later, just a quarter of an hour after the first touchdowns, heavy weapons companies were to land along with Battalion HQ and medical teams, as well as navy beach teams.

Just fifty minutes after H-Hour, and still before dawn, bulldozers, 40mm anti-aircraft guns, 75mm self-propelled assault guns and a number of jeeps were to join them. Then the reserve battalions would follow, and after that, at H-Hour plus 140 – at 4.40 a.m. – assuming all had gone well, anti-tank weapons, tanks and field artillery would come ashore.

On paper this was a sound plan, and always very much a best-case scenario, but from the outset the Texans suffered from the lack of off-shore naval support. Here, as per General Fred Walker's decision to forego naval fire support, there were no destroyers beetling up and down the coast pounding enemy positions, and while rocket landing craft were a boon, the extra firepower from a mass of 120mm-plus-sized guns would have been a huge help. Instead, in darkness flickering with the light of flares and fires, confusion and chaos soon reigned. Part of the 1st Battalion of the 141st landed too far south by around 500 yards, and although the first two waves of troops did achieve some surprise and were able to quickly push inland, the third wave met intense enemy fire from the hills around Agropoli and was both cut to pieces and swiftly isolated.

The 3rd 141st, meanwhile, landing next beach up on Yellow, ran into immediate fire but managed to move inland until meeting enemy troops 400 yards from the shore and into the modern village of Paestum. On Green and Red Beaches, where 142nd Infantry were landing, enemy opposition was less intense but still fierce. The darkness, the water, the fizz and zap of bullets and mortars, the strobe effect of flashes of fire and explosions, the smoke, and the fact that these men had never been in combat before, inevitably led to mayhem on the beaches. Assault teams lost one another, scattered by tracer and machine-gun fire, radios were swamped in the water, ammunition and mortar base plates accidentally dropped. A number of landing craft were hit and burning, drifting helplessly. From the hills and mountains beyond, and particularly from Monte Soprano, a massive curved line of bare strata five miles away in front of them, the gun flashes of German artillery were all too clear.

It was this mayhem that Captain Roswell Doughty was about to enter with his I & R Platoon of 141st Infantry Regiment. It had still been dark when he alighted his LCT – landing craft, tank – but by the time they finally stopped circling and turned for the shore, the first glimmer of dawn was rising over the immense landscape away to the east. They were speeding now, a line of landing craft separated by perhaps 100 yards, heading into the jaws of battle. Narrow strips of fog could be seen ahead, hugging the sea. Doughty thought it gave their advance to the beaches a rather nightmarish quality, especially as they neared, and either side of him landing craft disappeared then spectrally re-emerged. Doughty felt sombre. He could hear no fighting ahead despite three waves of infantry going in before them, but knew that signified very little. Green flares shot up into the sky. Away to the north, the distant thunder of guns. British warships, he thought. On they ploughed, getting nearer. There were twenty-five men on the landing craft and his own jeep, into which he now clambered. Outside, the sky brightening dramatically. Sea spray showering them. More flares – he wondered whether that meant enemy aircraft were about to descend on them. Away to his right, the hazy, jutting Agropoli peninsula, extending out to sea.

And then a destroyer signalled to them to stop.

Heavy resistance had been met on Blue and Yellow Beaches. They were to hold for the moment.

Tense minutes, ticking by.

Suddenly, up ahead, machine-gun tracers cut a dotted line, a visible Morse, bright against the dark backdrop of the coast with its low dunes, and beyond, in the distance, the hazy blue of the mountains rising. That was not good: if the MG tracer was coming from the dunes, that meant the enemy still held them. Where were the previous three waves of infantry, Doughty wondered? Then they were ordered to move on once more, to the shore and to Yellow Beach. Now artillery shells were hitting the water nearby, huge spumes rising high into the air, then mortar shells crashing around them too. Doughty crouched, vulnerable and powerless, praying no mortar would crash into their LCT. He braced himself.

A rasping, scraping sound as the LCT hit the sand. Clanking as the bow ramp lowered. The landing craft lurched forward, engines still running, then stopped, and with it the bow ramp. Doughty jumped from his jeep and, urging others to help, leaned into it, heaving, pushing, and suddenly it began lowering again. But they were not on the shore; they were still 200 yards away. A sandbar. Well, too bad. He'd have to do without the jeep. Jumping into the water, he could not touch the bottom, but managed to shed his assault vest, musette bag and helmet and plunged towards the shore, his only weapon his Colt .45 pistol. Machine-gun bullets fizzed and zipped over his head and mortars crashed around him sending columns of water into the air. His breathing heavy. Getting heavier with the exertion of trying to plough through the water as quickly as possible. A strange kind of exhilaration, betting his life like this against the enemy fire.

Then he was at the shore, crawling on the sand, and glancing back saw that the LCT had backed off the reef. Others from the craft were alongside him, drenched, covered in sand. They'd made it too. He knew he had to move quickly – and he didn't have far to go as the beach was only about 30 yards deep until it reached the edge of the dunes, which offered a low shelf of cover. He also knew those enemy guns had been zeroed on the shoreline. Lying there, they were sitting ducks. But he couldn't move. He couldn't bring himself to get up on to his haunches and make the dash to the edge of the dunes. Instead, he found a crater and paused, looking around him. Ahead was Monte Soprano, a curved, looming mass of almost bare rock above the mountain village of Capaccio, and one of the day's objectives. It seemed horribly far away. Out of touch. He wondered how they would ever reach it, with the beach under intense fire and also now, he realized, under attack by tanks. There it was, perhaps 1,000 yards away, inching forward, a low-profile tracked beast with a big gun. In fact, it was not a tank at all but a StuG – Sturmgeschütz – assault gun, tracked like a tank but with a fixed gun rather than a rotating turret. To his horror, he now watched it slew and, it seemed, point directly at him. Its machine gun opened up, bullets ripping through the air just above his head. Behind, an LCT burning, angry smoke billowing. An LCR fired a salvo, rockets screaming over. The noise, the confusion, the hammering of his senses. More smoke billowed as the rockets landed with a crash, and then there was an anti-aircraft gun, one of their own, barrels horizontal, that had somehow been landed and was firing at the StuG just as the haze began to disperse. Hastily, the StuG pulled back, but not before firing several parting shots at the gun. Doughty felt groggy from the seawater, the noise, the smoke, but he now saw a gap in the wire ahead, suddenly blasted open. A shell from the StuG?

'Captain Doughty,' yelled a voice near him, 'it's me, Hobday!'

Doughty looked round and saw one of the corporals in his I & R team.

'Let's get out of here,' Doughty said to him, getting up from his hole. He was sodden and covered with wet sand, but hurriedly squelched towards the gap. A flash of movement up ahead and a split second later the distinctive shape of a German helmet. Doughty threw himself to the ground, firing his Colt as he dived, just as the man brought his rifle to his shoulder then pitched forward.

'Hot damn, Cap'n!' said Hobday beside him. 'You got him!'

Doughty was a bit stunned, but they both got to their feet and pushed on through the wire and then ran along the edge of the dunes towards the anti-aircraft gun. He realized his teeth were chattering and his hands shaking. Being under fire – so intensely – for the first time and now killing another man – it was shocking. He spotted Colonel Richard J. Werner, commander of the 141st, by the anti-aircraft gun along with a number of other men. Several bulldozers from 531st Shore Engineers were miraculously already ashore, as planned, one pulling wire matting into place to create a roadway for vehicles while another pummelled a route through the dunes. The cacophony was immense. Their own guns, the enemy guns, rockets, mortars. Werner yelled orders and they moved through the marshy dunes. Here the ground was flat and lined by a number of shallow irrigation ditches, vineyards, and dotted with a few trees, umbrella pines, bushes and dry-stone walls, and a handful of farmsteads and stone houses. They found shelter behind a stone wall near a farmhouse just off the beach. A radio link was set up. The news: that shelling of Blue Beach was so bad the rest of the regiment was being diverted a few hundred yards to land on Yellow Beach instead, although that wasn't much better. That was the cause of the delay to Doughty's landing; he'd been among the first to have been diverted, a little way to the right to the southern edge of Yellow. Just off the beach, emerging through the smoke, was the Tower of Paestum, built in the Middle Ages and still standing after all these centuries – and despite finding itself in the midst of a new battle on the boundary between two assault beaches. The 1st Battalion had taken a hammering, but the decision to send follow-up troops to Yellow Beach meant the remainder were now isolated, cut off and lacking heavy weapons.

Doughty thought Colonel Werner seemed edgy, panicky even. Well he might be, though, with one entire battalion in danger of annihilation. Werner had already dispatched several officers to try and find them and establish a link, but none had yet returned, which was ominous. Now it was Doughty's turn.

About 7 a.m. The British were now also ashore, with 46th Division around Salerno not meeting much opposition, but 56th Division, further south, meeting heavy enemy forces. General Clark, still on board *Ancon,* sent a further signal to Alexander. The situation was generally favourable, he told his Chief. The 36th Division were having trouble, he reported. They had a toehold, but the Germans were fighting back. Clearly, the next few hours would be critical.

CHAPTER 9

Toehold

IN EBOLI, HAPPINESS AT the news of the armistice had burst as quickly as a pricked balloon. First shellfire could be heard, then the siren sounded, droning mournfully out over the town, its wail reverberating around the mountain backdrop. Lina Caruso felt a mixture of amazement and fright as she and her family hurriedly left their home and headed to a large cave dug almost underneath the castle; it was a mere 100 yards away from their front door, on the eastern side of the ridge on to which the castle had been built centuries before. Surely, she thought, the Allies wouldn't bomb them now they were friends? A number of others were sheltering in the cave, and soon after the Caruso family settled in they heard the first bombs falling. Someone shouted out, others wept. Another suggested the Germans would punish them for breaking the alliance. More people arrived, so that soon it was packed with as many as 200 sheltering there, the air suffocating. Lina felt overcome by the blackest melancholy. Every time more bombs whistled down she hugged her mother and sisters tightly. One crash was so close the cave shook. 'We thought we were dying,' Lina wrote in her diary, 'and we commended our souls to God.'

Bombs were then replaced by shells from the Northern Attack Force's gunfire, not that Lina was attuned to the difference. Then, at around 3 a.m., it stopped at last, only to be followed by what sounded like hundreds of planes flying over. A student near her suggested they all move away from Eboli for a few days, just until the Allies arrived. But where? No one was really sure. Somehow, Lina managed to fall asleep but woke up to discover the cave was almost empty – people had moved outside for some fresher air and to find out what was happening. Gunfire could still be heard, but she and her family decided to head home all the same. There, Lina went to her room and wept.

To the north, some 180 miles away in Rome, Generale Giacomo Carboni had had a long night. There had been orders to issue to his staff, and an uncomfortable discussion with Ambrosio, who had urged him not to allow his men to fire the first shot at the Germans. Carboni had brushed this off; at night, it was hard to tell who fired what. He had placed his troops on alert and told Ambrosio that if they all stood firm, the Germans might well pull out. They outnumbered them, after all.

He had then been summoned to see the King, who asked him whether his troops would contest the city if the Germans attacked.

'They will fight to the last round,' Carboni assured him, 'especially against the Germans.'

After this brief audience, Carboni had hurried back to Army HQ where he met Baron von Clemm, from the German Embassy, and promised him safe passage for him and his staff. No sooner had the perfumed Clemm left him than Carboni was told the Germans were now attacking all along the Granatieri Division's front to the south of the city. Carboni dashed to Roatta's office, who sat at his desk looking depressed and clutching a telephone intercept between General Westphal and the OKW. Westphal, it seemed, had reported that their paratroopers were disarming Italian troops already. The 3. Panzergrenadiers were also heading into Rome. Worse, the Germans had seized the largest Italian fuel dump in the area, out towards the coast near Ostia. It had been left totally unguarded. Why? How could this have been allowed to happen? The Piacenza Division was also fighting with 2. Fallschirmjäger-Division between Pratica di Mare to the north-east and Frascati to the north-west. The Piacenza were supposed to be blocking the northern approaches to the city. The reports, varying and contrary but mostly dismal, presented a confused and depressing picture.

Both Roatta and Carboni agreed that they should retaliate as swiftly and firmly as they could, and also implement the OP 44 directive, which they understood to have been issued to all garrisons already and which now merely needed activating. Carboni, having also issued instructions of his own to his troops to fight furiously against any German aggression, had decided to try and snatch a few hours' sleep. He'd not been to bed in three days and he knew he needed to be fresh and sharp in the morning.

No sooner had he lain down, however, than he was called to an urgent telephone call from Tenente Ettore Rosso, an engineer officer in the Piacenza Division, who had been busily mining a key road bridge near Monterosi, north of Rome. He explained that an armoured column from 3. Panzergrenadier-Division wanted passage across the bridge. He had stalled them, but they had only given him half an hour. Rosso wanted to know what he should do. Let them pass or bar their passage? Carboni ordered him to prevent them from crossing. Calling off, Rosso had quickly asked for volunteers to man a barricade while he hastily tried to link a detonator to the mines on the bridge, the minutes to the deadline ticking by. At the appointed hour the German column began to move forward on to the bridge, but no sooner had the first troops started to cross than Rosso plunged the detonator, blowing up not only the bridge and the first German troops but also himself.

By this time, news had reached Roatta and Ambrosio that Germans were advancing on Rome from the north and the south. Even Roatta now believed the city was lost. Prince Umberto was woken, then Badoglio, and finally the King and Queen. Just before dawn the King, wearing the uniform of the commander-in-chief of all the Italian armed forces, stepped into the courtyard of the Ministry of War, where his black Fiat 2800 limousine was waiting. Badoglio was also there and motioned to the King to get into the waiting car.

Vittorio Emanuele III hesitated. 'I'm an old man,' he said to Badoglio. 'What could they do to me?'

Badoglio told him it was vital they moved the monarch and the government to a safe location. The King reluctantly agreed and stepped into the car next to his Queen, Elena. Just before 5 a.m., the limousine left the courtyard and headed into the streets of the city. Soon after, Badoglio followed. They were abandoning Rome – and its people.

Meanwhile, Generale Carboni had been woken again, this time by Roatta. Back in Roatta's office at the Palazzo Caprara, the Army commander-in-chief ordered him to leave the Granatieri where they were but move the Ariete and Piave. The Ariete, one of the army's few armoured divisions, was the best division in Carboni's corps.

'We can no longer defend ourselves in Rome,' Roatta told him. 'We'd simply be trapped. Here is an order to move your corps to Tivoli.' Carboni was bemused. Tivoli was the new headquarters of the Comando Supremo, up in the hills, safe from Allied bombers. But it was nearly thirty miles east of Rome. What about the Granatieri, Carboni wondered, who by all accounts were already fighting to the south of the city? Roatta told him the Granatieri were no longer part of his command, and so no longer his concern.

'At least tell me what line you want me to assume,' Carboni demanded. 'And what you want me to do.'

Roatta scowled. 'I don't know, yet.' Roatta then told him he would receive further orders once he was established at Tivoli.

'Aren't you going to give me a written order?'

'No need,' Roatta replied. 'Not in an emergency such as this.' Then, snatching a piece of paper, he hastily scribbled instructions and handed them over. After that, Roatta, with Zanussi in tow, hurried out. Carboni watched them descend the great staircase and disappear out of the front entrance. They could hardly get away quickly enough.

Carboni was utterly exhausted. Having issued his orders to move the Piave and Ariete to his Chief of Staff, Colonnello Giorgio Salvi, he went to his nearby flat, gathered his things, and then, with his son and a young aide, Tenente Lanzi, headed off for Tivoli in his car. With his diplomatic licence plates, maintained by the SIM, he had little trouble getting through despite several roadblocks, both Italian and German. By the time they reached Tivoli the sun was up.

Barely a soul moved in the town. At the barracks, all was shut up; there was not a sign of the Comando Supremo nor of the Army Command, nor, for that matter, even a lone member of the Carabinieri. No one to give him fresh orders. A fruitless couple of hours followed as he motored through the hills looking for any sign of the high command. Lanzi, taking Carboni's car, had discovered Roatta on the side of the road to Avezzano, which was some fifty miles further on, with a puncture. The army chief was both truculent and uninterested in Carboni's predicament. Back in Tivoli, Carboni had eventually managed to get a line to Colonnello Salvi, only to discover that the orders to the Piave and Ariete had not been issued. Carboni could hardly believe what he was hearing. Sacking his Chief of Staff on the spot, he then began hastily ringing through the orders himself. The commanders of the Ariete, especially, were furious. At that moment they were fighting 2. Fallschirmjäger-Division; as one of the Italian Army's best-equipped – and experienced – armoured divisions, the Ariete had the weight of firepower to overcome the more lightly armed paratroopers. To disengage now would not be easy; it would also cost them the initiative they held in the fighting south of Rome. It was a terrible decision, and one that Carboni, abandoned by the Comando

Supremo in Tivoli, should not have made, despite the direct order from Roatta. But in that moment he was not thinking clearly. Three days and nights with almost no sleep were addling his thinking.

Far to the south at Salerno, the British landings had gone about as well as the Allies could have hoped for. The 46th Division, five miles south-east of Salerno, had come ashore almost entirely unopposed, while the biggest hiccup to 56th Division's landings had been some landing craft from 46th Division getting in their way because of mines in the water. The 56th Division had landed two brigades – about ten minutes late at 3.40 a.m. – each with two battalions up front and one in reserve either side of the Tusciano, a narrow river that ran down from the mountains through the hill town of Battipaglia and out to the sea. The first field artillery had arrived by 5.30 a.m. and tanks of the Royal Scots Greys half an hour later. More batteries of field artillery continued to land without a hitch.

By 7 a.m., the follow-up and third brigade of 56th Division was also heading to shore. Lieutenant Christopher Bulteel, a twenty-two-year-old platoon commander in the 3rd Coldstream Guards, was rather mesmerized to find himself out at sea and watching the sun rise over the mountains directly ahead of them beyond the plain. Gradually, the water around them turned from grey to soft green, while the peaks of the Amalfi coast mountains away to his left were suddenly magically lit up with a golden halo. The ships and landing craft glinted in the sudden and dramatic brightness. Ahead, the sun seemed to just touch the top of the smoke and dust along the shore, like a crown of gold. Everywhere he looked were ships and landing craft and launches scurrying from one vessel to another.

Bulteel had been plagued by the dead weight of fear in the days crossing the sea, but now a kind of excitement seemed to have drowned those feelings of dread. From Cornwall, in the far south-west of England, Bulteel had no great military ambitions and had only ended up with the 3rd Coldstream Guards because his father, another unenthusiastic soldier, had accidentally found himself serving with them in the last war. An unassuming fellow, with a genial face and thick, dark, wavy hair, Bulteel had joined the battalion in Libya and fought with them right to the end in Tunisia. He'd survived Medenine, the Mareth Line, and although briefly captured by the Germans at one point, he had swiftly escaped. For someone who had always considered himself entirely unsuitable for soldiering, he had turned himself into a much-liked, experienced and half-decent junior officer.

Now, with the rising sun beating down upon them, Bulteel found himself speeding towards the shore in a larger LCI, one of three carrying the battalion into battle. Above them a few black puffs of flak smudged the sky, but the noise of the landing craft, the guns and the din of battle was so great that he paid these shell bursts little attention. As they neared the shore, Bulteel could see men scurrying about on the beach, the smoke and dust now gone. He saw a man waving a flag at them and the vessel made its way to him. Closer and closer. The beach clearer now of smoke. A splash as the kedge dropped into the water, and then a lurch as the LCI grazed the sand and came to a stop so abruptly that they all stumbled forward. Ramps thundered down with a rattle and loud clang and they were running ahead, not into water but straight on to the beach, Bulteel still clutching two bottles of gin he and his fellows had meant to drink but had failed to.

Suddenly, a mass of gunfire very close. Looking up, he dropped the gin as four Messerschmitt 109s hurtled over, but they were past in a flash. Gathering themselves together, his men were ushered off the beach through taped lines in the minefield and on through the dunes. Past gunners, already firing their 25-pounders and sweating in the morning sun. Flat ground, stone walls, densely cultivated fields of rich soil, a deep chocolate-brown. Bulteel followed the last of the men down a track and into an orchard, where he found his No. 3 Company commander, Major Mervyn Griffith-Jones, already sorting the stragglers into their platoons. Most were brewing up tea in the safety of a dusty ditch, although Bulteel noticed a number of men going around the orchard collecting apples, their helmets now being used as trugs. Up ahead, several miles away, the sounds of small arms. Bulteel felt slightly discombobulated by the noise and the lack of information. No one seemed to know what was going on, so for the time being they stayed where they were, in reserve, until such time as they were called upon – hoping for some news of the battle, which, as far as Bulteel was concerned, seemed too close for comfort.

On his hill overlooking the bay, Leutnant Rocholl had watched dawn arrive quickly; it had been dark, then first light, and then suddenly the sun was up and there before him was the invasion fleet. The Allies might have wanted a force many times larger, but Rocholl, for one, was impressed. 'Our astonished eyes,' he scribbled, 'witnessed a magnificent spectacle.' Rocholl sent his armoured cars to recce forward while he moved his OP to the Italian battery position. He watched two landing ships unloading and even saw the first Allied tanks. Destroyers were firing and then also laying another smokescreen, so he could no longer see anything but the fog covering the sea.

Around 10 a.m., the smoke cleared enough for him to watch another landing craft approaching a smashed mole in Salerno harbour. A German 88mm anti-aircraft gun near Rocholl's own position opened fire, and he watched, mesmerized, as the LCT drew towards the mole, fountains of water erupting ever closer around it. Then a shell landed almost on top of the vessel, the stern dipped into the sea and Rocholl expected to see it sink. Instead, though, it turned round and went back towards the main invasion force. Soon after, shells began whistling over his own position. He wondered whether he'd been spotted, but then realized it was the 88mm flak gun they were targeting. The first salvo had landed short but the second was right on target. The entire battery was knocked out. Just like that. Guns, men, gone, thanks to that missile of death and destruction. In this duel, Royal Navy gunnery had proved more accurate than the Luftwaffe flak battery.

While Rocholl was left on his hill, warships were now targeting German gun positions all along the invasion front, and the British infantry below him, supported by ever-greater numbers of artillery and armour, were pushing inland. Even though intelligence over the previous few days had increasingly pointed to a landing at Salerno, the senior German command had still had doubts the previous evening; Kesselring, for one, thought the Allies might land further north of Naples, or even around Rome, despite the indications to the contrary. As a Luftwaffe man who had commanded an air fleet during the Battle of Britain, it is odd that he did not seem to consider the constraints of fighter range. Maybe he thought the Allies had more twin-engine P-38 Lightnings than they really had. Overestimating Allied materiel strength was a malaise that appeared to be prevalent among the senior German command, despite reconnaissance photographs and radio intelligence that should have given them a more accurate picture. Neither Kesselring nor anyone else seemed to wonder where the supposed extra airfields, aircraft, landing craft and warships were hidden. There was, perhaps, a hint of arrogance about it – a presumption, deep-rooted, that only by overwhelming enemy might could they possibly be beaten.

Kesselring was also deeply frustrated that Hitler, usually so determined to fight for every metre, appeared to be willing to abandon the southern half of Italy. He had clashed with Rommel numerous times since their destinies had become entwined in the Mediterranean theatre, and feared that his former subordinate and now, in Italy, rival, had somehow managed to gain too much influence over the Führer. Repeatedly, Kesselring had explained to the OKW that holding the numerous air bases in Apulia was vital now that the Allied strategic air campaign was increasing in intensity. It was all too obvious that if the Allies could wrench them from the Germans they would soon be using them for heavy bomber bases against the Reich. He simply couldn't understand why more of Rommel's eight divisions in the north had not been sent south.

If that was frustrating Kesselring, so too was the sudden situation in which he found himself, with the Italian armed forces to disarm, an Allied invasion south of Naples and the British moving along the toe of the boot. There was a lot to think about. Nor had the bombing of his headquarters the previous day helped at a time when he needed his communication network to be at its most efficient. The trouble was, now that it was under strain it was proving less effective than normal, and his senior commanders were often out of touch with one another at the very moment when they all needed to be in regular contact. Civilian telephone lines were not secure, Kesselring's own headquarters was barely functioning, and atmospheric disturbances across the mountains frustrated radio contact, strangely, most often during darkness. All the previous night, Kesselring had been preoccupied with the situation in Rome and had struggled to make contact with von Vietinghoff. As early as 8 a.m. it was clear to the 10. Armee commander, however, that the scale of the invasion at Salerno suggested another was unlikely. He had already agreed with Kesselring that, because of the refusal to send Rommel's divisions south, they would very regrettably have to abandon Apulia; but he was also aware that Hitler had planned to withdraw all forces north of Rome in the event of an Allied assault. This left him in a bit of quandary. Unable to confer with Kesselring, von Vietinghoff had to decide whether to meet the invasion at Salerno or pull back.

At XIV Panzerkorps headquarters near Naples, General Balck was certainly in favour of contesting the assault, but was also struggling to get hold of von Vietinghoff; in fact, he couldn't get hold of either 10. Armee or Kesselring, and although he was able to send a radio signal, he then had to wait several precious hours for an answer. Meanwhile, at the coalface, the commander of 16. Panzer-Division, Generalmajor Rudolf

Sieckenius, also had to decide what to do. They had been posted to the Salerno area a few weeks earlier with instructions to immediately destroy any enemy landing should it occur, and that was what Sieckenius planned. The division, though, had been destroyed at Stalingrad and, although reborn, many of the men were new to battle and a lot of tank crews lacked experience. Even those who had fought in France and the Soviet Union now found themselves in very unfamiliar terrain, with no experience of deploying armour in mountainous country such as this or, for that matter, of defending an amphibious invasion. In fact, the only divisions operating within the German Army to have done so were 15. Panzergrenadier and Hermann Göring in Sicily and, in August 1942, 302. Division at Dieppe. The German Army had fought in mountains and in deserts, in the steppe and through forests and across dense farmland; they'd fought in scorching heat and in freezing snow and rain, and yet for all that, they'd not fought anywhere much like Italy and had accrued little knowledge in repelling seaborne invasions. Even in Sicily it had been Italian troops, not German, that had confronted the Allied landings. Where one should deploy one's troops, whether on the beaches or further inland – there was no rule book for such things. The defenders in 16. Panzer had more than twenty miles of coastline to defend with just 17,000 men. A lot was being expected of them.

Even so, there were principles of defence no matter what one was defending, and from the moment they had been deployed 16. Panzer had hurriedly set to their task. OPs had been sited in the mountains and hills, along with radio stations and gun positions. Roads, bridges and the entire shoreline were mined and strewn with wire. Forward mortar and machine-gun positions were held back from the beach where they could be hidden in vineyards and groves; these were natural defences to exploit. None the less, no one had thought to lay any further beach obstacles, nor had there been much opportunity to build concrete bunkers; after all, they had only been there a fortnight.

As it happened, von Vietinghoff had decided to fight, not withdraw, approval for which was finally received from Kesselring's headquarters by around noon, although word had not reached either Balck or Sieckenius at this time. Nor had Balck yet been handed any reconnaissance reports, and so at this stage had no firm knowledge of whether any further Allied landings might be made. Hedging his bets, he ordered 15. Panzergrenadier, now to the north in the Caserta area, to be ready to defend the coast either side of the River Volturno, twenty miles north of

Naples. The only reinforcement Balck felt able to send that morning was the reconnaissance battalion of the Hermann Göring Division from Naples. This left 16. Panzer with a lot to do. Allied naval firepower was playing a very effective suppressive role, while forward positions were unable to hold the weight of numbers pouring on to the beaches.

'A report from Admiral Hall,' noted Clark in his diary, 'whose task force is supporting the 36th Division, states that he believes the 36th Division is making good progress but has not penetrated far enough yet to clear artillery fire off the beaches.' Still on board the *Ancon*, Clark was desperately trying to make sense of what was going on, dispatching various members of his staff on launches to investigate, but while he'd heard nothing from General Fred Walker, broadly speaking the news seemed encouraging, and, frankly, better than he'd feared. The major concern was the 36th Texans, but it seemed he could now start to breathe a little easier.

Captain Roswell Doughty, meanwhile, had been unable to reach the stranded 1st Battalion. Taking one of his men, Private First Class Charlie Lane, he had set off, pushing through some low-growing trees and a small vineyard beyond the area of dunes and marsh. Suddenly, an anti-tank shell screamed just over their heads and both men dived on to the ground. Much to Doughty's humiliation, he landed chest-first on to where someone had earlier emptied their bowels. So far, his experience of combat was proving utterly wretched. They soon heard sounds of men crawling nearby. Doughty froze. 'They're Mexicans,' Lane told him. 'Probably E Company.' An American machine gun barked, tracers careering into a stack of brush at the edge of the vineyard, setting it alight. Suddenly, a StuG started up and began backing off from its camouflaged position less than 100 yards away, its two machine guns ripping bullets as it did so. One of the Mexicans fired a bazooka, but the projectile simply bounced off the armour.

'Forgot to pull the pin,' commented Lane. Bazookas were hand-held anti-tank rocket launchers, very effective at close range. That was often the rub, however, because to get close enough to be effective obviously placed the firer in considerable danger. Here, though, with plenty of bushes and vines for cover, and with the StuG so close, the 2nd Battalion men had a better chance, and a second missile crashed into the enemy assault gun with an immense explosion. This was followed swiftly by several more as the ammunition within exploded. In moments, the StuG was engulfed in livid flames and thick, billowing black smoke.

Someone else had shouted, 'Tanks!', and, realizing they were pinned down and unable to move further southwards, Doughty and Lane scurried back and reported to Colonel Werner. It seemed the two officers sent earlier to locate the missing 1st Battalion before Doughty had both been killed. Word also arrived that Hersel Adams's forebodings had been proved right: he was another reported dead. Werner now ordered Doughty back to the beach to assist the radio team, who were trying to help direct fire for the offshore naval guns. The beach was still chaotic, with the dead washed ashore and burned-out and broken landing craft, boxes and detritus strewn everywhere. Doughty found Colonel Joe Crawford manning the set at the edge of the lagoon; he had been temporarily posted from the battle-hardened 1st Infantry Division to provide the 141st with an officer of proven combat experience. Doughty, for one, was glad to have him there, especially since he had little time for Werner. The lagoon marked the northern part of Blue Beach, where now, at last, it seemed a little calmer. At least it was until three Messerschmitts hurtled over, machine guns hammering and spitting up spurts of sand. Along the beach, as yet more unloading was going on, men dived for cover, anti-aircraft guns pounded and then, as quickly as they had arrived, the Messerschmitts were gone again.

The landings continued as a continual ferrying of troops and supplies on the beaches disgorged loads and scuttled back for the next round trip. Hitting the shore around noon was Corporal Bud Wagner, touching down on Red Beach at the northern end of the 36th Texans' landing area. Although Wagner was part of the 151st Field Artillery attached to 34th Division, all of the Red Bulls' four artillery battalions had been temporarily seconded to a strengthened Texan Division; the Allied way of war – and especially the American – was to use firepower as much as possible to try and limit the number of young infantrymen having to fling themselves directly into the firing line. Mark Clark and his planners had been determined that if they were to be restricted on the number of infantry divisions they could land, then they would partly compensate by having as much artillery and armour as they could possibly squeeze into the available landing craft.

Unlike the rest of the Texans, Wagner and his fellows had seen plenty of action and knew a bit more about what to expect, even though this was his first amphibious assault. They'd been shelled on the run-in and he'd also been staggered by the number of ships and vessels he could see all around him; he'd counted seventy-six.

Wagner was twenty-four and a farm boy from Hermantown, Minnesota. He and his older brother, Ray, had always worked on the family farm, although his father had also helped him set up a market gardening business back in the summer of 1938. Then, in October 1940, he'd registered for the draft and in April the following year had been called up. This had prompted some soul-searching for Wagner, as an uncle accused him of abandoning the family farm to needlessly fight against the Germans. Wagner did not want to leave his family or the farm, but he also felt strongly that it was both his duty and the right thing to do. Hitler and his Nazis had to be stopped.

As a Midwestern boy he ended up in a Midwest division, the 34th Red Bulls, but in an artillery battalion rather than infantry. The Red Bulls had not only been the first to be shipped overseas to Britain, in January 1942, but had been among the first into action too, part of II Corps in Northwest Africa. Wagner had become a cook with the 151st Field Artillery, but then, in early May, he had been asked if he wanted to become the Battalion Agent. The agent, or 'liaison agent', or even 'messenger', as they were variously known, was the link between the Headquarters Battery at Divisional HQ and the four artillery battalions within the division. It was the agent's job to base himself at the division, be on duty twenty-four hours a day and, equipped with a jeep, be ready, at a moment's notice, to deliver reports, messages or firing orders to his allotted battalion.

Wagner had jumped at the opportunity and had never once regretted the move. The chow at division tended to be pretty good, he loved his jeep – or 'peep', as he called it – and liked being at the centre of things, as well as the degree of independence the job afforded. Now he and his peep were about to be on Italian soil, and as he drove down the ramp and straight into the sea it never once missed a beat, despite the water sloshing over the hood. Between tasks as an agent Wagner had always made sure he looked after his vehicle, and now it was looking after him.

Once clear, he was directed inland; the fighting had progressed and by early afternoon 142nd Infantry were several miles from the beach; the Germans were starting to pull back now that the initial American landings had been successful. One armoured column of thirteen panzers had been moving along the road that ran parallel to the coast when it had been spotted by a lone 155mm howitzer that had been hastily brought into position. The gunners had hit the lead tank, then the rear one, and the eleven in between had then found themselves trapped by a low wall either side. One by one they'd been shot up in turn. A howitzer was designed to lob shells in an arc over a number of miles and mostly to fire indirectly – in other words, at targets that could not be seen by the crew manning it, such as over the far side of a hill, or beyond a village. But at very short distances, and with enemy tanks lining themselves up like targets at a fairground popgun stall, the howitzer had done a great job as a panzer killer. At any rate, such catastrophic losses encouraged the enemy to pull back, which, in turn, allowed men like Bud Wagner to quickly get off the beach and drive inland. 'Came about 1 mile inland,' he noted in his diary. 'Moved again to some ancient ruins.' These were the ruins of Paestum. The 36th Texans had allocated the ancient city as their assembly area. After all, it was a big space, surrounded by thick stone walls, and offered an ideal spot in which to gather supplies, men and equipment and then push on. There was a war to fight; worrying about the survival chances of a temple or two, no matter how significant, was not at the top of the Texans' priority list right now.

Meanwhile, Fifth Army's build-up continued, helped, especially in the Northern Attack area, by the array of warships and adapted landing craft. Not only were there LCRs, for example, but also LCFs – landing craft, flak – which were 152-feet-long LCTs with the bow ramp welded shut and a deck built parallel to the top of the sides. Bolted on to this higher deck were four pairs of Oerlikon 20mm cannons and four QF – quick-firing – 2-pounder pom-poms. The idea was to create a small but well-armed and highly mobile anti-aircraft vessel that could offer cover right up to the shore if necessary. Guns could be lowered to support operations on the ground, but LCFs were really for shooting down aircraft, barrels pointed skywards and ready should enemy aircraft streak over. With a crew of sixty men, they were a simple but ingenious addition, like the LCRs, to the Allied assault arsenal.

One of those supporting the invasion was LCF 12, commanded by Lieutenant Peter Bull, an appropriately bull-faced thirty-one-year-old. The war had brought the most unlikely people into uniform, and Bull was one such person. As a young man he had never imagined he could end up in any of the armed services, and had grown up without even a hint of the sea in his blood. Rather, Bull had been a young actor, but in October 1940 realized he was going to be called up and so thought he'd better volunteer first to give himself a bit more choice. He didn't like heights so that ruled out the RAF, while the army would involve a lot of walking, which didn't appeal, and he didn't feel his well-built physique was suited to battledress. On the other hand, he'd once played a Nelson-ian character in a show at the Coventry Rep, quite liked the current Royal Navy uniform, and so plumped for Britain's Senior Service having gone on a crash-diet eating mostly nothing but radishes. During train-ing he became great friends with another actor, Alec Guinness, but they were then separated. Bull had hoped he'd get a posting to coastal craft – he had quite fancied haring about in a fast motor gunboat – but he'd been told he was too old. He was also apparently too advanced in years to be sent to a destroyer. He was, however, the perfect age to be posted to a landing craft flotilla. Bull had been appalled, although in the eighteen months since his first posting he'd resigned himself to his fate. He'd also seen more action than he'd imagined he would, first at Dieppe, then the TORCH landings in North-west Africa a few months later, and since then Sicily too.

Now here he was, with sixty men under his charge, a raft of light anti-aircraft guns and a long, grey, flat-bottomed tin can to command. Dawn had found LCF 12 several miles off the coast, where they were ordered to stay. They'd barely seen an enemy aircraft so had been distant observers to the events unfolding on the shore until around midday, when they were ordered to close up to the coast. The nearer they drew, the more the smoke and haze cleared, and soon shells were screaming over. Not only could Bull see the passage of these missiles through the air, he could also spot the point from which they had been fired. He ordered the vessel to anchor just 100 yards from the shore. There they remained, watching the ceaseless unloading on the beaches, opening fire if ever an enemy aircraft appeared, but otherwise vulnerable observers to the mayhem of an amphibious assault slowly but surely unfolding before them.

In Tivoli, Generale Carboni had begun assembling a force of sorts when, just after midday, Generale Count Carlo Calvi di Bergolo had arrived with lead elements of the Centauro Division. The King's son-in-law, he should have been in Rome helping to defend the city. Instead, he calmly told Carboni that the Comando Supremo had gone south, behind Allied lines. Carboni was dumbfounded. 'But that means disaster,' he told Calvi. 'In Italy there are sixty divisions in a position to fight, and now there is no one to command them.'

Calvi shrugged and told Carboni he was no longer prepared to fight the Germans, only the Allies or the Communists. He meant the anti-monarchists. Carboni demanded he resign immediately. Calvi refused to do so.

What to do? Carboni had enough Ariete and Piave troops to surround and disarm the Centauro, but they were supposed to be fighting the Germans, not their own. Calls kept arriving thick and fast into the former Comando Supremo headquarters now operated by Carboni's skeleton staff, all from regional commanders wanting to know what to do. A dishevelled commander from Velletri arrived, forty miles away; his corps headquarters had been surrounded and his men disarmed; he'd managed to escape through a back window and make a dash for it but had only just got away.

Despite his fatigue, Carboni now suddenly realized with stark clarity what had been happening. Of course, OP 44 had never been issued. It was why Badoglio and Ambrosio had been so evasive about it. In fact, Ambrosio had instead issued an entirely separate order, No. 24202 of the Comando Supremo, specifically instructing that no hostile action should be taken against the Germans. Nor had Roatta ordered the Piave and Ariete out of Rome in order to better defend themselves in the hills. Rather, they were there to hold the road so that the King and the Comando Supremo could better make their escape. It all now seemed so horribly crystal-clear. Carboni, the spy master, had been duped. Italy had been duped. They had saved their own necks and in doing so had abandoned the capital, its people, and all hope of helping to save the southern half of the country, at any rate, from a vengeful German occupation. Fear and cowardice had trumped honour, duty and their moral responsibilities. Carboni was disgusted.

In fact, Calvi had already surrendered Rome to Kesselring. 'An old Fascist serving with one of the Italian divisions,' noted Kesselring rather contemptuously, 'told me they would offer no further resistance and were ready to talk.' Kesselring left the negotiations to Westphal, his Chief of Staff, who agreed to respect the Open City, withdrawing troops well north and south of the capital. Only a small number of German troops would be allowed to occupy the German Embassy, but also the telephone exchange and Radio Rome. How small was not specified. Westphal told Calvi he had until 4 p.m. the following day to agree. If not, he would send 700 bombers over to flatten the city. The Luftwaffe did not have that number, but that was neither here nor there. Calvi did not agree there and then, but Westphal and Kesselring were pretty certain they'd get their way.

In the meantime, von Vietinghoff had ordered 29. Panzergrenadier-Division north to reinforce 16. Panzer at Salerno. By evening Balck had also realized that the scale of the Allied assault meant a further landing was very unlikely. His entire corps could be flung into the counter-attack. Destroying the Allies and sending them back into the sea was now the committed aim of Kesselring, von Vietinghoff and Balck. The Germans were determined to fight back.

Down near the coast, the Allies had slowly but surely extended their beachhead without quite reaching their objectives. The two British divisions of X Corps, the 46th and 56th, had pushed inland between three and four miles on a ten-mile front; Christopher Bulteel and the 3rd Coldstream Guards, still in reserve, were now dug in along the edge of a tobacco field with a field of fire over an airfield which 201st Guards Brigade, of which they were part, had been due to capture that day. The Commandos, meanwhile had secured the Cava–Nocera road above Salerno, while Colonel Bill Darby and the rest of the Rangers were on the Chiunzi Pass and the heights either side. To the south, 142nd and 143rd Infantry had pushed as much as five miles on an eight-mile front and even nearly seven miles with the capture of Capaccio, nestling on the lower slopes of Monte Soprano. The 141st were still isolated, but well inland to the east of Agropoli. Roswell Doughty was just relieved to still be alive; it seemed to him scarcely credible that he'd not even been hurt. Bud Wagner had been so busy since landing, he'd barely stopped, ferrying messages and orders hither and thither. 'Running around for me until after dark,' he'd scribbled in his diary. 'Some resistance: machine-gun fire and shelling.'

The weak spot was the wide gap between the northern and southern sectors; neither the 36th Texans nor the Brits had managed to flank either side of the River Sele, the big dividing line, although men of the 142nd were within shouting distance. A further setback: the Germans had blown the bridge over the Sele on the main Highway 18 from Paestum to Battipaglia. None the less, Clark's men had survived the day. That evening, at 8.45, he signalled to Alexander again with a report on the size of the beachhead and the general situation. Five enemy tank attacks had been repelled. 'Units badly mixed due to sea mines restricting available beaches,' he wrote. 'Reorganisation taking place, and situation appears more favourable.' He was, he added, committing one combat team of infantry, armour and artillery from 45th Division immediately south of the River Sele that night. Neither of the two airfields at Salerno and Montecorvino, whose swift capture were seen as vital to success, had yet been taken. So, not as bad a situation as feared, but not as good as hoped. It was, though, a footing.

The key to the future campaign in Italy, however, was whether they could hold on to that toehold.

CHAPTER 10

Italy's Collapse

W HILE FIFTH ARMY HAD been landing at Salerno, Eighth Army had been pushing forward, every bit as slowly as Montgomery had predicted but far slower than Clark or anyone else within the Allied senior command would have liked. Those not in theatre were often quick to grumble about the pace of any Allied advance, especially political leaders back in Washington and London, or Chiefs of Staff. Such concerns were understandable, though; from thousands of miles away, lines on a map could appear deceptively small, and surely, with all that mass of Allied materiel, Eighth Army should have been able to get a bit more of a move on? The press, too, were quick to flip – ecstatic about victories one moment, frustrated the next. Needless to say, such criticism was born of impatience to finish the war as swiftly as possible; the Germans had suffered two terrible reversals in the Soviet Union, first at Stalingrad over the previous winter, and then, in July, at Kursk. In the Atlantic the U-boats, the German submarine force, had been defeated, Allied bombers were pummelling German cities, Sicily had fallen and Italy had signed an armistice. The tide had turned and yet there was a terrible feeling that perhaps Nazi Germany – and Imperial Japan, for that matter – might continue fighting to the bitter end. How many more lives would be lost before it was all over? How much of the world would be left in ruins? So if those trying to run the Allied war effort were in a little bit of a hurry to end the war, and showing their impatience at times, it was hardly surprising.

On the other hand, they weren't the ones on the ground trying to make headway in the narrow, mountainous, highly populated leg of Italy, and if shipyards back in the United States and Britain could only multiply the number of landing craft being produced, then the war here could be fought in a very different way and a lot more effectively. But there weren't enough and that was all there was to it, and so Eighth Army was having to progress across the toe, and then up the leg, along the winding, narrow mountain roads – routes that ran along precipices, over bridges, through tunnels, all of which were incredibly easy to destroy for German troops pulling back and trying to slow down their pursuers.

Captain David Cole and the 2nd Inniskillings had reached Bagnara, where the SRS had had their all-day stand-off, on 6 September. The bridge over the gully was still intact, but by holding up the British advance for a day, the engineers of the German 29. Panzergrenadier-Division, now slowly retreating from the toe of the boot, had been given more time to lay mines and set demolitions – demolitions encountered by the Inniskillings and the troops of 13th Brigade as they pushed on through the toe. Cole couldn't help feeling rather awe-inspired by the combination of immense natural scenery and the enormity of the Germans' capacity for destruction. Huge slices of road were missing, while bridges lay in scattered heaps hundreds of feet below. Much of their time was spent precariously inching around shattered cliff edges and up and down scraggy gorges. Vehicles had no chance – not until the sappers turned up – and repairing missing bits of road and even replacing bridges at often extremely remote spots did not always happen overnight despite the ingeniousness of the Bailey bridge, which could be assembled and placed over a gap in remarkably quick order. They were also repeatedly shelled as they followed the elusive 29. Panzergrenadiers. At 1.30 p.m. on the 7th, they had been halted by shelling and two men were wounded. Later that day, they abandoned the coast road and tried a different tack by moving cross-country. 'The country, which up to then had been close olive trees and just possible for transport,' noted the battalion diarist, 'now opened out a bit, but became quite impossible for transport owing to a thick undergrowth of brambles and bushes.' That 300-mile journey to Salerno had seemed even further that afternoon.

The Canadians, meanwhile, were pushing across the centre and arch of the boot. Hacking through the mountains were the Seaforth Highlanders of Canada, part of 2nd Infantry Brigade, all travelling on foot because their transport had yet to catch up. The Seaforths had crossed the Straits on the 4th, and even by the 7th were already operating on half rations, which meant one meal per day. Captain Roy Durnford, the battalion padre, was certainly finding the going pretty tough. Born in Frome in Somerset, England, he had emigrated to Vancouver in British Columbia and there had become a priest, volunteering for the Canadian Army Chaplain Service at the start of the war. Now aged forty, he was quite fit enough for this tramp through the toe of the boot, but, like all the men, was feeling by turns hungry, drenched with sweat and then, at night, freezing-cold. Still, he couldn't fault the views, which reminded him a little of British Columbia. 'Mountainous ranges, vast ravines,' he noted in his diary. 'Towns in morning seen, look beautiful among trees far down in plateau or valley beneath. Great river beds, sheer precipices, forests, sea on horizon to south, winding roads thread about, disappear and reappear.'

They were still in the mountains on the morning of 9 September, when news reached them of the Italian surrender. Durnford listened to the sound of English church bells tolling joyously on the BBC, broadcast on their radio set. The acting CO, Major Douglas Forin, told Durnford he reckoned they'd be back in England by Christmas. That was as maybe, but right now they already seemed a long way from nowhere, nor was there much sign of them moving for a day or two either.

Moving a little faster was 1st Brigade, who were attempting to clear the southern coast and get to Crotone as quickly as possible, where there was a major airfield. Airfields were doubly vital because, once in Allied hands, they were denied to the enemy and benefited their own air forces. Progress, however, was extremely slow. Farley Mowat, part of a stop-start-stop column of the Hasty Ps, could hardly believe the scale of the demolitions. And where there weren't demolitions there were mines.

At around 7 p.m. on the 9th, Mowat was directing a column of supply trucks off the road and into a stone-walled farmyard where they planned to leaguer – camp – for the night. The entrance was narrow, and as a truck turned in a little too sharply, Mowat worried he'd be pinned to the wall. He had just opened his mouth to yell at the driver when the rear wheel struck a Teller mine. Mowat was whammed back into the wall by the blast and then forward into the truck with such force that he was knocked out cold.

In his first conscious thoughts, he assumed he was dead. He felt no pain at all, just strangely euphoric, and blind except for a translucent haze before his eyes. He stumbled, seemingly disembodied, then sharply came to when, stumbling out of the haze, he tripped and fell full length over the body of a man whose head had been blown clean off his body. Then someone grabbed him, pulled him up and led him across the road. It was his friend Dicky Bird, and Mowat could see his mouth moving but couldn't hear the words. Bird hurried off and returned with some whisky, which he tipped into Mowat's mouth. This seemed to do the trick.

'My goodness gracious, Squib,' said Bird a little later, 'you should have seen yourself! You popped out of that dust cloud as white as a rat in a flour barrel and with the silliest expression on your face – like a girl who's just been kissed for the first time.' Mowat thought that it had very nearly been the kiss of death. The truck had been carrying boxes of mortars, but by incredible good fortune these had not exploded.

Those divisions of Eighth Army's XXX Corps were not the only DUKE forces now in Italy's boot. As part of their bacon-saving strategy, the King and Badoglio had offered, during the surrender negotiations, to open up the Apulian ports of Taranto, in the western heel, and Brindisi, on the southern Adriatic coast. Eisenhower and his team had been considering a landing at Taranto early on during the planning phase but had discounted it as being too far away, too risky and too draining of men, materiel and especially shipping. The offer from the Italians, however, prompted a dramatic and frantic rethink. Intelligence suggested that only 1. Fallschirmjäger-Division was in Apulia, and nothing more. The region was, unusually for Italy, mostly flat, making it considerably harder to defend. Taranto was a major port and one of the Regia Marina's main bases; it was where the British had carried out a daring and successful airborne raid in November 1940. Brindisi was also a significant port. Since one of the prime Allied aims was to swiftly capture the airfield complex around Foggia, which was only 125 miles to the north and still within the flat plain that dominated the south-east of the Italian boot, the Taranto operation suddenly looked a lot like it was worth the hassle.

Nothing could happen until the part of the Italian Fleet based at Taranto surrendered, but if the shipping could be hastily scrambled together then it was clearly too good an opportunity to miss. A plan was swiftly hatched. The 1st Airborne Division, which had been in theatre since Tunisia and which had played a part in the Sicilian campaign, would be brought directly into Taranto by ship, rather than parachuting. Since the port was very much intact, once the Italian Fleet left for Malta, as per the surrender agreement, Allied warships could simply swap places and the Airborne troops file off. Landing craft would not be needed. And once Taranto was secured, the Airborne troops could hurry to Brindisi.

Even better, V Corps, with its two infantry divisions, could also then be shipped straight to the Adriatic side and together they could hurry towards Foggia along with the Canadians, who, having taken Crotone airfield, could help clear up the central-southern part of the country. The 1. Fallschirmjäger had a reputation for being a tough nut to crack and had certainly fought tenaciously in Sicily, but there was a limit to what they could do to stop such a weight of Allied troops. What's more, with the capture of Taranto, a wing of four fighter squadrons could also swiftly be brought over too.

The code-name for the Taranto operation was SLAPSTICK, but the planning staffs quickly nicknamed it BEDLAM, so hurriedly was it organized. In the event, the first element of the Airborne Division, 4th and 1st Parachute Brigades, were brought in by the 12th Cruiser Squadron, which had been spared from AVALANCHE. Also hurriedly mustered was a covering force of the US cruiser *Boise* and the British battleships *Howe* and *King George V*; this meant they couldn't be at Salerno, but it was viewed as a comparatively small price to pay.

Despite the frantic three-day planning, the invasion force reached the edge of the harbour at 3 p.m. on the 9th, just as planned and the same day as AVALANCHE, and at the very moment the Italian Fleet was leaving for Malta; the King and the Comando Supremo clearly knew which side their bread was buttered and were not going to scupper the chance of a safe haven from the terrifying Germans. The 1st Airborne Division docked and began moving into the city without a shot being fired. By evening, Major-General George 'Hoppy' Hopkinson had established Divisional HQ in the very well-appointed Europa Hotel. SLAPSTICK, despite the bedlam of hurried planning, had been a great success. The King and the Comando Supremo could also breathe a little easier too.

In fact, General von Vietinghoff had already given orders for 1. Fallschirmjäger to withdraw northwards, which was the reason Taranto was empty of Germans. It was undoubtedly the only practical decision with the division still not at full strength after Sicily and with its component units spread all over the place. In large part, this was once again due to Hitler's meddling. The division was part of LXXVI Panzerkorps, which also included the 29. Panzergrenadier and 26. Panzer divisions. There were concerns that in the latter two units morale was declining, and so the Führer personally ordered Generalmajor Richard Heidrich, commander of 1. Fallschirmjäger, to strengthen the 'fighting will of all divisions, units and defensive measures with all means'. As a consequence, 3. Fallschirmjäger-Regiment was now attached to 26. Panzer-Division and 4. Fallschirmjäger to 29. Panzergrenadier. They were supposed to help stiffen both backbones and fighting power, but it had left the rest of the division horribly weakened. It was no wonder von Vietinghoff was withdrawing them, and in quick order.

Certainly, Leutnant Martin Pöppel wasn't sure what to think about this dispersal of the division, but he was pretty sure the leadership had slightly lost their heads. His machine-gun company had barely reached Apulia from their brief sojourn in Cosenza when the armistice was announced, so that was another spanner in the works. He thought the local civilians appeared glad their war was over but also somewhat reserved, unsure how to regard their German former allies as they passed through one dusty, poverty-stricken village and town after another. The Italian troops they encountered seemed to have given up the ghost. No efforts were being made to improve defences and he'd heard they'd only been given five rounds each.

The following day, Thursday 9 September, they'd moved east from their first camp on the Casa Iruna estate, until they were halted around seven miles north of Matera, a town forty-five miles north-west of Taranto which was perched on a hill at the edge of the plain. The countryside hereabouts was harsh, bare and sun-bleached after a long summer, and it was another hot day, the sky relentlessly clear and deep-blue. But no sooner had they stopped than they were told to move on again a further three miles. There they pitched camp in fields, waiting for further orders. News arrived soon after. 'The Tommies have landed in Tarent,' noted Pöppel, using the German name for the port, 'so things should be livening up a bit. Rumours and conjectures multiplying.' A short while later, at 4 p.m., new orders reached them: they were to head back to Casa Iruna, from where they'd come that morning. Pöppel was unimpressed; it seemed as though their superiors were in a total flap. Nor did his mood improve when, on reaching their old camp, orders arrived for yet another transfer. This time to Montescaglioso, ten miles to the south of Matera and perched on a sprawling flat-topped plateau emerging from a twin valley either side. Yes, 1. Fallschirmjäger were withdrawing, but with the arrival of the British at Taranto they also needed time to slow the enemy advance as much as possible. And that meant roadblocks and rearguards to buy the engineers a bit of time.

One of those combat engineers – or Pioniere, as the Germans called them – was Unteroffizier Jupp Klein, twenty-two years old and already a highly experienced combat veteran. Tall, broad-shouldered with a strong, square chin and piercing grey eyes, Klein looked, and was, as tough as old boots. From Wattenscheid in the Ruhr, the industrial heartland of western Germany, Klein had originally joined the Luftwaffe as a pilot but after qualifying had been posted to an air-sea rescue unit, which was not how he'd imagined his flying career would be spent. He'd wanted to fly fighters but, realizing that was not to be, decided to transfer to the Fallschirm-jäger instead.

His first posting was to Russia, where he'd been horrified by the scale of the slaughter. 'It was just terrible,' he said. 'There were trenches full of corpses.' In his first action, they'd been attacked by hordes of Red Army troops and they had mowed them all down. It had been such a shock. Once, he'd been in a trench and a mortar shell crashed near them. Klein ducked, but when he dusted himself down he realized both his comrades either side of him were dead. The previous winter, he'd found himself in a snow-covered trench in freezing conditions. 'There was ice below us and my hand gradually melted the ice,' he said, 'and suddenly I realized my hand was in the mouth of a corpse.' Such experiences had a profound and lasting effect. He wanted to live, wanted to survive the war, but one became fatalistic. After all, by the time the division was pulled out of Russia, there were only twenty men left in his company out of 150.

There had been a brief pause in Normandy, and then had come deployment to Sicily and bitter and heavy fighting first at the Primosole Bridge in the Plain of Catania, and then all the way back up to Messina. There hadn't been the wholescale slaughter he'd experienced in Russia, but Allied artillery and air power had been devastating. And now the fighting was about to happen all over again here in Italy.

The machine-gun battalion was now back up to full strength, but the division's Pionier-Bataillon was still cripplingly short of men; 1. and 3. Kompanien – Klein served in the latter – could muster no more than seventy men between them. Battalion headquarters had remained at Altamura, while the companies – such as they existed – were dispersed so they could get a move on with mine-laying and demolitions. Klein's 3. Kompanie was packed off to Monopoli on the Adriatic coast, around twenty-five miles south-east of the port of Bari.

There, Leutnant Kranefeld, Klein's platoon commander, decided the one Henschel and one Horch truck they had been left were not enough – even though the platoon was understrength. At any rate, they headed off

on a truck-scouting mission and at an isolated farmhouse soon discovered an almost new Fiat 7.5-tonner in military camouflage, carefully
hidden and covered in straw in a barn. With insults and curses from the
owner ringing in their ears, they cleared off the straw and drove it out of
the barn. 'Lt Kranefeld,' noted Klein, 'nearly passed out, he was so happy
at what we'd captured.'

Their success gave them something of an appetite for more 'truck
research' and so they planned to have a nose around Putignano, the next
town on the way back to Monopoli. Before they reached there, however,
Kranefeld halted their small column. Up ahead was a roadblock and at
first he thought it might be the Allied troops that had just landed. Then
they realized they were Italians. Unteroffizier Schleger was driving the
new Fiat and Kranefeld and Klein agreed that he should go first, driving
slowly towards the barrier, then, as he neared, accelerate and burst
through. The rest of the platoon, in their Henschel and Horch Kfz15 light
trucks, should follow.

The Fiat burst through the barrier as planned, but then the Italians did
something none of them had expected: they opened fire with a heavy
machine gun, raking the back of the Fiat. The Fiat slewed to a halt, while
the rest of the Pioniere frantically jumped out of the Henschel and Horch,
still 200 yards short of the barrier, and took cover – although not before
Klein's snipers had shot and killed the Italian machine-gunners. Suddenly there was a stony silence, except for the cries of the wounded and
dying men in the Fiat.

Moments later the battle resumed as successive Italians tried to man
the heavy machine gun but were picked off in turn. Another machine
gun opened up from a house 300 yards away at the edge of a vineyard.
Those manning it were swiftly sniped and killed too. The stand-off continued until Klein and Kranefeld worked out a plan. Two MG42 teams
would give cover while Klein and a couple of others worked their way
around to the side of the roadblock. Bullets spat, machine guns of both
the Italians and Germans hammering away, while Klein and his men
jumped over a wall and gave a long burst of fire. Only then did they realize how hopelessly outnumbered they were as machine-gun bullets fizzed
and pinged in return; they only just managed to duck down in time.

The situation was rapidly getting out of control, and with options of
how to extricate themselves swiftly diminishing, suddenly an Italian officer called out and began walking down the road clutching a white flag on
a pole. Klein kept a bead on him just in case, but it soon became clear the

major was quite distraught about what had happened and asked for a negotiator. Klein noticed he was wearing a German Iron Cross, First Class on his tunic breast.

The situation then rapidly diffused, although some of the major's men took exception to Klein's Italian Beretta submachine gun. The Battle of the Roadblock, however, was over; there would be no more violence that day. Kranefeld demanded the Italians withdrew first and the major agreed. Sure enough, they duly left, leaving only the major and a few of his men to help bury the dead. Schleger and his group had also been killed. And all because of a commandeered Fiat truck that was now shot to pieces and useless. After all he'd gone through in Russia and Sicily, it had seemed a gross tragedy that several of his fellows had been killed on a nothing road near a nothing town by people who had been their allies a day earlier. 'In the morning,' noted Klein bitterly, 'we'd been joking and laughing with each other. Now we were all sad and deeply horrified at this sudden turn of events – suffered at the hands of those we'd considered our friends against our common enemies.'

Klein and his fellow Pioniere might not have been issued with any orders to disarm the Italians, but elsewhere the systematic dismantling of the Italian armed forces was taking place. Just a day after Kesselring had shared a cordial conference with Ammiraglio de Courten, the Italian Fleet had begun leaving port and heading to Malta. While those sailing from Taranto had suffered no trouble, the fleet at La Spezia, on the north-west coast, had left port, with three battleships, four cruisers and eight destroyers, heading initially to Sardinia, from where they were to pick up further orders to make for Malta.

Off Sardinia, however, they discovered that the port of La Maddalena was now occupied by the Germans, and so Ammiraglio Carlo Bergamini was then told by a signal from de Courten to head to the Allied port of Bône in North Africa instead. When the Germans discovered they were heading south, they sent several Dorner 217s equipped with a new weapon – a radio-controlled bomb code-named the Fritz X. Bergamini initially thought the aircraft were the promised Allied escort, but at 3.37 p.m. the Dorners closed up and released their guided bombs. Despite intense anti-aircraft fire and evasive manoeuvres, the battleship *Italia* was hit and so too was the *Roma*, the bomb passing through her hull and exploding under her keel. A second Fritz X hit *Roma* at 4.02 p.m., causing both catastrophic flooding and a massive internal explosion as the magazine under number-two turret detonated. The pride of the Italian Fleet was doomed. All too quickly, the ship capsized and her back broke. Tragically, 1,393 men were killed, the crew swollen by some 200 of Bergamini's staff. The admiral was one of the victims. Only 596 survived.

Meanwhile, across Italy, Greece and the Balkans, Operation ACHSE was being put into action, with German troops swooping into Italian barracks and garrisons and ordering their former allies to hand over their weapons. At Salerno, while Leutnant Rocholl had been disarming the neighbouring artillery battery, their divisional commander, Generale Don Ferrante Gonzaga, had immediately issued orders to his unit commanders to resist any attempts by the Germans to disarm them. When German troops arrived at his headquarters, he refused to hand over his pistol. As they made to take it from him, he took it out and pointed it at them, declaring, 'A Gonzaga never lays down his arms!' Gonzaga came from a family with a long history of military service; he had also been decorated in the last war. His stance cut no ice with the Germans, however, who killed him at his desk with a burst of submachine gun fire.

Over 100 miles to the north of Salerno, at the small coastal port of Nettuno, Tenente Eugenio Corti had been as happy as the rest of his friends and comrades in the 2a Batteria of the 61 Raggruppamento di Artiglieria at the news of the armistice. Like many of the German units now in Italy, his regiment had also served on the Eastern Front; Corti had been among those who had served in the Italian Eighth Army north of Stalingrad and survived. A number of Germans had even joined the drinking on the night the armistice was announced, but the following morning the same Germans, now armed and organized, had arrived at the regimental barracks just to the south of Nettuno and opened fire from the gates with a pair of anti-aircraft guns. At the time, Corti and his great friend and fellow officer Antonio Moroni had been asleep at their digs in the town.

That afternoon, civilians looted the abandoned barracks. Corti and Moroni, remorseful at having been in bed and not defending the barracks, had finally decided to head up there on the evening of the 9th and saw columns of people still swarming over the camp and also tramping back along the roads to their homes in the Roman Campagna; this was the area of the ancient Pontine Marshes, drained and cleared under Mussolini, where, in the 1930s, a number of new towns had been hastily constructed. Corti now spotted one woman, overloaded with stolen goods, drop one of her bundles. She then cried out for someone to help her pick it up again. Corti noticed the bundle contained tent pegs, for which he couldn't imagine she had much use; he supposed it was better she had them than the Germans.

It was dark by the time they reached the barracks. The moon shone down upon the oaks lining the wide main courtyard. Not a soul stirred. Rubble littered the ground, and bloodstains too. Suddenly, a shadow emerged from one of the buildings and then the regimental paymaster appeared, an ageing former non-commissioned officer.

'There's still money in the pay box,' he told them, 'and therefore I can't abandon it. But I've been left without orders . . . What is happening in Italy? Give me some orders.' They did so, telling him to take the pay box, look after it, and when things settled down deliver it to the authorities. Then Corti and Moroni sadly turned round and headed back to their house in Nettuno, not sure what they should do now that the regiment appeared to be no more.

Corti had only been in Nettuno a week, having been posted from Bolzano, up north in the Tyrol region of the Alps. The town was a key military base because both the road and the railway ran down through the Brenner Pass, through Bolzano and then Trento and on until they cleared the Italian Alps and ran into the northern plains of the Po Valley. Through the Brenner, almost all German troops and equipment entering Italy passed; it was the lifeline, and why Hitler had been so determined to maintain strong forces there – forces he had been building up in the region even before Mussolini's defenestration. There was, as Kesselring had rightly pointed out to the OKW, sound military sense in holding the southern half of Italy, but if they lost the northern half, and especially control of the Brenner route, then they were finished in Italy. This was the borderland: the Alpine barrier that guarded the southern Reich. The mountains were a crucial natural defensive barrier, but men were needed there too, and with the announcement of the armistice it was essential that all Italian troops in the region were disarmed and disbanded as quickly as possible. That, for Hitler and his lackeys in the OKW, trumped the battles in the south.

Holding the Brenner was the 44. 'Hoch- und Deutschmeister'-Division, originally formed in Vienna in 1938 but destroyed with the rest of 6. Armee at Stalingrad. It was, then, another phoenix division, reborn, but with little surviving from its earlier incarnation except its number and snappy name. Nor were most of its men Austrian any more; commanding 3. Bataillon was Major Georg Zellner, who had been born in the tiny

German town of Vilshofen, between Nuremberg and Regensburg. A career soldier, Zellner had joined the Reichswehr in 1926, when, aged twenty, he had done well and been called for officer training; it was a feature of the German Army that no one could presume to become an officer. Rather one had to earn the opportunity to go to War School, serving in the ranks first, and proving both leadership potential and mettle. By the outbreak of war, Zellner was a company commander and went on to serve in Poland and France before being posted to the headquarters of the Oberkommando des Heeres or OKH, the Army Staff, at Zossen, just outside Berlin. After three years, and having avoided the slaughter in Russia, he had been posted back to the 44. Hoch- und Deutschmeister-Division in March as commander of 3. Bataillon. He and the division had been in Holland when Mussolini had been toppled in July, and were immediately posted to the Brenner. His battalion was now holding Brixen, about thirty miles to the south of the pass and twenty-five miles north of Bolzano. They'd been sent there, into this northern, Alpine part of Italy, because, as he noted in his diary at 1.30 a.m. on 9 September, the Italians from that moment on could no longer be trusted. It was Zellner's first diary entry.

Earlier that night, he had received orders to start rounding up and disarming Italian troops in the early hours before dawn on Thursday, 9 September. Coordinated operations in the entire region were to begin at 3 a.m. This would be the moment, Zellner scribbled, when 'the knot is untied'. Hopefully, Italian troops who had been out carousing would be caught snoring. He'd listened to the armistice announcement and heard Badoglio tell the Italians to offer resistance if the Germans attacked; he knew nothing of Ambrosio's passive order. Clearly, there was no other choice but to disarm the Italians. They might have surrendered to the Allies, but Germany had to fight on. About this Zellner was quite clear; it was a matter of national survival and of protecting families and homes. 'Germany must live,' he noted, 'so we will carry out the internment operations with good confidence for the coming battle and with confidence in my battalion.' It was a tragedy that it had come to this, but he hoped no great casualties would result.

Having issued orders and seen his men move out, he returned to his CP, conscious that this was a significant moment and that a Rubicon was about to be crossed. As he sat at his post in Brixen, alone in a small office, the clerks and battalion staff beyond in another room and with the night still dark outside, thoughts tumbled out. He thought of his home in

Regensburg, and of his loved ones: his adored wife Franziska, to whom he had now been married for eleven years, and their two children, Brigette and Gernot, still so young. They would understand, he hoped, as he prepared for combat for the first time in over three years, if the sacrifice had to be made. 'That it was only for them and for Germany, and it is worth it,' he wrote. Emotion welled within him. 'I also know that my wife's great love borders on the miraculous,' he added. 'I thank her, even if only in my thoughts, for everything.'

Out in the valley, the dismantling of Italian units had begun. Barracks, forest camps, mountain OPs – at each one Zellner's troops swept in, despite a numerical disadvantage of one to seven. He heard sounds of shooting and saw flashes of light in the distance from Bolzano to the south. Radio connections kept failing, as was so often the case at night in Italy, but eventually reports started arriving: the barracks, as well as Waldlager I and II, had been swiftly taken. Waldlager III was still fighting. Zellner issued new orders, then swallowed a Pervitin tablet – effectively crystal meth, or speed – to keep the fatigue at bay.

Outside, the day was dawning at last. Leaving his CP, he drove up to Waldlager I, where he heard a few shots still echoing around the mountains, but his men had the forest camp sewn up. Then to Varna, a few miles up the valley, where the operation was done by 6 a.m. 'The plan has proved successful,' he noted. 'I meet 11. and 3. Companies. All Italians captured, 1,050 men, 30 officers. Big haul. The prisoners are being collected.'

Zellner was both pleased and relieved that in his area the round-up had been so successful and with very few casualties. 'It was,' he noted, 'one of the most exciting days.' It was also good news for German ambitions in Italy, because despite some pockets of resistance from the Italian Alpini troops, the success of Zellner's 3. Bataillon was repeated elsewhere. With the Brenner secured, German supply lines into the leg had remained open.

Into this surreal vacuum of uncertainty, Filippo Caracciolo was heading south from his clandestine meetings with the OSS in Switzerland. He had reached Milan, where he had to change trains, in the early hours of 9 September. Outside the station he found the silence rather frightening, hardly anyone was about. The wreckage of a bombed-out building gleamed against the night sky, then he heard the chatter of a machine gun somewhere, from the city centre, he thought. He headed back to the station, where he saw pockets of people talking furtively or quietly sitting on the floor of the atrium, waiting. He found a seat by the ticket gate that no one was guarding any more. The trains were not running. Then they were. Eventually, at 4 o'clock, a train was formed that was heading to Rome. At first he was alone in his compartment, but with each stop more passengers joined him. 'Disorderly clothes, bitter and shocked faces,' he noted. 'At first the survivors are silent, they look around them with distrust, then, in an atmosphere that gradually warms, confidence grows.' He learned that everywhere Germans had gone into action, storming barracks, surprising unsuspecting Italian troops while they slept. 'Sporadic sparks of resistance,' he added, 'have been smothered in blood.' While Caracciolo's train falteringly stuttered on its way, first to Bologna and then on to Florence, the battle for Rome continued. Carboni might have been duped by the Comando Supremo, but he had managed to distribute weapons to the civilians of Rome before heading to Tivoli. More than 2,000 mostly young men were now out in the streets, clutching a wide selection of rifles and other weapons and following rumours of where more might be found.

A febrile atmosphere hung heavy over the city. In her family apartment near Trajan's Column, where she lived with her mother and younger brother, Carla Capponi had woken at dawn to the sound of shouts and clamour outside. The previous evening, after listening to Badoglio's broadcast, she and her mother had stayed up, wondering what on earth would happen next, but with artillery flashing across the night sky and the sound of fighting getting nearer, they began to fear they might soon find themselves in the middle of a battleground.

Getting out of bed, she hurried to the window, looked out and saw a group of men clutching rifles on the street below. Seeing her leaning out, they beckoned her to join them. Carla, an attractive and spirited, fair-haired twenty-four-year-old, decided there and then that she would do just that.

'Are you crazy?' her mother had said. 'They want men. What can a woman do?'

That she would soon find out. Hurrying down out of the apartment and into the street, she fell in with the group of young men and together they headed towards the Tiber, the great river that snaked its way through the city. They then walked on towards the Porta San Paolo, the ancient southern gate of Rome. Some of the men had hunting rifles, others pistols in their belts. The city sprawled further south than it had in Emperor Aurelian's day, but the twin towers of the Porta, despite a complex of roads passing either side of it, still marked the gateway to the heart of Rome, and beyond the roads, stretching east and west, were the third-century Aurelian Walls, still intact and still imposing. Carla and her new comrades paused by the Pyramid of Cestius, a vast edifice taller than the Porta San Paolo built into the walls to the west of the gate. Two Italian tanks stood by. Troops were busy preparing defences and more tanks manoeuvring into position.

One of the young men now asked her if she was looking for someone.

'No,' she replied. 'I'm looking to make myself useful.'

That was all very well, the man replied, but did she realize there was soon going to be a battle here?

'That's why I came,' Carla replied. She was, she added, a Communist.

'Ah,' replied the man, who confessed to being in the Action Party, 'a young Pasionaria!'

If Carla Capponi was a Communist, then it was not something she had ever before admitted to herself or anyone else. None the less, she had been politically aware since her teens. Her father had been a mining engineer but was opposed to the regime and had refused to join the Fascist Party. Those who did were issued with a *tessera*, a party card, and without one it was very hard to progress in a career, especially if working for the state civil service as her father was. However, he had stuck to the courage of his convictions, the price for which had been his career and ultimately, his life. Posted far from Rome and his family, in 1940 he had been killed in a mining accident. With the family facing financial ruin, Carla had given up hopes of university and taken a job as a secretary in a chemical laboratory, while her mother had begun giving language lessons. Finding the rent each month to pay for the large and rambling apartment in which they lived had been tough, but they had somehow managed, learning to scrimp and save and make every *lira* count.

They had also, almost by accident, become a refuge for those on the run; on the day after Mussolini's fall, an old school friend had asked if she and some other activists could meet at her apartment. Carla shared her father's abhorrence of Fascism and blamed the regime for his death; that first meeting in late July had marked the start of her clandestine political life. She hated the war, hated the Fascists and dreamed of a better, democratic Italy in which she would be free to live how she chose. Those were also the ideals the Allies wanted to bring to Italy, but on that Thursday morning they were still a long way from Rome. There was, though, an atmosphere of excitement and nervous anticipation down by the

Pyramid and the Porta San Paolo. She thought that if others were prepared to fight for Rome, so too was she. The prospect of living under the Nazi yoke when, just six weeks earlier, Fascism had finally fallen was hard to bear.

She and her young companions now headed on down the Ostian Way, the old Roman road that ran due south from the city walls, until they reached the Basilica Papale San Paolo, about a mile and a half south of the Porta San Paolo. In the park next to the church, beside the banks of the Tiber, a tented first aid post had been set up. Carla left the men and headed to the tent, where she saw rows of wounded. Only when she drew closer did she realize to her shock that they were all dead – already killed in the fighting for Rome. Bursts of machine guns and small arms could clearly be heard. The Granatieri di Sardegna Division – the Grenadiers of Sardinia – had been fighting the paratroopers of 2. Fallschirmjäger-Division since the first shots had been fired at around 10 p.m. the previous evening. The tragedy for Rome was that, had the Ariete remained engaged, the Italians could well have been able to keep the German attackers at bay.

Generale Giacomo Carboni, meanwhile, had accepted that it was now unlikely his corps could hold Rome, although he resolutely refused to accept that all hope was gone. In any case, the longer they held out, the better; after all, while his divisions were fighting, the Germans could not head south towards Salerno. Frustratingly, however, neither the Ariete nor the Piave were able to turn straight back to Rome; more fuel was needed first and getting it would take time – time that was fast running out.

Rumours and counter-rumours; messages arriving, often contradictory. Carboni was being flooded, but rarely with the information he so desperately needed. What had happened to Maggiore Briatore, who had been sent to Castellano to plead for a delay? Carboni had armed him with maps of the German dispositions. Why had the Allies not bombed them? Carboni, like every other Italian general, it seemed, believed Allied resources were limitless. Allied air power was currently focused on Salerno and, to a lesser extent, Taranto, not Rome.

Word now reached him that Calvi was negotiating with Kesselring. Carboni was determined to have nothing to do with such perfidy, but perhaps they could stall for time. Perhaps another Allied landing would be made near Rome. Perhaps the Allied air forces would appear. Perhaps the Granatieri and other troops and the popular rising would keep the Germans at bay. Perhaps, perhaps, perhaps. But Carboni was clutching at straws.

Late on the 9th, he finally tried to get a few hours' sleep. It was not to be. Calvi's Chief of Staff, Tenente-Colonnello Leandro Giaccone, a fanatical Fascist and Germanophile, arrived at the *pensione* where Carboni was staying and woke him. The Germans were at the gates of Rome. Kesselring was offering lenient terms, vowing to honour Rome as an Open City, but had threatened to pulverize resistance and bomb the capital if the terms were refused.

No, Carboni insisted, there could be no terms. 'At dawn,' he told Giaccone, 'I will take the divisions towards Rome and start the battle again. We must stop the Germans from moving south against the Allies.' The battle for Rome would continue.

CHAPTER 11

Build-up and Containment

F ELDWEBEL ROBERT GUGELBERGER HAD been scrambled soon after 6 a.m. on the morning of the 9th, by which time the pilots had all learned about the Allied landings. And, inevitably, it was to Salerno that they had been sent. They attacked from the south, swooping down low on the landing craft heading for the shore. 'I saw my two rockets,' he noted, 'landing right between two landing craft.' Soon, though, they were tussling with Spitfires, P-40 Kittyhawks and P-38 Lightnings. Gugelberger reported that they'd shot down four, with two losses of their own. In fact, the Luftwaffe was hammered that day. JG53 alone lost seven aircraft, including two Focke-Wulf reconnaissance planes blasted from the sky by their own troops; there had never been much coordination between ground forces and those in the air, but it was getting worse, not better, as time went on. In all, the Luftwaffe lost twenty-four that day – a lot when they were so starved of aircraft in Italy. By contrast, the Allied air forces had half that number shot down, but many more aircraft to call upon.

The following day, Friday the 10th, Gugelberger had been scrambled again. 'Shortly after lifting off,' he wrote, 'I crashed and my machine somersaulted several times. Unconscious, was very lucky.' Extricated from the wreckage, he was dragged clear, patched up and later flown in a Junkers Ju52 transport plane to a hospital in Foggia. Frankly, it was a miracle that he'd survived. All air forces suffered a considerable number of accidents, many fatal. Most were in training and could reckon on as much as 30 per cent losses due to pilot or mechanical error. In the Luftwaffe, however, that number was rising. The Messerschmitt 109, especially, was a difficult machine to master, but even once a pilot was at the front, and operational, the risks remained very high. Maintenance was not to the standard it could be due to lack of parts and fatigue. Too much was also asked of the pilots, who were not given anything like enough leave. At any rate, his departure left another hole in 4./JG53.

Meanwhile, swarms of Allied fighters and bombers continued to dominate the skies over Salerno. It was the combination of air power and offshore naval guns that had allowed AVALANCHE even to be considered, and a considerable burden was now being placed on the Mediterranean Allied Air Forces. If much was expected of the Luftwaffe's fighter pilots, the same was true of those in the RAF and USAAF now flying the long route from Sicily to the bridgehead. Lieutenant Smoky Vrilakas, for example, had been flying as much as Gugelberger, although on 7 September the entire 1st Fighter Group had moved from Tunisia to Catania on the east coast of Sicily, the scene of heavy fighting in July. No sooner had they arrived than they were told they would be practising night flying.

The explanation came when, on the evening of 8 September, they were briefed for a pre-dawn start to cover the invasion. None of them fancied it much, but early the next morning they taxied ready for take-off, the runway lit by two rows of trucks with their headlights on. It was all a bit makeshift, and just as Vrilakas was lining up there was an explosion at the far end of the runway. Vrilakas took off anyway, wheels up as he sped over the burning wreckage; a P-38 Lightning had struck one of the trucks with its wingtip, bellied and then caught fire. Fortunately, the pilot managed to get out and run for his life before it blew, but it was another aircraft lost without any help from the Luftwaffe.

Vrilakas might not have relished night flying too much, but Wing Commander Hugh 'Cocky' Dundas did not relish any part of the Salerno operation. A week earlier he'd been leading his wing of Spitfires, providing cover for the little ships and craft bustling back and forth across the Straits of Messina, and couldn't help thinking that it had been four long, hazardous years since the start of the war. Back on 3 September 1939 he'd been a nineteen-year-old trainee pilot, but in the intervening years he'd survived combat over Dunkirk, the Battle of Britain, fighter sweeps over France, the Tunisian campaign and Sicily. 'Now I was just twenty-three years old,' he noted, 'with the leadership of five squadrons of fighters and I felt I had done enough fighting to last me a lifetime.' He'd survived, but too many friends had not. Nor had a beloved older brother, John, a

Spitfire pilot in 609 Squadron, lost nearly three years earlier in November 1940. Dundas felt exhausted, and while he now had the experience and, he supposed, authority to match his rank, inside he still felt rather gauche and immature in almost every other regard. Really, all he'd done since leaving his teens was fly and fight. He wasn't alone, but that was hardly the point.

And he had really not been happy about this Salerno caper either. It was 175 miles from their base on Sicily, with every part of the journey over the sea, where, if one ditched, the chances of ever being found again were slight. That jarred at the nerves. To get there, they had been given 90-gallon drop-tanks – auxiliary fuel tanks that detached and dropped into the sea once the fuel in them was spent. Dundas had used them before and had not liked them; the fuel switch didn't always work smoothly and sometimes the tanks refused to be jettisoned. Going into combat with the extra drag they caused was not a laughing matter. So far, however, the first two operations had not been too bad: he and his fellows had got there all right, seen off some enemy planes, and returned to base without a glitch. The plan, he knew, was for the ground forces to capture two airfields just behind the beaches and then they would fly in and operate from there while a couple more were hastily cleared and prepared. They couldn't be in Allied hands soon enough as far as Dundas was concerned.

Lieutenant Jim E. Reed was another disgruntled fighter pilot, although his chagrin was more about still being in the theatre at all rather than flying over Italy per se. From Memphis, Tennessee, twenty-three-year-old Reed was flying with the 59th Fighter Squadron, part of the 33rd Fighter Group, and had been out in North Africa and then Sicily since the very end of 1942. He'd always been obsessed with flying since seeing P-26 fighters coming over from the Air Corps base at Memphis when he'd been a kid and later, while at college, had been accepted into one of the civilian aeronautical schools and had enjoyed flying every bit as much as he'd thought he would. When he graduated in the spring of 1941 he had immediately volunteered for the Army Air Force, and a little over a year later, with more than 300 hours in his logbook, found himself on his way to war. He still loved flying but he was sick of risking his neck in old P-40 Kittyhawks that were becoming badly outclassed by the latest Focke-Wulfs and Messerschmitts, and he was also sore that the goalposts kept shifting over what was considered a tour of duty. When he'd first reached North Africa, pilots were promised they'd be rotated back after thirty combat missions. Then it became after forty missions. In Tunisia he'd been grounded for three weeks with an infected thumb, which meant he got a little way behind some of his fellows, but then the tour was raised to fifty missions. By this time, while in Sicily, some of his pals were sent home, but as Reed neared the magic number the bar kept being raised again. Now it was sixty missions; it seemed he simply couldn't catch up.

Now the entire fighter group was at Termini on the north coast of Sicily, waiting to fly to Italy, and Reed, for one, was feeling restless. They'd only been there a day when a dead German airman washed up on the beach, a reminder of the dangers of flying over the sea. Then, on the 8th, they'd heard the news of the armistice and the following day reports of the landings and assumed they'd be back in action. But no orders had arrived. 'We just sat around and waited for news,' Reed jotted in his diary on the 9th. 'Not doing a damn thing but standing to move in a hurry,' he wrote the following day. It was frustrating, to say the least. And blisteringly hot in Sicily too, just to add to his worsening mood.

Meanwhile, more troops were arriving and also making their way towards the Salerno bridgehead, including all of XIV Panzerkorps. By that second morning, Friday, 10 September, General Balck was clear in his mind there could be no further Allied landings. 'My corps,' he noted, 'could now be committed to the counter-attack.' The 15. Panzergrenadier was ordered south from the Volturno area, which meant that Leutnant Hans Golda's relaxing fortnight of rest was over. That morning they packed up and moved out.

Also on the move was the Hermann Göring Division, which had been based around Naples. Neither division had far to travel in the big scheme of things – and certainly not compared with Eighth Army's 5th Division, the only other unit coming to help Clark's forces at Salerno, which was still hundreds of miles to the south. None the less, after the hammering it had taken in Sicily the HG Division was still licking its wounds and waiting for reinforcements. 'The division had only two Panzergrenadier battalions,' noted Oberst Wilhelm Schmalz, one of the HG's senior commanders, 'a pionier battalion, a reconnaissance battalion and about 30 tanks.' Additionally, the division still had some artillery – a single assault gun company of StuGs and three battalions of field artillery and three of anti-aircraft guns. This made it very badly understrength. A panzer battalion, for example, should have had four companies, each of twenty tanks – and eighty-two tanks in all including battalion headquarters. The division was also supposed to have two battalions of panzers, along with an armoured regiment of three battalions – the equivalent of a British brigade – as well as a Panzergrenadier regiment, which was motorized infantry. That was its fighting core, along with the additional artillery, recce, pioneer, anti-tank and signal units.

In other words, the Hermann Göring Division was operating at around 30 per cent strength. Nor was it an elite unit either, despite pretensions to the contrary from its namesake; rather, its current incarnation had been cobbled together from clerks, Luftwaffe ground crew and other odds and sods back in June, following the annihilation of a regiment bearing the same name in Tunisia. However, because it bore the Reichsmarschall's name it did tend to get the cream of whatever equipment was available; in Sicily, for example, a company of heavy Tiger tanks, the most powerful in the German arsenal, had been attached to the HG Division. All bar one had been lost in Sicily, however, and it hadn't received any more since reaching Italy.

On the plus side, a cadre of highly experienced officers and NCOs had been sprinkled in among the mass of ill-trained troops, including men like Oberst Wilhelm Schmalz, a forty-two-year-old cavalryman from Saxony and, by the summer of 1943, a man who had seen a huge amount of action. He was also a career soldier, having joined the Reichswehr in 1919, become an officer in 1923 and a company commander by the start of the war. He'd served in Poland, France, Yugoslavia, Greece and then the Eastern Front. He'd fought in blazing heat, torrential rain and freezing snow. In the Soviet Union, his unit had been part of the giant encirclement of Kiev when more than 770,000 Red Army troops had been captured. Schmalz certainly knew a thing or two about fighting in this current war. He was conspicuously professional in all he did, intelligent, quick-thinking and utterly imperturbable. Such experience could only be spread so far, but while the divisional commander, General Paul Conrath, tended to loiter at divisional headquarters and take something of a back seat, Schmalz was always at the front, the consummate fighting commander. Understrength they might have been as a division, but they had been ordered to advance down the Cava–Nocera road towards Salerno and hold it, and that was what Schmalz was determined to do, for this was the main road through the mountains from Salerno to Naples – the same route that had been secured by the Commandos. The key was to block any exits and hold the Allies in their bridgehead – and then kick them back into the sea.

Meanwhile, for 16. Panzer the task was now clear: to give a little ground if necessary but also to hold the Allies in the bridgehead until the promised German reinforcements reached the front. Little information had reached Leutnant Rocholl, however, who, as the previous afternoon had worn on, had begun to feel a little isolated on his hill overlooking Salerno and the bay. At 4 p.m. on the 9th he'd heard that 3. Kompanie had pulled back and taken up new positions at Fratte, just to the north of Salerno and guarding the way to the valley due north of the port. Rocholl had been a bit perplexed by this as they had not yet engaged the enemy at all. 'At any rate,' he scribbled, 'they were off, and with them our Heavy MG section. And so I was left on the ridge with my handful of men, armed with revolvers, sending an occasional message down to the armoured cars.'

Time wore on. They ate some grapes and watched the activity still going on below, and then suddenly a burst of machine-gun fire whistled past their ears. Incredibly, two Tommies had crept up to within 10 yards or so of their position; Rocholl and his men had not heard a thing until they'd opened fire. Managing to make a dash for it – there was plenty of rocky cover – they reached the armoured cars, where Rocholl paused for a brief moment. He'd not been given any orders to withdraw, but on the other hand his OP had clearly been discovered. Realizing that if they remained up there they were unlikely to survive the night, he decided they should clear out and set up a new OP.

They drove down off the hill and into Salerno, dark, silent and seemingly uninhabited. 'It is a ghastly feeling,' he wrote, 'to drive through a destroyed and dead city, where, however, one may find an anti-tank gun hidden round every corner.' But no one fired; the British hadn't captured it yet. He headed to a sanatorium that overlooked the town, not far from the Fratte road, but no sooner had he arrived than a priest accosted him and implored him not to shoot – 'A strange conception of war these Italians have!' – and then he received an order to join the battalion at the roadblock they had established at Fratte. It was now well after 8 p.m. and dark, but as they passed through the edge of Salerno a number of Italians shouted '*Viva Inglesi!*' and threw flowers. 'These had been our allies,' noted Rocholl drily, 'and now presumed that the British were already on the march.'

The British were on the march, but not as far inland as they would have liked. None the less, more Allied troops were being landed into the bridgehead, including the 179th Regimental Combat Team – RCT – from the 45th Thunderbird Division. An RCT was much like a British brigade – three infantry battalions, plus added artillery, combat engineers and other units. It was what the Germans called a Kampfgruppe. Clark had ordered them to land overnight just south of the River Sele, so on the flank of the 36th Texans.

More units had been landed in the British sector too, including 139th Infantry Brigade, part of 46th Division. Twenty-two-year-old Lieutenant Peter Moore, a platoon commander in B Company of the 2/5th Leicestershire Regiment, had been supposed to land mid-morning on the 9th, following the Hampshires and part of 46th Division's assault, but because of intense enemy shelling and because Green Beach hadn't been secured at that time, their LCI had turned round again. It was very possibly the same landing craft that Leutnant Rocholl had seen make a quick U-turn. As a result, not until late in the afternoon did B Company finally come ashore. By that time the beach was free of enemy fire and they all scampered down the ramp straight on to the sand. Following a track, they quickly hurried inland, past numerous vehicles and supplies, to try and catch up with the rest of the battalion, which had landed ahead of them and had been supporting the Hampshires to expand their part of the beachhead.

By this time dusk was falling. Immediately behind the beach the land was flat but dense with vineyards and olive groves. It was hot, and cicadas were whining and chirruping and insects buzzing and biting. Up ahead, artillery was still thundering and occasionally the hammer of a machine gun rang out. The light now faded rapidly and in no time Moore could barely see 10 yards ahead. In this dense, dark countryside no one spoke as they carefully moved forward for fear there were still Germans about, as they'd been warned. Reaching the road, Moore realized they had become separated from most of the rest of the company. A sign helpfully pointed towards 'Brigade Headquarters', and assuming that meant their brigade, the 139th, they followed it, turning down the coast road that ran parallel to the beach. Moore felt deeply on edge, as he knew the rest of the men did. Suddenly, up ahead, he heard footsteps. As one, the platoon crouched down, fingers on triggers.

'Who goes there?' came a low challenge from the gloom.

'Friend,' Moore replied.

'Mail fist.'

'Hearts of Oak,' Moore answered, correctly remembering the password.

He then realized he was talking to the Battalion CO, Lieutenant-Colonel Orr, who was with HQ Company and equally lost. Back they went down the road along which they had just walked until they bumped into the Ox and Bucks, part of 56th Division. Apparently, they'd just crossed no man's land. The Ox and Bucks weren't sure where the Germans were, but had earlier seen a Tiger tank. Or it might have been a smaller Panzer IV, but neither Moore nor any of his men – nor even Orr for that matter – were willing to be flippant about such reports. They hurriedly dug in at the edge of a vineyard, the dark, rich soil easy to scoop out even with the flimsy entrenching tools with which they'd been issued. Moore had fought with the battalion in Tunisia so had plenty of combat experience, but he couldn't help feeling on edge still. It was what one didn't know that made a man twitchy, and the confusion and uncertainty over where they were and what had happened to the rest of the battalion was enough to ensure a sleepless night of staring into the vines and not daring to smoke or even talk lest Jerry snipers be lurking somewhere nearby.

However, Moore not only survived the night but discovered that by morning the rest of the battalion had found one another and that they were whole once more. Orders soon arrived to move off. The brigade was to begin the advance on Naples, but first the Leicesters were to secure some high ground on their right flank, twin high points marked on the map as Points 236 and 419. This latter hill was the very same high ground on which Leutnant Rocholl had set up his OP. It was a hot climb, but when they reached the top there was no sign of the Germans, only the same magnificent views Rocholl had enjoyed. Joined by a FOO – a forward observation officer – to direct artillery fire, Moore watched as the FOO spotted German vehicle movements on the roads heading out of Salerno and radioed them to the gunners in the beachhead below. Soon enough, however, they came under fire themselves and the FOO was wounded and had to be stretchered back down the mountainside. A replacement arrived shortly and calmly continued the work of his wounded predecessor. Moore was rather in awe – of both their skill and courage.

Another who had landed the previous evening was thirty-five year old Sergeant Norman Lewis, an intelligence officer in the 312th Field Security – FS – Section, part of the British Intelligence Corps, but which, for some reason that was not at all clear, had been attached temporarily to Fifth Army HQ staff. With landing craft at such a premium, getting this eleven-man squad ashore without any defined role, task or specific orders was also something Lewis could not entirely understand. Then again, he'd only been posted to the 312th a week earlier, had yet to really get to know any of his fellows, and accepted the situation with a mild curiosity mixed with bafflement that had been a feature of much of his army career to date.

Before the war, Lewis had rather struggled to settle in life. He was clever, naturally adventurous and had married a Swiss-Sicilian, although by the time war broke out the two had separated, not least because Lewis's wanderlust had already seen him disappear off travelling, first in Spain and then in Arabia. Two books had followed; the first, *Spanish Adventure*, was published in 1935. Then war had come along and Lewis, with his ability to speak a number of languages, including Italian and Arabic, had been siphoned off into the Intelligence Corps. At the time of the TORCH landings he'd been posted to Algeria with 91st FS Section, and, as he'd quickly realized, being part of an FS team was not much about intelligence and not really that much about security either; rather, they were primarily linguists, there to liaise with the locals and bridge the gap between the military and the civilians.

At any rate, 312th FS Section had landed on Red Beach at Paestum – albeit minus their twelfth member and CO, Captain Cartwright, who had been badly injured in a car crash the day before they departed. They'd hauled their motorbikes off the landing craft, then started them up and ridden them over the wire mesh already laid out on the sand and made for the cover of the wood. The sun was setting over the mountains, their grey-blue folds providing a dramatic and timeless amphitheatre around the plain that lay immediately before them. Here and there, Lewis saw distant villages nestling tightly on hilltops and spurs, while thin columns of smoke rose windlessly like cypress trees marking the spot of earlier fighting – a still-smouldering tank or vehicle. At the wood's edge he saw the ancient ruins of Paestum, the still-intact temples glowing pink in the dying light of the day. 'It came as an illumination,' noted Lewis in his diary that night. 'But in the field between us and the temple lay two spotted cows, feet in the air.' A reminder, along with the rows of dead he'd seen laid out on the beach, that this was the front line. They moved back to the edge of the wood and settled down for the night.

Later, he awoke. The night was as dark as could be but he could hear movement nearby and a mutter of low voices. German voices. 'The voices died away,' he added, 'and I slept again.'

The following morning, thankfully still alive and not further disturbed

by enemy troops prowling around, he and his fellows set out to explore
the bridgehead. Over the past year he'd become somewhat seasoned to
war, but, he thought, the raw and untested Texans appeared a little jumpy.
Repeatedly they found themselves being pounced on by young 36th Division men pointing weapons and screaming for a password that no one
had thought to give them. Lewis began thinking that they were more a
threat than the Focke-Wulfs and Messerschmitts that occasionally hurtled over, machine guns and cannons rattling.

Meanwhile, Captain Roswell Doughty had managed to locate the missing 1st Battalion, having taken four men and pushed southwards out of
the known bridgehead. They'd passed several blackened hulks of enemy
tanks stinking of burned flesh and then, rounding some shrubs, they'd
come face to face with a German kneeling behind a fallen tree trunk
pointing his rifle. He had made them start, and they needed a moment to
realize the man was dead, a bullet through his head, frozen in position.
Picking their way forward, it soon became clear the enemy had pulled
back, and not long after they ran into Captain Herb Eitt of A Company,
part of 1st Battalion. Eitt told them they'd been caught in an open area of
fields, criss-crossed by drainage ditches, and had become pegged from
two sides. Eventually, however, they had forced the enemy back. Bazookas, he told him, had been a godsend.

After sending word back, Doughty pressed on, appalled by the carnage
he saw. One dead German appeared to have been blasted by shell fragments and was little more than a shattered mass of flesh and crushed
bone. More dead, charred to a crisp, lay in a tilted and wrecked tank.

Later, back at the Regimental CP near the beach, he interrogated a
number of prisoners, who confessed that they had been waiting back
from the shore rather than at the sea's edge; both sides were learning
valuable lessons about amphibious assaults. They also told him that the
offshore naval gunfire had been devastating and, perhaps more importantly, revealed that they had pulled back in order to deal with the perceived
greater threat from the British to the north.

With the interrogations over and news reaching him that Cicerale was
clear, he took his platoon on a recce in their jeeps to find another OP.
Monte Cicerale was the high point of a mountainous spur that stretched
towards the sea like a second, smaller talon to the Monte Soprano massif.
It was a few miles south of Soprano too, due east of Agropoli. A winding,
dusty road took them past fields ripe with tomatoes, melons and fig

Left: Air power was a vital part of the Allied way of war and by August 1943 they could call on vast forces. Here, bombs fall on Foggia, one of the prime strategic targets for the Allies when considering an invasion of Italy.

Below: The Germans spent much of the summer preparing for Italy's exit from the war. Here a column moves southwards.

Below left: Pilots resting between sorties at Cancello. It was hot, dusty and primitive on the ground, while in the air the pilots invariably found themselves hopelessly outnumbered. The Luftwaffe in Italy was a shadow of what it had been.

Below right: Fighter pilots of JG53 grab something to eat at their rough grass airfield at Cancello. Robert Gugelberger is second from the right.

Below left: P-38 Lightnings, as flown by Smoky Vrilakas – the only long-range fighters the Allies had in theatre.

Below right: A photocall after the Italian armistice was finally signed. From left: Brigadier Kenneth Strong, Generale Castellano, Major-General Walter Bedell-Smith and Franco Montanari, the official Italian interpreter.

Above left: A British Tommy gazes at the mass of landing craft lying ready in Messina. It certainly looked an impressive amount but was nowhere near enough for the task in hand.

Above right: Australian journalist Alan Moorehead crossed over the Straits of Messina on General Montgomery's assault craft. It was the day of invasion: 3 September 1943.

Left: American DUKWs drive on to the beaches of Calabria in Italy's toe. Matting has already been laid on the sand and bulldozers delivered. Dozers were vital parts of the Allied machinery and among the first vehicles ashore.

Below: The Italians barely fired a shot in Calabria and certainly these Italian soldiers look happy enough – prisoners of war but alive and out of the war.

Above: Carnage in Calabria. The town of Reggio and the coastal railway were hammered by Allied bombers and then artillery ahead of the invasion.

Left: Even civilians welcomed the Allies as liberators – despite the weight of bombs and shellfire that had fallen on their homes.

Above left: German engineers preparing to lay mines on the beaches south of Salerno. The Germans had never faced an amphibious assault before.

Above right: Tommies climb the steep slopes of southern Italy in the late-summer heat. This was terrain that totally favoured the defender and was terrible for the attacker.

Above left and right: Plenty of bombers had pummelled Italy before the invasion but artillery and the storm of war brought further devastation, as these two images demonstrate. There was little financial – or any – relief for those whose homes were wrecked and destroyed.

Right: Many Italian civilians were also chronically hungry. The relish on this boy's face, shoeless and wearing filthy rags, as he tucks into an Allied tin of food is all too evident.

Above right: The Allies quickly captured key airfields such as Crotone on the south coast. Messerschmitt 110s and fuel drums were abandoned by the hastily departed Luftwaffe.

Right: Because the Germans abandoned Apulia with barely a fight, the docks at Taranto were among those taken intact and so ready to use immediately by the Allies.

Above left: The 36th Texan Division landing at Paestum on D-Day, 9 September, the crusader *Torre di Paestum* clearly seen just inland.

Above right: Troops from the British 56th Division landing some fifteen miles to the north-west, but still south of Salerno.

Left: Texans on the beach. A landing craft burns but already the beaches are secure, although not without a fight.

Below left: Tommies of 46th Division move inland. The immediate bridgehead was flat terrain but ringed all around by hills and beyond, looming mountains.

Below right: Another packed landing ship approaches the coast.

Below left: US troops from 36th Division hit the beach as it comes under fire.

Below right: A British heavy machine-gun team firing just inland. Every move they made could be seen by German observers up in the hills, such as Leutnant Rocholl.

A British mortar team (**left**) amongst the vines just inland in the bridgehead. The vines and olive groves and flat ground made it difficult for the Allied troops to see what was up ahead, while the Germans (**right**) had the benefit of observers feeding information to their mortar crews.

British infantry moving forward through the vines.

German troops looking down on the bridgehead. Holding high ground was a vital advantage.

Rome was in German hands by 12 September. As this line-up shows, they were quick to demonstrate who was now boss in Italy's capital.

A Nebelwerfer, as operated by Hans Golda's battery, in action.

A curious feature of the Salerno battle was the number of Italian former troops simply trudging home through the middle of it.

Right: Allied air power played a critical role at Salerno. Here, B-17 Flying Fortresses take off amid the dust from an airfield in southern Italy.

Above left to right: A British wiring party and their jeep suddenly coming under shellfire. The first shell to land is close, then the second and third almost on top of them.

Left: US Rangers attacking through a smoke screen in the mountains near the Chiunzi Pass.

Below left and right: With every passing day, more German units reached the front, allowing them to mount a major armoured counter-attack on 13 September. Here, a Panzer III pauses near the bridgehead, while a column of artillery, including this 88mm, heads towards the battle.

Left: General Mark Clark addressing men of the 504th PIR. Clark was a very active presence in the bridgehead, and deserves much credit for his conduct during the battle.

Men of 5th Division clamber up a steep hillside as they inch north through the mountains.

A camouflaged Sherman tank passes by an American heavy machine-gunner of the 143rd Infantry during the push north from Salerno.

Above left: A British Sherman rumbles through the damaged edges of Salerno.

Above right: An all-too-familiar scene of a shattered town and a destroyed bridge. Bailey bridges were one of the most important pieces of equipment in the Allied arsenal and employed relentlessly.

Below left: Men of the 56th Heavy Regiment load a big 7.2-inch howitzer.

Below right: On the road to Naples, a British carrier, carrying a mortar team, passes through another town.

Above left: A four-day popular insurrection rose up in Naples at the end of September. Here, former Italian soldiers join the fighting.

Abover right: Allied bombing had caused immense devastation in Naples, but the Germans then made a very good fist of wrecking the harbour areas and destroying the water and electricity supplies too.

Left: This church was one of the victims of Allied bombing. Rubble and wreckage was everywhere in the city.

Right: Civilians still came out to welcome the liberators into their ruined city. Life was not about to improve any time soon for most Neapolitans, however.

Below left: With amenities shattered, the civilian population was also starving. This bare-foot boy – one of the *scugnizzi* – clambers over the rubble, precious fruit tucked under his shirt.

Below right: American troops pause on a Naples side-street to catch up on the news.

groves, but then they began to climb, passing groups of infantrymen and a number of dead Germans. Although they wore goggles, they were soon caked in dust; anyone watching their progress would have had no trouble following them. Nestling just below the summit was the village. They halted in this tiny community that time, it seemed, had forgotten, and then Doughty, taking a couple of men, headed up to the verdant summit, which was covered with low bushes and shrub. Although they were hot, sweaty and caked in dust, the view alone was worth the effort. There before them was the entire invasion front, the thin line of beach, the mountains enclosing them and the bay, heavy still with shipping. Below he could see bulldozers working to improve the beach exits and even supply dumps already piled high. He couldn't helping thinking the Germans had abandoned this spot too hastily.

They dug some slit trenches then ran wire back down to the edge of the village, and from there on down to the 1st Battalion switchboard a little further below on the Cicerale saddle. After checking in with the Regimental CP via the newly laid telephone line, Doughty headed back to the village. The southern flank of the bridgehead was now firmly in American hands.

Meanwhile, to the north, the battle for Rome was reaching its climax. With the fighting mostly to the south of the city, Generale Carboni had managed to drive in from Tivoli without a hitch, not at the head of the Ariete, although they were finally starting to get moving once more, but in his car with his special SIM-provided diplomatic plates. There he discovered that the eighty-one-year-old Maresciallo d'Italia, Enrico Caviglia, was now in charge. Caviglia was not only the highest ranking general in Rome, he was the highest-ranking soldier in all of Italy, a legendary First World War hero of the Battle of Vittorio Veneto who had had a long and illustrious career, albeit one that had seen him into retirement fifteen years before this current war had begun. Many had tipped Caviglia to take over from Mussolini; that he had not was partly because he was a decade older than Badoglio but also a Freemason, of which the King had taken a dim view.

The previous day, with the royal family and Comando Supremo apparently fled and vanished into thin air, Caviglia had realized he was the most senior general still in Rome and that some authority and leadership was urgently needed; such grave decisions could not be left to useless Fascists like Calvi di Bergolo. Caviglia had tried in vain to make contact with the King, unaware, as was just about everyone else, that Vittorio Emanuele and the Comando Supremo were on board the Italian corvette *Baionetta*, off the Adriatic coast and waiting for somewhere to land.

Since the King was indisposed, the marshal made an executive decision to grip the current situation; he had earned the right to a bit of respect, and certainly everyone was now doing exactly what he demanded without any whiff of dissent. And, despite his years, Caviglia had been quick to act, ordering placatory notices to be printed and pasted all around the city. 'Life goes on in its usual and normal rhythm,' ran the bill. 'Negotiations with the command of German troops posted in the zone are taking place for the transfer of these units north.'

Carboni found the old man sitting in his shirtsleeves and grimacing with disgust at the whole sorry state of affairs. He had, though, been swayed by Calvi's insistence that prolonging the fighting would only lead to the destruction of Rome.

'The Germans won't keep their word,' Carboni told him. 'We must fight as long as we can. It is our only card.' He explained that the Comando Supremo had run, that he still hoped the Allies might intervene, and that they should do all they could to prevent Kesselring sending reinforcements to Salerno. Carboni told him he wanted to reinforce the Granatieri and prepare to hold back the German attack from the south.

'All right,' growled Caviglia. 'See what you can do,'

That was all the authority Carboni needed. Now back in command of all forces in and around Rome, he issued a general order for all to attack any Germans trying to move into the city.

'Time 1300,' wrote Clark in his signal to Alexander that second day from the *Ancon*. 'Have just returned from personal reconnaissance of VI Corps sector. Situation there is good. Favourably impressed with morale of 36th Division.' Clark had first stepped ashore at Paestum around 8.50 that morning and, borrowing a jeep, drove off to visit Fred Walker, who had set up his HQ in a factory a couple of miles north-east of the Paestum ruins. Walker reported favourably. Contact had been made with the missing 1st Battalion of the 141st and they were making good progress with the hilltop village of Capaccio, beneath Monte Soprano, now firmly in their hands. Casualties across the division, however, had been pretty high – some 250 dead and unknown numbers of wounded. The rough rule of thumb was three to one wounded to dead; if true, that meant the equivalent of one entire battalion had been wiped out just on the first day.

Because the bridge over the Sele was not yet complete, Clark then headed back into the launch and headed off to see Dick McCreery, the rake-like British commander of X Corps. McCreery's CP was on board HMS *Hilary,* but it took them two and a half hours to find the converted passenger ship, and when they did finally locate her they discovered that McCreery had just headed to shore. Speeding off again, with Clark becoming increasingly frustrated at the time lost in faffing about, they caught up with McCreery en route, and together landed at Sugar Amber Beach. Another jeep was found and they motored off to see Major-General Douglas Graham, the 56th Division commander, at his CP a mile inland at the battered village of Pontecagnano. Together, they agreed to urgently start sending troops north up the passes to reinforce Darby's Rangers and the Commandos and to swiftly land another RCT, the 157th, from the 45th Thunderbird Division, on the north of the River Sele and on the right flank of 56th Division. With this resolved, Clark headed back to the *Ancon,* reasonably pleased with how everything was going. Monte-corvino airfield was also now in 56th Division's hands, although not yet usable because of heavy enemy fire nearby. Clearing those enemy troops was clearly a priority. A further landing strip was being constructed; with a bit of luck, both might be operational the following day.

Much to his annoyance, though, on his return to the ship he discovered that 157th RCT had been landed south, not north, of the River Sele, a mistake on the part of the navy. However, a Bailey bridge was being hastily constructed across the river in place of the one blown up by the Germans, so it was hoped they would soon be alongside the Brits and that the bridgehead would be whole all along the front in quick order. And with 157th RCT ashore, all landing craft could then concentrate on the additional build-up.

And build-up was very much the prime concern that second day. The rate of this was the key to the success of any amphibious assault. So long as the enemy could not be certain where a landing would take place – and despite the intelligence picture, the German senior command had remained uncertain – then tactical surprise could be achieved. And so it had, which was why, despite determined German resistance, Clark's men had secured a toehold. D-Day for AVALANCHE had, unquestionably, been a success. The danger period, though, was D plus 1, 2, 3, 4 and 5 and up to a week to ten days after the landing. The cat was out of the bag; the enemy knew what the Allies intended, and could now bring to bear the full weight of their resources in the southern half of Italy.

German senior command, having been caught badly on the wrong foot the day before, had now regained its balance. The shock of the armistice had passed; Rome looked set to fall imminently, Operation ACSHE seemed to be progressing satisfactorily, and they now understood Allied intentions. From the hills and mountains, 16. Panzer were still keeping the attackers at bay, but plenty more German units were now hurrying towards the bridgehead. Salerno, just a few days previously a rather sleepy Tyrrhenian port town, was now a magnet drawing German and Allied troops alike. As well as Balck's troops hurrying to block the routes to Naples, 29. Panzer-grenadier and 26. Panzer were also disengaging from Eighth Army and hurrying north. Kesselring and von Vietinghoff hoped that rearguard engineers would do their worst and hold up the British in the toe long enough.

This hurried redeployment of German forces meant that von Vieting-hoff's 10. Armee might very well have six divisions – even if mostly understrength ones – in and around Salerno before Clark's Fifth Army had four complete divisions ashore. Well, Clark had nothing like the three-to-one rule of thumb on the ground. In the race for the build-up of troops at Salerno, it looked like the Allies were losing. And that spelled serious trouble.

Meanwhile, in Rome, on that 10 September heavy fighting had taken place all through the morning and on into the afternoon, the sound of small arms and artillery echoing around the city. The truth was, Carbo-ni's efforts were too late; of the Ariete there was as yet no sign, not even of the fast column that he had ordered to rush straight to Ciampino air-field to the south-east of the city. Since Maxwell Taylor's departure on the 7th, Carboni had been constantly waiting for a salvation that had never been likely to arrive, but with every disappointment Rome's – and Italy's – fate became ever more firmly sealed.

And throughout the day the Germans were gradually closing in on the centre from the south. An atmosphere of confusion pervaded Rome, with troops falling back, dirty, hungry, spent, and civilians with rifles and pistols running, scampering, shouting; there was a mood of anarchy, as Germans and Italians alike looted shops. By the afternoon, the defenders holding the Porta San Paolo and the Pyramid were beginning to weaken. The barricades had been burned by German flamethrowers, while the Granatieri and the poorly armed civilians were running out of ammuni-tion. Dead lay on the streets.

Into this mayhem Filippo Caracciolo arrived, pulling into Termini Station in the early hours. He immediately headed to the Hotel Ambasciatori, mercifully still open, and was thrilled to have a bath and shave; it seemed like a long time since he'd last put a razor to his face. Once freshened up, he hurried to meet with his political friends. Rumours abounded about the King and Badoglio, although all agreed that they had shamelessly fled. Over breakfast on the Piazza Venezia, Caracciolo learned that the still-banned opposition parties in Rome had agreed, that morning, to work together and form the Comitato di Liberazione Nazionale – the Committee of National Liberation, or CLN – which would bind them, no matter their political differences, in opposition until such time as Italy was liberated and free, democratic elections could take place.

He and his friends were still at a cafe when they heard firing. 'We go out into the street,' he noted. 'People flee madly. Some trucks and two small tanks parade quickly along the Corso in the direction of Piazza Colonna. Rifle shots and bursts of machine-guns.' He and his friends agreed to split up, try and find some news of what was going on, then reconvene.

Heading off, Caracciolo found a number of Granatieri now scattered in the shadows of the trees along the edge of the Piazza Venezia and next to the Vittoriano, machine guns and rifles ready. An officer waved at him to get away, but he still managed to approach and talk to a young lieutenant. They'd been on watch all night, the lieutenant told him. No one knew what was going on and they were no longer getting any orders. Caracciolo wondered how much longer this could go on. He hurried on towards the Colosseum, questioning passers-by and shopkeepers. No one could tell him anything. Nobody wanted to know anything.

Meeting back up with his friends, they took a car south towards the Porta San Paolo. There they were mobbed by anxious young men asking for weapons and ammunition. Caracciolo admired them and their spirit, but where were the leaders? 'No organization frames them,' he jotted, 'no order regulates them.' Extricating themselves, they drove on. 'There is an atmosphere of absurdity and uselessness,' he added into his diary, 'that squeezes the heart.'

Carla Capponi had been helping the wounded all day, but she too now hurried back towards her home as the stand of the Granatieri and civilian fighters began to crumble. She had almost left it too late; as she reached the edge of the Palatine, the area of the surviving ruins of ancient Rome sacked centuries earlier by a different invader, she saw a column of Panzer

IV tanks rumble and clatter forward and come to a halt at the end of the Via dei Trionfi. Now the turret of the lead tank began rotating so that its gun was pointing straight towards the Colosseum and the Arch of Constantine, which stood at the end of the wide Vittoriano avenue. Suddenly the tank fired, not at those two landmarks but towards the Piazza di Santa Francesca, to the left of the arch. Ducking behind some oleander bushes, she then saw a retreating Italian tank. Moments later there was a crash – it was hit and stopped. She had a very strong feeling that the tank was about to burn, and then saw a young tank man struggling to pull himself clear. Without pausing to think she ran over, struck by how very small the tank was compared with the panzers at the far end of the Via dei Trionfi. Reaching the man, she began pulling him, but he was panicking, grabbing at her in his terror and making the task harder. Eventually he was clear and collapsed on top of her, both falling back on to the ground. By this time he had passed out, so, getting to her feet, she pulled his inert body to the oleander bushes in the hope of hiding him; earlier she had seen German troops shooting the wounded lying on the street and she feared this young boy would suffer the same fate. In any case, he urgently needed help. He was bleeding badly from a gash in his leg. Tearing off pieces of her dress, she used the strips to tie a tourniquet of sorts and bind the wound. German armoured cars were now nearing them, and she felt certain that if they saw him they would kill him.

The man began murmuring and muttering and asking if they were going to the cemetery. 'Calm down!' she told him. 'I'm going to take you to my house.'

Then she heaved him on to her shoulder; at first he was lighter than she had expected, but then suddenly became overwhelmingly heavy as the adrenaline dissipated. At the Temple of Venus and Rome she paused as a new burst of bullets pinged and clattered just above her head. How strange it was, she thought as she stumbled on, to be in the middle of a battle amid these 2,000-year-old monuments.

Somehow she managed to get him across the Forum and up to her apartment next to Trajan's Column, and there, despite her exhaustion, Carla and the porter carried him up all 128 steps to her apartment. She and her mother dressed his wounds, then put him to bed. Her part in the battle for Rome was over. It was for almost everyone else too.

A stone's throw away, Generale Carboni was now at the Ministry of War, those last threads of hope slipping from his fingers. Earlier that morning, on learning about the creation of the Comitato di Liberazione Nazionale, he had sent a mission to them, urging them to encourage a popular uprising. Around noon he learned that this plea had been rejected. By around 2 p.m. it was clear even to him that Rome was lost. At the ministry, Tenente-Colonnello Giaccone had arrived from Kesselring's headquarters with the latest terms, which had been updated and which were now presented to Maresciallo Caviglia. They were, inevitably, harsher than they had been the day before: the Italians were to accept the armistice terms by 4 p.m. or the Germans would immediately blast the city's water pipes, then send over bombers. This onslaught would be followed by a ground assault and the sacking of the city in another rerun from history. Furthermore, Kesselring now demanded that all Italian armed forces surrender not only themselves but their weapons too. Generale Calvi insisted that he trusted the word of the Germans and believed they would honour their pledge to keep Rome an Open City; Carboni, tearing his hair out in frustration, insisted the Germans could not be trusted one iota. A 'lively discussion' followed, but finally Carboni suggested that if Calvi was so certain the Germans would honour the terms, he should sign the document; Carboni, though, refused to have any part in it. Reluctantly, Calvi agreed. It would be his name on the surrender document. At 4.30 p.m., half an hour after the deadline expired, it was over. Rome was now at the mercy of the Germans. Soon after, Kesselring's troops poured into the city, marching in columns from different approaches, and by 5 p.m. the last guns stopped firing, the city suddenly, dramatically silent.

Rome, one of the Allies' prime objectives, was in the hands of the Germans. Kesselring could now focus all his attention on swiftly crushing the Allied landings at Salerno.

CHAPTER 12

Fritz X

A<small>S HANS GOLDA AND</small> his Nebelwerfer battery had headed south on 9 September, he'd had no idea what to expect. All he'd been given was a circle on a map, so he'd roared ahead in his car, a Kübelwagen, with some scouts. 'The sun is burning down on the wide asphalt road,' he noted as he neared Cava. 'Now drive slowly, this must be our area!' A guide stopped them soon after and assigned them their area off Route 18, the road that went south from Naples to Nocera, then cut through the Amalfi Mountains to Vietri and Salerno, then on to Battipaglia and to Paestum – right across the bridgehead. He got out and explored, tramping through the vineyards to the right. A little way up a drive was a large villa, boarded up and, it seemed, empty. Satisfied that this would make a good spot, he waited for his Werfers. One by one, the gun tractors – Sd.Kfz. 11 half-tracks – arrived, towing their smoke machines, the Nebelwerfers. Carefully, Golda placed each one in among the vines, lush with grapes; he and his men quickly discovered that they could open their mouths and pluck the fruit without using their hands. 'What a pity for this beautiful garden with its ripe fruit,' he noted, thinking of the carnage to come. 'But war has no mercy. According to its inexorable law, the best and most beautiful must fall if it serves its purpose.'

They were less than three miles from the jutting Amalfi coast, the pretty little town of Cava de' Tirreni directly in front of them in the valley that bisected the mountains. On their right, towering above, a huge 3,000-foot mountain, mirrored on the far side of the valley. Men seemed very small in these surroundings.

They slept amid the vines that first night, then through the next day began digging in, building defences around their Nebelwerfers and scooping out foxholes. Golda and his men were not supporting 15. Panzergrenadier, which had been sent around to attack down Route 88 from Avellino, but rather the Hermann Göring Division, which was advancing on a two-pronged front up to the Chiunzi Pass, still held by the Rangers, and also down Route 18 towards Cava and Vietri. Wilhelm Schmalz thought the landscape a nightmare place to deploy. Defending through mountains was one thing, attacking quite another, especially since the enemy held the heights and had OPs that could direct not only British artillery down the valley but, more significantly, Allied warships in the Bay of Salerno. His panzers were struggling to deploy in the narrow confines of the valley, while almost immediately his grenadiers came under heavy fire as they tried to work their way up the hills and mountains on both sides. 'The rugged mountains,' he noted, 'seemed to literally absorb the individual companies. There were gaps in the front everywhere.'

Golda and his men came under fire from out at sea on that second day in the vineyards, 10 September. They were still digging when the first shell whooshed in, a terrible, cacophonous, sucking scream through the air. 'A crash, a cloud of dirt!' scribbled Golda, 'Son of a bitch!' Someone was directing the fire; as an artilleryman he could tell. He looked up at the mountains. Yes, up there somewhere. The bastards! More shells hurtled in, whooshing, crashing, exploding, mountains of dirt and rock spewing into the sky and all around them as they crouched and cowered. *Jesus,* he thought, *if one shot hits our ammunition now, it's all over.* Then a pause. Golda had been crouching in his hole, like all his men. He couldn't see anything for the smoke and dirt. The sharp smell of gunpowder bit his eyes and nose. He yelled at his men – everyone all right? Shouts back. Yes, everyone OK. *Thank God.*

The only man struggling was Leutnant Dederichs, recently attached to Golda's battery. He was calling for a medic. What the hell was wrong with him, Golda wondered? He can't go on, the medic told him.

'What do you mean, no longer can?' Golda replied angrily. He looked down into Dederichs's foxhole and saw him squatting there, pale and trembling and saying he couldn't move. Golda was furious. Dederichs was supposed to be firing Nebelwerfer salvoes back at the enemy and so, standing over him, Golda bawled at him, deliberately making a spectacle of him in front of the men and reminding him of his duty as an officer. The men looked to their officers; they needed to set the standards. Cowering there – what signal did that give? Pulling him out, Golda sent him back, out of the way for the time being; he didn't want him contaminating his men at the very moment battle was joined. 'My boys listened, pulled themselves together,' noted Golda, 'then, as if in defiance, our salvoes rushed to the commanded target.'

Fighting in the valley intensified throughout the next day, Saturday, 11 September. Oberst Schmalz realized almost immediately that with only weakened and understrength companies and by attacking on two differ-ent lines, any kind of unified, coordinated battle and command was impossible. In Sicily he had played a masterful hand in the hills and mountains, blocking roads, delaying the enemy, using height to observe any attempt to advance which the British might make. Now, though, the boot was on the other foot. Attacking in this country was very difficult indeed.

The naval guns were playing a vital part in the unfolding battle and were obviously even more effective the moment Allied troops managed to get themselves on to some high ground. Colonel Bill Darby and the rest of the Rangers were still firmly fixed on the heights around the Chiunzi Pass and able to relay coordinates back; in the south, the 36th Texans were doing the same job from Monte Cicerale and Monte Soprano too. Cer-tainly, while Captain Doughty was stooging around the front with his I & R team he was repeatedly witnessing the effects of naval gunfire.

Leutnant Rocholl was also discovering the effectiveness of naval shell-ing. On the morning of Saturday, 11 September he was sent forward to discover where the enemy were. Pushing down Route 88 towards Fratte, he saw that their own roadblock had been destroyed, and soon after his armoured cars came under small arms fire. Mission completed, he imme-diately pulled back and awaited further orders at the northern edge of the village. The valley opened up a little further to the north but here was no more than 700 yards wide, huge peaks standing sentinel either side and jagged bluffs and ridges running down towards the village and the road into Salerno, a couple of miles to the south. With naval shells hurtling over at regular intervals, Rocholl parked up his armoured cars on the right-hand side of the road, where its course tucked behind a jutting and perpendicular outcrop of rock. 'The spotter for this firing,' he noted, 'was on a hill about 1 km away and could see us clearly, and obviously wanted to catch us.' But behind this bluff Rocholl and his men were safe. Even so, the shells were falling nearer and nearer, shrapnel and shards of jagged rock hissing past uncomfortably close, clattering against the side of their armoured cars and making Rocholl duck involuntarily, even though he was inside. Suddenly there was an immense crash as a shell hit the bluff directly above them, showering them with rock, dirt and debris through the open turret. 'This was a bit too much,' wrote Rocholl, 'and I ordered the armoured cars to withdraw under a bridge about 200 metres in the rear.'

Rocholl's experience amply demonstrated the twin benefits of such naval gunfire. The first was the actual damage it caused, but the second was how it hampered movement. Attacking at all was exceptionally hazardous when the only route forward was along a single road in a narrow valley. While German troops such as Rocholl and his men were taking cover, the Allies could be unloading more supplies on the beach.

Out on the USS *Ancon,* the war correspondent Quent Reynolds had also been impressed by the immensity of the naval fire. The *Ancon* was a command ship, so not heavily armed, although it had plenty of light anti-aircraft guns – four twin 40mm Bofors guns and fourteen 20mm cannons. 'The 20s fire very rapidly,' he noted. 'They go rat-rat-rat-rat-rat – pause for a moment then repeat.' The 40s, on the other hand, were heavier and more ponderous, with a duller sound. Reynolds found himself subconsciously tapping his hand, keeping time to the rhythm of the Bofors.

He'd been getting fed up with all the air alerts and desperate to feel dry land again, so the previous morning had managed briefly to get ashore. There he'd talked to a few soldiers, watched men stripped to their pants unloading, bodies glistening with sweat, and picked up some positive feedback from the Texan boys about Clark, who they all seemed to think was a swell guy. It had only been a brief trip, however, and he was soon taken back to the *Ancon*; because he didn't want to be cooped up, he spent a lot of time on deck. It was where he was now, on the morning of the 11th, standing at the rails alongside a fellow reporter, Sammy Schulman. Together they watched the light cruiser USS *Savannah* moving up behind them, its sleek lines glinting in the relentless sun until it paused abreast of them, only a couple of hundred yards away. General Quarters was being sounded again, but Reynolds had become a little blasé – he put on a tin hat and a life vest, but that was all. Enemy shells soon started screaming in like a bottled hurricane, fountains of water erupting uncomfortably close as they crashed and exploded in the water.

'I wish we were on the *Savannah*,' he said to Schulman. 'She, at least, was built to stand a beating. If we have many more near misses these plates of ours are sure to loosen up.'

He had barely said this when suddenly, without warning, a sharp sheet of flame thrust upwards from *Savannah*'s forward No. 3 turret. Reynolds and Schulman were frozen to the spot in disbelief. 'The flame must have shot eighty feet into the air,' he wrote, 'and then, as it receded, men who had been blown skyward, fell with it, mingling with the flame and the orange smoke that turned oily black as the flame died.' The *Savannah* continued to steam forward but her bow was now noticeably lower in the water. A livid orange ball of flame suddenly erupted from the turret, rolling then dying, replaced by immense clouds of billowing black smoke that shrouded the stricken ship. The *Savannah* continued forward, then turned and ran in front of them. Reynolds hurried to the other side as a further eruption burst from around the gun turret. A minute had passed and already Reynolds saw men on deck hosing the flames. Someone nearby said it was a Dornier that had dropped the bomb – a bomb with wings. Another had seen it too.

This was the Fritz X, which had sunk the *Roma* and was the world's first precision-guided weapon, a radio-controlled gliding bomb containing 320 kg of amatol which was released and directed to its target by a bomb aimer using a radio link aboard a twin-engine Dornier 217. No one who witnessed the attack could possibly doubt the brilliance of some of the Third Reich's scientists. Weaponry in this war really was developing at an astonishing rate.

Reynolds felt dumbfounded and sickened in equal measure. They'd made a lot of wisecracks about near-misses, but now no one said anything. 'Everyone, I think, felt useless,' he wrote. 'We'd just seen a great many Americans killed – we had no way of knowing how many – and we were all stunned.'

The Fritz X had hit the gun turret, then passed through three decks into the lower ammunition-handling room, where it exploded and blew a hole in her keel on the port side. For half an hour after, a succession of secondary explosions continued, but crews quickly sealed off the damaged area, corrected the list and kept her afloat. Even better, she was later able to set sail back to Malta. The losses were terrible, however: 197 men killed and fifteen more seriously wounded.

And her fifteen 6-inch and eight 5-inch guns were now out of the battle.

Throughout that Saturday and on into Sunday, 12 September, the Americans of VI Corps – both the 36th Texans on the right of the River Sele and the 45th Thunderbirds on the left – continued to expand the bridgehead. The Germans only had finger-holds in this deepest part of the plain. A key objective was what had been labelled Ponte Sele – where Route 19 crossed the river twelve miles inland from the sea, but while that, for the moment at any rate, was a step too far, Persano, a cluster of farm buildings on the southern side of the river seven miles inland, was taken, and then so too was Altavilla, which, as its named suggested, was perched on a ridge at the end of a saddle of hills ten miles from the sea. The town stood at only around 900 feet above the plain and was dwarfed by the 4,000-foot-high Alburni Mountains that rose behind it to the east, but it was another significant stretch of high ground with clear views over much of the unfolding battleground and which, like all other high ground in the area, offered a double effect: the side that occupied it could use it to their advantage and at the same time deny its benefit to the enemy.

Down in the plain, Corporal Bud Wagner felt as though he had barely paused, so furious had been their artillery fire. Constant messages about targets to relay had flooded in. 'Up at 5.30 a.m. and on a steady go until 10.30 tonight,' he scribbled in his diary on the 10th. 'Hardly time to eat.' He moved again that night, ten miles in, past abandoned German boxes and supplies; it had been encouraging to see how far the enemy had pushed back. 'Running around a lot,' he noted on the 11th, 'in fact, most of the day.' He came across a number of Italian soldiers trying to get home and now caught in the crossfire. He talked to one, who spoke a little English. The Germans had been rough on them, the Italian told him. 'Result:' wrote Wagner, 'hatred and no co-operation.'

Around him the din was constant and ear-splittingly loud, which didn't help anyone trying to make sense of what was actually going on. Certainly, Wagner found the unfolding battle extremely confusing, even though he was beetling about in a jeep and seeing more than the average soldier. 'Wish I could get some information,' he jotted, 'as to where, what and how we are doing.'

Another now trying to make sense of the mayhem was Pfc Frank Pearce, a twenty-eight-year-old combat engineer from Sulphur Springs in North-east Texas with dark, wavy hair, steel-blue eyes and Clark Gable ears. After school he'd joined his father selling automobile parts until, in October 1940, he and a few mates decided to join the local Texas National Guard; after all, it was only part-time and meant a few more dollars in their pockets. To their surprise, however, the division had been activated on to a permanent footing just a month later. For Pearce, it was an end to selling car parts and the start of full-time soldiering, and a journey that, almost three years later, had led him here to Salerno.

The 111th Engineer Combat Battalion, of which he was a part, had been split up for the assault, with each of its three companies attached to one of the three regiments of the division. C Company, to which Pearce belonged, was to support the three battalions of 143rd Infantry, the reserve regiment, which was why he'd landed later in the day on the 9th. Since then he'd been shelled, machine-gunned by Messerschmitts and, like Bud Wagner, had barely paused to take in or attempt to make sense of this colossal bombardment to this senses. During the night of the 11th he'd been up at the front, trying to get some sleep in a foxhole to avoid the shrapnel and bullets still fizzing about. The following day, Sunday 12th, he and his squad were ordered forward again to clear some mines. 'Artillery jeep hit one,' he noted. 'Blown to bits. Several killed.'

One of the reasons why the Americans were finding the plain in front of them less well defended than it had been on D-Day was because Generals Balck and Sieckenius believed the greatest threat lay in the British X Corps sector; after all, it was from there that the roads to Naples lay and thence ran on to Rome. For the British troops now ashore, the battle was as confusing as it was for the Americans. Lieutenant Christopher Bulteel and the men of the 3rd Coldstream Guards had been told to push forward towards the town of Battipaglia. This lay at the edge of the plain beneath two low spurs extending from the Monte Eboli massif, which climbed dramatically a little over two miles north-east of the town. Battipaglia itself was a junction of Routes 18 and 19, the two main thoroughfares through the battleground. Either side was a mass of small square and rectangular fields of tobacco and tomatoes, vineyards and olive and fig groves. This was rich, intensive agricultural land, but the flat terrain, interspersed with drainage ditches, stone walls and low-growing vegetation, made it hard to see what lay ahead unless one happened to be on the high ground overlooking it all. Needless to say, here in the British X Corps sector the Germans held the high ground, which was far closer to the sea than it was in the central part of the plain where the Americans in VI Corps were pushing forward. The proximity to the mountains in this stretch also meant there was far less room for manoeuvre; the fighting so far had been close and compact, the front line often uncertain because of the vegetation and lack of forward visibility.

A mile out of town on Route 18 to Salerno stood another tobacco factory, an obvious landmark to capture because it offered both a base and some cover. It was particularly significant because a mile and a half further on down Route 18 to Salerno stood the triangular expanse of Montecorvino airfield, orientated at 90 degrees to the shore, about three miles due west of Battipaglia and on the seaward side of Route 18. And it was securing the airfield, tobacco factory and Battipaglia itself that was the task of 201st Guards Brigade, of which the 3rd Coldstream Guards were a part.

It was noon on the 10th when Bulteel and the rest of the battalion had been told to push forward on the right of the 2nd Scots Guards, now assaulting the tobacco factory, wheel right along the road towards Battipaglia, then cross it and push on towards the mountains. The idea was to meet with the Scots Guards a couple of miles beyond and in so doing encircle the Germans there. In two days of fighting since, nothing of the sort had happened. They held the airfield but the Scots Guards were still short of the tobacco factory, and the Coldstream Guards only just across the road but no further. It was bitter, attritional fighting: one of snipers, machine guns and, most deadly of all, mortars. Those attacking had no real idea when a machine gun might suddenly spit out, while the defenders could not always see their attackers until they got quite close. Casualties were mounting, inevitably. At about 4 p.m. that day Major Michael Brodrick, one of Bulteel's great friends in the battalion, was killed when a mortar hit his tracked carrier. He'd been second-in-command of No. 3 Company when Bulteel had joined but had since taken command of No. 2 Company, despite being only twenty-three. Bulteel had barely had time to register his friend's death, however, convinced as he was that his own death must be imminent too. Nor was he alone in feeling increasingly worried about their precarious situation. Clearly, the plan was not working because they'd barely moved in twenty-four hours, nor did they the following day either. 'There were far more Germans than we anticipated and they were fighting savagely,' noted Bulteel. 'Even now we were only four miles from the beach.' He was also conscious that there could be no retreat; re-embarking was simply unthinkable. And so they were stuck there, among the tobacco plants and vines, unable to clear the Germans in front of them and with no space to fall back either.

On the night of the 11th the Scots Guards launched another furious attack around the tobacco factory, across the Coldstreams' front and down the road to Battipaglia where they planned to capture the cross-roads at the edge of town. It was a disaster. One company was almost entirely overrun and most taken prisoner. From two other companies, three officers were killed and five missing and a further one wounded; that was almost all the officers from two attacking companies cut down at a trice.

By the 12th, the entire brigade was ordered to simply hold on to what they had; they were not to retreat but nor were they to launch any more attacks for the time being. Bulteel was mightily relieved; they all were. Hasty digging in was now the order of the day, easy enough with the soft clay soil. 'We dug with a will and made good positions,' noted Bulteel. 'Then we waited for the Germans to attack.'

It was a similarly tough couple of days for Lieutenant Peter Moore and the 2/5th Leicesters. The division had occupied the shattered remains of Salerno on the 11th and its brigades then found themselves holding the town, as well as the roads leading out to Naples and Avellino, and also trying to hold the hills, Points 236 and 419, east of the town – where Leutnant Rocholl had held his OP at the start of the invasion. That night the Leicesters had been split, with two companies ordered to remain where they were on the hills while the other two, which included Moore's B Company, were sent off overnight to find the Sherwood Foresters who were holding the road at Fratte. Shelled as they climbed down the hill-side, they then came under heavy machine-gun fire pulsing straight down the road as they headed towards Salerno; as the town was now in British hands this was unnerving to say the least, but typical of the con-fusion of this close-quarters battle. Quickly they slipped into the vineyards either side of the road and pushed on, only to discover their No. 18 radio set was now on the blink, the Italian night-time atmospher-ics playing up once more. It was night and dark, and with no radio link they weren't entirely sure where they were, which added to the sense of isolation. On they went, moving as quietly as possible through the vine-yards and past deserted houses. Moore had rarely felt more tense, waiting for a German machine gun to open up at any moment. Occasionally flares shot up, crackling as they burst and slowly descended. Somewhere in the hills was a Nebelwerfer battery, the screaming salvoes moaning through the air as they hurtled over. None hit them, but it made the move more nightmarish.

At dawn they'd still not found the Foresters, so began frantically dig-ging in where they were, only later to discover they had gone right past them in the night. Later Moore watched a pair of Germans amble down a track up ahead of them, casually eating grapes and oblivious to the Tommies now dug in just a short distance in front of them. No one fired because Moore had told his men in 12 Platoon not to open up unless fired upon; he didn't want to reveal their position. Moments later, however, a Tommy gun a little further away tore apart the quiet and the two Germans were cut down. Clearly, there was no point in being discreet any more. 'We waited,' he noted grimly, 'for the inevitable attack.'

On the morning of Sunday, 12 September, General Clark finally moved his HQ to the shore, first to a large villa and then to Albanella Station, which was three miles inland next to the blown bridge across the River Sele on the southern side. Clark was not unduly concerned, but there was no question the British in their half of the line were feeling stretched. At the northern end of the front, 46th Division needed 56th Division to take some of the slack, but the latter had its hands full trying to take Battipaglia. McCreery thought the situation was under control, but reported casualties of 1,321 in his two divisions. Although an infantry division held around 16,000 men, only around half that number made up an infantry battalion, the prime fighting component, so the casualties lost in four days of fighting were significant. By the evening of the 12th McCreery had every one of his infantry battalions committed, which meant there was very little room for manoeuvre and a scenario in which big holes in the line might easily develop; a commander always wanted to keep his balance and have reserves. With this in mind, he asked Clark whether the 45th Thunderbirds might take over some of their front on the northern side of the River Sele. Clark agreed that the 179th RCT should move across. It would take place the following morning, Monday, 13 September.

By now, more German troops were arriving with every passing hour as they converged on this tiny corner of Italy. 'Elements of Hermann Goering, 15th Panzer Grenadier and 16th Panzer Divisions identified on 46th Division front,' Clark signalled to Alexander that afternoon, adding, 'Montecorvino airdrome cannot be used because of artillery fire.' Spitfires had landed at Paestum, however, but with tragic results. It had been impressed upon Cocky Dundas and the rest of the fighter groups how absolutely vital it was they landed on the beachhead as soon as possible, so two days earlier, on the 11th, after flying over the battleground, 93 Squadron had been ordered to come in and refuel between patrols. The squadron's CO, Squadron Leader Ken Macdonald, led the way but was shot at by the American troops below, so he pulled up and asked the controller, still operating from a command ship in the bay, to tell the army not to fire. Once assured this had been done, he came in again, only for his tail to be shot off by light flak. The Spitfire crashed and exploded, and Macdonald, a highly experienced pilot – and friend of Dundas – was killed. A second pilot was also hit and crash-landed but thankfully survived, while most of the others suffered some kind of damage. Near the beach at the time, Frank Pearce had seen it happen. The barrage had gone up and the two Spitfires had been hit, Macdonald's crashing less than half a mile from him. 'Do more damage than good,' he noted of the gunners.

Despite this, Dundas's group commander, George 'Sheep' Gilroy, ordered them to give it another go later that evening. He made the first landing, touching down safely, and then it was Dundas's turn. As he approached, however, there were a number of very loud bangs that sounded over the noise of his engine and a series of orange flashes from the neighbouring olive groves. He'd nearly jumped out of his skin. No sooner had he touched down than another salvo thundered. As he quickly discovered, a battery of medium guns was in the groves between the airstrip and the beach. Borrowing a jeep, Dundas hurried off to find the artillery commander and ask him to stop firing whenever aircraft were attempting to land. The artillery officer looked at him as though he were mad – as though the very thought of field artillery shooting down a Spitfire was absurd.

Thankfully, no further aircraft were shot down while landing at Paestum, but the truth was that the planned airfields had not been opened up as quickly as hoped. That was a big concern, because with more German units converging on Salerno the Allies needed all the air power they could get, and obviously if fighters were operating from the bridgehead itself they could spend the entire flight over the battleground rather than most of it flying back and forth from Sicily.

The Allies now faced two crises. The first was the expected counter-attack from the massing enemy forces, and the second was how to substantially increase the strength of Clark's troops as they braced themselves to confront this onslaught. 'In view heavy enemy reinforcements,' he signalled to Alexander in his message on the afternoon of the 12th, 'it now appears I must await further build-up before resuming offensive.' It was potentially more drastic than that. He had to await further build-up and hope his forces weren't kicked back into the sea in the meantime. On the afternoon of 12 September, that looked like a very real possibility.

In Bizerte, Alexander was certainly concerned. 'I am not satisfied with the situation at Avalanche,' he signalled to General Sir Alan Brooke, the British Chief of the Imperial General Staff, at 9 p.m. on the 12th. 'The build-up is slow and they are pinned down to a bridgehead which has not enough depth.' An imminent counter-attack was inevitable. Strengthening the bridgehead was rather out of Clark's hands; only the three service chiefs – Alexander, Tedder, Cunningham – and Eisenhower had the power to do anything about it, but it was not just a matter of clicking their fingers and issuing a few instructions. It was more complicated than that.

This was because the supply chain and build-up for AVALANCHE had been worked out very carefully beforehand and had already been set in motion. The scarceness of ships and landing craft, which bedevilled the Allied plans from the outset, ensured that loading schemes had been predetermined well in advance. Each convoy, each ship and landing craft, had loads allocated not just for D-Day itself but for the days and even weeks following and could not be easily altered at the drop of a hat. As a result of these constraints, Clark could not expect to receive a fresh infantry and armoured division before D plus 12 and D plus 17 – which meant not before 21 September at the earliest. With the Germans poised to deal a hammer blow, this was obviously far too late.

Eisenhower and Alexander had foreseen that this very situation might well occur. There were four US divisions waiting to deploy to Fifth Army. The 34th Red Bulls and 1st Armoured were in North Africa and the 3rd Infantry and 82nd Airborne in Sicily. The 3rd Division, which had fought in Sicily, wasn't yet ready, but the 82nd Airborne was and had been since the signing of the armistice; Alexander had placed it at Clark's disposal on D-Day, 9 September. Clark, though, had not wanted to use it right away because he hoped to deploy it to help with a breakthrough to Naples or crossing the Volturno. In the meantime, Alexander had managed to rustle together enough landing craft released from the toe and from the dockyards at Malta to quickly transport an entire RCT of some 4,000 men. In fact, these deployments could have been given the go-ahead as early as the 10th, when it was clear that objectives had not been taken as planned, yet even two days later Clark was still thinking of using the 82nd Airborne offensively somewhere beyond the Salerno bridgehead. An opportunity had unquestionably gone begging.

There were also eighteen precious landing ships in North African ports waiting to be posted to other theatres, but on 11 September Eisenhower was given permission by the Chiefs of Staff to keep them for a further month. These would take a bit of time to collect together, load and then embark, but they would certainly help if Clark's men could hold on over the next few days. The only other option was to try and increase the naval and air support. This Cunningham was able to do by ordering a number of warships being used in other operations, such as SLAPSTICK, to hurry to Salerno. Air Chief Marshal Tedder and General Spaatz, meanwhile, ordered a maximum effort from all their air forces, including the heavy bombers of the strategic air forces. Whether this would be enough, however, was another matter.

CHAPTER 13

Crisis

FELDMARSCHALL KESSELRING AND GENERAL von Vietinghoff had visited the Salerno front around 1 p.m. on the 12th and both were feeling in a bullish, confident mood. Rome was in their hands, 3. Panzergrenadier was now on its way safe to join the battle and the Allies were trapped in a semicircle in which the Germans held much of the all-important high ground. They had six divisions either fighting or reaching the front and elements of 1. Fallschirmjäger fighting with 26. Panzer and 29. Panzergrenadier. Most of these divisions were by no means under-strength either, only those that had been fighting in Sicily, like the Herman Göring, 15. Panzergrenadier and 29. Panzergrenadier; of those, the HG had received the least replacements because it was Luftwaffe, not army, and the pool of manpower was narrower. Furthermore, 29. Panzergrenadier had entered the fray in Sicily only halfway through the battle and had not suffered as badly as the other two, which had both faced the full brunt of the massive Allied invasion. So Kesselring and von Vietinghoff had reason to feel upbeat at the prospect of kicking four fully stretched and pegged-in Allied divisions back into the sea.

Kesselring's confidence was given a boost by rumours picked up by AOK 10s – the German 10. Armee – signals that the Allies in Salerno were preparing to evacuate. At 2.30 a.m. on the 13th, Kesselring was then passed radio reports that supported this. So at 8.30 a.m. on that Monday, when Balck and von Vietinghoff met, they both sensed that a golden opportunity lay before them. By around 11 a.m. they had thrashed out their plans. Most of their forces were not operating as complete divisions but rather as a collection of battle groups, each with components of infantry, armour and artillery, which gave them a certain degree of tactical flexibility. The HG's battle groups were to continue pushing down the valley to Vietri along the Naples road, but also, along with 15. Panzergrenadier, down the Avellino road and the saddle of hills to the east and south-east of Salerno. This was all in the British 46th Division's front. The main attack, however, was to strike into the heart of the Allied line, from Eboli, which lay midway along the plain, and either side of the River Sele. Although 16. Panzer was to strike out from Battipaglia, the main thrust, using a combination of five Kampfgruppen, and drawn from five divisions in all, would hurtle straight into the Americans of Dawley's VI Corps. One concern was the poor showing by the Luftwaffe so far, and they both urged Kesselring to insist that Luftflotte 2 – the air fleet operating in Italy – up their game. None the less, as their battle groups began to mass and move forward to their start lines, confidence was high.

Into this maelstrom flew 33rd Fighter Group from Sicily. 'Same old stuff, just waiting to get out of here,' Lieutenant Jim Reed had scribbled on the 11th. 'Doing nothing but waiting to move,' he added the next day. And they hadn't been able to leave base or even take a swim in the sea because they had been on standby to get flying the moment the orders came in. Then, suddenly, they were off. The crisis at Salerno meant that whether Paestum was ready or not, the 33rd 'Fighting Nomads' were going to have to fly in anyway. Reed's first flight there was escorting C-47 Dakotas loaded up with their equipment. Flying in was mayhem because it was at around 2.45 p.m., just as the fighting on the ground was intensifying. Naval guns were firing, the artillery was firing, flak guns were pumping and a certain amount of panic was going on down on the ground. Spitfires, with their elliptical wings, could never be anything but Spitfires, but P-40 Kittyhawks had a very similar wing shape to Focke-Wulfs and Messerschmitts and it was far easier, in the heat of the moment, to fire first and think second. And there were a fair few Luftwaffe fighters flying over the battlefront – one Messerschmitt 109 and one Focke-Wulf 190 were shot down over the beaches, but so too was Lieutenant Charles Franco, one of Jim Reed's fellows in 59th Squadron. Franco was killed – at low height there was very little sky in which to manoeuvre if hit. The P-38 Lightnings shot down another. 'Everyone seem to pick on the P-40s,' Reed scribbled in his diary. 'It's bad enough having to fly those beat-up crates.'

*

While the mayhem of battle was going on in the bridgehead, Italian civilians were desperately trying to work out what to do for the best. On the 12th, news had reached the Caruso household in Eboli that Germans were mining the castle that stood at the top of town right next to their street. 'We must flee,' wrote Lina Caruso. 'We decide to pack luggage – some blankets and some food – for any occasion.' Her mother thought it best to do as their neighbours, the Maffia family, were planning to do, but then, a short while later once the Germans had gone, they had a change of heart. After all, where would they flee to? The mountains? But where on the mountains? Would that be safer? With no government, there was no government advice. No one told them anything: about what was going on, about what the Germans expected of the civilian population of Eboli; Lina's father was still in Naples and they were used to him making the decisions. Telephone lines were down so they could not speak to him, and yet they now found themselves in the middle of a battle zone.

Throughout the day, Germans continued to drive up to the castle, then move out again. Were they really mining the place? Or were they looking for young Italians to press-gang as labourers? No one was quite sure. The Carusos' neighbour, an eighteen-year-old boy called Cosimo, tried to hide, was caught and was questioned by soldiers, a submachine gun pointed at his chest; they thought he was an escaped Italian soldier but he told them he was not and that he was only fifteen. At that, they let him go. Such incidents compounded the air of menace.

As night fell, the shelling grew heavier again and at around one in the morning the Carusos tramped off once more to the cave under the castle. 'We lie down dressed, full of worry,' wrote Lina. 'Ah, Papa, why aren't you here?'

The following day, the 13th, she saw an old friend, Tanino Cuozzo, in town, back from the army. With him was an Italian officer, although both men, having fled the Germans, were now dressed as peasants. They had come down from the mountain to look for food. Soon after, they parted company, but later they appeared at the Caruso home. The officer had a slight wound on his arm and Tanino hoped they might be able to dress it. While Lina's mother applied disinfectant, the young man told them some news. Mussolini had been sprung from captivity in the Abruzzo Mountains by German paratroopers two days earlier. A new Fascist puppet government was being formed in the north by the Germans with Mussolini as its head. The Brenner Pass was in German hands; Badoglio and the King were now refugees in Sicily. In Italy, he told them sadly, there was now complete anarchy. As if to prove the point, later that day ware-houses were broken into in Eboli and ransacked by civilians and Germans alike. 'No food is sold any more,' she wrote. 'There is no bread. It is only stolen.'

Southern Italy, it seemed, was now teeming with Italian servicemen, who, escaping from the clutches of the Germans, had taken to the back roads, hills and mountains in search of escape and freedom. Two such were Eugenio Corti and his friend Antonio Moroni. The disorder in Net-tuno had lasted until 12 September. Up until then, troops in the area had had their hands full in Rome; this distraction, and that of the battle around Salerno, had allowed many other Italian troops in the area to simply up sticks and scarper. In Nettuno, however, the officers had remained in town, paralysed by the lack of instructions.

Then had come the German order for the Italian officers to convene for what they called a 'clarifying report'. The Italian district commander, who had loosely held on to some vestiges of authority, had instructed them all to attend. Immediately, the Germans had disarmed them and roughly pushed them outside to waiting trucks. Corti, who had guessed that something of the kind would happen, had urged his fellows not to go along, but to no avail. Only his friend Moroni had listened. Having laid low that night, early the following morning the two men set out, now dressed in civilian clothes, planning to head for the Abruzzo Mountains There, Corti believed, in the south, in one of the remotest parts of the country, they would be safe. Perhaps there would be a partisan war, Corti wondered. Maybe they could join them. At any rate, returning north to Lombardy was clearly out of the question.

'I don't think that in Italy there will be time for a partisan war,' Moroni told him, but he agreed to head with him to Abruzzo. 'Because you were so right yesterday,' he added, 'regarding the German trap.'

Soon they saw a German roadblock ahead, so left the road and went round it by scurrying through vegetable plots damp with dew and across farmyards. Their hearts were heavy, all relief at the armistice gone. Both wondered whether their friends and comrades in the regiment would be shot. That day, they used the plentiful vineyards round about for cover, and walked eastwards with no small amount of trepidation. 'Because an unarmed nation in the hands of armed barbarians,' noted Corti, 'is a frightening prospect.' But no one stopped them, and by the end of that first day on the run they were nearing Velletri, having covered some twenty-five miles.

In fact, despite the very succesful German disarming of the Italians, much of Italy was now teeming with fleeing soldiers and also thousands of Allied POWs. There had been 79,543 Allied prisoners in camps in Italy on 8 September, but some 50,000 escaped over the following days as their guards simply packed up and left and before German troops could reach them. Many were subsequently rounded up, but plenty remained on the loose in what was effectively the biggest mass-escaoe ever.

Far to the south, the situation in VI Corps' sector of the bridgehead was becoming desperate. The 36th Texans had pushed quite a distance to the south-east, so that with the 45th Thunderbirds' shift to the north side of the river, they were now defending a thirty-five-mile front with battalions scattered and suddenly lacking cohesion. One battalion of the 142nd had even been shipped to help the Rangers in the Chiunzi Pass. In fact, Colonel Darby's Rangers had been doing just fine. The 3rd Battalion, on the left side of the pass, had most of the mortar teams and continued to pummel any attempts by the Germans to attack, while observers had become very adept at directing naval fire on the Germans moving up Route 18. So clear was their view that on one occasion they'd spotted Germans loading ammunition in Nocera and so directed ammunition of their own directly on to them, sparking a series of massive explosions. They'd watched the balls of fire erupt and then, a few seconds later, heard the thunderous detonations. Although the 1st and 3rd Battalions were in almost constant action, Darby had still felt confident enough to send his 4th Rangers to take Amalfi itself and block the coast road. So whether they needed a battalion of Texans was questionable. The Texans, on the other hand, certainly needed every man on that Monday, 13 September, with their battalions spread far and wide: to the south, in the hills around Agropoli; to the east, well beyond Monte Soprano; and still fighting for Altavilla, which had been taken the previous evening and then lost again, but which, after a further assault that morning was retaken once more. They did not clear Point 424, however, which lay a little further along the saddle beyond the town. That was a concern because they needed both town and ridgeline to be able to successfully cling on to this key spur for good.

It was the 45th Thunderbirds, however, who faced the full force of the German attack, which smashed into them at Persano, an otherwise inconsequential collection of farmsteads. The full weight of a motorized Kampfgruppe of 29. Panzergrenadier-Division, attacking from Eboli, swiftly overran the American battalion there. This was the first big crisis for Fifth Army because Persano was only a few miles from the coast and less than two from Albanella Station and Clark's HQ. As soon as he heard about the loss of Persano, General Mike Dawley rang Clark.

'What are you doing about it?' Clark asked him. 'What can you do?'

'Nothing,' Dawley replied. 'I have no reserves. All I've got is a prayer.'

This was not what Clark wanted to hear from his corps commander. Nor was it entirely true. Dawley's infantry might have been stretched and now fixed in position, but artillery and armour could always be redirected and, with the comparatively short distances involved, in pretty quick order. Now was not the moment to pray, it was the time to think clearly and act decisively.

Nothing, however, was stopping the juggernaut in the short term, for after leaving its attached companies of Fallschirmjäger to hold the position, the battle group swept on and encircled an entire battalion of Texans from 143rd Infantry. Attempting to lie doggo, the battalion commander tried in vain to call in artillery fire, but nothing could be done with the guns immediately available and almost the entire battalion was rounded up and put in the bag as prisoners of war.

The situation for Clark's men was critical, to say the least, and for the beleaguered Americans around Fifth Army's CP it seemed potentially catastrophic. The 45th Thunderbirds did, however, have two battalions of field artillery, which were both dug in along a road that overlooked the southern bank of the River Calore, which ran into the River Sele. The German Kampfgruppe was now trying to cross the Calore and strike south to the coast, so splitting the Allies either side of the Sele. The plan was to fold up the Texans now in the southern half of the front. This was extremely alarming for the Americans, and not least Mark Clark himself, because the area where the two rivers converged and into which the German armour was now pouring was less than two miles as the crow flies from Fifth Army's HQ.

No matter how desperate the situation might have appeared for the Americans facing this onslaught, the Germans were, in fact, now rather trapped, caught by the convergence of the two rivers and unable to ford the Calore because the banks were too steep; here, the river ran some 15 feet and more below. The river was utterly impassable. Such were the shortcomings of a hastily cobbled-together Kampfgruppe: a lack of reconnaissance, which would have told them the impossibility of getting armour across at this point.

The constraints of geography for the Germans were not at first apparent to either side, however, and it was now Clark, rather than Dawley, who was urgently issuing orders at the enemy armour's approach. The hastily cobbled-together defence line just in front of Fifth Army HQ. As trucks and other vehicles approached from the beaches, the drivers and support troops were hauled out of their vehicles, given weapons and told to join the stand. A handful of tank destroyers – lightly armoured but tracked fighting vehicles with anti-tank guns – were also hurriedly brought in. On one level it was crazy that with the United States' incredible materiel and manpower resources it had come to this, but so desperate did the situation appear that Clark even sent a regimental band to take hold of a very low rise a little way to the right of the field guns. And it was still hot even now that evening had fallen. Touring this urgent, makeshift line, Clark passed men glistening with sweat and covered in dust, but as the German battle groups surged south towards the junction of the two rivers, the Americans lying in wait opened fire.

Steep-sided riverbanks were not the only geographical feature to be helping the Americans now, however. From the southern bank of the Calore to the road behind which the American field guns were now lined – a distance of perhaps two-thirds of a mile – there were a series of terraces, each 20–30 feet high. This meant the German armour could not see the American artillery, and without a direct line of sight they were effectively useless. On the other hand, the US gunners were able to elevate the barrels of their field guns and, directed by hidden observers at the edge of these terraces, lob shells into the fields where the Germans were now caught.

As the enemy frantically tried to find a spot where they might ford the river, the gunners pummelled them at what was effectively point-blank range, pouring round after round into the mass of enemy armour now pinched between the junction of the two rivers. The noise was immense, the ground shaking, the air thick and sharp with smoke and fine dust. Canalized, the Germans were hammered. More than 3,500 rounds were fired by sunset, and by then the remnants of the enemy were falling back. After an hour of brief, frantic fury, the danger, for the moment at any rate, had passed. The Germans' armour might have been within spitting distance of the shore, but they could have been twenty miles away for all the good it had done them. Their very proximity had allowed them to be caught in a lethal kill-zone.

There was intense fighting elsewhere. At Altavilla the 36th Texans had been forced back again, although one company, cut off from the rest, remained in the town. Frank Pearce was hurrying up towards the town late in the afternoon when he and his squad were shelled. 'A shell went right over us and hit a few yards away,' he noted breathlessly in his diary. 'Pieces of it hit our vehicle but that only speeded us up. You should have seen us go up that mountain road. Lightning de luxe!'

While the strike into the hearts of the American lines was the prime plan, a renewed German effort around Salerno was also under way that evening. Leutnant Rocholl had been at battalion headquarters since pulling back from Fratte and had taken great interest in following the plans chalked up on the situation map. A night attack was planned to retake the saddle of hills on which he'd had his OP when the invasion had begun. Behind this ridge, running down from the north-east, was another valley emerging from the mountains, the Picentino. The idea was to take the ridge and hold it, which would then deny the enemy any observers up there and so allow a Kampfgruppe to sweep down the valley to the villages of Faiano and Pontecagnano. From there they would then be within spitting distance of the sea. 'But the plan failed,' noted Rocholl, 'because the CO of the Infantry Regiment was in charge and had too much confidence in himself and his Regt.' In fact, the Germans had come up against the two remaining companies of the 2/5th Leicesters still on the ridge. Dogged defence and well-directed artillery and naval firepower had created a brick wall through which the Germans could not pass. It was hard, attacking up hills and mountains.

Around the hinge of the coast, the Hermann Göring Division was also attacking hard towards Vietri, while 3. and 15. Panzergrenadier were, with elements of 16. Panzer, striking towards Salerno from the Avellino road. Facing this latest onslaught were the Sherwood Foresters and the other two companies of Leicesters. Peter Moore and his men were still dug in near Fratte, the steep sides of the mountains rising beside them. By this time, he and his men were increasingly hungry and parched; they'd carried no rations when they'd made their sudden overnight shift up the Avellino road and the water bottles were now empty. With the arrival of more German troops, Moore and his men also felt helplessly pegged in. Trapped, in fact. Trapped and constantly fired on. All day the enemy had kept up their fire. *Tung, tung, tung* – the sound of mortars being fed into tubes and then, moments later, *whoosh-bang, whoosh-bang, whoosh-bang* as they exploded around them. Shards of jagged metal, razor-sharp shards of rocks fizzing and zipping around them.

Rapid-fire machine guns hammering over their heads. Numbers of wounded rising. Dead too. Getting to the wounded was difficult because of the intensity of enemy fire. A burst from some of their Bren light machine guns and a flurry of their own mortars and men would scamper across, grab the wounded, and drag them back to the safety of a cave dug into the rock.

There had been no let-up all day, and Moore, a young Leicestershire man who had joined up with many local friends, began to resign himself to the worst; he simply couldn't see how they could hold on. He only hoped that whatever befell him would be quick. In this awful spot his only comfort was his paperback *Army Prayer Book*, which, while ducking down in his foxhole, he surreptitiously read. Outwardly, though, he tried to show an air of undaunted optimism to his men, cajoling them and trying to keep their spirits up. It wasn't easy. Later in the afternoon he heard the whirr of a piece of shrapnel and a sharp blow to his right leg. Soon, though, the pain wore off, and with everything else that was going on he forgot all about it.

Frantic signals had been going back and forth between Clark, his commanders and Alexander back at Army Group HQ now that the first main onslaught had been held. Eighth Army had been urged to hurry from the south with all haste. More warships were on their way. Air forces were all being directed to the Salerno front, and that evening the 504th Parachute Infantry Regiment was to be dropped around Paestum. In addition, further troops from the 82nd Airborne as well as the final RCT from 45th Division were on landing craft and heading their way, due to arrive the next day, Tuesday, 14 September. By the 18th, two RCTs from 3rd Division were also to join the bridgehead at Salerno.

Whether this would be enough and arrive in time was not at all clear. That night, the Salerno battle hung very much in the balance.

CHAPTER 14

Turn of Fortune

INCREDIBLY, CONSIDERING THE INTENSITY of the fighting, three airfields, built from scratch since the invasion, had now opened up within the Salerno bridgehead by the evening of Monday, 13 September. It was an astonishing feat and another sign of the enormously ambitious thinking with which the Allies were now conducting their war. In June, Alexander had told a reporter that the army, navy and air forces should be viewed as a brotherhood, inextricably entwined; and so despite the pressure on landing craft and shipping there had still been space for numerous dozers and graders with which to create near-instant airfields.

33rd Fighter Group were now flying frenetically from Paestum. Jim Reed had been scheduled to fly early on the 14th, despite being bombed and shelled throughout much of the previous night; he'd been bored and restless at Termini, on the north Sicilian coast, but now was closer to the front line on the ground than he'd ever been before. As it turned out, they hadn't got airborne on the 14th until 8.30 a.m. because of the immense amount of dust swirling over the airfield. When he was finally in the air, he'd been rather overawed by the naval bombardment pounding away out at sea and by the waves of medium bombers that had also flown over and pummelled the enemy positions. The next day, the 15th, Reed had again been flying early when Major Glenn Crast, the squadron commander, was shot down by a Focke-Wulf and killed; that had been the first of three enemy raids that day. A new kind of routine had developed: wake up to the sound of shellfire and often enemy aircraft too; fly amid too much dust and plenty of their own artillery and naval fire and hope they didn't collide with a passing shell; stooge about the sky, tussling with enemy aircraft;

pray not to be shot down by own side on landing; clamber out and leap for safety; pray not to get shelled; try and get some sleep; start over. So far, though, *Cloud Hopper* – his personal mount and a name suggested by Irene, his girlfriend back home – had come through unscathed.

By this time Montecorvino airfield, next to the Guards Brigade, was operational, even though, by any normal reckoning, it wasn't really at all safe for them to use; but this was an emergency and risks had to be taken. Cocky Dundas and a squadron from 324 Wing flew and occupied Tusciano and this time remained there, while 64th Fighter Wing took over Sele and 225 Tactical Reconnaissance Squadron made Asa their new home. Spitfires, dive-bombing Mustangs and P-40 Kittyhawks were now all within the bridgehead and able to significantly increase their time over the battleground. Also now ashore and joining Clark's HQ was fighter control, which would significantly improve the coordination between those on the ground and those flying above. It meant the naval Seafires from Force V could be withdrawn at last after what had been an especially intense four days of combat flying. More than 1,660 combat sorties had been flown on the 12th and a further 1,456 on that Monday. It was an extraordinary effort. The Germans called them 'Jabos', short for 'Jagdbomber', fighter-bomber. Suddenly the sky seemed full of them.

The Luftwaffe was still doing its best, however. Feldwebel Gerhard Waag had been sent up to Vicenza to scout for a new possible airfield for them to use in the north, should they need it, but also to pick up a new Messerschmitt 109, so had missed the invasion. By the time he rejoined his group they had been moved to Lucera, just to the north-west of Foggia. He had not been impressed. 'It is rather disconsolate at our base in Lucera,' he noted in his diary. 'No tents, no shade – huge clouds of dust whenever an aircraft takes off.' They were all filthy and covered in dust and no one felt particularly well. Nor was their ration supply system working, so all they were eating were local grapes. And they were supposed to fly combat missions from this dump.

Waag did too, twice the following day, 12 September. In two sorties he never even had a chance to fire and, returning back to Lucera after the second mission, it was getting late, dusk was falling and they slipped off course, so that by the time they landed all of them were almost flying on vapours. The frustrations continued the following day. 'We could not let ourselves become involved in the air battle,' he wrote, 'because Lightnings were flying high above us, just waiting for us to attack those below.' Really, if they couldn't engage the enemy there wasn't much point in them flying over the battlefront. Everyone was miserable. Still no mobile kitchen, so they had no food at all that day. It was all very demoralizing and so pointless. Fortunately for Waag and his fellows, someone higher up the chain agreed and on the 14th they were posted to Littoria near Rome. That day the Luftwaffe flew just eighty five sorties, a piddling amount.

Overnight on 13–14 September, Clark, still at his HQ at Albanella Station, had pulled back his lines to make them shorter, tighter and easier to defend. 'Retreated at 2 a.m. this morning before it was too late,' noted Frank Pearce. 'At 5 a.m. moved to left flank and set up defense. Well dug in. Machine-gun set up.' He and his company might have been engineers, but they were also combat engineers, and that meant fighting alongside the infantry when they needed to. Bud Wagner, meanwhile, managed to get four hours' sleep, which made a pleasant change – he'd got his head down at 3.30 a.m., having been careering around the battlefront half the night. The battalion had also moved back as part of the line-tightening, but he'd found it all right.

General Clark knew they were not out of the woods yet, but there was no doubt their position was looking marginally better, even though intelligence on the enemy strength was a little hazy. As planned, Colonel Reuben Tucker's 504th had successfully dropped near Paestum. Unlike in Sicily, they'd not been sent to the four winds and no naval guns had opened fire; they'd landed about as perfectly as could have been expected. This proved it could be done in future airborne operations, and at night too. The 505th PIR – Parachute Infantry Regiment – were also due in the following night, while the third RCT of the 45th Thunderbirds were now in landing craft and heading their way. More warships were also due to arrive that day – including five cruisers, hastily sent to Salerno by Admiral Cunningham.

At 7 a.m. Clark met up with Mike Dawley, and together they toured the VI Corps front in a jeep. Clark thought the men looked tired, as well they might be: combat was exhausting, and combat with almost no sleep was debilitatingly exhausting. Leaping out of the jeep time and again, he tried to talk to as many of the men as possible. 'There mustn't be any doubt in your minds,' he told them. 'We don't give an inch. This is it. Don't yield anything. We're here to stay.'

Yet there had been moments of doubt for Clark the previous day. He hadn't wanted to tell anyone other than a few key senior commanders – but he had warned them to be prepared to disembark. Of course, he hoped it would never come to it, but as an army commander he wanted to be prepared should the very worst happen. 'Rumours come in thick and fast,' Norman Lewis, still at Albanella Station, had scribbled in his diary the previous day, 'the most damaging one being that General Mark Clark was proposing to abandon the beachhead.' That was the trouble – rumours did always spread, but such caution was perfectly sensible. And the plans to defend the beachhead with all they had still stood; Clark was, though, breathing a little more easily this Tuesday. All depended on just how much the Germans could fling into the battle.

Rumours still abounded among the Germans too. Overnight the usual problems of atmospherics and the limited amount of aerial reconnaissance conspired to give von Vietinghoff's headquarters a faulty intelligence picture. Optimism – and confidence – were vital in attack, but problematic when they were totally misplaced. Fire for their counter-attack had been stoked by ill-founded rumours of an Allied evacuation, one Kesselring and von Vietinghoff still believed looked likely on the morning of the 14th. From those on the ground a different picture was emerging, however, with commanders such as Oberst Schmalz reporting brick walls of defence and the hellishness of being under constant air and naval assault. General Balck, for one, reported in good faith that he believed the British were reinforcing around Salerno. McCreery was, but only by scraping the barrel of his own resources already within the bridgehead.

As it happened, the front barely moved at all that day in the British sector, and although it seemed to men like Christopher Bulteel, still dug in near the tobacco factory, that the Germans were attacking constantly and from everywhere, he had just begun to grow a little in confidence. The enemy attacks were beginning to lessen in their fury and weight of fire. He prayed Eighth Army would soon arrive. Then, he felt certain, they would be saved.

But despite the repeated cajoling of General Alexander, Monty's men were still way, way down the boot, battling the endless mines and demolitions the Germans had left in their wake and struggling to build up supplies while on the move. David Cole and the 2nd Inniskillings only left Vibo Valentia that morning, which was still on the top of the toe. And 'Eighth Army' wasn't an army, it was 5th Division; the Canadians were still down south, and apart from the 1st Airborne at Taranto no further Eighth Army troops had arrived. So the notion of Eighth Army riding to the rescue was proving more potent to men like Bulteel than was reality.

However, the war correspondent Alan Moorehead had made it to the beachhead, after a madcap journey – one that had begun after he and a couple of other press men borrowed a Bedford 15-hundredweight truck and crossed the Straits of Messina on a Turkish ferry full of Arabs who had just arrived from Egypt. How this could be, no one was able to explain to him. Once across, however, rather than hugging the coast, Moorehead and his fellows moved inland. At one point they even over-took the retreating Germans, but because they were on their own they could double back, take wrong roads, twist and turn and find a way; it made all the difference not being in a long, cumbersome convoy. When they did finally near the beachhead they ran into some Americans about to destroy a bridge, but they zipped across it after waving and shouting that they were Allies. 'The run down to General Clark's headquarters at Paestum was sheer pleasure,' noted Moorehead. 'One felt like Red Riding Hood after she had escaped the wolf and finally slammed the door safely behind her.' Needless to say, the staff at Clark's HQ were astonished to see them.

Moorehead had reached the front at a moment of crisis. The din was extraordinary, the air full of screaming shells and aircraft roaring over-head. Everywhere was the detritus of war: upturned boxes, shell-holes, shredded vines and smashed buildings. It was hot, sticky, the air filled with dust and smoke. And yet the tide was turning. That day, during his tour of the front, Clark visited the forward troops of the 45th Thunder-birds and found them in decent heart and holding up well. Earlier that morning, the 179th's artillery had knocked out thirteen tanks. Confi-dence was growing.

Certainly, in the British sector, General Dick McCreery, the X Corps commander, also seemed reasonably content with the state of play. 'Noth-ing of interest to report during daylight,' he signalled to Clark at 5 p.m. All along his front, his battalions had dug in tighter and withstood the endless mortaring and machine-gun fire. It was bloody and attritional but the German attacks could not find a way through, not least because while it was one thing firing mortars, the moment they actually moved into the open they were hammered in turn, not just by the small arms of the infantry dug in ahead of them but by the terrific weight of naval and artillery fire, which was intensified in the narrow confines of the valleys running from Salerno; here attacking troops were canalized, the soil was thinner and rock shards more lethal.

Instead, for the second day, the greatest German effort was in the VI

Corps sector. Mark Clark was touring 141st Infantry's area and up towards the village of Albanella, where the 504th had moved into the line. From one of the low hills he counted eighteen panzers pushing through their lines. Hurrying back, he sent orders to move some engineers and an anti-tank gun unit he had seen earlier in the foothills below Monte Soprano and directed them on to the enemy infiltration. Once again, the wall of fire stopped the German armour in its tracks.

'Hot, terribly dusty driving,' noted Bud Wagner, who noticed it was easier for him to get through to his division than on the previous day. Their guns were firing constantly, the din immense. At one point in the afternoon he had to rush back to the beaches and hurry up the ammo supply. 'An unusual job for a messenger,' he noted, 'but we have fired over 1,000 rounds from the 105s.' Still at the front not far from Albanella Station, Frank Pearce spent the day in his foxhole. Enemy shelling had been horrible during the morning, then quietened down, but a further attack came his way later in the afternoon. 'Bullets and shells zooming all over,' he wrote. 'Shell skimmed by me and killed Sgt. Couch.'

Norman Lewis was still at Fifth Army HQ. He could barely comprehend the noise or the bizarre spectacle of seeing former Italian troops trudging down the railway track all day, right through the battle. A further German armoured attack towards them had been pummelled not only by American field guns but also by warships. Every time the big naval broadsides fired, not only could he hear them come over, he noticed that his shirt fluttered in the eddies of the blast.

At last, the light began to fade on that second day of the counter-attack. 'To the north,' noted Lewis, 'a great semicircle of nightscape had taken on a softly pulsating halo spread by a kind of ragged fireworks display, and occasionally a massive explosion opened up like a pink sea-anemone with wavering feelers of fire.' Crouching in his slit trench under the fluttering leaves of the olive trees around him, he watched the fires appear to come closer but then gradually fade. A little way away, Mark Clark, who had not changed his clothes in forty-eight hours, sensed a corner had been turned. 'I began to feel,' he wrote, 'that we would pull out of the hole into which we had fallen.'

That evening, A and B Companies of the Leicesters were relieved, pulled back to link up with the rest of the battalion once more. By this time casualties had mounted badly, and Peter Moore was not alone in being delighted to get out of there. Extricating themselves was not easy, however; darkness gave them some protection, but never enough. A Spandau – as the Allies termed German machine guns – might open fire at any moment. Mortars might rain down once more. Moore was also worried they would come under their own fire – troops were twitchy at night. Walking through vineyards in open extended order, Moore felt utterly exhausted, and when they did finally near their own lines they were greeted by a burst of Bren-gun fire. Throwing caution to the wind, the Leicester men then hollered who they were and thankfully the shooting stopped – and without a response from the enemy. Salvation! Moore had rarely been more relieved in his life. Four hellish days were over.

A little way to the north from the positions the Leicesters had held, Leutnant Rocholl had been given effective charge of his company as the commander was with the battalion commanding officer. With naval shells – and bombs – falling all around, he decided the better part of valour was to pull back to their pre-invasion CP at Penta, on the Avellino road, a small town about eight miles north of Salerno and not currently attracting the attention of Allied naval guns. Rocholl and his men reached Penta at around 9 p.m., and were looking forward to a quiet night. Guards were posted, Rocholl got his head down and was soon in the deepest of sleeps.

Soon after, however, he was awoken by one of the guards, 'Leutnant! Leutnant! Paratroops!'

Still half asleep, Rocholl hurried to the window and, with the departing aircraft still droning overhead, spotted perhaps fifty or sixty parachutes gently swinging towards the ground; in the moonlight he saw them all too clearly. Now wide awake, he ordered his men to hurry to their weapons. 'Soon fourteen 20mm guns,' he noted, 'and some 20 MGs were firing on the descending enemy.' Unbeknown to Rocholl, these were men of the 509th PIR, the second lift of the 82nd Airborne, who had been ordered to harass the enemy's supply lines north of the battlefield. Unlike the precision drop of the previous night, the 600 men of the 509th were scattered far too wide. What Rocholl was witnessing was some of those dropped too far south.

At any rate, Rocholl now ordered his armoured cars to block and patrol the main road and then led off a team for a search. But nothing was to be seen; the paratroopers appeared to have vanished. Finally they came to the last house in the village; finding the door locked, they began to force it. There was a burst of automatic fire from inside. 'So that's where they were!' noted Rocholl. 'One, two, three grenades were our prompt reply.' With a spurt of their own submachine guns they stormed inside to find ten or so American paratroopers, most of them wounded – the rest had escaped out of the back door, but it was too dark to try and follow them. Back at his company headquarters, the men and their equipment were thoroughly examined. Rocholl thought them excellently supplied, from their weapons to their silk escape maps, knuckledusters and generous supply of cigarettes.

Air Chief Marshal Tedder and General 'Tooey' Spaatz had promised an all-out effort from their heavy bombers and were as good as their word. Between Naples and Salerno, the roads and railways were pummelled as formations of B-17 Flying Fortresses droned over and dropped nearly 200 tons of bombs that day. The road between Nocera and Torre Annunziata, a coastal port near Pompeii, was completely destroyed. Medium twin-engine bombers also hit German concentrations around Battipaglia and Eboli. And escorting the bombers were fighter aircraft, which would provide top cover and then sweep down and shoot up ground targets themselves. Earlier that day, Smoky Vrilakas had flown his first mission as a flight leader; it had felt good to be able to use a little bit more of his own judgement and he had relished the extra responsibility. Over Salerno, they made radio contact with the ground controller, now ashore, who picked out targets for them to strike. Down they swooped, hammering away with their .50 calibre machine guns. Vrilakas was once again unscathed, and if there had been any Luftwaffe stooging around, he'd not seen them.

That night the RAF's Wellington bombers, the prime night-bombing force, struck again, surpassing any previous effort. Battipaglia was largely obliterated. So, too, much of Eboli. That night Lina Caruso and her family cowered once more in the cave; it had been a traumatic day as German troops had been seen swarming around the castle. One of their neighbours told them the Germans were looking for women to rape. This was almost certainly not the case, but that was not the point; Lina was terrified, and so were her sisters, who had started crying. All of them had hid, Lina in the toilet for more than three hours, until they'd heard the Germans had left.

Then they went down to the cave, but in some panic because an unexploded bomb had been discovered near the castle entrance. 'Flee! Flee!' someone shouted. Panic, screaming, running to the cave, then someone reported that it wasn't a bomb, merely a dropped mortar shell and, in its current form, quite harmless. The Germans had not intended to rape anyone; rather, they'd been using the castle as an ammunition dump. But what did Lina Caruso and her family know of such things? It had been a frightening day, and now, sheltering in the cave, they were forced to endure even more bombing as the Wellingtons thundered over as part of their maximum effort. Were they bombs or shells from the guns? Lina had no idea; but she could hear the whistle, then the explosions, over and over. 'Whistles and explosions, explosions and whistles,' she wrote. 'I hear nothing else.'

By the morning of Wednesday, 15 September, Clark's situation was looking suddenly and dramatically much better. The 509th drop might have been scattered, but a third regiment, the 505th, combat veterans of Sicily, had landed at Paestum in a drop that was as accurate as that of the previous night; the men had hurried off into the darkness to join their fellows at the eastern part of the bridgehead near Altavilla. Also now arrived was the 180th RCT, the final regiment of the 45th Thunderbirds to be deployed. These were vital extra numbers, easing the pressure on his entire front line. The bridgehead was also considered safe enough for Clark to receive visitors. Air Marshal Sir Arthur 'Mary' Coningham, one of the toughest air commanders around and a pioneer of Allied tactical air power, and General Alexander had sailed by destroyer from Palermo and now landed by motor launch. Alex, as always, looked immaculate and imperturbable, and seemed happy that the worst of the crisis was now over. Alan Moorehead saw the Army Group commander and was reminded of when Alex had turned up at the front the previous February, in Tunisia, and had spread calm assurance, confidence and singleness of purpose. He'd turned Allied fortunes around in a matter of days back then. Now Moorehead was watching him again, looking utterly unruffled. Moorehead reckoned that in a crisis there was no one better. 'He seemed to have that rare talent,' noted Moorehead, 'of seeing things clearly and wholly at a time when he himself was under fire, and when from all around the most alarming and confusing information was pouring in.'

In their conversations Clark did, though, raise concerns over Mike Dawley, who had not impressed him when the going had got tough. Alexander always believed it was vital that a commander should have complete trust in a subordinate commander – in their fighting spirit, their decision-making and their ability to act decisively; an army commander could not be everywhere, nor could he make localized decisions. So if Clark had doubts about Dawley, Alexander believed he should let him go. It was something for Clark to mull over, but having stemmed the German counter-attack they now had to turn the tide and win the battle.

In that task he and his men on the ground were being given incredible help by the naval forces, which had been pounding targets with ever-growing ferocity. Just on the 14th the USS *Boise*, having arrived from Taranto, fired some 900 rounds, while her fellow cruiser, the *Philadelphia*, fired around 1,000. That was a huge amount of steel hurtling over, each 6-inch shell weighing 130 pounds. Two British cruisers, *Aurora* and *Penelope*, veterans of the Mediterranean, had also reached Salerno Bay that morning, so that by the time the battleships *Warspite* and *Valiant* steamed in at around 11 a.m. on the 15th, the number of warships lending heft to the battle was considerable. 'A mass of shipping of all sorts,' noted Captain Bertie Packer, 'and the combined barrage terrific.'

In fact, on the afternoon of 14 September both battleships had begun the journey home to the UK for a much-needed refit. Packer was delighted for the crew – they'd been away for two whole years and he knew they all deserved a spell of home leave. Personally, though, he rather regretted leaving as his wife Joy was currently in her native South Africa, working as a reporter in Cape Town, and without her back in England he knew he'd just be kicking his heels.

Then, at 8 p.m. on the 14th, as they'd been steaming west, they were ordered to turn round and hurry to Salerno instead. So off they set at 23 knots, a decent lick. 'Roared thro' Messina Straits,' he scribbled, 'and were greeted by an air raid as we arrived in the middle of Salerno Bay near the landing beaches.' As no one had ever expected mighty battleships to be part of the plan, no provision had been made for liaison officers or FOOs; nor did Packer or anyone on *Warspite* and *Valiant* have a target list or bombardment maps. After some hasty conferring, FOOs were allocated and set ashore at around 2 p.m. The *Valiant* had fifty rounds of 15-inch shells while *Warspite* had eighty-eight, so it was agreed that they should fire half that day and half the following morning. At 5.20 p.m., and just one mile offshore so that the huge ship dominated the shoreline, *Warspite* opened fire on an enemy OP near Eboli, the great guns spitting fire and the recoil forcing the ship to rock in the water. Packer was rather pleased with the results, which by all accounts were very accurate. The only scare was when twelve Focke-Wulf 190s roared over. 'The ship was stopped,' noted Packer, 'and it was vital to keep exactly in the right place if the bombardment was to be accurate.'

Feldmarschall Kesselring had been eager for a fresh attack on the 15th, this time against the eastern part of the bridgehead, where the American airborne troops now held the line, but his plans had always been laced with an excess of optimism. Von Vietinghoff, on the other hand, was more of a pragmatist and recognized that the chance for a decisive victory had probably now passed – and said as much to his chief. Nor was General Traugott Herr, commander of LXXVI Panzerkorps, keen to launch another attack; that morning, 15 September, before receiving any instructions from Kesselring, he ordered his corps on to the defensive.

Further attacks were planned – Oberst Schmalz attempted an assault in tandem with 26. Panzer on the afternoon of the 15th, for example – but these were broken up by air and naval assault before they ever really started moving. They tried again the following morning, early on the 16th, against 201st Guards Brigade, but when they eventually got going were blasted by British 25-pounder field artillery. 'A gunner's dream,' noted the 65th Field Artillery's diarist. 'Plenty of targets, all in the open, lots of ammunition, and nothing coming back at us.' That evening, Balck reported that Schmalz's Kampfgruppe had not achieved their targets and that the enemy seemed stronger.

Certainly, by the morning of the 16th even Kesselring appeared to have accepted that it was time to withdraw. 'The effect of the heavy ships' bombardment and the almost complete command of the fighting area by the far superior enemy air force has cost us grievous losses,' Kesselring signalled. 'Therefore the present operation will be broken off.'

On this day, when the battle seemed to have turned for good, there was, however, one setback for the Allies. In the morning, HMS *Valiant* steamed off around the Sorrento peninsula to bombard Castellammare, while *Warspite* closed in towards Red Beach for a second shoot. No sooner had they weighed anchor than a number of Focke-Wulf 190s roared over, dropping single bombs that erupted with huge amounts of spray but otherwise did no damage. At 1.15 p.m., *Warspite*'s big 15-inch guns opened fire again, once more on enemy targets around Eboli. Thirty shells were fired in all, very accurately, and then she moved off again, threading her way towards the north of the bay for a second shoot.

More Focke-Wulfs now appeared, roaring out of the sun, again dropping bombs and once more without success. But no sooner had they disappeared than suddenly from the bridge those on *Warspite* sighted three glider bombs, Fritz Xs, coming towards them. Captain Bertie Packer knew what they were immediately, having already dodged one before. They were flying horizontally at around 8,000 feet and then suddenly they dived, absolutely vertically and at terrific speed. It was only a matter of seconds. There was absolutely nothing Packer or any member of his crew could do.

The first missed the starboard side by a matter of feet, but a split second later a second hit just to the rear of the funnel. The third also near-missed the starboard side. 'I was not thrown off my feet,' jotted Packer, 'but for a fraction of a second I had a kind of "black out" like when you take a hard toss at football or fall off a horse. But I could see and think perfectly clearly all the time.' Black smoke swirled from the turret, which was making a terrible noise; Packer thought it might completely collapse, and for a moment he feared the worst, that the great ship must surely sink. However, no one was losing their head or shouting wildly; rather, the crew all seemed remarkably calm. The anti-aircraft guns were still firing and then, incredibly, Packer discovered that the ship was continuing to run and the steering was working. A fire was now reported. 'Put it out!' Packer commanded down the voice tube, then added, more for effect than anything, 'if we can steam and shoot we'll carry out our final bombardment after all.'

This, however, was not to be, as he realized when further reports began coming in. Four boiler rooms out of six were flooded. Then the steering packed up and they began going round in a circle, but, alarmingly, also turning towards a known minefield. A minesweeper scurried up, shouting over its intercom to move away. 'I couldn't,' wrote Packer, 'for helm was hard over and finally the starboard engine room died out too.' An American tug, the *Orpi*, hurried over and managed to tow her out of immediate danger. There was now only one thing for it and that was to head straight to Malta, although the journey would be fraught to say the least. There were known to be U-boats about and *Warspite* would have to be towed by tugs. Maximum speed was no more than a brisk walking pace, and the ship was already beginning to list a little. Admiral Hewitt sent over a second tug and Packer called up the cruiser HMS *Delhi* and four destroyers, and off they set. 'We were making three-and-a-half knots,' wrote Packer, 'and had 300 miles to go.' A torturous journey lay ahead.

*

Despite *Warspite* limping off, it was clear by sunset that Clark and his men, with the help of Allied naval and air forces, had pulled off a remarkable victory in an operation that had been blighted from the outset by wider political pressure, insufficient shipping, a lack of planning time and the ludicrous machinations that surrounded the Italian armistice. Ironically, that same day a patrol from the 36th Texans made contact with leading reconnaissance troops from the Eighth Army at Vallo, twenty miles to the south. So much expectation had been pinned on this link-up since the landings, and yet when it finally happened the battle at Salerno had already been turned. The truth was that Fifth Army had landed at Salerno back on 9 September without anything like enough men, materiel and firepower to ensure success. At a time when the Allies were very sensibly trying to eschew any kind of high-risk, very damaging setback, AVALANCHE was about as high-risk an operation as could have possibly been conceived, spurred on by an Allied urgency to accelerate the war that was totally out of the hands of those expected to do the fighting on the ground.

Credit, rightly, was being given to the naval and air effort, but in many ways that was a given. The Allied naval forces in the Mediterranean were immensely experienced and the Royal Navy, especially, had always been Britain's most polished arm; after all, it had been the largest navy in the world in 1939 and its professionalism ran deep. Similarly, the Mediterranean Allied Air Forces had also developed into a huge and well-honed machine. At the very top it was led by people of immense experience – commanders who had been developing both tactical and strategic air power in the theatre for two years and more, and at a more junior level by group, wing and squadron commanders who were tough, combat-hardened and had learned about combat flying in multiple theatres. Cocky Dundas, for example, was a case in point. The air forces were also operating against a fading Luftwaffe that was no longer their equal in either numbers or skill. The task of the Allied air forces, then, had been a formidable one, but it was also a challenge to which they were more obviously able to successfully rise.

Fifth Army, on the other hand, had had the toughest task and was the least well equipped and experienced to deal with the onslaught that befell it. Much credit should go to Clark, untested as an army commander. It was true that he'd asked for Fifth Army, but at the time, early in the year, he could not have had any inkling about the circumstances in which it would first be tested. Since arriving off Salerno Clark had faced down the many challenges flung at him, handled his meagre resources well, been resolute in his decision-making and a very visible army commander too, scurrying about the battlefront, urging his men and never once flinching at the weight of enemy fire. 'This has been a great opportunity and privilege,' he wrote to Eisenhower on the evening of 16 September, 'and I appreciate your letting me bring my Fifth Army into action. We have made mistakes, and we have learned the hard way, but we will improve every day and am sure we will not disappoint you.' His humility was impressive: no crowing, no back-slapping but an acceptance that there could be no complacency as they moved on to the next battle. No one in the Allied high command could possibly feel disappointed by their achievements at Salerno. At no point so far in the war had Allied forces confronted such a density of German divisions – and yet they had stood firm and held all that had been hurled at them.

It was now their turn to pursue the enemy. The drive on Rome, one of the main prizes for which Italy had been invaded, had begun.

CHAPTER 15

Breakout

O N MONDAY, 13 SEPTEMBER, Harold Macmillan flew to Taranto as part of a mission to get in touch with Badoglio and the Italian government – such as it existed. Badoglio, the Comando Supremo and the King and royal family were, the Allies had discovered, now ashore in Brindisi. Eisenhower had been keen that Macmillan and his American colleague, Bob Murphy, should be part of this mission, but also Brigadier-General Maxwell Taylor. Another addition to the party was General Sir Noel Mason-MacFarlane, an old soldier hurriedly flown over from Gibraltar, where he was currently the British Governor-General.

They flew over from Tunis in a B-17 Flying Fortress, the pilot asking them where they wanted to go as though he were a cab driver in New York. Either Brindisi or Taranto, they told him.

'Aren't those in Italy?'

'Yes.'

'I think the Germans have got the aerodromes there,' the pilot told them.

'No,' they told him. 'We sent a brigade into Taranto and we think they have got Taranto.'

'Yes, but the aerodrome is at a place called Grottaglie, about twenty kilometres from Taranto, and how do you know who has got this?'

'Well, we can go and see. We try this first, and then Brindisi.'

As it happened, they were able to land at Taranto, although they were immediately swamped by Italian Air Force officers. Macmillan could remember some Italian, having once spent some time in Venice, and Maxwell Taylor had learned 'Italian in Twenty Lessons'. It turned out that

Mason-MacFarlane's batman, Bombardier Casey, could be understood the best, however. Apparently, the closest Germans were fifteen miles away. The 1st Airborne Division had pushed on out of Taranto and a large detachment had been sent to Brindisi and also Bari; both were in British hands within forty-eight hours of the landings. There had been only a couple of blights to SLAPSTICK. The first was when the mine-layer, HMS *Abdiel*, hit a couple of mines as it berthed and then sank in three minutes. More than 100 had been killed. Also dead was Major-General 'Hoppy' Hopkinson, commander of the 1st Airborne, and the first British general of the war to be killed in action; he was hit as he approached a German roadblock near the town of Castellaneta.

Despite these tragedies the heel of Italy was now in Allied hands, and after a night in a rather deserted Taranto and an understandably run-down hotel they had headed off to Brindisi, where they met the King but also Badoglio, Ambrosio and Roatta. Macmillan thought the King seemed nervous, rather infirm and shaky, but courteous. 'Things are not difficult,' he told Macmillan, 'only men.' Badoglio he rather liked. He thought him both honest and humorous; he might have been the latter, but the ageing marshal had been lying through his teeth repeatedly ever since taking over from Mussolini in July. He was less impressed by Ambrosio, and thought Roatta seemed clever but untrustworthy and 'a natural coward'. He'd got the measure of Roatta more than, perhaps, Badoglio. Overall, he detected an atmosphere of 'well-bred defeatism'.

The entire point of this first mission was to lay the ground for the implementation of the armistice agreement – the Long Terms. There was also Allied Military Government of the Occupied Territories – AMGOT – to establish and a need to work out how the governance of Italy might function as the Allies progressed up the leg. At what point did the Allies run the show, and when did territory devolve to the Italian government? None of this had been yet thought through. As Macmillan pointed out, the Brindisi party they were meeting could hardly be dignified with the name of government. The Italians, for their part, seemed braced for the terms, but also desperate to salvage some dignity. They wanted to be con-sidered formal allies too. As Badoglio pointed out, it would be hard for the Italians to stand up to the Germans and consider them now a common foe when, under the terms of the armistice, they – the Italians – were still regarded as a defeated enemy. 'Shall we,' Badoglio asked the mission, 'as we would like to do, in order to make clear the position to our people, declare war on Germany?'

Almost all these questions and issues, however, were left unanswered and unresolved on this first mission. But the dialogue had begun and after that first, tentative, opening round the mission flew back to Tunisia on Friday, 17 September. Clearly, there was a lot still to work out.

Although General von Vietinghoff had ordered 1. Fallschirmjäger-Division to withdraw from Apulia and the south, Leutnant Martin Pöppel and the rest of the Maschinengewehr-Bataillon had spent a week being sent from pillar to post – disarming Italians, setting up roadblocks, even laying a consignment of mines themselves. Since the supply chain seemed to be on the blink they were left to fend for themselves and for once given carte blanche to take whatever food they could get; there were very strict rules against pillaging, but these, it was accepted, were exceptional circumstances. In any case, the Italians had just stabbed them in the back, so sympathy was spare.

Pöppel and his fellows saw no British troops at all, although on 18 September, as they had been directed towards Grassano, a town at the edge of the mountains in the Basilicata region of the central south, they had been warned that the Canadians were nearby. Pöppel had ridden ahead on his motorbike with his submachine gun on his lap and ready to fire. He'd not been stopped. Demolitions and mine-laying had continued. A couple of days later, however, a Canadian prisoner was brought in. 'A pleasant little chap, twenty-three years old,' noted Pöppel. 'He claims they are by no means hungry for battle and don't know why they are fighting.' A sentiment that would have been echoed by many thousands more troops now in Italy, both German and Allied. Even to Pöppel, the constant haring around in this sun-battered and bleached, bare, poverty-stricken backwater of southern Italy seemed inexplicable.

Meanwhile, the division's engineers had left Bari and, on 17 September, were sent up to the Foggia area, the town at the heart of numerous airfields. Jupp Klein and his group were immediately sent to the main airfield on the south-west edge of the town by his 2. Kompanie commander, Oberleutnant Ernst Frömming, with instructions to destroy anything that could be used by the Allies. When they got there they discovered a large number of Junkers Ju88 twin-engine bombers lined up around the airfield, already destroyed. Not far from the airfield was a railway line on which stood a number of wagons of aviation fuel, also blown up. Klein and his men immediately assumed that this destruction had been caused by what he called the 'Badoglioputches' and Luftwaffe ground crew, who had seen no option but to blow them up as they'd evacuated the airfield. Possibly more likely culprits were Allied bombers, who had visited the Foggia airfield complex repeatedly.

What remained, however, were vast stacks of bombs, all of which now had to be detonated. Klein was incensed. They were all thinking about how much this arsenal might help them as they continued the fight in Italy. 'We almost cried because of what we were about to blow up,' noted Klein. 'With furious curses we prepared the detonators.'

With Taranto, Brindisi and Bari all now in Allied hands and with the port facilities intact, more troops could be shipped directly from Egypt into Eighth Army's ranks without the need for landing craft, vessels that were only required when landing directly on to beaches with no quayside available. On Saturday, 18 September, 8th Indian Division were preparing to ship out from Alexandria the following day on five transport ships. Most of the men were encamped near the city, and Corporal Harry Wilson stuck his head out of the front of his tent and gazed up at the stars and the searchlight beams sweeping the city sky. He felt excited as he tried to look into the future. So far he'd been incredibly lucky, but he sensed this couldn't be expected to hold. 'And the worst part of this war,' he wrote in his diary, 'was just beginning.' He had a kind of melancholy fascination with trying to assess the odds. 'But if the stars above knew my fate they gave no sign,' he noted. 'What was I to them but one of the many thousands of men stretched out beneath them! And once more I had to reflect on the indifference of Fate to individual fortune.'

Wilson was an Irishman, although when war broke out he'd been living in Bedford in England with his brother, who was serving in the RAF and based at nearby Cardington. Wilson had come over from Ireland and had been doing very little other than playing the piano at the Air Force Club and then realized, as the Germans were sweeping across France, that he'd run out of money and, feeling a wave of zeal to help stop Hitler, decided to sign up to fight. His brother suggested he join the RAF too, but he thought he might see more of the world in the army. On 17 May 1940 he joined the Royal Engineers in Northampton and ended up being sent overseas to the Middle East as a clerk in the Well-Boring Section, serving with 10th Indian Division.

Then, in the spring of 1943, he'd decided to try and retrain as a cipher clerk. Having secured a place on the course, he had managed to pass with flying colours and then was posted to III Corps Signals, part of Tenth Army in Lebanon. Then, in early September, despite Captain Selkirk, his boss at III Corps, pleading to keep him, he had been posted to 8th Indian Infantry Division HQ. This, Wilson had noted, had been the first time that anyone had wanted him for either his temperament or his ability and he'd felt rather flattered. At any rate, at the beginning of September he'd been posted, so that not only did he have a whole new team to get to know at Divisional Signals, but also an entirely new theatre as well: Italy.

The following morning, he and the rest of the company boarded a Dutch liner called the *Ruys* which, unlike a lot of civilian liners converted to troop transports, had retained some of its pre-war luxury. Wilson was delighted, and although a mere junior NCO had been invited to take lunch in the 1st Class dining room, where Javanese waiters served him vegetable soup, hors d'oeuvres, cold cuts of ham, tongue, veal and salad, and finally sweet melon slices, as well as bread and butter and coffee with cream. He'd rarely eaten a better feast. His table companions wondered whether they were being fattened up for the kill.

Meanwhile, those Eighth Army divisions already in Italy were slowly inching their way across the boot. The British 5th Division, in addition to linking up with the 36th Texans, had also made contact with the 45th Thunderbirds on the 20th. The Inniskillings were now a little way inland on the tails of 29. Panzergrenadier-Division as they pushed up on the right of Fifth Army. David Cole spent the days covered in dust, hurrying past cheering crowds in every village and town they went through, and although they rarely actually saw the enemy they were pursuing, Cole did spend one evening with some prisoners they picked up. 'It is evening. I am lying under a tree watching the sun go grandly down,' he wrote in a letter home. 'Under another tree a few yards away sit four cheerful Germans.' And they really were Germans, not men from eastern Europe conscripted into the German Army. One had ridden his motorbike straight towards their leading Bren carrier and surrendered, while the other three were deserters. They apparently seemed to believe the war was over and that the Nazis were finished. When one of them was asked if he was a Nazi, he roared with laughter as though the very notion was ludicrous. 'I wish,' added Cole, 'I could share his optimism about the state of mind of the German Army!'

On their right and advancing into the central southern part of the country were the Canadians, although now on a very wide flank from 5th Division. The Hasty Ps had taken the mountain town of Catanzaro on 11 September, after Lieutenant Farley Mowat had been sent to scout forward. Climbing up the mountain road from the coast, folds of immense, rippled, hazy blue mountains away to his left and a bleak, high plateau immediately below the winding road, he had turned what he thought likely to be the last hairpin before the town when he came face to face with an Italian anti-tank gun pointing down the road at him. Noticing a number of twitchy fingers fondling rifle and submachine gun triggers, he had been urged by the sergeant beside him to keep driving and bluff it out. Waving cheerily and pointing in the direction of the town, Mowat had done just that. Thankfully, no one fired, and he survived to see another day. And, warming to the bluff, he even told the Italian commandant that he was a special emissary from General Montgomery. The Italians appeared to fall for it too.

That same day, Canadian troops linked up with the 1st Airborne – a significant moment of sorts as it meant Allied troops were now joined coast-to-coast for the first time, but the Hasty Ps remained in Catanzaro for a few days waiting for supplies to catch up. As always when troops paused, furious letter-writing became one of the chief occupations. 'I think the end of the war just *may* be in sight,' Mowat wrote to his parents. 'In men and material we have the Jerries by the hind tit, and with the Russkies knocking at the western gates Hitler may surrender to our side.' He reckoned he'd be home early in 1944, although statistically he'd do well to survive that long; already he was one of the senior surviving lieutenants in the battalion. They'd not been in combat for even two and a half months.

His old A Company commander, Major Alex Campbell, also wrote home from Catanzaro. The country, he reported, was very beautiful, but like so many new to Italy he was shocked by the poverty he saw, which was worse in many ways even than in Sicily. 'The towns are dirty and the people all seem so starved and unhappy,' he wrote. 'It really makes us feel sorry for them.' He couldn't help feeling the Italians had been driven into the war against their wishes; it was a tragedy to see how emaciated the children were – and made him realize how lucky his two nephews were to be growing up in Canada. 'It makes us real mad at the Germans for all they have done,' he added, 'and when we catch up to them, there will be hell to pay.' The Seaforths padre, Roy Durnford, was also shocked by the squalor and poverty. 'A city of hunger, dirt and confusion,' he had written about Delianuova, the nearest town to where they were currently camped. He came across an old woman sitting alone outside the church, her eyes red and sore and flies buzzing around her incessantly, then noticed other similarly wretched women, haggard and obviously starving. He gave one of the women some food, which prompted her to weep with gratitude. 'No one seems to care for them,' he noted. 'The priests look well and show no sign of the weight this infinite sorrow brings to me.'

The reaction of Campbell and Durnford to the poverty in southern Italy was far from unique. Newsreels of Mussolini and marching Fascists in cities like Rome or Florence had made it easy to assume that Italy was as modern and bustling as London or any US city. Even Harold Macmillan was slightly taken aback to discover the simplicity of rural life. 'All the transport is horse- or mule-drawn,' he noted, then added, 'it is very hot, especially at night.'

At Salerno, Alan Moorehead was also moved by the plight of the ordinary Italians, who, it seemed to him, were desperately trying to continue with some semblance of normality amid the sudden typhoon of steel now blowing in around them. He had by now transferred over to the British sector and was following the fighting as it progressed up the valley towards Nocera. Climbing a low hill, he watched a farmer ploughing while mortars landed dangerously close by. He also saw women, bundles on their heads, still walking about through the shattered villages. He wondered whether the scale of death and destruction was so incomprehensible to them that their only response was simply to carry on as normal. More likely it was out of necessity. For most rural Italians, the margins of survival in the annual cycle were narrow, and if crops weren't sown or harvested it could have catastrophic consequences. They were continuing their lives because they had little choice. If they lost their homes and their livelihoods, would life be worth living?

The towns in the bridgehead were now wrecks. Battipaglia and Altavilla were utterly destroyed, a mass of rubble, dust and death, as though an earthquake had wrought the very worst level of carnage. When Christopher Bulteel and the 3rd Coldstream Guards finally reached the tobacco factory they found nothing but a charred ruin. Eboli, too, just a few weeks earlier one of the loveliest of hill towns, was also now largely reduced to rubble. Lina Caruso and her family had finally headed up the mountain on the 16th and watched their town being bombed yet again as they climbed. They had taken shelter, along with a number of others, at the Boffa Casino, a well-known local landmark in the mountain hamlet of San Donato, and several miles from Eboli. Tragically, it had proved no safer than staying put: they had only been there a day when a number of incendiary bombs were dropped around them which, as they were designed to do, then began fires. Two civilians were killed and a number of others injured, some very badly, and with no hope at all of getting to a hospital. A young medical student was doing his best for the wounded and others were helping, but the situation was desperate. One badly burned boy was taken to the stable next to the casino and laid in a stall. Lina was trying to help him when a horrifically burned man stumbled in. 'He is completely naked,' she wrote, 'stinks of burning, his belly and legs are burnt and bleeding, the skin hanging down. He carries his arms outstretched, full of sores and blisters.' Unsurprisingly, the man, Signor Caramanti, a father of four, died of his wounds soon after.

Lina Caruso could hardly comprehend how much their lives had been overturned in such a short space of time: the country overrun, her town destroyed, anarchy in the streets, incessant shelling, uncertainty and fear. She felt frightened nearly constantly: frightened that she would be blown to pieces or trapped by rubble, frightened that she might be raped by troops armed with guns and knives and who seemed totally alien to her; frightened of the future, if, indeed, there was a future to be had. The hardship and privations of sleeping in caves in the mountains toe to tail with many others, the lack of food and running water, and the sudden dramatic loss of everything that she had thought normal in life had been utterly shocking. 'Will we survive?' she wrote in her diary. 'Will we survive the many dangers, the many sufferings? Who knows?'

Bewildered and terrified Italians like Lina Caruso had little comprehension of what was going on, but the fighting was on the move and certainly away from the shattered wreck of Eboli. On the morning of Saturday, 18 September, General von Vietinghoff issued orders for his troops in AOK 10 to start withdrawing from Salerno. He and Kesselring agreed that they would pull back towards the River Volturno, but would try and hold the main routes north from the town for as long as possible to give the rest of their forces the chance to retreat in some kind of order. The Volturno, roughly fifty miles to the north, would be held until at least 15 October, because Kesselring now planned to create a series of four defensive lines that spanned the leg of the country. This would need a bit of time, and with his chief engineer, Generalmajor Hans Bessell, he planned an especially formidable position that would run from Minturno on the west coast to Pescara on the east and which at its heart would have the town of Cassino and, towering above it, the Monte Cassino massif. This dominated the mouth of the Liri Valley, through which Highway 6, the old

Roman Via Casilina, ran from Naples to Rome. It was the most direct –
and obvious – route to the capital. The road passed directly through the
town, which hugged the eastern side of the valley; this was why whoever
occupied the dramatic Monte Cassino massif above held a very strong
hand indeed. Kesselring wanted this to be as tough a nut to crack as possible, but it meant giving Bessell time. With every day that they could
keep the Allies at bay, the Gustav Line – as it was already being called –
would be increasingly formidable.

A new phase of the fighting in Italy was now under way. The Allies,
too, needed to sort out their plans and Alexander visited Clark again on
the 21st to explain how Fifth and Eighth Armies would advance either
side of the leg, with Fifth Army heading up the west and Eighth up the
east and along the Adriatic coast. Together they were now to be called
15th Army Group, and a truly multinational force it would be. The French
were currently clearing Sardinia and Corsica, but would in due course
join them in the leg. A Polish Corps was also working up in Palestine and
would move to Italy when it was ready.

And in the short term, divisions waiting in North Africa and Sicily
were starting to be shipped over as well as replacement troops. They were
desperately needed, both to bolster Fifth and Eighth Armies but also to
replenish those units that had taken a battering so far. The two British
divisions of X Corps, for example, had, in one week of fighting up to 16
September, lost 531 men killed, with 1,915 wounded and 1,561 missing –
which usually meant taken prisoner. That was over 4,000 and equated to
more than four entire battalions out of eighteen in X Corps. Those were
appalling numbers after such a short period, especially as the vast majority of the losses were infantry.

Among those that had been hurriedly allocated to the eighteen extra
landing ships now made available were 1,500 men from the 50th Tyne
Tees and 51st Highland Divisions, who had been expecting to join their
units in Sicily. When they arrived in Salerno and were told – without any
explanation – that they were instead to be replacements for the battle-
scarred 46th and 56th Divisions, a number of them were not at all happy.
Around 1,000 were fresh recruits, only recently arrived in theatre from
the UK, but some 500 were veterans of the North African and Sicilian
campaigns – men now recovered from sickness and wounds. In the rush
to get replacements to Salerno there had been a woeful lack of information given to these men – no explanations, no reasoning for the change of
units, and so around 300 of the veterans simply refused to join their

newly allocated battalions. After they obdurately remained in a field in the beachhead for four days, General McCreery addressed them on the 20th. He apologized, admitting that mistakes had been made, and appealed to them to help their joint cause. He also warned them of the consequences of mutiny in wartime. Some now agreed to fight, but 192 stubbornly continued to refuse. All of these men were charged with mutiny, with plans to ship them back to Algeria.

It was a reminder of the fragile hold Allied leaders actually had over their men. These conscripts were from a democracy and there would be no mass-executions for refusing to fight. Rather, they had to be persuaded to do so through a sense of honour, duty, loyalty to their comrades and, most importantly, by treating them as well as possible in the very difficult circumstances of war. They were not to be regarded as a commodity to be simply shuffled around, nor were they to be regarded as cannon fodder. Maintaining morale was absolutely paramount, because as all Allied commanders were keenly aware – and, after four long years of war, the British especially – an army with poor morale was no army at all.

As Fifth Army now began to move inland, they could bid farewell to most of the naval warships that had given such staunch support. The equivalent of 72,000 25-pounder and 105mm field artillery rounds had been fired by the naval gunners, an astonishing weight of fire. LCF 12 had been stationed just off the shore for the entire battle. Captain Peter Bull reckoned they'd shot down three enemy aircraft in that time; his nose was slightly put out of joint because around him the liberty ships and other freighters had begun painting their scores on to their funnels – a number of which Bull thought ridiculously out of all proportion to reality. 'They, fortunately being American,' he wrote tersely, 'did not have to get official credit, but the disparity was galling.'

On the other hand, American ships tended to be far better supplied with victuals than British ones, and now that life was a little calmer in the bay most mornings, Bull would send off some of the crew in their dinghy with a shopping bag to try and cadge some extra supplies. 'The larger ships,' he added, many of which were American, 'were generous with their refrigerated supplies and we did not do too badly.'

The crippled HMS *Warspite* finally reached Grand Harbour in Malta on 18 September after a horrendous journey. Casualties were, in the big scheme of things, light – six killed and twenty wounded – but the damage to the ship was extensive. Some 200 men working in shifts had to bail out seawater with buckets – back-breaking work at the best of times, but worse in the heat of late summer and in the belly of a battleship. On the evening of 17 September, Captain Bertie Packer decided it was time to say a few words over the intercom. The gist was that such an attack was a common hazard of war. 'We had done what we set out to do and had been hit,' he told them. 'We scared the hell out of the German Army and braced up our own soldiers.' They'd helped tip the scales. He was also full of admiration for their good humour and hard work. They would, he told them, get the Old Lady back to Malta.

And so they had, despite being tossed and wrenched one way and then another by the tide rips and whirlpools of the Straits of Messina; sometimes they sheered as much as 70 degrees to starboard and then back again to port. 'I was very tired,' Packer noted in his diary. 'Still, I was going strong and not allowing myself to think of sleep.' By the time they finally limped into port, Packer noted it was the second time he'd done so on *Warspite* in the past twenty-seven years – the last time had been after the Battle of Jutland. 'I <u>was</u> relieved,' he added, 'when we were securely berthed.'

Meanwhile, the 36th Texans were now out of the line and being given a chance to catch their breath after a bruising first taste of combat with nearly 1,000 casualties in their division alone. The number of dead and wounded had shocked Bud Wagner. One of his great pals, Ted Nelson, had lost a leg, six men in his artillery battalion had been killed and thirty wounded. 'My heart goes out,' he jotted, 'to those who were killed and their loved ones back in the States.' A makeshift cemetery had already been laid out, the dead marked with rough crosses, and he felt very thankful to still be alive. Incredibly, his artillery battalion alone had fired 10,504 rounds of 105mm shells, 25 per cent more than during the entire Tunisian campaign with the 34th Red Bulls – and in just eight days.

As a combat engineer, Frank Pearce had not been allowed to put his feet up, however. With the Germans pulling back, his unit were instructed to build bridges over the rivers and clear mines. On the 19th he helped move a Panzer IV from the road just below Altavilla. 'Burned,' he noted. 'Dead cattle and a few Germans (dead) still around. Trees all shot to pieces.' The next day he had to help clear more tanks and burned-out vehicles, which were now scattered all over the battlefield. And all the time, Italian soldiers tramped home, many, he noted, in rags and carrying large packs.

On the 21st, Pearce and his platoon were posted up to Altavilla, the town they had had so much trouble taking, although on pitching his tent the biggest threat came from the hordes of mosquitoes. The bites were bad enough, but these were malaria-carrying and cases were already rising despite the atabrine tablets they'd been given. The town was a wreck. Captain Roswell Doughty had driven up in his jeep on the 18th. During the climb he and his driver had rounded one hairpin to see an Italian woman sprawled face down on the road and beside her a little girl with long brown curls and a blue dress. Both were dead; it was one of the most brutal and upsetting sights he had ever seen, especially since they'd clearly been left there for a while. In the town itself he discovered a shambles with collapsed houses, shattered trees and dead animals everywhere. The Allies were liberators, but, as with Sicily, they also brought with them winds of immense destruction.

Intense fighting continued up the valleys leading out of Salerno. While following the action up the Avellino road, Alan Moorehead, calling in at McCreery's corps HQ, was handed a notebook found on the body of a young German officer. He'd served in the Aufklärungs-Abteilung – reconnaissance battalion – of 16. Panzer-Division and was called 'Leutnant Rocholl'. The young officer, so conscientious and courageous, had become one more casualty of what was already proving a brutal battle.

The dead were gone. They would fight no more, but the living had to dust themselves down, scramble up the hillsides and carry on. Lieutenant Peter Moore had had only a brief chance to write a letter to his parents on 17 September before heading back into the line once again. He congratulated them on their 26th wedding anniversary and updated them on the long list of injuries to the various young men in the battalion, all of whom his mother and father knew from home. Colin Stockdale had a poisoned leg and was in hospital in Sicily. 'Mike Moore has been injured,' he wrote, 'but not very badly. Richard is pretty fit but walking about with a tiny piece of shrapnel in his arm. I, of course, am as well as ever.'

He was not, however. Having moved back up into the line early in the morning of the 20th, this time up the Cava–Nocera Valley, he noticed his leg was starting to hurt – it was the shrapnel wound that happened days earlier. By the afternoon of the 21st it was agony and he had a high temperature. Although reluctant to leave his men, by the time he headed back down the slopes he could no longer walk and needed his platoon runner as a crutch. The MO took one look, realized he had septicaemia and immediately put him into an ambulance. On the beach he was transferred on to a lighter and then to a hospital ship. 'That evening,' he noted, 'it was like going to paradise after what we had been through.'

While the men of 46th Division were battling up the Cava Valley, 201st Guards Brigade had been sent up the Avellino road. This was Route 88, which climbed out of Salerno, past the narrow mouth of the valley at Fratte and then widened and continued to rise very gradually on up towards Avellino, the route snaking its way around low but prominent hills and lined on both sides by magnificent 3,000-foot-high peaks. A particularly troublesome feature, marked on the map as Hill 270, stood sentinel on the western side of the valley as it opened up north of Fratte.

Like every other British unit at Salerno, the Guards Brigade had been pretty bruised by their first fortnight on Italian soil. Casualties were mounting. A couple wounded one day, three the next, two killed. Chip, chip, chip. 'Padre found dead behind 3 Coy,' noted the 3rd Coldstream Guards war diary on 23 September. 'He was hit by a shell when returning from the forward companies.' A couple of hours later, a Guardsman and one further officer were wounded. They weren't even in the thick of the fighting, just holding a position.

On the 24th the Grenadiers led the advance, but then it was the turn of the Coldstream Guards: Hill 270 needed taking. The following morning, from the crest of a jutting spur, Christopher Bulteel and his company commander, Major Griffith-Jones, made a recce of the hill they were to assault at midday. It wasn't expected to be too challenging and thought to be only lightly held. As he looked out over the beautiful scenery ahead of him, Bulteel found it hard to imagine fighting there at all. 'The deep peace of the valley,' he wrote, 'green with its trees and vineyards that hid a little village completely save the tower of a church, all surrounded by a vast semicircle of steep mountains bare and bright in the morning sun – that peace could not be shattered, surely, by a modern battle?'

Inevitably, however, the attack was far harder than suggested, as it was always going to be when attacking up a steep hill defended by Germans with machine guns and grenades. To help the attack, the field artillery laid down a heavy stonk on to the hill first, and then once the barrage was over the Coldstreamers started their climb; No. 1 Company was on the right, No. 3 on the left, the men weaving through trees up a sunken track, guns pounding somewhere in the distance and birds still singing lazily on the boughs.

Progress good. Up ahead, the summit, quite close now. Nearly there.

Then suddenly, the rip of Spandaus shattering the calm. Bulteel and his men in No. 3 Company started running forward, past a little house nestling at the side of the hill into the trees, the firing increasing. Bulteel was struggling, his mind starting to cloud. Lots of smoke from a fire that had started. Men with strained faces as a burst of machine-gun fire spat through the trees. Lieutenant Raymond Nares's men joining his for a renewed assault; Nares wandering around with his pistol and blood oozing down both arms. Germans hurling grenades from their slit trenches. Nares coshing a German with his empty revolver. Prisoners coming in along with their own wounded, rescued as the flames surged, carried up the hill to avoid being burned to death. The stench of smoke, of gunpowder. Of death. Then digging in, the lack of water, the intense heat, and a counter-attack by the enemy that was seen off swiftly.

Bulteel was now feverish, and after being relieved he struggled to make it back down the hill again. It was raining – no, pouring – everyone was soaked and the last vestiges of summer were over. And Bulteel was shivering. But it wasn't the cold. It was malaria. He was yet another casualty for the battalion to try and fill.

The Americans of VI Corps, meanwhile, had also shifted shape a little. After consultation with Eisenhower, Clark had relieved Mike Dawley, who had been replaced by Lieutenant-General John Lucas, fifty-three years old but, truth be told, looking older. A career soldier and artilleryman, veteran of the last war, he had been in theatre for a while as Eisenhower's deputy and, in Sicily, also effectively as General George S. Patton's sidekick at Seventh Army HQ. Since the end in Sicily he'd taken command of II Corps too, and while he was short of senior combat command, he was hardly alone in that. Certainly, he had had a long and varied career and was widely liked and trusted for his perceptive intelligence and sound judgement.

Lucas had arrived at Clark's HQ at 10 a.m. on Monday, 20 September, still somewhat dazed by the rapid turn of events; he'd been commanding II Corps on Sicily just a couple of days earlier. He moved his CP to the edge of ruined Battipaglia and rushed around meeting his staff and also his division and regimental commanders. His first impressions of the countryside were that it was much like Sicily but with more cover, and he arrived just as two of his divisions, the 45th Thunderbirds and the newly arrived 3rd Division from Sicily, began pushing north in a much wider arc to that of the British, along roads and narrow valleys that wove through rugged mountains. 'The same old stuff,' noted Lucas in the diary he kept daily. 'The Sicilian campaign was worth a million dollars to me.'

Among those now battling northwards were the men of B Company of 1st Battalion, 15th Infantry Regiment, part of 3rd Division, and one young squad commander was none too impressed to be back in the firing lines. 'The Sicilian campaign,' jotted Corporal Audie Murphy, 'has taken the vinegar out of my spirits. I have seen war as it actually is, and I do not like it.' Born in Texas as one of nine children, his had been a tough, working-class upbringing. His father had walked out on them when Audie had been two and his mother had fallen ill and died when he'd been sixteen. Three of his siblings were sent to an orphanage but the rest scattered. Murphy decided to lie about his age and joined the army; he was still only eighteen, although with very fresh young looks and big brown eyes he barely looked as old as that – not even when wearing a battered uniform and tin helmet.

Murphy and the rest of his ten-man squad were currently sitting in a ditch near a road that ran along a valley through the mountains. The bridge up ahead over the stream had been blown and just beyond was a German machine-gun emplacement. It was their job to take it out. Crawling in a wide arc, they reached the stream, which was barely even a trickle, and were able to slip into the riverbed and then crouch along it without being seen. Murphy and two of his men began leapfrogging forward: one would cover, then the next would move forward, then the third would jump both. Now it was Steiner's turn, and he'd failed to spot where the Germans had cut a gap in the grass and weeds for clear firing until it was too late. A blurt of a Spandau and Steiner lurched forward, flat on to the stream bed, his body spasming, then still. Next it was Brandon's turn, but Murphy signalled to him to wait. Brandon thumbed his nose at the signal and moved up. 'I part the bushes quickly,' noted Murphy, 'spot the machine-gun emplacement and dig into it with a hail of lead from my tommy gun.' Brandon scampered past Steiner's body, and Murphy deftly shifted to a new position.

Now a German head cautiously raised itself from the MG post but Murphy was ready, fired a second burst, then dropped to his knees. Ahead, Brandon had reached the collapsed bridge and, pulling the pin from a grenade, hurled it into the Spandau nest, followed quickly by two more. Murphy watched Brandon crawl back, a fourth grenade in his hand, then get to his feet.

'Keep down, keep down!' Murphy yelled. 'Are you nuts?'

Ignoring him, Brandon lobbed the grenade towards the opposite side of the road from the bridge – at another foxhole. A further explosion, and the two men were then both scrambling up the back and running at the enemy positions. There they discovered five dead Germans.

'Jesus,' Brandon muttered.

Calling up the rest of the squad, they picked up Steiner's body and laid him by the edge of the road where he would be found. 'The bullet,' noted Murphy, 'ripped an artery in his throat.'

In the Cava–Nocera Valley, Leutnant Hans Golda and his men had not moved at all since reaching the front except that, rather than living in foxholes, they had shifted into a cellar of a nearby house and also a narrow ravine a few hundred yards behind. There had been no sign of the owners of the house, although it was fully furnished. Golda even found a drawer of underpants – they were pink, and for a lady not a man, but they were better than the filthy ones he had been wearing and so he put them on quite happily. 'The lady,' he noted, 'must have been a corpulent person.'

The house – and underpants – offered only comfort of a kind, however. When not sheltering in the house, the battery continued to fire. After sending off a salvo, a worrying cloud of smoke would mushroom around them and they would look up anxiously to see if any Jabos were circling. 'And when they fell,' he added, 'and we saw the bombs coming towards us, I can say that our arses were on fire!'

They had also felt the full weight of a naval bombardment. Golda had watched in something close to awe when the first had screamed over. 'There, not even 300 metres behind us,' scribbled Golda, 'just above the canyon, sparks, iron parts, dirt and chunks of stone are flying up into the air.' It had been terrifying, not that he had shown his fear. Golda and his men had retreated to the cellar of the house until things had quietened down.

Now, though, on 23 September, orders arrived for them to pull back. As they packed up he looked around and couldn't help feeling a little sad. The vineyards were torn and shredded. Some had burned thanks to the fire of their rocket mortars. A number of bomb craters pitted the site; peach trees and vines lay uprooted. 'A picture,' noted Golda, 'of misery and desolation.'

That same day, the men of 46th Division overran Cava and then pushed on, clawing back another half-mile each day. By the 27th they had captured two key high points at the mouth of the valley and were within touching distance of Nocera. Ahead stood the Plain of Naples, with only the giant volcano, Mount Vesuvius, blocking the way and dominating the landscape much as Etna did in Sicily. The roads to Naples, though, ran either side of the volcano and overnight the Germans began pulling back, the Salerno battle emphatically over at long last. Naples was now within the Allies' grasp.

CHAPTER 16

Naples

F ILIPPO CARACCIOLO FINALLY REACHED his home city of Naples on 15 September. It had been a torturous journey from Rome – stop, start, stop, start. Near Capua on the Volturno, the train had halted and apparently could go no further, and so Caracciolo then managed to get a ride on a donkey and cart before going a little further on the roof of a truck that took him as far as Aversa. From there, he supposed he would have to walk the rest of the way, but eventually managed to flag down a *carrozzella* – a horse-drawn hansom cab – and the driver agreed to take him as far as the museum. Entering the city, he crossed the Piazza Carlo III and spotted a swollen corpse, abandoned on the pavement.

'Yes,' the driver told him, 'that's a poor guy who went out to get water at night, before the curfew ended. He encountered a patrol, fled, and was shot.' The authorities ordered the body to be left where it had fallen for twenty-four hours.

Eventually, he reached his aunt's house at Vico Parete, 15. The family had all gone, but Vittorio, the porter, was still there and made him up a bed. 'He takes a tour with me through the abandoned rooms,' jotted Caracciolo, 'broken glass, dust and rubble, water seepage.' It wasn't so much the bombs, the porter told him, but the bombers. They make so much noise. Everything shakes. Naples had been visited by Allied bombers more than 200 times since the start of the war, and 180 times in 1943 alone. They'd been blasting the city to hell, but they wanted to liberate it.

The following morning, much refreshed, Caracciolo went off in search of friends, but was shocked to see the extent of the ruins. At almost every step he saw nothing but misery and devastation: collapsed houses, cluttered streets of rubble, piles of garbage. People were queuing around makeshift fountains because the water supply had been cut off. At every street he saw vehicles loaded with German troops. One had stopped and he watched its occupants; they were young, wearing tropical shorts and shirts. 'But the features are hard and contracted,' noted Caracciolo, 'they exhale a sadness without light.'

The 'authorities' were, of course, the Germans, but more specifically Oberst Walter Scholl, a fifty-nine-year-old cavalryman, who had spent most of the war either instructing or behind a desk and who, since 12 September, had been commander of the Naples Military Area. During the First World War he'd been ahead of General Balck by one rank; their paths had crossed occasionally ever since. Balck ordered the port prepared for demolitions, but he also wanted to ensure there was no popular uprising. Believing that the way to keep Neapolitans calm was through their stomachs, he had gone to some lengths to ensure enough food was reaching the city. He also made certain that any wounded troops from the front travelled round, not through, Naples, but that any replacements and vehicles should make a great show of passing through the city's very heart. Prisoners of war were also to be brought through, not round, and sometimes made to do so twice.

Civil administration, on the other hand, he left to Scholl, a humourless, uncompromising man of rigid efficiency. The day after his arrival Scholl announced to the city some new rules in five simple points. The first was crystal-clear in its messaging. 'Every single citizen who behaves calmly will enjoy my protection,' Scholl announced. 'On the other hand, anyone who openly or surreptitiously acts against the German armed forces will be executed. Moreover, the home of the miscreant and its immediate surroundings will be destroyed and reduced to ruins. Every German soldier wounded or murdered will be avenged a hundred times.' There was going to be a curfew from 8 p.m. to 6 a.m., and he was also announcing a state of siege. All firearms and ammunition were to be handed in. Anyone found in possession of one after twenty-fours had passed would be shot. His final instruction was that everyone should keep calm and act reasonably. Calmly and reasonably, these instructions were printed and slapped up as bill posters throughout the city.

Over the next few days, Filippo Caracciolo and his friends quickly adapted to the new lockdown rules; whoever was hosting dinner would find themselves with house guests for the night until the curfew was over.

In the background, almost, the Germans set about their destruction; on 22 September, Caracciolo heard explosions as German engineers blew up the nearby Bagnoli shipyards. Then, the following day, a new announcement was made: the entire coastal strip of the city was to be evacuated to a depth of 300 metres; this included some of the smartest streets, buildings and homes in Naples. The evacuation order caused mayhem as it had to be completed in just twenty-four hours and included the entire Posillipo area where Caracciolo had many friends, and which was another heavily populated part of the city. On the 24th he watched the exodus. 'They flee with tired faces,' he wrote, 'an absent gaze, bent under the weight of crates and suitcases. Many women cry.'

Amid all this upheaval, he was trying to galvanize his political colleagues to form a Neapolitan Committee of National Liberation. He wanted to be ready for when the Germans left; there might be a vacuum between their withdrawal and the arrival of the Allies. If so, surely there was a golden opportunity for the Neapolitan CLN to take over the government of the city. But his efforts were to no avail. 'The environment,' he noted, 'is shy and uncertain.' His friends and colleagues might have been wary of putting their necks on the line at this volatile time, but the people of Naples were not. Mounting anger was emboldened by news that the Allies were nearing, and reports and rumours of German withdrawals had prompted a number of Neapolitans to rise, exactly as Balck had feared. When, on the morning of Wednesday, 29 September, Caracciolo heard of barricades being erected in the Via dei Mille, he hurried over to see for himself. There he discovered a clutter of furniture, badly piled timber, slabs of stone and soil blocking the street. Young men, armed with old rifles, pistols and other weaponry stood guard. A little way up the street was an upturned German truck, the seat and door smeared with blood.

Caracciolo talked to some of the men and women standing by and realized that this uprising, this show of popular anger, was fuelled above all by resentment of the manhunt by the Germans for young men to be in their Organisation Todt, the labour corps. 'Wanting to escape the increasingly insistent raids,' jotted Caracciolo, 'thousands of men have hidden in the attics of houses, on roofs, in sewers, in the tunnels, and in the remains of ancient grain pits that form the unexplored tangle of subterranean Naples.' And now they had had enough and were fighting back.

Despite the mutiny at Salerno, 1,300 replacements had been incorporated into 46th and 56th Divisions, while further troops were on their way.

The 7th Armoured Division – the Desert Rats – were due to join X Corps, while other units, including more artillery, were also being shipped to Salerno. Among those landing on the 24th had been the 56th Heavy Regiment, Royal Artillery, veterans of the Tunisian campaign who had been rested for Sicily. The regiment was equipped with the big BL 7.2-inch howitzer, a beast of a gun that could lob a 202-pound shell the best part of ten miles. With the warships departing and with the Allies moving inland, these monster field guns offered a considerable amount of extra heavy firepower.

The Regimental Sergeant-Major – RSM – of the 56th was Jack Ward, a regular army gunner who had joined the Royal Artillery back in 1920, when he had been only eighteen. At the time he'd been a fitter in Eastbourne on the south coast of England, where he lived with his parents and siblings. The army had offered a career, but also the possibility of adventure. Now, aged forty-two, he was only a month short of twenty-three years in the army and very much the old man in the regiment; he was something of a figurehead to the men. Even so, for all his years of service through the 1920s and 1930s, his time in Tunisia – where he'd been lightly wounded – had been his first taste of front-line combat, just as it had been for most of the men he was now landing with at Salerno.

Almost immediately on reaching Salerno they were brought into the line, lumbering the big guns with their Scammell gun tractors up the Cava–Nocera Valley. 'Fourteen miles from Naples and still going forward,' he noted on 29 September, 'our guns are on the move and we are establishing our new positions about 5 miles ahead of our last position.' That would take them to Cercola, on the far side of Vesuvius and overlooking Naples and its bay. It was also an advance that had seen them average one mile per hour, such had been the congestion going along badly bombed and scarred roads.

Ward had been keeping a diary since they'd gone overseas, mainly to give to his wife, Elsie, when he got back home, or for her to have if he didn't make it. There was a lot of kicking one's heels in the army, so diary-keeping was also a means of passing the time in odd moments. More than that, it was a record of an extraordinary time in his life. Anyone out there fighting in Italy knew they were living through something extraordinary. That they were part of history in the making.

Ward, too, had been taken aback by the poverty of the Italians and the huge number of disarmed soldiers heading home. 'The people on the whole look pretty friendly,' he noted, 'but some look very sullen, only natural, I suppose.' That so many Italians had been crossing the battle-ground was, to a large part, down to General Balck. The official order might have been to round them up and put them on trucks and trains to Germany, but his XIV Panzerkorps troops had had no time for such operations. Moreover, as a veteran of the Eastern Front, where partisans had been a constant thorn in his side, he knew perfectly well that the best way to encourage a partisan war in Italy was to insist that young men work for Germany. Most wouldn't want to, so would run off and hide, and before they knew it the Germans would have a widespread partisan war on their hands. Much better to let them go home, where they would be the least trouble in the future. He had a very good point, although without labour Generalmajor Bessell was going to struggle to make the Gustav Line and other defences as strong as Kesselring hoped.

Certainly, Eugenio Corti and his friend Antonio Moroni were benefit-ing from Balck's policy. So far they had had little trouble in their trek across Italy and, having crossed the Liri Valley and climbed up into the mountains beyond, had seen few Germans and encountered mostly help and kindness. By 15 September they'd been in Subiaco, a small medieval town fifty miles from Nettuno, which stood at the intersection of two val-leys. There they paused at a Benedictine monastery, Santa Scolastica, where the abbot willingly gave them a map and some sage advice about walking across the mountains. 'Poor men,' he said to them when they bid him farewell, 'how I pity you! You, who are so young pay today for the ills committed mostly by others.' He then offered them one last piece of advice. 'Never hate anyone,' he said. 'Maybe the German who dies trying to hurt you, dies also for you.'

They continued on their way, walking through the mountains, sleep-ing in barns and mountain huts, meeting escaped British prisoners of war and mountain shepherds whose dogs still regularly fought with wolves. Corti began to believe that the Homeric world he'd read about in his youth still existed. This strange trek was opening his eyes to an Italy he had never known existed, one that in so many ways continued to follow the same rhythms and traditions its people had been observing since the Middle Ages. In between, as they passed through towns, they picked up news and rumours too. That Mussolini was back, running a new Fascist government in the north, that Germans were massacring civilians, and that the Allies were in Termoli on the Adriatic coast.

By 23 September they had reached the hilltop town of Pretoro, in the Abruzzo, from where they could see all the way to Ortona on the Adriatic coast and the sea beyond. Here one of Corti's companions-in-arms from Russia, Virgilio De Marinis, had a family home; to their great relief he was there and welcomed them to stay. They did, for six days, but then on Radio Rome they heard the news of drafts to establish work units for the Germans. In Pretoro a town crier also shouted this news, blowing a bugle as he walked the streets. It was time to move on, their blistered feet rested and ready for the next leg. Back in the mountains, they came across a group of New Zealanders, all escaped POWs. On 1 October they looked up and saw seventy-five Allied bombers, silvery against the sky, heading north. 'The valley,' wrote Corti, 'became filled with their thunder.'

On 24 September, the 8th Indian Division had pulled into Taranto. Harry Wilson was rather sorry his luxury cruise on the *Ruys* was over, but excited finally to be in Italy. It had seemed astounding to him that even though the Germans were only around twenty-five miles from Taranto they could glide into port unmolested and as casually as though they'd been tourists. At the harbour entrance was a large white statue of what appeared to be a saint, one hand raised in a benediction. Wilson stood on the rails watching them moor. Below was the dock railway and filthy warehouses with walls plastered with notices in German and Italian. On the quayside, British soldiers worked side by side with Italians, the latter wearing tattered shorts and vests in the morning heat.

The ship's intercom started issuing disembarking orders. Italians were ready for them, clutching baskets of grapes.

'What are they like, Mac?' Wilson called down to a Tommy.

'Buono,' he replied. 'Thruppence a pound! They'll give you as much as you want for a packet of fags. Go mad for fags!' He went on to tell him that champagne and vermouth was around six shillings a bottle. 'But damn all else. No food. Nothing! Bags of women, though!' The soldier whistled. 'Just the job. Fifty-four brothels here, all of them in bounds.'

Eventually, Wilson disembarked with Spiers, one of his fellow clerks. They waited for hours on the quayside for the promised transport, Wilson clutching the company ciphers box. Three Italian lads came over.

'Mussolini no good!' said one.

'You should have thought of that in 1940,' Wilson replied, but then threw him a cigarette. They'd landed at 8.30 a.m. but it wasn't until after six that evening that they finally got going, and even then they crawled snail-like through the city, which was clogged with military traffic; but eventually they were through and out into the countryside, although it was dark by the time they reached their divisional staging area, which had been set up at the edge of a vineyard. Having handed over the cipher box to a very relieved Company Sergeant-Major Walshall, Wilson discovered they were all expected to sleep together with only bush nets to cover them. Tired and hungry, he tied his to a gnarled olive tree and tried to get his head down, conscious that his brief taste of luxury was well and truly over.

The German abandonment of Taranto, Brindisi and Bari rather underlined how much German strategy in Italy was at sixes and sevens. Before the armistice, Hitler had backed Rommel's plan of abandoning the southern half of Italy and, had the Allies not launched AVALANCHE on 9 September, would that very day have ordered all German forces to pull back north of Rome. But then the armistice had been announced, the Allies had landed, and those plans, which had been gestating for several weeks, had been kicked into the long grass. Kesselring and von Vietinghoff had fought back at Salerno, but because of the earlier strategy championed by Rommel and backed by the Führer, nine full-strength divisions in three corps had remained in the north. Yes, they had then had a job to do disarming Italians and keeping pesky Croatians out of Istria, the borderland between north-east Italy and Yugoslavia, but that was nothing two or three of those divisions couldn't have handled; after all, only 44. Division, to which Major Georg Zellner's battalion was attached, was operating in the vital Brenner area. What were the others doing? Not a huge amount. And what's more, two further divisions had been on their way to join Heeresgruppe C. Had half of Rommel's troops been sent south, including the two panzer divisions in his arsenal, they could have given the Allies a run for their money not only at Salerno but also in Apulia.

Fortunately for the Allies, Rommel had a totally myopic approach to whatever command he held. In North Africa, he viewed his charge across Libya and Egypt as the key to the battle in the Mediterranean, if not the entire war, and his persuasiveness then had been allowed to prevail instead of Kesselring's far better strategy of securing Malta first. Now, in Italy, he could see no alternative to his plans for a withdrawal and stand in northern Italy. Had the roles been swapped with Kesselring, he would undoubtedly have been imploring Hitler to reinforce the south. Kesselring, for his part, had pleaded for some of Rommel's divisions but had been turned down, and with not enough troops for the task in hand, something had had to give – and that had been Apulia.

There was a sense that the timing of the armistice – and Fifth Army landings – had ended up benefiting no one, but there was no question that the withdrawal of 1. Fallschirmjäger-Division, already weakened by Hitler's insistence on spreading its units among other divisions, had been a massive boon to the Allies. Foggia was captured by the British 1st Airborne on 27 September, and with it thirteen precious airfields, all of which were in theory equipped to take heavy four-engine bombers. It would take a little time to move the strategic air forces across, with all the supplies, spare parts, fuel, ordnance and ground crew that would be needed, but at a stroke the Allies had a complex of bases from which they could further tighten the aerial noose around the Third Reich. Ploesti, Germany's only source of oil, was within even closer range. So too were aircraft plants in southern Germany and Austria. At the Quebec Conference, capturing these airfields had been a major factor in the decision to invade Italy, from where the POINTBLANK directive – to destroy the Luftwaffe – could be further prosecuted. In fact, three of the prime motivations for invading Italy had already been accomplished: the Allies had the Foggia airfield complex, Italy was out of the war, and they had drawn German divisions away from the Western and Eastern Fronts. So, judged by the goals the Allies had set themselves, the Italian campaign was already a notable success; the only objective that still eluded them was Rome.

For the landing craft-starved Allies, the almost cost-free capture of the three Apulian ports was a considerable own goal on the part of the Germans because it meant that DUKE divisions could be landed in large troopships directly on to the quayside, with no limit to the size of the ship being used. This ensured that the build-up of supplies would be quicker too, both for Eighth Army divisions but also for the air forces moving to Foggia.

While 5th Division and the Canadians were battling from the toe, more troops were being landed directly into Taranto, so that by the end of September Lieutenant-General Charles Allfrey had his entire V Corps ashore, because in addition to the 1st Airborne he could call upon the 78th 'Battleaxe' Division, which had fought in Tunisia and in Sicily, and the 8th Indian Division, one of three sent from the Indian Army to the Mediterranean, which, although it had last fought a significant campaign two years earlier in Iraq, Iran and Syria, was none the less combat-experienced, well trained and full-strength.

Now that 78th Division were in Italy, a plan was being hatched to bounce the port of Termoli, further up the coast beyond the thumb-like Gargano peninsula, in a quick and daring grab. The idea was to land overnight Paddy Mayne's SRS and two Commando units, now formed into a Special Service Brigade, and they would then secure the town and two key bridges just to the north of Termoli, including one over the main road north – Highway 14, the Via Adriatica. Then 78th Division would advance from the south and from a subsequent seaborne lift meet the Special Service Brigade men and push on north up the coast. The New Zealanders were now on their way to Italy, and the Canadians were also picking their way through the centre. This would allow Eighth Army to advance on a broad front, but with its main thrust along the coast. When they reached Pescara – hopefully in the not-too-distant future – they could then start crossing back over the mountains to Rome. That was the plan, at any rate, but along their path were a number of rivers and hilltop and coastal towns that needed crossing and capturing – the unavoidable geographical nuisance of fighting up a narrow country with a long, mountainous spine: because where there were mountains, rivers always flowed from them. And rivers always wanted to get to the sea. Inevitably, that in turn meant the Allies would repeatedly have to cross rivers that ran pretty much at 90 degrees to the direction in which they, as a fighting force, wanted to travel. Rivers were easy to defend and also required bridges, which were easy for the Germans to blow up before any Allied troops could use them. Reaching Termoli was one thing, but beyond lay the River Trigno, then the River Sangro, and then the Moro. And beyond these rivers and mountains, eventually, was Pescara.

Among the units earmarked for Termoli was the 38th Irish Brigade, whose three battalions had battled hard across Sicily and, in one of the more impressive actions of the campaign, had captured the mountaintop town of Centuripe. Now the Irishmen were on Italian soil once more, having landed directly into Taranto on 25 September.

One of the platoon commanders in the 1st Royal Irish Fusiliers was Lieutenant Lawrie Franklyn-Vaile, who had only joined the 1st Battalion in Sicily in August and so had missed the heroics at Centuripe. Units like the Faughs – as the Royal Irish Fusiliers were known (and pronounced 'Fogs') – still retained a core local identity, but all across the British Army Scotsmen now found themselves in Cornish regiments, Welshmen in Yorkshire ones, and Kentish men in Lancashire battalions as local recruitment was replaced by a larger, more nationwide system. There was also a sprinkling of servicemen from the British Dominions, who either travelled to join or who had found themselves in Britain when the war began and answered the call. One such was Lawrie Franklyn-Vaile, who had been born and raised in Melbourne, Australia, and had only moved to England in his twenties; he'd hoped there would be more opportunities for a young and ambitious journalist in London than there had been back home. He'd enlisted as soon as war had been declared and had been swiftly selected for officer training. Once commissioned, and a little older than most of his fellow subalterns, he had found himself posted to the training depot in Omagh, Northern Ireland, where he looked set to sit out the war as an excellent and much-respected trainer of new recruits.

The years in Omagh had been very happy. He adored his English wife, Olive, and together they had a daughter, Valerie, born in March 1942. On the other hand, he wanted to be tested, believing it was morally his duty to serve overseas, and so when offered the chance to join the Faughs in Sicily he took his chance. He had gone without regrets but with plenty of heartache; who knew when he might see his wife and daughter again? The wrench of leaving them was hard to bear. Sicily, however, had been a gentle introduction to his overseas service. 'I am writing this letter to you sitting under a lemon tree,' he had written in his first letter to Olive on 2 September. 'Above me the hot sun beats down fiercely although it is tempered by a slight breeze and below is a huge vineyard extending almost down to the sea. It all seems very faraway from England and it is amazing to think that it is only just three weeks since I left you.' There was no such thing as regular post for troops serving abroad, and already he was looking forward to receiving his first letter from her. 'In the meantime, precious, look after yourself and remember I love you more than anything in the world.'

By 1 October the Faughs had reached Barletta, a decent stretch up the Adriatic coast and around eighty-five miles south of Termoli. Franklyn-Vaile, who was now second-in-command of D Company, wrote to Olive on this day, letting her know he was now in mainland Italy. Barletta, on the sea, was pleasant enough, but, like almost everyone new to the country, he'd been taken aback by what he'd seen so far. 'Other Italian towns we have passed are very dirty and the stench is appalling,' he wrote. 'The sanitation seems to be of the most primitive kind and most of the people look very dirty.' But the majority of the Italians were friendly; on the drive up, if they ever stopped they were soon surrounded by swarms of people; he noticed a lot of children were suffering from sores. It was pitiful. By day they were plagued by flies and by night by swarms of vicious mosquitoes. They'd not fired a shot, but already the country was proving challenging.

On the other side of the country, Fifth Army continued to bulldoze its way north, while in Naples itself the popular uprising had continued in isolated pockets – in the Vomero district, another in Posillipo and also Chiaia; all over the city people were rising up, connected by a common wave of anger but little common authority or command. Oberst Scholl brought in tanks to attack one barricade, but he and Balck were now more concerned with making sure that the harbours, industrial facilities and anything else that could be of use to the Allies were mined and destroyed. This was a more time-consuming operation than it might have been because the OKW insisted on a complete inventory of every-thing in Naples that might be useful and demanded a daily report of all that had been destroyed. The Nazis had always been obsessed with paper-work, but very often the demands being made far away in Berlin or Rastenberg did little more than hamper the efforts at the front.

At any rate, with the Allies closing in, going after Italian insurgents became a secondary priority. Consequently, the Germans' approach was one of containment and using artillery to shell areas of the city instead, which only battered Naples even more. On the 30th, and with German headquarters under threat, Oberst Scholl even arranged a prisoner exchange; certainly, he was not planning to impose his 100-for-one rule.

Filippo Caracciolo, meanwhile, was still desperately trying to galvan-ize both the insurgents and the political underground to form a united command under the banner of the CLN. On Thursday, 30 September he was invited by some insurgents to attend a meeting in a church sacristy. A large number of people had gathered, including Aurelio Spoto, whom Caracciolo knew and who had been one of the local ringleaders in the Chiaia area, and Leopoldo Piccardi, who was – on paper, at any rate – a minister in Badoglio's government. There was a lot of shouting and a lot of anger. Piccardi appealed for calm and national solidarity, while the insurgents wanted revolution. Unity was needed in the face of the advan-cing Allies, but, Caracciolo believed, behind the CLN, not the Badoglio government. In the end, not much was decided and not much agreed. 'I leave the session with a sense of deep regret,' jotted Caracciolo. 'Naples and its anger, Naples and its insurrection, the suffering and blood of Naples, deserved quite different interpreters and quite a different fate.'

The next day, Caracciolo woke early to find Naples abuzz with cautious excitement and rumours that the Germans had abandoned the city. Guns still thundered in the distance and small arms could be heard, but he saw no German troops. Crossing a deserted Piazza Dante, however, his spirits sagged. 'It offers a bleak expanse of death, loneliness, horror,' he noted. 'Wide patches of blood, here already slimy with clot, there still very fresh, make the pavement purple.' Scholl, he learned soon after, had left at dawn, after a final prisoner exchange to ensure his safe passage. Then, at around 9.30 a.m., British armour of the King's Dragoon Guards and the Royal Scots Greys reached Naples, followed by men of the 82nd Airborne. Naples had been liberated. Just how liberated the population would be, however, remained to be seen.

CHAPTER 17

Termoli

'THE ITALIANS ARE GENERALLY hostile to us,' noted Oberstarzt – Chief Medical Officer – Wilhelm Mauss. 'To them we are the ones hindering them having their much yearned-for peace, waging war in their country; on the other hand, our necessary measures for warfare and defence do have an exceptionally hard and heavy impact upon them.' Mauss had some sympathy, but not a lot. He had just arrived back in Italy after a blissful home leave but was now resuming his former duties at XIV Panzerkorps. Quite apart from the importance of overseeing the supply, staffing and organization of military hospitals in the area, his position kept him at corps headquarters with access to the command and a privileged view and understanding of what was going on. He knew General Balck slightly, but he was friends with Hube, who was expected back from leave imminently. Mauss was looking forward to seeing him again.

Corps headquarters was in a chestnut grove in the countryside near Mignano, a small town straddling the same Highway 6 that ran through Cassino, ten miles to the north. The town was dwarfed by huge mountains, Monte Camino to the south and Monte Sammucro to the north, but also stood at the head of a long, low mountain, appropriately called Monte Lungo. The valley here forked either side of Lungo, although on the northern side, just west of Mignano, was a further, smaller, round mountain, also well named, Monte Rotondo. The Via Casilina, Highway 6, as well as a rail line, threaded its way through Mignano and then on through the narrow gap between Montes Lungo and Rotondo. This stretch, the Mignano Gap, was an obvious defensive strongpoint and as Mauss arrived was already being turned into a forward position of the

Gustav Line – a formidable obstacle for the advancing Allies before they even reached the main defences beyond.

Mauss was very happy with the corps camp; the setting and scenery could not be faulted. He felt rather like a grand pasha in his tent, erected alongside the rest of the Ia, the corps operations staff. On the floor was a real Persian carpet, there were electric blankets for his camp bed and a seat with a yellow brocade cover. He could hardly have asked for more. 'In peacetime,' he noted, 'many would pay a lot of money to enjoy this feudal romanticism.' Mauss was forty-four, with thinning hair, a trim moustache and spectacles, and a duelling scar on his right cheek from his student days. From Marburg, a university town in north Germany, he was bright, well read and intellectual, but also an ardent nationalist, views which he shared with his father. Defeat in the last war, in which he'd served as an artilleryman, had left a deep impression on him; and although afterwards he'd studied medicine, he had been determined to remain in the army. Needless to say, Mauss was also an enthusiastic follower of National Socialism.

Despite the beauty of his surroundings, Mauss had noticed a number of changes on his journey south and even in Cassino, where he had paused. It had recently been bombed by the Allies, although not severely, but all the shops now appeared to be closed, and the Italian pharmacy Mauss had used in the summer, when he'd been establishing hospitals in the area, was boarded up. He found it a little painful to see this pretty, charming town that he had got to know so well now looking so dead and empty.

He was also brought up to speed on the latest situation at the front. Naples had fallen but, he was told, not before all the harbour and industrial facilities were destroyed. Gas, electricity and water plants had also been blasted. This, he noted, would have a devastating effect on a city which during normal times had a population of nigh on a million and was the most densely populated in Europe. No hotel was usable and food supplies had also been cut off. It would be hard for the population, he knew, although not undeserved. What did they expect after so shamefully selling their German allies down the river? 'Elsewhere the surrendered territory is also being systematically destroyed,' he reported in the diary he'd been keeping since the start of the war. 'All livestock is now driven out or slaughtered, all stock which in some way have value for the war effort is moved to the rear. The country can no longer feed itself from the land, without the English help it must starve. The people must suffer severely for their treason.' It wasn't just a question of revenge;

rather, by adopting a scorched earth policy as they retreated, they hoped to make life more difficult for the Allies – the cost of feeding a starving nation, the possibility of some kind of Italian revolt; anything that slowed the Allies was fair game.

Early on Saturday, 2 October, the SRS had pulled into the small port of Manfredonia, which stood on the southern side of the strange, mountainous thumb that extended out from the Adriatic coast. There, Lieutenant Peter Davis and his fellows in the SRS spotted Lieutenant-General Sir Miles Dempsey on the quayside, talking earnestly with Paddy Mayne. Dempsey, the XIII Corps commander, had now shifted his HQ, like much of Eighth Army, to the eastern side of the country, but seeing him in discussion with Mayne, Davis knew that something was up. Before Dempsey had gone, Harry Poat was gathering the troop around him and confirming that they would be heading to Termoli, further on up the coast, that very night.

It was dark out at sea as, some hours later, they approached the town. Ever since the desert, there had been a question mark over how best to use the SAS, as it had been before its recent rename as the SRS. In North Africa they'd been dashing about, deep in the desert, and striking far behind enemy lines in daring hit-and-run raids. Such operations only really worked, however, in the vast and largely empty expanse of the Western Desert, so they needed to adapt to the new theatre in which they found themselves. Currently, though, they were being treated as Commandos – set up for quick *coup de main* strike operations; and in fact, for Operation DEVON, as the Termoli assault was code-named, Paddy Mayne's men had been banded together with Nos 3 and 41 Commando to form a new Special Service Brigade.

The plan was a simple one. They would hit the beach in landing craft just a little way to the north of the town. No. 3 Commando would clear the beach and form a bridgehead, while 41 Commando would head straight into the town and, with luck, capture it before dawn. The SRS, meanwhile, would push on and try to capture and hold two bridges over the River Biferno about two miles inland. The first carried the Via Adriatica northwards, the second a lesser road. No. 3 Troop was to take the first bridge, 1 Troop the second, and Poat's 2 Troop was to climb and secure a long rolling ridge, rising to around 300 feet, that ran from the south-west to the edge of the town and rather dominated the otherwise softly undulating coastal area around Termoli.

Peter Davis had a sinking feeling about the entire plan and was worried that his luck must surely be running out, but nerves were understandable. It was also a very dark, moonless night with rain, which didn't help, but as it happened they landed in pretty much the right place without a shot being fired, and after being gathered together by Harry Poat, 2 Troop were soon on their way. The going was bad, the rain making the ground slippery, and they struggled to clamber up the steep railway cutting that lay between the beach and the ground beyond. They all eventually made it, however, and soon after crossed Highway 14 and began climbing the ridge. The eastern sky began to pale, but they met no enemy at all, found their way easily enough and, to Davis's surprise and relief, by dawn they held the ridge as planned. 'It was scarcely possible,' he noted, 'to believe we were still technically behind enemy lines, so peaceful was the surrounding area.'

After Foggia, Jupp Klein had been ordered to take his group up to San Severo and then on to Termoli. Their task was clear: to lay mines, blow bridges and hamper the Allies in any way they could. Before San Severo, which lay at the northern edge of the Foggia Plain, they had blown a tree across the road and behind it set up a camouflaged 88mm flak gun they'd found abandoned at Foggia. Hidden in vineyards on either side, Klein and his men had soon after seen four British armoured cars advancing, recce troops of the 78th Battleaxe Division. The armoured cars approached, slowing down as they spotted the tree across the road. He'd instructed his men to hit the first and the last, because he wanted to trap the middle two and then take the vehicles for themselves. In fact, the men on the 88 hit the second with their first shot – they were not trained gunners, after all – and Klein watched in wonder as the armoured car commander was hurtled high into the air by the blast. A moment later a second round hit the third car with much the same result. Immediately, Klein's men rushed towards the other two, pulling the dazed Tommies from their hatches.

The captured men were in a state of shock. Klein offered a tot of grappa both to his men and to the Tommies and began questioning them. None of them told him much until one of the British suddenly blurted out, 'For heaven's sake, you all have English faces!'

'How do you think we should look?' Klein replied in English. 'Like Huns, with horns on our heads?' Rather stunned by this display of ignorance, Klein discovered that the man had been a teacher from Yorkshire.

They took the prisoners with them into the town, along with the two armoured cars, which they promptly recruited into their Pionier platoon.

A few days later, on Saturday, 2 October, the company reached Termoli, Klein and his men all tired after long days on the road north, but satisfied they'd managed to lay a large number of mines, blast several bridges and prepare a number of blocking positions. He was also glad to know they would now have a few days' rest; no one was expecting the Tommies to get this far any time soon. Billeted in a large room in a school, Klein and his platoon ate and drank and then sank into a weary sleep.

A few short hours later, however, he was roughly woken by one of the company messengers.

'Tommies are here, Herr Unteroffizier,' he said, 'and we should go with the platoon to make a counter-attack immediately!'

Klein thought he must be mad, but the messenger was insistent and so, cursing, they got themselves up. Outside the building, a burst of red tracer flashed past down the street. Clearly, the British really were in the town. Quickly, Klein pulled back inside, gathered his men together and then found Hauptmann Ernst Frömming, his company commander. There were also some naval troops and men from Oberst Ludwig Heilmann's 3. Fallschirmjäger-Regiment in Termoli – Klein reckoned as many as 200 in all. Still certain that no Tommies could get there by road for a couple of days at least, he assumed the plan would be to stay and fight and kick the Allies back into the sea. Climbing up from the port area, they were soon on the higher ground overlooking the harbour. As they'd moved, they had engaged the enemy and even managed to capture a few Commandos. Klein had no idea how many enemy had landed, but it didn't strike him as being a huge force. Strong leadership and determined fighting, Klein believed, and the British attack would likely collapse.

To Klein's disgust, however, Frömming now ordered them to fall back and abandon the town. Whether the small force of German troops in Termoli could have successfully fought back was a moot point, but Klein and his men were appalled. They'd not even tried. 'We broke away from the enemy,' noted Klein, 'and let the prisoners go after a while, since they would only have been a hindrance on our return march.'

They headed off along the southern finger-like ridge that ran from the town towards the hilltop village of Guglionesi, eight miles away to the south-west, but although they were abandoning Termoli now, on the morning of Sunday, 3 October, they were not leaving for good. Help was on its way. The 16. Panzer-Division, bruised at Salerno and but since then in reserve in the centre of the leg, were closest and Kesselring immediately instructed von Vietinghoff to send them with all haste to hurry towards Termoli and, with the Fallschirmjäger, take back the town. Salerno might have been lost, but Kesselring was determined to throw the Allies here back into the sea and reclaim the port.

Peter Davis's forebodings had not been so misplaced after all.

There was no question that a lot was being expected of 1. Fallschirmjäger-Division, which, at the end of September, was spread across the entire eastern side of the Italian leg, holding a mountain-top town here, setting up a roadblock there, laying mines and carrying out demolitions wherever they could, and generally trying to hold up the pursuing Eighth Army as much as possible. While the Pionier-Bataillon was in Termoli, for example, the Maschinengewehr-Bataillon was in the mountains of the Campania region, harrying the Canadians as they continued their own epic journey from the toe of the boot.

Jupp Klein wasn't the only one capturing vehicles either, because around 5.30 p.m. on 26 September one of Martin Pöppel's sergeants spotted four armoured cars winding their way towards them. Some 800 yards short of them, they turned back, but Pöppel's men opened fire, forcing the last in the line to stop. A small assault party was sent to round up the cursing Canadians and the Fallschirmjäger men then drove the car back to their own lines. 'Now we've got ourselves a fast little vehicle,' noted Pöppel, 'a first-class country car with a twin-barrelled machine-gun at the front and a super-heavy 15mm machine-gun at the rear. We're delighted with our motorised reinforcement.'

The hazards of this cat-and-mouse chase through the mountains were many, however, and not always caused by clashes with the enemy. Two days later, it started to pour with rain – they had seen it rolling in as night fell, a livid lightning storm on the horizon. But it quickly caught them up, and no sooner had Pöppel made a comment to his driver about the dangerous driving conditions in rain along these winding, narrow mountain roads than a lorry carrying a Panzerabwehrkanone – Pak – 40 75mm anti-tank gun turned over. The wounded were groaning, the convoy was now at a halt and the rain falling in buckets. Everyone was drenched. An ambulance was called up, and Pöppel asked for another truck to help pull out the lorry that had overturned. In the dark, the rain sheeting down, such incidents were extremely testing. They eventually managed to get going again and reached a main road, only for Pöppel's own vehicle to break down. One of his men managed to get it going again just a quarter of an hour later, by which time they'd had a tot of some unknown Italian herbal liquor. It was appreciated, but didn't stop them shivering in the wet and the cold. A little further up the road they came across 10. Kompanie from Heilmann's 3. Fallschirmjäger, and from them Pöppel was able to borrow an Opel Blitz truck and go back to pull out the overturned lorry. It was 2 a.m. by the time he rejoined the battalion near Roseto Valfortore, a small, remote village in the hill country on the western edge of Apulia.

They remained soaked, with no means of drying their clothes for much of the next day, but at last that night Pöppel got a good night's rest and woke with the sun in his eyes. 'One of those mornings that are never bettered,' he noted, 'that make you want to celebrate and forget this whole murderous business that's swamping the world.' Later, though, new orders arrived, signed off with the phrase 'good hunting'. Pöppel wanted to puke – he hated such glib phrases; more than that, it was a reminder of the grim reality: that they were all ordinary soldiers with a war to fight – and to try and survive. Their brief stay in this beautiful little Eden was over.

On the west coast, the Allies had moved into Naples. Frank Pearce drove down into the city on Saturday, 2 October, after finally leaving the Salerno area. Traffic was slow because all the bridges were blown and everything, it seemed, was passing over one single Bailey bridge. As they reached the city it began to rain, adding to the sense of desolation. 'In Naples we went down to the docks,' he noted. 'All twisted mess of wreckage and the buildings for blocks around a desolate mass of stones.' The people seemed glad to see them, mobbing their truck and asking for food. A humanitarian disaster was already developing. Neapolitans were beginning to starve, but also to die of thirst.

Norman Lewis reached Naples two days later. He'd been hospitalized with malaria, which was striking down as many men as battlefield casualties; on 27 September, the Chief Medical Officer of Fifth Army reported 2,122 cases and a further 1,250 other hospitalizations with fever. However, discharged by the American doctors a week later, he'd been given a US Army uniform – his battledress had been taken and, presumably, destroyed – and sent on his way. He then picked up a ride in an American truck that was heading to Naples. The journey wound its way through the shattered remains of Battipaglia, whose destruction Lewis blamed entirely on General Clark. He thought it resembled an Italian Guernica. An old man approached them and begged for some food. They got talking and he told Lewis that almost no one had been left alive, that the bodies were still in the ruins. Certainly, from the stench and amount of flies, Lewis could well believe it. Little attempt had yet been made to clear the rubble. 'So much so,' noted Lewis, 'that while standing by the truck talking to the old man, I felt something uneven under one foot, shifted my position, and then glancing down realized that what had at first seemed to be a mass of sacking was in fact the charred and flattened corpse of a German soldier.'

They drove on and eventually reached the edge of Naples, sweeping down into the Piazza Carlo III, just as Filippo Caracciolo had a couple of weeks earlier on his return to the city. There the truck pulled over, beside the enormous 350-yard-long Ospedale l'Albergo Reale dei Poveri, the Bourbon Hospital for the Poor. Several soldiers immediately came over and began lifting boxes out of the back of the truck, taking them up the steps into the building. Lewis thought he'd better lend a hand, his boots crunching on broken glass. Not a single pane remained in any of the windows of this huge edifice. Following the Americans inside, he found himself in a huge room crowded with troops but also with a row of Neapolitan women, sat about a yard apart, their backs to the wall, and each with a stash of tins beside them. Lewis looked at these women aghast; their faces were devoid of expression, as though numb to the ghastliness of what they had to do to get food.

One young soldier, goaded by his pals, eventually put a tin of rations down beside one of the women, unbuttoned his flies and then lowered himself on to her. 'A perfunctory jogging of the haunches began and came quickly to an end,' noted Lewis. 'A moment later he was on his feet and buttoning up again. It had been something to get over as soon as possible. He might have been submitting to field punishment rather than the act of love.' This was what liberation by the democracies looked like to Lewis: barely comprehensible levels of destruction and the subjugation of the civilian population by offering tins of food in return for sex and, no doubt soon enough, a dose of the clap.

The prospect of an outbreak of venereal disease was a concern, but it was just one of a very long list of dire problems in Naples. The existing civil authorities, such as they were, formally surrendered Naples on 1 October to Colonel Edgar E. Hume, the head of AMGOT for Fifth Army, and Brigadier-General Frank J. McSherry, the Deputy Chief of AMGOT in the Mediterranean theatre. McSherry was also responsible for the writing of policies, directives and instructions for AMGOT staff.

As Patrician of Naples and a senior player in the emerging CLN and also Action Party, Filippo Caracciolo had had a two-hour conversation with Colonel Hume the following morning, 2 October. Caracciolo warmed to him immediately – Hume, in his early fifties, had a good-natured face and appeared to be willing to listen. Naples was to fall under his jurisdiction; as the chief AMGOT officer in Fifth Army he had also become the new Governor of Campania, at least certainly until the political situation could be properly thrashed out with the Badoglio government. 'He is intelligent and full of honest good willing,' wrote Caracciolo, 'but totally unaware of the problems he is preparing to face.' Other officials were invited to join them, and they occasionally asked some perceptive questions, but also many that reflected their naivety.

Caracciolo tried to explain, as calmly as possible, the situation in Naples. There was enormous political unrest, with many young men wandering around with weapons, and the conditions in the city were terrible. Naples was home to more than 900,000 people, the third-largest in Italy after Rome and Milan, and more than half a million were still there despite the relentless bombing and round-ups by the Germans. The rumours of plague and pestilence had been exaggerated, but food was acutely short and the shops mostly empty. There was no electricity at all, and almost no water. The Germans had destroyed the main aqueduct in seven places and all the reservoirs, bar one, had been drained; that had only been saved by an Italian managing to cut the fuse set to demolish it without the Germans realizing. Only a trickle of water remained at a handful of hydrants, which were constantly besieged by queues of desperate people. The sewers were also badly damaged, and without running water were in danger of becoming clogged very quickly, then creating the perilous prospect of diseases such as typhoid and dysentery. The lack of electricity wasn't just about lighting and pumps; it also made the operation of flour mills impossible, thus depriving the population of the most basic element of their diet. The Germans had burned most of the city's hotels and destroyed all public transportation.

These, then, were just some of the problems that Colonel Hume and his staff had to try and overcome. Naples had become a modern-day Augean Stables; at any rate, the challenge was certainly a Herculean one.

The Canadians were getting close to the tails of 1. Fallschirmjäger Maschinengewehr-Bataillon. By 1 October, Leutnant Martin Pöppel and his company were at San Bartolomeo in Galdo, eight miles north-west of

Roseto Valfortore. Later that day they were shelled and at 8 p.m. the Canadians broke through on the battalion's right, capturing a Pak 40 and other equipment. A few hours later, the order arrived for Pöppel's company to withdraw. They slipped away from the village on foot to an assembly area a couple of miles further on where lorries were waiting to drive them away.

It was now cold and wet and Pöppel was exhausted, but by the 3rd his company had been put into reserve and they were able to rest up. That night he found some straw in a barn and managed to sleep right through. Only their own guns firing woke him at 6 a.m. the following morning. 'Blankets over my head,' he jotted, 'and back to sleep again.' Later that morning, feeling refreshed, he set off to see the battalion commander to organize some supplies for his men. His route took him through Gambatesa, a village perched on a narrow ridge; the road on the far side wound its way down via a series of hairpins, and while turning on one of these his right wheel hit a large stone, the car lost control and overturned down the bank running down from the side of the road. Pöppel was flung out of his seat and then hit a glancing blow in the pelvis by the car as it rolled past. 'A grab down there reassures me that everything is still there,' he wrote, 'but the left testicle has been forced out of the sac and is starting to swell and looks a disgusting blue.' Lying there, he couldn't help thinking what a damn stupid way it was to be put out of action. And he'd just been promoted to Oberleutnant too, and made company commander, with 180 men – on paper, at any rate – to look after. He was not quite twenty-three years old, but command would now have to wait. Eventually an ambulance arrived, jolting him all the way to a field clearing station and causing new agonies with every bump. There he was stitched up and then taken to Rome, where he was told that within a few days he would be sent by hospital train back to Germany. His time in Italy, for the time being at any rate, was over.

Meanwhile, on the Adriatic coast, the battle was about to be resumed at Termoli. By the afternoon of Monday, 4 October, Lieutenant Peter Davis and his section were back in the town after a quiet day patrolling the San Giacomo Ridge and seeing very little. Heavy rain had fallen constantly for around eighteen hours, which had made the experience miserable, but they found a barn in which to shelter. The entire SRS was now in the Villa Comunale, a large monastic-looking building dominating the Piazza Sant'Antonio which overlooked the narrow stretch of the city's beach below. Paddy Mayne's men had taken over the large ground floor and, with their task over and part of 78th Division having arrived, were expected to be shipped out later.

Davis had not been there long when Mayne asked him about the rumours of a heavy German counter-attack. A few shells had whistled over earlier that morning, Davis told him, but he had hardly regarded that as a major enemy counter-punch. Mayne was inclined to agree, but as the afternoon wore on more messages arrived reporting ever more enemy forces. An infantry brigadier then radioed asking Mayne for the entire SRS to help him strengthen the line. This Mayne was reluctant to do: he thought the strength of the enemy assault was most likely being exaggerated, and in any case was loath to risk his troops in a traditional infantry role. Eventually, however, two sections were sent off to help that evening, but not Davis and his men. Instead he took himself off to try and get some sleep.

If the German counter-attack appeared to have been something of a slow burner, that was because it was. The 16. Panzer-Division had been only forty miles from Termoli, part of its shift east, when news arrived that it was to head urgently towards the town; but a division and its many component parts could never move as one, so had begun arriving piecemeal in the early hours of 4 October. That day, with one Kampfgruppe advancing from the south-west and another from the north, they had begun shelling as artillery had arrived, moving along the high ground around the hilltop village of Guglionesi. They then tentatively pushed on, across a low saddle and up to San Giacomo, a small village on the ridge where Peter Davis and his section had been patrolling earlier. The plan was for the Germans to hold this key high ground and then, once all available forces were assembled, launch the counter-attack.

The heavy rain had brought few troubles to the Germans but had badly hindered the progress of the leading 78th Division troops coming up from the south and trying to cross the River Biferno, which reached the sea a couple of miles to the south of Termoli and cut across the British approach. The bridge carrying the Via Adriatica had been blown up by Jupp Klein's men before the launch of Operation DEVON, and so overnight on that Monday and into Tuesday, 5 October, sappers had been frantically trying to get a Bailey bridge across. They'd still not been able to finish this by morning, but six Shermans had managed to ford the river. In doing so, however, they had turned the crossing point into a morass of mud, so that no further tanks could make it over the river until the bridge was complete; one that tried had become bogged. These six tanks from the 3rd County of London Yeomanry, along with infantry of the 8th Argyll and Sutherland Highlanders, now attempted to clear the Coccia Ridge. This was part of a long, lozenge shaped ridge but was divided by a wooded ravine in the middle. The village of San Giacomo stood on the western side, which was the part of the ridge that Peter Davis's section had been patrolling. The Coccia Ridge was parallel but east of it, and on its top was a fairly flat plateau about two-thirds of a mile wide. Running from its northern end down towards the main coast road and the town itself were further folds and shallow, wooded ravines. Neither the San Giacomo nor the Coccia Ridge was particularly high – perhaps 250–300 feet above sea level – but they did dominate the surrounding area. The British plan on the morning of the 5th was to try and get a firm hold of the Coccia Ridge and then hang on until the rest of the brigade crossed the River Biferno and the 38th Irish Brigade arrived by sea later that night.

In the meantime, German artillery was shelling both the British sappers trying to bridge the Biferno and the build-up of troops south of the river; despite this, overnight the Argylls had managed to advance on to the northern end of the Coccia Ridge and also push on towards San Giacomo. At first light, however, the Germans, including the Fallschirmjäger of Hauptmann Steiner's Pionier-Bataillon, had succeeded in working around them and then forcing them to fall back. In the process, Jupp Klein and his men had picked up an abandoned anti-tank gun.

By around midday, the Pioniere had pushed on and were now heading down off the northern end of the San Giacomo Ridge. They could see the town clearly, just a mile or two ahead, while in front of them was the junction of the San Giacomo road and the Via Adriatica heading north. Not far away they also spotted a handful of British tanks moving forward using the road to San Giacomo as their axis – the ravines were too steep and too wooded to cross. These were the Shermans that had managed to ford the Biferno earlier. The task of Jupp Klein and his men was to knock them out, but it was far easier said than done. Supporting them they now had two StuG assault guns from 16. Panzer and also the captured anti-tank gun, but the challenge was how to bring these to bear. Klein's men were not trained gunners, and even the low profile of the StuGs would be easily seen by the Shermans as they attempted to move off the ridge. Feldwebel Kabinger now devised a plan. In their current infantry role, the Pioniere could move off the road and, using the western edge of the ridge, move forward without being seen. Behind them, however, the road from San Giacomo dropped into a small saddle in which the two StuGs could remain out of sight. Kabinger suggested that the Pioniere scurry forward with machine guns and fire at the Shermans, aiming for the hatches. That would make the commander and driver drop down inside, at which point they would be dependent on periscopes, which were never much use. And hopefully they'd be distracted anyway. While the Tommy tanks were focused on the machine-gun fire, the StuGs could move forward and, with men on the ground to help direct their fire, blast the Shermans.

Klein thought this a sound idea and, sure enough, as the machine guns started firing he heard the engine of the lead StuG roar into life, clattering and squeaking up the short slope of the saddle. A short moment later, a short, dry bang, and the first Sherman was hit, exactly as planned. Klein was over the moon, and even more so when, a little while later, a second Sherman was hit. 'Bright flames erupted from the tanks we'd knocked out,' noted Klein, 'and from time to time the ammunition inside detonated with a thunderous roar.'

They now realized that a number of British infantry, startled by the sudden loss of two tanks, were taking cover behind a haystack no more than 40 yards from the farmhouse to which Klein's platoon had pulled back. Immediately Klein directed their machine guns on to it. Their MG42s had an incredible rate of fire, which lost them accuracy, but they could certainly spew out a great weight of bullets over a comparatively wide area and in a very short time. Hand grenades were also hurled, screams and shouts could be heard, and Klein now yelled at the top of his voice for them to come out with their hands up. And so they did. Klein thought them to be Paratroopers, but they were the remains of a platoon of Argylls – about twenty in all.

News reached Klein that the StuGs were now pulling back to rearm and refuel and that some panzers would soon be joining them instead. Realizing that the remaining Shermans had withdrawn, Klein led his men down over the eastern end of the San Giacomo Ridge, passing the burning hulks as they did so, and then clambered up the short, steep slope of the Coccia Ridge beyond. The air was heavy with the smell of battle. Cordite, burning flesh, rubber and fuel. 'Even in Russia,' noted Klein, 'I had often had to take in that unmistakable stench.' It often gave him nightmares and made him think of the inevitable battles to come.

*

At the Villa Comunale, Peter Davis had been woken by the sounds of small arms and shellfire all too close at hand and Mayne's men had been put on half an hour's notice. The Germans were certainly closing in on the town. At 2.30 p.m. the SRS were suddenly ordered to hurriedly help hold a weak point in the line to the immediate west. Paddy Mayne took one group and headed off, while the rest were to load up into trucks now parked up just below the piazza. The vehicles were lined up, toe-to-tail, along a wall opposite a row of houses, and at 2.45 p.m. the men began clambering into them. To his delight, Davis saw that Sergeant Bill McNinch was driving the first truck he reached; he'd been out of the section with a bad foot but was clearly on the mend and helping with driving duties. No sooner had Davis's section loaded up than Johnny Wiseman, one of the desert veterans, arrived and told them his section was supposed to be in this particular truck. Davis muttered that he thought one truck was as good as another, but did as Wiseman asked and they moved to the vehicle in front.

Just at the very moment the men were all packed into the half-dozen vehicles, a deafening high-pitched shriek ripped the air apart; then came an immense detonation followed by a second and third air-sucking, all-consuming scream and explosion. Then two more swiftly followed, five in all. Davis watched a wall of a house collapse and felt the air violently drawn from around him as though his whole being was suddenly encased in this moment of devastation. Immense noise, smoke, dust. Figures of men stumbling through smoke. Air choking and thick. A rush for cover, the brain hardly thinking, hardly coping with such horror.

Slowly the dust began to subside and Davis realized that, incredibly, he was unscathed. The street, though, was unrecognizable. Huge chunks of masonry, a collapsed house, one of the trucks mangled and burning angrily. An Italian family had been standing in the doorway of the house as the shells had landed. The mother and father were dead, the girl had vanished and the little boy was prostrate on the ground, his intestines unravelling but still alive. Suddenly he got up and began running and screaming. Reg Seekings, one of the SAS originals and among the toughest of them all, caught him, took out his pistol and shot the boy; it was the only thing he could have done for him. The seventeen men in McNinch's truck had all been killed; each had been carrying a handful of grenades as the shell whammed into the vehicle. Half of Chris O'Dowd's skull was found caught on the telegraph wires above while his torso was discovered on the second floor of a building 60 yards away.

Johnny Wiseman had been yet to board his truck when the first shell screamed in so was also miraculously alive. With Davis and his section they began the grim task of trying to see what could be done. What looked like a slab of meat in a butcher's shop lay on the road until Davis noticed scraps of khaki cloth. 'Here lay a man with half his head blown off,' he noted, 'an arm lay there, and somewhere else an unrecognisable lump of flesh.' He could barely comprehend that a few minutes earlier these shattered pieces of human remains had been living, breathing young men. Nor could he understand how he'd survived. It seemed impossible.

Those still standing, numb with shock, did what they could – retrieving O'Dowd's piece of skull and scooping up remains – but there was still a battle to fight and they were needed. Mayne was calling for them. So, the survivors, Peter Davis and his section included, then hurried forward to join the rest of the squadron now helping to hold the line to the western edge of the city.

CHAPTER 18

Desolation

O N THE OTHER SIDE of the leg, Norman Lewis was witness to a different kind of desolation in Naples. He had now rejoined his colleagues of 312th FS Section in the Palazzo Ravaschieri di Satriano, on the Riviera di Chiaia near the seafront. A seventeenth-century baroque palace, it overlooked the narrow strip of public gardens of dusty palms and walkways, and beyond these the Bay of Naples. The FS Office had made its HQ on the first floor, at the top of a sweeping marble staircase. Lewis was delighted with these surroundings, although depressed by the state of the city. There were ruins everywhere, sometimes blocking an entire street, as well as bomb craters, abandoned and burned-out trams and other vehicles. Everything smelled of charred wood.

Labour was needed for the clean-up operation, but all Italians had to be vetted by Lewis and his colleagues as potential security risks. This task was made a lot easier because the Fascists had kept tabs on pretty much everyone, and they found all their files in the Questura – the central police headquarters. None the less, nearly all the information was mind-numbingly uninteresting and revealed nothing apart from a tendency to pursue sexual adventures and that most Italians were politically agnostic. A suspects' file had to be created, though, and that task was given to Lewis. It meant laboriously going through all the files left in the German Consulate but also sifting through an astonishing deluge of denunciations which now started pouring in. 'They were delivered in person,' noted Lewis, 'by people nourishing every kind of grudge, or even shoved into the hands of the sentry at the gate.' Most of the denunciations were clearly personal vendettas and nothing more; others were quite eccentric. One person accused a priest of having shown blue movies to Germans; another was reported because he had an obsessive fear of cats. Lewis found the work tedious in the extreme.

To make matters worse, their team was soon spread to the four winds – three were posted to the Sorrento peninsula, another to the town of Nola, and three more were tied down by other administrative duties, so that soon only four remained 'to confront the security problems of that ant-hill of humanity, the city of Naples itself'.

Yet progress of sorts was being made in Naples. Several electrical sub-stations were found to be repairable and work was under way to restore them as soon as possible. In the meantime, the engines from two Italian submarines found in the harbour were used to generate some power for pumping water. Port facilities had been restored so quickly that within six days 200 tons of food were being unloaded daily; it was nothing like enough, but it was a start. The United States was the most technologically advanced nation in the world and had brought plenty of that know-how to the war; brilliant engineers had been swiftly brought in to weave their magic. Miracles of modern engineering and ingenuity were taking place.

Furthermore, the rain that had now struck Italy was helping the Nea-politans. Downpours were allowing civilians to collect water in pans, and also helped flush out much of the sewer system. Pumping machinery had been given emergency repairs by Fifth Army engineers in record time. Among those helping were combat engineers like Frank Pearce. 'Past two days we have been working at docks cleaning it up for use,' he jotted on 5 October. 'Ships sunk all over the place and all buildings ruined.' They'd help set up a water line, but people were still fighting over it despite best efforts to marshal the queues. The following day, 6 October, a delayed mine blew up just as he and a friend were driving through the city in their jeep – it had happened only a block away. 'Debris filled the air, big chunks of pavement and dust,' he recorded. 'Civilians running and screaming. No one hurt. Blew hole about fifty feet wide, fifteen feet deep. We're lucky.'

At Termoli, meanwhile, the battle had reached a critical moment. That night, 6 October, at around 10 p.m., and with a perimeter around Ter-moli still holding to the west and north, the 38th Irish Brigade landed and the men were hurriedly sent forward to reinforce the Special Service

Brigade of SRS men and Commandos. For Lawrie Franklyn-Vaile, now promoted to captain and second-in-command of B Company, this was to be his first taste of front-line combat.

In fact, they'd joined the battle at the very moment British fortunes were changing. Just fifteen minutes after the attack on the SRS men the Bailey bridge across the Biferno had been completed, and since then many tanks had rumbled across the river, the Country of London Yeomanry later bolstered by the arrival of the Canadian Three Rivers Regiment, which had been rushed forward to help. Fighter-bombers of the Desert Air Force also swept over and hammered the German positions so that by nightfall the British had managed to get back on to the Coccia Ridge once more. The plan was to counter-attack early the next morning.

By first light on Thursday, 7 October, Jupp Klein and the Pionier-Bataillon were dug in on the Coccia Ridge alongside a company of grenadiers from 16. Panzer. Not for the first time since the battle had begun, Klein felt that a golden opportunity to strike had gone begging the previous afternoon. They'd had the Tommies on the back foot. Shermans knocked out and the rest pulling back. Termoli had been right there, in front of them, almost within touching distance, ripe for the plucking! A determined and massed drive would have surely seen them win the day.

Platoon sergeants, however, did not always see the wider picture and 16. Panzer, which had barely paused after facing the full brunt of Salerno, were struggling not only with casualties but also with malaria. General Sieckenius had been able to see what Klein could not: that they had simply not had enough troops or firepower to drive home their earlier successes the previous day. And if the 16. Panzer command had sensed that the town was out of reach then, the door had been most definitely closed by the morning of the 7th, as the rain of British fire now hurtling over demonstrated all too clearly. Klein himself was lucky to be alive after a mortar shell landed near his foxhole and knocked him unconscious.

'They've got Unteroffizier Klein!' he heard one of his men shout just as he was beginning to regain his senses.

'You might have thought so, but I'm still alive!' he'd yelled back.

Around mid-morning, after a heavy barrage, the British attacked, anti-tank guns firing first from hidden positions in the treeline at the eastern edge of the plateau. Near Klein, several scout and armoured cars were hit and burst into flames and then suddenly Shermans were emerging too, infantry scurrying behind, the tanks blasting their main guns and spraying machine-gun fire. The Pioniere let rip with their MG42s but the neighbouring grenadiers quickly hoisted a white flag. Klein was appalled. The air was now filled with screaming shells, the burst of explosions, the whirring and hissing of bullets. Again and again, over the radio, the Pioniere screamed for the support of some anti-tank guns. None came to help them. Under the weight of this assault they could not hold their position and they now upped and ran, falling back to the wooded ravine behind them and between the two ridges of San Giacomo and Coccia.

It was inevitable that San Giacomo would soon be overrun, so they fell back again, this time four miles to Guglionesi. By the time they got there it was clear that the battle was lost; that afternoon, at 4.35 p.m., General Herr, the LXXVI Panzerkorps commander, issued the order for a general withdrawal. The Germans were not getting their hands back on Termoli.

'I have just had my first battle experience,' Captain Lawrie Franklyn-Vaile wrote to his wife the following day, 7 October, reassuring her that he had come through all right. 'A bullet whisked across my hand and left a slight scar.' He had found the experience rather grim but also quite exciting. At one point the Germans had launched a sudden counter-attack at the very moment his company commander, Dennis Dunn, had been back with the CO. Suddenly, Franklyn-Vaile had realized that B Company were in danger of being cut off and that he needed to act decisively. 'We had the pleasant experience,' he added, 'of crawling down a shallow ditch with bullets zipping over our heads and banging up against a brick wall behind.' At the end of the ditch they had to get up, one at a time, and make a dash for it. Much to his relief, he didn't lose a single man. He was also very relieved to discover that in the heat of battle he had been able to think clearly and not have the slightest feeling of panic. Until tested, one simply didn't know how one would respond to finding oneself in the thick of it.

The prisoners they brought in looked a dejected lot and were only too happy to talk – not the hardened Nazis he'd been led to expect. 'It is curious how impersonal one feels,' he wrote, 'no feelings of hate towards them, just a matter of doing the job on hand.' He told his wife not to worry – he had faith in his lucky star and felt sure he would come out all right. How much comfort such reassurances were to her could only be guessed at.

Miraculously, Peter Davis and his entire section survived the battle unscathed; it could so easily have been them that had been blown to bits had Johnny Wiseman not intervened. That alone prompted some soul-searching. In all, the SRS lost nearly 30 per cent of their number in the battle, losses they were not used to taking. Termoli itself was battered, blasted and largely deserted, another beautiful town that had been bedevilled by the war, while the surrounding battleground was scarred and butchered; San Giacomo was all but destroyed. A couple of days later, before they were shipped out, Davis visited the blown bridge over the Via Adriatica – one of the two they had originally been sent to secure on the first night. Shattered, blackened vehicles littered the area. Where the river had been forded a Sherman stood, abandoned, bogged down in the mud. The fields were worn with tank and vehicle tracks and innumerable shell-holes. A hundred yards from the ford, another Sherman stood leaning over perilously, one track off and its turret, a mass of twisted steel, on the ground beside it. Next to this, a row of white crosses. What a desolate scene it was.

On 5 October, it had been Renie Clark's birthday. 'I give you Naples for your birthday,' her husband, General Clark, cabled her. 'I love you, Wayne.' He had always used his second name with family and close friends. That same day, Alexander flew in and was given a tour of Naples and the port facilities. Already the harbour had been entirely cleared of mines, debris pushed out of the way, and half-sunken ships ingeniously used to create the bases for temporary jetties and piers. Tour over, they then discussed future plans for Fifth Army. The 34th Red Bulls were now in the line, and so too was the British 7th Armoured Division, which meant Clark had around 100,000 combat troops. Their plans were for McCreery's X Corps to advance to the Volturno along the fertile and flat coastal plain, with the Triflisco Gap just east of the town of Capua as the boundary with VI Corps. Now under General Lucas, the Americans would close up to the Volturno through the hilly and mountainous terrain north of Caserta and on the Brits' right flank. Then they would launch attacks across the River Volturno. Clark favoured a broad-front assault wherever possible, the idea being that by punching in multiple places at the same time, the sheer weight of attack would be too much for the enemy, who, at some point, would give way. This could then be hastily exploited. Getting across the Volturno, which was a sizeable river between

40 and 60 yards wide, was to be done as quickly as possible. Neither Clark nor any of the Allied commanders, however, had counted on the first week of October being quite so debilitatingly wet, or reckoned how much this would affect progress.

The Allied way of war was to use industrial power, global reach, technology and mechanization to do as much of the hard yards of fighting as possible and to limit the number of men who were forced to fight at the coalface of war. It was an entirely sensible approach and far less wasteful of life than the way in which the Axis forces and Soviet Union approached the conflict. Infantry, especially, but also armoured troops were the most vulnerable, which was why the Allies placed such emphasis on air power and firepower. Filippo Caracciolo had been invited by Colonel Edgar Hume to visit the Salerno bridgehead and had been staggered by the scale of Allied mechanization. He thought the road looked like a stream of metal. 'Motor vehicles of all kinds, of all sizes, proceeding in uninterrupted theory, almost wheel to wheel, from the landing beaches to the unknown destinations of combat; armoured cars, troops transports, command cars, radio cars, tool wagons, workshops, barrel wagons, ambulances, kitchens. Gigantic trucks bear the weight of diggers and cranes.' He'd realized that Fascist propaganda, which had derided the boasts of Americans about their industrial might, had got it entirely wrong.

Yet impressive though this mechanical arsenal was, it was not designed to operate along dirt roads turned to mud by excessive rain and by excessive use. The moment a column came across a blown road, for example, a detour had to be made, usually hastily cleared by dozers and graders, but essentially earthen and not metalled. The combination of rain and lots of heavy vehicles soon turned such tracks into quagmires. The numerous rivers, some small, some deep and wide like the Volturno, could dry up completely in summer or certainly be fordable, but not now. Every one had become a raging torrent, so much so that very often the engineers built temporary bridges, only for them to be swept away again.

'Rained some,' noted Bud Wagner on 2 October. 'Rained again,' he jotted two days later. 'Are in a muddy spot,' he wrote on 9 October. 'Had to find the 151st first thing and the 125th. Several trips out also tonight. Raining. Nothing but mud.'

Battling through this dismal autumn weather was the recently arrived 100th 'Nisei' Battalion, attached to the 133rd RCT of the 34th Red Bulls Division. Although led by white officers, the 100th Battalion was otherwise made up entirely of Hawaiians of Japanese-American ancestry, most of whom had originally joined the Hawaiian National Guard. There were around 120,000 Japanese-Americans in the US, most living on the west coast and in Hawaii. Two-thirds were full citizens and had been born and raised in the States, and although intelligence services had immediately arrested some 3,000 suspected subversives, this was not enough for the wider public. Paranoia and suspicion quickly reached fever pitch, and in response to this the majority of Japanese-Americans were subsequently rounded up under drastic legislation swiftly imposed by the federal government and detained in camps for the rest of the war.

There were exceptions, however, and not least the Hawaiian Provisional Infantry Battalion, which had sailed to Oakland, California and been renamed the 100th Battalion, albeit an orphan formation not assigned to any parent unit. Its men had proved outstanding recruits during training, and so in August 1943 the 100th had been shipped overseas to Oran in Algeria. Its commander, Lieutenant-Colonel Farrant L. Turner, had been given the choice of having his battalion assigned to guard duty in North Africa or being shipped to Italy. Turner immediately volunteered the 100th to combat duty and they were then attached to the Red Bulls.

'Do you think you can trust them to fight?' Major-General Charles 'Doc' Ryder, the commander of 34th Division, had asked Turner during their first meeting in Algeria.

'Absolutely,' Turner had replied.

'Good. That's all I want to know.' They were in, replacing the 2nd Battalion of 133rd Infantry, which was currently serving as Eisenhower's personal guard in Algiers.

Among the first recruits to the 100th had been Sergeant 'Isaac' Fukuo Akinaka, a thirty-two-year-old Japanese-Hawaiian whose father had left Japan back in 1898 and been joined by his wife-to-be ten years later purely on the basis of a posted photograph. Fukuo Akinaka was the eldest of three sons, and although his father practised the Shinto religion and his mother was a Buddhist, Akinaka had become converted to the Mormon faith and even been ordained. Although proud of his Japanese heritage, he was an equally proud American and had volunteered for the draft in December 1940, joining the National Guard for a year. His twelve months had been due to end on 8 December 1941. Then had come the attack on Pearl Harbor and that had been that: he was in the army for good, and with no regrets.

He'd been nicknamed 'Isaac' at school and it was a name he'd always liked, so he decided to stick with it and used it on his draft papers and any other official documentation; it was another way of identifying himself as both an American and a Christian. Devoted, determined and assiduous in all he did, Akinaka had arrived in Italy as a technical sergeant in the Communications Platoon of Battalion Headquarters Company. On the morning of 29 September the battalion had been leading the division on the advance to Benevento, a sizeable town forty miles north-east of Naples which had been repeatedly hammered by Allied bombers since the spring. They'd just passed through the village of Castelvetere when the lead troops had been fired upon by machine guns and mortars. Spotting the enemy MG nest, Sergeant Joe Takata had charged it, firing his Browning automatic rifle – BAR. As he'd been shooting, a piece of shrapnel hit him in the head. Isaac Akinaka had been on the walkie-talkie handset radio when Takata had been hit – the first casualty in the 100th – and he immediately called out for stretcher bearers and relayed the news to Captain Isaac Kawasaki, the battalion medical officer. Kawasaki had hurried off immediately, saying, 'Where my men go, I go!' Akinaka had been much impressed by this.

A couple of days later they led the way again into the shattered remains of Benevento. They'd advanced twenty miles in twenty-four hours, battling rivers of mud and driving rain much of the way. General Clark, though, had been much impressed by his new battalion. 'Efficiency of Bn very good,' he signalled to Eisenhower on the 8th. 'Quick reaction to hostile opposition. Employed all available weapons unhesitatingly.' He'd also recommended Sergeant Takata, who had subsequently died of his wound, for a posthumous Distinguished Service Cross. 'Morale high.'

By 7 October, all of Fifth Army's divisions had reached the southern banks of the Volturno; Clark had hoped that the Brits would be able to quickly get across on the night of 9 October, but more torrential rain put paid to that, and with the floodplains on the approach to the river now a morass of mud there was no hope of launching an attack immediately. The old JG53 airfield of Cancello, just south of the Volturno, was now little more than a swamp. No vehicle could get close to the river; no bridging could be carried out; no tanks would be able to support the crossings. Even the infantry were liable to get bogged down. 'We have had terrible rains here which have not helped my tactical situation,' Clark wrote in a letter to his mother on 10 October. 'It is clear today and I hope it will stay that way for a few days to permit me to get out of the mud.'

The heat and dust of summer had gone. What's more, the enemy might have fallen back, but the Germans were showing no sign of handing the Allies an easy route to Rome. Rather, on 4 October, in a sign that his thoughts were starting to shift, Hitler ordered Kesselring to now fight for every metre south of Rome. Plans to retreat to the north, championed by Rommel, had vanished on the air as swiftly as the summer sun had turned to debilitating rain.

CHAPTER 19

The Volturno

'GENERAL CLARK TRIES TO make suggestions only,' noted General John Lucas, the new VI Corps commander, in his diary, 'but he always wants speed and becomes impatient sometimes when I can't give it to him.' If Clark was a little impatient, that was because he had his own superiors breathing down his neck, as did Montgomery. The invasion of Italy – conceived in August in the heat and sun of a Mediterranean summer and based on dubious intelligence that Hitler planned to swiftly retreat north of Rome – had been launched on the understanding that its objectives would be quickly achieved, that the capital would be in Allied hands in a trice and that it would be a limited operation to keep Allied troops in the fight on land until the second front opened up in northern France early the following summer. Having the Germans contest every inch of the way, with Allied armies slogging their way through mud, rain and all manner of blown bridges and mine-strewn roads, had not really featured in the planning phase – a phase that Clark had been a witness and party to. The President and Prime Minister wanted swift results, and the Chiefs of Staff wanted swift results, and that meant being in Rome by Christmas. Clark, understandably, felt the heat.

Montgomery was less affected by this because he had always single-mindedly refused to be bullied or cajoled by anyone; and since taking over Eighth Army in August the previous year, had always allowed Alexander, first as C-in-C, Middle East and then as his Army Group commander, to take whatever flak was being thrown their way from above. He was wise and experienced enough to realize that the best-laid plans rarely stood up to the test. Clark, though, was new to army command; only on 2 October was his permanent US Army rank confirmed as brigadier-general. Up until that moment he would have reverted to being a humble colonel once the war was over. So of course he wanted to do well. He wanted to do well for the United States, for the Fifth Army – which he had created – and, naturally, for himself. There were very, very few generals without ambition.

Yet as Lucas was discovering, the scale of German demolitions, combined with biblical levels of rain, made even advancing along a road challenging – and that was without the Germans shooting at them. Heading north through hills and mountains, as VI Corps was doing, meant there were innumerable spans to cross: it might be over a trickle, or a raging torrent, or just a culvert. Or rather, there might have been bridges, but now they were all gone. Near Acerno, for example, the road threaded its way through the mountain, but where there had once been a neat, 25-yard bridge there were now only the crumbled struts of a stone arch. Engineers had to bring up cranes and lengths of wood and build scaffolding from either side of the mountain brook 40 feet below. Rubble had to be cleared and planking laid across the top of the scaffolding. Then it might just be ready to use again, although steady nerves were required of those in the first vehicle to cross over this hastily built, rickety-looking structure. And that was being repeated over and over and over again. American engineers had never been so busy.

Clearly, vehicles were no longer enough and Lucas's staff had already had to send men out to procure any mules, donkeys and ponies they could find as his divisions struggled north through the mountains. Purchasing these animals was one thing, but finding the men to run the show was quite another. The Allied armies, the US Army especially, were designed to be entirely mechanized; farm boys now ploughed with tractors while the boys from the cities drove Fords and Cadillacs. The German Army, by contrast, had always had a large number of horses – its manuals all included notes about handling them; and because Nazi Germany had been so under-mechanized before the war and its farming so inefficient compared with countries like the US, Britain and Canada, there were men with knowledge of horse-handling at every level. Suddenly, in the mountains and rain of Italy, German forces had a transportation advantage over the materially and mechanically rich Allies that they'd not before experienced.

Lucas had visited Benevento on 5 October. 'The town near the river is merely a mass of rubble,' he noted, 'and smells horribly from the bodies buried in the masonry.' A Bailey bridge was being placed across the River

Calore and another planned further up. The levels of destruction he had so far witnessed in Italy had been disturbing. 'There can be no doubt in any soldier's mind as to what we are fighting for,' he jotted in his diary. 'Anyone who has seen these miserable people standing amid the rubbish of their destroyed homes or digging in the rubble for bodies of relatives or friends must know that this must not happen to America.'

He was also horrified to learn that new types of booby traps had been discovered in a vineyard where a tripwire between the grapes detonated an S-mine. The Germans had many different types of mines. Some were anti-tank devices such as the Teller mine, which would only be triggered by something heavy crossing it. Others were anti-personnel. The S-mine, or Schü-Mine, came in different forms. One held explosives within a wooden box, making it hard to discover using detectors, which were designed to pick up buried metal. Other S-mines had explosives contained in metal canisters and were designed to blow off a foot or, in the case of the Schrapnellmine, the explosive would launch into the air and detonate at waist height. Mines were, obviously, a defensive weapon, which was why the Allies, going forward, rarely had much opportunity to lay them, and why the Germans, as they withdrew, used them so liberally. The trouble with laying them in such numbers in a population of over 40 million, however, was that all too often it wasn't Allied troops that detonated them but local civilians. 'Who would think of that except a Hun?' Lucas jotted about the tripwire in the vineyard. 'Much more apt to kill some poor Italian child than one of us.' On the other hand, it was mostly Allied bombs and shells that had destroyed Benevento and pretty much every other ruined village and town, and which were responsible for a far greater number of civilian casualties.

Nor was there any denying that mines and booby traps were very effective. In Russia the Red Army would clear minefields by sending a mass of troops across them, but the Allied commanders treated the lives of their young soldiers more preciously, so the practice was to carefully clear an area first before sending troops forward. This saved lives but sucked up time. Oberst Wilhelm Mauss felt slightly uncomfortable about the number of mines and booby traps – devil's gardens – they laid, but on the other hand, statements he'd seen made by Allied POWs about how such devices severely hampered movement were testimony to their effectiveness. 'This proves that the destructions, which seem to be so horrific,' he wrote, 'have a military justification after all.'

*

The US 3rd Division had reached the southern banks of the Volturno, with the 1st Battalion of 15th Infantry nearly opposite the village of Triflisco. Here the mountains dropped steeply almost down to the river on the southern side, while north of the river was a tail of low hills. The Volturno passed through this narrow 300-yard-wide gap. Corporal Audie Murphy and his squad reached here in the rain but found an abandoned German position – a sandbagged post at the very foot of the rock face, no more than a couple of hundred yards from the riverbank. Behind it was a cave dug into the rock, the northern buttress of the Monte Tifata massif. There was no reason for the Germans to be there now – they'd all fallen back the other side of the river – but it must have been a shelter for troops on an OP on the ridge directly above them.

Inside, the cave was inky dark and smelled foul. 'The sour stench of decaying food and mouldy clothing,' noted Murphy, 'tells us that the Germans have been up to their usual job of bad housekeeping.' Striking matches, they looked around for booby traps but found none, and so each of them marked off an area of the earthen floor and settled down. They had been ordered to remain there, holding the post, until relieved. The Triflisco Gap was the narrowest point, the obvious place to attack, and because it was so obvious General Truscott decided to mount a feint there, while the main assault took place at multiple crossing points further east up the river.

'So we're pigeons?' said James Fife. 'The damned decoy?'

'I guess you could call us that,' Murphy replied.

Murphy's squad was composed of the different kinds of peoples that now made up the United States of America. Fife, for example, was a Seminole Native American from Red Mound Township, Oklahoma; Kerrigan was Irish; Antonio was Italian and Joe Sieja was a Pole. Different peoples, different cultures. And they were now in Italy, with the rain pouring down and about to take part in a battle to cross a wide and fast-flowing river.

The next morning it was still raining. From behind the sandbags, they peered across the Volturno. The poplars shimmered in the rain, while beyond, on the rising shrub-covered rock, there was not a sign of life. They had to be there, though, Murphy was certain. He now spotted a shrub that didn't look right so, borrowing a Garand rifle, took a few potshots. Sniper bullets fizzed into the sandbags in reply, but then it went quiet again.

None of them liked this position. It felt like a trap. Antonio was particularly put out. He'd wanted to come to Italy, but had written to his father that the country stank. His father had always told him that Rome was the place – that was the real Italy. 'The real Italy. Rome,' said Antonio. 'We ain't goin' nowhere but to another sonofabitchin' mudhole crawlin' with lice.'

The British of X Corps were slowly but surely rolling northwards too. On Fifth Army's left flank they were emerging north of Naples into the narrow, flat coastal strip, which, with the rain, produced just as many headaches as did travelling through mountains. On 3 October the 56th Heavy Regiment left Cercola and began to move northwards. 'Saw the sight of a lifetime last night,' noted RSM Jack Ward, 'Naples burning on one side and Vesuvius throwing out red hot ash on the other.' They passed through towns and villages, the roads nothing but mud, and although there were plenty of Italians watching them and clapping, there were also many refugees. 'Very foot weary,' noted Ward, 'and looking fed up with life.'

The regiment was by now moving forward every day and by the 7th within range of the River Volturno. 'In fact,' added Ward, 'we are at present shelling villages by the river.' All the towns and villages they'd passed through so far had been damaged, and some largely obliterated. 'Passed one yesterday,' he jotted, 'where the railway station and town bombed and shelled to blazes and trains wrecked.' That had been the handiwork of the bombers during the height of the Salerno battle.

Two of their batteries – eight guns in all – were in position just south of the river by the 8th. 'There is going to be a devil of a scrap to get to the other side of the Volturno,' he scribbled in his diary. As RSM, one of his tasks was to recce new firing positions, and as they'd made their way back from this task they'd been shelled, and then some enemy planes had dive-bombed them. It had not been pleasant. The rain was also making it very difficult to get their heavy 7.2-inch guns into position – each one weighed more than ten tons. 'All our vehicles are bogged and will have to be towed out,' he noted, then added with some exasperation, 'What a game.'

In the wake of all this destruction, Italian civilians were trying to pick up the pieces of broken lives. Lina Caruso and her family had returned to their home in the ruins of Eboli on 23 September. The trees that lined the avenue running up to the castle had all been shattered and stunted, and the rubble of collapsed homes and buildings blocked many of the streets.

The church of San Francesco had been destroyed, so too the magnificent town hall and the school, and even the sports field was now pockmarked and cratered. Their own home was, thankfully, still intact, so too the castle; but three-quarters of Eboli had been crushed as though by a giant fist from hell. News drifted in: that the Allies were closing in on Naples. Then that the city was in Allied hands. Finally, they heard from her father; a young lad had walked from Naples and handed them a letter. 'He promised to come and see us as soon as possible,' noted Lina, 'and he railed against the cruel Germans.'

Meanwhile, Eugenio Corti and Antonio Moroni were continuing their journey to Brindisi. On 3 October they had reached Ripalimosani, a mountain village in Molise, not far from Campobasso. It stood at the top of a valley and had been built, like so many of these villages, into the side of the hill, surrounded by vineyards, olive groves, chestnuts and baby oaks; its main feature was a pretty church with a tall, thin bell tower. Villages such as Ripalimosani were remote, isolated and had been largely untouched for centuries, their inhabitants eking out an existence as sharecroppers, giving half of their profits to a usually absentee landlord, the *padrone*, and keeping the rest. Such farmers were known as *contadini*. The system had remained unchanged for centuries.

It was evening when Corti and Moroni reached Ripalimosani. The rain was driving into them and they were soaked. The top of the gorge was covered by patches of low cloud, but suddenly there was the village, looking as though someone had thrown a handful of gravel on to the side of a slope, with each stone a small house. They knocked on the door of the first house they came to, interrupting the family dinner; they were welcomed in all the same, the mother of the house heating some water in copper basins in which they were then encouraged to wash their feet. Meanwhile, a second dinner was prepared for them. The family sat with them while they ate.

'Just think,' said one of the men, 'here there's never been war, never,' and within days we'll be in the middle of it.'

'What will happen?' said one of the women. 'May the Virgin Mary help us!'

Corti began to suggest there had been wars here once; he was thinking of the Visigoths.

'Not here where we live,' he was told, 'never, they say.'

They wondered again what they should do; if their home was destroyed, they wouldn't be able to afford to rebuild it.

Corti tried to reassure them. It might miss them altogether; and if not, he was sure it would pass quickly. 'May the Virgin Mary help you,' Corti told them, 'like you helped us.'

'You are a good soldier,' said the mother. 'The Virgin Mary will bring you home.'

Later they were given a load of quilts and blankets and stretched out on the brick floor of the kitchen. Suddenly, a hearth cricket started chirruping. They couldn't help thinking about what an extraordinary country of contrasts Italy was. Their trek across Italy, begun as an attempt to flee the Germans, had become a rather wondrous pilgrimage of discovery.

At XIV Panzerkorps headquarters, General Hans-Valentin Hube had returned from leave, which meant Balck's brief tenureship was over and he could return to Germany and allow his broken ribs a chance to mend. Oberstarzt Wilhem Mauss was delighted Hube was back and immediately hurried to see him and give him an update on the medical situation in the corps from 8 September to 5 October: only 323 dead, but 1,232 wounded, a further 628 missing, and in all the various field hospitals a total of 6,107 wounded and 7,726 sick; malaria was responsible for the majority of the latter. Together, the numbers of sick and wounded amounted to more than an entire division's worth of manpower.

The following day, Saturday, 9 October, Mauss attended a division commanders' meeting at the corps headquarters near Mignano. These included General Conrath of the HG Division, Generalmajor Gräser of 3. Panzergrenadier and Generalmajor Ernst-Günther Baade of 15. Panzergrenadier. Baade was one of the more flamboyant German generals – a former Olympic cavalryman, Afrikakorps veteran and aesthete, he had a penchant for wearing kilts and liked to carry a claymore at his side. He was also an extremely capable, much-respected and inspirational commander. Hube himself was also vastly experienced, brought out of the Stalingrad pocket on Hitler's express orders and against his wishes; not for nothing was he known as 'Der Mann'. Also attending was Generalmajor Bessell, there to report on his construction works. Tactics were discussed, but all were agreed that the plan was to hold up the Allies as long as they could at the Volturno – the 'Viktor' Line – and to make the 'Bernhard' position as strong as possible while Bessell continued work on the Gustav Line. In fact, it was clear that the Bernhard Line, which would join the Gustav Line halfway across the leg and would span the valley at the Mignano Gap, had the potential to be a formidable position, largely because the valley was so narrow with the long hulk of Monte Lungo running down the middle. The Allies, moving up through here, would be canalized and that would make it very tough for them to get past easily.

Meeting over, the assembled generals were invited to stay for dinner in the mess tent. Mauss loved such evenings: good food and wine shared with comrades at their picturesque camp, the valley air clean and fresh, and plenty of convivial conversation. It reminded him of the hunting picnics he used to enjoy in the good old days.

Leutnant Hans Golda and his Werfer-Regiment 71 had been posted up to Minturno, on the coast at the mouth of the River Garigliano, which ran down from Cassino to the sea. There they were on alert for further Allied attacks from the sea, but of course none came. One day they thought a Jabo was heading for them and they all ran for it, only for the aircraft to plunge straight into the ground just a little behind them, but not before Golda had spotted the black cross on the fuselage. 'So, another German fighter less!' he noted. A dull bang, a jet of flame against the sky and a dense, swirling cloud of smoke billowing over the crash site. They hurried over to find the fighter drilled into the ground and the shattered remains of the pilot. Once the flames had died down they buried the body, placed a cross over it and fired a volley of honour.

Since then, Golda had been thoroughly enjoying himself. They found a well-appointed villa at the mouth of the river and decided to make the most of this brief holiday, including swimming in the sea. 'We ran into the water,' he noted, 'frolicked like fish and rejoiced like exuberant children.' Golda set up shooting competitions using bottles as targets, and they also went on fishing trips using grenades. They ate well, drank well, had fun and caught up on sleep. Their week there was quite the tonic.

Then came orders to deploy to the Volturno – not the rest of the regiment, just his 7. Batterie. Golda knew this reflected well on him and his men, and he was, in a way, flattered. On the other hand, he'd have far rather remained enjoying their little holiday than head back into the firing line. Reaching the front near the town of Capua, he reported to the regimental commander of the artillery unit to which they'd been seconded and set his firing positions behind the banks of a canal that ran roughly parallel with the Volturno but two miles behind. Apart from the dyke on either side of the canal, here the land was flat – a few rows of dead-straight trees, the odd farmhouse, but otherwise waterlogged pasture which was grazed by a large number of buffalo. Around 300 yards in front of the canal was a low-walled yard behind a row of poplars. This he made his CP, where he set up both a radio and ran a field telephone wire back to the Werfers.

Nearby, though, was the airfield of Grazzanise, only a few miles from Cancello on the southern side of the Volturno. Golda was horrified to count twenty-three fighters, all burned and all with fuel barrels beneath them and the sign of a single bullet hole. Elsewhere, they found a mass of abandoned barrels – 600 in all – many of which were only half empty. Just as Jupp Klein had been incensed by what he'd discovered at Foggia, so too was Golda now. 'Here everything was abandoned to destruction,' he wrote, 'because some mindless rags did not do their duty.' He was so furious he wrote and dispatched 'a very rough' report.

There was no more time for exploring, however. The British had drawn up to the Volturno, the ding-dong of shelling had begun and Golda and his battery were now busy responding to the fire orders that were coming in.

'Rain, rain, rain,' noted General Lucas. 'The roads are so deep in mud that moving troops and supplies forward is a terrific job. Enemy resistance is nearly as great as that of Mother Nature.' The osmosis effect of impatience from the very top had seeped all the way down to corps level and Lucas was now feeling anxious about getting over the Volturno. A postponement had been just as well, because 45th Division, on the 34th Red Bulls' flank, had struggled to reach their crossing points. The 45th Thunderbirds had had the toughest approach as they'd tried to use winding mountain tracks and trails that were in no way fit for a modern mechanized army. The main roads were still mostly dirt and also quagmires, while a further issue had been the amount of civilian traffic. Italians in rural communities rarely left the confines of the village but they did when armies were battling across them. The number of refugees, often with carts and animals blocking the road, had been a further debilitating factor. Roads clogged with fleeing civilians had hampered French and British troops in France in 1940; they were hampering American forces now.

Everyone was getting a little tetchy, although this was hardly surprising. Major-General Troy Middleton, the commander of the 45th Thunderbirds, felt that too much was being expected of his men. They were all tired; they'd been in action for a month and morale was on the dip. Lucas didn't think they were as exhausted as Middleton claimed, although this was largely because he couldn't afford them to be. He needed them for the Volturno crossing but promised Middleton they'd be pulled back and replaced by the 36th Texans once this operation was over.

With all the rain, General Clark now planned to assault all along the Volturno on the night of Tuesday, 12 and Wednesday, 13 October, when, if the forecasters were right, there would be a pause in the rain. The day before, on 11 October, and with the sun out, Lucas climbed a hill on the southern side of the river with General Lucian Truscott, the 3rd Division commander. The 3rd Division OP was in a farmhouse, and from there much of the Volturno Valley lay spread out before them. The mostly tree-lined river itself snaked through lush, vividly green farmland. Steep mountains and hills ran close to the southern side of the river, but on 3rd Division's front there was a notable floodplain on the far side, sometimes a mile or two deep, sometimes further, but rising from this was a series of hills, some isolated, others the low humps of the mountains behind them. A little way to the east was where the 34th Red Bulls were due to cross, which Lucas could see clearly too. There, the hills on the far side, 200–300 feet high, rose almost straight from the northern banks of the river. Dotted along these hills were little villages, church towers overlooking their flocks of houses. Small, normally peaceful backwater communities; but now, though, OPs from which the Germans on the far side could direct mortar and artillery fire. There was no doubting the strength of the Volturno as a defensive position. Lucas couldn't help feeling they'd lose a lot of good men crossing it and taking the hills beyond.

By the 12th Audie Murphy and his squad had been at their post for three days, and while they still had some rations they had run out of water and were horribly parched. Everyone was getting ratty and starting to quarrel, but there was no getting to the river – they'd been exchanging fire through the slit in the sandbags out front and knew that if they tried to make a dash to the river's edge they'd be dead men. That night, they agreed, one of them would have to do it. The thirst was torturing them.

Murphy didn't know that the attack across the river was due to be launched that very evening. None of them did. He was dozing when suddenly he heard, in his dreams then his consciousness, the telltale *brrrrrp* of a German MG42. Up immediately, Sieja had beaten him to the tunnel, and as they emerged they realized that no one was on watch as they should have been. Gazing through the slit in the sandbags they saw, in the evening gloom, that Antonio was down, out in the open, writhing on the ground. The terrible thirst, and being pegged into this grim, dank cave, had got to him and so he'd made a dash for the river.

'Come back, you crazy fool. Come back!' Murphy yelled.

Antonio managed to get up, still clutching his canteen, wild terror in his eyes. Taking a step, his leg bent double, the bone thrust through the flesh and he stumbled forward on the stump. Murphy frantically looked for the enemy gunner but couldn't see him. Now came a second burst, a tearing rip that tore into Antonio's midriff and cut him down. *The kraut is a butcher*, thought Murphy.

Joe Sieja screamed, 'Gah damn sonsabeeches,' and started around the sandbag, but Murphy grabbed him, only to be kicked back. Murphy lunged at him again; this time Sieja was throwing punches. Murphy hit him in the stomach then caught him in a headlock and yelled for Tattie Lipton and Kerrigan to help. Eventually Sieja calmed down. All were in a state of shock, but soon afterwards Murphy found the Pole sitting in the cave with his head in his arms. A candle flickered in the dim, musty light.

'Goddammit, man,' he said to Sieja, 'it would have been no use. Antonio was already dead.' Sieja neither moved nor replied, so Murphy went back to the firing position and peered once more through the slit in the sandbags. 'Antonio lies in the mud with his leg double beneath him,' he wrote. 'He has come home to the soil that gave his parents birth.'

'Time 2045,' noted Jack Ward, 'and the battle for the Volturno is on.' Regimental HQ was based in a large, grand country villa, a summer palace, rumour had it, belonging to the King. It stood two and a half miles south of the Volturno near the coast and had barracks attached as well as thick stone walls; Ward thought it an ideal place. 'From an OP on top of the house,' he wrote, 'I can see what looks like a sea of fire reaching for miles. What a do!'

The British had begun their attack ahead of the Americans, although VI Corps artillery joined in the opening barrage. General Lucas was in his CP at Maddaloni, a small town near Caserta. Both towns were backed by an impressive arc of jagged mountains. Passes zigzagged their way up and led down to the Volturno, the mountains acting like a backdrop of high rock from which the American divisions would be launching their attack. Even from the southern side of the mountains Lucas could hear the rumble of the artillery and saw the night sky flashing and flickering. He thought the majesty of this immense firepower a fearful but also exalting thing to behold.

'Tonight we cross the Volturno,' he wrote in his diary at 10 p.m. that Tuesday. 'Have been working on it for days. I have done all I can and now I'm in the hands of God and my subordinates.' Yet he couldn't help feeling anxious, and nervous about the responsibility on his shoulders. 'A solemn thought,' he noted, 'that your name on an order means the death of many men.' But every man had his part to play; his was to command three divisions, the private's was to try and get across the river. It was just the way it was.

Twenty-five miles to the north, Wilhelm Mauss was in his tent when he heard the distant thunder of guns. The sound swelled until it became a long, rolling roar. It reminded him of the barrages in the last war, what they'd termed a 'rumbling'. It continued, on and off, for hours more and could still be heard at midnight. Mauss lay in his bed in his pasha-style tent, aware that twenty-five miles away their troops were in mortal danger, crouching in their foxholes, knowing they could be hit at any moment. 'Should one sit here calmly at all?' he wondered. 'Wasn't it a great gift in that we had been able to lie in a bed here and sleep warmly and softly while others must fight, bleed and die?'

Later that night, at 1 a.m., the VI Corps artillery opened up along their own front, initially firing high explosives. A deafening, ground-shaking roar as shell after shell was flung across the river, pummelling the hills beyond. Then, at 1.55 a.m., the gunners began mixing smoke shells with high explosive for the final five minutes of the hour-long barrage. Now the infantry were slugging across the mud, carrying light assault boats, slipping down the bank into the fast-flowing water. Flares whooshing into the sky, bursting and crackling, thick, swirling smoke. Some battled the currents and waded across the river – about 5 feet deep – to anchor guide ropes on the far side. Enemy machine-gun fire ripped through the air despite the barrage, but the infantry were starting to make their way on to the far bank – not just on 3rd Division's front but also on the 34th Red Bulls' four crossing points too, further up the river and along a six-mile front from Limatola to the junction with the River Calore.

Here, the grenadiers of 3. Panzergrenadier soon fell back. Further east yet, the 45th Thunderbirds were already over the Calore and, because the Volturno turned north on the right flank of the Red Bulls, did not have to cross it at all. They were, however, still part of the assault, attacking key high ground including Monte Acero and pushing up to the next Volturno tributary, the River Titerno.

By dawn the Americans were going well, with bridgeheads over the Volturno. Audie Murphy and his squad were finally relieved from their post and later that morning crossed the river. The British, however, were not having such successes. At Capua, 56th Division had failed to establish a bridgehead while 7th Armoured managed only a toehold at Grazzanise; here the Hermann Göring Division had put up stiff resistance. Only 46th Division, on the coast, facing 15. Panzergrenadier, had managed to get both brigades across. 'Our planes join in in the morning at dawn,' jotted Jack Ward, 'can hear machine-gun fire so the PBI are on the job, our guns are firing now.' The house was shaking from the fire of the artillery. Ward was always grateful that he was a gunner and not infantry – the Poor Bloody Infantry, the 'PBI', always had the worst of it he reckoned. He was not wrong. Shellfire, mortars and bullets repeatedly proved what a fragile thing the human body was.

Hans Golda and his battery were opposite the Desert Rats at Grazzanise, although with the weight of the enemy assault in 46th Division's sector near the coast he was ordered to hurriedly send a troop towards Castel Volturno. Golda, though, was feeling the increased pressure from the British there; through his field glasses he could see that tanks had been landed on the north shores, and, having directed a number of salvoes towards them, the response was swift and devastating. 'He had finally spotted us,' noted Golda. 'I was horrified to see the fountains of dirt coming up right between the launchers. I feared for my boys. They were lying almost without cover.'

Suddenly, one of his men shouted, 'Herr Leutnant, Wöste is dead!' For a moment Golda closed his eyes, barely able to believe it. Heinrich Wöste was his best driver, the son of a farmer. Golda found him in his foxhole, still clutching his pipe, but with half his head ripped off by a piece of shrapnel. 'We were shaken,' noted Golda. 'My men sat distraught in their holes.'

Even before the main attack began it had already been decided to make 46th Division's crossing the main effort. This was because the flat, waterlogged ground was too soft for any vehicles; the only way they could get forward was by using roads, but this canalized the attackers into the enemy's most heavily defended areas. None of the attacking divisions in Fifth Army had ever made a river assault before and it was clear there had not been anything like enough bridging provided beforehand; Lucas reckoned he'd been given enough pontoon bridging for two crossings per division, but both the 34th Red Bulls and 3rd Division had crossed in six places. This shortage was partly because of the competition for shipping space, but also lack of experience. It was an important lesson to be learned.

Despite this, General Clark could feel pleased on the morning of 13 October, and when Alexander arrived with Air Marshal Coningham that morning he was able to report favourably. Also joining the conference at Clark's CP was General Montgomery, who had flown in from the Adriatic front. There was much to discuss, not just the battle raging at the Volturno but also future plans and what resources they could expect in the weeks and months ahead. Later, Clark took Alexander and Coningham to visit 3rd Division and then Lucas at his VI Corps CP. Lucas was feeling like a cat in a box, itching to get up to the front but not daring to in case he was needed; it did not do to have commanders wandering off when urgent decisions had to be made. He, too, could be feeling some relief; it was his first major action as a corps commander. 'The big Chief seemed immensely pleased with what we are doing,' he jotted in his diary of Alexander's visit, 'and expressed his great admiration for the American soldiers.' Then he added, 'he is one of the most charming men I have ever met.' Charm was of high value in a multinational coalition force that found itself operating in such challenging circumstances.

Over the next two days, despite vicious fighting, Fifth Army managed to continue to expand the bridgehead. It rained again on the 14th, but from the news Jack Ward was receiving the battle seemed to be going well; their guns had been firing almost constantly, the big shells whooshing miles over the battlefront. They were shelled in turn that day, but no one was hurt and three enemy shells that landed in the courtyard turned out to be duds. 'The battle is going very well,' he jotted on 15 October, 'Jerry made a counter-attack last night, saw PBI had heavy losses, but regained ground later. We shall be on the move before long, I think.'

The 34th Red Bulls were certainly pushing forward. 'Crossed the Volturno on a pontoon bridge,' scribbled Bud Wagner on the 15th. 'Not too bad, but a little scary.' The division had done well, clearing the high ground and taking the villages of Caiazzo and Villa San Giovanni and extending into the hills beyond. He had seen plenty of enemy planes overhead – Messerschmitt 109s and Focke-Wulf 190s – although their boys had put up plenty of ack-ack. One fellow had got scared and left his jeep in the middle of the road, blocking the way, and so Wagner rushed over and drove it clear before heading back to his own and driving on.

Either side of the river was now a hive of activity: trucks, artillery, jeeps all moving across the pontoon bridge and expanding the bridgehead, a division on the move once more.

The carnage of battle was all about them. Churned-up roads, blasted trees, hillsides pockmarked with craters, abandoned boxes and detritus. A fug of smoke, cordite and fumes that not even the rain had dissolved. Further along, Triflisco had become a mass of rubble, while to the east of the hills, in the coastal plain, Capua, a town once rich with Renaissance and baroque gems, was now also largely in ruins. Grazzanise, too, was all but wiped from the earth.

Still at the front was Hans Golda and his 7. Batterie. The previous evening he had held a council of war with his men and suggested they regularly move their Nebelwerfers in an effort to avoid the worst counter-battery fire. His boys thought this an excellent idea, so early on the 15th he sent one of his trusted NCOs, Unteroffizier Heinrich Bornemann, to recce some potential firing sights. A little while after, Golda was in their farmhouse when he heard the Kübelwagen arrive back, then moments later, Fingler, the driver rushed in, wild-eyed and jabbering. Golda hurried out only to find Bornemann still sitting in the car but without his head. 'From the stump of the neck blood oozed thickly,' recorded Golda, 'ran over his uniform and dripped on to the sand.' Golda was still staring, dumbstruck with shock, when Eisele, Bornemann's inseparable friend, came out and, moaning with grief, lifted out the body. Fingler was still in a terrible state, with bits of Bornemann's brain and tufts of hair stuck to his tunic. Apparently, they had been at a crossroads when they were caught by enemy fire. Bornemann had slumped on to him and he'd nearly lost control. He had managed to push the dead man back, wipe the worst of the gore from his face and drive on at full throttle.

That night, Golda had been unable to sleep, feeling deeply the burden of responsibility for his men. He vowed never to leave them, and always to lead them to the very best of his ability. 'Then I was seized with intense pain over the death of my two boys,' he wrote, 'and wept bitterly, help-lessly under my blanket.'

By that time, the British had built up enough strength on the northern side of the river around Castel Volturno, while the Americans had taken a series of key heights, including Monte Acero in 45th Division's sector. General Hube asked permission for his corps to pull back, and as it was now Friday, 15 October, the date Kesselring had stipulated until which the position should be held, von Vietinghoff agreed. The Allies might have crossed the mighty Volturno, but up ahead were yet more mountains, more rivers and a mass of engineers and conscripted labourers working round the clock on the defensive lines Kesselring was preparing sixty miles south of Rome.

At XIV Panzerkorps headquarters near Mignano, Oberstarzt Wilhelm Mauss was contemplating this new shift of the front. He might have had a level of uncompromising steel about him, but he fully understood the tragedy and absurdities of war. He was also a somewhat aesthetic man; like many educated Germans, he had profound love for and appreciation of nature and marvelled at the world's beauty – and for humans' capacity for violence and destruction. At his pasha's tent at Hube's headquarters, he couldn't help feeling contemplative that noontime on Saturday, 16 October. Mountains rose either side, vast, immutable and magnificent. On the lower slopes, the colours of autumn. Glancing around him, he spied the many terraces, thick with silvery olive and fruit groves. 'Chestnut trees and oaks mix with the fruit trees a little further,' he jotted, 'and form a dense fleece, which shines in the different tones of green.' Here and there, small villages, largely unchanged – and untouched – in centuries. Somewhere, a little way away, a church bell tolled the hour.

Further beyond were yet more peaks, even higher, shimmering in the background, a soft blue-violet. So beautiful. And such a romantic landscape, yet he couldn't help feeling wistful. The Volturno had been crossed by the Allies and he knew Hube had already given orders to fall back to the next line, here, that ran right across the valley floor at Mignano. They would hold them before falling back a few miles more, to the next line of defence, already being called the Gustav Line. This meant that here, in this lovely, timeless spot, the storm of war would soon roll in. 'It will eat itself into these slopes and mountains,' he wrote sadly, 'and move through the valleys with noise and destruction turning peaceful villages into ruins.' It would, he knew, be especially brutal here, because this is where they planned to make their strongest stand. Glancing at the mountains to the south, he wondered where the enemy would place their OPs. Their guns would boom and echo and crash around the valley where he now stood, and their own guns would reply, and those chestnuts and oaks and olive and orange trees would be shattered and ripped to pieces along with the villages and towns in their path.

One day. The war couldn't last forever. 'New life will again flourish here,' he scribbled, 'old ruins will be overgrown and the scars will heal in order to rebuild lavishly again. Although much life of any kind might have been destroyed, new life will come into its place, as it always was and for ever will be.'

Mauss might have taken some comfort from his musings into the future, but they would provide little solace to those living in this Eden right now, in the middle of October 1943.

Winter was coming.

PART III

Winter

CHAPTER 20

Despair

A T THE BEGINNING OF October, there had still been hope among the
Allied leadership that the Germans would fall back all the way to
the Pisa–Rimini Line 200 miles to the north of Rome in fairly quick
order. On 7 October, however, Eisenhower had a rather dramatic change
of view, with the news reaching him that Germany was sending more
divisions south to join Kesselring's forces. That suggested that the Germans had every intention of fighting south of Rome and very little of
adopting delaying actions only. The mathematics didn't look great either,
since Alexander's 15th Army Group were still due to lose a number of
divisions at the end of November for Operation OVERLORD, the cross-
Channel invasion, currently scheduled for May next year. Total Allied
divisions in Italy were expected to be fifteen by mid-October, seventeen
a month later but only sixteen by Christmas. In contrast, the Germans
might have as many as twenty-six divisions in Italy by then. They had
helpfully decided to evacuate Sardinia and had had a fighting retreat
against the French in Corsica, so the islands, both potential targets for
the Allies in the summer, had landed in their laps without much of fight.
On the other hand, what the Germans didn't have in Sardinia or Corsica
they could put into the mainland Italy pot, which was precisely why
they'd hurriedly bailed out from those two Mediterranean islands.

Suddenly, Eisenhower had realized with depressing clarity that there
would be no swift capture of Rome. Already, it was time to start managing expectations. 'Clearly,' he told the Combined Chiefs of Staff on 9
October, 'there will be very hard and bitter fighting before we can hope to

reach Rome.' So was there a case for holding a line at the Volturno and Biferno and calling it quits with their designs on Rome? Eisenhower – and Alexander agreed with him – thought not. They'd committed to setting up strategic air forces around Foggia, and Naples was clearly the key supply base on the Tyrrhenian coast, but the Volturno Biferno Line offered insufficient depth; rather, the minimum acceptable position, they reckoned, was still around fifty miles north of Rome. What's more, Eisenhower believed, and so did his senior commanders, that the best help they could give OVERLORD here in Italy was to push the Germans all the way back to the Po Valley in the north.

As things stood, seven Allied divisions were to be withdrawn and also 170 heavy bombers – still currently operating from North Africa – plus most troop-carrying aircraft and almost all landing craft, except a skeleton number that could lift, at a push, one division. Alexander's troops on the ground now faced the prospect of attacking an army superior in numbers and in terrain that favoured the defender in every single way. Sure, the Allies had a massive advantage in air power, but, as the recent rains had demonstrated, they might as well not be there at all when it was raining buckets and the skies were bruised with ten-tenths cloud. Autumn had been like late summer; now, it seemed, the weather had turned to winter overnight.

And as if Eisenhower didn't have enough to worry about, Churchill was now demanding the release of troops to help his ill-conceived operations in the Dodecanese. The Prime Minister had hoped to capture and hold the Greek islands off the Turkish coast, but British troops had already been driven off Cos and looked likely to lose Leros too. It was an almost Hitlerian design – trying to do too much with too little – but Eisenhower had no manpower to spare. They couldn't do everything, and in the Mediterranean, Italy, rightly, was the priority.

In early October, Alexander moved his command HQ to Italy, setting up shop near Bari, and then set out plans for 15th Army Group. The objective now was to secure further airfields, centres of communications and ports and reach a general line at least fifty miles north of Rome. 'If we can keep him on his heels until early spring,' Alexander signalled ('him' being the Germans), 'then the more divisions he uses in counter-offensive against us the better it will be for OVERLORD.' It was clear that the heady ambitions with which they'd invaded Italy over a month earlier had already begun to be substantially adjusted.

Hitler, meanwhile, had still been prevaricating as he so often tended to do. Both Kesselring and Rommel had been summoned to the Wolf's Lair at the end of September, after the Führer realized, too late, the terrible folly of having let Foggia go. Kesselring once again argued for strengthening the south and making a stand along the Bernhard and Gustav Lines, which, he assured Hitler, were going to be formidable. Here, he pointed out, the leg of Italy was at its narrowest and he reckoned he would only need eleven divisions, including two in reserve in case of Allied amphibious outflanking operations. Rommel, on the other hand, would need thirteen to twenty divisions to defend the northern Apennines; he argued, though, that the southern strategy was too easy to outflank and supply lines too vulnerable to attack from the air. The Führer, not for the first time, settled for a fudge. Kesselring was to hold the line south of Rome for as long as possible, and Rommel was to oversee the construction of a defensive line in the northern Apennines – the Pisa–Rimini Line he'd been advocating all along. Since Mussolini's fall, it had been Rommel who'd had Hitler's ear regarding strategy in Italy. Now, for the first time ever since the two had become both colleagues and rivals in the Mediterranean, it was Kesselring who was edging ahead.

For the Allies, the logistics of operating in Italy were mind-bogglingly complex. For every ship there were conflicting claims for space. The entire US II Corps, for example, experienced in battle in Tunisia and Sicily, was still sitting waiting in Sicily but couldn't be deployed for want of shipping. So, instead of arriving and slotting into Fifth Army as had been assumed, they remained where they were twiddling their thumbs and the whole of British X Corps, which logically should have gone to help Eighth Army, remained under Clark. The reality was that troops were competing for shipping space and the logistics chain with bulldozers, cranes and graders, and they were competing with more Bailey bridges and other bridging equipment, and they were competing with demands from the air forces, who wanted to hurry up and start operating from airfields around Foggia. Miracles really had been achieved in Naples, which was now, in the middle of October, unloading 3,000 tons a day, but inevitably it was never enough.

And it was the PBI, as Jack Ward called the infantry, who suffered the most because they now faced the reality of the stretched Allied war effort and the operational challenges. The Canadians were a case in point. The Seaforths, part of 2nd Brigade, finally caught up with the Germans on 5 October at Foiano di Val Fortore, about as remote a village as it was possible to imagine, lying in a narrow V-shaped valley. By this time they'd travelled around 375 miles already. Now, directly in front, rose a high ridge of hills from which the enemy started shelling them and which they were ordered to capture. 'Everything is MUD,' noted Padre Durnford on the 7th. 'We have had 53 casualties in 2 days.' Five men had been killed and Captain James McMullen was missing, but because they were still under enemy fire Durnford couldn't get forward to bury them. It rained all that night. Everyone was soaked, everyone was bitterly cold. By the following day, the casualty list had risen and McMullen was confirmed as among the dead. Despite not being right at the sharp end, Durnford still found himself under near-constant mortar and shell fire. At one point, a sniper fired a bullet that went through the sleeve of an officer standing right next to him. 'Go forward and bury four in morning and seven in afternoon,' jotted Durnford on the 9th. 'Terribly shattered bodies.' He held makeshift services at both. 'Men in tears,' he added. 'Ghastly experiences.'

The Hasty Ps, meanwhile, part of 1st Brigade, had travelled more than 400 miles into the central southern mountains of Molise, chasing the tails of Fallschirmjäger rearguards. This area was also incredibly remote, its villages and towns all perched on top of hills and mountains, each of which was linked by interminably winding dirt roads and tracks. Up here, it was hard for either German or Canadian troops to discern any obvious reason for slogging their guts out in the rain and risking their lives. The German paratroopers must have felt a long way from home, but this corner of Italy truly was a heck of a distance from Canada.

'This is a lovely war,' Major Alex Campbell had written at the end of September. 'The Italians don't want to fight and we can't catch the Germans. The weather is lovely except at night. Then it rains, and how it rains.' Chasing the enemy up and down the mountains, he reckoned he'd already lost at least twenty pounds in weight since landing.

Certainly, by the end of the first week of October Farley Mowat, for one, was unimpressed by this mountain chase. Occasionally they exchanged some fire, and one time two of Mowat's men had an actual physical tussle with some German paratroopers in the village of Sant'Elia a Pianisi. This remote spot stood 2,000 feet above sea level, served by one track in and one track out. Sent on a scouting patrol by Mowat, they'd run into the Germans, been taken prisoner, but then, in the dark and the rain, jumped on their captors and escaped. After one firefight the Hasty Ps

came across several dead paratroopers, and, as battalion intelligence officer, Mowat had to search each of the bodies. On one they found an
unfinished letter to a friend; bodies were always checked for papers, letters and any potential intelligence, all of which was then passed up the
chain. 'The Führer has ordered us to hold Rome at all costs,' the German
had written. 'This shouldn't be too hard if you have any idea of the kind
of country here. It is made for defence and the Tommies will have to
chew their way through, inch by inch and we will surely make it hard
chewing.' It was not the kind of letter Mowat wanted to read.

The wet weather and the terrain and lack of decent sanitation were
also taking their toll. Able Company, as the Canadians called A Company, were now without Alex Campbell, who had succumbed to a
particularly bad case of jaundice and had been evacuated to a hospital in
North Africa. He was, he told his mother in a letter home, facing a month
in hospital then a further month convalescing. 'It is a long time,' he noted,
'to be away from the job.'

Campbell might have gone for the time being but the battalion kept
going, even though losses were not being sufficiently replaced. On 14
October the Hasty Ps pushed into Ferrazzano, another town perched on
a crag-like rock just to the south of the much larger regional town of
Campobasso. The Hasty Ps had taken over from the 48th Highlanders,
who had driven the Germans off the crag but not actually systematically
cleared the town. So a platoon of the Hasty Ps was sent to do the sweeping, led by Lieutenant Gerry Swayle, a bespectacled and rather earnest
recent arrival who shared with Mowat a love of birds and poetry. It was
first light when they parked up their vehicles in the town square, and
Swayle sent off his platoon sections to different parts of the town to search
the place. Swayle and Mowat, meanwhile, headed to the castle, the new
boy carefully gripping his Tommy gun, while Mowat, with studied sang-
froid, slouched behind him. Suddenly, as they neared the castle's entrance,
there was a grinding of gears and a car roared out of the main courtyard,
and as it went past a German in the front seat aimed his submachine gun
and let out a burst of fire. Mowat felt a hard blow on his back, the force of
which knocked him to the ground, where he waited for a second burst to
finish him off. Instead, Swayle opened fire, pouring a magazine into the
enemy vehicle which swerved, screeched and crashed into a house, tip-
ping over and with it the two occupants, who slumped out dead. Swayle
then rushed over to Mowat, who he assumed had been hit. Mowat had

assumed so too, but taking the small pack off his back he realized the bullet had been absorbed by a tin of bully beef. A lucky escape.

The same day the Germans abandoned Campobasso and so the chase began again, the Germans laying mines, booby traps and occasionally leaving rearguards to try and slow the Canadians down. The Hasty Ps were ordered to clear out three villages, all on outcrops of the high mountain plateau north of Campobasso. Able Company were to clear Montagano, and the Carrier Platoon to occupy the tiny hamlet of San Stefano, perched on a mountain at 2,080 feet and overlooking the narrow Biferno Valley below. Mowat, with only a jeep patrol, was told to take Ripalimosani, at the top of a gorge that then ran all the way down off the high plateau to the Biferno.

Driving into Ripalimosani, Mowat and Doc Macdonald, his only companion, were greeted by the peeling of the church bells and ecstatic villagers, including, presumably, the same people who had welcomed in Eugenio Corti and Antonio Moroni barely a week earlier. It seemed the Virgin Mary had protected them after all, as the village was untouched; it had been saved, even though a German patrol had apparently pulled out only an hour earlier. Yet while Mowat was being welcomed as a liberator in Ripalimosani, the Carrier Platoon had been driven back from San Stefano by a combination of mines and mortar fire, which was why Gerry Swayle's platoon was sent up to clear the place the following morning.

'Ask for the Spumanti,' Mowat told Swayle, having enjoyed this drink in Ripalimosani and expecting himself and his platoon to be equally feted.

But there were no cheering locals, only German machine guns and mortars, which ambushed them as they approached. Swayle and every man in the leading section was killed. The village was not taken until 20 October, four days later, and this time by two companies with machine guns and 4.2-inch mortars in support. Mowat helped with the burial party. It was cold and wet, but despite this the bodies had all bloated and didn't look like men any more. Someone handed Mowat Gerry Swayle's broken spectacles and for the first time since landing in Sicily his eyes began to fill with tears. He was starting to understand that he was not immortal, that none of them were. 'A young guy named Swayle came up to us three weeks ago,' he wrote in a letter home, 'fresh out of Blighty, and before he really knew what in hell it was all about, he ended up a pile of perforated meat along with seven of his men. Why him? Why them? And when will it be you? That's the sort of questions you ask yourself.'

*

Yet while the Canadians were slogging across the bleak and lonely mountains of Molise, 8th Indian Division had been stuck at their staging area
near Taranto doing very little. Harry Wilson thought the surrounding
countryside not so very different from the Middle East with its endless
olive groves, vineyards and bare landscape. Even the lizards were the
same. He was getting on well enough with the cipher team, although dis-
liked the CSM, who was something of a martinet, which didn't really work
with the bunch of misfits in ciphers. Captain Asquith was their CO, an
Indian Army man through and through, but also an alcoholic, so inevitably nicknamed 'Squithy'. 'Squithy never bothers us and we all like him,'
noted Wilson, 'except perhaps CSM Walshall who, I think, would prefer
him a little stricter and more sober.' It was Walshall who really ran the
show. Sergeant Brown considered himself a civilian in uniform, which,
frankly, they all were other than Asquith and Walshall; Sergeant Fisher
used to be a bus conductor before the war and had a chip on his shoulder
about being less literate and learned than the others; Wilson thought he
could be a bit 'peculiar' at times. Spiers he liked a lot because he was quick-
witted, sharp-tongued and very entertaining. Corporal Heales was a
schoolmaster in civilian life but was pleasant enough and liked to quote
Shakespeare and Horace from time to time. Lance-Corporal Griffiths was
a Scot and very quiet. Finally, there was Lance-Corporal Kenison, whom
Wilson had first met in Syria. 'He is one of the most even-tempered per-
sons I've ever known,' he noted. 'Very obliging too. A ladies' man, I should
think.'

On 6 October they finally moved north, rumbling along in a convoy of
trucks, past endless olive groves and through dusty villages and towns.
Girls waved and blew kisses and threw grapes as they thundered by. One
hurled bunch caught Spiers a stinging blow on the side of his head.

'The one who fired that,' muttered Spiers, 'must have been a Fascist.'
They halted at another stretch of open countryside – a vast expanse of
olive groves, vines and almond trees, where they were promptly drenched
by rain for the next few days. 'Mud, muck and pools everywhere,' noted
Wilson. 'It lies inches deep on the floor of the truck. At meals we eat
standing, or perhaps I should say, sinking.'

On 18 October they finally moved again, heading north to relieve
78th Division in the line. They got going at 9.30 a.m., all loaded into a
truck, with Asquith up front with a bottle of whisky carefully placed
under his seat. Wilson was a little worried about their driver, an Indian
who seemed rather timid out of the truck but once behind the wheel

became something of a demon; he managed to uproot two olive trees just reaching the assembly area. Eventually they were on their way, the driver's aggressiveness kept in check by dint of being part of a long convoy. In addition to the large signs announcing the names of Corato, Canosa and Cerignola, there were also now a mass of British signs along the way. 'In town tonight – mosquitos – malaria' and 'The missing link! Salvage supplies it!'

They reached Foggia. 'It was in little pieces,' jotted Wilson, 'completely smashed by our bombers.' The power station at the entrance of the town was wrecked and the tram system ruined. Civilians were everywhere, picking through the rubble and debris. Wilson couldn't help remembering Mussolini's boast about Italy's military might and its 7 million bayonets. 'The mills of God,' he noted, 'grind quickly sometimes.'

They reached the new Divisional HQ the following day, 19 October. They were about ten miles from the front and close enough to the coast to be able to see the sea. The signals and cipher lorries were parked in the shade of a large haystack while a white farmhouse had been occupied by the division staff. 'I'm writing on a table (Squithy's personal table), outside the cipher lorry,' jotted Wilson, 'and the sun is shining gloriously. Birds are warbling and the only sign of war is an occasional burst of gunfire in the distance.' The good weather continued and Wilson marvelled at their new location with its smooth, velvety hills, ancient towns and villages perched on ridgetops. The peace was shattered by a horde of bombers heading over escorted by Spitfires, and also too many wasps. They dug slit trenches and were warned to disperse as much as possible from around the cookhouse. New passwords were issued. The challenge was 'Jack Hobbs' after the famous England cricketer, and the answer 'Surrey and England', on the basis that no German could possibly know it because, as heathens, they didn't play cricket.

On Fifth Army's front the Germans were falling back, although not entirely quietly. Jack Ward crossed over the Volturno to recce some new positions and hadn't been there five minutes when shells started crashing around, although fortunately not very accurately. The next day the whole regiment moved up through Capua – 'just a mass of ruins' – and, having set themselves up, supported an attack that night by the Guards Brigade. Then on the following afternoon, 22 October, they were shelling a town on the side of a mountain. 'Through glasses,' he noted, 'I could see the shells landing amid the houses.' Later that night, the Guards put in another attack and took their objectives. While this was going on, Ward could see and hear a big German air raid over Naples, bombers flying over, anti-aircraft guns pumping shells into the sky, distant flashes and the rumble of explosions. At one point he heard cannon fire in the sky above them, and a moment later a twin-engine German bomber came down in flames, crashing only 100 yards from one of their battery's guns.

A couple of days later, on 25 October, they were off again, this time to Sparanise, the very town he'd spied through his binoculars while they were shelling it. Their firing had obviously been effective because now Sparanise was just a mass of bricks and mortar. 'Had to get Italians to help clear the road,' he noted, 'to allow our vehicles to come up to our RHQ, which is a much-shelled block of flats, empty of course, but functioning.' They remained in the wrecked remains of Sparanise for several days. 'Hard fighting going in on all the 5th Army front,' he jotted, 'but we are pushing them back. Wonder when and where another landing will be made, shall have to do something before long, at this rate it will take until Xmas to get to Rome.'

Bud Wagner was experiencing much the same, although further inland into the mountains where the 34th Red Bulls were continuing their advance. 'We had to move again,' he wrote on 19 October. 'I really don't mind. Maybe we will still be home for Christmas. The guys always say to that, "Sure, maybe if we don't stop a bullet – but which Christmas?"' On 12 October, after a period of training for the 36th Texans, Captain Roswell Doughty took a jeep to Naples. 'Everywhere along the route were signs of the war's devastation,' he noted. 'Factories and large mercantile buildings appeared to have been dynamited by the retreating army and the few Italians we saw were a pitiful sight.' As the Red Bulls pushed north, Bud Wagner found himself driving through the remains of Alvignano, a linear town at the edge of the hills in the floodplain of the Volturno as it flowed south. The place was totally shattered. 'Germans blew buildings deliberately,' he noted, 'to block roads.' It was easy to blame the Germans – after all, they were the bad guys, the Allies the good, come to liberate Italy and beat the Nazis, but once again it was Allied firepower that had done most of the damage. The Germans did not waste explosives; they might try and block a road, but there was no reason to flatten a one-horse out-of-the way place like Alvignano. This was the problem with the Allied way of war when applied to a highly populous country. Few, if any, on the Allied side thought of themselves as anything but liberators; their cause was a crusade that was to free the world of Nazism and its terrible ideology; but it was an odd kind of moral high ground because it was causing so much destruction, killing and maiming plenty of civilians and wrecking lives. What levels of carnage were acceptable for the Allies to still be the righteous ones?

The trouble was, the comparative paucity of Allied infantry was making the Allies even more dependent on artillery than they might otherwise have been. If commanders didn't have enough boots on the ground, then they needed to make up for it with shells and bombs. Of course, it was hard on the ordinary Italians, and most seeing this destruction and human misery could not help feeling some compassion for their plight, but no one in the Allies' camp had asked Italy to enter the war. No one in Fifth Army or Eighth Army, slogging their way through the mud, rain and mountains and through these scenes of devastation, wanted to be here. The Italians had got themselves into this mess and all the Allied armies were doing was trying beat the Nazis, win the war and get home with as few casualties as possible. That late October, it was beginning to dawn on men like Jack Ward, like Bud Wagner, like Farley Mowat that this war in Italy still had a horribly long way to go. So if the way to move forward, and get closer to Rome, was to shell a town and save the PBI a tougher scrap than it might otherwise encounter, then that was what had to happen. And when they finally reached these shattered godforsaken wrecks of former villages and towns and there was rubble in the way, then it was the survivors of the town who had to lend a hand. There was sympathy, but only so much. This war was making decent, gentle men harder of heart.

Yet most Italians in these remote towns had never asked to go to war either, and while it was true that a lot of Italians had supported Musso-lini, it had to be remembered that he came to power on the back of another national catastrophe, the Great War, in which the Italians had come out on the winning side but still seemed to have lost so much. And in any case, what did these provincial Italians know about politics? Italy had one of the highest rates of illiteracy in the West, and also more regional dialects than any country in Europe. Lawrie Franklyn-Vaile was invited to supper with some Italians near Termoli and was surprised by how little they knew of the war; they were completely ignorant of what was happening in Russia, even though an entire Italian army had fought and died there, and were unaware that Naples was now in Allied hands.

'Asked why they went to war with America,' noted Franklyn-Vaile, 'they shrugged their shoulders and blamed the politicians.' So how were the people of Sparanise or Alvignano or even Eboli to blame? What had they done to deserve this apocalypse?

Now that there was a continuous front across Italy, the southern third of the leg came, for the time being at any rate, under AMGOT; yet Allied bombing and shelling, combined with German destruction as they retreated, meant that this southern part of the country had ceased to function in any normal sense of the word. The transportation network, for example, was shattered, with 75 per cent of Allied-occupied Italy's pre-war trains, 85 per cent of its coaches, 90 per cent of its trucks and lorries and 87.5 per cent of its merchant fleet all destroyed by the war. Mountain communities such as the village of Ripalimosani were largely self-contained and the effects of this devastation were less keenly felt, but in the cities normal, functioning everyday life had totally collapsed.

In Naples there was now a small but regular supply of electricity, but this was carefully rationed according to priority, with military requirements coming first, then hospitals, flour mills and the water system. It was nowhere near enough. Food was also catastrophically short, partly because not enough was being shipped in but also because of the difficulties of distributing it. On 8 October, one Neapolitan, Vincenzo Lionetti, penned a letter to his landlord, who had clearly fled the city, explaining that he and his family had been without bread, water, gas or electricity for ten days. 'I can't tell you what our poor beautiful Naples has become,' he wrote. 'I swear on the bones of my daughter that even writing this makes me want to cry for all those atrocities committed by those German cowards.'

There was no question that the Germans were largely to blame for this misery, but the Allies were hardly beyond reproach. Planners at Allied Forces HQ in Algiers, desk-wallahs with mostly a very limited understanding of the country that was being invaded, had simply not appreciated the scale of the challenges. Sicily was underpopulated compared with the mainland, and at the time of the campaign Germany and Italy had still been allies; towns had been left in ruins, but in the main cities there had still been electricity and running water. Mills had been functioning again swiftly, and although there had been numerous problems and Sicilians were still suffering, what was now happening in southern Italy was on an altogether different scale for which the Allied planners had not been sufficiently prepared. Sicily was also smaller, and Allied shipping had not been under quite the same pressure then as it was now.

Travelling out of Naples in the second week of October, Norman Lewis had been astonished to see thousands of Italians, mostly women and children, all along the roadside searching for edible plants. When he paused to speak to some, they told him they had left their homes before dawn and had walked up to three hours to reach the places where there were still some plants that could be eaten. The people he spoke to were mostly collecting dandelions; others were trying to net small birds. A day later he saw children desperately trying to prise limpets off rocks along Naples' seafront. The Allies had still not allowed any boats to go out and fish, even though the bay had been cleared of mines; why not was hard to fathom. Butchers' shops that had reopened were selling only scraps of offal and off-cuts: chickens' heads and intestines, gizzards, calves' feet and windpipes. 'Little queues wait to be served with these delicacies,' noted Lewis. 'There is a persistent rumour of a decline in the cat population of the city.'

On 22 October, a young teenage girl appeared at his office. Her eyes were downcast and he noticed she was shaking; he'd seen her before when he'd visited a peasant house near Aversa where Italian deserters had sexually assaulted the women. The girl, who had struck him then as extraordinarily pretty, had been among the household. And now here she was, quivering before him, handing him a letter from her father. Because of the high levels of illiteracy in Italy, Lewis guessed it had probably been written by the local priest. The girl's father explained that he'd noticed that his daughter had made a favourable impression on Lewis. 'This girl, as you know,' the letter continued, 'has no mother, and she hasn't eaten for days. Being out of work, I can't feed my family. If you could arrange to give her a good square meal once a day, I'd be quite happy for her to stay, and perhaps we could come to some mutually satisfactory understanding in due course.' Lewis understood exactly the kind of 'understanding' her father had in mind.

Given a pass on 20 October, Frank Pearce was quite astonished by the transformation in Naples since he was last there helping to get the port facilities up and running. The place seemed to be teeming with people once more. 'Sure changed,' he wrote. 'Streets full of people peddling wares. Water is on. Drank lots of wine. All kinds of people. Lots of prostitutes. Pimps everywhere. Streets and buildings are filthy. Never saw so many kids.' The change did not signify an improvement to the lot of those living there, however, but rather that half a million inhabitants had started to emerge from the caves and shelters in a desperate effort to eke a living or some food from servicemen who had come from a world of comparative plenty. Very few would choose prostitution for a living; it was a potential means of survival in a world that had been entirely turned on its head. Filippo Caracciolo was also despairing at what was happening to both the country and his home city. He noticed the sullen faces of Neapolitans, struggling with hunger and the lack of water. 'Garbage accumulates and decomposes in ever-larger and more numerous deposits,' he wrote. 'The battered sewers give an acrid stench. To all the miseries suffered, the epidemic has not yet been added, but it seems that cases of typhus and even smallpox are spreading.' Typhus was on the rise, caused less by the lack of water than of soap; it was borne by lice. The Allies' solution was to douse civilians with DDT, a toxic insecticide. Notices were put up requesting people to present themselves at various delousing centres, mostly public piazzas. There they were to hand over their clothes in exchange for some simple new clean ones and get sprayed at the same time. Roswell Doughty witnessed this humiliation and was horrified by what he saw. 'A cloud of dust, mostly DDT,' he noted, 'was rising from the central area where GIs stripped to the waist were using motors and hoses to blast DDT onto the poor Italians.'

Caracciolo was also frustrated by the lack of political movement. Giuseppe Pavone, a sixty-six-year-old retired general, had joined the Action Party and, with Caracciolo, was trying to organize new Italian combat formations called the Volontari della Libertà – the Volunteers of Liberty. 'But we proceed slowly,' jotted Caracciolo, 'because the days are consumed with smoothing out the thousand difficulties that arise from relations with the Americans, from relations between ourselves, and from relations with the first volunteers.' The obstacles continued, not least because the only way a force of Italian troops could effectively be brought into the line was with Allied equipment and, more importantly, Allied training; Italian troops so far in the war, for the most part, had not impressed the Allies with their grasp of modern soldiering. Why train Italians – which would take months – when there were already Allied troops in theatre, fully equipped, fully trained, and many even combat-experienced? The troubles of shipping were nothing compared with the challenges of equipping and training Italians from scratch. And, frankly, from an Allied perspective, there were simply other priorities. On the other hand, Caracciolo believed that the creation of the Volunteers was vital for Italy's rehabilitation. The brick walls confronting him remained solidly high, however. 'Here, everything proceeds in the greatest confusion,' he noted, 'between excessive bureaucracy, constant friction with Allied officers, and insuperable difficulties in provisioning and transport. And how to advance a cart with square wheels.'

CHAPTER 21

Questions of Morale

ON 13 OCTOBER, BADOGLIO issued a declaration of war on Germany, and with it Italy shifted from being a defeated enemy to becoming a 'co-belligerent' with the Allies. This was largely meaningless as the Italians had no troops with which to fight and no money with which to fund a new Regio Esercito – Royal Army – but certainly it was the intention of Eugenio Corti to reach Brindisi and hope he could one day fight for Italy alongside the Allies. He and Antonio Moroni were now in Allied territory and enjoying the feeling of waking up each morning knowing no one would be attempting to hunt them down. They were seeing AMGOT notices in which the greatest threats were of fines or, *in extremis*, jail sentences. 'We would no longer hear talk of executions and more executions,' he noted, 'and this fear – which makes man nothing more than beast – would no longer hang over us.' Lingering over one such notice, he repeatedly thanked God from the bottom of his heart. Even so, that strangers were now running the country was a humiliating feeling that ran deeply.

They reached Bari then pushed on, heading to Manduria, near Taranto, where Corti had learned that his brother, Achille, was stationed with what was left of the army. Sure enough, he found him – Achille held out his hand when they saw each other again, but Corti hugged him. Together, the three of them went to a tavern that promised to serve meat – which was surprising since the Allies usually cleared out all supplies with their occupation lire. 'Only later,' noted Corti, 'was it discovered that it was dog meat the restaurant served.'

Soon after Badoglio's declaration of war, Corti and Moroni finally reached Potenza, where they presented themselves at the garrison command. From there they were sent to a 'reorganization camp' in Guagnano, soldiers once more, albeit in an army which less than two months earlier had been over a million-strong, but which now barely existed. Their long odyssey across Italy, however, was over.

Also in Apulia was the war correspondent Alan Moorehead. In Taranto he discovered the shops open once more, Italian and British sailors moving about together and the harbours thick with shipping; the Royal Navy was busy mounting small raiding operations against Greek islands now garrisoned by Germans and up and down the Balkan coast. Brindisi was shabby but busy too, and now the seat of both the monarchy and the Italian government. Badoglio held a press conference, recounting the tale of Mussolini's fall and talking of his own position – borne with the weary resignation of an ageing soldier who was aware that he should be in retirement but had stepped into the breach out of a sense of duty and honour. 'He had a kind of *dolce far niente* demeanour,' noted Moorehead, 'something between deprecation and regret and patriarchal dignity.' Badoglio emphasized the wickedness of Mussolini and the pain and suffering he had brought on Italy – Italy, which now stood shoulder to shoulder with the Allies. Moorehead wasn't fooled by this, however, for all Badoglio's apparent regret. All of them, he thought – the King, Badoglio, Ambrosio and Roatta – were living a lie behind a rather absurd façade. 'There was a curious cardboard quality about all these figures,' wrote Moorehead, 'a strange kind of toy-like respectability which was quite unreal and bore no relation towards the original objects or the spirit of the invasion.' It was as though they were claiming that all Italy's ills had been caused by Mussolini, but Moorehead, for one, refused to swallow it; all of these men had earlier thrown in their lot with Fascism, had worn its uniforms and medals and accepted its riches. The King had even signed the declaration of war against Britain in June 1940. 'They were at the top of affairs in Italy,' added Moorehead, 'not because they loved Italy but because they had accepted Mussolini.' And at a time when leadership, courage and duty to their people had been so desperately required, they had cut and run like the feckless cowards they were.

Yet these were the people the Allies now had to deal with, and together they were working towards a settlement for the Allied-occupied southern half of Italy. Harold Macmillan had been briefly back to England, but on his return had been struck by a fever – not malaria but some other 'organic' disease, he was told by the doctor. He managed to pull himself out of his sickbed on Wednesday, 13 October, first to see Eisenhower and then to take part in a conference about plans for Italy. Macmillan had been giving considerable thought to what they should impose, but in a nutshell it was to create a Control Commission in Brindisi to advise and help organize the Italian government, and then gradually wrap up AMGOT in Sicily and Calabria and elsewhere in stages as the Allies advanced up the leg. These territories would be returned to the Italians as soon as could be arranged, but the Control Commission would be there to help and also ensure that the Italians continued to adhere to the armistice terms. 'I think we got what we wanted,' noted Macmillan that night. 'It is a *huge* task, and we must set about it without delay.' He did, though, believe that Eisenhower was a considerable asset to moving things forward. Persuaded by the concept of a Control Commission, Ike agreed to propose this to the Combined Chiefs of Staff. 'He will always listen to and try to grasp the point of an argument,' noted Macmillan. 'He is absolutely fair-minded and, if he has prejudices, never allows them to sway his final judgement. Compared with the wooden heads and desiccated hearts of many British soldiers I see here, he is a jewel of broadmindedness and wisdom.'

There was still, though, the question of what the Italian government should be, which in turn was directly linked to the future of the monarchy. Count Carlo Sforza had returned from exile and was a political heavyweight and an obvious person to bring into Badoglio's government. Filippo Caracciolo visited him near Brindisi but Sforza, like the rest of the Action Party, wanted the monarchy overthrown and would not countenance joining a government under Badoglio unless the King was gone. Caracciolo then headed to the Allied Military Mission, now ensconced in the International Hotel, where Colonel Cecil Roseberry, an SOE officer working at the Military Mission, tried to convince him to help soften the stance of the Action Party. Refusing to cooperate with the King, Roseberry told him, only increased the political confusion. This in turn undermined the efforts of the Allies, who needed Italian political cooperation; frankly, the least the Action Party could do was show a bit of gratitude for the lenient way the Allies were treating them. The CLN, Roseberry told him, would have the full support of the Allies, just so long as they collaborated with the King. It was, he said, the duty of everyone in the Action Party and the CLN to huddle round what already existed. Post-war, that was a different matter – they could do what they liked.

Caracciolo listened, but he knew that neither Sforza nor any in the Action Party – or indeed the three largest parties in the CLN – would countenance keeping the King in power. To do so would strengthen the King's authority and legitimize a monarchy and those around it who had for too long propped up Fascism. Both Sforza and Caracciolo regarded the King much as Moorehead did: as the morally bankrupt figure he was. That Italy was in such a diabolical mess lay, in a very large part, at the feet of the King. What message would it send, if men like Sforza and others agreed to serve under his rule? And so the stand-off continued, with the King refusing to fall on his sword and Badoglio unable to form a credible government. But if the plans outlined by Macmillan came into being, then increasingly, as the proposed 'King's Italy' increased in size and scope, that credible government would become ever more important.

In the north of Italy, life was now more draconian than it had been under the Fascists. Mussolini was back in power, the head of the RSI, the Repubblica Sociale Italiana, although he was little more than a puppet dictator, humiliated and shorn of any real power. His new capital was the small lakeside town of Salò, on the shores of Lake Garda. Real power lay, of course, with the Germans, under the authority of Rommel and Rudolf Rahn, the ambassador to the RSI, and especially Obergruppenführer and General der Waffen-SS Karl Wolff. The latter was a smooth-talking and highly intelligent charmer, who was the Höchste – highest – SS Polizei-Führer in Italy and in charge of all security in German-controlled Italy. In the wider organization of the SS, he was also on a level peg with Obergruppenführer Ernst Kaltenbrunner, the head of the Reich Security Office, the Reichssicherheitshauptamt or RSHA, as joint second most senior SS officers under Heinrich Himmler. This made him very powerful indeed. By the end of October, Wolff was effectively running the show in northern Italy, keeping Mussolini's authority to a minimum and ensuring that any decision by the RSI was carefully monitored. Wolff was not a brutal sadist like some senior figures in the SS, but there could be no mistaking life in the north for freedom. Young men were expected to either 'volunteer' for labour work in Germany or join SS-Polizei battalions, or the new Fascist militias such as the Guardia Nazionale Repubblicana, the GNR. All of these forces, as well as the Carabinieri, came under Wolff's overall authority, and he ensured they were very visible from the outset. While most Italians in the north desperately tried to keep their heads down and stay out of trouble, for any young men the choice was clear: you were either for the Fascists and the Germans or against them. And if you were in the latter camp, and actively resisting in any way, you would be executed if caught. Just as the Allies were reluctant to spend time and effort on training and equipping the Italians wanting to fight the Germans, there was no enthusiasm for the Germans to equip and train Italians to fight the Allies. 'The only Italian Army that will not be treacherous,' declared Feldmarschall Wilhelm Keitel, the Chief of the OKW, 'is one that does not exist.' Mussolini repeatedly asked to be allowed to create a new army but was equally repeatedly turned down. Instead, able-bodied Italian men were to be used as labourers, or in the SS Polizei battalions and the GNR.

On the flip side, people were not starving and there was running water and electricity. Food was not abundant and conditions were far from good, but whether it was better to starve yet be 'liberated' or have something in the stomach but live under the cloak of oppression was not an easy question to answer.

For German troops at the front, motivation remained important and was linked to morale. To a certain extent, it didn't matter whether morale was poor because in a totalitarian state such as Nazi Germany soldiers at the front simply had no choice: if they tried to run they would be shot. Hans Golda was, for the most part, a cheery and mild-mannered fellow, yet he'd rejected all Leutnant Dederichs's excuses for refusing to get out of his foxhole at Cava and had handed him over to the regiment, knowing full well that the lieutenant might well be shot for cowardice or at very least be flung into prison.

Yet morale did matter, even in the German Army. There needed to be enough men prepared to lead by example, to foster a sense of pride, honour and comradeship to keep the show going because, as Jupp Klein had discovered at Termoli, even troops in 16. Panzer-Division, a unit with an illustrious wartime record, had immediately hoisted a white flag the moment British pressure became too great. It was also why Golda had come down so hard on Dederichs.

There were also large numbers of men conscripted from eastern Europe serving in AOK 10: Poles, Czechs and men from the Baltic states. Many did not share the motivations of German troops and furthermore they were treated differently, and not in good way. They served in the German Army on probation, and although eligible for gallantry awards could not be promoted until their trial period in the ranks was over.

Morale was generally poor because they had often been coerced into fighting and were treated as second-rate soldiers. Time and again, Nazi ideology got in the way of sound military sense.

The war had also shifted for the Germans this year, 1943. After the catastrophic reversal at Stalingrad, the propaganda minister, Joseph Goebbels, had delivered a speech warning that what lay ahead was total war. Germany now faced serious dangers, which every German needed to confront with complete commitment. 'How should I interpret all the events and happenings?' Georg Zellner wondered. 'Everything happens as fate decides and you are just a pawn in the game. This realization helps me to look to the future with confidence. Come what may. You have to bear everything with a strong heart.' He knew that his mother, who was living in Regensburg near his wife and children, all under the threat of Allied bombings, felt the same way. It didn't mean they had become fatalistic, but rather they were people who still had both feet on the ground. As a battalion commander, that helped Zellner lead from the front and instil similar notions in his men.

Naturally, linked to this was the motivation for fighting. If the war was lost, then why bother? Because they were part of a struggle to save Germany, and because the alternative was too awful to bear. And because, as Zellner believed, they were pawns in a giant game that was totally beyond their control. For Wilhelm Mauss – and for men like General Hube and his Chief of Staff, General von Bonin – a vital motivation was the profound belief that they were part of some bigger, esoteric force that was directing them and for which they had to be worthy: the righteousness of Aryan superiority. 'The white race,' wrote Mauss, after a lengthy philosophical discussion in the XIV Panzerkorps headquarters mess, 'by spirit, ethic and body, absolutely must remain on top.' Christianity, they believed, because of its origins in Judaism, had lost its right to exist. 'Whatever the attitude of each individual may be,' penned Mauss, 'one thing is clear. The thinking German soldier does not wander around in mercenary mindlessness in the fifth year of war, but senses the tasks and feelings within, to spiritually build anew, and create in order to help his people and humanity to rise. This is simply not seen in Bolshevism or Americanism in their flat materialistic attitude, but in an ethical aspiration for a higher development.'

How much the ordinary German soldier aligned himself to this kind of Nazi pseudo-spiritualism was neither here nor there; it was allowed to filter down, and so long as enough commanders believed it, and enough lower-level officers and NCOs were committed to upholding those gelling factors of duty, pride, honour and *esprit de corps*, as men like Hans Golda and Jupp Klein were, the Germans would continue to fight in Italy.

Motivation and morale were far more ticklish issues in the Allied armies, however. There was still capital punishment in the US Army, but no one had yet been executed for cowardice in this war, and there was no such thing at all in the British Army or, for that matter, those of the Commonwealth forces. The prospect of mass desertions and a total collapse of morale were issues that Allied commanders took very seriously indeed. General Spaatz had been sufficiently worried about morale in his air forces to write to his boss, General Hap Arnold, about it in September, just as an extra all-out effort was being demanded to help the situation at Salerno. 'Our frequency of operation in spite of all efforts to hold it down to a minimum,' he wrote on 15 September, 'is continuously greater than the replacement rate warrants, and crews are becoming war weary faster than replacements will arrive to relieve them.'

Spaatz was talking about bomber crews especially, but this cut to the nub of the challenge facing Allied commanders in Italy. Up until AVA-LANCHE the Allies had become increasingly risk-averse, and very sensibly so; after all, there was no point in suffering reverses if they could be avoided by bringing overwhelming force to bear. That was partly to ensure victory but also to maintain morale; the two were inextricably linked. AVALANCHE had proved that the Allies were, if necessary, prepared to undertake high-risk ventures, but now, having pulled off that particular operation, troops in Italy were still being expected to do more than had been asked of them in the past – and at a time when the tide of the war had turned and they were supposed to be winning. If the bulk of Allied assets were heading elsewhere, what was in it for their troops battling over mountains and through the mud in Italy? This was true for Americans such as Audie Murphy's squad, but they'd only been in the fight since July. The British, however, had been in this war since 1939. There were troops in Italy who had fought in France in 1940.

It was why simple things like the regular rotation of divisions were so important, why a three-battalion brigade was designed to fight with no more than two up and one in reserve. At Salerno, brigades – and US regiments – had been fighting with all three battalions in the firing line. That was an exception, but how many more exceptions were there likely to be in Italy when manpower was at such a premium? Just one extra

effort! One more push! Until the next time – because once the rules had
been changed it was always easier for commanders to do it again.

Suddenly, small comforts took on even greater importance, whether
they be adequate leave and rest camps or that most basic tool of morale,
letters from home. Montgomery wrote to Alexander about Eighth Army
mail being too slow on 23 September. 'Nothing,' he wrote, 'has such
adverse effect on morale as lack of mail from home.' He urged intervention at the highest level. Certainly, Farley Mowat was very browned off by
the paucity of post arriving from Canada and grumbled about it repeatedly. Jack Ward carefully numbered every letter he got, by airmail or by
ship. 'Received No. 69 air letter from Mum and one from Mitch yesterday,' he recorded on 10 October. He then had to wait a week to receive
Nos 72 and 73, the latter taking only eleven days to reach him, which was
pretty good going. Of Nos 70 and 71 there was yet no sign; they often
came out of sync. A couple of days later a number of newspapers arrived,
dated from the end of July and early August. This was part of a scheme
that had been set up in August in Britain – the public were asked to return
Sunday papers for dispatch overseas. It all helped keep that connection to
home.

For Lawrie Franklyn-Vaile, correspondence with his wife was a vital
part of keeping his spirits going. 'At long last a letter has arrived from
you,' he wrote back to her on 10 October. 'If I have read your letter once,
I must have read it twenty times.' Her letter, though, had prompted even
more questions than it answered, which was the frustration of having a
correspondence from far away when one never knew how long it would
be until the next letter arrived. Money was tight in the Franklyn-Vaile
household, so his captaincy was a promotion in more ways than one. 'It
means an extra £6 10/-,' he told her, although he warned her that this
might take a while to reach their bank account. She wasn't to start cash-
ing cheques just yet.

He was, though, acclimatizing to life at the front, although they were
living at a standard he would never possibly have considered in civilian
life. Company HQ was an old cowshed north of Termoli; they'd all been
bitten alive by fleas. His toes were raw from tramping about too much
and not having a chance to wash his feet or change his socks. On the
other hand, he was making firm friends, especially with Dennis Dunn,
the company commander, and John Glennie, one of the younger platoon
commanders. Glennie had told him he had made a good impression with
the men, which pleased him enormously. 'Everything tends to be more

violent out there,' he wrote. 'Life is painted in richer and darker hues and one's loves and hates are all of a much more vigorous nature.' He once again hoped his wife would not worry too much about him; there was an awful lot of time when they were not in contact with the enemy at all. 'I do feel,' he added, 'that wives have very much the worst end of the stick – you read accounts of battles and wonder whether we are participating in them.'

The fighting had been a little quieter on the Adriatic front following the end of the fighting at Termoli, with the Germans withdrawing behind the Sangro and Eighth Army reaching the southern banks on 8 October. It had even been a little calmer on the western side as Fifth Army chased north. It was, though, only a brief pause as the Allies pulled up to the next defensive line. With the days drawing in, temperatures falling and the Germans dug in for the long haul, neither Lawrie Franklyn-Vaile nor any other Allied infantryman now in Italy would be twiddling their thumbs for much longer.

CHAPTER 22

A World Turned Upside Down

T HE BATTLEFRONT WAS STILL shifting, but both sides were now drawn up across the leg of Italy. The 1. Fallschirmjäger-Division was whole again, while more divisions were being sent down from Rommel's Heeresgruppe B, the first of which to arrive was 94. Infanterie-Division, which now held the coastal front along the Garigliano. Next in line was 15. Panzergrenadier, then 3. Panzergrenadier and, further into the mountains, another new division, the 305. Infanterie. The HG Division, which had suffered the most in Sicily and been in the fighting since Salerno, was now pulled back to rest and refit. Reichsmarschall Hermann Göring, OB of the Luftwaffe, took especial interest in the division that bore his name so both new troops and equipment were heading their way; it helped when the second most powerful Nazi was your patron.

Hube was also suddenly and unexpectedly posted on Hitler's orders, much to Wilhelm Mauss's dismay. The doctor regarded Hube with something close to hero-worship and had also planned a birthday celebration for him on 29 October, but it was not to be; Hube had been summoned by the OKW at 1 a.m. in the morning of 24 October and by 7 a.m. was gone. 'A superb man both as a soldier and as human,' noted Mauss. 'We will miss him.'

Mauss also decided that the time had come to move out of the tented XIV Panzerkorps camp. The front was obviously approaching. 'Last night,' he wrote on 27 October, 'the artillery duel rolled so strongly that one had the feeling that one could hear shells impacting on us any moment.' The pressure from the Americans on 3. Panzergrenadier's front was now so strong, they were about to be pulled back behind the Bernhard

Line. What's more, it was miserable camping in such rain – it had rained 'cats and dogs' all night and by morning everything was wet in his tent. So he moved, along with the whole of corps headquarters, to Roccasecca, nestling at the foot of Monte Caira in a tiny tucked-away valley, about ten miles north-west of Cassino. Here he found and requisitioned some houses at the far end of the village, with views of the mountain rising immediately above him and the simple village church. Mauss was thrilled with his find: two big stone houses with walls thick enough to be fortresses. There was enough room for the entire corps staff and he was delighted to discover that the owners had left an impressively learned library; he found a copy of Goethe's *Italian Journey*, which he began reading immediately.

Yet while Mauss was now feeling much better about his situation, the same could not be said for those living in what was about to become the eye of the storm. Between Mignano and Cassino, on the slopes of Monte Sammucro and overlooking Monte Lungo, Monte Rotondo and the Mignano Gap, was the mountain village of San Pietro Infine, another sleepy rural community that time had largely forgotten. Like so many Italian mountain villages, its stone houses had been built rather on top of one another, somehow stuck on to the mountain side, its stone-paved lanes and alleys winding up the slopes. Around the village were terraces of vines and olive and fruit groves, wares that were mostly sold locally in Mignano and the surrounding towns. There was no running water, but there was a village well and also a fountain, where the people would do their washing. Most families had a few animals, such as cows for milk and a few chickens, sheep or goats. These would live on the ground floor and the family above, the livestock helping to heat the family in winter. Cooking was done over a stone fireplace, much as it had always been done. There was a timelessness about San Pietro. It was a tight community where everyone knew everyone and in which the sixteenth-century church was the focal point that bound them all.

The first German troops arrived in the village in early October and told the villagers they had to vacate their homes because the front line was about to run right through the middle of it. Benedetto and Enrichetta Pagano lived in Via Vico Valle in the lower part of the village, and were at home with their four-year-old daughter, Antonietta, preparing some lunch when they heard a commotion going on out in the street. Germans were systematically banging on the doors of each house, ordering the families within to gather their belongings and leave. People were

crying and shouting; the Germans had weapons and were roughly pushing the Sanpietresi – the villagers – out into the streets. Enrichetta was
understandably very distraught, but they hastily gathered blankets and
bedding, spare clothes and what else they could. All valuable items, such
as jewellery, Benedetto hid in his inside jacket pocket, as he'd heard the
Germans were notorious for pillaging. After closing all the window shut-
ters and making sure the fire was completely out, Benedetto ushered his
wife and daughter out and bolted the door. Seeing how distressed Antonietta was, he scooped her up in his arms and followed the exodus. Some
had relatives elsewhere, but the Sanpietresi were such a closed community that most had no choice but to head for the higher ground on the
slopes of Monte Sammucro above the village. Young and able-bodied
men were forced to work as labourers, while the animals were commandeered by the Germans. For the Pagano family and for many others in
this backwater, an uncertain and perilous existence had begun in which
the elements were potentially as dangerous as the Germans now swarming over their village.

A dozen miles to the north in the upper Rapido Valley and lying under
the shadow of the mighty Monte Casale was the village of Vallerotonda, a
mountain community not so very different from that of San Pietro, but
which nestled in the heart of the mountains and was surrounded by rising
peaks. Like so many such towns, from a distance it looked like something
from a fairy tale: perched impossibly, one building seemingly on top of
another. In early October the Germans had arrived and had begun both
garrisoning troops but also preparing work on the defensive lines. Then
two German troops were shot and killed – apparently by an Italian. At
least the Germans assumed so, and swarmed into the village that evening.
After blowing up several houses, they warned the villagers that they had
twelve hours for the perpetrator to turn himself in. If he refused, they
vowed to shoot up to 100 women and children in the piazza. But none of
the villagers knew who had killed the two soldiers, let alone where he was.
Fortunately, the mayor, Salvatore Ettore, managed to persuade the Germans not to carry out the threat, but the majority of the able-bodied men
were rounded up. Most of the rest of the town decided to pack up and take
to the mountains as those of San Pietro Infine had done.

That was also the decision of the di Mascio family, who lived in the tiny
hamlet of Cardito on a verdant high plain beneath the mountains. San
Pietro and Vallerotonda might have been remote places but Cardito was
even more so, linked to the outside world by a mule track and nothing

more and enclosed by a ring of immutable mountains; it seemed incredible to these few families, normally so untouched by the modern world, that the storm of war should be about to roll through their tiny corner of Italy. And yet up here word spread quickly, and with the news arriving from Vallerotonda the di Mascio family decided to lock up their home and head out of the village, first to the mountain plain beyond. Pierino di Mascio was just fourteen at the time, one of six children. An uncle and aunt and their family were also joining them – Domenico and his wife Angelina, and their three sons. Angelina had been brought up in Glasgow, in Scotland, but had returned and married, and was now very heavily pregnant with their fourth child. They were all *contadini*, poor sharecroppers like almost everyone else, and to head out of their homes in winter, and, in the case of Domenico and Angelina di Mascio, with a baby about to be born, was not an easy decision for them to make, but one born of understandable fear and the calculation that it was the lesser of two evils.

There had been something of a pause on Eighth Army's front since Termoli while Montgomery waited for supplies to catch up so that he could attack on what he called 'a sound wicket'. He planned to attack across the River Trigno near the coast with 78th Division and 8th Indian – in its first action since arrival – and then, further inland, towards Isernia, with the Canadians and 5th Division. The Irish Brigade, however, were to try and cross the Trigno early, ahead of the main attack, and secure a bridgehead on the far side.

Although the Faughs had spent the intervening time mostly being bitten alive by mosquitoes and fleas, they had had a brief chance to pause for breath. Lawrie Franklyn-Vaile had been thrilled to receive a letter from his wife, Olive, on 19 October, which she'd only written on the 6th, so it had reached him quite swiftly. The previous letter had been dated 22 September, so he was a little anxious as to whether she was writing regularly or whether her letters had simply got held up. 'I hope you are managing to write every couple of days and airmails at that,' he wrote, 'as letters here are water to a man dying of thirst.' There could be no news too small or inconsequential as far as he was concerned, and he loved hearing about little Valerie, their one-year-old daughter, although he did admit this prompted some heartache at times. Olive was considering mating their two dogs, Sadi and Sylva, and Franklyn-Vaile thought this an excellent idea. 'Let me know what you think about it,' he wrote, 'but I am certain we would do well financially (eventually) on them.'

The Faughs were currently near Petacciato, just to the north-west of Termoli, roughing it out in flea- and louse-infested barns, with the rain hammering down and the mud getting thicker and more gelatinous every passing day. When thrown together in such intense circumstances, men were not only dependent upon one another in a way that would be totally alien in normal civilian life, but were also spending almost every minute of every day together, sharing mortal danger and privations alike. Inevitably, deep friendships could be made very quickly. It was not unusual for men to find a kind of 'soulmate' within their immediate unit, and since he'd joined B Company, Franklyn-Vaile had become such close friends with Lieutenant John Glennie that the two had agreed to write letters to their respective families. 'He is a grand friend and I think you have the imagination to realize the need for friendship out here,' he wrote to Olive on 22 October. 'Life would indeed be miserable without it and John and I, thrown together by circumstances, have achieved a very deep friendship and understanding.' Glennie was only twenty-one, eleven years younger, and a slightly bluff Northern Irishman; in many ways they were an unlikely pair. But he made Franklyn-Vaile laugh and was ever cheerful. 'I think you would like his Ulsterism and high spirits and liveliness,' he wrote to Olive, 'but at the same time he has a touch of shyness and small boy aspects that make him very endearing.'

Franklyn-Vaile was writing about his friend that day as he waited to go into battle. They'd marched through the night, reached their positions in the early hours of the morning, dug in, and then received orders at 3.30 p.m. that afternoon to prepare to assault the River Trigno that night.

Eight miles to the north, the Benedictine monks at the Abbey of Monte Cassino were also trying to make sense of the storm that was beginning to whip into the valley below and on the mountains around them. A sense of imminent peril hung heavy in the air. Theirs was a quiet, ascetic existence, dedicated to prayer, contemplation and work, whether within the abbey or without, tending crops and livestock and producing honey, oil and wine. They were not a silent order but did keep hours of silence in which to think and read. The time given by God was not to be wasted but used in God's service. Rather like the village of San Pietro Infine, the Benedictines existed within a highly self-contained community. Intellectually and spiritually rich they may have been, but the machinations of the modern world were largely alien to them.

Benedict of Nursia had founded his second abbey here around the year 529; the first abbey had been sacked by invading Lombards in 570, and the second, built in the early eighth century, was again destroyed, this time by Saracens in 883. A third was established in 949 and became one of the most important monasteries of the Benedictine Order, but was already in decline when an earthquake struck and reduced it to rubble in 1349. Once again it was rebuilt and, in the sixteenth century, considerably enlarged. Despite being overrun by Napoleon's troops in 1799, the mostly sixteenth-century abbey church was repaired and rebuilt once more. This building, originally established more than 1,400 years earlier, dominated the surrounding countryside, a huge, white-stone and magnificent edifice to the Glory of God, perched on an outcrop at the very end of the Monte Cassino massif. It stood sentinel over the Liri Valley below, could be seen for miles, dazzlingly bright when the sun caught it, and a truly breathtaking and awe-inspiring sight from the little town of Cassino nearly 1,700 feet below.

While one of the reasons why Benedict had chosen the site was because of the beauty of its setting, it also made sense to build such an abbey high up where both buildings and monks would be safer. Lombards, Saracens and French revolutionary troops had all brought their own waves of destruction, but for the current generation of Benedictines this latest approach of war was troubling in the extreme. Padre Abate Gregorio Diamare – the Most Reverend Father Abbot – had complete authority over the abbey and those living there, but in practice he fathered his flock with a light touch. Gregorio was seventy-eight and had been abbot for thirty-four years; he knew little of wars, and certainly not modern ones with bombers and artillery capable of firing devastating shells miles on to mountainsides. So, now that war was sweeping towards them, he struggled to know what to do for the best.

The first Allied bombing raid on Cassino had been on 10 September, the day after the Salerno landings, prompting an influx of refugees, including from the Suore Missionaries della Carità – the Sisters of Charity – whose building had been badly damaged, but also from the town, so that suddenly there were more than 100 extra mouths to feed. That same day, a German aircraft had hit a support wire for the cable car that ran from the town to the abbey, so that was now out of action. Further air raids had occurred on 4 and 10 October, cutting off supplies of water and electricity. The monastic community had tried to continue their way of life as much as they could, but they all sensed that worse was to come.

On 14 October they had been visited by Oberstleutnant Julius Schlegel, an art historian currently serving in the HG Division. Witness to this meeting was Dom Eusebio Grossetti, a thirty-three-year-old monk and priest who, prompted by Schlegel's visit, decided to keep a diary of these extraordinary and disturbing times. 'I come in the name of peace,' Schlegel told the abbot, then confided that the German military high command was now preparing a powerful defensive line – the Gustav Line – which would run across the Monte Cassino massif. The abbey would therefore soon find itself on the front line. He advised the monks to leave the abbey and, as a practising Catholic, implored the abbot to save the abbey's artistic and cultural heritage. Schlegel offered to oversee their removal to a safe place.

The following day, the abbot called the community together. 'The meeting was extremely difficult,' noted Dom Eusebio. 'Nobody wanted to recognise the extreme gravity of the situation.' In the end, they agreed not to hand over the archive of codices and manuscripts but would entrust the main library to the Germans. Other treasures, including those of the Prince of Piedmont and of San Gennaro, were hidden in the underground passages of the abbey, while the monks also dug and prepared places to hide some of the most precious silver and gold.

Two days later Schlegel returned, again stressing that they should evacuate, and promised to return with soldiers and vehicles to remove the art treasures and library. This they duly did, a convoy of trucks arriving and packing up works of art and the abbey's library over the course of several days and nights, and German photographers and film cameramen from the propaganda services recording everything. 'Great upset and confusion overall,' noted Dom Eusebio, 'while the whole monastery is caught up in preparations.' Boxes and boxes were being loaded on to the lorries. It was so very difficult to know what to do for the best. If they declined the German offer and everything was destroyed it would be a catastrophe. On the other hand, could the Germans, about whom they knew very little but who had done nothing to demonstrate trustworthiness, be trusted? They all felt so ill equipped to make a judgement and had no idea whether they had made the right or wrong call. On the morning of 17 October, the first three lorries drove away. 'Everything will be destroyed,' the abbot said to Dom Eusebio, in a state of deep distress. He was openly weeping. Two days later, the abbot handed over a suitcase of sacred relics to Oberstleutnant Schlegel, telling him he was entrusting him with the most precious artefacts they had. The German gave his solemn word that they, and all the other treasures, would be safe in Rome.

The monks had to pray to God that Schlegel would be as good as his word.

The final truckloads left on 3 November, following a Mass at the High Altar, for which Schlegel had repeatedly asked and which was attended by a number of German officers, including General Conrath of the HG Division. This, too, was filmed, giving the monks an uncomfortable feeling that they had been made unwitting pawns in a bigger game. Most of the monks also departed, as had been urged by Schlegel, along with the various women's religious communities and civilians who had been recently staying there. Just thirteen monks, including the abbot and Dom Eusebio, remained. After the last truck departed, it was agreed with the Germans that two guards would be sent to prevent any pillaging or ransacking by troops or civilians. Dom Eusebio took the opportunity to ask one of the German officers whether the abbey would be safe. 'He expressed his personal opinion,' noted Dom Eusebio, 'that the Anglo-Americans would not bomb Monte Cassino, above all for political reasons.'

Later, a little after midday, he recorded the first Allied shells to fall on Cassino, on the Via Casilina down in the valley below. The dark clouds of war were inching ever closer.

Over on the other side of the leg of Italy, the Faughs had made their crossing of the Trigno and created a small bridgehead as planned. Overlooking the river on the southern side at this coastal edge of the line was a dominant ridge, but the far side was pretty flat, one of the reasons why it was a tricky position for 16. Panzer to defend. Once across, however, the Faughs had dug in and been shelled almost constantly. Lawrie Franklyn-Vaile thought the worst aspect of being shelled was the complete impotence he felt, and this experience, combined with a lack of food and woefully little sleep, was having a wearing effect on his nerves, leaving him tired and depressed. He reckoned he'd had no more than four hours' sleep in ninety-six hours. 'Indeed, yesterday,' he wrote, 'when I was by myself, I actually cried a little as I felt so done in.' He had then got a grip of himself, taken an aspirin and, grabbing a blanket, lain down under a tree, where he'd slept for six hours until roused by his batman bringing him a mug of tea. He woke feeling like a new man, but not five minutes later a shell whooshed in and landed 5 yards from where he'd been sleeping. 'Lesson learnt,' he noted, 'never sleep outside a slit trench.'

That night a German patrol tried to enter their area, but they heard them early, opened fire and the enemy retreated. Then it was B Company's turn to send a patrol forward and Franklyn-Vaile decided to go himself, really just to test his nerves. They didn't find anything, but the patrol had been a success as far as he was concerned, as he'd proved to himself that he could handle the tension and the fear. 'The only good thing that can be said for war,' he added, 'is the spirit of comradeship it produces. No finer friend than Johnny has ever existed and for once I have someone I can occasionally lean on.' He was writing this on 26 October, the day before his thirty-third birthday. Perhaps, he wrote, on 27 October 1944 he would be back at home with his beloved wife and daughter.

First, though, he had to survive the following night's attack, a horrid way to spend a birthday, scheduled to begin with a divisional artillery barrage at 11 p.m. Right on cue, the guns opened up.

The usual ear-splitting din. Shells whooshing and screaming over. Ground shaking. Flashes of light behind as the guns rippled. Bursts of flame ahead. 11.06 p.m. Forward companies move off to the start line – a line that only exists on a map. A Company on the right, B Company on the left. Infantry moving forward, two platoons up, one in reserve, and two sections up, one behind. Each section spread out to minimize casualties from mortars and shells. Darkness but not dark because of the explosions, because of flares crackling overhead. Almost a strobe effect. Pause, crouch, up, move on.

Then suddenly a burst of enemy machine-gun fire, bullets tearing across the sky so rapidly that the rip of the firing is almost one sound. Twenty-three bullets per second per gun. Tracer criss-crossing, enemy shells and mortars raining down on them in turn. Confusion, senses pummelled. The noise. The shaking ground. Men falling. Hard to keep going in this.

B Company was taking hits. In the confusion, Lawrie Franklyn-Vaile bumped against Johnny Glennie and together they decided to try and rally what men they could and push on. Crouching, crawling, making the most of the ground, they inched forward, making good progress. Franklyn-Vaile felt bizarrely calm and completely in control. He wasn't scared at all. Nor, it seemed, was Glennie, who was able to laugh and joke amid this mayhem. A fizz, and Franklyn-Vaile was hit with a glancing blow on the face. He groaned and in a moment Glennie was beside him. But he was OK. A nick, a bit of blood. Nothing more.

Now they were in a field and rather exposed. Hard to know exactly where they were. Glennie was hit in the arm, but not badly, and with the help of another, Franklyn-Vaile quickly bandaged him up. Clearly, they were going nowhere, the enemy fire was too intense. Time to pull back, but getting out of this field was not going to be easy. Suddenly, another burst of machine-gun fire and Glennie fell on his side, gasping, 'I have been hit in the chest.' Bullets fizzed and zapped all around them, but in a panic Franklyn-Vaile somehow managed to pull his friend clear and into some kind of cover. It was dark but still flashing, pulsing with light. Hurriedly sending off some of his men for some stretcher bearers, Franklyn-Vaile now lay with him in the field.

'You know I am here, Johnny?'

'I do, Frank,' Glennie replied. Franklyn-Vaile tried to fill the holes, but his friend was losing a lot of blood. 'Are you still there, Frank?' he asked. 'Don't leave me, will you?' Of course he was not going to. Glennie cried a little and began calling for his mother. This was it, the life slipping away, out in the middle of a muddy field in a totally unremarkable part of the Italian coastline.

Then he was gone, dead in Franklyn-Vaile's arms.

'I could have stood anything out here with the exception of Johnny's death,' he wrote from a field hospital a few days later. 'No one ever had a better friend and there is now a huge void which I don't know how I can possibly fill.'

CHAPTER 23

Continuous Pressure

OBERSTARZT WILHELM MAUSS WAS worrying about his family back
home in Hanover, which on the night of 8–9 October had been hit
by more than 500 RAF bombers. Nearly 4,000 buildings had been completely destroyed, 30,000 damaged and more than 1,200 people killed. It
was no wonder Mauss had been anxious for news. On 19 October, after
an agonizing wait, he heard from his wife that she was all right, although
she reported that much of the centre had gone, including the railway
station, post office and city hall. Later that night, he heard via the
Wehrmachtsbericht – the daily OKW-issued media communiqué – that
there had been a further raid on Hanover, although it had caused less
damage than the raid ten days earlier. That was hardly the point. 'Again
one worries for one's family,' noted Mauss. 'When will this ordeal come to
an end?'

Allied air power had been on his mind again a couple of days later,
when, with the sun shining, he was outside as enemy aircraft roared overhead. He felt so very helpless, especially if they came at night when there
was little chance of being able to see them or get any sense of where they
were heading. 'The Tommies were very active in the air today with the
good weather,' he wrote. 'They especially severely attacked Cassino.' With
the feverish work going on along both the Bernhard and Gustav Lines,
the area around Cassino had become a prime target for the Allied
bombers.

Certainly, throughout the second half of September, even after the
Salerno bridgehead was secured, Jim Reed and the 33rd Fighting Nomads
had been flying whenever the weather allowed. On 23 September Reed

had flown his seventy-ninth combat mission, this time a bombing run on a road and town inland. 'We ran into a lot of very, very accurate flak and we had to scatter everywhere,' he noted. 'We didn't hit very much.' Everyone made it home, which was something of a wonder to him. This should have been his penultimate flight, but yet again the criteria had changed, a reflection of the shortage of pilots in the theatre and the second-class status Italy was getting compared with England. He flew his eightieth the following day, this time a comparatively straightforward stooge around Capri, but it felt like he was tempting fate, and each time he flew he became increasingly convinced he was on borrowed time and that he'd never quite make it home. Then the weather intervened and he didn't fly again until 6 October. So that was eighty-two. As long as they didn't move the goalposts yet again, that left him just eight missions to complete his tour.

Wing Commander Cocky Dundas, on the other hand, was not flying to a specific number of missions, so was only too happy to fly a little less. He and his 324 Wing had moved to Capodichino on the edge of Naples on 10 October. It was one of the days on which it had been pouring with rain, and although he and his fellow pilots had been happy at the thought of moving into houses rather than tents they soon had a change of heart. Dundas was depressed by the state of the decaying city, the hordes of filthy, tattered people begging and scavenging for food and the lack of any kind of amenities. They tried to make themselves as comfortable as possible, but he reckoned they would have been better off in tents near the edge of the airfield. At any rate, sickness levels soon rose, although maybe the malaise Dundas personally felt was more to do with his state of mind. He was feeling physically and mentally exhausted; there'd been a time when getting into a cockpit had given him an incredible thrill, but now he found he had to force himself to fly. In the evenings he did his bit as a wing commander, touring the messes and adopting an image of cheery bonhomie, but inside he was feeling all done in.

With the Luftwaffe down to only 350 or so aircraft throughout the Mediterranean, the role of the tactical air forces was now primarily to provide standing patrols in case enemy aircraft did show up and shoot at potential ground targets. The weather, though, was seriously limiting what they could do, which was ominous for the Allies; during the final phase of the Tunisian campaign and throughout the battle for Sicily, Allied tactical air forces had ruled the roost. They gave such an enormous boost to the troops on the ground, particularly by limiting the enemy's ability to move by day, but also striking at targets just behind the lines. Poor weather, as well as the shortening days, was already severely restricting their effectiveness and as a result taking away a huge advantage the Allies had over the Germans.

The strategic air forces were still mainly operating from the balmy skies of North Africa, however, and there they would remain until teams of engineers had sufficiently licked the Foggia airfields into shape after the hammering they'd given them when they'd been held by the Luftwaffe. Medium bombers, on the other hand, were now moving into airfields at Crotone in the toe and around Taranto and also in Sardinia and Corsica, which gave them greater opportunities to strike enemy targets in northern Italy and even into southern France; Allied troops might still have been far to the south of Rome, but Allied air forces were getting closer to the Reich and, once the Foggia airfields opened up, would be tightening the ring even more so.

The heavies, however, could still reach railway marshalling yards and, by staging in Italy, even German aircraft factories. Joining the 2nd Bomb Group at Tunis was Lieutenant T. Michael Sullivan, a replacement bombardier from Elgin, Illinois. Having joined the Army Air Force in April the previous year, when just eighteen, he had completed his training and then been shipped overseas on 23 September in a large sixty-five-ship convoy to Casablanca. Reaching Morocco on 11 October, he'd managed to watch the movie *Casablanca* in the town itself, then set off in a C-47 Dakota along with fourteen other aircrew for the final leg. Bad weather could strike North Africa too, however, and they were forced to pause in Algiers for a night before finally reaching the 2nd Bomb Group on 18 October and being posted to the 429th Bomb Squadron. 'Came by truck to my bomber base,' he noted in his diary. 'Burned planes and tanks all over. Live in tents. No conveniences.' If Sullivan had been a bit taken aback by such basic surroundings, he quickly put his concerns to one side. 'Damn good so far,' he noted three days after his arrival; he was relishing being part of a real squadron and itching to get going. First, though, he was being put through night school, attending classes in meteorology and navigation. It wasn't anything he hadn't already learned and was really more of a refresher, part of the acclimatization process, than anything else. On 22 October, he flew a practice mission over Sicily and southern Italy with Lieutenant John C. Goodfellow's crew on a B-17 Flying Fortress they'd named *Wolf Pack*. All went well, and so Sullivan was cleared to begin the fifty combat missions that constituted a tour in the Mediterranean theatre for American aircrew.

On the 23rd they flew to Grottaglie, near Taranto, where Harold Macmillan et al. had landed more than a month earlier. This was now a B-25 medium bomber base where they were to spend the night, each man having flown in with his flying kit, mess kit and a bedroll. 'Ate a rotten supper,' Sullivan noted. 'Slept on marble floor in operations.' It was perhaps not the best preparation for a first mission, particularly when it was hardly a straightforward 'milk run' but rather an attack on the seven Luftwaffe plants at Wiener Neustadt in Austria, which, according to Allied intelligence, were now producing 20 per cent of all German single-engine fighters and 40 per cent of all Messerschmitt 109s. Enemy fighters and intense flak over the target could be expected. More than 200 heavies were scheduled for the mission, with fifty P-38 Lightnings escorting, Smoky Vrilakas among them. Escorting the strategic air forces meant operating for longer and at higher altitudes, so the P-38 Lightnings were now given drop-tanks with extra fuel, but also more oxygen and electric suits – Vrilakas hated them as some parts of his suit burned his skin, while in other patches it didn't work at all.

The weather once again was not great, with ten-tenths cloud, but despite this the formation managed to form up over Foggia. By the time they'd reached Austria the force had become badly strung out, which was not good when keeping in tight formation was key to effective defence. Fortunately, the bad weather also prevented the Luftwaffe from getting airborne. By the time they reached the Wiener Neustadt plants, visibility was almost non-existent and only a mere five B-17 Flying Fortresses managed to drop their bombs anywhere near the targets. 'Impossible to see target,' noted Sullivan. 'Washout mission.' It had been a lot of effort on the part of Twelfth Air Force for almost no gain, but from a personal point of view, at least Sullivan had got his first mission under his belt and with a big 1,000-mile raid too.

A few days later, on 29 October, T. Michael Sullivan flew with a different crew to hit a ball-bearing factory in Turin in northern Italy, but the Flying Fortress developed engine trouble and they had to turn back. Bad weather scuppered his next trip, due for 5 November. 'Another combat mission called off,' he noted a day later. 'Bad weather.' He whiled away the time by sleeping, reading and writing letters. And the next day, Sunday 7 November, it was the same, bad weather calling off a renewed attempt to

hit Turin. That same Sunday he learned that one of his friends from training had been killed on a second strike at Wiener Neustadt less than a
week earlier. Sullivan was cut up to hear the news. 'He was an old friend
and a swell kid,' he wrote. 'I'll pray for him.' Whether it concerned tanks
and vehicles or fighter planes and heavy bombers, the advent of winter
was not helping Allied plans.

Generalleutnant Fridolin von Senger und Etterlin had been a little surprised to have been given command of XIV Panzerkorps. Just turned
fifty-two, von Senger, a former Rhodes Scholar at Oxford University, was
a highly intellectual career soldier and, unlike the vast majority of senior
Wehrmacht commanders, had never truly supported National Socialism.
He was a proud German, however, and had always taken his military
duties seriously; he had done well in France in 1940 and had commanded
17. Panzer-Division in the Soviet Union. Having been attached to 6a
Armata headquarters during the Sicilian campaign, von Senger had then
been posted to command the German garrison on Corsica. After the Italian surrender, German commanders had executed thousands of Italian
troops of the Acqui Division on the Greek island of Cephalonia, and
had demonstrated an equally brutal approach to Italian resistance elsewhere in Italy and the Balkans. Von Senger had refused to do any such
thing in Corsica – for which he'd confidently expected to be sacked.
Instead, having managed to evacuate most of his troops from the island
largely unscathed, he'd been applauded and now promoted.

He joined the corps headquarters at its new digs in Roccasecca and
quickly discovered that there was something of a schism between those
in the Panzerkorps who were North Africa veterans and Rommel
supporters – such as his Chief of Staff, von Bonin – and those who were
not, picking up the same streak of animosity towards Kesselring that
Balck had discovered. Von Bonin favoured Rommel's planned withdrawal to the north and believed that Kesselring's insistence on fighting
south of Rome had caused needless slaughter, while other divisional
commanders thought it was wrong to squander any ground at all. These
factions von Senger would have to try and reconcile over time. Immediately, though, he now had six divisions in behind the Bernhard Line, a
position which Hube had chosen and which, von Senger knew, his predecessor felt was stronger than the Gustav Line still being developed
behind it. As the new XIV Panzerkorps commander was aware, however,
the quality of the troops was key to successfully holding ground and so

he wasted no time in heading out on a tour of inspection to see how his men were deployed.

While von Senger was touring the front, the troops on the ground were bracing themselves for the onslaught they knew would come. Hans Golda was not happy. Werfer-Regiment 71 had been sent forward just north-west of the Mignano Gap and, together with the other two batteries, had dug themselves into excellent firing positions, established CPs and built up ammunition. Then had come orders for his 7. Batterie to move further forward almost as far as Monte Lungo. 'This fucking shit!' Golda railed. 'The others squat in impeccably built positions and we are the stupid ones yet again.' With no small resentment, off they went to the area marked on the map. On his left Monte Sammucro rose up 3,000 feet; on his right was the even more dominating Camino massif, while directly ahead was Monte Lungo, the valley snaking either side. Behind, the low saddle of Monte Trocchio, guarding the entrance to the Liri Valley. It was hard not to feel a little small surrounded by all these magnificent mountains. He set up his battery near the railway line as it brushed the southern slopes of Monte Lungo and about 500 yards in front of the Stazione di Rocca d'Evandro rail halt. In front, a stream passed underneath the railway; both the embankment and the hedges and trees here offered some decent cover. What's more, just behind was a stone farmhouse. 'We haul all the junk into the room above us,' he noted, 'support the ceiling, reinforce the thin walls, shore up the door with thick logs, create a narrow entrance for ourselves, leaving only a narrow window to the rear and make the room into something liveable.'

On 24 October there had been a Commanders' Conference in Tunis with Eisenhower and the three service chiefs, which Harold Macmillan had attended. The meeting broke for lunch, and after the meal Alexander offered to drive Macmillan around the northern battlefields they had fought over in Tunisia in April and May, visiting the Medjerda Valley and climbing over Grenadier Hill and Longstop, landmarks that had witnessed vicious fighting. 'It was most interesting,' noted Macmillan, 'and gave one a great insight into his methods and the essential clarity of his thought.'

That same clarity of thought had been evident in an appreciation Alex had written in anticipation of the Commanders' Conference. It provided a summary of the events so far but then looked at the German situation, which showed they currently had nine divisions at the front and many more in the north. In contrast, the Allies' own build-up was dropping badly from 1,300 vehicles a day to 2,000 a week. This reduction was being exacerbated by the decision to move the Strategic Air Forces into Foggia as rapidly as possible. As ever, the lack of shipping, especially landing craft, was the biggest problem. 'The reduction in craft, already decreased by wear and tear,' Alexander noted, 'has been so serious as to preclude us from taking advantage, other than with minor forces, of the enemy's inherent weakness, which is the exposure of his two flanks to turning movements from the sea.' He argued that despite the enemy's superiority in divisions, a stabilized front south of Rome could not possibly be accepted. 'The capital has a significance far greater than its strategic location,' he added, 'and sufficient depth must be gained before the Foggia airfields and the port of Naples can be regarded as secure. This being so, the seizure of a firm defensive base north of Rome becomes imperative.' Nothing had made him change his mind about the need for a decent cushion north of Foggia.

In any case, to go on to the defensive would entail surrendering the initiative to the Germans. It would also expose the Allies to a major counter-attack by potentially vastly superior numbers. As Alexander had stated very clearly when taking over as C-in-C Middle East the previous August 1942, there were to be no more reverses. That was an even firmer mantra by October 1943. 'The obvious present German intention,' he continued, 'is to hold a line south of Rome, where the country favours defence and allows no scope to the deployment of our superiority in armour or artillery. Coming bad weather will limit the employment of our air forces, as indeed it has done already.' He feared they were about to be committed to a long slogging match in which, even if it was successful, they might be so exhausted by the end that they were more vulnerable to a powerful German counter-attack from the north.

This had been discussed at length at the conference. All were agreed on the need to keep fighting and maintain the initiative. Rome absolutely remained the goal, and as soon as possible. The following day, 25 October, Eisenhower cabled the Combined Chiefs of Staff, envisioning a two-fisted assault – Eighth Army to strike towards the high ground north of Pescara on the Adriatic and then threaten Rome from the east, and then Fifth Army to launch a frontal attack directly towards the capital, but combined with an airborne drop near Rome and an amphibious operation just as soon as enough landing craft could be assembled. That would mean keeping landing craft for a little longer, but Eisenhower's plans for 1943 remained the same: Rome before Christmas.

*

Meanwhile, Fifth Army continued its slow advance to the Bernhard Line, which was now known by Clark's men more simply as the Winter Line. Approaching the position, Fifth Army had to negotiate yet more demolitions, an upper Volturno that had become a raging torrent, 45,000 mines in the approach to the Bernhard defences and a further 30,000 immediately before it. Lucas's VI Corps were once again running up against the River Volturno, which was turning into something of a bad penny that kept dogging them all the way. This was because it began in the mountains north-east of Cassino, ran southwards then south-west of the town of Venafro, before wiggling south-eastwards until dog-legging westwards to the sea – which was the stretch the Allies had crossed in October. Now, though, the 34th Red Bulls had to cross it again to capture Venafro and get into the hills and mountains beyond.

It was the end of October. That left only two months of the year. Rome by Christmas! But, of course, time was running short, just as the days were shortening. On the morning of 29 October, Lucas showed General Clark his plan for crossing the Volturno a second time. Admittedly, it wasn't anything like as deep here but was wide, still quite shallow with plenty of gravel banks and bars. It was, however, very exposed to the hills beyond – where the Germans now were. Clark liked the sound of Lucas's plan, but the Red Bulls were still a long way behind and he was clearly feeling impatient. In the army newspaper the *Stars and Stripes*, Lucas had seen an article which claimed that the Germans were fleeing before them. 'No German yet has ever fled,' he noted. 'They are fighting a stubborn, determined and skillful rear-guard action and they never flee.' New field orders were issued on this day. The Red Bulls were to cross the Volturno east of Venafro then seize the high ground north of the town, while the 45th Thunderbirds would pass through the 34th and take Venafro from the south – a quiet, pretty town with a notable Romanesque church nestling below the hills behind it. From the upper Volturno Valley, this normally beautiful panorama was a demoralizing sight: vast, rugged mountains climbing steadily higher into the distance. 'The prospect,' noted Lucas, 'was not pleasant.'

The next day, Alexander visited the front as he was wont to do. Lucas took him and Clark to 3rd Division's front as they approached the Mignano Gap, a little to the south-east of Venafro. As they motored north from Lucas's CP near Caserta, they passed through the battered town of Pietravairano. Here they were slightly held up because two young children had just been blown to bits by a German booby trap. 'Damn the

German,' muttered Lucas in his diary. The town backed on to a saddle between two long, razor-crested peaks that barred the way to the upper Volturno Valley, but the Army Group commander was anxious to climb up and see the battleground ahead for himself. An important OP had already been established up there and the views were breathtaking – all the way to Venafro and the Mignano Gap and the towering peaks beyond – both in terms of beauty and the sheer enormity of the task before them. Lucas, though, was deeply concerned that both Alexander and Clark were wandering about with no regard at all for their safety, while the infantry and artillery observers were crouching under their camouflaged positions, being within range of enemy guns.

Yet Lucas was also worried because there was pressure to press on harder and faster. Progress was slower than everyone would have liked. Clark was urging him to push the 34th Red Bulls swiftly across the Volturno, insisting that the enemy were no longer there. 'But I still think we should do the thing right and not run the risk of a mouse trap,' he noted. 'Why inflict unnecessary casualties on my men? And, why risk a bloody nose when, by sound tactics, it can be avoided?' In fairness to Lucas, this was very much the approach the British had adopted ever since Montgomery had taken command of Eighth Army in August the previous year, and it was rooted in sound sense. Monty would have applauded this sentiment. But political pressure was coming from above to push on, not get bogged down. To be in Rome before Christmas. The entire Italian campaign had begun with the Allies' normal cautious, heavily front-loaded approach to war being flung to one side. The Winter – Bernhard – Line and Gustav Line behind were like a huge, metal, double-locked door, and with every passing day another bolt was being added, making the barrier to the golden Liri Valley beyond that much tougher. So, yes, Clark was well aware that much was being expected of the men in his army, but this was not a time for caution. It was the time to smash a way through before it was too late. In other words, to take more casualties now in order to suffer fewer later.

Even so, Lucas was not prepared to berate Doc Ryder and his 34th Red Bulls and they were late crossing the Volturno south of Venafro; their attack on 2 November was postponed by a day, although 3rd Division was doing better and drawing up towards Mignano. Finally, the Red Bulls and 45th Thunderbirds crossed the Volturno on 4 November, a further day later than planned. 'This is a heart-breaking business,' noted Lucas.

'An advance of a few miles a day, fighting a terrible terrain and determined enemy, building bridges, removing mines, climbing mountains. The men get punch drunk, but we must keep on going. Continuous pressure is the answer.'

All the Allied commanders were telling themselves this. Whether they believed it or not, however, was another matter.

CHAPTER 24

The Winter Line

O N 25 OCTOBER, LIEUTENANT Jim Reed had flown his eighty-ninth combat mission, a fighter sweep around and north of Naples. His eighty-eighth had been a nightmare – the bombers they'd supposed to be escorting had turned home due to bad weather and then they'd flown straight into the storm. Somehow, he'd managed to get back to Paestum and, miracle of miracles, safely land in the mud. If he'd become convinced his luck was sure to run out, that mission had done nothing to persuade him otherwise. But then again nor had this eighty-ninth mission, because just after he'd narrowly escaped being hit by flak well north of Naples his engine started cutting out. He'd hardly been able to believe it, but although he'd been waiting for disaster to strike all the way back to Paestum, *Cloud Hopper* had looked after him – or rather, he'd looked after *Cloud Hopper* – and he'd touched down and jumped on to dry land once again.

And then that had been it. Eighty-nine was all that was asked of him; he'd made it through after all. He and Lieutenant Tom Lamb, who was also tour-expired, got up early on Friday, 29 October and hastily packed so as to be ready to go at a moment's notice. He could barely believe he'd completed his tour after all. 'After saying goodbye to nearly everyone,' he noted in his diary, 'we got off just after dinner and head for Naples.' They stayed the night there, then the following morning were off, via Foggia, Catania in Sicily and Tunis – all the places he had flown and fought in the year since he'd left the States. Jim Reed was on his way home, his combat flying days over.

The DUKE pilots of 324 Wing, meanwhile, were still living in the wreckage of Naples. On the evening of 2 November, Cocky Dundas was visiting the pilots in one of his squadrons who were billeted in a house on the hillside down from the airfield and towards the harbour. While he was there the air raid siren rang out, the distant roar of bombers could be heard, and then the customary anti-aircraft barrage opened up. None of the pilots made any effort to head to a shelter and Dundas carried on drinking downstairs while several others were upstairs watching. Suddenly, a Ju88 bomber thundered over at low level firing its guns. By chance, a bullet hit Freddie Mellors of 111 Squadron in the neck and he collapsed on to the floor dead. It was a reminder that there were many different ways in which a man could end up getting killed in Italy.

One way was in a traffic accident. There were macadamed roads in the cities and the main highways were asphalted, but the vast majority were *strade bianche*, designed for very occasional motor vehicles but mainly horse-drawn and hand-drawn carriages. Despite producing Alfa Romeos, Fiats and Lancias before the war, Italy had been among the least automotive nations in western Europe, with an average of one motor vehicle for every ninety people, and most of these were in the large cities. These roads were not designed for the more than 3,000 vehicles that made up an Allied infantry division in the second half of 1943.

On 1 November, 8th Indian Division HQ moved again, this time to San Felice del Molise, a few miles south-east of the River Trigno. It was raining again, and the wiggling, winding mountain roads – little more than tracks – which had been subject to the usual demolitions were simply not suitable for big 3-ton trucks and larger. Before the journey to San Felice, Captain Asquith of the cipher team had warned his men that the route would be treacherous; apparently, an acting provost marshal had been killed at a certain point when his jeep ran over the edge, while a tank had also come off the road, injuring two. Their same aggressive Indian driver was behind the wheel, which did nothing to improve Harry Wilson's confidence, and they all spent the entire journey fearing their imminent demise. All were grateful that their back wheels had been equipped with skid chains, but they were still held up en route as various vehicles came off the road, rolled into ditches and had to be pulled out. At the particularly dangerous spot where the provost marshal had died, their driver kept hugging the edge of the road insanely close to the cliff. Spiers and Wilson were anxiously looking out the back when they suddenly saw a void under their right-hand rear wheel as the truck leaped a culvert.

'Jesus wept!' said Spiers, looking as white as a ghost.

Somehow, they made it safely to San Felice, where once again they began to dig in, especially as they were now much closer to the front line than they had been. They were also next to the divisional artillery, which woke up Harry Wilson at 4 a.m. It was his first experience of having shells whistling over his head. 'They soughed through the air making a noise like a train steaming through a tunnel,' he jotted. 'The din was appalling and the echoes added to it.' He and Spiers had a cigarette each then reckoned they'd got accustomed to the racket and so went back to sleep. 'I reckon you get used to anything in this world,' he added.

That morning, medium bombers roared over hammering the German ridgeline beyond the Trigno, and more flew over later. Guns, bombers, Spitfires too, barrage again, in sequence. Then shells started crashing around from the other direction, although none had yet landed at Division HQ. A novice under shellfire, Wilson had looked around hoping everyone else would be hurrying to take cover but no one did, and so they carried on working. 'But I felt as insecure,' he wrote, 'as an earthbound fly under a poised swat.'

With Fifth Army closing up to the Bernhard Line, the vision Wilhelm Mauss had had of the villagers becoming ravaged by war was about to become tragically fulfilled. Most of the Sanpietresi who had taken to the mountain had since returned and instead were now living in a series of caves at the western end of the village. A sharp cliff of perhaps 30 feet marked the village boundary as it overlooked a narrow and shallow gorge that ran down from the mountain. The limestone here was soft tufa and comparatively easy to cut; a fingernail could easily score a line in the rock, and with picks, shovels and hard toil it did not take too long to hollow out a series of caves at the foot of the cliff.

Living a troglodyte existence in these makeshift caves were a number of families from San Pietro, including Benedetto and Enrichetta Pagano and their children, but also Serafino and Antonia Masella and their young son and daughter. Serafino was a cobbler, but like most of the men from the village his sole occupation now was one of survival and ensuring they kept themselves hidden from the Germans, who were still rounding up the local menfolk and forcing them to become military labourers.

Water was collected at night or by the women from a stream a little further down below, but the privations were many and made worse by the persistent fear, uncertainty and anxiety over the welfare of their children. No one knew whether they'd ever be able to return to their homes and whether, after the fighting, they would even have homes to which they could return. One thing, however, was certain as the thunder of artillery grew ever nearer: the fighting was drawing closer.

This of course meant that, apart from occasional air raids by the Luftwaffe, the battle had now passed well to the north of Naples, but the city and its citizens still faced a long road to recovery and life was as perilous and uncertain for many Neapolitans as it was for the Sanpietresi now huddled in their caves. Still trying his best to alleviate some of the misery was Sergeant Norman Lewis, although he was far from sanguine and outraged to be told that counter-intelligence funds were to be reduced to just 400 *lire* – the equivalent of £1 – per section member per week. These funds were vital for paying informers in the battle against the already rampant black market and other crimes and misdemeanours. Lewis was well aware that most of the informers he'd got on his lists would still work for him because they had little choice, but it was for these skin-and-bones civilians in his pay that he felt so disgusted. After all, occupation money cost next to nothing to print.

One of his informers was called, simply, 'Lattarullo' and on 1 November he called on Lewis to tell him the latest long list of black-market operators. The poor fellow looked even weaker and hungrier than normal and, even when sat down, began swaying with his eyes closed. After taking down the names Lattarullo gave him, Lewis decided to take him for a meal. They set off together, walking through the broken, crumbling city. Piles of masonry were everywhere and had to be negotiated, while Lattarullo was so weak with hunger he had to frequently stop to gather his strength. The stench out on the streets was appalling – shattered drains were part of the problem, but because the drains were broken, both excrement and rubbish simply ended up on the street. In no more than 200 yards, Lewis was accosted three times by child-pimps. Lattarullo was offered a cut-price coffin. All the shops were shut except for the bakers, who offered no bread but instead *torrone* and marzipan, made from stolen Allied sugar. A collapsed building in the Vico Chiatamone proved something of a choke-point, but because of this a sanitary post had been set up where every passer-by was sprayed with DDT.

They eventually reached a restaurant where they sat down and ordered macaroni. Yet more boys begged and cajoled, the *scugnizzi* of the city, although no one made much effort to whisk them away; they were like persistent flies. Then, suddenly, six little girls appeared, aged, Lewis guessed, between about nine and twelve years old. They had all had their hair cut short like convicts and were weeping and clinging to one another as they bumped and banged into tables. Everyone ignored them and their pathetic begging and crying. Suddenly, Lewis realized they were all blind. Lattarullo then explained that the girls were from an orphanage on the Vomero, where conditions were rumoured to be very bad. Apparently, they'd been brought down here on a half-day's outing.

Seeing these tragic girls caused something of a Damascene moment for Lewis – although his conversion was not to the righteousness of God and a holy cause but to one of profound pessimism. 'These little girls,' he wrote, 'any one of whom could be my daughter, came into the restaurant weeping, and they were weeping when they were led away. I knew that, condemned to everlasting darkness, hunger and loss, they would weep on incessantly. They would never recover from their pain, and I would never recover from the memory of it.'

This was the terrible reality of the war in Italy. How simple it had been for the Allies in North Africa, where there were vast deserts in which few others lived. There, one army could fight another army in a clean war that damaged little but their own souls and their own machines. Here, in this so densely populated city, the full horrors of a modern war were laid bare for anyone who cared to look. Most didn't, because the reality was too awful to contemplate and because those fighting this new, brutal European war were already hardened to its horrors. Life had become cheaper, the misery of starving Italians too commonplace and the challenges facing the storm-wrecked south of Italy simply too great to be easily overcome. The war had ripped through the road north like an earthquake, leaving in its wake villages and towns reduced to rubble and hundreds of thousands with no home, no food and no hope. This was the price of liberation from the Nazi yoke. And the price of exiting a war.

On the right-hand flank of the Americans of VI Corps were the British 5th Division, who had been the first to land in Italy from across the Straits of Messina in the distant summer days of 3 September. Captain David Cole and the 2nd Inniskillings had battled their way up the Tyrrhenian coast, then been shifted to the centre to complete the line between the Americans and the rest of Eighth Army, joining the now continuous front on 25 October. Since then, they'd been pushing through the mountains and hills. The pattern was much the same most days: send patrols out, get fired upon, work out enemy strength, call up some artillery and push forward on a scale appropriate to the size of the enemy defence. Usually, the Germans then fell back fairly swiftly as they gradually headed towards the Bernhard Line. The conditions were appalling, so 13th Brigade's battalions would take turns helping the mud-immobilized artillery. Near Roccamandolfi, at the edge of a lush, fertile valley, but backed by mountains and ridges, Cole caught glimpses of Allied fighter-bombers streaking through the valley at low level, hammering with their guns at a column of German transport; sadly, these glimpses were symptomatic of the fleeting nature of Allied tactical air power over the battlefront. The terrible weather ensured it could never be more than that.

From Roccamandolfi they had to climb two more peaks of the Matese Mountains. By early morning on 2 November they had reached the tiny village of Castelpizzuto, 2,500 feet above sea level but lying in a cultivated bowl surrounded by towering peaks. David Cole was admiring the cold but fresh mountain air and rare, clear, sunny sky as he made his way towards Advanced HQ. His path took him up a steep meadow, past a farmstead with chickens clucking freely, when suddenly, with only the briefest warning, a salvo of shells screamed in. He and the handful of men he was with flung themselves on to the ground and moments later the shells erupted, mushrooming mud, stone, grit and smoke into the air. By a strange lottery that Cole had long ago given up understanding, not one of them was hurt. Two days later the battalion entered the town of Isernia, their objective, Cole still happily unscathed.

By the beginning of November Eighth Army had crossed the River Trigno and was now, after the capture of Isernia, drawn up in a line alongside Fifth Army. With Alexander and his HQ now based in Bari with easy air access to both Army HQ he took more direct control and decided to adopt his favourite tactic of the two-handed punch, in which his forces would strike on one side, draw enemy reserves, then strike again on the other. This was the joint directive Mark Clark had received on 9 November. The first punch – Phase I – was to be by Eighth Army, smashing its way across the River Sangro, the next major obstacle. It would then push on to Pescara and Avezzano. Alexander hoped this first assault would draw 26. Panzer from XIV Panzerkorps, to which it had recently been switched, back into the fold of LXXVI Panzerkorps on the Adriatic side. Then Clark's Fifth Army would attempt to blast its way through the Bernhard and Gustav Lines and reach the town of Frosinone, which was thirty miles north-west of Cassino on the road to Rome. This was Phase II, and was certainly ambitious; but the prize had always been to be in Rome by Christmas, so with that giddy goal rather on everyone's minds, there was no point in proceeding with anything other than forthright confidence. But there was also a Phase III: an amphibious operation south of Rome in the Anzio area, possibly supported by an airborne landing too. The limited landing craft available were being retained until 15 December, but Clark's team were to begin planning for Phase III on the assumption that more landing craft would – somehow – be secured.

All along the front, more troops were moving up into the line. Now that Eighth Army had crossed the River Trigno, 8th Indian Division were on the move again, still to be brought into the battle properly but holding the left flank of the 78th Battleaxe Division. Harry Wilson and Division ciphers passed through Montefalcone on 8 November, the target of their guns the week before. The narrow pass into it had been bombed, shelled and then finally completely demolished by the retreating Germans, so the cipher staff got out of their truck and walked. A grey-haired, rather refined gentleman approached them. 'My three houses gone,' he said in English. 'All finished!'

'What's he worrying about?' said Sergeant Fisher. 'I haven't even got one house, let alone three.'

It then began to rain again, torrentially, and with thunder and lightning too. They camped for the night at Palmoli, and Wilson woke up the following morning with wet legs as during the night he'd slipped down the slope. They then moved on toward Furci, another tiny ridgeline village just a few miles south of the River Sangro, although not before Indian engineers had bulldozed and ploughed a new road across the hillside ahead of them. Once again, Wilson and everyone else in the convoy had to clamber down and walk while the trucks slid and wheels spun and the sappers threw down stones and branches in an effort to make the wheels grip. They eventually reached Furci at 4 p.m.

Two days later, Wilson saw that bill notices had been pasted on the walls of the village, written in Alexander's name as the Military Commander of the Occupied Territories. The notice began by apologizing for the Allies having to occupy Italy and bring it under martial law. But all citizens would be properly treated if they respected the law. All Italians should accept Allied currency. There were then a number of offences which carried the death sentence, for while the British no longer had capital punishment for desertion, it held for other crimes, not least rape or attempted rape of any Allied nurses, but also any attacks on Allied troops. Weapons, war materiel and radio sets were to be surrendered by 15 November. There was also a curfew imposed from sunset to sunrise. Anyone trying to leave Italy by boat would be fired at. These orders were really not very different at all from those posted up by Oberst Scholl in Naples. Just as Wilson had finished reading the notice, a number of P-40 Kittyhawks roared over at low level to attack German positions on the far side of the Sangro, and he noticed that the old women of the village and the children all hurried back into the safety of their homes.

On Monday, 15 November 8th Indian Division HQ was on the move again as its fighting units prepared to enter the battle for the first time. The ciphers staff moved out in convoy at 6 p.m., by which time dusk was descending. No one dared put on headlights. 'The rain was over,' noted Wilson, 'but the sky was full of murky cloud, which was spectacularly lit up at close intervals by the vivid flashes of the front-line guns.' There was nervous chatter as to how their driver might cope in the dark, but at least they were topped and tailed by other vehicles and crawling at a snail's pace. Then, around 8 p.m., the wind folded back the cloud, revealing a wondrous full moon that bathed them in a milky pale light. Wilson nodded off, woke up to eat some biscuits and drink some beer, then dozed once more. When he awoke again they had stopped. Where they were he had no idea, but the artillery were firing again, their flashes flickering and rippling across the countryside.

On 6 November, Hitler had appointed Kesselring as the German OB – supremo – in Italy. Even a month earlier, when he'd backed Kesselring's plans to fight south of Rome, he'd still intended Rommel to take overall charge, a move that was widely expected by Jodl, Warlimont and the planners at the OKW. Rommel had been expecting the announcement too. Instead, on 24 October, Kesselring had been summoned to see Hitler, and clearly his particular brand of optimism and positivity at a time when the Führer had very little to cheer about had cut through most effectively. Rommel, much to his deep chagrin, was sent off to inspect the Atlantic Wall, while Kesselring's Heeresgruppe C was enlarged to cover all of Italy. In addition to AOK 10 he was also given a second army, AOK 14, under Generaloberst Eberhard von Mackensen, who had formerly commanded 1. Panzerarmee in Russia.

With this sudden and dramatic clarification of command came a renewed interest from Hitler in the Italian campaign, which was good for Kesselring insofar as it meant that more troops and supplies were on their way, but bad because it would inevitably reduce his room for man- oeuvre. With von Vietinghoff away sick, AOK 10 was temporarily being commanded by General Joachim Lemelsen, another Russian veteran, so that both XIV Panzerkorps and the Tenth Army now facing the Allies were being commanded by new boys. Nor were they happy with the situ- ation. Clark might have been bitterly disappointed by the lack of breakthrough, but Fifth Army's hammering of the Bernhard Line had been costly to the Germans. Neither von Senger nor Lemelsen thought much of 3. Panzergrenadier, and 15. Panzergrenadier was badly in need of a chance to rest and refit. Lemelsen proposed pulling back to the north of the Mignano Gap, which would effectively mean withdrawing to the Gustav Line behind, but predictably Hitler refused to countenance such a withdrawal; Kesselring should have just done it without referring it upstairs, but because of his new appointment was anxious to get off on the right foot.

Meanwhile, Lemelsen also recognized that on the left flank of the line, along the Adriatic, huge danger lurked. Only two divisions were holding the line: 65. Infanterie, also full of 'Ost' battalions – conscripts from east- ern Europe – and 1. Fallschirmjäger. Lemelsen had the battered 16. Panzer in reserve behind, but this was a rather spent force; he did also have two more divisions on their way, 26. Panzer, which had only ever been temporarily switched to von Senger's command, and 90. Panzer- grenadier, which had been holding Corsica. What really worried Lemelsen was whether these would arrive before Eighth Army smashed a way through. Time was of the essence.

Forty miles to the north, Fifth Army was preparing for another swing of the battering ram as the Germans fell in behind the Bernhard Line, their strongest defensive position so far. 'Jerry is going back to the River Garigliano,' noted Jack Ward on 2 November, 'and I expect will make a stand there.' The 56th Heavy Regiment had moved and were in a village near Teano. He'd never seen filth like it. 'The worst sight I have ever seen was a baby in arms,' he jotted, 'just looked like a piece of skin and bone with a head of an old man. Tensed me up to see it.'

General Dick McCreery, the X Corps commander, had been braced for a big scrap on Monte Massico, a 2,500-foot massif overlooking the coast, but the Germans withdrew almost without firing a shot, which meant 46th Division, on the left flank, were scurrying along the low-lying coastal region. Suddenly, on 2 November, they were at the River Garigliano, and 7th Armoured was now switched to this coastal stretch where Hans Golda and his men had enjoyed a week after the Volturno and where, it was hoped, they could better use their armour. A much tougher nut, however, was the mighty bulwark of Monte Camino, another 3,000-foot peak towering over the southern side of the Mignano Gap; it and Monte Sammucro on the other side formed two matching bastions guarding the entrance to the Liri Valley and Cassino beyond.

It was 56th Division, and specifically – to begin with, at any rate – the 201st Guards Brigade who were given the task of trying to take Monte Camino. The 56th Heavy Regiment were giving them support from the town of Grottole seven miles from Camino. The town was another shambles, the Germans having blocked either end with demolished buildings. Ahead, the Guards were picking their way up the rough mountainside. 'This, by the way, is 4.30 p.m. Sunday afternoon,' noted Ward, 'and raining like the devil. Thinking of the home fire and time for tea.' No post had come in; he reckoned it must be difficult for the mail to reach them with all the bridges blown.

Despite the artillery support, the sound of which was now crashing and reverberating around the mountains, the Guards were struggling to make much headway. The Guards Brigade included three battalions as good as any infantry in the British Army. They were well equipped and well trained, but not trained in mountain warfare; none of the British or American divisions were, yet it was precisely the kind of training they needed. As von Senger knew, 15. Panzergrenadier had a decent amount of experience behind them and had positioned their men in good, mutually supporting positions. The combination of well-placed mortars and machine guns and OPs on the high ground feeding information to artillery further back made this a very tough position indeed. Allied troops were still getting plenty of artillery support, but under leaden skies there was precious little help from the tactical air forces, while the infantry had to attack uphill, carrying everything with them, against an enemy that was already in position. Here the ground was horribly rough: thin soil, scrub, scraggy rock and occasional terraces, the odd stone farmhouse and remote settlement such as Camino village itself. This was bare, tough terrain. How were men supposed to advance effectively when every movement was being watched, and when they were exposed to constant, withering, stone-splintering, shrapnel-spraying fire? The Allies' superior scale of artillery counted for a great deal, but not necessarily enough to enable the poor bloody infantry to clear a mountain the size of Monte Camino, with all its folds, ravines, escarpments and places for a well-organized enemy to position and hide itself.

Meanwhile, Hans Golda found himself stuck at his OP on Monte Lungo. His battery of Nebelwerfers were still down near Stazione di Rocca d'Evandro, but linked by field telephone wire was a post about a third of the way along the southern side of Lungo. They had climbed up a shallow wooded ravine, and above this, near the top, he and his men had built a small log bunker. He had watched American trucks and other vehicles rumbling up the road from the south-west and had also followed the fighting on Camino. It was hellish: endless artillery firing, the whistle and screech of shells, the explosions and clouds of smoke. The sound retorting around the valley. Allied shelling was also pummelling Monte Lungo and their positions behind. All Golda and his men could do was watch, huddle together, pray they never got a direct hit and hope for the best.

On the other side of the Mignano Gap, the American 3rd Division was also trying to push a way through to the top of Monte Sammucro. Lucas's and Truscott's idea was not to even try squeezing through the gap on the valley floor, but to outflank Mignano entirely by crawling high over Sammucro and the smaller Monte Rotondo. At least 3rd Division had gained some experience of mountain warfare in Sicily, although the peaks here were of an entirely different scale.

The task of clearing Rotondo was given to 15th Infantry. Audie Murphy thought it a nightmarish place to try and fight offensively. The narrow trails, which would often pass by sudden, plunging drops or narrow gorges, challenged even the most sure-footed mules. Murphy discovered that in this terrain the Germans were next to impossible to spot until they were almost upon them and the enemy opened fire. The ground was slippery and difficult to move over, especially when laden with kit, and visibility was often difficult because of low cloud that could descend like a dropped shroud. Despite the difficulty of fighting here, Rotondo was none the less eventually taken on 8 November in a two-pronged assault. While 15th Infantry attacked first from the south on to the lower Hill 193, which nestled next to Rotondo, drawing the enemy fire, 30th Infantry then struck from the eastern flank. It was, though, a dent in the German positions rather than a major bite into the line.

The Ranger Force, meanwhile, had arrived back at the front, reaching

Venafro at 1.30 a.m. on 9 November. Colonel Bill Darby had looked up in awe at the huge peaks looming above him monstrously in the moonlight, but it was up on to those peaks that he and his men – save the 3rd Battalion, which had yet to move up – were heading. Up they went, picking their way through the plentiful olive groves on the lower slopes and then up old goat trails to the twin peaks of Monte Croce and Monte Corno, two more massive 3,000-foot-high crests, taking over positions for the 45th Thunderbirds. Corno stood on the left, south-western side, Croce on the right, a series of ridgebacks rising up to one long, razor-like ridge, the two peaks connected by a slightly lower saddle. On the far side the mountains dropped steeply to the valley below. 'Active patrolling in the Venafro sector' was what was written in the Ranger diary, plus communiqués with the usual military understatement, but very quickly Darby realized they had a heck of a job on their hands, even with the support of the Chemical Mortar Battalion once again and a handful of 75mms down on the lower slopes from the Rangers' Cannon Company. For the first couple of days they were trying to hold too much with too little; it was freezing-cold, especially at night, and the men were clinging to roughly made stone sangars because there was almost no soil up there to dig. 'There was no spirited or desperate fighting,' noted Darby, 'just hide-and-seek action.' But casualties were mounting – three men killed here, five wounded there – from the lethal weapons of the infantry: machine guns, mortars and grenades. On Corno, his men were clinging to a ridge that ran at 90 degrees to the main crest of the mountain; and to the left was a plunging, almost sheer drop. German troops were just the other side of Corno's highest point, a bare-stone knoll no more that 200 yards away. Separating both sides were wire, mines and guns laid down to fire the length of the ridge.

Darby called for help and was sent the 509th PIR, still in Italy but soon to deploy back to Britain; they took over Monte Croce while the Rangers clung on to Corno. Now Darby felt he could focus on making life as difficult for the enemy as possible. On the other side of the mountain in the valley below lay the tiny village of Conca Casale, the Germans' base for operations on the mountain. From up on Corno, Darby and his men could see every movement and they realized there was only one trail up to the summit from the northern side – a goat track that ran east then cut back up the ridgeback to the top. As soon as anyone moved out of Conca Casale the mortar team were warned, and when the Germans were half-way up mortars would rain down upon them.

By the middle of the month, Darby and the rest of his men were thoroughly fed up with this. The cold, the rain, the lack of any cover on his bare-topped mountain – it was debilitating. 'Static warfare,' noted Darby, 'broken only by patrol action was nerve-wracking.' Enemy shelling was persistent and when the rain came down they often found themselves in low cloud, which up there meant fog with very limited visibility, further stretching their nerves. Really, what were they doing up there? They were supposed to be marching on Rome, but apart from the odd night-time patrol down to the village on the other side the Rangers were not moving a jot.

Further up the front, the 34th Red Bulls were doing well in the hills to the north-east of the Mignano Gap, above the lower Volturno Valley. Having crossed the raging river, they pushed up into the hills around Pozzilli where they came up against 3. Panzergrenadier-Division. Von Senger had been making the rounds of his new divisions and was near Pozzilli when the Red Bulls were making an attack. He was shocked by what he considered the utter uselessness of the forward troops' deployment, which, he could see, consisted of individual, weakly protected and completely unconnected strongpoints. 'Such positions,' he noted, 'frequently are more like traps than defensive installations.' A lot of the division's units were made up of troops from occupied territories in eastern Europe – Poles, men from the Baltic states, Czechs and Slavs – and von Senger felt the division had a big problem with morale, in part because they were not treated as well as German troops and lacked any obvious motivation. 'This difference in treatment,' noted von Senger, 'based on racial principles was not conducive to good morale.' Yet again, Nazi ideology was hampering military logic. This was just another example.

The 100th 'Nisei' Battalion were part of the 34th Red Bulls' attack on 5 November when they were ordered to capture a series of three hills, marked 590, 600 and 610 on the map. Just as von Senger had feared, the Japanese-Americans of the 100th Battalion swiftly wiped out three enemy outposts. Isaac Akinaka was now a medic; he'd heard that more medics were needed and, having been mightily impressed by Captain Kawasaki when he'd helped attend the wounded Sergeant Joe Takata on the road to Benevento, had asked to join him. Kawasaki's fearlessness had not diminished. On the morning of the 6th, the captain had led Akinaka and a stretcher party up to the hills when the heavy scream of shells screeched over. A shard of shrapnel tore over Kawasaki's calf while Akinaka, hugging the ground for dear life, yelled curses at the enemy.

The conditions up there were every bit as terrible as they were for the Rangers. There were now night frosts and some of the men took to wearing the jackets of dead German troops over their own at night. On 8 November, German smoke shells reduced visibility to about 30 yards on the top of Hills 600 and 610. The 100th Battalion boys waited for an enemy attack but none developed. Slowly, as the smoke lifted, word reached the battalion CP on Hill 600 that around seventy Germans, carrying machine guns and mortars, were moving across their front 500 yards to the south. Almost all were killed, wounded or taken prisoner by men of 133rd Infantry's 1st Battalion, dug in a little way away. The loss of these 3. Panzergrenadier men was a stark example of the difference between experienced troops and those less well trained and struggling with issues of morale.

Isaac Akinaka was sorry to lose Captain Kawasaki but was kept busy not just with their own casualties but also the enemy's. On one occasion it took him more than three hours to get a wounded Pole down the steep and slippery hillside to the aid station outside Pozzilli. At one point they paused and Akinaka pulled out his knife, intending to cut off the man's insignia as a souvenir. 'He turned white and almost fainted,' noted Akinaka. 'He thought I was going to kill him.' The 100th Battalion came down from the hills on 11 November, Armistice Day, which marked the end of the Great War twenty-five years earlier. 'At the going down of the sun, we will remember them,' noted Jack Ward in his diary. 'If the man in the street had done so, I wouldn't have been writing this and those poor bloody infantry wouldn't be chucking away their lives like they are doing at this minute.'

Less than twenty miles to the north, Wilhelm Mauss was also musing on the significance of the date and the terrible humiliation of surrender and the catastrophe that befell Germany as a consequence. It might, he conceded, happen again; so far they had held firm, but victory had eluded them. 'We are still in the centre of heaviest battle on all fronts,' he wrote. 'But we know now what we must expect from the enemy should they win and so our people stand earnestly and with closed ranks, prepared for everything, behind their Führer and trusting in him.'

CHAPTER 25

Slow Death

Leutnant Hans Golda was having a miserable time at his OP on Monte Lungo. Food was reaching them only every third day. They were all soaked, and even when it wasn't raining it still dripped inside their little log bunker. The mud level on the floor increased so they added more stones, but that didn't really work. Then the temperatures dropped and they were both wet and really cold; fires up there were out of the question, until eventually they thought to hell with it and built themselves a stove using a large jam tin and a piece of piping. They took turns reading a novel out loud to keep themselves entertained. In between, they continued relaying instructions to the firing position back down in the valley.

In the battle that raged, however, neither side was making much headway during that first part of November. 'Enemy attacks continue at all points of main effort,' ran the XIV Panzerkorps war diary for 8 November. 'Our own attack, launched south of Monte Camino, makes little headway. Enemy troops launch new attack at the right wing of the 3. Panzergrenadier Division and capture Monte Rotondo.' Even as battles were going on, officers and clerks were typing up reports, memos and unit war diaries, already beginning the work that would follow in the years to come, tidying up the battles into their most basic forms in which bare facts were recorded for posterity. 'The enemy defended from strong-points throughout the period holding tenaciously to high ground,' ran the sitrep – situation report – for US VI Corps. '3rd Infantry Division repulsed 2 counterattacks this morning capturing 41 PW believed to be from 3rd Bn 29 PGR.'

But for most of the men caught up in these battles, the fighting they experienced was about what was happening in the immediate patch of ground on which they found themselves – ground dictated by men very much higher up the chain of command. Whether they were fighting somewhere that, years later, would be remembered or entirely forgotten was, in the moment, neither here nor there. They only knew what they were experiencing at the bottom end of this enormous, life-sucking whirlwind of violence.

After the capture of Monte Rotondo, Audie Murphy's B Company of 15th Infantry were ordered to take over Hill 193, a rather square hill nestling on to the edge of its much larger neighbour and around which the Via Casilina, Highway 6, ran. It was an unenviable place to try and capture because on its south-western flank was the long saddle of Monte Lungo, still held by the enemy. It was dark, but as they got going Murphy heard German voices away to his left – presumably a patrol coming from the direction of Lungo along the Via Casilina. Murphy fired his rifle and the enemy troops appeared to fall back. That was something, but now the Germans knew the Americans were there.

Murphy and his squad hurried up the slope, which climbed gently along a low saddle between Rotondo and Hill 193 on their left, and soon found that they were isolated once more and on their own, separated by the confusion of night from the rest of the company. They'd barely gone 400 yards when in front of them they came across an old lime kiln and a quarry the size of a large tennis court about 12 feet deep. Cut into the right-hand side of the quarry wall was a cave from which a jutting slab of rock protruded. This offered ideal – and dry – shelter for the night, and so with one man nestled behind the jutting rock at the cave's mouth and armed with a BAR, the light machine gun, the rest tried to get their heads down.

Early the following morning, however, by which time they were all very much awake, they spotted a German patrol coming down the slope from Hill 193 above the quarry, the silhouette of their distinctive helmets clearly visible against the pale streaks of dawn. Seven men, led by a veteran; Murphy could tell by his composure, by the way he paused repeatedly, looked around, not liking the situation at all. From their positions in the dark recess of the cave the Americans were hidden from view. Carefully, the squad flicked off the safety catches on their weapons. Fife, the Cherokee, was on the BAR with its twenty-round magazine, lying by the slab of rock extending from the cave and the quarry's side.

Murphy watched the enemy troops slowly move forward. His mouth went dry, his muscles tightened, heart heavy in his chest. The German patrol leader paused and seemed to be looking straight at them. Could he see them? It seemed not. Relief, but heart still pounding. Mouth like sand. Murphy wondered when Fife was going to fire.

'What's the Chief going to do?' Kerrigan whispered beside Murphy. 'Shake hands with the krauts before he shoots them?'

Then at last the sharp rattle of the BAR, one magazine's worth of bullets, the enemy dropped, and the rest of the squad jumped up and ran forward, up out of the quarry and on to the track above. Four of the Germans, stunned by what had happened, immediately raised their hands but three lay on the ground, wounded, bullets having punctured their middle parts. 'From the ripped bodies comes only the sound of gasping,' noted Murphy. 'Shock for the instant stifles the pain that will soon stab through the flesh.'

Suddenly, a single enemy howitzer fired from Monte Lungo, the strange screech of the shell rising, hurtling over their heads, the retort echoing around the hills, then crashing into Monte Rotondo above them.

'Reveille,' muttered Kerrigan.

While the prisoners were taken to Company HQ, the rest stayed with the wounded, waiting for the medic to arrive with stretchers. That was the curious thing about situations such as these: one moment Murphy's men had been trying to kill the enemy, the next they were looking after their wounded. One of the men was much older than the others, almost too old, Murphy thought. The other two were youngsters. Murphy ordered his men to get the three men into the cave and watched as Joe Sieja and Snuffy, another in the squad, lifted the old man. A pool of blood had collected in his trousers and it now poured out in a stream. Murphy looked down at the third man as he stared at the sky, breathing roughly. He loosened the youngster's collar.

'Danke,' mumbled the young German.

Artillery fire grew heavier, but they were safe enough where they were in their narrow valley and with their cave. The morning wore on, and still there was no sign of any medics; American troops took priority. Pain now swept over the wounded men. One of the youngsters began openly weeping. Murphy and his men dressed their wounds, but there was little they could do. The old man had a bullet in the left lung. 'Superman,' Kerrigan said to him, 'you should have been home with your grandchildren.'

The German asked for water, but he had three bullet holes in his stomach and they knew a man with belly wounds should not drink. Lipton and Kerrigan argued over whether they should give him a drink. 'Aw, let

The first Allied supply ships reach Naples on 10 October. This was already turning into an engineers' war and miracles had been performed to get Naples operating again so quickly.

The ferocious heat of September was suddenly and dramatically replaced by relentless rain. It made a tough job for the Allies even tougher.

Above left: A British tank crew from the Desert Rats, the 7th Armoured Division, eat a liberated chicken. The contraption at the back of their Sherman is to enable them to wade through rivers. **Above right**: The Luftwaffe fought on, just, but in the air the Germans were hopelessly outmatched and outnumbered. Wreckage of a Messerschmitt 109 lies where it crashed to the south of the Volturno.

Left: Tommies crawling through a sugar beet field near the Volturno River.

Right: Men of the 34th Red Bulls cross the Volturno on a hastily built pontoon bridge.

THE ENGINEERS' WAR

Left: If any one picture encapsulates the challenges faced by fighting up through Italy, it is this. German engineers such as Jupp Klein were quickly becoming masters of demolishing roads and bridges where it would cause maximum problems for the Allies.

At every turn, yet another blown bridge had to be fixed. Many an Allied engineer – not to mention commander – must have repeatedly thanked the British Donald Bailey for his design, but it was American engineers, especially, with their arsenal of machinery and speedy can-do approach who became the masters of repair and construction, whether it be a bridge, new road or restoring the docks at Naples.

Left: British troops advancing across one of the many irrigation ditches in the flat coastal plain near Cancello and Capua during the Volturno battles.

Above left and right: Infantrymen hack into the rock. There was little scope for digging down very far, so stone sangars – rough stone-wall shelters – around existing rock formations were the best shelter most could hope for, which is what this Bren gun team have done here, taking cover behind a pile of stones. The Abruzzo Mountains loom in the distance.

Above: A Fallschirmjäger clips his MG42 on to a stand. These beasts could fire at a rate of 1,400 rounds a minute, but it was mortars that were the most lethal weapons in the rocky mountain terrain.

Below left: Troops from the 34th Red Bulls move through the village of Caiazzo on the northern side of the Volturno. For once, it wasn't raining.

Below right: The generals confer at Lucas's OP at Pietrovairano on 30 October. John Lucas was a bit nervous at the way Alexander moved about quite openly, the others following his lead, as they were still within enemy range up there and the artillery observers nearby were all dug in and camouflaged. *From left to right*: Truscott, Alexander, Clark, Lemnitzer and Lucas.

Above left: An American half-track and gun cross a pontoon bridge over the Upper Volturno. Beyond are the mountains which mark the start of the German Bernhard Line.

Above right: A German Panzer III moves up through another blasted Italian town. There wasn't much *vincere* – victory – for anyone here, just the misery of mud, shattered towns and shattered lives.

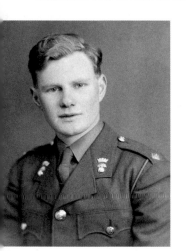

Far Left: John Glennie, Lawrie Franklyn-Vaile's great friend in the Faughs.

Left: 8th Indian Division gunners manhandle a 6-pounder anti-tank gun into position.

Below left: The floodplain on the northern banks of the Sangro where the New Zealanders crossed. It's easy to see why progress slowed in these conditions.

Below right: British trucks moving up. The white tape denotes a channel cleared of mines, which meant more traffic over that ground and which then churned it up even more.

Left: New Zealanders near the Sangro move up through a mine-cleared lane.

Right: No sooner had the Upper Volturno been bridged than it was swept away again by torrential rains. It was the same for the Sangro crossings.

Below left: A British mule train getting ready for loading at the foot of Monte Camino.

Below right: A GI picks his way across a shallower part of the Upper Volturno near Venafro.

Below left: It's hard to believe, but these exhausted men are from the 3rd Coldstream Guards – survivors of the first attempt to take Monte Camino in November 1943.

Below right: It's all shoulders to the wheel as these American gunners try to move a big 155mm howitzer through the mud. The Allies were battling the Germans, the mountains and the mud and rain as they made their first assault on the Bernhard Line.

Above left: Tommies hurriedly run across the road between Mozzagrogna and Lanciano on 1 December 1943. A knocked-out German Panzer III lies on the edge of the road while another vehicle up ahead burns. In the distance on the left are the snow-capped Maiella Mountains.

Above right: Yet more flooding of the Upper Volturno, vehicles pulled across by wires.

Left: Men of the 180th Infantry out of the line. Recuperating sufficiently from mountain combat was difficult, to say the least, in these conditions.

Below left: Laying mines and booby traps was a cheap and easy way of confounding the progress of the Allies and the Germans laid millions of them. Here, American infantrymen wait while an engineer disables a mine.

Below right: An American mule train heading up Monte Sammucro.

Above left: German dead and battle debris lie scattered on the slopes where the Red Bulls were fighting north of Venafro.

Above right: Italian troops on the southern end of Monte Lungo. They were not the best trained or equipped, but looking at the landscape it's not surprising the Germans, dug in on the top of the ridge, cut them to pieces when they first attacked.

Above left: Misery in the mud and mountains. **Above right**: What a terrible terrain on which to fight. The bare rock made artillery and mortar fire many times more lethal because there was no soil to absorb the explosion and both shrapnel and shards of rock were then sprayed all around. And there was very little cover when attacking. This Guardsman clambers up the slopes of Monte Camino.

The 15th Air Force finally began moving to Foggia at the end of November but conditions were hardly conducive to heavy bomber operations.

Orsogna under fire.

Above left: Guardsmen near the summit of Monte Camino, December 1943.

Above right Major Roy Durnford conducts a burial ceremony near Ortona.

Right: A paratrooper from the 509th PIR passes one of the knocked-out Shermans sent down this road into San Pietro.

Right: Rosa Fuoco, killed in the village square in San Pietro while trying to get desperately needed water in the early hours of 13 December.

Above: A dead Fallschirmjäger in Ortona. The scattered photos, including one of Hitler, were placed there after by the Canadian photographer, although the blood-stained letters, from his family back home, were really those of this dead boy.

Below left: The ruins of San Pietro after the battle. **Below right**: Canadians run for cover in the mud and blasted landscape south of Ortona.

him have a drink,' said Snuffy eventually. 'He's gonna die anyhow.' So they gave him a drink. Soon after, he lost consciousness.

Later, in the afternoon, the company runner arrived, although only once Sieja, on the BAR, had given him cover.

'You bring mail?' Sieja demanded after the runner had caught his breath. No, he hadn't, but he had brought news that the battalion commander had been badly wounded. And what about the medics, Murphy asked him? Not until the morning, the runner told him; they were up to their necks with their own. The rain began to fall again, harder and harder. The wounded Germans were still alive but muttering feverishly.

'The poor bastards,' said Lipton, softly. 'What is death waiting for?' They all wished they would die quickly rather than have to watch their agonies, listen to their mutterings and ravings. Murphy felt exhausted. His bones ached and the muscles around his eyes twitched. He wondered whether the war would ever end. Sitting in that cave with three dying Germans, the rain sheeting down and artillery fire still thundering around them, it seemed all too clear it never would.

Darkness fell once more. The old man was becoming delirious, quiet one moment then suddenly trying to get up, raving madly. As the hours wore on, one of the younger men joined him. Murphy thought the two dying men were having some kind of ghostly conversation. On it went, these terrible death throes, this ghastly protracted end.

'They kill us too,' said Sieja, trying to make himself feel better.

By dawn two of them had finally died, mouths open, dead eyes staring glassily.

The rain had stopped and the sun caused steam to rise from their uniforms. Still no medics reached them, still they were stuck where they were, the second cave in which they'd been abandoned since arriving in this godforsaken country. In the afternoon the third German took a long breath, exhaled with a big sigh, and died.

Another night, the moon shining its milky light. The dead looked green, unearthly. Lipton turned them over; they weren't sure why they hadn't done so right away. Murphy was still only nineteen. He was too young for this awfulness, but how could they not contemplate their own fate? They all knew it might just as easily have been them dying slowly in a cave surrounded by Germans.

Dawn came eventually and quietly too until suddenly the air was alive with shells screaming over – but their own artillery's, not the enemy's.

*

Leutnant Hans Golda had been relieved on Monte Lungo and been back at the 7. Batterie firing positions when the heavy shelling that Murphy had heard screaming over started to land around them. 'We pressed ourselves into the corners,' he noted, 'and then there was a hell of a crash, we were shaken up, there was dense smoke in the room and we could barely breathe.' A dull rumbling followed and then all was quiet around them. When they emerged, they were astonished by their good fortune: the entire house had collapsed, except for the room they were in and one next to them, which had remained intact.

Yet while relentless shelling obviously took its toll, Fifth Army had been unable to create a decisive breakthrough at any point along its front. General Clark had begun his assault on the Winter Line with the knowledge that Rome still remained the goal – for the political prestige, for the importance of moving the front sufficiently north of Foggia and Naples, and for ensuring the Allies maintained the initiative. Yet it was so frustrating to think that there was a backlog of 40,000 vehicles waiting to be shipped because the strategic air forces were taking precedent, and it was even more galling to think that they were slogging their way through mountains and over raging torrents because they lacked landing craft. He was very aware that he was pushing his divisions hard, but what else could he do? Time was against them. Yet he had also just been handed details of a survey about the attitudes of enlisted men and their views on morale. Not enough consideration was given to the need to rest; the survey reflected a widespread view that certain troops were doing all the fighting – yet it was also clear that these put-upon and abused GIs were invariably from the units of the troops being questioned. Slowness of mail was another big complaint. 'Many men do not have a clear understanding of what they are fighting for,' the survey concluded. 'There is a definite lack of understanding concerning the whole situation and they do not know their role in the war.' And how could they, sitting behind a rock in pouring rain on some remote mountain of southern Italy? Or as they pushed a jeep through 2 feet of thick mud?

Clark responded by sending round a memo to all his senior commanders asking them to make sure they paid particular attention to the welfare of their troops. 'It is incumbent,' he wrote, 'upon every commanding officer of a Fifth Army unit to minister continuously to the mental and physical well-being of his command. If proper thought and action is taken in this regard, the present high morale of the Fifth Army can be not only maintained but improved.' Well, perhaps, but how were they going to improve the morale of Audie Murphy and his squad after spending two days in a cave, under shellfire and with three Germans dying beside them? Were a few choice words of encouragement going to boost morale?

The truth was, this current battering of the Winter Line wasn't going especially well, and there was no doubting that the best way to improve morale was to start winning some decisive victories. On 12 November Clark had a disquieting meeting with General Dick McCreery, whose 56th Division had been struggling on Monte Camino. As McCreery pointed out, the division had been in constant action since the landings at Salerno and had suffered debilitating casualties, especially among officers and NCOs. At the present time, these were not replaceable as there were simply no reserves left in North Africa or, yet, in Italy. He was sorry to say this to Clark, but his depleted battalions were tired out and despite their best efforts had not been able to gain and secure Monte Camino.

This, in a nutshell, was the fundamental problem of the Allied effort in Italy since the planning of AVALANCHE: there was simply not enough of anything to do the job properly. It wasn't McCreery's fault, it wasn't Clark's fault and it wasn't Alexander's fault either. It was down to those heady aims, set out at Allied conferences over the summer when all had been going well, which had created a level of expectation that had not taken into account two vital factors: what would happen if the Germans chose to significantly reinforce Italy and make a stand south of Rome; and the debilitating effects of winter weather on the highly mechanized and air power-heavy Allied way of war. By August 1943, the Combined Chiefs of Staff had already forgotten how badly things had gone initially in Tunisia when the cold, rain and mud had bogged them down and the Germans had reinforced and defended more tenaciously than any of the Allied high command had thought likely. The knock-on effect on Allied global shipping that had been caused by the Tunisian campaign taking many months longer than planned was still being felt.

Now, in Italy, the very same mistakes had been made again, only this time it was worse because there was a wider strategy that had to be stuck to, which meant shipping schedules could not be easily altered. What's more, the current winter in Italy was far worse than anything in Tunisia, the terrain far harder through which to attack, and the enemy far more numerous and more determined.

No matter that the overestimations of the Italian campaign lay at the hands of others, Clark felt bitterly disappointed that his army had been unable to break through decisively. On 9 November, Alexander had issued him with a directive to launch a renewed assault at the end of the month, and with this in mind, and with 56th Division battered and bruised and his three American divisions also pretty beaten up, on 15 November he reluctantly decided to call a halt to offensive operations for the time being. A pause was needed, and a rethink about how they might force a way through. On the plus side, more divisions had arrived: 1st Armored, a veteran unit of North Africa, for whose deployment Clark had argued vociferously, and so, too, finally, the rest of II Corps. Fifth Army was growing, but it needed to if it was going to batter and bludgeon a way through the Winter Line and beyond.

'The Anglo-American advance continues slowly, I would say exasperatingly,' noted Lina Caruso. 'If we keep going at this pace, Rome will still find itself German in the New Year.' In Eboli, she and her family were no longer threatened so much by bombs and certainly not shellfire, but now they faced starvation. 'There is no wheat, there is no bread.' What food there was now cost more than most people could afford; chestnuts were as much as 16 *lire* a kilo, bread as much as 70 *lire* a kilo. She had no idea how they were going to survive.

In Rome, Kesselring's promises had amounted to nothing, just as Generale Carboni had known would be the case. The city was now entirely run by Germans in cahoots with Fascist lackeys. SS Polizei troops regularly marched up and down the streets and occupied former Italian military barracks. Obersturmbannführer Herbert Kappler had also been sent to Rome to oversee the round-up of Rome's estimated 12,000 Jews. The Germans had emptied the Banca d'Italia of 110 tons of gold reserves, and Kappler, aware that the SS intelligence services were short of funding, demanded 50 kilos of gold from the city's Jewish elders while he waited for instructions about what was to be done with them all. The majority of Rome's Jews lived in a ghetto and were mostly impoverished rather than the wealthy capitalists of Nazi ideology, so there was little chance of finding the money. The Jewish elders had appealed to the Vatican, however, and Pope Pius XII had authorized a loan, which together with the donations of wedding rings and other small items enabled the scales to tip 50 kilos and Kappler's demand to be met.

Kappler had been expressly ordered to round up the city's Jews and send them north to the death camps, but feared that in Italy, with very few Jews and little systemic anti-Semitism, this would cause trouble they did not need. Instead, he agreed with Kesselring that they should be used as forced labour. This had prompted a severe rebuke from his boss, Obergruppenführer Ernst Kaltenbrunner, the head of the RSHA, the Reich Security Office. Soon after, Hauptsturmführer Theodor Dannecker was sent to Rome to put some steel into Kappler and carry out the deportations. Dannecker had become something of a fireman for such operations. He'd been the man who had overseen the round-up of Paris's Jews and of those in Bulgaria and so, having arrived in Rome, he wasted no time. The operation began at 5 a.m. on 16 October and by the end of the day 1,023 Jews had been arrested, three-quarters of them women and children. Most, however, and especially the menfolk, had already fled, tipped off about rumours they would be conscripted for labour rather than heading to camps in the Reich.

Meanwhile, Carla Capponi had decided to join the Gruppi di Azione Patriottica, known more simply as 'GAP'. This was an embryonic armed resistance operation set up by the CLN in Rome's Military Council which was run primarily by the Action Party, Socialists and Communists. GAP Centrale was the group operating at the heart of the city, with a number of teams, or squads, each with between three and six combatants. 'We have decided to methodically inflict upon the Germans whatever blows possible,' announced the Action Party's underground newspaper *L'Italia Libera*. Not only Germans but Fascists too would be 'taken out of circulation'.

Now with the code-name 'Elena', Carla Capponi had so far been doing little more than gathering intelligence and distributing underground publications. She had, though, met and swiftly fallen in love with a fellow GAP Centrale partisan, Rosario Bentivegna or 'Paolo' – a youthful-looking twenty-one-year-old medical student and member of the Italian Communist Party, the PCI. Meeting at the Capponi flat near Trajan's Column, where he had come to deliver some pamphlets, the two had soon begun arguing. 'It was,' noted Bentivegna, 'love at first sight.'

Elena, as she had become, was, however, frustrated that female partisans were only deemed suitable as couriers and lookouts and was determined to get a weapon of her own. On Sunday, 10 October, she and Paolo had been on a crowded bus and she found herself standing near a member of the GNR Fascist militia. His back was towards her but she could see his Beretta pistol at his waist, loose in its holster. 'I used the crush of passengers,' she wrote, 'to get as close as I could, got one hand on it, slipped it into my jacket pocket and he was none the wiser.' Then, the next time the bus lurched, she slid the spare ammunition clip off his belt too. Only then did she realize that a fellow passenger, a rather startled-looking man, had seen the entire theft. Sticking her hand in her pocket, she pressed the Beretta into the man's side and without a word pushed him to the exit and together, at the next stop, they stepped off Paolo followed, unaware of what had happened, and as soon as they were clear of the bus the man made a dash for it and jumped on to a passing tram. She could see the GNR man wondering in panic where his pistol had gone, but the bus moved off and Paolo, now understanding what was going on, took Elena by the arm and hurriedly led her away. But she'd got away with it – her very first prize of the war.

From Monte Cassino, Dom Eusebio Grossetti was following the daily developments with growing alarm. Shelling in the valley below had now markedly increased, while the rain was so heavy on 15 November that part of the Rapido, which ran down to Cassino and then into the Garigliano, had flooded the surrounding plain. German soldiers also arrived to dismantle the cable car, much against the monks' wishes. 'Misery and hunger increase every day,' he noted on 19 November. 'God continues to test these poor people.' Dom Eusebio and the other monks also watched in horror as the Germans began systematically blowing up parts of Cassino town. The railway lines and a bridge on the bend as the line turned behind Monte Trocchio – which guarded the mouth of the Liri Valley – were detonated; Dom Eusebio saw the flames erupting from the explosions. On 21 November they started blowing up buildings too. 'The mines used to blow up the villa of T. Varrone, behind the railway station,' he recorded, 'were huge and shook the ground. I suddenly saw a very high column of thick, yellowish smoke and debris rising up into the air for several hundred metres and I immediately felt an immense blast.'

It was all so bewildering, so upsetting. The following day, Monday, 22 November, Dom Tommaso Carfora, a priest from Acerra near Caserta, who had been hiding in the mountain village of Villa Santa Lucia, arrived looking for sanctuary, having had to flee the Germans; he was in danger of being shot. News also arrived that three people, two men and a young boy, had been shot and killed by Germans in Terelle, a village on the slopes of Monte Caira; apparently they had been trying to escape being taken for labour and were cut down as they tried to run. How were they to make any sense of this? More grief and despair followed. On 25 November, German troops arrived to requisition animals and take away some of the men who were tenants and servants of the abbey. 'The seizing of one poor man was particularly heart-rending as his wife is ill and they have ten young children.' Fortunately, the man managed to run away, but from that moment on he had become a fugitive. Later that afternoon, a young girl, one of the daughters of their tenants, was assaulted and possibly even raped by a soldier. In the evening a German lieutenant arrived demanding to see the abbot; Dom Eusebio joined them to act as an interpreter as he could speak German. The lieutenant wanted to post a Luftwaffe officer to the abbey to use the observatory – only, he claimed, so he could observe the clouds and weather. That was all. Dom Eusebio didn't believe a word of it and nor, it seemed, did the abbot, who refused the request; it would, he told the officer, instantly change the status of the abbey.

In between, the monks tried to continue their lives which they had dedicated to God. 'The air raids in the area,' noted Dom Eusebio, 'did not cause us to run to the shelter, relying on the monastery's immunity from attack. We could see the artillery fire down on the plain without any overwhelming sense of apprehension.' In the evening they watched the bombardment from the infirmary, all wondering what might happen and what lay in store for them next.

Meanwhile, large-scale engineering works were going on to make the Foggia airfield complex a base fit for strategic heavy bomber operations; it had been a priority for supplies since its capture at the end of September. Most of this work was being carried out by American USAAF engineers and included the laying of an aviation fuel pipeline from Manfredonia on the coast to Foggia by an Engineer Petroleum Distribution Company. Incredibly, this 20-mile-long pipeline was completed by 25 November and could handle 160,000 gallons of high-octane fuel every week; its creation not only saved offloading time but also freed up a large amount of rail and road freight from fuel transport commitments. It was an impressive feat.

Certainly, contributing to POINTBLANK remained the prime reason for committing the Mediterranean heavy bomber forces to air bases in Italy; it was this additional benefit that had persuaded General Marshall of the benefits of invading Italy in the first place. 'Spaatz and I,' Eisenhower had signalled Marshall in September, 'believe that at times, at least, greater intensity of air effort against Germany will be attained with less loss if substantial portion of heavy bomber effort is applied to airfields in Italy during the winter months.' This note had been written back on 18 September, however, when it was still hot and dry and dusty and not raining cats and dogs. Yet despite the turn in the weather the Allies were now committed, and Spaatz and Eisenhower suggested that a further air force, the Fifteenth, be created especially for such independent strategic air operations against the southern Reich from the Foggia airfields. This would allow the Twelfth Air Force, already in theatre, to become a purely tactical air force and focus on supporting ground operations. The six bomb groups of XII Bomber Command were to make up the core of the new air force but would now receive a further fifteen direct from the United States, so that by March 1944 it would grow to twenty-one bomb groups.

This was an extraordinary new commitment being proposed by two senior American commanders and ran counter to all those concerns Marshall had voiced in May about Italy sucking up more men and materiel than anyone wanted. Even a single bomb group represented a considerable commitment. Each one, for example, had four squadrons of eighteen heavies, so there were seventy-two per group. That would make the Fifteenth a 1,500-strong air force with a personnel of more than 50,000 men.

Both General Ira Eaker and Air Chief Marshal Sir Arthur Harris, the commanders of Eighth Air Force and Bomber Command back in Britain, objected to this plan, fearing they would be competing for resources with the proposed Fifteenth; but the Allied strategic air campaign was also reaching something of a crisis just as the campaign on the ground was slowing in Italy. Operation POINTBLANK, the planned destruction of the Luftwaffe, could only be achieved if bombers hit German aircraft factories, but they were deep in the Reich and beyond the range of fighter escorts. During the second week in October the crews of the Eighth were butchered as they tried, for the second time, to hit key German plants in Schweinfurt and elsewhere. The trouble was, clearing the skies of northwest Europe was an essential prerequisite for Operation OVERLORD because it was vital that in the run-up to the cross-Channel invasion the Allies did all they could to slow down the German ability to reinforce Normandy. That could only be done by blasting bridges, roads, railways and marshalling yards – and this was only possible using medium bombers operating at low level. Unless the skies were clear of Luftwaffe fighters, they would be slaughtered.

So now, at the beginning of November 1943, the campaign in Italy was affecting plans for OVERLORD in multiple ways: by drawing German troops away from both the Eastern and Western Fronts, but also in terms of POINTBLANK, because from Italy the heavies could hit targets out of reach from Britain. The problem, though, was that establishing the strategic air forces in Italy was competing with the campaign on the ground for the very precious shipping and long logistical tail. While it had been a very good thing to capture the Foggia airfields quickly, it made sense to focus on one thing at a time. The rain was already coming down in Italy, and there had to be a question mark over how effectively the heavies would be able to operate from mostly dirt airfields in winter. Surely it would be better to focus on the ground forces first, ensure that Rome was captured and the line advanced well to the north; this would then create a stronger safety net for Foggia, and then, in turn, build up the strategic air forces, which, after all, were already operating quite effectively from North Africa where the weather was far drier and more consistent. In other words, if shipping was so limited it might be better to undertake one task properly where the immediate riches promised much, rather than try to fulfil two competing tasks at the same time, which would inevitably have a particularly adverse effect on the build-up of 15th Army Group.

This was very much the position of Churchill, but also that of Air Chief Marshal Sir Charles Portal, the British Chief of the Air Staff, who had been all in favour of strong strategic air forces in Italy if they could quickly get bases in northern Italy. He was less sure, however, how effective they would be operating much further south around Foggia; General Ira Eaker also wanted the nine bomber groups due to reach Italy in November, December and January to be sent to England instead, where there were plentiful air bases with asphalt and concrete runways. The British presented their concerns to the US Chiefs in Washington on 29 October but they were brushed aside, with General Hap Arnold insisting that the build-up would not interfere with that of the ground forces. This was nonsense; it already was. General Marshall also reminded the British that Eisenhower, the theatre commander, had asked for the strategic air forces to be brought into Italy in September. What's more, with the recent catastrophic losses suffered by Eighth Air Force over Schweinfurt on 14 October, Marshall stressed the urgency of now getting the heavies into Italy as quickly as possible.

And so the die was cast. On 1 November 1943, Fifteenth Air Force was formally activated, with General Jimmy Doolittle as its first commander and 'Tooey' Spaatz as overall theatre commander of the USAAF.

In the meantime, however, the heavies were still operating from North Africa and proving that the earlier perceived better Mediterranean weather was not always quite so advantageous as had been thought. Lieutenant T. Michael Sullivan's stumbling start to his combat career had continued, for example, and was of no fault of his own. On 9 November his crew suffered a flat tyre, so that was another trip aborted. The next day, engine trouble kept them grounded. There was no flying for the next three days so on the 13th he hitched a ride in a British truck only for it to crash and roll four times. Sullivan managed to get off quite lightly with just a bashed right arm and a sprained left leg. The next day, Sunday, 14 November, was his twentieth birthday. 'I'm out of my teens,' he jotted. 'I feel as if someone beat me with a baseball bat. Can scarcely walk.'

Finally, on 22 November, he flew his second mission, this time to bomb the naval base at Toulon in southern France, although yet again, despite stooging around for six hours, he simply couldn't see the target and so they eventually had to turn tail and head back for base. However blue the skies might have been when they took off from Tunis, over Europe it was winter – and proving to be a particularly bad winter as well. Navigation aids were improving, but not fast enough for the Allied strategic air forces in the Mediterranean. How much flying they would be able to do once they got to Foggia and were part of the new Fifteenth Air Force was suddenly looking like a very moot point.

CHAPTER 26

The Sangro

T HE GERMAN BERNHARD LINE at the Sangro was not along the river itself, which was wide, gravelly and not particularly deep even when the water levels were high and in full flow, but around three miles back, running along a roughly 600-foot-high ridge parallel to the river. Needless to say, the Germans had blown all the bridges and mined the entire area in between, but the landscape was much like that of the Trigno – as flat as a board on the coastal strip on the northern banks of the Sangro until it gradually began to rise once more. Montgomery's plan was for the 78th Battleaxe Division to attack along the coast with 8th Indian on its left flank and then the New Zealanders – new to Italy and about to join the battle for the first time – about a dozen miles inland. Initial operations were to begin on the night of 19–20 November to create bridgeheads over the Sangro, and then the main assault would be launched the following night: three divisions, supported by most of Eighth Army's artillery and a maximum effort from the Desert Air Force. Montgomery also planned to use considerable amounts of armour; the Germans clearly assumed that the ridge was too steep for tanks, and aerial reconnaissance had showed the enemy were short of anti-tank guns. Bridges would be made across the Sangro, but initially the plan was to simply ford it – not just with infantry, but with the tanks as well. Against the weak 65. Infanterie-Division, this looked like a sound and winning plan: massed infantry, operating with armour, supported by immense firepower from both artillery and tactical air forces. It was the kind of long-tail, 'big-war' approach that Montgomery favoured and which absolutely played to Allied strengths.

While the bulk of his forces were going to attack close to the Adriatic coast, he also sent a diversionary force to attack Castel di Sangro in the upper Sangro Valley. This was the 3rd Brigade of the Canadian Division, which up until that point had had a relatively quiet time of things. The Sangro Valley here was a lush, green bowl almost entirely surrounded by mountains, the river snaking its way to the north-east towards the coast through the interlocking spurs of yet more peaks. Castel di Sangro itself was dominated by a 1,000-foot-high very steep hill on which was perched a ruined medieval castle and a chapel, marked on Canadian maps as 'Point 1009'. Defending it were men of Oberst Heilmann's 3. Fallschirmjäger-Regiment.

The Canadians attacked at 1 a.m. on the morning of 23 November, but had been lured into something of a trap because Heilmann's men in and around the castle had kept silent in an effort to avoid the worst of the Canadian artillery and only opened fire once the attackers were halfway up the hill; the lead company of the West Nova Scotias were cut to pieces. Inevitably, it was pouring with rain too, but at first light there was a thick mist which did at least enable the survivors to slip away to safety. A second attempt was made on the 24th, before which time the artillery managed to fire some 5,000 rounds on to the castle hill in just one half-hour period. That night the Fallschirmjäger quietly withdrew into the hills behind, and by the 25th the Canadians had managed to create a six-mile-wide bridgehead over the Sangro about a mile deep.

Amid this rain and fighting further inland, preparations continued for the main event. Great efforts had gone into keeping the presence of the New Zealand 2nd Infantry Division secret, not that the men of 24th Battalion were particularly aware of this. They had landed at Taranto on 9 October, undergone some night training and played a lot of rugby, then slowly worked their way northwards. By 14 November they were near Lucera, in the Foggia Plain, then on they went again, trundling north. Roger Smith, a lance corporal in A Company, thought the entire journey utterly miserable. The weather had been foul – cold, with sleet-like rain – and they'd bounced about in the back of the trucks, weapons between their legs, freezing, uncomfortable and damp. On 16 November, as dusk had fallen, they'd been ordered out and told to march the rest of the way. This was all part of the secrecy plan, but it just seemed wretched as far as Smith was concerned.

A farm boy from Waikato near Auckland, Smith, now twenty-four years old, had joined the battalion in June 1942 and had fought through the Alamein battles, all across Egypt and Libya and into Tunisia, where the New Zealanders' campaign had ended at Enfidaville. Since then they'd been training and refitting in Egypt, a period that was much needed after such a long campaign, until finally being packed off to Italy as the shipping convoys slowly but surely caught up with the troops available all around the Mediterranean. The New Zealand Expeditionary Force – NZEF – had first joined Britain's war effort in Greece and, like the other Dominion nations of the British Empire, the country had so far made a contribution to the war effort that was out of all proportion to its tiny population. Little more than 1.5 million people lived in New Zealand at the start of the war and by October 1942 its army had stood at 131,000, around 19 per cent of its entire adult population. This figure did not include the considerable numbers flying in the RNZAF or Royal New Zealand Navy.

2nd Division comprised numbered battalions, each one drawing its men from a different area in New Zealand. The 28th, for example, was the Maori battalion, entirely made up of volunteers and its companies recruited on a tribal basis. The 24th Battalion was composed of men from Auckland, in the North Island, and was part of 6th Brigade, to which the 25th – mostly from Wellington – and 26th – drawn from the South Island – Battalions were also a part.

The 24th Battalion men were now at the edge of the Sangro after two nights of clandestine marching, by which time Montgomery's plans had already gone awry due to the weather – which had made the New Zealanders' approach march so grim. On 16 November, when patrols had been due to begin, the Sangro had been too high and fast-flowing to cross. The water levels were better on the 19th, so patrols had begun nearer the coast but not on the New Zealanders' front, where the levels were still way too high. So it wasn't until the night of the 21st that the first New Zealand patrols were ordered to recce across the Sangro – the night on which, according to the original timetable, the main assault should have been made on the ridge three miles beyond. But there was nothing that could be done about it; if the weather was preventing them from doing what they needed to do, that was all there was to it. They would have to adjust timings, pray that the rain would stop, and hope for the best.

On 24th Battalion's front, a twelve-man patrol from A Company, specifically from Roger Smith's platoon and led by Lieutenant Garth Turbort and Sergeant Ted Yearbury, was to be sent across the river, with engineers joining them to clear the inevitable mines. They followed Turbort along a muddy track, having dropped down from the higher ground on to the Sangro's floodplain. Smith was carrying the Bren light machine gun with a haversack of extra magazines on his hip, and as they trudged forward he realized his eyes were gradually adjusting to the thin, night light, although he still couldn't see much, only impressions. At least it wasn't raining. They passed through the company holding their forward defence line and then they were at the banks of the Sangro itself. Here they were split, Turbort taking one half, Yearbury the other, which included Smith, who was told to lie down and wait with the Bren, giving them cover. Smith could see little – a faint sheen from the water – and could only hear faint splashes, but where the engineers were, or where Yearbury and the others had gone, Smith hadn't a clue. Then, lying there, his chin resting on the wooden stock, he couldn't help himself – and fell asleep.

He woke suddenly with a boot kicking hard into his ribs.

'Now I should cut your bloody throat, just like a Hun would!' hissed Yearbury in his ear. 'Get up you dozy bastard.' Smith immediately jumped to his feet. He had never felt more ashamed. He liked Yearbury – they all did. He was one of the great characters of the platoon and of A Company, repeatedly demoted for boozing and brawling but repeatedly promoted again because he was such a damn good soldier and because the men all loved him. Smith knew the sergeant had every right to be livid. 'Can I trust you with the weapon,' Yearbury demanded, 'or will you roll over in the bushes, snoring like a hog any minute?' But then he softened and grinned. 'No, I guess you'll be all right, Rog. Only for God's sake, remember that's what could happen, only more so.'

They moved off and rejoined Turbort a little further up the river. Suddenly there was a loud explosion behind them, the force of which flung them flat on to the ground.

'What the hell was that?' asked Turbort.

'Mines,' said Yearbury. 'We're right in the middle of them. I can feel a tripwire beside me.' This was a terrible situation. They were in the middle of not just a minefield but a devil's garden, where tripwires were laced between the mines.

'Stay quite still, everyone,' said Turbort. 'Can you feel anything, Rog?'

Smith couldn't so he carefully inched backwards, where he found one of the men unconscious and with a gash on his head. The engineer officer told Turbort he would have to push on with the job in hand. He suggested the rest of them slowly and carefully move backwards, clear of this devil's garden. Turbort sent a couple of men forward with the engineer officer, but then John Barnes, another in the patrol, said, 'My rifle is hooked on something, sir. I can't get free, it feels like wire.'

'Don't move,' said Yearbury, 'don't even breathe. I'll see if I can ease it.'

Smith could hear slow, careful movement and Yearbury's quiet voice – but then two sharp and shocking explosions shattered the quiet. Brief flashes of white momentarily lit the night sky. Then silence. Smith barely dared think about what might have happened. Eventually Turbort called out.

'There's three of us here, sir,' replied one of the men from further back. They didn't think they were among the mines, but couldn't see anything forward at all.

'Five missing,' muttered Turbort. 'Christ!' And two wounded, one with a gash in his head, the other with shrapnel in one of his legs. Turbort decided that he and Smith should get themselves out along with the two wounded by dropping into the water. The water was icy-cold, waist-deep and the current fast, and by the time they were in line with the others Smith was exhausted, numb from the middle down, and all of them were gasping. Back on the bank, they gathered themselves together and Turbort gingerly went forward until he felt the first tripwire, then called out. No response. He waited, listening, but there was nothing, and so reluctantly they took the two wounded to the RAP – Regimental Aid Post – and then headed to Company HQ, feeling sick in their stomachs and fearing the worst for the missing men.

The following morning, cold, stiff, tired and miserable, Smith joined Turbort and a pair of Zambuks – medics – to look for the five missing men. Smith knew in his heart that they were dead, and yet it also seemed impossible to think of Yearbury, especially, as no more. Down the slopes they went, along the muddy track, totally different now in the early-morning daylight, then, through some bushes, there they were amid a scene of desolation. The minefield was obvious now – about 10 yards wide and 50 long, wires connecting the protruding prongs of mines only roughly buried. The previous night they'd crossed over one corner where there were now two craters, one small, one much larger. 'Four crumpled bodies,' noted Smith, 'battered beyond recognition, lay around the large crater.' The Zambuks carefully picked their way over, collecting identity disks and paybooks, but Yearbury wasn't among them. Then Smith saw him; he must have been blown right over their heads. He was face-down on a sandbank, 15 yards out in the river. It seemed so impossible to think that this boozing, fighting, funny reprobate was gone. 'A myth was exploded,' wrote Smith. 'The indestructible was destroyed. Death, who had passed a dozen times, had paused this once, to leave a disembowelled, limp rag doll, swirled by the muddy waters of the Sangro.'

Unteroffizier Jupp Klein was now based at the mountain village of Gamberale with the snow-capped Pizzi Mountains behind. The 1. Fallschirmjäger-Division might have been as one on paper but they certainly weren't in practice, having been given an absurdly lengthy front to hold. On the other hand, the division's engineers had been ruthlessly efficient with their demolitions, mines and booby traps and every conceivable road and track leading to the Sangro Valley from the south had now been covered. Gamberale was not far from the key town of Castel di Sangro, in the centre of the leg, through which the key Highway 17 passed on its way north. The town itself was held by Oberst Heilmann's 3. Fallschirmjäger, while the Pionier companies were spread out from Castel di Sangro across this sector of the Bernhard Line.

Gamberale felt a long way from the war – a village 1,000 feet above the valley, perched on a bare-rock bluff, with yet more mountains towering behind. How could the war possibly reach this remote corner of Italy? Yet it had, because here was another outpost of the HKL – the Hauptkampflinie, the main defence line of the Bernhard position; certainly, Gamberale offered a stunning OP over the Sangro Valley stretching below. In truth, though, Klein was rather grateful for the pause. He and his company had been on the go constantly; and it had been this relentless pressure to blow bridges, lay mines and then hurriedly move on that had led to a tragic accident.

A week earlier, he and his men had been laying a number of Schü-mines in a field. With the pressures of time, they were not bothering to make minefield maps, but this meant they needed to be particularly careful; normally they weren't required to be since the Pioniere were always the last of the rearguards. They'd finished laying around fifty on their side of a gap in a hedgerow and had taken a wide and circuitous route back to their vehicles when they heard the dull explosion of a mine detonating. At first, Klein couldn't understand it – surely the Tommies weren't here already? But with a feeling of mounting dread he and his men hurried back, and as they neared they heard loud shouts and voices. His worst fears were quickly realized: some reconnaissance troops had come into contact with the enemy, which had forced them to fall back in a different direction than intended. A mule carrying a wounded paratrooper had stepped on a mine; the beast had taken most of the damage but the wounded man, lying across the animal, had had his legs shorn off.

It was getting dark, but there was a moon and the sky was clear, so Klein managed to crawl through the minefield with some white tape to mark his route, reach the recce troops and help them get clear. Then he returned for the wounded man, who was moaning near the hedge, the ragged dead mule beside him. After tying tourniquets around the stumps of his legs he gingerly pulled him clear. 'It was a terrible ordeal for the wounded man,' noted Klein, 'who cried out in pain. He felt wretched and cursed the war once again for all its terrible cruelties.' Once clear, they wondered what to do, but soon realized that the closest medical help was at the advanced aid station, up over the hill behind them a couple of miles further; their truck was too far away, so the quickest route was simply to jog there. Klein volunteered, hoisting the man on to his shoulders. The poor fellow was now dropping in and out of consciousness, but Klein talked to him all the way, trying to soothe and encourage him.

It was completely dark by the time he reached the aid post and he was angry to find no guard there. Eventually, a medic arrived and Klein berated him: where had he been? He had a wounded paratrooper with him who needed urgent attention!

'What can I do with a man who's dead?' the medic replied. He peered again. 'The man is stone dead.'

Klein was devastated. 'Although I had seen many a hard death of a comrade in Russia and also in Italy,' he noted, 'I was stunned. It didn't seem real. I had run for my life to save this man, and now he was dead.'

Over towards the Adriatic coast, Captain Lawrie Franklyn-Vaile had rejoined the Faughs on 4 November. The medical team had wanted to evacuate him to a base hospital but he had refused, thinking it would be far better to get back among the men and keep himself busy rather than lie in bed with dark thoughts. He was, however, initially sent to help with B Echelon, the supply and administrative part of the battalion responsible for transport, food and bringing up ammunition, mail and all the support for the rifles companies; it wouldn't be for long, just until he was properly fit again.

The entire battalion was still reeling from the dreadful night attack over the Trigno, in which twenty-six had been killed and many more wounded – and most from just two companies. His dead friend, Johnny Glennie, was especially on Franklyn-Vaile's mind, however. It was left to him to go through Glennie's kit, pack up his few possessions and send them home, in this case to a large family in Northern Ireland. Franklyn-Vaile also visited his friend's grave and was shocked to discover Sergeant Leslie Farbrother buried a few yards away. He knew Farbrother had been wounded but had spoken to him and had thought he'd make it all right; only later did he learn that the sergeant had had both arms and legs amputated. Farbrother had been just twenty-seven and had a young son he'd never seen, and now never would. Only three men in Glennie's platoon were still standing, and he'd heard that two other officers he knew in the Inniskillings had also been killed. 'Honestly, Olive,' he wrote, 'it is a simply ghastly business, you just cannot conceive at home how bad it is – good life after good life goes. Men who have been out here all the time say that the fighting here is very much worse than in N. Africa or Sicily.'

He rejoined B Company a few days later, by which time the battalion was in a new position near San Salvo, which, because the front had moved, was now well behind the lines. The casualties prompted a significant change-around of officers, but new men arrived too – there were two subalterns joining on 15 November, and two more old faces returning from stints in hospital. No matter how bad the hit, the battalion continued, perhaps not at full strength, but by jiggling numbers and by shifting people here and there, the beleaguered A and B Companies became a functioning fighting force once again.

By the middle of the month, Franklyn-Vaile and two other officers were billeted in a small farmhouse. Dried tobacco leaf hung from the ceiling above them and rats could be heard scuttling about at night. The rain continued and mud was everywhere – it was simply impossible to avoid tramping it into the house, and although the appalling weather was horrible for both sides, from a military point of view it was a great benefit to the defending Germans and a terrible hindrance to the Allies. 'The ghastly wastage of life,' one of his fellow officers said to him, 'makes one wonder how much it is all worth.'

He couldn't help grieving for his lost friend and had called together the survivors of Glennie's platoon, thanking them for their support on that terrible night. The following day he was censoring letters and one of the men had written home about this brief chat. 'He was very nice,' the fusilier had written about Franklyn-Vaile, 'and we all felt very sad and sorry for him because they were real mates and always knocking around together. In their spare time you never saw one without the other. The

Captain has changed a lot since he came back from hospital – he is very quiet now and we know he misses him an awful lot.' It was heart-breaking. A few days later, Franklyn-Vaile heard that another friend had been killed; of the six officers that had left Saltfleet in Northern Ireland together in July, four were now dead.

Outside, the rain continued and it was now getting dark by about 5.30 p.m. Franklyn-Vaile was also suffering from what were known as 'desert sores' – he had one on his left hand, one on his right wrist, another on his right elbow and a large one on his leg. He wasn't alone. Lots of servicemen had them. 'No one really knows what is the cause,' he wrote, 'our MO thinks it is partly the perpetual tin food and lack of variety, the sweat and dirt that gets into any cut and they develop if one is feeling at all "run down" in health.'

He would have to put up with them for the moment, because on 19 November the weather improved, water levels in the river began to fall and they moved forward again, ready for the assault on the Bernhard Line the far side of the Sangro. Also moved up were 8th Indian Division, to start their preliminary operations over the river. 'We're going a thousand yards south-east of Paglieta,' Captain Asquith announced to his cipher staff, then added with his usual relish, 'The latter part of the route is under fire.'

The sky was sullen and bruised, but it still wasn't raining. Paglieta had been captured ten days earlier. They moved off through Scerni, ten miles to the south; the road now was dense with military traffic. Their truck skidded slowly past lines of tracked carriers, 25-pounders with their quads and limbers, and swerved to avoid lines of pack-mule companies; the irony of the highly motorized and technically advanced Allied armies becoming dependent on medieval mule trains was impossible to miss. A column of Gurkhas, clutching Bren and Tommy guns as well as entrenching tools, headed past in single file, walking faster than the cipher team's truck was moving. A smell of mule, fuel, mud and dampness hung heavy in the air. 'The cipher boys stayed very quiet, as if in deep thought,' noted Harry Wilson. 'I lay back watching the rectangular view presented by the back of the truck. Contrasting scenes melted into one another.' They trundled on, the town behind them, past woods and then ditches and embankments and occasional stone farmhouses.

At 10.30 p.m. they passed the gun positions, already firing. The din was immense. Great orange flashes lit the sky. They went through a village, still and ghostly quiet. Camouflaged troops skulked along the edge of the road, moving to their start lines, small orange dots of cigarette ends like fireflies. Eventually they reached Paglieta, silent and deserted, and stopped at a farm just outside. 'Our driver,' noted Wilson, 'spoiled a perfect night's work by knocking down half a farmhouse gate as clean as a whistle.'

It then rained heavily all the following day, so the big attack, code named Operation ENCROACH, was postponed by forty-eight hours. Since the enemy were not supposed to know about the existence of 8th Indian Division they were still on radio silence, and during a quiet moment Wilson and Lance-Corporal Kenison went on a recce for a comfortable billet. Finding two decent houses deserted, they began to have a nose around and were delighted to discover some very comfortable-looking beds. They decided they would sleep there that night and pocket anything of value. Kenison gathered a handful of Fascist literature, which he passed on to Asquith, while Wilson took an image of Virgo and a decorated soup plate. Later, after they had returned, the owners walked back in on them. 'Instead of being grateful to find their house still standing,' scribbled Wilson, 'they began ringing their hands and crying to heaven because a few articles were missing.'

'Give them nothing back,' Kenison said to him firmly. 'They're dirty Fascists and that fellow fought against us for I saw his uniform in the drawer.'

Wilson agreed. 'These people declared war against us,' he wrote, 'and I don't see why it shouldn't cost them a soup plate and an image of the Virgo.'

Montgomery had issued a printed order of the day in which he exhorted his men to give the enemy a 'colossal crack', but the torrential rain which fell that Saturday was a bitter pill for Montgomery and all in Eighth Army. Small bridgeheads had been made across the river the night before, but rather than attacking in these terrible conditions, every effort had to be made simply to get enough weapons and supplies across to ensure they kept those fingerholds. Any hopes of using large amounts of armour on the ridge had to be swiftly shelved, when, after further biblical downpours on Tuesday, 23 November, flood water from the mountains swept down and overwhelmed the three bridges the sappers had laboriously created over the previous three nights. Suddenly, the river, instead of being 50 yards wide, had become more than 300 and the bridges were left rather forlorn in the middle of a wide expanse of fast-flowing water. A new plan had to be made. The 8th Indian Division would try to take the ridgeline village of Mozzagrogna on 26 November and Santa Maria Imbaro two days later; 78th Division would then clear the ridge to the coast with or without armour, but most likely now without. Yet again, it was the PBI that was suffering the most. Meanwhile, the Indians were going to seize a ridge that ran quite close to the northern bank on the New Zealanders' front, after which 2nd (NZ) Division would launch its own attack at last. But, having taken the ridge as planned, the Indians were then cut off and isolated by the rapidly rising water in the Sangro. Yet another plan had to be made, which would discard any subtlety. Using all available air and artillery, a massed assault would be made on 28 November.

During this lull, Kesselring himself visited the front and immediately ordered the defences around Mozzagrogna to be strengthened. Although 16. Panzer-Division was still in reserve, a Kampfgruppe was ordered forward opposite the New Zealanders, while towards the end of the month more troops were arriving, including the leading units of 90. Panzergrenadier and 26. Panzer; the movement of this division back across the leg was so far the only part of Alexander's plan that was working. The tragedy for Eighth Army was that, had it attacked, as planned, on 20 November, it would have encountered only the weak 65. Infanterie-Division, which it would almost certainly have swept aside. The road to Pescara and Avezzano would have been blown wide open. Now, though, three DUKE divisions were going to find themselves attacking four of the enemy. The rain was not only sweeping away bridges, it was also carrying with it Allied hopes.

None the less, the weather did at last start to improve. The 27th was dry and, incredibly, some 100 tanks were moved across the river. That evening the Indians took Mozzagrogna, although they were driven out of the village again by enemy infantry and assault guns from 26. Panzer-Division. From 8th Indian Division HQ, Harry Wilson watched wave after wave of Boston and Baltimore bombers then P-40 Kittyhawks roar over relentlessly, and by dusk there were twelve bombers every fifteen minutes. Reports were reaching them in the cipher truck that scores of dazed and helpless prisoners were being escorted to the rear. Then, at 10 p.m., every gun on the front – 312 of them – opened up another immense barrage. 'The cipher truck rattled and the explosions were flung from one part of the sky to another,' noted Wilson, 'which looked like a glowing cinema screen.'

The next day, Sunday, 28 November, was also clear, allowing the tactical air forces to fly over in force. That day Eighth Army did well, consolidating gains and allowing General Allfrey, the V Corps commander, to try his tanks on the ridge at last. All day the artillery and support from the air had been immense, and that night the 8th Indians retook, and this time held, Mozzagrogna, while 78th Battleaxe launched a combined infantry and armour attack on the ridge early on the morning of the 29th – and were completely successful. Allfrey's gut instinct had been right; once the tanks had clambered up on to the ridge they discovered no anti-tank defences at all. British gunnery, combined with near-constant strikes by the Desert Air Force, proved just how potent Allied forces could be when the wind was in their sails and the sun was out.

The New Zealanders, meanwhile, crossed the Sangro at around 10.30 p.m. on the night of 27 November, walking on to a gravel bank in a bend in the river and wading across in icy water that went up to their chests. On the far side, Roger Smith and his mates in Lieutenant Turbort's platoon waited for the rest of the company, taking off their boots and wringing out their socks. The artillery opened up, flickering the sky, shells whooshing over in concentrations on identified strongpoints, and then the men were up, heading along a track, while D Company took Point 122, also known as Pylon Hill, which rose sharply at the end of a low ridge. With 25th Battalion on their right, Major Ted Aked's A Company now led the way, Smith – a new section commander and carrying Ted Yearbury's Tommy gun – being uncomfortably aware there was now no one between him and the enemy.

It was night and dark, and the New Zealanders were swarming over the countryside north of the Sangro, an area of undulating hills, small woods and fields, little villages and isolated farmhouses. Germans were expected, but not in any strength this close to the Sangro. Roger Smith, up front, Tommy gun at the ready, was conscious of how still the night was. Artillery was firing, but it wasn't the constant thunder that had started some of the desert battles. Suddenly he heard whistling, and not any old tune but 'Lili Marlene', a German song that everyone had known in North Africa. A moment later he saw the silhouette of the distinct German coal-scuttle helmet. Smith swung his Tommy gun and pulled the trigger but nothing happened. Cursing to himself, he immediately realized that the cocking-handle was only halfway forward. Hastily, he re-cocked and pushed the magazine in until it clicked, as the German, stopping as soon as he'd heard the click of the bolt, tugged at his belt and threw a grenade. He then leaped for the side of the road but was caught mid-air when Smith fired his Tommy gun and at the same moment the

Bren opened up. The German never stood a chance. A moment later, though, the grenade went off, wounding one of the men in the leg, although fortunately not fatally.

Despite the noise of this brief, dramatic engagement they neither saw nor heard any more enemy troops so continued on their way until they reached their objective, which was a pyramid-shaped hill called Colle Marabella. For once, timing with the artillery was perfect, for soon after they neared it another concentration of shells whooshed and crashed over, and then it was their turn to attack, two platoons of A Company sweeping up and around the hill. A machine gun sputtered and Smith heard someone shout, 'Come on, get stuck into the bastards!' Turbort's platoon attacked a barn the far side of the hill. One of the enemy troops fired a submachine gun from a window without any accuracy and then Turbort pumped an entire magazine of thirty rounds from his Tommy gun in turn. 'Come out! Come out! Tedeschi. Kamerad!' he shouted, and moments later the double doors of the barn tentatively creaked open and half a dozen terrified enemy troops emerged.

The A Company boys pressed on, climbing the hill. There was more Spandau fire, but it was half-hearted and they reached the crest easily. Smith noticed a haystack silhouetted on the skyline and with one of his mates went over to investigate. They began kicking it when suddenly four enemy scrambled out; it was a camouflaged machine-gun post complete with a low trench that zigzagged back to the reverse slope. Two 50mm anti-tank guns were captured, which the A Company men quickly adopted since they could expect no heavy weapons themselves until the Sangro was bridged. So far, it had all been very easy.

CHAPTER 27

The Good Cause

Hans Golda and his battery had managed to recover the lost wheels of their Nebelwerfers, clean the mud off the tubes and get them back in working order. Morale was also improved by the indefatigable Gefreiter Beecken, who had been a baker before the war and continued to bake passionately whenever he had the chance. The men in his battery had managed to scavenge plenty of olive oil and flour on their withdrawal from the Volturno and now, at the end of November, Beecken had not only salvaged the oven from the shattered farmhouse but had, with Golda's permission, recruited two assistants to help him produce loaves of bread and pancakes, so that a delicious aroma filled their ruin. 'Boy, oh boy,' noted Golda, 'it was a feast every time he started baking and the whole battery came back to life.' Golda reckoned that after Beecken had been baking the only sound that could be heard was the chewing and smacking of lips. German rations were notoriously bad so Beecken was a very popular man, not least with Golda himself. Amid the deprivations of their waterlogged, mud-filled and shell-blighted conditions, some good food went a very long way indeed.

And there was some good news for Golda too. He had been sitting in his bunker when one of the radio operators burst in to tell him he'd been promoted to Oberleutnant – first lieutenant – despite already having 134 men under his command. Golda was thrilled, and what pleased him even more was that his men seemed so genuinely delighted for him too. 'Like wildfire,' he noted, 'the message jumped from bunker to bunker: "Our old man has become Oberleutnant!"' Golda was not yet thirty.

The pause might have allowed Golda and his battery to fill their stomachs a little, but the brief respite along the front here also coincided with Kesselring's appointment as supremo in Italy, and he wasted no time in ordering south many of those divisions that had been tantalizingly out of reach for him while Rommel had been running the show in the north. The 305. Infanterie-Division was one, 94. Infanterie-Division another, but also on its way was 44. Division, which, on 22 November, began its journey south by train, and which included Major Georg Zellner and his 3. Bataillon. There was a huge downpour of rain in the night but Zellner woke at 5 a.m. and early that morning saw sunshine spread over the Apennines. 'First air raids,' he noted. 'We stop in Foligno. We stretch our legs. We can't go any further as there is no water for the machines and the electrical system is disrupted by bomb damage.' A night of drinking too much wine and discussing politics followed – after which Zellner vowed never to talk about politics again; it was pointless and only put him in a bad mood. They finally moved off once more at 3 a.m. and by the time he woke up again they were passing through beautiful countryside. How lovely it must be in peacetime, he thought. 'People beat each other to death over ideas that survive on the basis of the act of beating each to death,' he mused in his diary. 'And after the war, no one will know why they waged war. All the misfortunate will accuse the present generation. The widows and orphans will curse those responsible. But, life will go on, the next generation will have forgotten everything. New "buts" will emerge. The youth will again become enthusiastic about war and the new misfortune, a war, will begin again.'

They reached the front on 25 November. It was raining cats and dogs again, but Zellner wasn't complaining – it meant no Jabos overhead. They then marched on foot to Ceccano, a small town that lay in a plain between the mountains. The area was stunning, Zellner thought, and the town looked charming at a distance. 'But the poverty and misery here cannot be expressed in words,' he noted. 'Fifteen people live in a room that would certainly not be a goat shed in our country. It is simply unbelievable that people can live like this.' Some of his Russia veterans said the poverty was worse than in the Soviet Union. The fate of Italy was still on his mind a few days later when he was summoned to a conference in Rome. He had passed columns of refugees all day on the trip to and from the capital and it made him wonder if Germany would share the same fate if it lost the war. 'So, when we see images like these,' he added, 'we always come back to the firm resolve to fight until our homeland is secure.' On a personal level, he could hardly bear to think what losing would mean. 'Everything,' he noted, 'would melt away into nothingness. So, we fight on for the good cause.'

Thursday, 25 November was Thanksgiving Day for the Americans. On Fifth Army's western side of the leg, Frank Pearce and his platoon in the 111th Engineers had been repairing the road from Venafro to San Pietro on the 24th and could see phosphorous shells hitting Monte Sammucro. That night, in the darkness, he marvelled at the amount of guns firing. 'Must be lots here in the valley,' he scribbled, 'as the whole valley can be seen by gun flashes.' The following morning a truck turned over in a ditch near him, and although no one was killed two of the boys broke legs. This Thanksgiving Day, he realized, was the third anniversary of him joining the army and here he was, on a cold mountain in Italy getting rained on. Even so, he was given a turkey supper. 'Big rain,' he added, 'so turkey and water.'

Bud Wagner, meanwhile, a little further north of Venafro, began the day changing a flat tyre on his jeep; it rained much of the day but that afternoon, before it got dark, he did get a Thanksgiving Day dinner at division: beef steak, rice and proper coffee. 'Even in this situation,' he noted, 'probably the worst times I've ever been through, I'm still able to count my blessings.'

Above Frank Pearce, on Monte Corno, even the Rangers were able to get a hot turkey dinner, brought up specially thanks to the mule teams and kitchens that Bill Darby had ordered go as high as practically possible. This meal was eaten hastily while preparing to stave off enemy attacks. Soon after, a fighting patrol had captured ten prisoners. 'One of the prisoners,' noted Darby, 'said that they had been in position for just four days and under our heavy mortar fire had been cut from eighty to forty men in that time.' It had been relentless over the past two weeks they'd been up there. Two days earlier, on 23 November, Darby had received no fewer than nine signals at his mountainside CP in just one hour between 9.25 a.m. and 10.25 a.m.

0925   Captain Shunstrom reports that E Company has captured two prisoners, one of who was shot trying to escape.

0958   Muleskinner killed by shellfire and mule hit in leg – mule destroyed.

1002   Enemy small arms heard.

1004   E Company suffered casualties by heavy shellfire, wounding four, one missing, and one known dead.

1007   Enemy shot green flare on left flank: meaning enemy [the Rangers] has broken through, according to a prisoner.

1008   Enemy shell has hit own position – a cave under rock.

1015   Prisoner says they have had quite a few casualties in last few days. Is now carrying papers of lost comrades. New replacements coming in daily.

1023   Enemy machine-gun fire heard.

1024   Enemy attacking right flank of E Company. Call for mortar fire on forward slope.

And so it went on, every hour, every day. Static, not mobile warfare. Fifth Army was gaining inches and yards, not giant leaps. Rome was still 100 miles away.

General Mark Clark was spending the last days of November both reorganizing his front and preparing for round two of Fifth Army's attempt to reach Rome by Christmas. The British 7th Armoured Division had been sent back to England for OVERLORD, and so too the 82nd Airborne, although the 504th PIR had remained for the time being. He now had II Corps but also the new 1 Special Service Force – six battalions of American and Canadians trained in Commando-style operations. They weren't Army Rangers and they weren't Commandos either; they were something rather unique, but all volunteers, and as such motivated, supremely fit and well placed to use their initiative, attributes that made special forces such as these stand out above the ordinary rank and file. Then there was also the Italian 1. Raggruppamento Motorizzato, the 1st Motorized Group, a 5,500-strong brigade now under Fifth Army. Adding to Clark's international coalition was the arrival of 2e Division d'Infanterie Marocaine, the advance party of the Corps Expéditionnaire Français. This corps, commanded by Général Alphonse Juin, was trained in mountain warfare, so although an unknown quantity as far as Clark and Alexander were concerned, it was none the less just the ticket – on paper, at least.

On 23 November, Alexander visited Clark and motored up to the front. Inevitably, it was raining as they reached the CP of the 36th Texan Division, now back in the line. Thick, sticky mud greeted their arrival, but they managed to get through and then later push on up Highway 6, the Via Casilina, to have a better look at the terrain of the Winter Line. They soon came under shellfire, one after another screaming over and landing disconcertingly close.

Later, Clark headed to Caserta to inspect the 6th Grenadier Guards, one of the battalions that had tried to take Monte Camino earlier in November. The battalion should have been 845 men-strong, but it currently had just 315 in its number – and it was about to be flung at Camino again. This was the debilitating effect the Italian campaign was having and was atypical of the Allied approach to war, in which normally units were regularly rotated and kept up to strength. That perennial issue – shipping – and the Allied strategy higher up the chain was being felt most harshly by the infantry battalions who were expected to simply do more with less.

In no other theatre was more demanded of Allied front-line troops. They were not being supplied with the normal levels of materiel or replacements. The conditions were appalling: the mud, the rain, the freezing temperatures, disease, the inability to deploy armour, mechanization and air power. In the valley floor the mud was knee-deep. Even in the jungle or on Pacific atolls, the men could at least dig in. In the mountains the soil was thin or non-existent, making mortars and shells even more lethal and shelter harder to come by. Alexander had been so taken aback by the conditions at the front that he'd even suggested to Clark it might be better not to launch the next phase; after all, Eighth Army had not had the decisive breakthrough as planned. Clark wasn't having any of that; if Alexander wanted him to hold fire, then he needed it in writing. As it happened, the Army Group commander was already coming down with jaundice. It helped explain the somewhat jaundiced view. Malaria, jaundice, head colds and flu were all taking their toll, not just on the troops at the front but on commanders too.

So Clark continued with his plans, issuing Operations Instruction No. 11 the following day, 24 November. There were to be three phases. Phase I, the appropriately named Operation RAINCOAT, would see the capture of Monte Camino by the Brits of X Corps and the slightly lower peaks of the Camino massif, Monte La Difensa and Monte Maggiore, by II Corps. Then, in the second phase, the 36th Texans with the 504th PIR would take Monte Sammucro and Monte Lungo in the centre of the valley. Further north up the line, the 34th Red Bulls and the Moroccans would push on into the mountains. Phase III would be the full-throttle drive into the Liri Valley, and then, with a fair wind, on to Rome.

On Wednesday, 24 November Harold Macmillan, along with his American counterpart, Bob Murphy, flew to Cairo for the latest Allied conference, code-named Sextant. Macmillan was glad to be getting away, as even in Algeria the weather had been beastly in recent weeks and almost as cold and wet as Italy. This was to be the first course in what was to become a mammoth meal of talks, for the second part would see them shift to Tehran for Eureka, their initial joint conference with Stalin and the Soviet Union, while dessert would then see the American and British delegations return to Cairo to bring future strategy to something of an agreed head.

Landing at around 5.30 p.m., Macmillan was driven to the Casey Villa, as it was known, which for the time being had been transformed into No. 10 Downing Street, the Prime Minister's official residence. On arrival he was greeted by Churchill's doctor, Lord Moran, but also various private secretaries and was ushered through a raft of typists, detectives, Marines and Sawyers, the PM's valet – the entire circus. He was immediately summoned to see Churchill, who was in bed, surrounded by red dispatch boxes and smoking a big cigar. Macmillan thought he seemed in good form, and he was kept there for an hour, talking mainly about de Gaulle and the French rather than Italy. How to handle the prickly de Gaulle and the French Comité français de Libération nationale was just one of many issues that needed discussing in Cairo. Certainly, the broader strategic situation had changed considerably since the Combined Chiefs had last met at the Quadrant Conference in Quebec. The Red Army had now crossed back over the Dnieper River in Ukraine, the scene of a humiliating encirclement back in September 1941, and moved the Eastern Front a further 250 miles since Kursk in July. The tide was emphatically turning against Japan in the Pacific, which was greatly encouraging the Americans to maintain this initiative with greater commitment. Tied into this was a determination to keep the Chinese afloat, which was why the Generalissimo, Chiang Kai-shek, had been invited to Cairo. There was a suspicion by the Americans that the British were still not fully committed to OVERLORD, but there was also concern from the British that the Americans were going to miss opportunities in the Mediterranean in favour of South East Asia and China. Supporting China, the British chiefs believed, was largely a wasted effort, while a major effort into Burma and South East Asia could wait for the time being, at any rate.

None the less, Italy and the Mediterranean had dominated the opening of the second plenary meeting of the Sextant Conference earlier on the morning of the 24th. In his opening words, President Roosevelt had quickly come to the nub of the matter. 'The logistic problem,' he said, 'is whether we can retain OVERLORD in all its integrity and, at the same time, keep the Mediterranean ablaze.' Churchill had agreed. The Italian campaign had flagged; they did not have sufficient manpower to force the Germans back. The weather had been bad, and the departure of seven divisions had played badly. The build-up of the strategic air forces had also contributed to the slow progress. The main objective, he maintained, remained Rome. 'For whoever holds Rome,' he said, 'holds the title deeds of Italy.' The British campaign in the Dodecanese had failed, but he still believed it was worth driving the Germans out and hoped there could be an assault on Rhodes, which was so close to the Turkish coast. Bringing Turkey into the war would certainly be a huge benefit and was a particular pet strategy of the Prime Minister's. 'The effect on Hungary, Rumania and Bulgaria would be profound,' he said. 'All this might be done at quite a small cost, say, two divisions and a few hundred landing craft.'

He then turned to OVERLORD, stressing that his zeal for this vital operation had in no way diminished. 'OVERLORD remains top of the bill,' he told the conference, 'but this operation should not be such a tyrant as to rule out every other activity in the Mediterranean.' He would like to a see a little flexibility in the employment of landing craft; more were being built in Britain and he hoped the seventy LCTs currently under construction could be increased further. These opening remarks, however, were just that; much depended on the conversations to come with Chiang and the Chinese and then, especially, in Tehran with Stalin and the Soviets. Macmillan attended the meetings the following day, 25 November, and the massed gathering at the Kirk Villa, where Roosevelt was staying. At midday, everyone gathered on the lawn beneath a cloudless sky in lovely, gently warm weather. 'Here there was an indescribable scene,' noted Macmillan, 'of all the American and British officers of whom one had ever heard.'

While the Americans remained as resolute on OVERLORD as they ever had been, their rigid approach to strategy stopped with the cross-Channel operation. Rather, with regard to just about every other theatre, they assumed the kind of opportunistic policy so favoured by the British. It was to bolster his plans for supporting China that Roosevelt had invited Chiang Kai-shek. Backing the Chinese and supplying them with vast amounts of war materiel was a key part of the President's strategy, albeit one not shared with quite the same enthusiasm by the American chiefs. Macmillan had been rather intrigued to meet the Generalissimo but especially Madame Chiang, who – rather unorthodoxly – had accompanied her husband. 'Madame Chiang excited great interest among the British – rather less, I think, among the Americans, who have by this time seen and heard quite enough of her,' he noted. 'I gather she gives herself great airs and behaves like an Empress.' And the Americans had made it clear they held no truck with imperial aspirations.

With Chiang present, it was no surprise that once OVERLORD and Italy had been discussed, the Sextant talks were dominated by discussions about the war against Japan. Ahead of the conference, Roosevelt had already promised Chiang there would be amphibious landings in South East Asia to help reopen the Burma Road. This would then allow supplies to reach China overland rather than by flying them in over the Himalayas, which was the only current supply route and which was far from ideal; it was dangerous flying over the world's highest mountains and air freight could not deliver as much as transportation overland, especially when it had to reach remote airfields in Assam first. Where the shipping was going to come from for such further amphibious assaults was not clear, as none of the Americans were suggesting it should be taken from operations in the Pacific.

At any rate, the Allies were increasingly committed globally: to supplying the Soviet Union, to supplying the Chinese Nationalists, to operations throughout the Pacific and in South East Asia; to Italy, to a growing strategic air campaign against Germany, and to OVERLORD. Something would have to give. First, however, with the hors d'oeuvres and starters out of the way, the Chiefs of Staff had to meet the Russians in Tehran for the next course.

Macmillan was not attending this leg of the conference marathon and so headed back to Algiers, but while these high-level talks were going on and battles raged across Italy's leg, the political situation in Italy rumbled forward too, almost as slowly as the Allied advance. The thorny status of the monarchy was at the forefront of such deliberations. Even the most ardent monarchist would struggle to regard the King with generosity, but from Harold Macmillan's perspective the character of the King and his past history was not something over which the Allies should get involved, no matter their private individual feelings. Rather, he was convinced it was up to the Italians themselves, because while there were very good reasons for getting rid of Vittorio Emanuele, not least because of his earlier support of Fascism and entering the war, the pro-monarchy navy and merchant navy were working well with the Allies and most of the Italian embassies around the world were also supportive. It wouldn't reflect well on the Allies to have enforced an abdication. As it happened, Roosevelt and Churchill were also agreed on a non-intervention policy, at least until Rome was in Allied hands, so for the time being, at any rate, it looked like the King was going to remain – no liberal government would serve under him and Vittorio Emanuele was clearly not about to resign. An impasse had developed which the Italians would have to resolve themselves.

A plan had been agreed for the governance of Allied-occupied Italy, however. The area immediately behind the front line – twenty-five miles or so – would be run by AMGOT and was to be directly under military rule, with Alexander as the Military Governor. Behind this front-line area, however, would be Allied Control Commission territory. Here the King and royal government would govern, albeit with the indirect control of the Commission. The plan was to progressively hand back Sicily, Calabria and the south to the Italians as the Commission became more organized. However, how different this set-up was from that of the Germans and the RSI in the north was something of a moot point. On paper, the Badoglio government might be governing, but the Commission had complete control over all Italian armed forces and war materiel and was also authorized to exploit whatever Italian resources there were to the full and make first claims on these over and above the needs of civilians. The Badoglio government had also been obliged to provide 180,000 men to be employed by the Allies in manual labour and a further 45,000 for use in military rear areas. Allied-based military *lire* had to be honoured and the Commission also took control of banking and business, and any foreign exchange and overseas trade. The difference was that the Allies were not shooting people for disobedience, but they were most definitely placing military needs over those of Italian civilians.

There was, however, now a further strand, which had been suggested by Stalin during Allied talks in Moscow in October. This was the Advisory Council, which would include members from the United States, Britain, the Soviet Union but also the Free French; it was clearly a level too far, but in an atmosphere where the Soviet Union were now friends for the duration, the Allies agreed to let the Russians in as a placatory gesture, albeit a rather weak-handed one. Harold Macmillan, who was Britain's member of the new Advisory Council, flew into Brindisi on Thursday, 2 December, where he was met by the Vice-President and Deputy Vice-President of the Political Section of the Control Commission, who reminded him of how top-heavy the Control Commission had become in such a short time; already, some 1,500 officers and 4,000 further staff were working for it, running around, doing everything in duplicate – for the Americans and the British – and wasting precious resources that could have been better deployed at the front.

The first meeting of the Advisory Council was held the following day, 3 December, and attended by Andrei Vyshinsky, the Soviet representative and formerly the mastermind behind Stalin's purges of the late 1930s. Macmillan found him charming, although he was aware that he was talking to a man who'd not think twice about putting a bullet in the back of someone's head. The day was dominated by Vyshinsky trying to get more Soviet influence and showing lots of interest in Italian politics, but very little about the thorny issue of economics and supplies. 'Free speech is all right,' Vyshinsky told Macmillan over dinner after the meeting, 'so long as it does not interfere with the policy of the government.'

On the Adriatic coast, the Irish Brigade had been in reserve, but had crossed the Sangro and tramped forward as the line advanced. 'Am writing this under rather uncomfortable conditions,' Lawrie Franklyn-Vaile wrote to his wife on the 27th, 'so you will have to excuse the scrawl. It is a bright sunny Sunday afternoon, but we are all very dirty, unshaven and generally the aspect is not unduly peaceful.' He had just received a letter from John Glennie's mother, written before she'd heard the news of his death. 'I feel he is so young to have to face all the horrors of war and so innocent,' she had written. 'God grant you will both be spared to come safely through and remain together to the end.' He had barely been able to read it.

They might have been in reserve, but had then spent several days and nights in the concentration areas, which was precisely where most of the artillery were, so sleep had been very hard to come by. Then they waded across the river, dug in, and finally moved off again, following the London Irish. From Mozzagrogna to the coast and for the next few miles north, the plateau on to which they'd climbed was scored with a number of narrow gullies, mostly covered with trees and bushes, that wiggled their way to the coast. In many ways, these gullies were rather like giant trenches; it was why, on the morning of the 29th, the Faughs, while waiting to be ordered forward, took cover in one of these strange gorges just below Santa Maria Imbaro and the village of Fossacesia. Without warning, several shells landed right into the gully, killing nineteen and wounding twenty-seven, including the medical officer. It was terrible bad luck, but more than an entire platoon had been wiped out.

And it was freezing-cold and supply lines were not as they should be. 'We had another icy cold night without any blankets, greatcoats or food,' noted Lawrie Franklyn-Vaile, 'and the following day went into a big attack.' For once, the battalion had an easy time, sweeping through the village of Fossacesia, which had earlier been taken by the London Irish, and pushing on to capture a monastery that had been their objective. This was 65. Division's area and that day the Faughs captured a mass of booty, including a commander's car and twelve machine guns, but also over 100 prisoners. In all, more than 1,000 prisoners were taken, including 65. Division's commander. Really, the division had all but crumbled, and those not captured, killed or wounded were, on that last day of November, falling back in disarray.

It had been the combination of Allied artillery and air power that had broken 65. Division; when these worked properly in tandem, half-trained German troops simply had no answers. A combination of lower-level medium bombers and fighters had been over the Sangro front on the 27th, but the following day had seen the greatest effort from the Allied air forces, when they'd flown more than 500 sorties over the battlefront. Each single combat mission was one sortie – so that ensured a near-constant presence. 'Enemy air force has attacked in unheard of proportions,' AOK 10 signalled to Kesselring's headquarters that day. 'Our losses in blood and morale are increasingly high.' Kesselring had already sent Generalmajor Hans-Günther Baade, an old hand from the Afrikakorps days, to take over 65. Division, but when he spoke to Lemelsen, the acting 10. Armee commander confessed that the scale of Allied artillery and air power had been truly overwhelming. It was no wonder that 65. Division had struggled. Even Baade reckoned it surpassed anything he'd witnessed in North Africa. 'With Montgomery,' Kesselring told Lemelsen, 'you can count on that.'

Late on the 29th, Generalmajor Fritz Wentzell, Lemelsen's Chief of Staff, spoke to his opposite number at Kesselring's headquarters, General Westphal. The Allies' total control of the air, Wentzell said, and the weight of artillery fire was so heavy that absolutely nothing could move. 'It is simply impossible to do anything,' Wentzell told him, 'he has everything concentrated right there. One cannot make a counter-attack; the troops would be wiped out. Our losses are enormous.' The 2. Bataillon of 145. Regiment had been destroyed, Wentzell told Westphal. The next evening,

30 November, Lemelsen personally rang Westphal and reported that four entire battalions had been totally destroyed – including all three of 145. Regiment. It had simply ceased to exist.

The brief break in the rain had showed just how devastating a powerful, modern, firepower-heavy Allied army could be when properly integrated with close air support; not only had an infantry division of nearly 13,000 men been effectively destroyed, the ferocity of Eighth Army's attack had clearly spooked the German command too. In the first three days of battle, the eleven regiments of field artillery had fired a staggering 145,770 rounds. 'I bet Jerry is sorry he started this war,' Harry Wilson noted in his diary after listening to three days of relentless shelling and air attacks. Clearly, the Allies did have enough to smash their way through – but only when the weather was on their side. And that was the rub.

Both 8th Indian and 78th Divisions had made good progress, but so too had the New Zealanders. On the left flank of Eighth Army's attack, 6th Brigade had found their advance from the Sangro a great deal easier thanks to the barrage of artillery and Jabos. By the 30th they had reached Castelfrentano, six miles to the north. One of the demoralizing aspects of fighting in Italy was the looming bulk of ever more mountains. The eight-mile stretch between the Sangro and the next river, the Moro, was rolling hill country, but Route 84, the dirt road heading north along which 24th Battalion were advancing, was overlooked the entire way by the immense peaks of the Maiella Mountains and the 8,000-foot Monte Amaro, snow-capped, breathtakingly beautiful but barring their route north. At least by this time the Sangro had been bridged, and after capturing a two-storey villa at the edge of the town which overlooked the road into Castelfrentano, 24th Battalion attacked on 1 December with the support of both Shermans of 4th Armoured Brigade and the division's artillery. That day, Roger Smith and his platoon were supporting three Shermans as they entered the town. Route 84 was like a fish-hook, sweeping west before crossing the railway line below the town and then climbing gradually eastwards up the ridge, at the top of which stood Castelfrentano, its church and tall, thin bell tower overlooking its summit. Route 84 had to turn a sharp 90-degree corner to reach the centre, and the lead Sherman had just started to make this turn when there was a crack – a solid-shot anti-tank round hit the wall of the house next to the tank and wailed its way on down the ridge.

The Sherman hastily pulled back, something at which these tanks were very adept, and the commander clambered out and had a look around.

Together with Smith and the rest of the platoon, he realized that behind the house was an alleyway which rejoined the road into the town a little further up, behind the anti-tank gun that threatened their approach. After getting back into his tank the commander closed his hatch, swivelled the tank, and lurched forward. 'There was a clattering crash,' noted Smith, 'a squeal of tracks above the roar of the motors and the Sherman disappeared into the house in a most impressive manner, enveloped in a cloud of dust and debris.'

Suddenly, Smith noticed some Italians watching this from the arched entrance of a storeroom: a man, his wife leaning against him for support, a shawl across her anguished face, and three terrified young children clutching their parents' legs, watching in horror as their house was destroyed. After the first Sherman had passed through, the second and third followed, rubbing salt into their wounds. The woman now buried her head in her husband's shoulder as he stroked her hair. The children began crying, so their parents scooped them up and tried to comfort them. But how could they? Their home lay demolished. How could it be explained that this was done for liberty, for their freedom? That their house had been destroyed for the good cause of helping the Allies? This, once again, was the problem of fighting a war in a narrow country of 44 million people. 'You are in the way or out of the way,' noted Smith, 'a yard or an inch can spell the difference between life and death, destruction or deliverance. It could have been bombs, it could have been shellfire, but it happened to be a Sherman tank.'

The Germans pulled out that night and by dawn on 2 December Castelfrentano was in the New Zealanders' hands. Capturing the town was all well and good, but barring the way to the mountains beyond was the next German defensive position, yet another dominating ridgeline that ran behind the River Moro from Ortona on the coast to Orsogna fifteen miles inland. This latter town, perched on the edge of an impossibly dominant and steep ridgeline just four miles north-west of Castelfrentano, was the New Zealanders' next objective.

Now, though, the Germans were behind the Moro, a much stronger defensive position, with three divisions in line, not one, and with 1. Fallschirmjäger also being brought into the fray. It was December, and would be Christmas in barely three weeks. Rome still seemed a very long way away indeed.

CHAPTER 28

RAINCOAT

W HILE THE ALLIES' WAR leaders were discussing future strategy in such balmy conditions, the battle had been raging along Eighth Army's front, both sides struggling under considerably less clement skies. Harry Wilson and 8th Indian HQ crossed over the Sangro on 4 December on the latest Bailey bridge to span the river. Below them as they trundled over, the water ran deep and fast. The battlefield looked grim and scarred, strewn with wrecked vehicles, tanks and guns and the blackened remains of innumerable mules and horses. Wilson noticed hundreds of little crosses marking the graves of the dead. 'Mossogrogna was in ruins,' he noted, 'the streets rubble-strewn. Trees that had prettily adorned the roads had been blown up by the roots snapped across like sticks, or barked and chipped by machine-gun bullets. There were graves everywhere.' The Division HQ was established in a farmhouse and Wilson went for his usual explore, soon discovering a dead German sitting upright in a hedge but with both legs shot away. His dead face looked fair, handsome and wore a smile totally at odds with his circumstances. 'I reckon those legs of his went as far as Cairo,' a passing infantrymen said to Wilson.

Yet despite these horrors, Wilson was still able to marvel at the innate beauty of the country. A couple of evenings later, a patch of snow-white mist crossed the face of the moon hanging low in the sky, which then caused a strange halo of red, violet and green that lasted several minutes. 'Underneath this beautiful phenomenon,' noted Wilson, 'the German artillery was constantly shelling the New Zealand front. The rumble of the guns echoed along the mountain range like the noise of a great wind howling into the mouth of a giant cave.'

Needless to say, the Faughs and the rest of the Irish Brigade did not have it so easy for long as 90. Panzergrenadier- and 26. Panzer-Divisions began launching counter-attacks. Lawrie Franklyn-Vaile was called up to immediately take command of A Company when its commander, Toby Jewell, was wounded on 2 December. After a day trying to reorganize the depleted company they were ordered forward again on the 4th, crossing down and up yet more snaking gullies until reaching San Vito that night, a village that overlooked both the sea and a plunging wooded escarpment. On they went, moving forward in tandem with Shermans of 4th Armoured Brigade down the escarpment until they finally reached the ridge that overlooked the River Moro, only a mile beyond San Vito. Up ahead, no more than three miles away, was Ortona, a fishing port. Briefly, they were the most forward troops in the entire Eighth Army – until A Company was pulled back into reserve.

Early the following morning, however, it became clear that there were still German rearguards on this eastern side of the Moro, and B and C Companies were ordered forward to clear them off for good. It was a scrappy, confusing day of difficult fighting in which the Faughs lost yet more officers and men. Major John McNally, who had been Franklyn-Vaile's B Company commander, was wounded, so Major Richard Wood took command of both companies but was then killed by a mortar shell. At one point, enemy machine-gun fire was being fired straight on to Battalion HQ. 'Take what's left of your company up as quick as you can, Lawrie,' the CO told Franklyn-Vaile, 'and clear the ridge.' Doing as ordered, they crept forward, linking up with B and C Companies that evening.

The next day, now dug in, they were subjected to heavy mortar fire, that weapon of perennial danger for the infantryman. Six more were killed during that first Tuesday of December and thirty-one wounded. Chip, chip, chip. An officer here, a few fusiliers there. This was what happened when in action, even on days of comparative quiet at the front. Finally, the battalion was relieved at 9 p.m. on 5 December. One of Franklyn-Vaile's men in A Company, Lance-Corporal Ginger Rhodes, aged nineteen, was killed in this fighting. His best friend, the ten-man section commander, was so distraught at Rhodes's death that he went a bit mad, jumped up and began shouting and shooting wildly. One of the men had to knock him unconscious and take him back to an aid post. 'That is war, Olive,' Franklyn-Vaile wrote the next day, 'stripped of all the nice wireless and newspaper talk. We certainly hated the Hun yesterday – one man waved a white flag then shot down two of our men.' The strain, he told her, had been appalling. 'We are all desperately tired,' he added. 'I have not had a change of clothing for about three weeks and feel absolutely filthy. Last night, I took my boots off for the first time in 9 days.'

Now at the front was Ernie Pyle, already a legendary war reporter and equally beloved by his readers back home and the men he wrote about. Pyle wrote for the Scripps-Howard syndicate, which ran huge numbers of newspapers all across the United States, and before the war had become something of a pioneer by travelling around and writing very affectionate and personal pieces about the everyday folk he came across. Taking this same approach to writing about the war had won him a huge legion of fans. War reporters came and went – Quent Reynolds had shipped out after Salerno, for example – while 36th Division had also recently been entertaining the photographer Margaret Bourke-White, but Pyle, especially, won friends by facing danger and talking to the boots on the ground rather than making a beeline for the generals. Aged forty-three years, prematurely grey and looking at least ten years older, he was also somewhat neurotic; but he was empathetic, genial, and the one reporter every soldier, sailor and airman hoped to meet and be written up by.

Pyle had reached Naples in November, but no sooner had he arrived in the city than he felt an overwhelming urge to get out again, and so he got a ride north to see what was going on in Fifth Army. One pile of rubble after another marked where small Italian towns and villages used to be. The roads were atrocious and military signs littered the route. Even in the countryside, the telltale signs of fighting were never hard to spot – a broken olive tree, a handful of dead and swollen cattle, a straw stack burned down. Shell-holes and craters on a hillside, scraps of discarded equipment – a helmet, rifle or ammunition box. A lonely, recently dug grave. These things littered the fields he passed.

He also discovered that sympathy levels for the Italians were quite low. While riding in a jeep he got talking to an American of Italian extraction, who told him that despite his connection to Italy he wanted nothing to do with the people. He could speak Italian, and had discovered that when he did he was always given a sob story about how starved they were and complaints about why the Allies weren't feeding them faster.

'I look at it this way,' he told Pyle, 'they've been poor for a long time and it wasn't us that made them poor. They started this fight and they've killed plenty of our soldiers, and now that they're whipped they expect us to take care of them. That kind of talk gives me a pain. I tell them to go to hell. I don't like 'em.'

Pyle stopped with a battery of big 155mm howitzers a few miles back from the front-line infantry in the upper Volturno Valley and it rained almost all the time he was there, the countryside vividly green as a result. Italians continued to try and farm around the American artillerymen, moving herds of cows or pigs right past them. Grubby children waited at the battery kitchen hoping for leftovers; Pyle was struck by how untroubled they seemed by the war going on around them until aircraft thundered over, at which point the children, especially, always ran for their lives.

On his first night there, under canvas amid the mud, he slept fitfully as the guns of both sides continued to boom. 'We could hear the shells chase each other through the sky across the mountains ahead, making a sound like cold wind blowing on a winter night,' he wrote. 'Then the concussion of the blasts of a dozen guns firing at once would strike the far mountains across the valley and rebound in a great mass sound that was prolonged, like the immensity and the fury of an approaching sandstorm.' The closer guns made the ground tremble when they fired and the breath of the blast would ruffle the canvas of his tent.

There were four guns in each battery, three batteries in a US Army artillery battalion and three battalions in a regiment. At Pyle's battery, each gun was dug into a pit around 3 feet deep and the front of this scrape lined with sandbags. Poles were erected over which camouflage netting was strung. On one side of the gun pit was a stack of black powder cases and on the other a stack of shells. Powder charges, on the other hand, were kept well clear and brought in one at a time. They were all operating in thick mud and it was all too easy to slip. Artillerymen did a lot of lugging around: the powder, the shells, clearing the shell casings and then, several times a day, unloading more shells and powder when the ammunition truck came up. All the guns were linked by field telephone to the battery's executive post, which in turn was linked to the battalion CP. The battalion received their orders from the division CPs and by men like Bud Wagner, beetling about in their jeeps and delivering instructions. Targets were relayed to divisions and then battalions by observers several miles ahead in OPs on the mountain. As a result, the artillerymen on these 155s never saw their targets at all.

Supper was early now that it was nearing midwinter – at 4.30 p.m. – and an hour later it was dark. 'There was nothing to do, no place to go,' noted Pyle, 'and even inside the big tents the candlelight wasn't conducive to much fun.' So unless they had night firing to do, the crews were generally asleep by 8.30 p.m. Guards were changed through the night to keep a watch but also to be on hand should firing instructions come in. They would be night firing, however, once Fifth Army's offensive began again.

The Faughs, and the whole of 78th Division, were about to be relieved by the Canadians. Farley Mowat, still battalion intelligence officer, had gone with Major Bert Kennedy, the acting CO, to a divisional briefing at Campobasso on 25 November. A brigadier from Eighth Army HQ was there to give them the form. 'As you may have guessed, gentlemen, our objective remains Rome,' he told them. 'Can't let the Hun spend the rest of the winter there all nice and comfy-cosy. So, we shall jolly well turf him out.' The Yanks, he said, were going to burst through into the Liri Valley, while Eighth Army would make a colossal crack, grab Pescara, then cross over to Rome. It all sounded so very easy. The Canadians were going to spearhead the way once the initial breakthrough had been made.

Two days later, Mowat and Kennedy took a jeep up to the Sangro front. Kennedy had been captured by the Germans but had escaped and spent twenty-five days on the run, rejoining the battalion just as the CO, Lord Tweedsmuir, had gone sick with jaundice. Fortunately, Kennedy had arrived in time to step into his shoes, and just as the battalion was out of the line in Castropignano, yet another remote village perched on a hill which overlooked the Biferno; it was a stone's throw from San Stefano, where Gerry Swayle had been killed. The men had renamed it Castelpigface, although it was a pretty enough place, if a little cold and damp. Mowat was still thoroughly browned off, though. 'I hasten to disillusion you about the climate,' he had written to a friend, 'but it must be the worst in the whole bloody world.' He told him that the first travel agent he saw back home with a poster of Sunny Italy was going to get a rock through the window.

And nothing about his drive with Kennedy to the front did anything to cheer him. 'Everything that was not solid rock seemed to be turning fluid,' he noted. 'Lines of olive trees gnarled by a hundred winters stood gaunt as gibbets on dripping ridges above vineyards that had become slimy swamps.' In the villages they passed through it seemed to him that even the little stone houses had shrunk under the weight of relentless rain and sleet. Once at the front they were given a tour, and, seeing the number of vehicles motoring slowly through thick, syrupy mud halfway up each wheel and the dejected, grey atmosphere and levels of destruction, it was clear they would not be galloping to Pescara any time soon.

A couple of days later, on 1 December, the battalion moved out of Castelpigface, a long column of trucks and other vehicles heading to the Adriatic coast. Once they'd crossed the Sangro they halted and the take-over process began. Mowat met a liaison officer from 78th Division who was almost in tears. 'Haven't any of the high mucky-mucks looked at their frigging maps?' he said. 'There'll be half a dozen Sangros before we get to Pescara – if we get to Pescara. Thank God you're taking over, Canada. We've *had* this show!'

The Hasty Ps were ordered to relieve the Faughs on the afternoon of 5 December after the padre, Captain the Reverend J. F. Goforth, had held a voluntary church service for the men. Farley Mowat had gone forward with the Faughs' intelligence officer. Rain pelted down. Files of Faughs were coming out of the line, Lawrie Franklyn-Vaile among them. 'Their faces were as colourless as paper pulp,' noted Mowat with mounting dread, 'and they were so exhausted they hardly seemed to notice the intense shelling the coastal road was getting as they straggled down it.'

The Faughs might not have been noticing, but Mowat was. The pervading and rancid smell of cordite hung in the air. His heart pounded and jolted in his chest without rhythm. He began to shiver, although he was not cold. Everything told him to stop, turn round and run. Pulling out a cigarette, he offered one to the Irish lieutenant, who lit a match in cupped hands. But Mowat turned away. 'For in that instant,' he wrote, 'I realised what was happening to me. I was sickening with the most virulent and deadly of all apprehensions . . . the fear of fear itself.'

They walked on, reached the ridge and lay on their stomachs among some sodden bushes. Low cloud obliterated the view. This was a strange landscape: a series of plateaus, rather than ridges, gently undulating but rather flat, on which stood villages, farmsteads and endless vineyards, olive groves and meadows. Scoring these plateaus, one after the other, were a series of gullies, mostly quite narrow and verdant – covered with acacia, baby oaks and low-growing bushes. Mowat could see little but ahead lay the Moro Valley, plunging steeply perhaps 200 feet from the edge of the plateau. Tracks wove their way down past more vineyards and olive groves to cross the Moro itself, no more than 10–15 yards wide, but below deep, steep banks, and then climbed back up to a series of villages – Villa Rogatti, the hamlet of La Torre, and San Leonardo, which on a fine day could be seen very clearly, a collection of white and stone houses sleepily huddled together. The valley itself was only two-thirds of a mile wide. From where Mowat crouched, the coast was a mile distant, if that. Ortona, their initial objective, could be clearly seen, perched on the edge of the sea, a little way to the north. So close one could almost touch it.

Yet, as was so often the case in this ancient land, the landscape favoured the defender. Crossing the valley, already zeroed by enemy artillery and mortars and teams of machine-gunners, would be brutally tough. Beyond them, beyond those villages, were the gullies – narrow gashes into the plateau covered with trees and vegetation. Ideal for placing mortar teams. Each of these gullies, some long, some quite short, ran towards the sea and against the flow of the Allied advance. And for all the support of the artillery behind them and even tanks, taking this ground was really a job for the infantry: men who would have to thread their way off the plateau, down into the valley and up the far side, and hope there would be enough of them still standing to prise the enemy from their positions.

Also now up on the southern side of the Moro were the Seaforth Highlanders of Canada. Captain Roy Durnford, the padre, had been shocked by the scenes of desolation as they'd neared. 'The river and banks are profuse with battered remains of war and a completely ruined bridge,' he noted. 'Dead strewn about – all German. God help our lads.' For those entering this war-torn landscape there was a terrible, gnawing sense of approaching hell. Either side of the Bailey bridges over the Sangro were immense furrows of mud as well as battle debris. Durnford crossed the river on the 3rd and immediately saw large numbers of new crosses. A barrage was in full swing, and ahead stood San Vito. Durnford thought the remains of the village and the surrounding landscape were worse than anything he'd seen in terms of absolute devastation.

The changeover was complete that evening and in the Hasty Ps' sector complete by 7.30 p.m., and, as Farley Mowat discovered when he reported back to Bert Kennedy, they were due to attack straight away, that night, and silently too, without any artillery softening up the enemy first. General Chris Vokes, the division commander, believed that a silent, stealthy attack was their best chance of success. Vokes had only taken command at the end of September when Major-General Guy Simonds became yet another to succumb to jaundice. He was a professional soldier, taciturn and with a reputation for pushing his men particularly hard.

Kennedy, frantic at the speed with which they were expected to be ready to launch this assault, now ordered Mowat to head back again and find a suitable crossing point over the river. The thought of such a patrol was making Mowat sick to his core; he knew that four months earlier he'd have been eager for the chance and that even two months ago he'd have undertaken it without too much thought. But not now. Orders, though, were orders. Collecting some scouts, he willed his way forward and together, scrambling down the vine-covered slopes, they safely reached the river, waded along its overflowing banks until they found a fordable spot, then scampered back up again. Not a shot had been fired, not a single enemy soldier had been heard. Mowat had survived.

Vokes's plan was to launch three battalion assaults. The Hasty Ps would be on the right, near the mouth of the Moro, close to the sea and the main Highway 16 heading north. In the middle would be the Seaforth Highlanders of Canada aiming for the village of San Leonardo, perched on the plateau the far side of the valley; and then on the left, the Princess Patricia's Canadian Light Infantry – the PPCLI – would attack the next settlement along on the north side, Villa Rogatti. Three crossing points, three bridgeheads, and from there they could push forward across the plateau and take Ortona. Vokes had identified a crossroads that stood above the south-west end of a particularly long gully just to the south of the town as a key objective. Here, the track north from the plateaus and gullies crossed the main lateral road that wound its way towards Orsogna, and, immediately parallel to the road, the railway line. Vokes code-named this objective 'Cider'.

Behind the Canadians, back on the Sangro, the torrential rains that had accompanied them on their journey north had caused the river to flood and all three pontoon bridges had been swept away. The engineers would have to start all over again, but a more immediate concern was the halt in supplies this caused. The Canadian 3rd Brigade hadn't even reached the Moro front yet.

None the less, at midnight the attacks began. Able Company, Mowat's old crew from Sicily, were without Alex Campbell, who was recovering from jaundice. Mowat watched them head off, his old platoon leading the way. Down they went, into the valley, and then silence. No artillery, no firing. The rain continued; it could be heard beating a drum on the leaves and on the track. Then suddenly, starkly, cutting across the night, the buzz-saw of machine guns, flares crackling overhead and fire from the enemy artillery, shells screeching and sucking their way across the valley.

The battle for Ortona had begun.

*

RSM Jack Ward was at RHQ of 56th Heavy Regiment to the south of Monte Camino and Monte La Difensa, the southern bastion of the Bernhard Line on the western side of the peninsula, on 1 December. That night, at 10 p.m., their guns were going to be firing in support of X Corps' attack on the mountains and their hopes of breaking through the German defences and crossing the Garigliano. 'It's the first day of the month, a new moon, and a grand night tonight,' he noted, 'so here's luck to us all, as we shall want it. I feel we cannot fail and once over the river, into Rome.' Everyone knew that the Eternal City remained the goal. Just one more push – break through the door in front of them and the road would roll out before them. Well, that was certainly the plan, although even the 56th Heavy Regiment was suffering at present, less from battle casualties than from illness – and specifically jaundice; it was currently under-strength by around 100 men. Everything, it seemed, was working against the Allies at present.

None the less, Clark now had considerably greater forces amassed than he had a month earlier. This wasn't just because the Bernhard Line had been recognized as a tougher nut but also because those extra divisions and materiel had been shipped to Italy, and the Fifth Army engineers had performed miracles to improve Naples' docks, build bridges and repair roads all the way to the front. During the first attempt on Camino, there had been 180 guns supporting 56th Division. Now there were 820 for the opening bombardment due to begin at 10 p.m. that night, 1 December, including those batteries of 155s that Ernie Pyle was with.

It opened up as planned. 'The firing was absolutely terrible,' noted Dom Eusebio, up at the abbey of Monte Cassino, 'and continued very heavily at intervals.' 'The major battle has commenced,' recorded Wilhelm Mauss. 'After the usual heavy artillery barrage yesterday, the English have stormed Monte Camino.'

In all, the Allied artillery fired a staggering 11 tons of shells per minute on some targets, and 1,329 tons in just seventy-five minutes in four separate concentrations each laid on to targets 500 yards square. Over the next few days, X Corps' artillery alone fired 3,800 tons, each shell thundering over, sucking the air as it hurtled through the sky, crashing amid an explosion of metal, rock and earth. The ground pulsing, buildings shaking, dust, debris, carnage.

Battles were confusing, terrifying and extremely violent, and often the fog of war descended with astonishing speed, particularly in Italy that winter. For all those involved, and on both sides, the battles now raging in Italy were sheer bloody awful. There was a reason why the campaigning season of old had occurred during the summer months and, really, those military traditions still stood; except that in this awful global conflict there was not the patience for that, while also an underlying belief prevailed that in modern times technology should be able to circumvent tedious matters of shortening days and worsening weather. It couldn't, though, not really. Ever since British and then Allied fortunes in the war against the Axis powers had started to turn in their favour in the second half of the summer of 1942, an obvious pattern had started to emerge in which great strides were made by the Allies in summer, followed by progress slowing and grinding almost to a halt during the winter, and then things picked up again. Already, in December 1943, there were very clear signals that the Allied war machine was struggling to function properly. The pragmatist might have recommended pausing, building up strength and having another go once the snow had thawed, the ground dried and green buds sprouted from the trees and hedgerows once more. On the other hand, if the Allies took their foot off the throttle, even when in low gear, the Germans could spend the winter building increasingly formidable defences – so much so that not even the best weather would be enough.

No, they had committed to Italy, and they would have to keep going, chipping away, swinging the sledgehammer at the rock face.

This was why the Allied armies were now fighting right across the leg of Italy – but because of the weather the job was so much harder and so much more deadly for the infantry, who were the ones who had to clamber out of their foxholes and actually advance and take the land that was occupied by the enemy. When artillery was firing and the skies were full of aircraft, that task was easier because their presence meant the Germans had to crouch in their own foxholes and keep their heads down. It also prevented them from easily moving about by day, so any supplies would have to come up by night, which added to their exhaustion, and exhaustion ensured that they were less well able to fight.

Without this immense fire support, however, infantry had to pick their way forward at night – or by day – and hope they could find a way through, even though spotters could help enemy artillery find their targets, even though it was easier for the German infantry to man machine guns and mortars. Infantry would generally attack with one or two companies up front. Around 10 per cent would always be LOB – left out of battle – to help form the cadre of a new unit if the worst happened. Each company would then have lead platoons and platoons also in reserve, and sections of ten men in the lead and following behind. Men would move forward and try not to bunch up, but at night, or in thick smoke, this was easier said than done. Most were reluctant soldiers, didn't want to be there, and were waiting to be led and told what to do; that was true of professional armies but certainly of mostly conscripted ones. The men who led them forward, who urged them to keep going, were the NCOs, particularly the platoon sergeants, and also the junior officers – the lieutenants commanding platoons, and the majors and captains who ran the company. Because they were leading and showing the men the way, they were often the most likely to be killed and wounded. This was why the Guards Brigade simply hadn't been able to keep going on Monte Camino during the attempt to take the massif in November – so many senior NCOs and officers had been killed or wounded that there was no one left to lead the rest. It was utterly brutal. Casualties among the infantry in Italy were proportionally higher than they had been during the slaughter on the Western Front in the last war. A single mortar shell, for example, or a well-aimed burst of machine-gun fire might wipe out half a section – or squad – of ten or even more. Meanwhile, it wasn't any fun sitting in a foxhole being shelled and mortared and trying to force back the enemy either.

The experience of the 3rd Coldstream Guards on the renewed assault on Monte Camino was a case in point. Lieutenant David Helme was ten days short of his twenty-third birthday and a platoon commander in No. 4 Company when, on 3 December, he and his men began climbing up towards Bare Arse Ridge, as one part of Camino had been named. From the valley floor, Camino looked mighty indeed but reasonably conical. This, however, was an illusion, because like almost every mountain its summit was merely the highest point of a series of peaks, high knolls, plunging rock faces, saw-edged ridgelines, crevices and ravines. Immediately to the north-eastern side of Camino, for example, the mountain dropped savagely steeply by several hundred feet and again on the other side, albeit into a high mountain plateau of cultivated terraces and a small hamlet of farmhouses called Colle. Just south of here the mountain plunged sharply again. To the west of the farmed plateau, with its stone walls, tracks and normally pleasant pastures and terraces, and less than a mile as the crow flies from the Camino summit ran a 2,000-yard-long paddle-shaped ridge, largely bare except for patches of scrub and strewn with rocks and loose stone. The western side sloped less severely than the brutal drop on the eastern saddle. This was the appropriately nicknamed Bare Arse Ridge. To reach its southern edge required a ferociously steep climb up mule tracks and over crumbling, rocky and scrub-covered terrain. Bare Arse itself, as its adopted name suggested, was mostly just rock and sparse scrub, with plunging drops, loose rock everywhere, and a series of progressively high knolls, each of which was a defender's dream because of the view it gave of any approaching attack. What's more, the narrowness of the ridge and its severe slopes either side, but especially on the eastern edge, meant any attack was hamstrung by the canalizing effect of the terrain. Troops such as those in the Guards Brigade were rapidly getting used to fighting in such a challenging landscape but they were not actually trained in mountain warfare. Rather, they were expected to adapt on the job.

It was a night climb with heavy packs of food and ammunition and took them twelve and a half hours, so was a severe test. They were horribly exposed up there and the troops ahead of them were delayed, so they then had to manoeuvre themselves on to the reverse slope of Bare Arse, off the ridgeline itself, so they might keep out of sight of the enemy. Helme and his men remained there all day and much of the next day too, waiting for the rest of the battalion to join them. It rained constantly, the droplets from above spattering on to the rock, on to their tin helmets, their greatcoats and gas capes. There was no escape from it on this exposed, high, boulder- and rock-strewn slope. Once darkness fell, the battalion attacked two features, Points 683 and 615 – nearly 1,400 feet up – which meant dropping down off Bare Arse and crossing a narrow valley in which the tiny village of Formella was nestled, and then up to an even narrower saw-edged ridge, but one that was thick with scrub and small trees and vegetation. And all this at night and in the rain. Lieutenant John Hamilton, the Patrol Platoon commander, had been up there in the first Battle of Monte Camino the previous month, so he and his men led the way. It took them all night to get close to these knolls. 'My boots (from Fortnum and Mason),' Helme noted in his diary, 'were torn to shreds by the end of the march.' That was not surprising: this landscape would challenge the toughest of boots.

It was just getting light on the morning of the 5th when they reached their objective and they found themselves right in among the enemy rearguards. As they were taking position, an MG42 opened up and mortar shells began crashing around them. Helme's own No. 4 Company took the brunt of this as they were still in the open. Three men were wounded, including Sergeant Curry. Another man was shot in the arm. They then learned that both David Forgan, the medical officer, and the padre, Captain Levis, had been killed the previous evening by a shell. Getting the wounded evacuated was near-impossible because they were constantly under observation and snipers fired the moment anyone tried to move. 'Eventually,' scribbled Helme, 'we flushed one Hun and I shot him. Great satisfaction.' Their situation, though, was 'disquieting', because they now found themselves stuck on a mountain salient without any communications with any other unit except by lamp, which no one seemed able to answer, and also without their 3-inch mortars because the base plates had been lost in the climb. There was no soil and they couldn't dig in, so instead they used rocks to create sangars – effectively stone walls around them. Then two of Helme's greatest friends in the battalion, John Hamilton and Major Geoffrey Clark, were killed; Hamilton had taken out a party of Bren gunners and a mortar observer to a point 300 yards to their left. Unbeknown to any of them, three German snipers had crept into a position between this new post and the left-hand platoon and started taking potshots. Hearing the firing, Hamilton hurried back, stumbled on the sniper post and was shot dead. Helme was devastated.

By this time the battalion was out of water, so they had to stretch out groundsheets and gas capes to catch rain. There was no chance of shaving, but Helme did manage to have a bit of a wash in water that had collected in a shell-hole. The following day, 6 December, the Scots Guards and Grenadiers moved through them at dawn, to attack the Acquapendola Ridge, which ran forward from Bare Arse and Point 685, but more or less parallel, and which was a further mile and a half west as the crow flies. Another artillery barrage fired over them and as they attacked Acquapendola Ridge the Coldstreamers also gave covering fire. The ridge was successfully taken, which greatly improved the battalion's situation up on the mountain. Helme, though, got hit in the head by a mortar fragment – he was lucky. 'Slightly stunned,' he noted, 'but nothing bad. Strong sweet tea in the RAP very welcome.'

They were now on emergency rations, however, because the mule trains simply hadn't been able to reach them. The officers did what they could to keep the men going; Helme was very impressed that their CO, Colonel George Burns, made sure he visited every position, making jokes with the men. 'His beard,' noted Helme, 'was even longer than mine.' Rations finally reached them on the 7th and on the 10th even bundles of mail made their way up there. All the men were wet, cold and fed up, so getting some letters cheered them enormously. Regular mail really was one of the golden keys to maintaining morale.

Battles in these conditions were every bit as confusing for the commanders as they were for the men slogging their way forward. Whether commanding an army, corps or division, a general could expect a mass of different information arriving near-constantly, much of which was hard to piece together. Or sometimes units were cut off entirely, just as the 3rd Coldstream Guards had been, making it impossible to know what the hell was going on. The same happened to units of the 15. Panzergrenadier troops on Monte Camino on 2 December; not until late on the 3rd was contact established with Corps HQ. Nor had von Senger been entirely clear where the main weight of the Allied attack might come until a day after Fifth Army's guns had started the battle with their latest night barrage. Clambering over the rock-strewn slopes of Monte Sammucro on 2 December to visit a battalion up there, von Senger had realized that the answer lay towards Monte Camino. 'What I observed filled me with surprise and dismay,' he noted. 'A heavy barrage was directed by enemy artillery on the opposite side of the valley against the positions on the northern slopes of the Camino massif.' Not since the last war had he witnessed a bombardment of such intensity.

At his shattered battery command post, Hans Golda and his men found themselves repeatedly under attack from Allied bombers and Jabos whose bombs were falling horribly close. As they whistled down, Golda and his men dived on to the ground. A dull roar, the ground trembling, the air sucked from their lungs and choking dust and debris. 'When we looked up,' he noted, 'we were very, very pale, but otherwise healthy.' Their bunker was desolate and the remaining walls of the house had collapsed but, although coughing and spluttering, they had all survived yet again.

On the 4th, the rain that had blighted David Helme and the 3rd Coldstreamers had continued, heavily, into the next day, causing the Rivers Garigliano, Rapido and Liri to flood. Golda's fire position was deluged and in no time three of his Nebelwerfers had become submerged. Soon their bunker was also full of brown, gurgling broth. The water subsided the following day. Of their three Nebelwerfers, only the tube barrels could be seen – everything else was stuck in the mud. 'We could not salvage anything from the drunken bunker,' he noted. 'Likewise, the ignition machine and the ignition cable were with the devil.' His battery would not be firing the Nebelwerfers for the time being.

Von Senger believed it was time to pull back. Behind them, the bridges over the Garigliano had either been destroyed by Allied shelling and bombing or swept away by the floods, which meant 15. Panzergrenadier was in danger of being cut off. The British and American troops on the Camino massif were also clearly making progress too. On 5 December he asked for permission to withdraw, and the following day General Lemelsen told Kesselring that the Camino massif could no longer be held. Kesselring, however, then referred back to Hitler, who predictably refused to countenance any retreat. So the forward units of the Hermann Göring and 15. Panzergrenadier clung on to the Camino positions for a couple of days more. Only on 9 December was the southern bastion of the Mignano Gap finally in Allied hands. RAINCOAT, as the second battle for Monte Camino had been code-named, had been a success, despite the rain, the cold and the mounting casualties. The 3rd Coldstream Guards were just 598 men-strong by 12 December. They'd lost 30 per cent on Bare Arse and its neighbouring ridges. How many more would they lose before they reached Rome?

CHAPTER 29

Valley of Death

Across the leg, ferocious fighting continued at Ortona and Orsogna, battles that were every bit as messy, brutal and destructive as those raging on Fifth Army's front. Near Ortona, the Canadians' three crossing points had mixed results; the silent night attack on Villa Rogatti on the left by the PPCLI did well and the hamlet was captured swiftly. In the middle, the Seaforth Highlanders could barely make a foothold at all, so San Leonardo remained hopelessly out of reach. On the Hasty Ps' front, Bert Kennedy reckoned he could get his men across the Moro Valley with the help of artillery, heavy 4.2-inch mortars, and from a squadron of British Shermans placed on the ridge behind them. Charley Company set off at 2 p.m. after twenty minutes of screaming, pounding shellfire, by which time smoke covered much of the valley. With the mortars tonking away just ahead of their advance, Kennedy hoped C Company might be able to force a way through. Watching their assault was Farley Mowat, who immediately realized to his horror that the enemy dug in opposite were returning fire with equal ferocity, pounding the valley floor with shell after shell, immense fountains of earth, stone and steel hurtling into the sky. Dog Company was then also sent into this inferno, disappearing spectrally as the smoke enveloped them. So too did the tanks which had begun working their way down.

After an hour of silence from both companies, Kennedy became increasingly distraught; it had been his suggestion that they try crossing this accursed valley again that afternoon and he feared two companies had been slaughtered in the carnage. The difference between advancing into the valley of death in front of them now or over no-man's-land twenty-five years earlier was negligible. Only the terrain was different. Kennedy ordered Mowat and a runner to investigate, then decided to lead the way himself. Down the valley sides, through shattered trees, shattered olive groves and shattered vineyards. The ground trembling. Above, the overwhelming din of battle. The air thick with cordite and smoke. Sharp on the throat. Stinging the eyes. There was the river, narrow, but flowing fast. Wade across. Water icy, numbingly cold. Scramble up the far side, hands covered in mud, knees slick with mud. Mud everywhere. Where the hell was everyone? Mowat struggling, his brain screaming at him to turn and run.

The tanks were bogged down and couldn't move; they would have to do without armoured support. Somehow they found Charley Company, sheltering in a cave at the foot of the valley. The company commander was missing and the shaken sergeant could tell them little. Clearly, the situation was hopeless and Kennedy wanted to call them back, but he didn't have a radio. So back they went, back up to the ridge, Mowat feeling as though he were drowning, plunging into the mire, his lungs gasping, his brain scrambled. Sinking. They cleared the ridge intact, however, and Kennedy marched them down the road, only for them to be bracketed by enemy shells. Something struck Mowat's boot and the concussive effect of the shell knocked him face-down in the mud. Dazed, he looked up. Ahead, Kennedy was on his knees, shaking his head while behind something – someone – was screaming in his ears. Not a shell but a human scream. Then he saw him: the runner, a young lad whose name he'd never known, body humping jerkily, his severed leg a little distance away. As Mowat looked on this ghastly image, a boy reduced to roadkill, the runner gave one final shriek of despair and pain then collapsed, dead.

'Get up, Mowat!' yelled Kennedy. 'Goddamn you! Up!'

Mowat protested – he'd been hit in the leg, he told him – but Kennedy grabbed him and pulled him to his feet. Another salvo of shells whooshed over and crashed nearby but, crouching, they stumbled on, got clear of the ridge and when some Baker Company men spotted them they helped Mowat to the first aid post.

'Good lad, Squib,' Kennedy told him. 'You've done OK.'

Mowat had been hoping he'd got a 'Blighty' – a wound sufficiently severe that he'd be shipped back to Britain – but the bit of shrapnel in his backside was pulled out and the wound on his foot was negligible. All he needed was a new pair of trousers and boots. By this time, the remains of Charley Company were straggling back to their side of the escarpment, but there was still no word from Dog Company. Kennedy, refusing to allow one of his companies to remain stranded, now ordered Able and Baker Companies into the fray too, and also the dismounted Carrier Platoon. Mowat was told to accompany him as he led the way. This time, they crossed the river and managed to reconnect with the missing D Company – a defunct radio, as so often, was the problem. By dusk the battalion had cleared the escarpment and then began digging in on the far side, a tentative foothold in their hands.

The night brought more misery – the grinding and squeaking of enemy tanks nearby, flares crackling and bursting regularly, shells continuing to screech and burst. On both sides, soldiers stumbling through shredded vines, firing weapons with a panicky abandon. Mowat was sent back yet again, this time to fetch what was left of Charley Company, and returned once more, reporting to Kennedy up on the northern ridge. Padre Roy Durnford had been up to the front repeatedly to try and bury the dead. 'We are shelled constantly,' he jotted. 'A barrage of artillery is being heard north of us and on our left the like of which has surely never been heard before.' Nor had he ever seen mud like it – from A Echelon, the battalion supply base, right to the front. 'Go up line to front,' Durnford wrote on the 8th. 'D. Wilson killed. We are up against fierce odds. War has never been so savage as it is now for us. Narrow, hair-breadth escapes are common among us all. Nerve-wracking in the extreme.'

For the men on the ground it was often hard to make much sense of what was going on, yet everyone recognized that the battle was rapidly turning into what the men called a 'meat grinder'. The success of the PPCLI couldn't be exploited because the engineers decided it was impossible to bridge the Moro below Villa Rogatti. Instead, further attempts were made to clear San Leonardo and expand the toehold eked out by the Hasty Ps. General Vokes agreed to shift his entire front to the right and the 8th Indians took over the area around Villa Rogatti; their engineers promptly bridged the Moro there, which they wittily named Impossible Bridge. A renewed assault on San Leonardo and the original goal – the crossroads code-named 'Cider' – was launched at 4.30 p.m. with a barrage by 350 guns that had been somehow massed together, pummelling an area only a few miles wide. An immense, preposterous din, an earthquake beneath the feet, the plateau beyond pitched and turned and tossed, San Leonardo just the latest Italian village to be reduced to rubble.

Cowering under this onslaught was Grenadier Werner Mork, twenty-two years old, but looking younger with his mop of flaxen hair. Brought up near Bremen in northern Germany, he'd served in North Africa and more recently Sardinia and Corsica, and had moved across to the Adriatic front with the rest of 90. Panzergrenadier-Division in October. Recently, Mork had been serving in the quartermaster's office – the B Echelon, or support team – which was where he'd liked it. He'd enjoyed being stationed on the coast and had become friends with a slightly older raven-haired Italian lady who ran a flour mill just to the north of Ortona. He had also been expecting some leave because he was engaged to his childhood sweetheart and had been told that the marriage licence – effectively permission to go home and wed – would be authorized at any moment. Unfortunately, his old company commander, Leutnant Tscheschow, whom Mork loathed, had returned and demanded he return to the front lines, and so his cushy quartermaster job, along with his visits to see the lovely miller, came to an end. Instead, he found himself dug in on the plateau to the north of the Moro with the rest of 12. Kompanie of 2. Bataillon, 200. Panzergrenadier-Regiment.

His task was Number 3 machine-gunner, a role for which he had not been trained, not that it required much training. He shared a foxhole with the other two in the team, and when firing it was his task to pass up belts of ammunition and to scurry back and get more tins of the stuff when they ran out. The motto, drummed into them all, was 'If one falls, another must replace him.' 'The one important thing,' noted Mork, 'was there had to be three men on each machine-gun. You learned fast or died, it was that simple.' Like Farley Mowat, Mork was also starting to struggle badly with combat fatigue; his tank of courage was simply running out. He'd nearly been killed by an air attack in Tobruk in North Africa and it had made him a little bomb-happy. In Sardinia and Corsica life had been fairly gentle, and it had been easy enough here at Ortona too up until now. Everything had changed with the Canadian attack. Day and night, it seemed, they had been pummelled by Allied shelling. And all they had to protect them was a hole in the ground.

Not far away, a dozen miles to the south-west, the New Zealanders were in the midst of another tough fight at Orsogna. The town was strung out on a 1,300-foot-high ridge overlooking the Moro but with steep, plunging cliffs running down into the valley below. There were three very good reasons for trying to snatch this precariously perched town in quick order. Taking Orsogna would help the capture of Ortona, because the main lateral road that ran roughly parallel with the Moro, but on the ridgeline, connected the two, so it could be used to roll up the German position from the east. It would also provide a base – a jumping-off point, in effect – for the next drive north towards the towns of Chieti, Pescara and Avezzano. Finally, it was a very dominating position and there was a very good reason to get the enemy off it and take it instead. An attempt to quickly snatch the town on 3 December had been stopped short, but a renewed assault, Operation TORSO, was launched on 7 December, with 24th Battalion approaching on the southern road that ran from the east up on to the Brecciarola Ridge, and 28th Maori from the Ortona road, which reached the town along a further ridgeline that led to Orsogna from the north-east. A half-mile out of town the road passed the town cemetery, so inevitably this route became known as Cemetery Ridge.

Roger Smith and Lieutenant Turbort's platoon had managed to join the rest of the battalion in reaching the eastern edge of Orsogna, but only after taking considerable casualties. The town, like San Pietro and elsewhere, had been emptied of civilians by the Germans and was held by units of 26. Panzer. The place already looked a wreck. Turbort's platoon managed to storm a villa on the edge of town they named the 'Pink House' and dug in around it, but without enough tanks to support the infantry and with the Germans bringing up StuGs and Panzer IVs overnight, it was clear the New Zealanders' toehold was not going to become much more than that without substantial reinforcements, particularly armour. The trouble was, because of the town's precipitous position, the only real way in for any Shermans was via the roads running along the two ridges. Canalizing tanks, in a line, toe to tail, was a sure way of getting them knocked out by enemy anti-tank guns in very quick order.

Despite their vulnerable position, Smith and his fellows dug in around the grounds of the Pink House. Ordered to take his section into an orchard in front of it, Smith suddenly felt his foot catch on some wire. A cold chill swept over him and goosebumps ran up his back to his head.

'Hold it, you blokes,' he called out. 'I've struck a tripwire and an "S" mine, sir.'

Turbort now ordered him to stay dead still for a couple of minutes while the rest of the men tentatively walked backwards. 'Rog,' he said, 'it's over to you and if you do happen to pull it, drop onto your face. If you're close enough to it everything ought to go over the top of you.'

It was small comfort. Pins and needles soon numbed his foot and his leg began to tremble. Eventually, with the last of the men behind him clear, he leaned down, checked the wire wasn't caught in a lace or anklet and then stepped back. Nothing. He waited for his pins and needles to lessen in case he stumbled and collapsed on to some other device, and only when some feeling had returned did he gently, oh so carefully, move backwards.

The following morning, after a night dug in around the Pink House and fending off repeated attacks, they were pulled back. By that time Smith was suffering from concussion after a Panzer IV tank shell had struck the house just above his head. But he, like most of the battalion, had got off quite lightly. Yet for the time being, at any rate, the New Zealanders had been unable to force a way through and clear this imposing town for good. The plans to roll up Ortona from the west would have to be put on hold.

Across to the western side of Italy on Fifth Army's front, the 34th Red Bulls and 45th Thunderbirds were pushing up into the mountains north of the Mignano Gap. 'Raining all day,' noted Bud Wagner on the 4th. 'Raining again,' he noted two days later. 'Raining most of the day. Another flat tire,' he jotted on the 7th. The Red Bulls were due to be relieved by the Moroccans soon, so a number of French officers had been coming and going, but all the while the division's guns kept firing. The 151st Field Artillery Battalion, of which Wagner was part, had fired a staggering 33,000 rounds since landing at Salerno.

Opposite the Red Bulls in the line was the 44. Hoch- und Deutschmeister-Division, and Major Georg Zellner wasn't only feeling blue, he was feeling angry too. A feature of the Wehrmacht was its tactical flexibility – the speed with which it could cobble together battle groups of different units. Sometimes, though, it was counterproductive, because they ended up fighting with penny packets, flinging one unit into the fray after another and so losing any kind of unit cohesion. This was what was happening to Zellner's 3. Bataillon, which had reached the front and immediately been seconded to 305. Infanterie-Division. '11. Kompanie replaces 1. Kompanie tomorrow,' he scribbled. '10th is to relieve the day after tomorrow.' These were now attached to 577. Regiment, but his 9. Kompanie had been sent to bolster 578. Regiment, a different unit in 305. Division. 'I have a stinking rage,' he ranted, 'because my battalion is being sold out, drip by drip.'

By the 5th, Zellner's battalion had been brought back together and into its parent 44. Division, and he was now at the front and in direct command again. Here, tracks passed through high mountain valleys towered over by endless peaks, shrub-covered spurs and ridges. This was a normally remote but majestic mountain wilderness, but it was also part of the Bernhard Line, defended by the Germans and now being attacked by the Americans of VI Corps. Zellner's battalion command post wasn't even a farmhouse but rather just a foxhole. 'Constantly under fire,' he scribbled. 'Dead, wounded. Four of us lie in a hole in the ground and can hardly move. Artillery fire day and night.' By this time the line between 44. and 305. Divisions was under threat. The 44. Division was on Hill 769, a spur of the 3,000-foot-high Monte Casale, which overlooked the narrow, winding valley between the town of Filignano and the village of Cerasuolo from the southern side. The 305. Division held the north side, but the Americans of 45th Thunderbird Division, pushing from Filig-nano, were battling Zellner's men hard for this stretch of high ground to the south of the valley. On the 6th, Zellner saw American scouting parties approaching, but these were successfully pushed back. The rain beat down; Zellner and his men were all soaked, although his men were putting up a new roughly made command post, which offered some shelter. Enemy artillery fire screeched over all day. 'In the evening,' he wrote, 'we sit crammed together in our hole and think about home. We have no friends any more. The war seems like nonsense to us. 10 p.m. Rations arrive with mules. A couple of bottles of wine also do us good. But the mood doesn't get any better. We try to sleep but don't succeed. Artillery fire.'

A little further to the south, the 36th 'Texas' Division was trying to clear that other great bulwark against the Mignano Gap, Monte Sammucro, and with it the village of San Pietro Infine. This was the very village that Wilhelm Mauss had been looking at from his pasha tent a little under two months earlier when he'd imagined the war soon raging through this spot; now his predictions had come so horribly true. San Pietro was reached from the valley via a track that led off the Via Casilina; heading back out towards the American lines, it snaked more or less horizontally along the mountainside of Sammucro, wound its way behind the great hulk of the mountain to the hamlet of Vallecupa and larger village of Ceppagna and eventually to the town of Venafro, the launch base for the 45th Thunderbirds and Darby's Rangers. The Texans were trying to spread themselves across an entire eastern swathe of Sammucro, with 143rd Infantry advancing along yet another brutally steep ridgeline that overlooked the Via Casilina below and up to the summit. The 141st, meanwhile, had taken over the lower slopes and Monte Rotondo, where Audie Murphy and 15th Infantry had been.

The CP of the 141st was in a house a little way back from Rotondo at the edge of Mignano, but Captain Roswell Doughty had created an OP further up the mountainside, reached by a trail that wound its way through the many terraced olive groves of the lower slopes. It was in full view of the enemy observation posts on Monte Lungo, so he and his men only accessed it by night. A natural outcrop of rock offered narrow crevices through which they could peer with a telescope, while a little bit of camouflage was created by branches from olive trees. Having learned his lessons from the British back at Salerno about siting an OP, he also created a dummy position 100 yards away with a very obviously tramped path leading into it. This proved a sensible move, because during their first day there enemy guns repeatedly tried to hit the decoy OP. From here, they were able to develop a pretty clear picture of the German strength in and around San Pietro, marking up numerous machine-gun posts and the movement of enemy troops. It convinced Doughty that this was not going to be an easy place to take, even though the American artillery was systematically reducing the place to rubble. The Germans were simply too well dug in around it; and as Hans Golda had proved, a house might be destroyed, but much could be done with the rubble and the cellars below. Reducing a village didn't necessarily mean that the enemy presence was being reduced as well.

On 5 December, Doughty was called down to the Pink House because he and his men were to act as guides for the Raggruppamento Motorizzato, 1st Motorized Group, the first Italian troops to be sent in to fight for the Allies. Their task was to clear Monte Lungo, instead of the 36th Texans as had been originally planned. It was likely to be a tough job, but no more so than any other launched against the Bernhard Line. Inserting them into the fray here meant that the bulk of the Texans could fight on their right flank, over Rotondo and Sammucro. Doughty and a few of his men waited for them at dusk, although they were not expecting them until it was dark, the only time it was safe to move. 'I had just about reached the spot we'd chosen to meet the Italians,' noted Doughty, 'when we heard the damnedest racket I'd heard in a long time.' Trundling down the road was a long column of trucks with no obvious blackout lights. When they pulled up, Doughty saw they all wore black cockerel feathers in their helmets. 'Any thought of moving into the lines by stealth went glimmering,' he added, 'as the sound of the trucks, with mufflers blaring, was enough to wake the dead.'

No matter what he told the Italians, he simply could not get them to

and found guilty of misconduct in the presence of the enemy; they'd each received sentences of between five and ten years' imprisonment. Then two journalists had taken up the story and written pieces that were highly sympathetic to the convicted men. Fortunately, these had been intercepted and stopped, but desertion was a serious problem because what usually kept these enlisted men fighting was the fear of letting down their pals. That forty men had bunked off was no small matter; and five to ten years in prison was, Clark thought, totally inadequate. 'I cannot impress upon you too strongly,' he wrote to Lucas and also to Lieutenant-General Geoffrey Keyes of II Corps, 'my views as to the serious nature of the offense of misbehaviour before the enemy. It strikes at the very foundation of battlefield discipline and each case gives aid and comfort to our enemy.' He followed this with a visit to General Charles W. Ryder, the Red Bulls' commander, who was in hospital with shingles. Clark thought Ryder an excellent combat commander, but told him he had been too easy on regiment and battalion commanders who were not up to the job. This had led to a weakening of morale. The Red Bulls were coming out of the line but, as Clark was aware, their casualty figures were no worse than those of the 45th or 3rd Divisions. And so he told Ryder, in no uncertain terms, that once out of hospital he needed to ruthlessly purge the division and get it back on track. If this was not done, Clark told him, he would be removed as division commander.

Meanwhile, Fifth Army continued its hammering of the Bernhard Line, just as on Eighth Army's front the Canadians, New Zealanders and 8th Indians continued to try and force a way through the German wall. It was now the second week of December, and over the past two weeks of fighting the front had moved no more than a few miles. Rome was still many miles away.

CHAPTER 30

The Tyranny of OVERLORD

P RESIDENT ROOSEVELT HAD STOPPED in Palermo because he was finally on his way home from the Cairo and Tehran Conferences – discussions that had considerably clarified Allied strategy, but which had also left a number of ongoing question marks too. It turned out that Roosevelt had already promised Chiang Kai-shek an amphibious operation to capture the Andaman Islands as a stepping stone to the reinvasion of Sumatra and Malaya, and also renewed efforts to reopen the Burma Road, captured by the Japanese the previous year and up until then the only land line for the Allies into China. Roosevelt was the biggest champion of keeping China in the war.

At Tehran, Stalin had a couple of surprises up his sleeve. First, he offered to go to war with Japan once Germany was defeated. That was good for the British, who still adhered very strongly to the Germany-first strategy. He had then made it clear that of all planned operations, OVERLORD was top of the list for the Soviet Union, but surprised the Americans and British by recommending a two-fisted approach to the invasion of France with landings in southern France as well as across the Channel; in his experience, pincer movements were generally more effective than those launched on a single axis. Certainly, the great turnaround of Red Army fortunes at Stalingrad testified to the sound thinking behind this principle. By the time the Tehran Conference drew to a close, it was agreed that OVERLORD and an invasion of southern France, code-named ANVIL, should be launched at the same time in May the following year, 1944. The various other loose ends and fine detail were then raked over by further talks between the Americans and British in Cairo at the beginning of December.

British arguments for not getting involved in an operation in the Andamans had been given a lift by Stalin's pledge to join the war against Japan; this was because the Soviet Union could give far more help on that score than the Chinese ever could. It was also clear that the landing craft needed for an amphibious assault in South East Asia would most definitely affect OVERLORD because there was no question of cutting back assault craft for the wider Pacific campaign. So Roosevelt reluctantly agreed to renege on his pledge to Chiang, using as an excuse Stalin's intervention and the British argument that defeating the Germans as soon as possible was the best way to help China. It was also decided that ANVIL would be a two-division assault with ten more American divisions following up directly from the US. An operation against Rhodes was considered desirable but not essential, which meant it would almost certainly now fall off the shelf unless there was some unexpected development that dramatically changed the situation.

As far as the strategy for Italy was concerned, however, the capture of Rome remained the priority and it was agreed that sixty-eight landing ships – those most precious of assault craft – would now remain in the Mediterranean until 15 January 1944. That meant an amphibious operation south of Rome could, in theory, still be launched this side of Christmas. Stalin had also asked for the name of the commander for OVERLORD and the Americans nominated Eisenhower, to which the British readily agreed. A man whose stature had grown considerably since his appointment as Supreme Allied Commander in the Mediterranean back at the Casablanca Conference, Eisenhower had proved a truly adept coalition commander. His departure from the theatre was as strong an indicator as any of the prioritization of OVERLORD, and as a man close to both British and American chiefs he would be much missed in the Mediterranean.

His imminent departure also underlined how much the campaign in Italy had been affected by the tyranny of OVERLORD, as Churchill had termed it, from the very outset. The battle on the ground had always been playing second fiddle – from the restrictions of assault craft, to the rigid insistence on withdrawing the seven divisions earmarked before the invasion had been launched, to the priority for the strategic air forces. Now, in a further upheaval, the Supreme Commander was off too, plus, presumably, many of his inner team. While there was now an ongoing – but still limited – commitment to Italy as a theatre, the essence of Alexander's warnings six weeks earlier had not changed. As his detailed appraisal of 24 October had made clear, there was both opportunity in Italy but also substantial threat too. He'd estimated that the Germans could bring to bear between twenty-four and twenty-eight divisions in Italy, and with the comparative proximity to the Balkans and the southern Reich it would be easier for the Germans to reinforce Italy than it would be for the Allies, with their limitations of shipping.

Alexander had not predicted how the Germans might respond or how they might choose to use what resources were left to them, but there was a very clear and present danger that the Allies could face a serious counter-punch in Italy. His prognosis might have appeared a little overly gloomy in late October, but he had wanted the Combined Chiefs to wake up to the reality of the situation on the ground. It was all very well giving the strategic air forces primacy, but the rain that was now thundering down on his troops was falling around Foggia too. Strategic air forces were operating from North Africa and already striking the southern Reich as well as targets in southern France. Admittedly, there were some bad-weather days in Tunisia, but nothing like as frequent or as severe as those in Italy. Clearly, there was a huge advantage to operating the heavy bombers from Italy, much closer to the southern Reich; but, rather like the Rhodes operation, it wasn't strictly speaking essential, especially if the strategic air forces reached Foggia and then found themselves grounded by the mud and rain. It might have made more sense to reinforce 15th Army Group first, make the strongest possible all-out assault on Rome, and ensure that the Allied situation was one that could not possibly be reversed.

As it turned out, his warnings in late October had since proved more prescient than they might at first have seemed, because once Kesselring had been made supremo in Italy, it was clear his attention would be dedicated to the fighting in the south. And so it had proved, with the arrival of new German divisions across the front by the beginning of December. And, as Allied intelligence could accurately prove, there were now twenty-five German divisions throughout Italy and twenty-four in the Balkans and Greece; the Allies had sixteen. Since one of the prime strategic reasons for invading Italy had been to draw enemy divisions away from the Eastern Front and also north-west Europe, this part of the plan was going swimmingly well. On the other hand, the dangers were all too obvious. A reverse in Italy was unthinkable, but nor was it a good idea to allow Alexander's forces to be so whittled down that they spent the rest of the year – and on into the spring – achieving little except losing ever more men and materiel in an attritional stalemate in the mud and mountains. The British, especially, had a pathological fear of allowing the war to descend into the static slaughter of the Western Front, yet that spectre was already starting to become a reality here in Italy.

The strategic and operational rigidity with which the Italian campaign had been launched had not helped Alexander's armies at all. For example, there had been no question of any flexibility over the seven divisions earmarked to be sent back to Britain for OVERLORD by the end of November, even though three of those had been engaged in the fighting at the time of their withdrawal. To move them had meant pulling them out of the line and replacing them, which, of course, required a massive logistical effort. Getting them back to Britain also involved no small amount of shipping – shipping that might be used elsewhere. By insisting on this, the Allies were somewhat shooting themselves in the foot. Could there have been another way? The 82nd Airborne was clearly needed for OVERLORD, but were all the other divisions earmarked? This had not even been considered.

Then there was the mission creep of the strategic air forces. It had been accepted that the capture of the Foggia airfields was one of the main reasons for invading Italy, but with the creation of the Fifteenth Air Force the Americans substantially enlarged the scale of what they'd been planning. The six heavy bomber groups originally earmarked for Italy had swollen to twenty-one, alongside seven long-range fighter groups and one reconnaissance group. The shipping required for twenty-one bomber groups was considerably greater than what was needed for two divisions, while the maintenance of such a force required as much as it took to keep the entire Eighth Army in the field. Double standards were creeping in, because while the American chiefs were worrying that Italy might become a long-term drain and then affect OVERLORD, it was they who had then given full backing to dramatically increasing the build-up of strategic air forces in Italy – and this shift of goalposts was currently largely at the expense of the beleaguered ground forces.

This, then, was the paradox: they were increasing the scale of Fifteenth Air Force because POINTBLANK – the Allied air plan to destroy the Luftwaffe ahead of OVERLORD – was not going well enough from air forces based in Britain alone, and because the aim was primarily about clearing the skies over north-west Europe ahead of the cross-Channel invasion. So the build-up around Foggia was also, really, about OVER-LORD. Just to get the airfield complex ready for heavy bombers to operate there was a massive logistical commitment; yet since its capture at the very end of September furious preparations had been under way, clearing the damage caused by Allied bombers, improving runways, bringing in fuel, stores, ordnance, anti-aircraft defences and creating the kind of tented cities needed to keep a mass of heavy bombers operational. It wasn't so much a case of the strategic air forces trumping the needs of the armies as that of their needs arising concurrently. However, this meant that the limited shipping available was spread more thinly and so came at the expense of Fifth and Eighth Armies. The emphasis on getting the airfields at Foggia up and running as quickly as possible was slowing the ground campaign in Italy and, in turn, risking the timing of the cross-Channel invasion. Muddled and contradictory thinking had been allowed to creep in. It had made sound sense to make the capture of the Foggia airfields a priority, but the strategic air forces could have remained where they were in North Africa for longer, which would have ensured that the logistic chain was dedicated to getting the ground forces north of Rome as quickly as possible. Building up the heavy bomber force at the expense of the ground forces was patently a false economy, because the Allies were trying to attempt too much all at the same time with too little. By only backing Alexander's armies half-cock and forcing him to juggle divisions in and out of the front line, they found themselves in a situation where a ghastly stalemate looked quite likely and a catastrophic reversal had to be considered. What's more, for all the effort being spent on preparing Foggia, there were still no heavies flying from these airfields as November gave way to December, and although their move there was imminent, the terrible weather was likely to affect them every bit as much as it was the tactical air forces. Another reason, then, to have waited a bit longer and prioritized the build-up of the ground forces first.

The lesson here was very obvious: the campaign should have been either properly and wholeheartedly backed from the outset or not undertaken at all. Had more assault craft been made available in September and October, when they were still in theatre from their HUSKY commitments, there was a high chance the Chiefs of Staff might not now be haggling over dates for their return. What's more, there had been an increase of around 32 per cent in landing craft production by the US Navy, but mostly of the new LCT Mk 7, soon to be renamed 'landing ship, medium', or LSM. These would be ready by the spring of 1944, in time for OVERLORD, but in fact were almost exclusively heading to the Pacific. But they needn't have been. This was a strategic and operational choice. 'Once undertaken,' General Marshall had told the Combined Chiefs in May, 'the operation must be backed to the limit.' That principle was being applied to OVERLORD, and also now to the campaign in the Pacific, but not, it seemed, to the Allied Armies in Italy – forces which had been committed to an ambitious campaign in August but most definitely without the proper full material backing Marshall had advocated. And it was the armies, the Poor Bloody Infantry, who were paying for it. With their blood.

'7 p.m., saw PM,' noted Harold Macmillan on 7 December. 'He was in bed. He is tired, but triumphant since at the last moment his policy – his strategical policy – has triumphed. The Far East adventure is postponed, and all will be concentrated (as far as may be) on the Mediterranean and north European campaigns. If reasonable material is made available again for the former, we may make some progress even during the winter.' With Eisenhower heading to Britain, however, a new Supreme Commander was needed and an adjusted command that included the entire sweep of the Mediterranean. Churchill thought it likely that Bedell-Smith would go with Ike, but he wanted to know Macmillan's views and particularly about who might take over from Eisenhower. It would be a Brit this time, and it was General Henry Maitland Wilson who was being strongly recommended by Brooke. Wilson was a big man – tall and broad-shouldered – and, perhaps unsurprisingly, known to most as 'Jumbo'. He'd been in the Middle East theatre since commanding British forces in Egypt and then Greece in 1941, and had then been made General Officer Commanding – GOC – of British forces in Palestine and Trans-Jordan, had overseen the successful battle for Syria and later commanded Ninth Army in Syria and Palestine. When Alexander had taken command of 18th Army Group in February 1943, Wilson had become C-in-C Middle East. He was widely liked, knew the Middle East and Mediterranean theatre intimately, and had proved himself adept at handling polyglot DUKE forces. He was not, however, Macmillan's choice, and since he'd been asked for his views he gave them frankly. Wilson was sixty-two and Macmillan thought him too old and too set in the Middle East mire to undertake the drastic reforms needed to unite the 'Augean Stables' of Algiers, Cairo and Italy. More to the point, he thought

Alexander would be a better choice in every way: younger, more dynamic, highly regarded by the Americans and already in Italy.

Churchill wanted Macmillan to repeat all he'd said to him to Brooke. The Resident Minister and CIGS caught up with each other the following day. Brooke made it clear he was not happy about Macmillan's interfering and spent nearly an hour trying to persuade him why Alex should remain where he was. 'The argument of the CIGS,' noted Macmillan, 'is that A's talents, which are mainly tactical, would be wasted in the sort of pro-consular job of Supreme Commander in the Mediterranean.' Brooke unquestionably had a point, but Macmillan was not persuaded, had been in theatre for a long time, and in his judgement Alexander was the better choice. Brooke was incensed; clearly, he railed in his diary, Macmillan had no understanding about the functions of the Supreme Commander. 'Why must the PM consult everybody,' he grumbled, 'except those who can give him advice!'

The debate rumbled on as they left Cairo and flew to Tunis. Eisenhower wanted Alexander as his land commander for OVERLORD, but Brooke preferred Montgomery. Churchill was determined to visit Italy, and Alexander arrived in Tunis on 12 December to join the talks with Brooke and Eisenhower and then escort the PM to Brindisi and a tour of the front. For his part, Alexander was entirely sanguine about remaining as Army Group commander, which Brooke had expected from him, and which was some relief. There were also signs that Churchill was coming down with something; that morning he had a temperature and he was dissuaded from travelling on to Italy, so instead Brooke accompanied Alexander on his own – albeit with mounting concern for the Prime Minister, whose temperature was now a concerning 102 degrees. Lord Moran, his doctor, was worried it might be pneumonia.

Luftflotte II, the only German air forces left in Italy and now based in the north, was losing aircraft at an attrition rate of 19 per cent, which was unsustainable unless substantially reinforced; and with the Allied bombers of the USAAF Eighth Air Force and RAF Bomber Command hammering the Reich from England, most of the Luftwaffe's replacement aircraft and aircrew were being sent to defend it. Apart from occasional Luftwaffe raids on Naples, the Allies now had almost complete mastery of the skies over Italy – the lack of Luftwaffe was a constant source of frustration for the Germans battling on the ground, as Wilhelm Mauss and Georg Zellner's diaries repeatedly made clear.

On the afternoon of 2 December, Air Marshal 'Mary' Coningham held a press conference in Bari, in which he told reporters that the Luftwaffe had lost the air war in Italy. 'I would consider it as a personal insult,' he told them, 'if the enemy should send so much as one plane over the city.' Coningham was a brilliant and inspired air commander, yet there was a touch of hubris about his comments because that same afternoon a lone Messerschmitt Me 210 twin-engine reconnaissance aircraft flew over Bari, spotting a mass of Allied merchant vessels crammed into the harbour.

The pilot's subsequent report prompted Feldmarschall Wolfram von Richthofen, commander of Luftflotte II, with Kesselring's support, to send an all-out effort of 105 Junkers Ju88 bombers to strike the port that evening, flying in low and scattering *Düppel*, tinfoil strips, to confuse radar, which had been first used by the British – code-named 'window' – during the destruction of Hamburg at the end of July. Most of the ships in harbour had yet to be unloaded, and one of the first bombs to fall at around 7.25 p.m. hit an ammunition ship, causing such a massive explosion that glass windows seven miles away were shattered by the force of the blast. A fuel pipeline on one of the quays was also hit, gushing fuel into the sea, which then caught fire.

Carnage followed. The anti-aircraft defences were totally insufficient, no fighter defence had been scrambled and the freighters in port were so tightly packed that the German bombers could hardly miss. A staggering twenty-seven precious merchantmen and one schooner were sunk in the holocaust that followed and a further twelve damaged. Thirty-four thousand tons of supplies went to the bottom of the harbour. Among the ships lost was the Liberty ship *John Harvey*, which had been carrying, among other supplies, 2,000 mustard gas mortar bombs, for although the Allies had never yet used gas in the war, they always had supplies of the poison to hand should the Germans play dirty and use it first. Tragically, as the *John Harvey* was hit a large amount of these mustard gas mortar shells leaked liquid sulphur mustard into the water already slick with oil. A number of sailors leaping from stricken vessels then found themselves in the sea and exposed to the poison, much of which mixed with the oil, caught fire and produced noxious fumes. Within a day, 628 patients fished out of the harbour were suffering from blindness and chemical burns. In all, some 1,000 seamen and another 1,000 civilians were killed in the attack. It was a disaster for the Allies: the loss of vital shipping, the loss of supplies, the loss of life, and the potential risk of the Germans discovering they had mustard gas in their arsenal. For this reason, news of the attack and especially the release of the gas was suppressed. It could not have happened at a worse time and showed that while the Luftwaffe was most certainly a much-depleted force in Italy, it still had a sting in its tail.

At the time, Fifteenth Air Force was still in the process of making the move to Foggia. The Fifteenth's HQ, activated at the Lycée Carnot in Tunis, began moving to Italy on 22 November, and was finally completed on 3 December. Moving the HQ was one thing, but that was just the start, because then the bomb groups themselves had to head over and roughly fifty ground crew were required for every ten-man bomber crew. That figure did not include the cooks, clerks, quartermasters and truck drivers needed to keep such a complex show effectively on the road. The plan was for the four bomb groups of B-17 Flying Fortresses and two fighter groups to be the first to move to Foggia, while two groups of B-24 Liberators and one of fighters were to be based in Apulia in the heel of Italy. Four bomb groups of twin-engine medium B-26 Martin Marauders were also to move to Sardinia. This enormous logistical operation was, needless to say, made more complex because of the short winter days and vagaries of the weather.

The 429th Bomb Squadron and the rest of 2nd Bomb Group had begun packing up in Tunisia on 2 December, while Lieutenant T. Michael Sullivan's co-pilot and the squadron ground crew left that very day. Sullivan and the rest of his crew were scheduled for a mission on 3 December, but it was cancelled due to bad weather over the target. And cancelled again the next day. And the day after that. On 6 December they did fly a mission, hitting rail bridges at Grizzana Morandi near Bologna in northern Italy. The weather was lousy all the way, though, and when they got to the target it was completely hidden by low cloud; but they ducked back down the Adriatic coast on the return leg and landed at Bari, stayed there overnight and then headed back to Tunisia the next day.

The next two days the weather once again prevented any flying, which rather underlined the potential hazards of operating from Italy in winter. Finally, however, on 10 December, Sullivan struck his tent in Tunisia, completed packing, and with the rest of the squadron flew to Amendola, around twelve miles east of Foggia. Here the plain was as flat as a board, the distant hills of Gargano looming to the east. The airfield itself already had some PSP – perforated steel plating – tracking laid down but no asphalted runway, and all around it were a mass of aircraft: medium bombers, P-38 Lightnings, P-47 Thunderbolts and Spitfires too. Most of the ground was wet and muddy, however. Although Amendola was a pre-war Italian air-field, what limited buildings were there had already been taken and so the crews were whisked off in jeeps and trucks to a camp five miles away. Needless to say it was raining, and Sullivan and his crew could hear the guns at the front even though they were as much as eighty miles away.

The next day, he and a few others explored the area. Their campsite was in an olive grove on a large estate; the main farmhouse had been taken over by 2nd Bomb Group HQ while a small chapel was requisi-tioned as a medical dispensary. Not far from the house were a number of cellars and grain stores carved down into the limestone – Sullivan was surprised by how extensive they were, but less impressed by their new surroundings. 'Continued setting up camp,' he noted. 'Food unbearable, constant rain, our tent leaks, expect to be bombed and strafed any minute.' Welcome to Italy.

They were due to fly on a mission on 13 December but it rained again, so the mission was scrubbed. Sullivan still thought the food was inedible, but at least a letter from his father had caught up with him. Finally, they flew on 14 December, this time to hit Eleusis airfield in Greece. Over the target there was ten-tenths cloud, so they were diverted to hit Kalamaki airfield instead. One B-17 Flying Fortress was shot down, and the flak was heavy. 'Damned rough mission,' noted Sullivan; he reckoned all operations were going to be tough from now on. Certainly, the moment the weather improved they were swiftly sent off to bomb further targets. Bolzano was hit the next day and Padua the day after that. On 19 Decem-ber, Sullivan and his crew were sent on a POINTBLANK mission to the Messerschmitt aircraft plants at Augsburg. It was a big effort from the Fifteenth, with some 250 heavies plus fighter escorts. 'Bad weather,' jotted Sullivan. 'Never saw target. Plenty of heavy and intense flak.' Flying over Bolzano they had been pounced on by thirty-five enemy fighters, and a running air battle had ensued for an hour during which three Flying For-tresses were shot down – one of which was Lieutenant Henry Vogel's crew, on their last mission before being sent home. 'No. 3 engine on fire,' noted Sullivan, 'all of crew out, I think.' In fact, Vogel had lost two engines to flak and the left wing had burst into flames. They had then been strafed, the radio compartment was on fire, and he could no longer control his ship, so Vogel had ordered them to bail out. Several of the crew had been hit and only five out of the ten managed to get out safely. Sullivan was right: these were proving to be tough missions.

*

On the Adriatic coast, the awful battle for Ortona had been turning into a proper meat grinder for both sides. So much was being expected of the men battling in the mountains either side of the Mignano Gap, but an enormous amount was being asked of those now pitched in combat just to the south of Ortona. Somehow, the Hasty Ps had held on to their fragile bridgehead on the ridge by the coast road, on the north side of the Moro and to the east of the battered village of San Leonardo. Over thirty-six hours between 9 and 10 December they had held off no fewer than eleven counter-attacks, all of which had cost considerable blood to the Germans of 200. Regiment, but which had also chipped away at the Canadians too.

Then, on Saturday, 11 December, new orders arrived for them to break out of their bridgehead and attack north. The assault was to be launched at 4 p.m. that afternoon, while it was still just about light, and despite the suicidal nature of the order it was merely a diversion from the main event, which was an attack by 3rd Brigade from the ruins of San Leonardo. 'Once again,' noted Farley Mowat, 'we were to be the goat in the tiger hunt.' He was at Battalion HQ on the ridge, a collapsed shed, peering out over the sea of mud, blasted farm buildings, burned-out tanks and the flotsam of battle and shattered vines. A scene of utter desolation, made worse by the grey of a winter afternoon sky. Suddenly, something moving caught his eye, and training his field glasses he spotted two huge pigs eating the bloated corpse of a mule. He knew they would be just as happy to gorge on dead soldiers.

A squadron of Sherman tanks arrived at 3 p.m. and to Mowat's horror Kennedy ordered him to accompany them on foot and to be the point of liaison with the infantry. It wasn't until 5 p.m., though, that the attack finally went in and, just as the Hasty Ps had expected, there was no sign from the Germans to suggest they thought this was a diversion. Artillery and mortars came crashing down; the raucous din was so immense that Mowat could hardly hear the engine of the Sherman behind which he was crouching. Meanwhile, Baker and Charley Companies, up ahead, disappeared, enveloped by the smoke and fog of war.

In fact, the attack went better than Mowat, for one, had feared, because the German infantry had already pulled back in their sector; and because of the mud, the shelling and mortar fire were less lethal than normal. Even so, when a salvo of shells whooshed in and crashed nearby, Mowat fell on his face in the mud and at that moment something snapped within him. Getting to his feet, he turned and hurried back, past the ruined building where the newly promoted Lieutenant-Colonel Bert Kennedy was sheltering and on to the pockmarked coast road heading south. He'd not gone far, however, when Franky Hammond, commander of their anti-tank platoon, speeding forward with a jeep and a 6-pounder, stopped and grabbed him by the arm.

'Drink this!' he told Mowat, thrusting a rum-laced bottle of water in his hand. Mowat drank. 'Get in the jeep,' Hammond then ordered. 'Now show me the way to BHQ.'

This seemed to snap Mowat out of his fear-induced stupor. He did not desert that evening after all.

General Vokes, the 1st Division commander, still aimed to reach the crossroads code-named 'Cider', and while the Hasty Ps were launching their diversionary attack along the coast road sent both 2nd Brigade and the newly arrived 3rd Brigade – joining the rest of the Canadians from the operations around Castel di Sangro – into the fray. To reach the 'Cider' crossroads they had to cross another of the strange, narrow, wooded gullies that so marked this landscape, although this particular one, stretching far to the south-west of Ortona, was named simply *The* Gully. They tried to attack directly across it, but the Germans, hidden until this point, appeared from the depths of The Gully as the leading Canadian infantry approached and stopped them in their tracks. Four counter-attacks followed the next day as the rain came down once again. It was the turn of the Canadians to attack once more on 13 December, and again they got nowhere. Nor were these men from 90. Panzergrenadier-Division any more but paratroopers of 3. Fallschirmjäger-Regiment, who, like the Canadian 3rd Infantry Brigade, had been moved up from the Castel di Sangro sector of the upper Sangro.

The Seaforth Highlanders, part of 2nd Brigade, were in as bad a shape as the Hasty Ps. Padre Durnford had gone up to the front on the 13th and found Charley Company. He offered cigarettes around and noticed that most of the men were struggling with shaking hands. More heavy shelling. He moved on and discovered Battalion HQ in a small barn. 'Al Mercer looking strained,' he noted. 'Sid Thompson grim. Murdock ill. No burials possible.' Word arrived on the radio that the house where he'd been talking to the C Company boys five minutes earlier had just suffered a direct hit, with many wounded. He hurried off to help. The remains of San Leonardo were being shelled again, and a little while later one of their ammunition trucks was hit. It erupted into a livid ball of flame and billowed thick, black smoke. The next day, Durnford found himself trying to give solace to one of the medics from the RAP who completely broke down in front of him.

Meanwhile, General Sir Alan Brooke had flown into Bari with Alexander on 13 December, the questions over future command in the Mediterranean still unresolved and with the Prime Minister's health in free-fall. It had been a frustrating fortnight, because although there was backing for the Italian campaign, that commitment remained limited, and it was also increasingly clear that British influence on global strategy was waning. As coalition partners, it obviously made sense for Britain and the United States to pool resources and work to an agreed and common goal, which was the point of the various joint strategy conferences; but it was still the prerogative of the United States to use their resources in the way they thought best. Brooke – and the PM – had rather assumed that, once committed to Italy, they could manipulate the Americans to their way of thinking regarding the Mediterranean. The British were now discovering that, having paid lip service to US strategic aims in the first eighteen months of the coalition, the American chiefs were increasingly determined to fight the war how they thought best, and although winning it as quickly as possible was still very much a shared aim, the Allies were not united on how that should best be achieved.

Despite the strain of the previous couple of weeks, Brooke was none the less thrilled to be setting foot on European soil for the first time since he had evacuated France in June 1940, and having spent the night at Alexander's HQ near Bari he flew up to see Montgomery after a gentle loop around the battleground of Hannibal's great victory at Cannae in 216 BC. Flying in a captured German 'Storch', a small, light reconnaissance aircraft, Brooke toured the Sangro front and then landed on a short strip near the mouth of the river, where he was met by Montgomery. Brooke thought the Eighth Army commander seemed in need of a rest or a change. Monty grumbled about the course of the campaign and belittled Clark. Brooke also had the impression that Alexander was not grasping the campaign with both hands either. 'Monty is tired out,' he wrote in his diary that night, 'and Alex fails to grip the show.'

Accusing someone of lacking 'grip' was an oft-cited complaint from British generals when things were not going entirely to plan. In fact, Alexander had given several perceptive appreciations of the situation and had repeatedly lobbied for greater support using a combination of carrot and stick to try and cajole Eisenhower, but mainly the Combined Chiefs, into helping his beleaguered forces. He had come up with about as good a two-fisted plan of attack in November as could be expected with the resources available and it was not obvious what else he could do. He'd provided a very clear set of aims but also outlined the potential risk facing the Allies in Italy. To make matters worse, he'd been suffering from jaundice, for which he'd not really taken to his bed; Alex Campbell of the Hasty Ps, twenty years younger than Alexander, had had a month in hospital and a month convalescing for his bout. There could be no such rest and recuperation for Alexander.

Rather, Brooke's concern about a lack of grip was really a reflection of his own dissatisfaction with how far the Italian campaign was going awry. As the senior military general in the British armed forces, it was he and his fellow Combined Chiefs who were not gripping the situation. It wasn't the fault of Alexander, or Montgomery, or Clark that they had been so poorly served by the Combined Chiefs. Nor was it the commanders in 15th Army Group who were deciding what landing craft and shipping was available, or who were insisting that the strategic air forces should have the priority of the logistic chain. They could only do what they could with what they had been given and, frankly, that was simply not enough for the truly monumental task in hand.

What's more, Alexander had been telling the Combined Chiefs nothing less than the truth when he predicted the discrepancy in the number of divisions. The division was the unit size by which the scale of armies was judged at this time. It was true that the Allies had more artillery and considerably more air forces than the Germans, and substantially greater numbers of vehicles. The trouble was, the combination of the weather and the terrain was limiting the use of vehicles and aircraft, and so it was being largely left to the infantry to do the hard yards – the PBI as Jack Ward referred to them. In other words, the huge material advantage of the Allies was being offset by the rain, mud and mountains. As a result, the playing field was levelling considerably.

A little bit of context was needed when comparing Allied divisions with German ones, however, because by this stage of the war, from October 1943, Wehrmacht infantry divisions were starting to be remodelled into smaller forces of 12,300 rather than the 17,000-strong they had been up until then. However, those changes hadn't yet been applied to all the divisions in Italy and the Panzer and Panzergrenadier divisions were still on the normal establishment of 13,725 and 13,876 men respectively. Establishment figures on paper and what was reality were not always the same, however; the Hermann Göring Division, for example, had been badly understrength by the time of the Salerno landings, but then had been brought back up to something close to full strength after the Volturno crossings. Divisions arriving at the front in Italy for the first time were also either at or close to full strength. Even 1. Fallschirmjäger had been injected with a number of replacements since September.

None the less, relentless action soon whittled down German combat strength, and unless divisions were pulled out of the line and given a chance to refit, the attritional effect soon became debilitating. Yet this was also true of Allied divisions. On paper, an Allied infantry division was around 16,700 men-strong, so about the same as the 17,000-strong establishment of a standard German infantry division but larger than the newly created formations, in which the three regiments that represented their combat strength had been reduced from three to two battalions each. At this time, in December 1943, most German and Allied divisions at the front in Italy had a similar establishment. They also had a remarkably similar combat strength too, because unlike operations in North Africa and Sicily, where divisions were withdrawn and swiftly replenished and brigades and battalions rotated in and out of the line, on both sides they had so far been more consistently committed in Italy.

Before Clark launched his assault on the Winter Line he had reliable intelligence that 305. Infanterie-Division had a fighting strength of 6,700 and 29. Panzergrenadier 7,460; 15. Panzergrenadier had 6,660 and 94. Infanterie-Division 7,430; all these were three-regiment divisions. Fighting strength referred to the number of combat troops – which, in an infantry division, meant primarily its rifle companies. Since the establishment infantry strength of an Allied infantry division was 7,605 infantrymen, the difference was slight, because the full 16,000-plus men in an Allied division also included engineers, artillery, service troops and so on. But in terms of infantry, the current difference in numbers between an Allied and German division was negligible, and this was significant because the battle being waged was largely an infantry one. Taking the 201st Guards Brigade in British 56th Division, for example, the three battalions were back at full strength on 3 November, but a month on, after the debilitating first Battle of Monte Camino, were notably down in numbers. The 3rd Coldstream Guards began Operation RAINCOAT with 745 men, exactly 100 fewer than they should have had. By 12 December they were down to 598 men, so around 30 per cent understrength; the

Grenadier Guards, on the other hand, were already at only 315 men before RAINCOAT was even launched, so were 63 per cent under-strength. Losses among American divisions were consistently similar. The 1st Battalion of 143rd Infantry, for example, was down to just 340 men after the fighting on Monte Sammucro. Because of the huge backlog of vehicles, and because the rain repeatedly led to flooding and the wash-ing away of temporary bridges, and because of the time it took to repair demolitions, the forward infantry units simply weren't being replaced at a level the Allies had considered acceptable at any other point in the war.

The military rule of thumb might have been a manpower advantage of three to one as a bare minimum in any attack, but here in Italy, where the mountains and terrain and weather so heavily favoured the defender, that figure needed to be higher. Normally, Allied armies could operate with less front-line infantry than, say, the Germans or the Red Army, because they were very well supported both technologically and mechan-ically; but that model wasn't working anything like as effectively now, in winter, in the mountains and mud of Italy.

The trouble was, even taking establishment figures for divisions at face value, the Allied armies did not have a three-to-one advantage. At the coalface it was closer to parity, although precise numbers depended on at what stage of the fighting comparisons were being made. With this in mind, that the Allies were making any headway at all was hugely impres-sive, especially since they were unable to fight in the way that had been successfully developed over the previous twelve months in North Africa and then in Sicily.

This fire-heavy, methodical way of war had proved very effective since it had been more consciously introduced in August 1942 and dovetailed well into broader principles of using steel rather than flesh wherever possible. The shortcomings of this approach had been exposed in recent weeks. The Allied infantry now needed to adapt swiftly and become more tactically flexible for the mountains, mud and flooded ground over which they were now fighting. The infantry could still call on the artillery, who would be firing from behind the lines, but now expected less direct sup-port from tanks and other armoured fighting vehicles.

In this new scenario, junior infantry leaders were the 'match winners'. 'It is not enough to train a section commander to lead a platoon,' ran a further assessment of the fighting in Italy, 'they must be trained to take command of a platoon and company respectively, should their commanders become casualties.' These were the same principles that had been a feature of German NCO and officer training before and earlier in the war – what was known as *Selbständigkeit der Unterführer* – the independence of the lower command to make decisions on the spot and, at the drop of a hat, to be able to immediately take charge at one or more rungs up the command ladder.

That was all well and good, but these were largely conscript armies and the vast majority of men didn't want to use their initiative and go the extra yard that was needed. A detailed report of the fighting in Sicily had shown that in a platoon of thirty-seven men, most of the firing was carried out by only around half a dozen troops. Most conscripts simply wanted to keep their heads down and try and somehow get through without being riddled with bullets or blown to pieces. And yet there were signs that the infantry were learning. It was no mean feat to attack up a mountainside and drive off the enemy, as had been achieved by 56th Division, the Special Service Brigade and 7th Infantry on the Camino massif. Then, on the night of 8 December, the Texans of 143rd Infantry had managed to clear the summit of Monte Sammucro, the bulwark on the northern side of the Mignano Gap. This in itself was an astonishing achievement because the route to the peak was immensely tough and, if anything, worse than Camino. From their starting point in the upper Volturno Valley near Venafro, mule tracks led up to the lower slopes but, once again, anyone advancing was canalized by ridiculously steep ridges which climbed over jutting knolls and abutments of jagged rocks. In numerous places, the climb involved using both hands as well as feet. All the time, the enemy were crashing down mortars, sniping and firing machine guns. Yet, somehow, they reached the top, a point at which three ridgelines converged. With this, the Bernhard Line was just starting to crumble and all that was now stopping Fifth Army from pushing through were the enemy positions on Monte Lungo, at San Pietro Infine and on the reverse, western slopes of Sammucro.

After completing his tour of Eighth Army's front, Brooke then planned to fly over and visit Clark the following day. During this first visit to the Italian front he was already concluding that the best way to unlock the front was with greater use of amphibious power, something that had been blindingly obvious before they had even launched AVALANCHE. Brooke might have been right that Monty was tired, but his accusations of a lack of grip at the top were unfair unless directed at the Combined

Chiefs themselves. Rather, Alexander's armies were actually performing heroically well considering the true state of play at the battlefront. It was neither the Allied armies nor their commanders that were the problem in Italy.

But there was a further crisis developing, not in Italy but in Carthage in Tunisia, from where news had reached Brooke that the Prime Minister was now gravely – and life-threateningly – ill.

CHAPTER 31

Death of a Village

Pierino di Mascio had been rather enjoying the adventure of living in the mountains. After initially moving just beyond their village of Cardito, the families from Cardito and Vallerotonda had now settled far higher in the mountains, in a ravine known as Collelungo that cut down between the towering peaks of Monte Cavallo and Monte Marrone. The refugees, taking some comfort from the safety of numbers, had settled on the banks of a gushing, babbling mountain stream. Despite being more than 3,000 feet up, here the steep sides of the ravine were covered in beech trees, but next to the banks of the stream were some hollows and flatter ground, surrounded by large boulders and rocky outcrops. These offered some shelter, which could be further fashioned with branches. The area was a small, almost entirely enclosed bowl. Beyond, the mountains either side of them could be glimpsed, and there was a sense of the ravine dropping away from them; but really it felt very secure and hidden, the ground dense with falling beech leaves where fires could be lit to give them warmth and on which food could be cooked. Here they felt protected from the battles raging beyond.

The di Mascio family had made themselves a rough dry-stone shelter, covered by wood and leaves. They'd also brought some sheep up with them to milk. For the teenage Pierino, the days were spent playing with his siblings and other children, hunting for food and keeping a watch for any movement beyond this hidden enclave. 'Everyone, especially us children,' said Pierino, 'was quite used to it. We felt like we were playing.'

At the beginning of November, three former Italian soldiers and, curiously, one Greek had joined them as they were unable to get through the lines safely. A few days later a former Commando officer, Lieutenant Alfred Burnford, also joined them. He had been captured during the Tobruk raid back in 1941, then, after the armistice, had been taken by the Germans and put on a train to Austria from which he'd escaped through the floor of the wagon along with two others. By the time he reached the mountain camp he was ill and suffering, having survived on the run since September and walked all the way from the Po Valley in the north of the country.

By the time Burnford reached them, the first snows had fallen. Seeing some Italian men and women, he had shouted out to them then collapsed. When he awoke he was being nursed by Angelina di Mascio, very heavily pregnant, who, from her Scottish upbringing, could speak to Burnford in English, albeit in a broad Glaswegian brogue. Settled in a stone den under an overhang, Burnford had gradually built up his strength again, and when he finally decided to make a move and try and break through into Allied lines he promised to get word to her family back in Glasgow that she was safe and well.

Angelina di Mascio had given birth up there on the mountains on 28 November and named the girl Addolorata – 'grief' in Italian, a reflection of the traumatic circumstances in which the baby had been born. Yet despite these brutal conditions, and despite the sound of guns echoing around the mountains and the proximity of war, the German troops they saw from time to time were friendly enough. They hoped that before long they would be back in their homes; these were hardy mountain people but it was tough up there, in winter, now with snow all around them. It was no place for a baby to be brought into the world.

On Thursday, 9 December Frank Pearce had been behind Monte Rotondo and watched the dismal sight of endless ambulances and jeeps taking out the wounded and dead. The fighting had been intense over the previous few days and he knew it must have been hell up there on Sammucro. 'Mortars doing lots of damage,' he noted. 'Boys sure looked tired and dazed.' It was dispiriting to see. The following day the mountains had been covered in low cloud, a shroud over the men clinging to the heights up there. 'We are not making much progress as it is hard to root them out of these mountains,' he jotted. 'They are always looking down our throats. Cost in lives heavy.'

General Clark was bitterly disappointed that his men had not cleared the Winter Line yet, but plans were afoot for a renewed effort on Monte Lungo and towards San Pietro. He was unquestionably a hard taskmaster, but really his men had already done incredibly well. Sometimes a fresh set of eyes was needed, and these came in the form of Generals Arnold and Spaatz who, with their entourage, were taken up to the front by Clark on the morning of 11 December. They parked their column of five jeeps and climbed a hill so they could look over the Camino massif, from where they could better appreciate the depth of this huge series of mountains, something that was not at all obvious from the south. They then motored on until they reached the southern side of Monte Rotondo and walked on foot a few hundred yards to the foot of Lungo. Shells whined over and crashed worryingly nearby, but Clark appeared unfazed as he led them to an orchard where a Sherman tank had recently been blown to bits after striking a mine reinforced by several hundred pounds of TNT. 'The tank had been demolished,' Clark reported in his diary, 'and bits of bodies of the crew were scattered about.' Nearby, engineers were making a bypass around a destroyed bridge. For these high-ranking visitors the awfulness of the fighting here was laid bare, but so were the immense challenges. More surprising than the lack of success was that Clark's Fifth Army was now close to breaking through this bastion. Traditional theories of military practice suggested they should barely have made a dent.

By this time, General von Senger had already accepted that the Bernhard Line was lost, but without Kesselring's permission there could be no general withdrawal and so his men, suffering every bit as much as the Allies, had to remain where they were. This meant there was a further battle to be had for Monte Lungo and the battered San Pietro. The 36th Texans were still the division in line, now part of Lieutenant-General Geoffrey Keyes's II Corps. It had been Keyes who had sent the Italians up on to Lungo, which had been a terrible idea; Lungo, although much lower than the surrounding mountains, had steep sides and, rather like the New Zealanders at Orsogna, the Italians had found themselves canalized by the long length of its ridge. Certainly, it was not the place for testing green troops of questionable quality.

At any rate, General Fred Walker, the Texans' commander, had planned a coordinated and large-scale assault which would see the 504th PIR and 143rd Infantry push beyond the summit of Sammucro and so effectively outflank San Pietro, while 141st Infantry, this time supported by Shermans of the 753rd Tank Battalion, would aim directly towards San Pietro. The idea was that the assault on Sammucro would take place overnight, the joint infantry and tank would attack the next morning and, all things being well, San Pietro would be pinched out in a pincer assault from two sides as a result. But that was not all, because at the same time 142nd Infantry would attack Lungo from the south, up the gorge that Hans Golda had used to establish his observation post; and with the Camino massif in their hands this was now a viable approach. Finally, the Italians would support the Americans on Lungo with a renewed attack from its eastern edge.

Joining 143rd Infantry for this night assault was Ernie Pyle, who had bid farewell to his gunners and headed closer to the front instead. Pyle had seen a few things in his time, but he'd been pretty shocked to find the troops living in almost inconceivable misery. The knee-deep mud at the valley floor, the freezing temperatures on the mountains, the thin snow now drifting over them this December. He found the men dug into the stones, trying to find some kind of cover and shelter in the little fissures and chasms of the rock. Up on Sammucro the wind never stopped blowing, so exposed was it, and in December it was particularly biting. The slow advance was not the fault of the men battling their way north, he wrote. 'It was the weather and the terrain, and the weather again.' They would get to Rome, he had no doubt, but the path was cruel. 'No one who had not seen that mud,' he noted, 'those dark skies, those forbidding ridges and ghostlike clouds that unveiled and then quickly hid the enemy, had the right to be impatient with the progress along the road to Rome.' That was nothing less than the truth.

Pyle was attached to a mule-pack outfit, new additions to the modern and normally entirely mechanized US Army. The mule-skinners – the men who led them up and down the mountain – were Italians from Sardinia but the packers were American, from an artillery unit, and based around a stone farmhouse in an olive grove on the southern side of Sammucro. There were about eighty mules in all, supplying a battalion of 143rd Infantry up on the mountain. There was nothing doing by day – it was too dangerous – so everything had to be loaded on to the mules in the afternoon and be ready by last light. Then off they would go, picking their way up a mountain path, one man per mule and a load of extra men beside to help the mules and to repack any loads that came loose. A typical eighty-mule convoy would include water, K rations – three individual packaged and often unpalatable daily meals – rifle, Tommy gun and machine-gun ammunition, telephone wire, mortar shells, cigarettes and first aid equipment; a mule could carry as much as 200 pounds. Extra socks, mail, gas capes and heavy winter jackets were also taken up. Pyle noticed that the mail was the most tragic cargo because every morning lots of it would come back again, unread and undelivered because the recipients had already been killed or wounded.

Pyle was in awe of what these mule teams were doing, and he was also in awe of the men fighting up there. How could he not be, when looking up at those jagged ridges and a mountainside strewn with loose rocks and boulders? He realized that mountain fighting wasn't like fighting anywhere else. Up there, where the soil was so thin or non-existent, rocks were such a big part of it. The men hid behind rocks, slept under the lip of rocks and, tragically, were often killed and wounded by rocks, because every time a mortar shell landed it wasn't just metal fragments that were sprayed but also shards of rock. Sometimes shells landed nearby and caused even bigger showers of rock fragments. At other times landing shells caused little landslides, or the kind of large rocks to fall that could stave in a man's skull or shatter a leg. The boys told him that a big rock falling down the mountainside sounded like a windstorm coming. One time, Pyle was at the top of a mule trail where there was an old stone building now being used as an aid post. He was standing around with a bunch of others – a dozen medics, wiremen, packers and a few lightly wounded – when the familiar whine and whoosh of shells coming in made everyone duck. Fortunately, no one was hurt as it landed 100 yards away. 'For twenty seconds afterwards,' wrote Pyle, 'big and little pieces of shrapnel tinkled and clattered down upon the rocks around us with a ringing metallic sound.'

Across the peninsula, the meat-grinding battle of Ortona continued as the Canadians inched towards the 'Cider' crossroads on the far side of The Gully. All along this ridgeline, separate battles were playing out as the landscape, thick with smoke, often low cloud and rain and the literal fog of war, made orientation very difficult. The southern slopes of The Gully were steep and of thick, soft clay: banks that were easy to dig into but also almost impossible to hit by shellfire because of the angle of the shell's arc. Even mortars, which had a steeper plunge, struggled to hit the southern bank. Further west, at the extremity of The Gully, German artillery had the ground liberally mined and zeroed, while on the ridge beyond to the north further troops were dug in with machine guns. These fired over the top of The Gully at any approaching attack.

So it was a formidable defensive position, not that it felt that way to Grenadier Werner Mork. He had remained dug into his foxhole amid the splintered remains of a vineyard on the northern side of The Gully, more or less opposite the Hasty Ps on the eastern side as the Canadians had launched one attack after the other. Crouching behind his two comrades, helping to man the MG42 slung over the lip, Mork alternated between

intense fear and a strange calm. Most of the time they were simply waiting and hoping not to get a shell with their name on it.

Yet on 12 December they found themselves being shelled again and
then, as they crouched while the rain of soil and grit clattered around
them, they heard screams. Shortly after, one of their fellows, an Obergefreiter, slithered across the mud and slipped into their foxhole. He had
news – Oberfeldwebel Müller had been hit; shrapnel had ripped open his
belly. Müller was dying and their hole was filling with blood; the Obergefreiter wanted their help to get Müller out.

Mork was distraught. Müller was a popular NCO – always good-
natured, funny and a highly respected soldier. In Sardinia, Mork had got
to know him well – they'd shared many an evening over a bottle of wine.
'Now he was dying,' noted Mork, 'in a filthy hole without any help.' It was
daytime, not safe to get him to an aid station, and there was absolutely
nothing they could do for him. They all felt terrible and frustrated by their
inability to do anything. All soldiers feared this kind of stomach wound
because they were nearly always fatal. Müller didn't die quickly. Darkness
fell and his screams rang out across the desolation – screams of pain, of
despair, for his mother, for his wife. 'It was truly awful to have to listen to
his screams calling out to the others,' wrote Mork, 'and the awful sounds
he made, but then came deliverance as the cries became one heart-breaking
whine and then finally there was peace.' It was the early hours of 13
December, the moon was up and casting a soft glow over the battlefield.

Shocked and upset, Mork worried he'd never erase Müller's cries from
his mind. He and his comrades were also conscious that they were rather
isolated. The shelling had stopped and they wondered whether this meant
the enemy infantry would attack. No orders had reached them – their
foxholes were not connected. They were now four men in one hole in the
ground, a single machine gun among them and out of touch with the rest
of the company. 'All that we could do now,' noted Mork, 'was sit back and
wait to see what would happen.'

In the caves cut into the rock below their now ruined village, the people
of San Pietro were suffering from the intense cold and the appalling deprivations, but now it was a terrible thirst that was proving their greatest
enemy. Until the battle had begun more than a week earlier they'd been
able to draw fresh mountain water from a stream that ran 100 yards
below them, but that was no longer safe. To their shock and horror, two
women, Mariantonia Mastanuono and Angela Ferri, wives and mothers

both, had been machine-gunned by Germans while attempting to reach the stream, so for several days no one else had dared try. There were, however, still some cisterns in the village, which caught rainwater for washing and for animals, but the Germans had contaminated them with dead animals. Even so, thirst had driven a few villagers to creep out at night and try and find some water in the cisterns that still survived. Finally, one was discovered on the night of 13 December. It was, though, quite a way away – on the other side of San Pietro, towards the eastern edge of the village, near the Piazza Municipio, which meant that anyone trying to reach it had a fair stretch of open ground to cover first.

But the villagers in the cave were desperate, and not least the Pagano and Masella families. Serafino Masella, for one, could not bear to see his wife and children suffering so terribly from such debilitating thirst and so decided to try his luck. Nor was he alone, for his sister-in-law, Rosa Fuoco, also decided to go with him as well as a number of others. It was early in the morning, barely light. If there were Germans about, they saw none. Carefully, they crept through the ruins of the village, clutching their jugs and pots. The cistern's owner, however, was unhappy that his water source had been discovered and that it was now surrounded by desperate villagers. He wanted the people to leave – it was too risky having this many people here, and the water needed to be more carefully rationed. Serafino tried to reason with him, and beside him Rosa also began arguing with the man. Voices rose. Then grew louder.

From a distance, American troops saw dark figures in the first light of the morning massing in the village square. As far as they were aware, only Germans from 29. Panzergrenadier-Division were in the village. And so they opened fire. Serafino was knocked backwards by the blast of a shell, hit his head on a wall and fell unconscious. Rosa was struck by a single bullet to the heart and killed instantly. Serafino came to. Choking smoke filled the square. His eyes stung. His head hurt, but so did his legs. He got to his feet, stumbling. Bodies lay all around, some on top of each other. He grabbed one, then another, trying to shake them back into life, then stumbled forward, aware he needed to get away, get back to the caves, despite his legs being shredded by shrapnel. But he had to keep going. Back to safety. Crouching, stumbling, then crawling, he reached a path. And then exhaustion and pain overwhelmed him and he collapsed.

Not until later in the day was he found – by Lucia, his brother Bernadino's wife. His family had been worried almost senseless; only a handful of those at the cistern had made it back. Of Rosa there was no sign; Sera-fino had not seen her. Heated child's urine was used as an antiseptic to dress his legs, but that was the limit of the medical care available. In the dank, stinking caves his family and the other San Pietresi could barely comprehend the new tragedy that had befallen them.

That same day, 14 December, the Rangers finally came down off Monte Corno. For the past month they'd been practising ever more adventurous means of getting to the enemy on the far side of the ridge. Back on 29 November, they had had a go at blasting the Germans off the mountain by blowing up the summit. 'We sent for 800 pounds of TNT,' noted Bill Darby, '300 feet of cord, 500 feet of wire, safety fuzes, friction tape, a long rope, electric and non-electric caps, firing reel, an exploder, twelve bags of sand, cap crimpets, and fuze lighters.' It was something of a rushed job, but at 3.30 p.m. on the 30th they plunged the detonator and there was an immense explosion, with rock, stone and splinters spread far and wide; but at the same moment the Germans launched an attack of their own from a different direction, prompting a furious exchange of fire. Small arms chattered, mortar shells blasted and a lot of people were shouting and yelling, but after a couple of hours, with darkness falling, the fighting died down again. At first light the following morning it was clear that the situation was still much the same and that the summit of Monte Corno looked as resolutely immense as it had always done.

The next idea was to sneak out at night and put a loudspeaker near to the German positions. The Rangers then surrounded it with mines and ran a wire back. Snipers and a machine gun were trained on it for the moment the enemy tried to take it. No one did, and so a variety of music blared out on and off through the day and night. On their last night up there, the Rangers broadcast a propaganda talk and played Viennese waltzes. It seemed both sides had come to enjoy this little light entertain-ment rather than find it an irritation.

Now they were finally off the mountain, however. During the thirty-five days the 83rd Chemical Mortar Battalion had been up there they'd fired a colossal 38,000 4.2-inch mortar shells. The Ranger Force had been up there for nearly five weeks – almost as long as the entire Sicilian cam-paign and more than a month of close, attritional fighting in which no ground had been lost but none gained either. Darby had lost 40 per cent of his men high up there on that bare-arsed rock.

*

Another losing too many men was Major Georg Zellner, a little to the north and still trying to hold the mountains west of Filignano against the best the 45th Thunderbirds could throw at them. His companies were continuing to be chewed up piecemeal and all of them were suffering from the relentless American artillery fire and, whenever the weather allowed it, enemy aircraft in considerable numbers. On 11 December, from his command post on the forward, eastern slopes of Monte Casale, he had watched the Jabos circling and diving at will. 'It is enough to make you weep,' he wrote. 'So far, we haven't seen a single German plane in the sky.' He was existing in a small, narrow hole in the ground, which meant that whenever there was a chance to sleep it had to be done sitting up. 'The day like before,' he noted on 12 December. 'No joy, only suffering. It is almost boring to write about it.'

His men, clinging to the slopes of Colle Vecchio to the east of Monte Casale, were being whittled down with every passing day. His 11. Kompanie was in particularly dire straits, but breakthroughs by the Americans had to be counter-attacked and plugged; and when the 11. Kompanie positions looked to be in danger of being overrun he had to urgently send in two groups from 10. Kompanie. This seemed to calm the situation and overnight mules arrived with much-needed rations and were able to take back some of the wounded. Zellner was exhausted, but after eating some food, with a curse on the war, he tried to get some sleep. '6 a.m. Drum fire rouses us from sleep,' he noted. 'The earth trembles. We cannot move.' At around 9 a.m. the shelling subsided, but all communication with his companies was cut; when it was fixed he learned that 11. Kompanie had been largely wiped out, with just one officer and nine men left from around 130. The Gebirgsjäger – mountain troops – were apparently scattered; they would have to pull back, but the enemy infiltration still needed to be sealed and for this the regiment sent every spare man they had: Russian Cossacks, men from the bicycle platoon and engineers. They managed to seal off the breakthrough once again, but Zellner then learned that their neighbours to the left and right were now pulling back, so that night they too withdrew to Monte Casale. The disengagement succeeded, although the battalion had a tough climb to the top of Casale, Point 1395. 'At 6 o'clock,' he jotted, 'in new position. A black day. Dead tired. I sleep for 1 hour.'

General Fred Walker's plan to launch a massed assault to take San Pietro from multiple directions and with different, but strict, timings was fine on paper, but there were a lot of different moving parts, each dependent on the other. The old adage about the plan being the first thing to go awry the moment contact was made with the enemy was a cliché because invariably it proved to be the case. The first part of his battle plan was a night attack off the summit of Sammucro by 1st Battalion of 143rd Infantry to take three rocky knolls to the west, which would then, effectively, get them in behind the Germans in San Pietro. To reach the westernmost one of these meant dropping steeply down from the summit, across a grassy saddle, then up again to the rocky pimple beyond – a pimple on to which the Germans were firmly clinging. Simply moving down towards it at night required deft sure-footedness and considerable concentration; but under fire and while trying to shoot back in turn, it was almost impossible. It was also a moonlit night, which cast a shroud of pale light over the mountain and made visibility reasonable but also covered much of the mountain in deep shadows. The Americans could see clearly enough to move forward down from the summit, but the enemy remained hidden behind rocks, crevices and fissures, and after the Americans had advanced some two-thirds of the way to their objectives the Germans opened up, machine guns cutting through the night air, tracer criss-crossing the mountainside, mortars crashing and spewing shards of metal and rock in a lethal spread. And the wind was still biting across this bleak mountain expanse.

Below the mountain, the mule-skinners and medical teams could hear the battle up on the mountain above. Ernie Pyle was still with them; over the past few days he'd noticed that when men came down off the mountain they tended to look ashen-faced, unshaven, grimy and ten years older than they were. Nor did they smile much. And no one was smiling at the goat shed at the foot of the mule trail from Sammucro in the early hours of Wednesday, 15 December, when the body of Captain Henry Waskow was brought down, the B Company commander of 143rd Infantry. In the light of the moon, Pyle had seen the mules slowly picking their way down the mountainside, the beasts and their skinners bathed in a creamy, soft glow. Dead men had been coming down all night, slung over the backs of the mules. The Italian mule-skinners wouldn't accompany the fallen so Americans had to, and even they didn't like unlashing the bodies; an officer mostly did this grim work himself. Pyle watched, silent, as the first that night reached them. 'You feel small in the presence of dead men,' he wrote, 'so you don't ask silly questions.' Who the first dead man was, he didn't know. They slid him off, stood him for a moment, laid him on the ground in the moonlight shadow of a stone wall then left him there, alone, while they returned to the goat shed, smoked and chatted quietly. An hour later, several more arrived.

'This is Captain Waskow,' one of the men said in a quiet voice as the mules halted. He'd been killed by shrapnel from an exploding shell hitting him in the chest. He was laid down next to the other dead man, and then three more, so there were five in all lying there, uncovered, next to the stone wall. One soldier stood in front of Henry Waskow.

'God damn it!' he said out loud.

Another came over. 'God damn it to hell anyway!' A third man wandered over; an officer, Pyle thought. The man stood in front of Waskow, staring for a moment. 'I'm sorry, old man.'

A further soldier came over. 'I sure am sorry, sir,' he said, his voice almost a whisper.

Waskow was just twenty-five, from DeWitt County in Texas. He'd been B Company commander in the 1st Battalion, and clearly was an exceptional young man: a scholar, handsome, committed to his men and universally adored by all who had known him. Pyle reckoned he'd never met an officer quite so beloved and rather felt as though he was intruding on their grief, but was compelled to watch this tragic but deeply moving scene. Now he saw the first man squat down beside the dead captain and take Waskow's hand. 'And he sat there for a full five minutes,' noted Pyle, 'holding the dead man's hand in his own and looking intently into the dead face. And he never uttered a sound all the time that he sat there.' Then, eventually, he straightened Waskow's collar, arranged the tattered edge of his uniform, stood up and walked off down the track in the moonlight.

'PM is definitely worse,' recorded Harold Macmillan on 14 December, 'and has got pneumonia and they fear pleurisy.' Lord Moran, his doctor, seemed very worried; Churchill did little exercise, drank large amounts, ate rich food and was rarely without a cigar smouldering between his lips. Getting pneumonia – all too often a killer – was cause for extreme concern. The following day, Macmillan noted that Churchill was worse and his pulse irregular. His son Randolph arrived, and Macmillan was worried he'd do more harm than good by talking to his father about French politics, a subject guaranteed to get his blood up. Then, at 6 p.m., the PM suffered a heart attack – only a mild one, but even so this renewed their worst fears. Moran told Macmillan frankly that he had thought Churchill would die the previous evening, but he had pulled through and was still alive that evening, 15 December, despite new concerns about his heart.

Few, it seemed, were having a comfortable time in the Mediterranean at present, and certainly not along the Italian front. Up at the abbey of Monte Cassino, the monks were following the events in the valley and around them with growing concern. Military emplacements were being constructed on the mountain and worryingly close to the abbey. The abbot had taken this up with the local German commander, Oberst-leutnant Pollack of 29. Panzergrenadier-Division, and told him the Germans would be shamed before the world for what they were doing, having made so much propaganda about how they'd saved Monte Cassino. A couple of days later, some German officers from Kesselring's headquarters arrived to tell the abbot they would impose a 300-metre zone around the abbey, within which all military personnel would be forbidden. That was something, and on the 14th Dom Eusebio saw the Germans placing signs warning that beyond, on the abbey side, was *verboten* on the authority of OB Süd – Kesselring. 'This morning,' noted Dom Eusebio on the 15th, 'I measured the distance from the monastery walls to Cavalletto of the cable car, which was exactly 300 metres.' There he was pleased to see a large notice saying 'Monte Cassino – Neutral Zone.' There were still armaments at a cave at kilometre 8, however, which was within the zone and which he reported to the abbot, who in turn informed the Germans. 'Every now and again,' noted Dom Eusebio, 'there are violations of the neutral zone.' In between, he and his fellow monks began sowing crops in the fields around the abbey, listened to the relentless fire of the artillery and watched an incredible amount of Allied aircraft thundering over. Dom Eusebio was no military man, but even he now understood that skies clear of rainclouds meant skies thick with Allied aircraft.

These same aircraft were giving Wilhelm Mauss and the rest of XIV Panzerkorps headquarters a torrid time. 'It is gradually becoming uncomfortable here,' he noted. 'A wave had hardly passed when the next appeared already.' The walls and windows of the houses were constantly trembling, but later Mauss was up on the mountain when he saw the Jabos arrive and swoop down again. It was, he thought, a gruesomely beautiful image, but at the same time his heart cramped with anger at the ineffectiveness of the German flak. Especially evil was the news that his field hospital at Sora had also been hit by Allied bombs. The next day he visited Sora and saw that not a single pane of glass in the hospital remained in one piece. There was nothing for it but to move the hospital and all the patients to a new site in Fiuggi, thirty miles to the north-west. Mauss was incensed – the hospital had had a large red cross painted on the roof. Finally, after a long day, he arrived back at Roccasecca. 'My house looked amazing,' he noted. 'Not a window intact, curtains ripped, pieces of glass everywhere, paintings fallen from the walls etc.' It was time for another move for corps headquarters too. 'Overall,' he added in his diary on the 15th, 'it isn't looking good at the front.' Soon, he thought, it would be time to move from the Bernhard to the Gustav position.

Soon – but not just yet, as the 36th Texans struggled to make much head-way up on Monte Sammucro. Not only Captain Waskow was killed that night; plenty of others were too and many more wounded. By dawn, 1st Battalion of the 143rd had been reduced to just 155 'effectives' – men still standing and able to fight. Their three objectives remained firmly in enemy hands. Despite this setback, a planned tank attack down the road from Ceppagna and Venafro went ahead anyway. Sixteen Shermans and a single British bridge-laying Valentine travelling toe to tail were always likely to struggle and especially so along this winding mountain road, which cut through the terraces of olive groves and so was straitjacketed by a stone retaining wall on the right and a vertical drop on the left. Tanks were most effective when working hand-in-glove with the infantry and when they had room to manoeuvre. On the other hand, Keyes was anx-ious to bring some extra firepower to bear for the hard-pressed infantry, and the tanks of 1st Armored Division were otherwise sitting behind the lines twiddling their thumbs. The II Corps commander reckoned it was worth a punt, and Walker was prepared to go along with the plan.

For the assault on San Pietro, the two platoons of 753rd Tank Battalion were to be accompanied by 141st Infantry, but there was no getting around the canalization: those tanks simply had to hope they were still in one piece by the time they reached San Pietro. Really, it wasn't so very different from the New Zealand assault on Orsogna – an attack that had failed. Predictably, the tank attack didn't really work, and especially not without the assault from 143rd Infantry attacking down the mountain and keep-ing the German defenders distracted. Remarkably, the leading tank, which was odds-on to be the first to get knocked out, survived, but seven were destroyed by mines or artillery fire and four were disabled along the way. By evening on that Wednesday, 15 December, the surviving tanks and infantry were within touching distance of the edge of the village but simply couldn't force a way through. Mortar fire seemed to have almost no effect at all on the already wrecked village, and the leading American troops were too close for their own artillery to start raining down shells. Hidden in the wreckage, the 100 or so German defenders were able to cover every approach with anti-tank fire, their own mortars and the savagely rapid-firing MG42s.

Even so, the battered 36th Texan infantry pushed on under the cover of moonlight, scurrying and scampering between the shattered olive groves, picking their way through the rubble and destruction, using grenades and Tommy guns to clear the first few houses. Infantry need support, however, and by this time 2nd Battalion of 141st Infantry were down to about 130 men. It was not enough with which to attack an enemy in such a strong defensive position, and so before dawn those still standing fell back to the safety of the walled terraces.

The situation was desperate. A village in ruins, the dead left where they lay. The Germans defending the wreckage were on their last legs, so too were the battered Texans, whittled down to a skeleton force in this brutal landscape over which to do battle. It was remarkable that any of them were still prepared to fight, yet on the morning of Thursday, 16 December both the remnants of 143rd Infantry on Sammucro and 141st lower down, attacking the village from the east, renewed their attacks. Neither attack made any headway.

However, just at the moment when it seemed as though this latest assault on the Winter Line was doomed, 142nd Infantry, the third of the Texans' infantry regiments, successfully climbed up on to Monte Lungo from the south in a silent night-time assault. Taking the enemy completely by surprise, by mid-morning on the 16th much of Monte Lungo was finally in American hands, with the Italians, attacking from the eastern end, sealing the deal. That afternoon, von Senger was finally authorized to pull his men back to the Gustav Line. 'Another battle on mountain,' noted Frank Pearce. 'We are at its foot. Germans trying to take it back. Mortars going all night. Artillery going strong.'

But it wasn't the Germans counter-attacking. It was heavy firing to mask their overnight withdrawal.

In the eerie quiet, the Americans moved into San Pietro on the morning of Friday, 17 December. At the eastern edge of the village the road had been so badly damaged that the terraces had collapsed and it was impassable to vehicles; a German six-wheeled truck stood on its nose at the edge of a collapsed section of road, riddled with bullets and shrapnel damage. A dead German machine-gunner lay not far away, his weapon beside him. The road itself was littered with debris – shrapnel, rock, the detritus of battle. Slowly, carefully, the Americans pushed on into the village. Not a shot was fired; it seemed that the Germans had really left after all. The Piazza Municipio was strewn with stone and rubble. Lying on her back, her water pail still looped over her arm, lay Rosa Fuoco. She had been just thirty-two, caught in the crossfire of war. Her dark hair was flecked with grit, her mouth open and a piece of stone rested between an eye and her nose. Her thin clothes, barely enough to keep the cold at bay, and bare legs were covered in dust and grit and a single bullet hole stained her chest. All around her, San Pietro lay in ruins. Half of the church's dome had gone, like a skull caved in. The narrow streets were piled high with rubble, the air was heavy with smoke, death and decay. Not a single house remained untouched. Fate had dictated that San Pietro be sacrificed by the savage storm of war, yet amid these ruins, as American engineers began sweeping for mines, the San Pietresi started emerging from their caves. Serafino Masella was in a bad way, but he was still alive, as were his wife and daughter – Antonietta was four years old that very day. What a day to have a birthday! And medical help was, at last, on its way, as were rations and water. The Americans now found themselves surrounded by the villagers, the women kissing their hands, thanking both God and GIs alike for saving them. It had been the Germans who had evicted them and the Germans who had chosen San Pietro as a key focus of their Bernhard Line; but it had been American shells that had destroyed the village and the Americans who had killed Rosa Fuoco and others in the Piazza Municipio. Now here they were, their destroyers but also their liberators.

CHAPTER 32

Try and Try Again

'P M MUCH BETTER TODAY,' noted Harold Macmillan on Thursday, 16 December. 'His pulse is steadier, and the lung is clearing a little.' The medical experts seemed to think he was through the worst, so that was one crisis for the Allies that appeared to be clearing up. The next, though, was not far away as already Churchill's gains at Cairo and Tehran appeared to be unravelling on the ground in Italy. The Germans were pulling back to the Gustav Line, but that threatened to be an even stronger defensive position than the Winter Line. Von Senger's forces had taken an absolute hammering – as Georg Zellner, for one, would readily testify – but so too had the American and British infantry. Nor were the Canadians and 8th Indian making much headway at Ortona. It wasn't Rome that was out of reach – Pescara, fifteen miles up the coast, was still a leap too far as things stood, as was the Liri Valley beyond Cassino.

On 16 December, General Brooke left the Adriatic and with Alexander flew across the leg to Naples. It was a fine day for a change and Brooke was fascinated to see Vesuvius smouldering away and even more so, once on the ground, to visit Naples and view the astonishing work that had been carried out by Fifth Army engineers since the port had been captured. A brief tour of Pompeii followed and then he motored on to visit General Clark at his Fifth Army HQ. 'I had a long talk with him about the offensive on his front,' noted Brooke, 'and do not feel very cheered up as to the prospects for the future from what I heard from him.'

The next day, the same Friday that San Pietro fell, Brooke and Alexander visited the front, climbing up Bare Arse on the Camino massif on horses and conferring with Dick McCreery. From up there they were able to look out over this beautiful corner of Italy made ugly by war. Across the Mignano Gap there was Monte Lungo and, towering over it, Sammucro, scenes of such bitter fighting. Nestling low against the mountain stood the broken remains of San Pietro, now at last in American hands. Beyond, up the valley, was the low saddle of Monte Trocchio and then, on the far side, the wide, open Liri Valley. And beyond that, far away behind the distant peaks, was Rome, the Eternal City, the capital of Italy, a place that was to have been in Allied hands before Christmas. And there, brightly white in the winter sunshine, perched magnificently at the edge of the highest massif of them all, stood the abbey of Monte Cassino. It was obvious then to Brooke, as it was to Alexander, that before them stood a formidable nut for them to crack. Really, it was hard to think of a better defensive position.

That night there were further discussions at Clark's HQ near Caserta. The Fifth Army commander was frustrated that his army had not got further, but the previous day had already issued new orders for Phase III of his Operations Instruction No.12, which had been the basis for this current battle. Now, rather than surge on into the Liri Valley and to Frosinone and beyond, more limited objectives were given. In the first instance II Corps was to capture Monte Trocchio, the gateway to the Liri Valley, then II Corps and X Corps were to cross the River Rapido as it joined the River Garigliano and push on over the Liri. Meanwhile, VI Corps was to continue to attack and continue battling through the high ground to the north of Cassino. Clark had issued no timings yet because there were other things to sort out first, not least the thorny issue of what to do about Operation SHINGLE, the planned amphibious landings south of Rome.

The next day, 18 December, Clark flew down in his Piper Cub to Pomigliano near Naples to meet with Eisenhower and Bedell-Smith, both of whom were still in theatre but soon to be heading to Britain. After driving to a villa in Naples, Clark put his cards on the table. As he'd discussed with Alexander, he reluctantly recommended that SHINGLE be cancelled. It wasn't that he thought an amphibious operation was a bad idea, it was more that it would mean launching by 10 January at the latest, because the assault craft all had to leave the theatre by the 15th. His infantry divisions in line at the moment were on their knees; only 3rd Division had been out of the action in this current battle and he needed them – he certainly couldn't afford to pack them off for amphibious training. Eisenhower accepted his judgement on this, for since there was going to be no immediate breakthrough at Cassino, it would clearly be absurd to land a single division far behind enemy lines when there was absolutely no certainty at all of when a link-up might be made with the rest of Fifth Army. 'I will continue planning SHINGLE Operation,' he signalled to Alexander later that afternoon once he'd left Eisenhower, 'in the hope that craft can be made available at a later date when it will be possible to execute this operation properly, coordinated and supported by the remainder of the Fifth Army.' Then he added: 'I urgently request that every effort be made to secure the necessary craft to mount this operation at a later date.'

In the meantime, Fifth Army's guns kept hammering, patrols went forward and the engineers continued mending bridges, building bridges, repairing roads and clearing mines. Frank Pearce, as part of the 36th Texans' engineers, went up to San Pietro that day. 'Worse torn up country I've seen,' he noted. 'Still lots of bodies scattered around.' He saw one dead German with his head blown off and an Italian civilian. The smell was not too good. Clearing the mines and booby traps was quite a task; he found one particularly elaborate devil's garden which he only just managed to avoid tripping into. Later he discovered two wounded Germans in a cave under the village. 'One bad,' he noted, 'with head & arm all shot up.' The blackened remains of the Shermans on the road in was also a reminder of the ferocity of the fighting. One of his pals, Felix Gus, was killed that day in San Pietro by low-flying Luftwaffe fighter planes making a rare appearance, so the fighting wasn't entirely over. Lieutenant Evans was also killed by a cannon shell blowing off his arm; he'd only been at the front a few days. Eight others were wounded.

Clearing the dead from the mountains and ruins of San Pietro was taking time; it had been impossible while under fire and it was a big task to pick over the entire battered and broken landscape. The stench was pervading the ruins and surroundings, a constant, unavoidable smell that got into the nose and lungs along with the residual smell of smoke, cordite and charred remains. 'It seems the Grave Registration hasn't enough men,' added Pearce. 'Can't be helped. Any of us are liable to get it any day but we never worry about that any more.' Fatalism had begun creeping into them all.

Hans Golda and his 7. Batterie were now back behind the Rapido at a small village called San Angelo. It was only a mile or so south of Cassino at the mouth of the Liri Valley and all three batteries were dug in behind a low hill next to the village cemetery. There was a cave in the side of the hill, which would provide an excellent shelter but was full of animal dung, so they decided to burn it wearing their gas masks to hide the smoke and the stench. It was too damp, though, and so they had to clear it by hand with shovels and entrenching tools. Then word reached Golda that at last he had been given some leave – he was actually going home to Vienna for three weeks!

On the evening of 19 December, Major Georg Zellner and what was left of his battalion were also ordered to pull back to the Gustav position. They'd all been unable to shave for two weeks, let alone wash, so they were filthy, bearded and a very sorry sight as they reached the now empty Vallerotonda. Sixty per cent of Zellner's 3. Bataillon had become casualties in the month's fighting in the mountains. A couple of days later they were told they were now being attached to 29. Panzergrenadier-Division, which, after being in action since the beginning of September, was finally being pulled back for a rest and refit. Then, on the 23rd, they were told they were to hold a stretch of the Gustav Line instead – still nominally attached to 29. Panzergrenadier. As Zellner recced their new areas he came under heavy and sustained Allied artillery fire and found himself repeatedly flat on his stomach in the mud. 'So, now we are deployed again,' he jotted, 'in front of Monte Cassino.' He had rather hoped to have been out of the line for Christmas, but it was not the German high command's way to carefully marshal and look after their troops. At least he received some mail and greetings from home en route to this new deployment.

In fact, Kesselring had been reckless with his troops from the outset. Having zealously insisted on fighting for every metre, he had won the attention of Hitler at long last and come out on top in his personal duel with Rommel; but now that he was in the Führer's spotlight he was discovering how difficult it was to steer clear of it. Lemelsen had wanted to withdraw to the Gustav Line back in mid-November, but that request, when put to Hitler, had been turned down. Lemelsen again was all for pulling back from the Moro too, but instead LXXVI Panzerkorps had to fight on and on, giving ground only when those holding it were either virtually annihilated or physically unable to hold on any longer. By the time 9. Kompanie of 3. Bataillon Panzergrenadier-Regiment 129 had pulled back off Monte Camino, for example, there had been just sixteen men still standing; Zellner's 10. Kompanie had been so badly abused on the mountain that it had been reduced to just ten men. This was absurd and represented a gross mismanagement of the manpower available. It was driven, though, by Hitler's rabid refusal to allow his commanders to pull back and by Kesselring's determination to do as he was ordered to the letter. To lose almost two entire divisions – 65. Infanterie and 90. Panzergrenadier, for example, at Ortona – was an appalling waste of lives. Withdrawing in some kind of order and allowing AOK 10 time to build up far greater strength in depth would have been a much more sensible use of the assets the Germans had available. Normal military practice was to trade space for time, but Kesselring was trading men instead, and with no obvious or clear end strategy.

Instead, the German units were flung into the meat-grinder with mounting desperation – penny packets pushed into the fray to firefight one crisis after another. Von Senger had been as horrified as Lemelsen. It was all very well making the Allies fighting tooth and claw, but there had to come a point where the loss of manpower outweighed the disadvantage of losing territory, especially since strategically they'd given up southern Italy's greatest asset, the Foggia airfields, without really a fight at all. Why allow so much valuable manpower to be chewed up south of Rome when the Allies already had one of their most important objectives pretty much scot-free?

The use of 1. Fallschirmjäger-Division was a case in point. Despite the amount of combat this division had seen since the start of the war, there were still a decent number of highly experienced veterans among its number, of whom Jupp Klein was one. It was made up only of Germans and Austrians as well, all volunteers, and there was an *esprit de corps* within their unit that was missing from many others, all of which made them among the best German troops fighting in Italy. Yet they had so far not been allowed to fight as a single division; because they were so obviously better than most other units they were used to firefight and plug gaps, but because they were always being deployed in pieces rather than as a whole they were never as effective as they might be. That was the paradox. One of the principles of warfare – and one the Germans had religiously adhered to at the start of the war – was concentration of force, and yet this had not been applied, least of all with 1. Fallschirmjäger-Division. Jupp Klein's platoon continued preparing demolitions and mines inland, while two companies of engineers were sent to Ortona along with 3. Regiment, which a few weeks earlier had been holding the line at Castel di Sangro. Another regiment was at Orsogna. Effectively, they were operating as isolated and independent battle groups, but most certainly not as a cohesive whole.

Twenty-one-year-old Siegfried Bähr had been recovering from malaria with a number of other Fallschirmjäger at Campo di Giove, in the centre of the leg and twenty miles north of Castel di Sangro. As part of their rehabilitation they had been working on the defences of the Gustav Line there and Bähr, for one, was quite enjoying it; the landscape was stunning, and although the work was hard they were not being shot at or shelled and were well fed with barbecued meat and wine each evening. He had been looking forward to spending Christmas there when, on 15 December, a truck arrived, they were ordered to clamber in and told they would now be joining the battle at Ortona.

As the truck trundled eastwards they began to hear the rumble of artillery, which grew steadily louder the closer they got. It was a little after midnight when they stopped close to the coast. As Bähr jumped out he could see clouds flitting across the moon and glimpsed the stars, while the moon reflected its silvery light on the sea. 'I was thrilled by this sight,' noted Bähr in his journal, 'yet also unspeakably sad. Why did such a bloody war have to break out between the peoples?' They were at the edge of Ortona itself. A dead man lay abandoned nearby, while the town appeared to be nothing but ruins. Bähr tightened the strap of his helmet and with the others made his way into the shattered town.

On the same day that Siegfried Bähr was taken to the Ortona front, the Canadians finally took Casa Berardi, a three-storey farmhouse at the western edge of The Gully, albeit only with the suicidally brave actions of Captain Paul Triquet and the thirteen other men still standing in his company of the Van Doos, the French-speaking Royal 22e Régiment. Earlier attempts had not been helped by the totally inaccurate maps that had been issued, and only after rigorous patrolling had been carried out to accurately identify enemy positions were they able to make any headway; this was because the patrolling had allowed more accurate shelling and mortaring. A couple of days of better weather, effective armour and infantry cooperation and the considerable sacrifice of young Canadian infantrymen had at long last unlocked the German position, because once the Casa Berardi bastion had fallen it was then possible to start unfolding The Gully from its flank.

Even so, the fighting for The Gully was far from over, but now Montgomery had 8th Indian on the Canadians' flank and had started to bring over 5th Division next to the New Zealanders, so he had four divisions in the line and they were not now as badly depleted as those of the Germans. They were still making only marginal headway, however, all along

Eighth Army's front. The New Zealanders had another go at Orsogna in the early hours of 15 December. Roger Smith was among the 10 per cent LOB so missed this fight, which was just as well for him. It was freezing and raining icy showers when the attack was launched, but Orsogna was better defended and the Germans had more anti-tank guns than the previous time the New Zealanders attacked. The usual mishmash of German units, some from 1. Fallschirmjäger, others from 26. Panzer, were badly mauled, but after five days of battle Orsogna remained in German hands and the New Zealand 23rd Battalion, for one, had lost 40 per cent of its rifle companies, and twenty-five tanks were knocked out in just one day's fighting. Attritional stalemate was the result.

Captain David Cole and the 2nd Inniskillings, meanwhile, had been based at Castel di Sangro before the move east. 'The place has been more or less obliterated and the house I am in is one of the few that is intact,' he wrote to his parents, 'or, I should say was intact.' Just before he penned his letter two shells struck, blowing clean holes through the walls. The entire house shook, everyone was covered in dust and plaster, and Cole's batman, who'd been brewing tea at the time, was blown right out of the door. Miraculously, though, no one was hurt. A couple of days later the remains of the town, the mountains and the bowl-like valley of the upper Sangro were covered in deep snow, and that largely brought an end to the fighting there for the time being. This same storm had snowed in Jupp Klein and his platoon at the mountain village of Gamberale too.

Meanwhile, 8th Indian Division HQ was now at Frisa, a small village perched on the ridgeline on the southern side of the Moro, which meant it was within range of the German guns. On 14 December the 17th Brigade Signal Office was wiped out by a salvo of Nebelwerfer mortars – seven were killed and many more wounded, a grim event that rather put the wind up Harry Wilson, for one. The division cipher truck was parked against a haystack and close to a compost heap, while the Signal Office was by a hedge along a track. 'I don't like the look of things at all,' noted Wilson. 'Poised up on the Frisa Ridge, it makes me edgy.' On the night of the 19th, German planes stooged over and attacked the guns now down in the valley, but at around 10 p.m., while Wilson and Spiers were on night duty, two bombs exploded worryingly close by. Grabbing his coat, Wilson hurried out of the lorry, intending to take shelter in his new slit trench, but instead tripped over the camouflage netting and fell on his face into the compost heap. Picking himself up and feeling both frightened and foolish in equal measure, he took cover and tried to calm down.

'The bombers went but the 105s in the valley then began firing and the Germans started lobbing back Nebelwerfers – named 'Sobbing Sisters' and 'Moaning Minnies' by the troops because of their mournful scream. 'If this is war,' noted Wilson, 'give me peace.'

At Ortona, the attacks on The Gully continued. General Vokes had already rather shot his bolt, because eight out of his nine infantry battalions had been committed and all had been either decimated or severely mauled. Despite this he was not for giving up, and nor was Montgomery, and behind the biggest and most concentrated barrage yet another frontal assault had been launched on the 18th. Again, the infantry had been unable to break through and it wasn't until evening on the 20th that at long last the 'Cider' crossroads, halfway along The Gully on the northern bank, was in Canadian hands. There was an awful pointlessness to this ongoing battle. The German 65. Infanterie- and 90. Panzergrenadier-Divisions had largely ceased to exist. '90. Panzergrenadier-Division can no longer be attributed as a fighting force,' noted the LXXVI Panzerkorps war diary on 12 December. 'Current positions can only be held by bringing in new battalions.' It was questionable, though, whether sending in Oberst Heilmann's 3. Fallschirmjäger was achieving any more than hurling good after bad, but once again it was the destiny of General Richard Heidrich's 1. Fallschirmjäger-Division to be AOK 10's firefighters. 'Wherever Heidrich is, all is well,' Lemelsen had signalled to Kesselring on the 14th. 'The others, they simply let themselves be crushed.' That, however, was hardly the fault of the men being crushed. Wehrmacht training had suffered many cuts in recent times, and because most of Germany's young men had already been slaughtered in western Europe, in the Balkans, in North Africa but especially in the Soviet Union, the cupboard was now largely bare. Most troops in Italy were teenagers, middle-aged men or eastern European conscripts, and nearly all were undertrained. They were being slaughtered because Kesselring – and Lemelsen – kept sending ever more troops into a situation that was, by any normal reckoning of warfare, already totally hopeless. This was the price of having Hitler's spotlight shining on the Italian front. So, apart from the threat of being shot for desertion, what was the motivation for conscripted Poles and Czechs, for example, to fight for Führer and Fatherland? They were cannon fodder and knew it, and were currently suffering a more intense and sustained artillery bombardment than at any other front, including in Russia.

Incredibly, however, by 21 December Lemelsen was actually planning a counter-thrust in the Ortona sector. More penny packets were being flung into the breach: the Aufklärungs-Abteilung – reconnaissance battalion – of the HG Division was sent over, while 3. Panzergrenadier, a spent force after fighting from Salerno to the Bernhard Line, was moved to Orsogna, alongside the battered 26. Panzer. 'First objective,' Lemelsen wrote to Kesselring in an outline of his plans, 'break the western side of the enemy's defence with the envelopment from the south and with the attack from the west. Second objective: destruction of the enemy attack group with an offensive from the Adriatic and an attack from the Ortona area in the direction of San Vito.' This, though, was pure fantasy. Alexander feared losing the initiative if the front stagnated and the Germans were able to bring considerable numerical advantage to bear, but that had yet to happen. By this time Kesselring had twenty-five divisions in Italy, but ten of those were still in the north. The idea that the Germans could counter-thrust now, after a month of debilitating battle, with fewer guns than the Allies, no air power to speak of and by throwing in a regiment here and a battalion there was absolutely absurd. Did experienced men like Lemelsen really believe it possible to turn the tide here? Or was this purely a matter of paying lip service to the known wishes of the Führer and his insistence on fighting for every metre?

Yet not only were the Germans pointlessly throwing ever more men into the slaughter; that same accusation could also be levelled at Montgomery and Vokes, as it was now crystal-clear that Pescara was not going to be reached by the Allies in 1943, and certainly not Rome; the men were starting to refer to Vokes as 'the Butcher'. The dead now lay strewn in the mud and mire all over the battlefield after weeks of fighting. Across countryside that just a few weeks earlier had been a sea of pale yellow and orange vine leaves and citrus and olive groves heavy with fecund fruit there was now mud and carnage, and the ever-present stench of decay: of lingering smoke and cordite, of the dead, bloated and abandoned, of faeces. Just in front of the Hasty Ps' positions there were some 170 German dead, and those had all been killed before 11 December. The question had to be asked whether there was anything much to be achieved. At earlier moments in the war, the Allies would have called off the fighting by now; but here in Italy, with the clock ticking and with the schedule so behind and expectations so high, commanders appeared compelled to keep going, to try and try again. Ortona was turning into the worst meat-grinder of the entire Italian campaign to date.

Werner Mork and his three comrades had remained in their foxhole at the eastern end of the plateau above The Gully but then, that night, had seen Canadian troops to the left and right of them, advancing not in a wide arc but in columns. All four were keenly aware that they could have very easily mowed them all down with their MG. 'But we didn't,' noted Mork, 'because we knew this would mean death to us.' With a sinking feeling, they realized their positions must have been overrun but somehow, in the night, they'd missed the orders to pull back – the runner simply hadn't called on them in their foxhole; he must have assumed they were dead. Now they were cut off and behind enemy lines. It wasn't a comfortable feeling. Whispering, they discussed whether they should surrender or try and make it back to Ortona. They decided to attempt to reach their own lines, but figured their chances would be better if they each tried to go it alone.

That night, having kept their heads down in their foxhole through the day and with darkness now fallen, they disabled their machine gun and one by one crept out. When it was Mork's turn he set off, crawling and crouching, his ears acute to every noise. On many occasions he heard low voices – presumably Canadians – so crept away as quietly as he could. Occasional shellfire and bursts of small arms cut through the night air, but after two weeks of fighting the battlefield was, for once, quiet, both sides pausing before the next phase began – the battle for the town itself.

Eventually he managed to reach the German outposts, where he was challenged but did not know the password of the day. 'With great difficulty,' he wrote, 'I managed to convince the sentries that I was not an advanced element of the enemy, but just a poor lost corporal in the Wehrmacht.' Mork had made it and, having been debriefed by the local commander, was given a seat on the next transport to the rear. There he discovered his old comrades in the regiment's supply unit, all of whom had been told he was among the dead. He had been very lucky.

The Hasty Ps were pulled out of the line on 19 December, having been in constant action since their first attack across the Moro on the night of the 5th. Generally, Allied front-line infantry and armour was rarely in the thick of it for more than four days, perhaps six at the most, because by that point exhaustion and casualties were invariably too great to continue. Here at Ortona, such norms had been thrown out with the bathwater. Companies had, however, been released one at a time for rotation through the mobile bath units that had been brought up to San Vito. But even here there was no escape, for on 16 December San Vito was unexpectedly shelled, killing five and wounding fifteen more from a single platoon as they were bathing.

Moving to the remains of an olive grove near what used to be San Leonardo, the Hasty Ps assumed that this was the first stop on their way to the far rear. The brief window of fine weather had vanished and the exhausted survivors and the handful of replacements – thirty had reached them on the 15th – began fashioning loose shelters amid the latest deluge of rain. Farley Mowat wasn't too bothered about the rain, however; he was just happy to be out of line. He'd survived, and yet he felt a wreck. That day he sat and wrote to his parents. He'd not written recently, he told them, because what could he say? He didn't want to tell them a lie, but nor did he want to write about how he was really feeling. 'The damnable truth,' he wrote, 'is we are in really different worlds, on totally different planes, and I don't *know* you anymore, I only know the you that was. I wish I could explain the desperate sense of isolation, of not belonging to my own past, of being adrift in some kind of alien space. It was one of the toughest things we have to bear – that and the primal, gut-rotting worm of fear.' Too many of his pals had died and he'd seen too much, been knocked off his feet by shells and by mines, lived in mud and filth and surrounded by endless destruction and misery. 'Too difficult trying to find the sense and meaning in any of this . . . Pray God we get a decent break. We need it more than you could ever know . . .'

They were still at San Leonardo when a single heavy-calibre shell screamed in with a tearing, air-sucking sigh and slammed into the RAP. Mowat was some distance from it, but the concussion still buffeted him and a searing hot wind coursed through his nostrils. A huge cone of soil and debris was flung into the air and when it subsided all that remained was debris and bits of both the RAP and Charlie Krakauer, the indefatigable battalion medical officer. While the mess was being cleared up, the CO, Bert Kennedy, was summoned to a 1st Brigade 'O' group – an orders group, or plan-of-action meeting – and as usual Mowat accompanied him. There they learned that they were not being sent to the rear, but rather were to mount an attack to the west of the town to draw off any German reinforcements while 2nd Brigade fought through Ortona itself.

'What's the word, Squib,' Al Park asked him on their return, 'are we going into reserve?' Park and Mowat had trained together in Scotland and had both been in Able Company; they were close friends. Park, now Able's second-in-command, had aged ten years since Sicily. No, Mowat told him – they had another date with the Tedeschi first.

'Ah well, what the hell?' Park replied. 'Who wants to make old bones? See you in Valhalla, chum.'

The attack went in early the following morning, the infantry advancing Passchendaele-style behind another massive artillery barrage, the reverberations of which seemed to be pounding as rhythmically as Mowat's increasingly heavily thumping heart. They were advancing in open country, Ortona away to their right, the landscape dotted with farm buildings but also drainage ditches. Later in the afternoon, Kennedy sent Mowat to find a squadron of Shermans that was due to be supporting them, and he was picking his way through the mud and between the drainage ditches and had just paused by a stone farm building when a salvo of Nebelwerfers screamed in and landed 50 yards away. The blast knocked him off his feet and in through the doorway directly on to a prone figure that gave a loud gurgling belch. There was a sickening stench. Gathering his wits, Mowat realized he'd fallen on to a dead German paratrooper, and then saw there were two more sprawled in the mud and manure, and a fourth, still alive, sitting against the wall.

Mowat stared at the man, convinced he was about to be killed, but the German made no move at all.

'Vasser . . . haff you . . . vasser?' he asked.

Slowly Mowat got to his feet, then realized that the German's left hand was clutching the stump where his right had been. 'Dark gore was still gouting between his fingers and spreading in a black pool about his outthrust legs,' wrote Mowat. 'Most dreadful was a great gash in his side from which protruded a glistening dark mass which must have been his liver.' He was young, pale-eyed. Plaintively, he asked again for water, but Mowat didn't have any – he only had rum in his water bottle. He tried to tell him – nein wasser, only rum – but the boy looked at him so pleadingly that he relented. Holding the bottle to the young man's lips, he watched him take spasmodic gulps then drank some himself. Not long after, the boy died.

Leaving the dead, Mowat continued on his way, located the Shermans and got a ride on the back of one to join Baker Company, who were forming up to mount a new attack. Sliding off the tank into the mud, his legs collapsed and then so did the rest of him. For a brief while, Mowat was out cold.

Major Alex Campbell was finally back with the Hasty Ps, rejoining Able Company on Christmas Eve. He'd enjoyed the rest camp although he was impatient to get back to the company. On the other hand, it had allowed him to send home some presents for Christmas, and he'd also remembered to send a card to his beloved niece, Janalyn. 'I hope Santa Claus will be good to you this Christmas,' he wrote, then added: 'You better stop growing so fast or I won't have any little girl to play with when I come home. I love you. Alex.'

He was marching along the road from San Vito with a new column of replacements when he spotted Farley Mowat, recovered after his brief collapse and being driven in the commander's jeep in the direction of the village. Mowat was cheered to see him; his old Able Company commander looked as big and indomitable as ever.

'Farley!' Campbell called out. 'Still here? And not a general yet? Must be all that verse you write. Bad for promotion.' He then handed a piece of paper over and told Mowat he had been 'versifying' too. 'Read this when you get time,' he said, 'and tell me what you think.' Mowat took it, tucked it into his battledress then fell in beside him and the men he'd been due to collect himself. There were 140 of them, straight from Canada – an entire company's worth, and despite the freezing sleet they were chatting easily and a number of them singing. This lessened as they neared the wreckage of San Leonardo and stopped altogether by the time they reached the battle-scarred salient that had developed to the west of Ortona. A new salvo of shells screamed over as they neared Battalion IIQ, and by the time the shelling stopped seven of the new boys were either dead or wounded. They'd not even fired a single bullet.

But by this time, the fighting in Ortona had only just begun.

CHAPTER 33

Merry Christmas and a Happy New Year

T HAT THE ALLIES HAD not yet reached Rome was a source of bitter disappointment to Carla Capponi and the partisans of GAP Centrale. They had been instructed by the Military Council of the CLN to rid the city of Fascists, and Carla's boyfriend, Paolo, had been involved with three others in a gunfight on 21 November, killing two men. Afterwards, the four Gappisti had headed to the Capponi flat, where Paolo had felt shaken by what he had done. After this, however, the Military Council instructed them to start targeting Nazis. This would, they knew, bring severe reprisals, but it would also raise the profile of the movement to the outside world. It was certainly a high-risk strategy, however, and the benefits of killing Germans in the city were questionable. An alternative was to disrupt, sabotage and gather intelligence. But they were young and angry, and these were the orders of the Military Council.

The first target for GAP Centrale was a Wehrmacht officer who had been spotted daily walking from the Hotel Ambasciatori on the Via Veneto to the Ministry of War, which was only a short distance away. He always wore his Wehrmacht uniform but also carried a bulging black briefcase. Four Gappisti were to make the hit on the evening of 17 December: Carla, Paolo and two others, code-named Giovanni and Maria. None of them had seen the man before but his route, uniform and briefcase were to identify him to them. The plan was for them to fall in behind him, acting as two pairs of lovers, and then shoot him. They agreed that they would fire at the first intersection on the Via XXIII Marzo.

On cue he appeared as they'd been told he would, and they began following him. Carla – or Elena as she was now – had her Beretta in her coat pocket. This was her first armed action and she told herself that the man in front was a Nazi officer, armed, and was simply someone whose life she had to take; that was all there was to it. She hesitated at the first road crossing, but they kept going and on the other side Paolo said, 'At the next cross-street, you shoot, you'll do it as soon as you're off the pavement.' As they neared the next crossing they closed towards the officer and, just as he was about to step on to the road, Paolo said, 'Now!'

Elena pulled out her pistol, fired, and the German collapsed, crying out, 'My God! I'm dying! Help me!'

Paolo bent down and picked up his briefcase and then all four of them hurried across the street towards the Piazza Barberini. Then suddenly there were some GNR officers hurrying towards the scene, but looking frightened, and they asked the group what had happened. Elena told them someone had been shooting in the Via XXIII Marzo and the GNR men hurried off. Only then did Elena realize she still had her Beretta in her hand. She felt full of anguish at what she had done. It was, after all, quite a thing to kill a man in cold blood.

The German died on the way to hospital; his briefcase revealed plans and blueprints of power and communications grids linking anti-aircraft sites in and around Rome. The following day, 18 December, a second GAP attack was made on a favoured trattoria of German and Fascist officers, which left eight German soldiers dead. That same evening, Paolo and Elena carried out a bomb attack outside the Cinema Barberini, which held twice-weekly showings exclusively for German troops. Paolo, on his bicycle, threw a kilo of TNT with an eight-second fuse at a truck loaded with soldiers after a visit to the cinema. A further eight soldiers were killed in this attack. The next day Gappisti bombed the Hotel Flora, headquarters of the German Command in Rome. Much of the ground floor was devastated.

While the Rome partisans were carrying out these attacks, Filippo Caracciolo had had his plans to create a Corpo Volontari della Libertà kicked into the long grass by the Allies. This was because they would have to be equipped and trained by the Allies, all of which took time, money and effort. The British were already funding and training Eugenio Corti and others in the Regio Esercito, so to add a further militia group of dubious military value was simply not something they were willing to sanction. It was hard enough getting properly trained and equipped troops to the front as it was. Even so, Caracciolo, who was not a military man, was bitterly disappointed, not least because the take-up had been very encouraging and training – by Italians – had already begun at the Bagnoli Barracks. Without material and financial support, however, it was, as a scheme, dead in the water. 'The disbandment order,' noted Caracciolo, 'extinguishes a flame and kills hope – one of the few throbbing hopes on our grey horizon.' Nor was he and the CLN making much headway politically either, despite public demonstrations against the King and government in Naples and elsewhere. As a leading member of the Partito d'Azione and a notable Italian aristocrat, Caracciolo had been trying to mediate a solution to the current political impasse. At the beginning of December he had had another meeting with Badoglio in Brindisi. 'I find him tired, querulous, disheartened,' he noted. 'The mask of old age has grown heavy on his face.' Badoglio was not budging over the issue of the King: Vittorio Emanuele was refusing to abdicate, claiming that standing down would not help Italy at this moment of crisis, and the old marshal insisting it was his duty to stand by his monarch. 'I object to him,' wrote Caracciolo, 'that no one is allowed to stand as judge in the conscience of others.' So for the time being, at any rate, the status quo remained: the CLN refused to support the Badoglio government while the King continued to rule, and Vittorio Emanuele remained where he was, serving not the people but himself and his feckless family and entourage in Brindisi.

Meanwhile, many Italians in the south continued their battle for survival. 'Poor us,' wrote Lina Caruso from the remains of Eboli, 'we starve to death!' A meagre bread ration of 100 grammes had been introduced by the Americans, but within a month the soft white bread they had been given had been replaced by a black and hard loaf instead and she worried that even this would soon be taken from them, for it was rumoured there was no more flour and an American steamer bringing promised provisions had also, apparently, been sunk. 'So,' she added, 'for Holy Christmas, no more flour.'

At Ortona, the battle for the town itself was now under way. Siegfried Bähr had been at 2. Bataillon's headquarters in a building opposite the large Aragonese Castle at the northern end of the town where he was set to work as a radio-telegrapher. Only one battalion was currently holding Ortona, but a company of Pioniere had blown up both ends of a series of streets and left others open in an effort to corral the Canadians into carefully prepared killing zones. The piles of rubble were laced with booby traps, while the paratroopers were able to use their machine guns very effectively; each Fallschirmjäger-Gruppe of ten was issued with two MG42s rather than the single one that was standard for all other infantry. It meant that buildings either side of the narrow streets were used as MG positions, and placed on different floors too. They also made liberal use of snipers. Roads were mined and cellars and roofs knocked through so they could move easily from one building to another without venturing into the street. As the Canadians began moving into the town, Bähr was sent forward with the rest of 5. Kompanie and by 23 December was in a building near the main square. Ortona, a small, ancient port perched on low cliffs overlooking the Adriatic, had been home to 10,000 people, but Bähr had not seen a single civilian and it was already largely wrecked, having been bombed three days earlier and shelled relentlessly. Within its narrow streets the raucous din of battle was terrible, the whine, wump and crash of shells and almost never-ending chatter of small arms, sharp and jarring. Manning his radio, Bähr felt a jolt and renewed sense of panic every time someone warned of a tank approaching. One Sherman rumbled close to their positions but was knocked out by Leutnant Heidorn firing a Panzerfaust, a single-shot hand-held anti-tank weapon being used in Italy for the first time.

The trouble was, that was the only one they'd been issued and now they had no more anti-tank weapons at all. More tanks inched forward, the infantry crouching behind. The turret swivelled then the gun fired, the shell crashing into the building. Smoke, dust, bricks, stone and masonry tumbling. Room by room, house by house the 5. Kompanie men were forced back. One man after another was wounded or killed, but Bähr stuck by his radio, passing on messages, reports and orders, carrying it with him as they retreated down the street. Only when it grew dark did a bit of calm return.

The following morning. Christmas Eve. Shells screaming in and exploding, gunfire in the streets. A tank thundered by, then fired. Feldwebel Erwin Walz, due to be commissioned, cried out and collapsed bleeding. He died soon after. 'The world is full of deceit and mockery,' noted Bähr. 'Christmas. All around again are screams of pain and death.' Bähr thought about his family back at home and many others decorating their Christmas trees, just as he himself had done before the war. If only they knew in Germany what was happening here in Ortona! Ten men had been killed already that day and three more wounded. Bähr radioed for more reinforcements, but all he was told was 'Resist! Resist!' 'Again we have to abandon some houses,' he noted. 'Houses? Ruins.'

They moved to a new house, setting up the radio on the ground floor. That night, having survived the day, he and his fellow radio operator, Heinz Kersten, drew up two armchairs left there, a small sofa and a coffee table, while in the cellar they found sugar and a barrel of wine. Having lit the fire, they warmed and sweetened some wine. 'An almost Christmas-like atmosphere reigns,' he jotted. 'Our thoughts fly home . . .'

At 1.30 a.m. the food carriers arrived, and with a treat too – Christmas parcels, each containing a small Christmas bun, chocolate, almonds and oranges. 'We sip our sweet mulled wine and "celebrate" Christmas,' jotted Bähr. 'For Heinz, a promotion to Unteroffizier has arrived, while I become Obergefreiter. We rejoice, talk again about what's happening at home and reminisce.'

'Wet, dismal, murky, muddy day,' jotted Harry Wilson on Christmas Eve. A few days earlier, he'd received a Christmas card from his mother. 'I hope you are happy and well,' she had written, 'and that you like your surroundings better than you did last year, and that you will have a very happy Xmas – the best yet.' He had reckoned there was a good chance he'd be spending Christmas Day in a hole in the ground with a small cross above it, but in fact he was still alive as the 24th drew to a close. Spiers called by and gave him half a bottle of whisky, but warned him not to drink it all at once. Wilson drank the lot immediately and went to sleep quite contented. 'With a thousand bottles of this stuff,' he wrote, 'I could see this war through without any bother at all.'

A few miles away in the salient west of Ortona, Farley Mowat spent the night of Christmas Eve in the farmhouse that was now the Hasty Ps' Battalion HQ. He'd been down in the cellar when he remembered Alex Campbell's poem, so pulled it out of his battledress. It had been written in pencil, and every time a shell landed the kerosene lamp flickered and dust shook from the ceiling, which, combined with Campbell's loopy handwriting, made it hard to read. None the less, he managed to make sense of the seventeen lines of simple, honest and rather touching verse:

> When neath the rumble of the guns
> I lead my men against the Huns,
> I am alone, and weak, and scared
> And wonder how I ever dared

Accept the task of leading them.
I wonder, worry, then I pray:
Oh God, who takes men's pain away,
Now, in my spirit's fight with fear,
Draw near, dear God, draw near!
Make me more willing to obey,
Help me to merit my command.
And if this be my fatal day,
Reach out, oh God, thy helping hand.
These men of mine must never know
How much afraid I really am!
Help me to stand against the foe,
So they will say: He was a man!

Early the next morning, Able Company was sent to clear a group of Fallschirmjäger who had infiltrated the Canadian salient overnight. It was 7 a.m. Mowat was still at Battalion HQ and tried to follow what was going on through the headphones of a radio set, but Able was off air so it wasn't until some wounded arrived that he learned what had happened. It was a sergeant with a gash in his leg who told him. The 7 Platoon had begun the attack but had been caught by the enfilading fire of three machine guns. At this point, instead of trying to outflank the position, Campbell then leaped up from his position, gave a bellow and charged straight at the enemy, firing his Tommy gun as he did so. He'd barely gone a few paces before he was riddled with bullets, his body falling into the mud and jerking until the life drained from him.

Mowat was still struggling to take in what the sergeant was telling him when the blanket screening the cellar doorway was pulled back and two stretcher bearers pushed in carrying Al Park, alive, but only just; he had a bullet wound to his head. As Mowat looked at his pale, ghostly face and the blood-stained bandages around his friend's head, he felt tears well and then stream down his face. It was Christmas Day, 1943.

Hans Golda was at home, in Vienna. 'My boy just lay in the bathtub,' he noted, 'and kicked and smiled at his Dad.' For a few precious weeks, he could forget the war. There were no air raids, he could move freely and spend time with his beloved wife and son. He was lucky, but for everyone else at the front the war continued with its usual fury. Perhaps not for Wilhelm Mauss, though, who also had an enjoyable Christmas, although he would have dearly loved to have been at home with his family as Golda was with his.

Mauss had spent Christmas Eve investigating some disused hotels above Guarcino on the Campo Catino which he hoped might serve as a field hospital for 5. Gebirgsjäger-Division, which was moving south and into the line. 'A fabulous journey,' he noted, 'with wonderful views into the landscape.' It was a steep climb in their car as the road wound its way up the mountain, but at 4,500 feet the snow started to fall and soon after they could go no further. In the evening they held a Christmas celebration at the new corps headquarters near Frosinone, singing 'Stille Nacht' and other carols. Mauss gave a short talk; the previous Christmas the corps had been in the ruins of Stalingrad. He spoke of the Christian and German meaning of Christmas, the celebration of love and hope. He wanted to still find reason to feel confident on this dark night and continue to believe in the German future even though it was the fifth wartime Christmas.

A little way to the east, just to the north of Cassino town, Georg Zellner and his depleted battalion were holding the new Gustav Line positions on the Monte Cassino massif. He thought it an impossible place to be, and they were living in holes in the ground and among stone scrapes and sangars, unable to budge by day because of American artillery fire. Only at night could they risk moving about; he felt they'd become rats. Nor could they make fires because they could be seen. 'So we spend the day brooding silently,' he noted. On Christmas Eve, once it was dark, a mule train arrived with Christmas mail and gifts and also a tree, but this brought few cheers and he remained at his command post listening to the howling of the shells as they continued to be hurled over. At midnight, things quietened down a little. 'We drink red wine,' he jotted. 'By Hindenburg light we sing the Christmas carol. Then we lie down. The first Christmas in the field is over. A thousand thoughts of home move me.' Shelling woke him in the morning, and around midday intensified. 'The day has nothing Christmassy about it at all,' he added. 'We curse the war, but it is no use. It goes on in the old madness of the people.'

It was the 45th Thunderbirds and the 2e Division d'Infanterie Marocaine keeping up the pressure on the German lines to the north of Cassino, but the 34th Red Bulls were now out of the line and in a rest area near Caserta, which meant Bud Wagner, for one, was having a better Christmas than many. He sent off some packages first thing, got himself a shave and a haircut and later even had a turkey supper. The day was rounded off with a film, *Rhythm of the Islands*. Frank Pearce, on the other hand, was still at the front, and his company was effectively acting as infantry because the rifle companies were so depleted. 'Some companies,' he noted, 'have as few as eighty men.' That meant 50 per cent strength. Great efforts had gone into ensuring that even those at the front received their turkey supper, however, and so Pearce at least ended the day with a half-decent meal inside him. Even so, he couldn't help thinking about how strange this Christmas was; he was a long way from home.

'Had quite a good Xmas,' noted RSM Jack Ward, who was still on the Garigliano front. 'I got the Xmas feeling by opening my Xmas parcel, also airgraph Xmas cards.' He was pleased because he received a lot of the things he was short of, such as spare socks. 'Our guns done a lot of shooting Christmas Eve,' he jotted, 'but bit of a lull on at present, expecting a big show any minute.' At Regimental HQ a cabaret was laid on, with a sing-song, and Ward held a whist drive too, which went down well.

Up at the abbey, now unwittingly at the centre of the new front line, General von Senger, a devout Catholic, had attended Mass on Christmas Eve, and returned again for the Mass held in the crypt on Christmas morning. 'Christmas at war,' noted Dom Eusebio. They were worried by the repeated infringements of the 300-metre zone, and after the service he took the opportunity to speak to von Senger about these violations. 'I expressed our confidence that the protection zone would be respected,' recorded Dom Eusebio. 'He did not reply.'

There was little sense of confidence, hope or Christmas cheer at Ortona, which had descended into a bitter street battle. The Canadians had not been trained in urban operations and the number of snipers and hidden machine guns had taught the tank men of the Three Rivers Regiment to simply pummel every building. Pushing behind and alongside them were the Loyal Edmontons – the Eddies – and the Seaforth Highlanders, the battalion that had first tried to storm San Leonardo a lifetime ago at the start of the battle. Liberal use of Brens, Tommy guns and grenades was the only way in fighting that had been floor by floor, not just house to house. Rather than risk tripwires and booby traps on the ground floor, they were soon discovering that it was better to knock down walls that hadn't already been blasted, lob in grenades and clear each house like that. At no point, though, did the Fallschirmjäger show any sign of throwing in the towel; men of the Seaforths came across one Fallschirmjäger who had been blinded by shrapnel but was still waving his weapon. 'I wish I could see you,' he yelled in English, 'I'd kill every one of you.' They were starting to call Ortona the 'Stalingrad of the Adriatic'.

'Jerry sending shells over,' jotted Major Roy Durnford on Christmas morning. 'Deathly chatter of machine-guns. Rumbling of falling buildings, roar of guns.' He had headed to the church of Santa Maria di Costantinopoli at the southern end of the town. Tables had been set for the companies to sit at and have a Christmas meal, and roses and violets placed in small cups of water to add a little cheer. 'Shells whine and explode,' he scribbled. 'Holy Night. The meal for C Company. Brigadier and Colonel cheered. The faces of new recruits . . . Orders to leave for the front – a few hundred yards forward. A Coy returns from front. Weary, strained, dirty.' He collected them for carols in the cloisters, which he was careful to make voluntary, then they repeated the meal again. And the entire occasion was repeated another time when B Company came in, and finally again when it was D Company's turn. The fighting in Ortona, Durnford reckoned, followed a quickly established routine: 'We shave same house, exchange grenades and shoot at his head if out of window and he at ours.'

There had not been a lull all day, nor on Boxing Day either. By the morning of the 27th, Siegfried Bähr learned that they had just sixty men left in 2. Bataillon. Once again he heard the rumble of tanks, the clatter and squeak of tracks, then the pause, followed by the shot of the main gun and the explosion and rumble of masonry that followed. Canadians were crawling over the roofs, through the upper floors. He could hear machine guns crackling, hand grenades bursting. Oberfeldwebel Sabludowski was killed by a grenade – another NCO in his company gone; he had been Leutnant Ewald Pick's best friend. 'The battle rages on,' noted Bähr. 'Leutnant Heidorn stands in the archway of a gate and secures a clear path with his machine gun. Suddenly a hand grenade falls in front of his feet and he quickly retreats. The Tommies are already in the same house on the upper floors. The Leutnant runs up a half-destroyed staircase. We hear gunshots, hand grenades explode . . . We have to leave the house, the Leutnant has fallen.' No, not fallen, Bähr then thought, that was a stupid word to describe it; after all, someone who fell over could get up again, but Heidorn wouldn't. He was dead, no more, lying in a growing pool of blood amid the dust and debris of yet another shattered house, in a nondescript street in a small coastal town halfway up the leg of Italy.

They scuttled to a new building, Bähr holding the radio link by a blasted window, the rest of the men looking at him and wanting to know what they should do, and when reinforcements might come. 'Absolutely resist!' was the instruction, repeated yet again. But how? And what with? Leutnant Pick looked dejected. He asked Bähr for a cigarette, then lit it with a trembling hand. Suddenly, without saying a further word, he dropped his machine gun and stepped out of the house and into the piazza outside. Bähr and the others watched, aghast. At the fountain, Pick stopped and crouched, smoking his cigarette, then pointed at a Canadian on the second floor of a building across the square. 'All weapons,' Pick shouted, 'fire at will.'

From their building, Bähr and the others yelled at him to come back, but then a shot rang out and Pick collapsed. He had been the last standing officer in 5. Kompanie. Only once darkness had fallen did Bähr and another man scamper out to fetch him. He'd been shot in the lung, but was still alive. What a waste. Carefully, they took him to the aid post but he died there soon after, in the early hours of 28 December. Bähr hurried back and then a radio message arrived that, at last, they were to fall back. 'In the middle of the night, in single file,' noted Bähr, 'we leave Ortona, heading north, stumbling on the slope of a vineyard, almost in the direction of the homeland.' They crossed another gorge, then followed the coastal road until they reached a railway tunnel, which was the new battalion command post. Trucks were waiting. After destroying the road, they headed out. Bähr sat huddled in the back, cold and exhausted, as the vehicle drew away from the ruins of Ortona, unable to fully take in the extent of the many dead left there but aware of his own good fortune at surviving.

The Battle of Ortona was over.

Up in the high mountain valley of Collelungo, beneath Monte Cavallo and Monte Mare, the villagers from Vallerotonda and Cardito were still praying that the fighting would soon pass. Shelling was heavy on the 27th, but in the evening a number of German troops from 100. Gebirgsjäger-Regiment, part of 5. Gebirgsjäger-Division, arrived and were happy to join the Italians around the fire and share some of their mutton broth. One of the soldiers handed over some dark bread and said in broken Italian that it was for the children; he had four of his own back home. The soldiers told them the Americans would probably arrive the next day. It snowed that night, heavily, from around 5 o'clock.

The following morning, the snow was thick on the ground but a fire was lit early and the refugees huddled around it. Then German troops appeared again, but this time they were newly arrived from 15. Panzergrenadier-Division, yet another bizarre deployment of penny packet formations as Lemelsen juggled his depleted formations. Now, the friendliness shown by the Gebirgsjäger had gone. Moving down the slopes into the refugees' small, sheltered bowl between the beech trees on the banks of the mountain stream, some began setting up a machine gun which was pointed directly at them. Panic and fear started to spread among the Italians. Fourteen-year-old Pierino di Mascio couldn't understand it; the Germans had always been quite affable up until this moment. Pierino's father, Antonio, shouted to his family, 'I have all our documents, ID cards and money in my jacket, if one of us survives.' He then hugged his wife, Teresa, Pierino's mother, who was also clasping the youngest of their children, Domenico, aged just one year old on Christmas Day, to her chest. Some of the women fell to their knees and began praying. Babies and children started to cry. Angelina di Mascio, the girl brought up in Glasgow, was breastfeeding tiny Addolorata, then dropped at the feet of the German sergeant who appeared to be in charge and screamed for mercy. The sergeant kicked her in the face, pulled out his pistol and shot first her and then the baby, the sound echoing around the valley.

Then the machine gun opened fire. Pierino was in the middle of the group and ran towards a large boulder by the stream's edge. His two sisters were also hiding there, in a tight crevasse. Bullets spattered, the saw-like sound harsh and jarringly loud in that tight space, chips of stone spitting and people dropping. There was nowhere for anyone to run – the stream was at their backs, the slopes of the ravines and the large rocks were in front and around them. 'They were killing everyone,' said Pierino, 'then they went around and shot those that were still alive.' Pierino's uncle, Domenico, was clutching his son in his arms; the Germans shot them both. They'd been right in front of Pierino and fell back, covering him. There was absolutely no way of escaping and he was convinced he was about to die. Something whistled through his hair and he turned and fell on top of both of his sisters, Antonietta and Angelina. All three passed out; it was this that saved them. When Pierino came to, he found himself under several bodies and covered in their blood. He began to cry but then heard Domenico, still alive, urging him to be quiet. His sisters came to as well and they held each others' hands and remained where they were, not daring to move. Only when darkness fell did they finally emerge. By then Domenico di Mascio had died, along with forty-one

others, including Pierino's parents and other siblings, apart from Angelina, and the three Italian soldiers and one Greek. Needlessly murdered.
Why? To stop them talking to the Americans and approaching Moroccans? But what could these simple mountain folk tell them that was of
any value? It was so senseless, so cruel. So unnecessary.

Numbed with shock and grief, he carried Angelina, who was only
three, and together they ran, leaving the dead behind. Pierino was in a
kind of stupor; he wasn't able to think clearly or comprehend what had
happened, but they managed to reach the road near Cardito. They saw
some Germans, but now they treated them kindly and gave them bread.
'Then they put us on lorries with other civilians, mainly children,' said
Pierino, 'and we started our long journey.'

'Last day of the year,' jotted Jack Ward on Friday, 31 December, 'and it's
raining like hell in the usual way.' It was a fitting end to the year in Italy, a
campaign that had begun in a hurry but with no small amount of expectation, and which had descended into a savage storm of destruction amid
the mud, darkness and desolation of a brutal modern war in this mountainous country.

Wilhelm Mauss was feeling reflective about the year that had passed.
'It has been the most difficult one of this war for us so far,' he wrote. 'Over
it lie the dark shadows of Stalingrad, Tunis. Within it the Badoglio-Italy
cowardice that spitefully attacked us in the back.' There had been the
enormous sacrifices on the Eastern Front, the loss of the U-boat war in
the Atlantic and the burden placed on the homeland by the heavy 'terror
attacks' by Allied bombers. He was grateful to God for sparing him and
his family and he prayed He would help aid the German population and
Fatherland, its leaders and his loved ones in the future. 'Thus I once again
salute the departing year 1943,' he added, 'and will now direct my gaze
towards 1944 erect and with confidence.'

Twenty miles away, at the front, Georg Zellner was also jotting down
his final thoughts of the year. His battalion had been moved again, this
time across the Rapido to the forward positions of the Gustav Line
around Cervaro and San Vittore; this put them closer to the American
guns and patrols nearby on Sammucro and around San Pietro and Monte
Lungo. He was feeling ill with a chest infection, stomach cramps and
flatulence. It was hardly surprising; the cold, the wet, the poor diet, living
in a hole in the ground and being shelled repeatedly was not conducive

to good health. The doctor had given him a vitamin injection but so far it hadn't made any noticeable difference.

Work was going on all around him to strengthen a number of bunkers, but Zellner was almost too exhausted to care. Apart from a couple of days in Vallerotonda, he'd been on the front line since reaching the front more than a month ago. 'Plague of lice and fleas,' he had written on the 29th. 'Dead and wounded by mines. The artillery fire continues with its monotonous regularity. There is not a square metre that is not shelled. It is unbelievable what an artillery effort we are facing. And yet the front holds. The suffering is great.' Through the night and into the next day, the shelling continued: the high screech like a wind tunnel, the crash, the explosion of stone and metal, the concussion and tremor of the ground. On and on and on, relentlessly. His 9. Kompanie had received a direct hit on 30 December. More men killed and wounded. The radio out. That night he slept fitfully, then he woke and thought of home. 'And outside,' he jotted, 'rides death.'

Now it was 31 December. A young, wounded artillery officer joined them at the bunker, then lay down next to Zellner and moaned in pain. Where was the Luftwaffe? Not a sign of them, only Allied Jabos circling about. Later Zellner finally decided to take off his boots, because, he realized, an incoming shell wouldn't care if he was wearing them or not. He cursed the valley. He cursed the poets who talked of the beauty of war; if he ever met one, he swore he would punch them in the mouth. He thought of his family at home in Regensburg – his wife, his children, oblivious of the cruelty at the front. 'Cassino and Cervaro,' he wrote, 'cities and sites of horror run through my mind. And if the war were to be brought home, it would look the same there. An unthinkable thought when I compare Cassino with Regensburg. But the war would know no mercy there either.' Then he thought sadly of an incident earlier that day in the ruins of Cervaro itself. Three of his soldiers had raped a fifteen-year-old girl. 'Man becomes an animal,' he scribbled. 'The girl stood stark naked as we snatched the prey from the three men.' There had been wild, frightened desperation in her eyes, and all three of the men bore scratches and bite marks, but which had only increased their frenzy. 'Now they will probably be shot,' he added wearily. 'What is a human life, after all?'

A lieutenant from the Texan Division checks the papers of a dead German near San Pietro on 17 December 1943. The dead man's MG42 lies beside him.

Postscript

B Y THE END OF 1943, it was clear that the Italian campaign had gone horribly awry for the Allies. The long descent from the giddy optimism at the end of the Sicilian campaign in August had reached its terrible end as the Allies drew up towards the Gustav Line, the German defensive position that stretched all the way across the leg of Italy from Minturno on the Tyrrhenian coast to just north of Ortona on the Adriatic. Ever since the invasion in September, the Allies had been aiming to be in Rome by the right side of Christmas. What would follow that imagined triumph had not really been considered, but there was now a realization that the fighting in Italy could not merely be a useful stopgap before OVERLORD. It had become something bigger, more drawn-out. A greater commitment. A larger drain on resources. Everyone fighting in Italy at the end of 1943 knew, with a sense of terrible dread, that there were plenty more battles to be fought in 1944. The savage storm sweeping up through Italy would continue to blow.

The casualty figures were sobering. In Fifth Army they stood at 29,716 dead, wounded and missing since the landings at Salerno, the equivalent to two entire divisions, and more than three divisions' worth of infantry. Eighth Army had lost 6,453 men in December alone, and a similar figure to Fifth Army since September. The German 10. Armee lost 13,362 men in December. These were substantial numbers and did not include those out of the line with illness.

The end of the year marked a shift in the campaign as both sides paused for breath before the Allies launched an assault on the Gustav Line. For the Allies there was a notable change at the top. Not only did Eisenhower go, so too did his Chief of Staff, General Bedell-Smith, and also Montgomery, who had been at the helm of Eighth Army since August 1942 but was now heading back to Britain to take command of Allied land forces for Operation OVERLORD. In his place came General Sir Oliver Leese, a desert war corps commander under Monty, who signalled to Mark Clark the moment he arrived at Eighth Army HQ on that last day of the year. 'Am delighted and honoured to be serving alongside your Army,' he wrote. 'Shall be coming to see you as soon as possible.' When Leese took over, it was to find an Eighth Army battered and exhausted and in bad need of a break. So, too, was Fifth Army, but it wasn't to be given one.

Historians, for the most part, have tended to point the finger of blame for the disappointments of the Italian campaign in 1943 at the Allied commanders, and especially Alexander, Montgomery and Clark. Considering they spent much of the campaign battling with overly ambitious expectations and insufficient supplies, it is odd that they should have become the focus of incredibly harsh criticism ever since. Clark, especially, deserves far greater credit for the success of Fifth Army at Salerno and, as a novice army commander, for getting his beleaguered army as far forward as he did. Crossing the Volturno and then smashing a way through the immensely strong Bernhard Line were no small achievements bearing in mind all that was against him. He really is due for a rehabilitation of his reputation just for this part of the Italian campaign alone. And despite General Brooke's gripes about of a lack of grip, it is hard to see what Alexander could have done differently in the circumstances. It is all too easy to forget that three of the four aims of the campaign were achieved, and in quick order: Italy was forced out of the war, huge numbers of German troops were redirected to Italy, the Balkans and Greece, and the Foggia airfields were swiftly captured. Only Rome eluded them.

That wasn't the point, however. The Italian campaign had been conceived as a useful time-filler and beneficial diversionary effort ahead of OVERLORD, and that it had been viewed in such a way was dangerous, arrogant and did a great injustice to those on the Allied side who fought there. As Marshall himself had asserted back in May, committing to a campaign needed full, not half-hearted, commitment. Frustration that it was now going to run on and continue to be a drain on precious Allied resources was casting a shadow over those pre-invasion boxes that had been successfully ticked. Yet if there was a black mark against the achievements of the Allies in Italy, the finger should be pointed towards the

Combined Chiefs of Staff and at Roosevelt and Churchill. Italy was hastily conceived by committee and something of a fudge, and because of that they had been hoisted by their own petard. The Americans, especially, were critical of any mission creep, yet were guilty of doing just that with their expansion of the strategic air forces in Italy. The successes of the summer of 1943 had encouraged a degree of hubris at the top and a lack of clear-headed thinking, which in turn led directly to the ruins of San Pietro and mud and mire of Ortona.

Historians have marvelled at the willingness of the Germans to keep fighting, but they had little choice in the matter and had the threat of instant execution to keep them sticking to it. The Allied troops, on the other hand, would not have been shot for desertion, and I continue to be in awe of how they kept going. Why should a Texan boy be fighting up a mountain in a desolate corner of Italy? Or a New Zealander be wading across the icy Sangro? It is astonishing that they did so. The lot of the infantryman in Italy was simply appalling. Casualty rates in this campaign were worse, on average, than they ever had been in the First World War. Of the forty or so front-line combatants in Italy I have talked to over the years, just one survived unscathed. It makes me shudder to think about it.

On the other hand, the Germans have been rather lauded for their heroic defence and dogged determination to keep fighting to the last man. In fact for the most part, German commanders, and Kesselring especially, managed their forces poorly, eschewing lessons of concentration of force and allowing divisions to be chewed up to the point of annihilation over and over again. It was true that they lacked air power and the number of guns the Allies enjoyed, but they variously had greater amounts of manpower in Italy and superb defensive terrain. Kesselring and his commanders could – and should – have handled their armies better even with the control freakery of Hitler hovering over their shoulder. Kesselring is often seen as something of a 'good' German – smiling Albert, who was just an honest soldier trying to do his best. History has been too generous to him; he commanded in Italy with utter ruthlessness, as the first months of the war there amply demonstrated.

Most of those who feature in this account then found themselves embroiled in the ongoing battle that unfolded into 1944. Of the Americans, these include Bill Darby, Roswell Doughty, Frank Pearce, Bud Wagner and Audie Murphy, as well as the airmen Smoky Vrilakas and T. Michael Sullivan. Jim Reed was rotated back to the States before Christmas 1943 and so survived the war. I interviewed Jim at some length in 2003, and fascinating to chat with he was too.

Of the DUKE servicemen, most also had further battles to fight: whether political, as was the case for Harold Macmillan; in the realm of civil affairs, as Norman Lewis was to experience; out at sea, as for Peter Bull; in the air – Cocky Dundas was not finished in Italy yet – or in the mountains and misery of the ground war, as was the case for David Cole, Roger Smith, Farley Mowat, Roy Durnford, Lawrie Franklyn-Vaile, Harry Wilson and Jack Ward. Ward's diary, which he kept almost every day during 1943 and would keep going as the New Year dawned, appears to have been largely written for his wife. It came up for sale in 2022 at Blackwell's Rare Books and so, after taking a deep breath, I bought it. At the time of my blind purchase I had no idea whether it was going to reveal much, but I need not have worried because his character emerges very clearly on every page – a thoughtful, rather gentle and highly observant middle-aged man, taking the privations and levels of destruction and death he witnessed with stoic fortitude. Harry Wilson's diary lies in the Imperial War Museum archives, and although he was not charging into battle he was an extraordinary witness to the war – both its awfulness and its absurdities. Sadly, the IWM have no details at all about him, so all that is left remain his words – but very rich and enlightening words they are.

Christopher Bulteel never returned to the war, and later became a highly successful and regarded headmaster. Peter Moore returned to his battalion in the summer of 1944 and fought all the way through to the end of the war. David Helme was badly wounded in the head early in 1944, but later rejoined his battalion in Italy. Post-war, he went to Oxford, got his degree and spent most of his professional career working for Lloyds of London. Peter Davis survived the war, later settling in South Africa. In 1994, aged seventy-four, he was shot dead at his home in a case that has never been solved. After safely sailing back to England, Bertie Packer became Chief of Staff to the C-in-C of the Mediterranean Fleet and post-war commanded the 2nd Cruiser Squadron before becoming Fourth Sea Lord in 1948, for which he was knighted. He retired to South Africa as a full admiral in 1953 but died in 1962 aged just sixty-seven.

Quent Reynolds continued as a journalist after the war and later became a television presenter. He also famously sued a right-wing Hearst journalist, Westbrook Pegler, for calling him 'yellow' and an 'absentee war correspondent' and won the case, but died aged only sixty-two, from cancer, in 1965. Alan Moorehead later reported on the war in north-west Europe, and post-war continued in journalism but also wrote a number of highly acclaimed histories, biographies and travel books. He died aged seventy-three in 1983. Ernie Pyle covered D-Day and the Normandy campaign but, tragically, was killed by a Japanese machine-gunner in Okinawa in April 1945.

Many of the Germans also found themselves trapped in Italy at the start of 1944; Wilhelm Mauss, Georg Zellner, Hans Golda and Jupp Klein were all still at the front. Getting an accurate picture of what and how German combatants were thinking can be challenging because post-war memories were often understandably distorted. Reading their remarkably honest thoughts, as they wrote them on the day in question, has been revelatory in many ways, clearly showing the conflicted nature of their part in a war that they all knew was going badly wrong. Fear of what would happen back home should the war be lost was a clear motivator. Gerhard Waag and Robert Gugelberger also survived, as did Siegfried Bähr and Werner Mork and also Martin Pöppel, who after recovering from his nasty wound went on to serve in Normandy. Hermann Balck later became a field marshal and emerged from the war with his reputation as a superb military commander intact.

Of the Italians, the diaries of Lina Caruso, Filippo Caracciolo and Dom Eusebio Grossetti also continued to be written as the war in Italy bludgeoned its way into January. Eugenio Corti remained in the army, while in San Pietro Antonia Masella greeted the New Year in the rubble of her home and with her husband, Serafino, still in hospital. Benedetto and Enrichetta Pagano's war was far from over: in January 1944 Enrichetta stood on a mine that had not yet been cleared, lost her leg and soon after her life before Benedetto, hurrying from the ruins of the village, could reach her. Generale Carboni was allowed to live freely, although his military career was over. After the war he was vilified for his actions in Rome around the time of the armistice but was acquitted. He does, I think, deserve a more balanced and nuanced assessment. He died in 1973.

The war in Italy is largely forgotten today, except for the battles of Cassino and at Anzio, which were to follow in the first half of 1944. Who remembers Ortona now, or the Volturno? Or even Salerno, that astonishingly high-risk venture? All that pain, all that misery, all that destruction has become a footnote, as though it barely happened at all. Does it matter, though, that this part of the war in Italy has been pushed into the shadows?

Well, I rather think it does. At the time of writing, another European war has been raging and tales and images of that conflict are eerily and tragically similar to what happened in Italy in 1943: the villages and towns destroyed, the extreme violence, the blackened hulks and the countless lives turned upside down and ruined forever. History does not repeat itself, but patterns of human behaviour do and lessons from the past need to be learned. Was the anguish of Georg Zellner, Lawrie Franklyn-Vaile and Farley Mowat really for nothing?

I have been studying the long and terrible Second World War for some years now, but nothing has moved me in quite such a profound way as researching and writing this book. Perhaps it's because, for the first time, I've used mostly contemporary sources: diaries, letters, signals and memoranda, and photographs taken in a split second. Rather than hearing the memories of those times fifty, sixty or even seventy years on, my cast of very real characters have been drawn from the testimonies they recorded at the time. I have deliberately tried to avoid any forward projection and to write purely in the moments, hours and days in which the events described were taking place. None of those writing diaries and letters knew when Rome would fall. None of them knew when the war would end. I have found it difficult not to be swept up in their experiences, their suffering, their anxieties, their fears, and it has been impossible not to care about their fates. For me, these men and women, long dead most of them, have come very much back to life, their characters bursting off the pages of what they wrote and recorded. It's been fascinating and rewarding, and I hope that anyone who reads this book will find themselves similarly drawn to these people, who, despite living through experiences that took place many years ago, still feel achingly familiar in many of their thoughts, feelings and fears. The past is not such a foreign country after all; or rather, certainly not when looking at the Second World War.

The terrible tragedy for Italy and all those who found themselves caught up in this campaign was that by the beginning of 1944 it still had fifteen very long months to run. The massacre of Vallerotonda would be repeated elsewhere, more villages and towns would be razed to the ground, many more soldiers and servicemen would be killed and wounded in the mud, rain, heat, dust, snow and ice of a second summer and winter, and although the German forces in Italy would be the first to unconditionally surrender to the Allies, that would not happen until 2 May 1945.

So what had been entered into as a short, limited campaign for some quick but rich rewards turned into exactly the long-drawn-out and bloody brutal battle that General Marshall had feared but had none the less sanctioned. Only by looking at those first months, however, and the descent into awful attrition to which it so quickly fell does the rest of this long war in Italy start to make any sense.

In many ways, Wilhelm Mauss was right when he sat outside his tent in early October 1943 gazing at the loveliness of the mountains and the valley at the Mignano Gap. Nature has woven its magic, the area is as stunning and lovely as he described it, the scars of war long gone and the terrible battles that raged there for the most part, but not entirely, forgotten. San Pietro Infine, for example, was never lived in again. Not really. Instead, a new village was built afresh a little lower down, closer to the main road and railway line, and so the remains of the old village stand there, still broken, even more tumbledown, trees and ivy crawling through the stonework and rooms where for so many centuries the Sanpietresi lived, loved, laughed, cried and died. It's a haunting, melancholy place to walk around, but visit the other side of the valley, climb the road to Camino, and one is given a sense of what San Pietro must have been like with its narrow, winding cobbled streets and alleyways and houses so close they almost touch.

Touring around the battlefields today, though, it's impossible not to feel a mixture of awe and wistfulness. Standing in Sant'Elia, for example, 2,000 feet above sea level, where the Hasty Ps exchanged shots with the retreating Fallschirmjäger, it's hard not to wonder about the madness of fighting in this mountainous country. It's so remote, even today. So too is Ortona, for that matter. The Moro Valley is lovely now, the terrible desolation long gone, and covered with vineyards, olive groves and fecundity, distant bells chiming. San Leonardo has been rebuilt and, like so many villages and towns utterly destroyed by the war, has lost the charm it must have once had, but Casa Berardi looks much the same, no longer battle-scarred, while the 'Cider' crossroads has become a roundabout with a Sherman tank plonked in the middle. Ortona itself still has a few scars for those who know where to look but otherwise it is a small, attractive coastal town, rebuilt, mostly in its original style, expanded, naturally, and with very little to suggest it was once a scene of such terrible violence.

In the heart of the town, however, and under the shadow of the beautifully rebuilt cathedral there is a small, triangular open area, the Piazza degli Eroi Canadesi. A Canadian maple leaf has been created on the ground, but at the edge of two roads stands a memorial, a bronze sculpture of a Canadian medic crouching beside a fallen soldier. The wounded man has an arm outstretched and his tin hat has fallen from his head. It's a beautiful work of art, heart-rending and profoundly moving. There is no glorification of war here, no triumphalism, just a scene of deeply touching pathos. As I looked at it, walking around and gazing at the sculpture, I found myself thinking of Alex Campbell, that great brave bear of a man, dying less than a mile from this spot, and of Farley Mowat and Roy Durnford, but also of the many other combatants from so many nationalities who had somehow, in the great stirred-up soup pot of war, found themselves battling through this land; and I thought, too, of those civilians whose lives were tossed up into the air and spun around in this terrible, savage storm. Guns were booming elsewhere in Europe as I stood there in the warmth of that October day, and it was impossible not to shed a tear for all those lost and broken lives, then – and now.

And so, I did.

APPENDIX I

Timeline of Events

1943

August ————————————————————————

TUESDAY, 17
Axis evacuation of Sicily complete
Short Terms agreed as basis for surrender negotiations for Italy
Report arrives from Madrid of Italian desire to surrender
Allied air forces attacking targets in southern Italy

WEDNESDAY, 18
Post-HUSKY plans approved

THURSDAY, 19
General Bedell-Smith arrives in Lisbon for talks with Generale Castellano
9th AF B-17s hit Foggia airfields
Medium bombers raid Sapri and Salerno

FRIDAY, 20
17th and 320th BGs hit marshalling yards at Caserta

SATURDAY, 21
B-26s of 319th and 320th BGs hit railyards at Villa Literno

SUNDAY, 22
Bombers target marshalling yards at Salerno

MONDAY, 23
B-26s raid Battipaglia

WEDNESDAY, 25
Major Allied bombing raids on Foggia complex
Zanussi arrives in Lisbon

THURSDAY, 26
Medium bombers attack Grazzanise and Cancello

FRIDAY, 27
Sixty-eight B-17s attack Sulmona and mediums attack the marshalling yards at Benevento and Caserta
Generale Castellano returns to Rome with Short Terms

SATURDAY, 28
Bomber attacks on Sardinia and Terni

SUNDAY, 29
Bomber attacks on marshalling yards at Torre Annunziata

MONDAY, 30
Bomber attacks on marshalling yards at Civitavecchia and Viterbo, and also other targets in southern Italy, including Catanzaro and Aversa
Final revision of Operation ACHSE
16. Panzer arrives near Salerno

TUESDAY, 31
Bomber attacks on marshalling yards at Pisa, Cosenza and Catanzaro
Castellano arrives for final negotiations at Alex's HQ

September

WEDNESDAY, 1
Badoglio accepts principle of Short Terms

THURSDAY, 2
B-17s attack marshalling yards at Bologna

FRIDAY, 3
4.30 p.m. Italians sign armistice
Operation BAYTOWN
XIII Corps of Eighth Army crosses Straits of Messina
B-24s raid Sulmona marshalling yards
Air forces covering Eighth Army's crossing of Messina Straits

SATURDAY, 4
Conferences at Alexander's HQ
Eighth Army moving inland

SUNDAY, 5
Cancello airfield heavily hit by 150 bombers
Allied bombing operations continue

MONDAY, 6
Italian Five Parties Meeting in Milan

TUESDAY, 7
Congress of Italian Five Parties in Florence
Cancello hit again – fourteenth 'Reich Party Day'
Brigadier-General Maxwell Taylor's secret mission to Rome

WEDNESDAY, 8
Italian armistice announced
11.30 p.m. minesweeping of channels to beaches begins off Salerno

THURSDAY, 9
Operation AVALANCHE
Uncle Sector Beaches: 46th Division
Sugar Sector Beaches: 56th Division
Allied landings at Salerno
0121 Enemy shore batteries open fire – *LST-357* hit with fifty casualties
0130 LCAs for Sugar Sector lowered
0145 Uncle Sector lowering position
0203 Rangers and Commandos in landing craft
0213 Rangers head to shore
0215 Naval barrage at Uncle Sector
0217 Commandos head to shore
0225 Sweeping of channels completed
0245 Uncle Sector force told to proceed
0315 Second destroyer barrage in Uncle Sector
0317 Naval barrage of Sugar Sector begins
0320 First Rangers landing craft touch down
0330 H-Hour – Commandos touch down
0333 LCRs fire rocket salvos
0335 First LCAs touch down on Roger Sector
0340 First men of 56th Division touch down on Sugar Sector
0630 CS15 arrives for offshore bombardment

Operation SLAPSTICK
Taranto occupied by 4th Parachute Battalion

Operation ACHSE begins
King Vittorio Emanuele and Badoglio flee Rome

FRIDAY, 10
German evacuation of Sardinia and Corsica begins
Salerno reinforced
Popular insurrection in Rome

SATURDAY, 11
Rome in German hands
XIV and LXXVI Panzerkorps hurried to Salerno
10 a.m. USS *Savannah* hit by Fritz X in Gulf of Salerno

SUNDAY, 12
Salerno battle
A.m. General Clark moves HQ to shore
Noon German counter-attack on Altavilla
USS *Boise* arrives to replace *Savannah*
Mussolini sprung from the Gran Sasso by Germans

MONDAY, 13
Salerno battle
6.30 a.m. 143rd Infantry attack launched on Altavilla
8 a.m. von Vietinghoff and Balck conference
1st and 2nd Battalions 504th PIR jump near Salerno
General Dawley considering evacuation of VI Corps
ABC orders cruisers *Aurora* and *Penelope* to Salerno
1.30 p.m. German counter-attack launched
4 p.m. German attack on 157th Infantry
2/143rd destroyed
5 p.m. 15. Panzergrenadier attack on Altavilla
5.30 p.m. Germans nearing coast in centre of line
6.30 p.m. Sieckenius and Herr planning encirclement around Paestum

TUESDAY, 14
0030 Germans attack 201st Guards Brigade
8 a.m. German command conference
Salerno battle German counter-attack
ABC orders cruisers to help transport troops
Warspite and *Valiant* ordered to Salerno

Overnight 2,100 men of 505th PIR dropped at Paestum
Overnight 2/509th PIR dropped near Avellino
Overnight HG-Division attack led by Schmalz against 128th Brigade

WEDNESDAY, 15
Salerno battle
German counter-attack against Americans fizzles out
Warspite and *Valiant* arrive
1 p.m. HG-Division take Point 419
4 p.m. two Schmalz Gruppe attacks checked
General Alexander visits beachhead
Leading units from Eighth and Fifth Armies link up south of Salerno beachhead

THURSDAY, 16
Salerno battle
6 a.m. Panzergrenadiers attack against 201st Guards Brigade
3 p.m. Schmalz Gruppe attacks again
Mutiny at Salerno by men of 50th and 51st Divisions
General von Vietinghoff accepts defeat at Salerno
2.10 p.m. HMS *Warspite* hit by Fritz X
Evening 504th PIR dropped near Altavilla
Evening von Vietinghoff's appreciation

FRIDAY, 17
End of Salerno battle
6.15 a.m. Kesselring authorizes retreat to Volturno

SATURDAY, 18
A.m. AOK 10 begins withdrawal from Salerno area

SUNDAY, 19
Allies pushing out of beachhead

MONDAY, 20
Dawley sacked as VI Corps commander
VI Corps drive towards Oliveto and Acerno

TUESDAY, 21
Alexander's First Plans for winter in Italy

WEDNESDAY, 22
Bari occupied by Eighth Army

THURSDAY, 23
Fifth Army advance from Salerno begins

FRIDAY, 24
Eighth Army crosses River Ofanto

SATURDAY, 25
X Corps pushing beyond Cava de' Tirreni

SUNDAY, 26
VI Corps thirty miles inland

MONDAY, 27
Foggia and surrounding airfields captured by Eighth Army

TUESDAY, 28
First major rainfall and heavy winds

WEDNESDAY, 29
Eighth Army reaches River Fortore
Rain

THURSDAY, 30
Rain
Avellino captured by US 3rd Division

October

FRIDAY, 1
Naples falls to Fifth Army
Early October Germans occupy San Pietro Infine
Alexander begins review of strategy
16. Panzer ordered eastwards to bolster 1. Fallschirmjäger-Division

SUNDAY, 3
Battle of Termoli
SRS and Commando force land at Termoli

16. Panzer sent to Termoli
11th Infantry Brigade crossing Biferno to south of Termoli

NIGHT, 3–4
36 Infantry Brigade unloading at Termoli

MONDAY, 4
Rain
Battle of Termoli
Hitler orders Kesselring to hold Italy south of Rome

TUESDAY, 5
Battle of Termoli
Fifth Army reaches River Volturno
Catastrophe for SRS in Termoli

WEDNESDAY, 6
Battle of Termoli
16. Panzer falls back to River Trigno

THURSDAY, 7
Rain

SATURDAY, 9
Rain
45th Division first attack on Volturno
2nd New Zealand Division lands at Taranto

SUNDAY, 10
Allies operating from Capodichino airfield near Naples

MONDAY, 11
Rain

TUESDAY, 12
Fifth Army crossing River Volturno

WEDNESDAY, 13
Fifth Army crossing River Volturno
Italians declare war on Germany

THURSDAY, 14
Rain
Fifth Army crossing River Volturno
Oberstleutnant Schlegel visits Monte Cassino and tells the Father Abbot that
the front line will pass through the abbey

FRIDAY, 15
Fifth Army crossing River Volturno
Eighth Army reaches Vinchiaturo

SATURDAY, 16
Rain

SUNDAY, 17
Rain

MONDAY, 18
Harold Macmillan persuades Eisenhower to propose Advisory Council for Italy

TUESDAY, 19
Holy relics of Monte Cassino abbey handed over to Germans

WEDNESDAY, 20
Delayed-action bombs left by Germans detonating in Naples
Germans retreat across River Biferno

FRIDAY, 22
Eighth Army crossing River Trigno

SATURDAY, 23
Luftwaffe air raid on Naples

SUNDAY, 24
General Hube leaves Italy

MONDAY, 25
Fifth Army pushing northwards

WEDNESDAY, 27
Discussions in Bari between Italians and Allies

THURSDAY, 28
Rain
Generalleutnant Fridolin von Senger und Etterlin takes command of XIV
Panzerkorps

FRIDAY, 29
Allied bombers in North Africa bomb Turin

SATURDAY, 30
British 5th Division attacking towards Isernia
Further bombing of Turin

SUNDAY, 31
OKW issues summary of Italian treachery

November

MONDAY, 1
US Fifteenth Air Force activated
Fifth Army fifteen to twenty miles north of River Volturno

TUESDAY, 2
Luftwaffe bombs Naples

WEDNESDAY, 3
1st Armored Division arriving in Naples

THURSDAY, 4
Germans start pulling back to Gustav Line on Adriatic Coast

FRIDAY, 5
First Battle of Camino

SATURDAY, 6
First Battle of Camino

SUNDAY, 7
Rain
First Battle of Camino
Luftwaffe air raid over Naples

MONDAY, 8
Heavy rain
First Battle of Camino
Eighth Army reaches River Sangro

TUESDAY, 9
First Battle of Camino

WEDNESDAY, 10
First Battle of Camino
Allied Control Commission officially starts
26. Panzer switched to western side of the leg

THURSDAY, 11
First Battle of Camino

FRIDAY, 12
First Battle of Camino
Heavy shelling in Liri Valley

SATURDAY, 13
First Battle of Camino

SUNDAY, 14
First Battle of Camino
Monte Rotondo taken by Americans
Heavy storm in night

MONDAY, 15
First Battle of Camino
Heavy storms
36th Division returns to Fifth Army front

TUESDAY, 16
Fifth Army preparing to attack Bernhard Line

WEDNESDAY, 17
US 3rd Division pulled out of the line

THURSDAY, 18
Most of 82nd Airborne Division starts shipping to UK

FRIDAY, 19
Eighth Army preliminary operations over Sangro
First frostbite cases on XIV Panzerkorps front

SATURDAY, 20
Heavy rain halts Eighth Army operations
Germans blow up railway lines and railway bridge at Cassino
Cable car wires from Cassino to Monte Cassino cut by Germans

NIGHT, 20–21
Eighth Army patrols across Sangro

SUNDAY, 21
Kesselring confirmed as Oberbefehlshaber Süd
First attack on Fascists in Rome by GAP partisans

MONDAY, 22
Sextant Conference starts in Cairo
Fifteenth Air Force HQ starts moving to Foggia

TUESDAY, 23
Sextant Conference continues
Bad weather continues to hamper Eighth Army operations

WEDNESDAY, 24
Sextant Conference continues
German demolitions in Cassino continue

THURSDAY, 25
Sextant Conference continues
26. Panzer and 90. Panzergrenadier move to Adriatic
Thanksgiving Day in US
Civilians sheltering at the abbey of Monte Cassino taken by the Germans
44. Infanterie-Division reaches front near Cassino

FRIDAY, 26
Sextant Conference ends

SATURDAY, 27
Night – Eighth Army assaults River Sangro

SUNDAY, 28
Eureka Conference begins in Tehran
Battle of Sangro

MONDAY, 29
Eureka Conference continues
Battle of Sangro
New Zealanders take Castelfrentano

TUESDAY, 30
Eureka Conference continues
Battle of Sangro

December

WEDNESDAY, 1
Eureka Conference closes
Battle of Sangro
Turin bombed by Allies

THURSDAY, 2
Operation RAINCOAT – Second Battle of Camino
Battle of Sangro

FRIDAY, 3
Battle of Sangro
Operation RAINCOAT – Second Battle of Camino
Eighth Army pushing north towards River Moro
New Zealanders attempt to capture Orsogna
Fifteenth Air Force HQ move to Foggia complete

SATURDAY, 4
Wet and cold
Operation RAINCOAT – Second Battle of Camino
Germans flood Rapido Valley
General Freyberg calls off attack on Orsogna

SUNDAY, 5
Sunny morning
Battle of Sangro
Operation RAINCOAT – Second Battle of Camino

Italian 1st Motorized Group attack southern end of Monte Lungo but are repulsed
Canadians take over positions of 78th Division on southern side of River Moro

MONDAY, 6
Operation RAINCOAT – Second Battle of Camino
Ortona – Canadians cross the Moro and capture Villa Rogatti
Seaforth Highlanders with narrow bridgehead at San Leonardo
Hasty Ps attacking further east
8th Indians take over Villa Rogatti

TUESDAY, 7
Operation RAINCOAT – Second Battle of Camino
Germans decide to give up Monte Camino
Renewed American attack on Monte Lungo and against San Pietro
5. Gebirgsjäger reaches front
Ortona – General Vokes issues orders for further crossing of the River Moro

WEDNESDAY, 8
Operation RAINCOAT – Second Battle of Camino
Ortona battle
Summit of Monte Sammucro captured by 36th Division

THURSDAY, 9
Operation RAINCOAT – Second Battle of Camino
Ortona battle

FRIDAY, 10
Operation RAINCOAT – Camino and Monte La Difensa taken and cleared
Ortona battle

SATURDAY, 11
Churchill ill with pneumonia in Carthage
Ortona battle

SUNDAY, 12
Germans agree a 300-metre no-fire zone around abbey of Monte Cassino
Ortona battle

MONDAY, 13
Battle of San Pietro
Ortona battle

TUESDAY, 14
Churchill critically ill in Carthage
Night – assault on northern side of Monte Sammucro by 143rd Infantry
Ortona battle

WEDNESDAY, 15
143rd Infantry unable to clear all of Sammucro
Renewed assault by New Zealanders on Orsogna – ends in failure
Night – Texans attack Monte Lungo
Casa Berardi captured by Canadians south of Ortona

THURSDAY, 16
Morning – 142nd Infantry clear Monte Lungo
7.15 p.m. AOK 10 authorizes retreat to Ortona

FRIDAY, 17
Monte Sammucro falls to Americans
San Pietro captured by Americans
Brief pause in fighting at Ortona

SATURDAY, 18
Clark advises the cancellation of Operation SHINGLE
Ortona battle renewed

SUNDAY, 19
Fifteenth Air Force bombs Augsburg
Continued fighting south of Ortona

MONDAY, 20
'Cider' crossroads finally captured west of Ortona
Battle of Ortona town begins
Orsogna bombed

TUESDAY, 21
Battle of Ortona town

WEDNESDAY, 22
Battle of Ortona town
Churchill much better

THURSDAY, 23
Battle of Ortona town

FRIDAY, 24
Battle of Ortona town

SATURDAY, 25
Christmas Day
Churchill conferring with commanders about future operations
Battle of Ortona town

SUNDAY, 26
Cold and wet
Battle of Ortona town

MONDAY, 27
Battle of Ortona town

TUESDAY, 28
Battle of Ortona town ends – Germans pull back
Vallerotonda massacre at Collelungo
President Roosevelt agrees to retention of shipping in Mediterranean until
5 February 1944

THURSDAY, 30
General Montgomery hands over Eighth Army to Lieutenant-General Oliver
Leese

FRIDAY, 31
Last day of year with Fifth Army drawing up to Gustav Line and Eighth Army
north of Ortona

General Sir Harold Alexander gives a briefing to war correspondents on 23 October 1943.

APPENDIX II

Order of Battle: Allied and German Armies at the Beginning of December 1943

Allies

US FIFTH ARMY
General Mark Clark

US VI CORPS
Lieutenant-General John Lucas

34th 'Red Bulls' Division
45th 'Thunderbirds' Division
2e Division d'Infanterie Marocaine

US II CORPS
Lieutenant-General Geoffrey Keyes

36th 'Texas' Division

BRITISH X CORPS
Lieutenant-General Richard McCreery

46th Division
56th Division

ARMY TROOPS
US 3rd Division
US 1st Armored Division

BRITISH EIGHTH ARMY
General Sir Bernard Montgomery

V CORPS
Lieutenant-General Charles Allfrey

2nd New Zealand Division
8th Indian Division
78th 'Battleaxe' Division

XIII CORPS
Lieutenant-General Sir Miles Dempsey

1st Canadian Division
5th Division

TOTAL: thirteen divisions

German

AOK 10
Generaloberst Heinrich von Vietinghoff

LXXVI PANZERKORPS
General Traugott Herr

65. Infanterie-Division
26. Panzer-Division
1. Fallschirmjäger-Division
90. Panzergrenadier-Division

XIV PANZERKORPS
Generalleutnant Fridolin von Senger und Etterlin

305. Infanterie-Division
44. 'Hoch-und-Deutschmeister' Infanterie-Division
29. Panzergrenadier-Division
15. Panzergrenadier-Division
94. Infanterie-Division

XI FALLSCHIRMJÄGER KORPS

Hermann Göring Panzer-Division
3. Panzergrenadier-Division

AOK 14
Generaloberst Eberhard von Mackensen

ADRIA-KOMMANDO

16. Turkistan Infanterie-Division
71. Infanterie-Division
371. Infanterie-Division

LI GEBIRGSJÄGER KORPS
Generalleutnant Valentin Feurstein

278. Infanterie-Division
188. Gebirgsjäger-Division

LXXXVII KORPS
Generalleutnant Gustav-Adolf von Zangen

356. Infanterie-Division
334. Infanterie-Division

IN PROCESS OF ARRIVING IN ITALY

4. Fallschirmjäger-Division
16. SS-Panzergrenadier-Division
362. Infanterie-Division

TOTAL: eighteen divisions plus three arriving

ROMA ← NAPOLI
Km.192 Km.38

Two Tommies digging in at the side of a road in the Volturno Valley, the road sign a reminder of just how far they still had to go to reach Rome.

Notes

Abbreviations used in notes

BA-MA   Bundesarchiv-Militärarchiv, Freiburg

FMS   Foreign Military Studies, US Army Heritage and Education Center, Carlisle, PA

NHB   Naval Historical Branch, Portsmouth

TNA   The National Archives, Kew

USAHEC   United States Army Heritage and Education Center

WSC   Winston Spencer Churchill

1 The Burning Blue

17   'The training here . . .': Arnold to Spaatz, 20/8/1943, Spaatz Papers

17   'If we can establish . . .': Spaatz to Arnold, 24/6/1943, ibid.

17   'I am confident . . .': Spaatz to Arnold, 14/7/1943, ibid.

18   'This has become standard . . .': Gerhard Waag Diary, 26/8/1943, cited in Jochen Prien, *Jagdgeschwader 53: A History of the 'Pik As' Geschwader May 1942–January 1944*, p. 672

18   'It was horrible to watch': Gerhard Waag Diary, 27/8/1943, cited in ibid., p. 672

23   'I sat quietly . . .': Robert A. 'Smoky' Vrilakas, *Look Mom – I Can Fly!*, p. 107

2 Conundrums

24   'What most scares me . . .': Pasqualina Caruso, *Vivere per raccontare, diario di guerra 1940–1945*, 4/9/1943

25   'Lord, Lord . . .': ibid.

25   'By now, Italy is a land . . .': ibid.

27   'I knew that the King . . .': Pietro Badoglio, *Italy in the Second World War*, p. 42

29   'The war continues . . .': cited in Militärgeschichtliches Forschungsamt, *Germany and the Second World War*, Vol. VIII, p. 1117

33   'The fearful price . . .': Winston Churchill, *The Second World War*, Vol. V, p. 514

34   'The wish might have been . . .': cited in Robert W. Coakley and Richard
      M. Leighton, *Global Logistics and Strategy, 1943–1945*, p. 66
34   'The only limit . . .': General Marshall in *Trident Conference Papers and
      Minutes of Meetings*, p. 327
34   'Why should we . . .': cited in Michael Howard, *Grand Strategy*, Vol. IV,
      p. 502
35   'boldness and taking . . .': ibid., p. 503
35   'All being said and done . . .': WSC to Alexander, 22/7/1943, Alexander
      Papers, TNA WO 214
35   'The moment is now approaching . . .': Churchill, Vol. V, p. 35
38   'Where is Mussolini?': cited in Harry C. Butcher, *My Three Years with
      Eisenhower*, p. 337
40   'maintenance of unremitting . . .': TNA CAB 121/154
41   'it looks as if . . .': cited in F. H. Hinsley, *British Intelligence in the Second
      World War*, Vol. 3, Part 1, p. 107
42   'C-in-C South-East has given . . .': cited in Walter Warlimont, *Inside
      Hitler's Headquarters 1939–45*, p. 371
42   'Kesselring hasn't got the reputation . . .': ibid., p. 364
43   'a game of cops and robbers': ibid., p. 373
44   'destruction measures': cited in *Germany and the Second World War*, Vol.
      VIII, p. 1119

3 At General Clark's HQ

51   'old fashioned': Mark Clark Diary, 4/8/1943
51   'It is obvious . . .': ibid.
51   'The question remains . . .': ibid.
52   'I feel very strongly . . .': Alfred D. Chandler Jr. (ed.), *The Papers of Dwight
      David Eisenhower*, Vol. II, No. 1174, p. 1324
52   'It would be better . . .': cited in Mark Clark Diary, 11/8/1943
54   'Great opportunities lie ahead . . .': ibid., 30/8/1943

4 BAYTOWN

56   'Today is Sunday . . .': David Cole, *Rough Road to Rome*, p. 84
56   'Now at last . . .': ibid.
57   'enjoy a period . . .': Farley Mowat, *And No Birds Sang*, p. 145
57   'It seemed to us . . .': ibid., p. 147
57   'You should see all the boys . . .': Alex Campbell, letter to Mary, September
      1943, 58A1 281.3, Canadian War Museum
58   'Reveille sounded . . .': RG24 15073, Library and Archives of Canada
58   'Just a short line . . .': Alex Campbell, letter to Sarah Campbell, 1
      September 1943
58   'Will Tedeschi . . ?': Mowat, p. 151
60   'The confusion and folly . . .': Harold Macmillan Diary, 26/8/1944
63   'Good morning . . .': Field Marshal Alexander, interview with Sidney
      Matthews, USAHEC

63   'Why, there must be some mistake! . . .': ibid.
64   'Then they ran screaming . . .': Alan Moorehead, *Eclipse*, p. 24
64   'A kind of upward . . .': ibid., p. 25
69   'One had the impression . . .': ibid., p. 27
70   'Toiling up the mountain . . .': Cole, p. 88

5 Uncertainty

72   'A brief flash . . .': Robert Gugelberger Diary, 29/8/1943 in Prien, p. 674
72   'A hole three metres . . .': Robert Gugelberger Diary, 1/9/1943, ibid.,
       p. 676
73   'I had far exceeded . . .': Robert Gugelberger Diary, 4/9/1943, ibid., p. 681
73   'Unable to land . . .': Robert Gugelberger Diary, ibid., p. 682
75   'As a foolish prophecy . . .': Bertie Packer Diary, 3/9/1943
77   'Tell your section . . .': cited in Peter Davis, *SAS: Men in the Making*, p. 129
77   'Now get cracking . . .': ibid., p. 131
78   'I honestly do not . . .': ibid., p. 135
79   '*The cunning devils . . .*': ibid., p. 139
80   'Everyone seems cheerful . . .': Filippo Caracciolo Diary, 4/9/1943 in
       Filippo Caracciolo, *43/44 Diario di Napoli*
81   'You know, sir . . .': Peter Davis, p. 158
82   'Whatever we do . . .': Martin Pöppel Diary, 23/8/1943 in Martin Pöppel,
       Heaven & Hell: The War Diary of a German Paratrooper
83   'A real Strength Through Joy . . .': ibid., 4/9/1943
83   'But these Italian . . .': ibid.
85   'As always in these times . . .': ibid., 5/9/1943
85   'Cordial farewell . . .': ibid., 6/9/1943

6 Mistrust

86   'ticklish business': Alexander, interview with Sidney Matthews, USAHEC
86   'But of course . . .': ibid.
87   'From confidential information . . .': Howard, *Grand Strategy*, Vol. IV, p. 531
90   'I know you wish . . .': cited in Peter Tompkins, *Italy Betrayed*, p. 149
94   'By D + 7 . . .': ACNS(F) Telegrams, Operation AVALANCHE, NHB
94   'How do you like our plan?': cited in Quentin Reynolds, *The Curtain Rises*,
       p. 281
94   'We may get hurt . . .': ibid.
95   'Apprehensive?': ibid., p. 282
96   'If I announce . . .': cited in Tompkins, *Italy Betrayed*, p. 165
96   'You seem to fear . . .': ibid.
97   'Let's hope . . .': cited in ibid., p. 167

7 Bluffing

98   'I was considered an Italophile . . .': FMS C-103, p. 12
103   'We do our best,': Harold Macmillan Diary, 8/9/1943
104   'It only remained . . .': ibid.

104   'As you gentlemen know . . .': cited in Tompkins, *Italy Betrayed*, p. 175
104   'Failure on your part . . .': Howard, *Grand Strategy*, Vol. V, p. 532
104   'There is no doubt . . .': Tompkins, *Italy Betrayed*, p. 176
105   'We are fucked . . .': cited in ibid., p. 178
105   'Italian troops . . .': AOK 10, Kriegstagebuch, 8/9/1943
106   'If we act . . .': cited in Tompkins, *Italy Betrayed*, p. 179
106   'They say that Radio London . . .': Pasqualina Caruso Diary, 8/9/1943
106   'Joy overflowed from our hearts . . .': ibid.
106   'His voice trembles . . .': Filippo Caracciolo Diary, 8/9/1943
107   'I finally feel it . . .': ibid.
107   'I can only say . . .': Harold Macmillan Diary, 8/9/1943
107   'the biggest bluff in history': ibid., 9/9/1943
107   'Initial operations . . .': ACNS(F) Signals, NHB

8 AVALANCHE
112   'In this spot . . .': Herbert Rocholl Diary, cited in Moorehead, p. 45
112   'At first the news . . .': Herbert Rocholl Diary, cited in ibid., p. 44
113   'They threw their weapons . . .': ibid.
113   'So what now?': Bertie Packer Diary, 8/9/1943
113   'Our low barrages . . .': ibid.
113   'One sod dropped . . .': ibid.
114   'General Quarters . . .': cited in Quentin Reynolds, p. 292
114   'We could see . . .': cited in Moorehead, p. 46
118   'At writing this . . .': Mark Clark Diary, 9/9/1943
121   'The finest compass . . .': William O. Darby with William H, Baumer, *Darby's Rangers*, p. 138
122   'But fortunately . . .': cited in Moorehead, p. 47
122   'One could hear . . .': ibid.
122   'Tommy with his landing . . .': ibid., p. 47
125   'Captain Doughty . . .': Roswell K. Doughty, *Invading Hitler's Europe*, p. 39
125   'Let's get out . . .': ibid., p. 40
125   'Hot damn . . .': ibid., p. 40

9 Toehold
127   'We thought we were dying . . .': Pasqualina Caruso Diary, 9/9/1943
128   'They will fight . . .': Tompkins, *Italy Betrayed*, p. 182
129   'We can no longer . . .': Generale Giacomo Carboni, *L'Armistizio e la Difesa di Roma*, p. 46, and Tompkins, *Italy Betrayed*, p. 188
132   'Our astonished eyes . . .': Moorehead, p. 47
136   'A report from Admiral Hall . . .': Mark Clark Diary, 9/9/1943
136   'They're Mexicans . . .': Doughty, p. 42
139   'Came about 1 mile . . .': Bud Wagner Diary, 9/9/1943 in Bud Wagner, *And There Shall Be Wars,* p. 294
141   'An old Fascist . . .': Albert Kesselring, *The Memoirs of Field Marshal Kesselring*, p. 185

142   'Running around for me . . .': Bud Wagner Diary, 9/9/1943
142   'Units badly mixed . . .': Mark Clark Diary, 9/9/1943

10 Italy's Collapse

145   'The country . . .': TNA WO 169/10233
146   'Mountainous ranges . . .': Roy Durnford Diary, 7/9/1943
147   'My goodness gracious . . .': Mowat, p. 157
148   'fighting will of all . . .': cited in Ben Christensen, *The 1st Fallschirmjäger Division in World War II*, Vol. II, p. 348
149   'The Tommies have landed . . .': Martin Pöppel Diary, 9/9/1943
150   'It was just terrible . . .': Jupp Klein, author interview
151   'Lt. Kranefeld . . .': Joseph Klein, *Fallschirmjäger*, p. 64
152   'In the morning . . .': ibid., p. 67
153   'A Gonzaga never . . .': cited in Hugh Pond, *Salerno*, p. 21
154   'There's still money . . .': Eugenio Corti, *The Last Soldiers of the King*, p. 39
155   'the knot is untied': Georg Zellner Diary, 9/9/1943, BA-MA MSg 1/2816
156   'That it was only . . .': ibid.
156   'The plan has proved . . .': ibid.
156   'It was one of the most . . .': ibid.
157   'Disorderly clothes . . .': Filippo Caracciolo Diary, 9/9/1943
157   'Sporadic sparks . . .': ibid.
157   'Are you crazy?': Carla Capponi, *Con cuore di donna*, p. 96
158   'No, I'm looking to make myself . . .': ibid., p. 97
160   'At dawn, I will take . . .': Carboni, pp. 43–4, and Tompkins, *Italy Betrayed*, p. 199

11 Build-up and Containment

161   'I saw my two rockets . . .': Robert Gugelberger Diary, 10/9/1943 in Prien, p. 687
161   'Shortly after lifting off . . .': ibid.
162   'Now I was just twenty-three . . .': Hugh Dundas, *Flying Start*, pp. 161–2
164   'We just sat around . . .': Jim Reed Diary, 9/9/1943 in James E. Reed, *The Fighting Nomads*, Vol. II
164   'Not doing a damn thing . . .': Jim Reed Diary, 10/9/1943
164   'My corps could now . . .': Hermann Balck, *Order in Chaos*, p. 305
164   'The division had only . . .': Wilhelm Schmalz, *Kampf um Salerno*, BA-MA MSg 2/13110
166   'At any rate . . .': Rocholl in Moorehead, p. 48
166   'It is a ghastly feeling . . .': Rocholl in Moorehead, p. 49
166   'A strange conception . . .': – and next two quotes – Rocholl in Moorehead, p. 49
167   'Who goes there?': Peter Moore, *No Need to Worry*, p. 106
169   'It came as an illumination . . .': Norman Lewis Diary, 9/9/1943 in Norman Lewis, *Naples '44*, p. 12
169   'The voices died away . . .': ibid., p. 13

172   'Life goes on . . .': cited in Robert Katz, *Fatal Silence*, p. 38
172   'Time 1300 . . .': Mark Clark Diary, 10/9/1943
175   'We go out into the street . . .': Filippo Caracciolo Diary, 10/9/1943
175   'No organization . . .': ibid.
177   'lively discussion': Carboni, p. 47

12 Fritz X

178   'The sun is burning down . . .': Golda, BA-MA MSg 2/4335, p. 21
178   'What a pity . . .': ibid., p. 22
179   'The rugged mountains . . .': Schmalz, *Kampf um Salerno*, BA-MA MSg
       2/13110
179   'A crash, a cloud of dirt!': Golda, p. 22
179   'What do you mean . . .': ibid.
180   'My boys listened . . .': ibid.
180   'The spotter for this firing . . .': Rocholl in Moorehead, p. 50
181   'This was a bit too much . . .': ibid., p. 51
181   'The 20s fire very rapidly . . .': Reynolds, p. 307
181   'I wish we were . . .': ibid., p. 327
182   'The flame must have shot . . .': ibid., pp. 327–8
182   'Everyone, I think . . .': ibid., p. 329
183   'Up at 5.30 am . . .': Bud Wagner Diary, 10/9/1943
183   'Running around a lot . . .': ibid., 11/9/1943
183   'Result: hatred . . .': ibid., 12/9/1943
183   'Wish I could get . . .': ibid., 11/9/1943
184   'Artillery jeep hit one . . .': Frank Pearce Diary, 12/9/1943 in John
       A. Pearce, *A Private in the Texas Army*, p. 35
185   'There were far more . . .': Christopher Bulteel, *Salerno, September 1943* in
       D. C. Quilter (ed.), *'No Dishonourable Name'*, p. 17
186   'We dug with a will . . .': ibid., p. 177
187   'We waited for the inevitable attack.': Moore, p. 109
187   'Elements of Hermann Goering . . .': Mark Clark Diary, 12/9/1943
188   'Do more damage . . .': Frank Pearce Diary, 11/9/1943
188   'In view heavy . . .': Mark Clark Diary, 12/9/1943
189   'I am not satisfied . . .': cited in C. J. C. Molony, *The Mediterranean and the
       Middle East*, Vol. V, p. 299

13 Crisis

192   'Same old stuff . . .': Jim Reed Diary, 11/9/1943
192   'Doing nothing . . .': ibid., 12/9/1943
192   'Everyone seem to pick . . .': ibid., 13/9/1943, and written 'seem' singular
193   'We must flee . . .': Pasqualina Caruso Diary, 12/9/1943
193   'We lie down dressed . . .': ibid.
194   'No food is sold any more . . .': ibid., 13/9/1943
194   'I don't think . . .': Corti, p. 42
194   'Because an unarmed nation . . .': ibid., p. 41

195   'What are you doing about it?': Mark Clark, *Calculated Risk*, p. 200
197   'Pieces of it hit . . .': Frank Pearce Diary, 13/9/1943
198   'But the plan . . .': Rocholl in Moorehead, p. 51

14 Turn of Fortune

201   'It is rather disconsolate . . .': Gerhard Waag Diary, 11/9/1943 in Prien,
       p. 687
201   'We could not let ourselves . . .': Gerhard Waag Diary, 12/9/1943 in ibid.,
       p. 688
202   'Retreated at 2 a.m. . . .': Frank Pearce Diary, 14/9/1943
202   'There mustn't be any doubt . . .': Clark, p. 204
203   'Rumours come in . . .': Norman Lewis Diary, 12/9/1943, p. 16; NB Lewis
       lists this as 12 September but he's actually writing about 13 September, for
       which there is no entry
204   'The run down . . .': Moorehead, p. 39
204   'Nothing of interest . . .': cited in Molony, p. 313
205   'Hot, terribly dusty . . .': Bud Wagner Diary, 14/9/1943
205   'Bullets and shells . . .': Frank Pearce Diary, 14/9/1943
205   'To the north . . .': Norman Lewis Diary, 14/9/1943, p. 17
205   'I began to feel . . .': Clark, p. 207
206   'Leutnant! Leutnant!': Rocholl in Moorehead, p. 52
206   'Soon fourteen 20mm . . .': ibid.
206   'So that's where they were . . .': ibid., p. 53
207   'Flee! Flee!': Pasqualina Caruso Diary, 14/9/1943
208   'Whistles and explosions . . .': ibid.
208   'He seemed to have . . .': Moorehead, p. 40
209   'A mass of shipping . . .': Bertie Packer Diary, 14/9/1943; NB it's written up
       as the 14th, but the entry covers two days including the 15th
209   'Roared thro' Messina Straits . . .': ibid.
210   'The ship was stopped . . .': ibid.
210   'A gunner's dream . . .': TNA WO 169/9490
210   'The effect of the heavy ships . . .': cited in Appendix H, RN Battle
       Summary No. 37
211   'I was not thrown . . .': Bertie Packer Diary, 16/9/1943
211   'Put it out!': ibid.
211   'I couldn't for helm . . .': ibid.
211   'We were making . . .': ibid.
213   'This has been a great . . .': Mark Clark Diary, 16/9/1943

15 Breakout

214   'Aren't those in Italy?': Harold Macmillan Diary, 13/9/1943
215   'Things are not difficult . . .': ibid., 16/9/1943
215   'a natural coward': ibid.
215   'well-bred defeatism': ibid.
215   'Shall we as we would like . . .': ibid.

216   'A pleasant little chap . . .': Martin Pöppel Diary, 20/9/1943
217   'We almost cried . . .': Klein, p. 74
217   'And the worst part . . .': H. A. Wilson Diary, 18/9/1943 (both quotes)
218   'It is evening . . .': Cole, p. 101
218   'I wish . . .': ibid.
219   'I think the end . . .': Mowat, p. 165
219   'The towns are dirty . . .': Alex Campbell, letter to mother, 15/9/1943
219   'It makes us real mad . . .': ibid.
219   'A city of hunger . . .': Roy Durnford Diary, 10/9/1943
220   'All the transport . . .': Harold Macmillan Diary, 17/9/1943
221   'He is completely naked . . .': Pasqualina Caruso Diary, 17/9/1943
221   'Will we survive?': ibid., 18/9/1943
223   'They, fortunately . . .': Peter Bull, *To Sea in a Sieve*, p. 113
223   'The larger ships . . . .': ibid., p. 114
224   'We had done what we set out to do . . .': Bertie Packer Diary, 17/9/1943
224   'I was very tired . . .': ibid., 18/9/1943
224   'I was relieved . . .': ibid.
224   'My heart goes out . . .': Bud Wagner Diary, 17/9/1943
224   'Burned. Dead cattle . . .': Frank Pearce Diary, 19/9/1943
225   'Mike Moore has been . . .': Moore, p. 112
226   'That evening . . .': ibid., p. 113
226   'Padre found dead . . .': TNA WO 169/10167
226   'The deep peace . . .': Bulteel in Quilter, p. 179
228   'The same old stuff . . .': John Lucas Diary, 24/9/1943
228   'The Sicilian campaign . . .': Audie Murphy, *To Hell and Back*, p. 15
228   'I part the bushes . . .': ibid., p. 16
228   'Keep down!': ibid.
229   'The bullet ripped an artery . . .': ibid., p. 16
229   'The lady must . . .': Golda, p. 23
229   'And when they fell . . .': ibid.
229   'There, not even 300 metres . . .': ibid., p. 25
229   'A picture of misery . . .': ibid., p. 24

16 Naples
231   'Yes, that's a poor guy . . .': Filippo Caracciolo Diary, 15/9/1943
231   'He takes a tour . . .': ibid.
232   'But the features . . .': ibid., 16/9/1943
232   'Every single citizen . . .': www.storienapoli.it/2020/10/05/walter-scholl-nazisti-napoli/
233   'They flee with tired . . .': Filippo Caracciolo Diary, 24/9/1943
233   'The environment . . .': ibid., 28/9/1943
233   'Wanting to escape . . .': ibid., 29/9/1943
234   'Fourteen miles from Naples . . .': Jack Ward Diary, 29/9/1943
234   'The people on the whole . . .': ibid.
235   'Poor men, how I pity you!': Corti, pp. 53–4

236 'The valley became filled . . .': ibid., p. 72
236 'What are they like?': H. A. Wilson Diary, 24/9/1943
240 'I am writing this letter . . .': Lawrie Franklyn-Vaile letter, 2/9/1943
240 'In the meantime . . .': ibid.
240 'Other Italian towns . . .': ibid., 1/10/1943
241 'I leave the session . . .': Filippo Caracciolo Diary, 30/9/1943
242 'It offers a bleak . . .': ibid., 1/10/1943

17 Termoli

243 'The Italians are generally . . .': Wilhelm Mauss Diary, 3/10/1943 in Hans-Jörg Mauss and Roger de Rijke, *The War Diary of Dr Wilhelm Mauss*
244 'In peacetime . . .': ibid., 9/10/1944
244 'Elsewhere the surrendered . . .': ibid., 4/10/1943
246 'It was scarcely . . .': Peter Davis, p. 181
246 'For heaven's sake . . .': Klein, p. 77
247 'Tommies are here . . .': ibid., p. 82
247 'We broke away . . .': ibid., p. 86
248 'Now we've got ourselves . . .': Martin Pöppel Diary, 26/9/1943
249 'One of those mornings . . .': ibid., 30/9/1943
249 'In Naples we went down . . .': Frank Pearce Diary, 2/10/1943
250 'So much so . . .': Norman Lewis Diary, 4/10/1943, p. 23
250 'A perfunctory jogging . . .': ibid.
251 'He is intelligent . . .': Filippo Caracciolo Diary, 2/10/1943
252 'Blankets over my head . . .': Martin Pöppel Diary, 3/10/1943
252 'A grab down there . . .': ibid., 4/10/1943
255 'Bright flames . . .': Klein, p. 90
255 'Even in Russia . . .': ibid., p. 91
257 'Here lay a man . . .': Peter Davis, p. 198

18 Desolation

258 'They were delivered . . .': Norman Lewis Diary, 6/10/1943, p. 27
259 'to confront the security . . .': ibid.
259 'Past two days . . .': Frank Pearce Diary, 5/10/1943
259 'Debris filled the air . . .': ibid., 6/10/1943
260 'They've got Unteroffizier Klein!': Klein, p. 92
261 'I have just had . . .': Lawrie Franklyn-Vaile letter, 7/10/1943
261 'It is curious . . .': ibid.
263 'Motor vehicles of all kinds . . .': Filippo Caracciolo Diary, 4/10/1943
263 'Rained again.': Bud Wagner Diary, 2/10/1943; 4/10/1943; 8/10/1943
264 'Do you think . . .': Thomas D. Murphy, *Ambassadors in Arms*, p. 120
265 'Where my men go, I go!': cited in Isaac Fukuo Akinaka, *The Life History of Isaac Fukuo Akinaka*, p. 40
265 'Efficiency of Bn very good . . .': Mark Clark to Eisenhower, 8/10/1943
265 'We have had terrible rains . . .': Mark Clark letter to mother, 10/10/1943

19 The Volturno

267   'General Clark tries . . .': John Lucas Diary, 2/10/1943
268   'The town near the river . . .': ibid., 5/10/1943
269   'There can be no doubt . . .': ibid., 12/10/1943
269   'Who would think . . .': ibid., 5/10/1943
269   'This proves that the destructions . . .': Wilhelm Mauss Diary, 11/10/1943
270   'The sour stench . . .': Audie Murphy, p. 23
270   'So we're pigeons?': ibid.
271   'The real Italy . . .': ibid., p. 28
271   'Naples burning on one side . . .': Jack Ward Diary, 3/10/1943
271   'Passed one yesterday . . .': ibid., 7/10/1943
271   'All our vehicles . . .': ibid., 8/10/1943
272   'He promised to come . . .': Pasqualina Caruso Diary, 13–14/10/1943
272   'Just think . . .': the conversation is recorded in Corti, pp. 74–5
274   'So, another German fighter less!': Golda, p. 26
274   'We ran into the water . . .': ibid.
275   'Here everything was . . .': ibid., p. 28
275   'Rain, rain, rain . . .': John Lucas Diary, 10/10/1943
277   'Come back, you crazy fool.': Audie Murphy, p. 32
277   'Gah damn sonsabeeches.': ibid., p. 33
277   'Goddammit, man . . .': ibid.
277   'Antonio lies in the mud . . .': ibid.
277   'Time 2045 . . .': Jack Ward Diary, 12/10/1943
278   'Tonight we cross . . .': John Lucas Diary, 12/10/1943
278   'Should one sit here . . .': Wilhelm Mauss Diary, 13/10/1943
279   'Our planes join . . .': Jack Ward Diary, 13/10/1943
279   'He had finally spotted us . . .': Golda, p. 29
279   'Herr Leutnant . . .': ibid.
279   'We were shaken . . .': ibid.
280   'The big Chief . . .': John Lucas Diary, 13/10/1943
280   'Jerry made a counter-attack . . .': Jack Ward Diary, 15/10/1943
281   'From the stump . . .': Golda, p. 30
281   'Then I was seized . . .': ibid.
282   'Chestnut trees and oaks . . .': Wilhelm Mauss Diary, 16/10/1943
282   'It will eat itself . . .': ibid.
282   'New life will again . . .': ibid.

20 Despair

287   'Clearly, there will be very . . .': DDE Papers, Vol. III, No. 1328, p. 1497
288   'If we can keep . . .': cited in W. G. F. Jackson, *The Battle for Italy*, p. 138
290   'Everything is MUD . . .': Roy Durnford Diary, 7/10/1943
290   'Go forward and bury four . . .': ibid., 9/10/1943
290   'This is a lovely war . . .': Alex Campbell letter, 30/9/1943
291   'The Führer has ordered . . .': cited in Mowat, p. 167
291   'It is a long time . . .': Alex Campbell letter, 8/10/1943

292   'Ask for the Spumanti . . .': Mowat, p. 185
292   'A young guy named Swayle . . .': ibid., pp. 186–7
293   'Squithy never bothers . . .': H. A. Wilson Diary, 30/9/1943
293   'He is one of the most . . .': ibid.
293   'The one who fired . . .': ibid., 6/10/1943
293   'Mud, muck and pools . . .': ibid., 7/10/1943
294   'It was in little pieces . . .': ibid., 18/10/1943
294   'I'm writing on a table . . .': ibid., 19/10/1943
294   'just a mass of ruins': Jack Ward Diary, 20/10/1943
294   'Through glasses . . .': ibid., 22/10/1943
295   'Had to get Italians . . .': ibid., 25/10/1943
295   'Hard fighting going in on . . .': ibid., 28/10/1943
295   'We had to move again . . .': Bud Wagner Diary, 19/10/1943
295   'Everywhere along the route . . .': Doughty, p. 74
297   'Asked why they went to war . . .': Lawrie Franklyn-Vaile letter, 19/10/1943
297   'I can't tell you . . .': Collezione Bonelli, Museo di Napoli
298   'Little queues wait . . .': Norman Lewis Diary, 9/10/1943, p. 29
298   'This girl, as you know . . .': ibid., 22/10/1943, p. 39
298   'Sure changed.': Frank Pearce Diary, 20/10/1943
299   'Garbage accumulates . . .': Filippo Caracciolo Diary, 7/10/1943
299   'A cloud of dust . . .': Doughty, p. 76
299   'But we proceed slowly . . .': Filippo Caracciolo Diary, 14–15/10/1943
300   'Here, everything proceeds . . .': ibid., 18/10/1943

21 Questions of Morale

301   'We would no longer . . .': Corti, p. 81
301   'Only later was it discovered . . .': ibid., p. 89
302   'He had a kind . . .': Moorehead, p. 55
302   'There was a curious cardboard . . .': ibid.
302   'They were at the top . . .': ibid.
303   'I think we got . . .': Harold Macmillan Diary, 13/10/1943
303   'He is absolutely . . .': ibid., 18/10/1943
305   'The only Italian . . .': cited in Richard Lamb, *War in Italy 1943–1945: A Brutal Story*, p. 86
306   'How should I interpret . . .': Georg Zellner Diary, 10/10/1943
306   'The white race . . .': Wilhelm Mauss Diary, 17/10/1943
306   'Whatever the attitude . . .': ibid.
307   'Our frequency of operation . . .': cited in Richard G. Davis, *Carl A. Spaatz and the Air War in Europe*, p. 257
308   'Nothing has such adverse . . .': TNA WO 214/62
308   'Received No. 69 . . .': Jack Ward Diary, 10/10/1943
308   'At long last a letter . . .': Lawrie Franklyn-Vaile letter, 10/10/1943
308   'It means an extra . . .': ibid.
308   'Everything tends to be . . .': ibid., 17/10/1943
309   'I do feel that wives . . .': ibid.

22 A World Turned Upside Down

310   'A superb man . . .': Wilhelm Mauss Diary, 24/10/1943
310   'Last night . . .': ibid., 27/10/1943
311   'cats and dogs': ibid.
313   'sound wicket': Molony, p. 455
313   'I hope you are managing   ': Lawrie Franklyn-Vaile letter, 19/10/1943
313   'Let me know . . .': ibid., 22/10/1943
314   'He is a grand friend . . .': ibid.
316   'I come in the name of peace': Dom Eusebio War Diary, October 1943, in
        Eusebio Grossetti and Martino Matronola, *Monte Cassino under Fire: War
        Diaries from the Abbey*
316   'The meeting was . . .': ibid.
316   'Great upset . . .': ibid., 18/10/1943
316   'Everything will be destroyed': Dom Eusebio War Diary, October
        1943
317   'He expressed his personal . . .': ibid., 3/11/1943
317   'Indeed, yesterday . . .': Lawrie Franklyn-Vaile letter, 26/10/1943
318   'The only good thing . . .': ibid.
319   'I have been hit . . .': ibid., 4/11/1943
319   'You know I am here, Johnny?': ibid.
319   'I could have stood . . .': ibid.

23 Continuous Pressure

320   'Again one worries . . .': Wilhelm Mauss Diary, 19/10/1943
320   'The Tommies . . .': ibid., 21/10/1943
321   'We ran into a lot . . .': Jim Reed Diary, 23/9/1943
322   'Came by truck . . .': T. Michael Sullivan Diary, 18/10/1943, in T. Michael
        Sullivan, *Life in the Service: Echoes of the Army*
322   'Damn good so far . . .': ibid., 21/10/1943
323   'Ate a rotten supper . . .': ibid., 23/10/1943
323   'Impossible to see . . .': ibid., 24/10/1943
323   'Another combat mission . . .': ibid., 6/11/1943
324   'He was an old . . .': ibid., 7/11/1943
325   'This fucking shit!': Golda, p. 33
325   'We haul all the junk . . .': ibid.
325   'It was most interesting . . .': Harold Macmillan Diary, 24/10/1943
326   'The reduction in craft . . .': cited in WSC Vol. V, p. 218
326   'The capital has . . .': ibid., p. 219
326   'The obvious present German . . .': ibid.
327   'No German yet . . .': John Lucas Diary, 29/10/1943
327   'The prospect . . .': ibid.
327   'Damn the German.': ibid., 30/10/1943
328   'But I still think . . .': ibid.
328   'This is a heart-breaking . . .': ibid., 1/11/1943

24 The Winter Line
330 'After saying goodbye . . .': Jim Reed Diary, 29/10/1943
332 'Jesus wept!': H. A. Wilson Diary, 1/11/1943
332 'They soughed through the air . . .': ibid., 2/11/1943
332 'But I felt as insecure . . .': ibid.
334 'These little girls . . .': Norman Lewis Diary, 1/11/1943, p. 49
336 'My three houses . . .': H. A. Wilson Diary, 8/11/1943
337 'The rain was over . . .': ibid., 15/11/1943
338 'Jerry is going back . . .': Jack Ward Diary, 2/11/1943
338 'The worst sight . . .': ibid., 4/11/1943
339 'This, by the way . . .': ibid., 7/11/1943
341 'There was no spirited . . .': Darby, p. 157
342 'Static warfare . . .': ibid., p. 160
342 'Such positions . . .': FMS C-95b
342 'This difference in treatment . . .': ibid.
343 'He turned white . . .': Akinaka, p. 40
343 'At the going down of the sun . . .': Jack Ward Diary, 11/11/1943
343 'We are still . . .': Wilhelm Mauss Diary, 11/11/1943

25 Slow Death
344 'Enemy attacks continue . . .': FMS C-95b
344 'The enemy defended . . .': cited in Mark Clark Diary, 8/11/1943
346 'What's the Chief . . .': Audie Murphy, p. 38
346 'From the ripped . . .': ibid., p. 39
346 'Reveille': ibid.
346 'Superman . . .': ibid., p. 43
348 'We pressed ourselves . . .': Golda, p. 37
348 'Many men do not . . .': Mark Clark Papers, Memos & Reports, 8/11/9143
348 'It is incumbent . . .': ibid.
350 'If we keep going . . .': Pasqualina Caruso Diary, 6–7/11/1943
351 'We have decided . . .': cited in Katz, p. 86
351 'It was love at first sight.': Rosario Bentivegna, *Achtung Banditen!*, p. 58
351 'I used the crush . . .': Capponi, p. 125
352 'Misery and hunger . . .': Dom Eusebio War Diary, 19/11/1943
352 'The mines used . . .': ibid., 21/11/1943
353 'The seizing of one . . .': ibid., 25/11/1943
353 'The air raids . . .': ibid., 28/11–2/12/1943
353 'Spaatz and I . . .': DDE Papers, No. 1265, 18/9/1943
356 'I'm out of my teens . . .': T. Michael Sullivan Diary, 14/11/1943

26 The Sangro
360 'Now I should cut . . .': Roger Smith, *Up the Blue*, p. 117
360 'Can I trust you . . .': ibid.
360 'What the hell was that . . .': this section all from ibid., p. 118

361   'Four crumpled bodies . . .': ibid., p. 121
361   'A myth was exploded . . .': ibid., p. 122
363   'It was a terrible ordeal . . .': Klein, p. 111
363   'What can I do . . .': ibid., p. 112
364   'Honestly, Olive . . .': Lawrie Franklyn-Vaile letter, 6/11/1943
364   'The ghastly wastage . . .': ibid., 15/11/1943
364   'He was very nice . . .': ibid.
365   'No one really knows . . .': ibid., 21/11/1943
365   'We're going a thousand yards . . .': H. A. Wilson Diary, 19/11/1943
365   'The cipher boys . . .': ibid.
366   'Our driver spoiled . . .': ibid.
366   'Instead of being grateful . . .': ibid., 20/11/1943

27 The Good Cause

370   'Boy, oh, boy . . .': Golda, p. 39
370   'Like wildfire . . .': ibid.
371   'First air raids . . .': Georg Zellner Diary, 23/11/1943
371   'People beat each other . . .': ibid., 24/11/1943
371   'So when we see . . .': ibid., 27/11/1943
371   'Everything would melt . . .': ibid.
372   'Must be lots . . .': Frank Pearce Diary, 24/11/1943
372   'Big rain . . .': ibid., 25/11/1943
372   'Even in this situation . . .': Bud Wagner Diary, 25/11/1943
372   'One of the prisoners . . .': Darby, p. 167
372   '0925 Captain Shunstrom . . .': ibid., pp. 162–3
375   'The logistic problem . . .': The Sextant, Eureka and Second Cairo
       Conferences, p. 383
376   'For whoever . . .': ibid., p. 385
376   'The effect on Hungary . . .': ibid., p. 386
376   'OVERLORD remains top . . .': ibid., p. 387
376   'Here there was . . .': Harold Macmillan Diary, 25/11/1943
376   'Madam Chiang . . .': ibid.
379   'Free speech is all right . . .': ibid., 2/12/1943
379   'Am writing this . . .': Lawrie Franklyn-Vaile letter, 27/11/1943
380   'We had another . . .': ibid., 6/12/1943
380   'Enemy air force . . .': BA-MA RH 24-76/7
380   'With Montgomery . . .': ibid.
380   'It is simply impossible . . .': ibid.
381   'I bet jerry . . .': H. A. Wilson Diary, 28/11/1943
382   'There was a clattering crash . . .': Smith, p. 141
382   'You are in the way . . .': ibid., pp. 141–2

28 RAINCOAT

383   'Mossogrogna was in ruins . . .': H. A. Wilson Diary, 4/12/1943
383   'I reckon those legs . . .': ibid.

383   'Underneath this . . .': ibid., 7/12/1943
384   'Take what's left . . .': Lawrie Franklyn-Vaile letter, 6/12/1943
384   'That is war . . .': ibid.
385   'We are all desperately . . .': ibid.
385   'I look at it this way . . .': Ernie Pyle, *Brave Men*, p. 118
386   'We could hear . . .': ibid., p. 99
387   'There was nothing to do . . .': ibid., p. 101
387   'As you may have guessed . . .': Mowat, p. 201
387   'I hate to disillusion . . .': ibid., p. 192
387   'Everything that was not . . .': ibid., p. 202
388   'Haven't any of the . . .': ibid., p. 203
388   'Their faces were . . .': ibid., p. 204
388   'For in that instant . . .': ibid.
389   'The river and banks . . .': Roy Durnford Diary, 2/12/1943
391   'It's the first day . . .': Jack Ward Diary, 1/12/1943
391   'The firing was . . .': Dom Eusebio War Diary, 2/12/1943
391   'The major battle . . .': Wilhelm Mauss Diary, 3/12/1943
394   'My boots . . .': David Helme Diary, 4/12/1943 in Quilter, p. 195
395   'Eventually, we flushed . . .': ibid.
395   'disquieting': TNA WO 169/10167
395   'Slightly stunned . . .': David Helme Diary, 6/12/1943
395   'His beard . . .': ibid.
396   'What I observed . . .': FMS C-95b
396   'When we looked up . . .': Golda, p. 40
396   'We could not salvage . . .': ibid., p. 38

29 Valley of Death

399   'Get up, Mowat!': Mowat, p. 210
400   'We are shelled constantly . . .': Roy Durnford Diary, 7/12/1943
400   'Go up line to front . . .': ibid., 8/12/1943
401   'The one important thing . . .': cited in Andrea di Marco, *Assolutamente Resistere!*, p. 138
402   'Hold it, you blokes . . .': Smith, p. 153
403   'Raining all day . . .': Bud Wagner Diary, 4–7/12/1943
403   'I have a stinking rage . . .': Georg Zellner Diary, 1/12/1943
404   'Constantly under fire . . .': ibid., 5/12/1943
404   'In the evening . . .': ibid., 6/12/1943
405   'I had just about . . .': Doughty, p. 91
405   'Any thought of moving . . .': ibid.
407   'You and your Fifth Army . . .': Mark Clark Diary, 8/12/1943
407   'Feel down in the blues . . .': Bud Wagner Diary, 8/12/1943
408   'I cannot impress upon you . . .': Mark Clark Diary, 10/12/1943

30 The Tyranny of OVERLORD

414   '7 p.m., saw PM . . .': Harold Macmillan Diary, 7/12/1943

415   'The argument . . .': ibid., 8/12/1943
415   'Why must the PM . . .': Brooke Diary, 8/12/1943
416   'I would consider it . . .': cited in Guy Faguet, *The War on Cancer*, p. 70
418   'Continued setting up . . .': T. Michael Sullivan Diary, 11/12/1943
418   'Damned rough mission': ibid., 14/12/1943
418   'Bad weather . . .': ibid., 19/12/1943
418   'No. 3 engine on fire . . .': ibid.
419   'Once again . . .': Mowat, p. 218
420   'Drink this!': ibid., p. 221
420   'Al Mercer looking strained . . .': Roy Durnford Diary, 13/12/1943
421   'Monty is tired out . . .': Alanbrooke, *War Diaries, 1939–1945*, 14/12/1943, p. 499
424   'match winners': The War Office, *Notes from the Theatres of War No. 20: Italy 1943/44*, May 1945, p. 63
424   'It is not enough . . .': ibid.

31 Death of a Village

427   'Everyone, especially . . .': cited in Costantino Jadecola, *Vallerotonda*, p. ??
428   'Mortars doing lots . . .': Frank Pearce Diary, 9/12/1943
428   'We are not making . . .': ibid., 10/12/1943
429   'The tank had been . . .': Mark Clark Diary, 11/12/1943
430   'It was the weather . . .': Pyle, p. 142
430   'No one who had . . .': ibid.
431   'For twenty seconds . . .': ibid., p. 151
432   'Now he was dying . . .': Mork cited in Di Marco, p. 142
432   'It was truly . . .': ibid.
432   'All that we could do . . .': ibid., p. 143
434   'We sent for 800 pounds . . .': Darby, p. 169
435   'The day like before . . .': Georg Zellner Diary, 12/12/1943
435   '6 a.m. Drum fire . . .': ibid., 15/12/1943
435   'A 6 o'clock . . .': Georg Zellner Diary, 16/12/1943
436   'You feel small . . .': Pyle, p. 154
437   'This is Captain Waskow . . .': ibid., p. 155
437   'And he sat there . . .': ibid., p. 156
437   'PM is definitely worse . . .': Harold Macmillan Diary, 14/12/1943
438   'This morning I measured . . .': Dom Eusebio War Diary, 15/12/1943
438   'Every now and again . . .': ibid.
438   'It is gradually . . .': Wilhelm Mauss Diary, 14/12/1943
439   'My house looked . . .': ibid., 15/12/1943
439   'Overall . . .': ibid.
440   'Another battle . . .': Frank Pearce Diary, 16/12/1943

32 Try and Try Again

442   'PM much better . . .': Harold Macmillan Diary, 16/12/1943
442   'I had a long talk . . .': Alanbrooke, *War Diaries, 1939–1945*, 16/12/1943, p. 500

444   'I will continue planning . . .': Mark Clark Diary, 18/12/1943
444   'Worse torn up . . .': Frank Pearce Diary, 18/12/1943
444   'One bad . . .': ibid.
444   'Can't be helped . . .': ibid., 21/12/1943
445   'So, now we are deployed . . .': Georg Zellner Diary, 23/12/1943
447   'I was thrilled by this sight . . .': cited in Di Marco, p. 193
448   'The place has been . . .': Cole, p. 125
448   'I don't like the look . . .': H. A. Wilson Diary, 19/12/1943
449   'If this is war . . .': ibid.
449   '90. Panzergrenadier . . .': BA-MA RH 20-10/76
449   'Wherever Heidrich is . . .': BA-MA RH 24-76/2
450   'First objective . . .': BA-MA RH 20-10/79
451   'But we didn't . . .': Mork cited in Di Marco, p. 144
451   'With great difficulty . . .': ibid.
452   'The damnable truth . . .': Mowat, p. 223
452   'What's the word, Squib?': ibid., pp. 224–5
453   'Vasser . . .': ibid., p. 227
453   'Dark gore . . .': ibid.
454   'I hope Santa . . .': Alex Campbell letter, 5/12/1943
454   'Farley! Still here?': Mowat, p. 233

33 Merry Christmas and a Happy New Year

456   'At the next cross-street . . .': Capponi, p. 153
457   'The disbandment order . . .': Filippo Caracciolo Diary, 9/11/1943
457   'I find him tired . . .': ibid., 1/12/1943
457   'I object to him . . .': ibid.
457   'Poor us . . .': Pasqualina Caruso Diary, 23/12/1944
458   'The world is full . . .': Di Marco, p. 195
459   'Resist! Resist!': ibid., p. 196
459   'An almost . . .': ibid., p. 197
459   'We sip our sweet . . .': ibid.
459   'Wet, dismal, murky . . .': H. A. Wilson Diary, 24/12/1943
459   'I hope you are happy . . .': ibid., 20/12/1943
459   'With a thousand bottles . . .': ibid., 24/12/1943
460   'My boy just lay . . .': Golda, p. 43
461   'A fabulous journey . . .': Wilhelm Mauss Diary, 24/12/1943
461   'So we spend the day . . .': Georg Zellner Diary, 24/12/1943
461   'We drink red wine . . .': ibid.
461   'The day has nothing . . .': ibid.
462   'Some companies . . .': Frank Pearce Diary, 25/12/1943
462   'Had quite a good Xmas . . .': Jack Ward Diary, 27/12/1943
462   'Christmas at war . . .': Dom Eusebio War Diary, 25/12/1943
463   'I wish I could see you . . .': R. H. Roy, *The Seaforth Highlanders of Canada*, p. 272
463   'Jerry sending shells over . . .': Roy Durnford Diary, 25/12/1943

463   'Shells whine and explode . . .': ibid.
463   'We shave same house . . .': ibid.
463   'The battle rages on . . .': Siegfried Bähr Diary, Di Marco, p. 197
464   'All weapons . . .': ibid.
464   'In the middle of the night . . .': ibid., p. 200
465   'They were killing . . .': cited in Jadecola, p. 24
466   'Then they put us . . .': ibid.
466   'Last day of the year . . .': Jack Ward Diary, 31/12/1943
466   'Over it lie . . .': Wilhelm Mauss Diary, 31/12/1943
466   'Thus I once again . . .': ibid.
467   'Plague of lice and fleas . . .': Georg Zellner Diary, 29/12/1943
467   'And outside . . .': ibid., 30/12/1943
467   'Cassino and Cervaro . . .': ibid., 31/12/1943
467   'Man becomes an animal . . .': ibid.

Postscript

470   'Am delighted and honoured . . .': Mark Clark Diary, 31/12/1943

Selected Sources

PERSONAL TESTIMONIES

Author Interviews

Berkieta, Stanislav
Bradshaw, Sam
Calvocoressi, Ion
Dills, Chas
Ellington, Edward 'Duke'
Harris, Reg
Howard, Michael
Klein, Jupp

Ortscheidt, Helmut
Piesakowski, Tomasz
Potts, Maggie
Reed, James E.
Rubnikowicz, Wladek
Saidel, Ray
Walters, Ed 'Bucky'
Wyke-Smith, Ted

Canadian War Museum

Coombs, William D.
Dunn, Hunter
Medd, A. Bruce

Go For Broke National Education Center Oral History Project

Hamasu, Mitsuo
Miyashiro, Takeichi
Sumida, Leighton

Imperial War Museum, London

Harding, Field Marshal Lord John
Hazel, Edmund
Nutting, Ivor

Matthew Parker Papers

Cunningham, Clare
Eggert, Werner
Langelüdecke, Kurt

National World War II Museum, New Orleans

Dumas, Floyd
Gilbert, Lawrence
Goad, Roy
Hayashi, Shizuya

Hughes, Lowell
Pierce, Wayne
Tweedt, Vernon T.

Rutgers, The State University of New Jersey

Cloer, Russell W.

Second World War Experience Centre, Otley, Lancashire

Bowen, H.
Chaudri, I. A.
Frettlöhr, R.
Ivy, R.

Kaeppner, G. R.
Talbot, G.
Thorman, R.

US Air Force Historical Research Agency, Maxwell, Alabama

Quesada, Elwood R. 'Pete'

US Army Heritage & Education Center, Carlisle, Pennsylvania

Bonesteel, Charles H.
Gay, Hobart

UNPUBLISHED REPORTS, DIARIES, LETTERS, MEMOIRS, PAPERS ETC.

Moore, Peter, 'Khaki and Gown: Memoirs 1940–1949'
Obermeier, Leonard, Letters, c/o Joe Hudgens
Trousdell, Philip J. C., Diary
Ward, Jack, Diary
Woodhouse, W. J., 'Memories of an Old Soldier' c/o Pete Connor

Archivio Diaristico Nazionale, Pieve Santo Stefano

Affricano, Wanda, *Diario 1943–1946*
Bauco, Viviano, *Diario 1944–1945*
Bocci, Stefania, *Sfollamento*
Branco, Domenico, *Diario di Guerra Anni 1943–1944*
Brcic, Fedora, *Sono Stata da Paola*
Buciano, Concetta, *Diario di Guerra*
Costigliola, Domenico and Capolongo, Carmela, *Mio Caro Mimi*
Curti, Clelia, *Diario*
Di Pompeo, Carrado, *Diario dedicato alla mia dolce Antonietta*
Fargnoli, Mario, *Preludo di Guai*
Giuliani, Mario, *Diario di una Fuga*
Levi, Bianca, *Chi non ha sentito stringere*
Nonno, Giuseppe, *Memorie della Guerra*
Orlando, Vincenzo, *Sulla frontiera di Cassino*
Paolisso, Irene, *Un Diario*
Verna, Elda, *Diario di Guerra*

Bundesarchiv-Militärarchiv, Freiburg

Eggert, Ernst, MSg 2/7283
Franek, Fritz, MSg 1/1398
Golda, Hans, MSg 2/4335
Goldscmidt, Karl, MSg 2/6303
Schmalz, Wilhelm, MSg 2/13109

Sikta, Hans, MSg 2/5520
Zellner, Georg, MSg 1/2816 and 2817

AOK 10, Kriegstagebuch

Canadian War Museum, Toronto

Campbell, Alex, Letters
Durnford, Roy, Diary

The Citadel Military College of South Carolina, Charleston

Clark, Mark, Papers

Collezione di Gaetano Bonelli, Museo di Napoli

Vincenzo, Lionitti, Letters

Dwight D. Eisenhower Presidential Library, Abilene, Kansas

Bedell-Smith, Walter, Papers
Butcher, Harry C., Diary 1943

82nd Fighter Group Website (82ndfightergroup.org)

Abberger, Tom, Diary

Go For Broke National Education Center (goforbroke.org)

Akinaka, Isaac Fukuo, *The Life History of Isaac Fukuo Akinaka*

Imperial War Museum, London

Baxendale, J., Diary
Clark, Norman, 'War Dispatches'
Cowles, B. R., Diary
Deane, D. H., Diary
Doble, M. L., Diary
Drury, K. R., 'One Man's Memories'

Leese, Oliver, Papers
Montgomery, Bernard, Papers
Parkinson, J. E., Diary
Turner, Rev. E. A., Diary
Tweedsmuir, Lord John, Papers
Wilson, H. A., Diary

Irish Brigade Website (irishbrigade.co.uk)

Franklyn-Vaile, Lawrence, Letters

Library and Archives Canada, Toronto

Vokes, Chris, 'Crossing of the Moro and Capture of Ortona'
Hastings and Prince Edward Regiment War Diary
Seaforth Highlanders of Canada War Diary
Three Rivers Regiment War Diary

Library of Congress, Washington DC

Patton, George S., Papers
Spaatz, Carl, Papers

Liddell Hart Centre for Military Archives, King's College, London

Alanbrooke, Alan, Papers
Green, Henry, Diary
Howson, John, Papers
Kirkman, Sidney, Papers
McNeil, John, Papers
Nelson, John, 'Always a Grenadier'
Penney, Ronald, Papers
Sprot, Aidan, Memoir

McMaster University Library, Ontario

Mowat, Farley, Papers

National Archives, Kew

War Diaries

AMG War Diary
1st Battalion, Royal Irish Fusiliers
2nd Battalion, Royal Inniskilling Fusiliers
2/5th Battalion, Leicestershire Regiment
2nd Battalion, Scots Guards
2nd Regiment, Royal Horse Artillery
3rd Battalion, Coldstream Guards
4/16th Punjab Regiment
6th Battalion, Royal Inniskilling Fusiliers
17th Field Regiment, Royal Artillery
30th Field Regiment, Royal Artillery
56th Heavy Regiment, Royal Artillery
185th Infantry Brigade
X Corps War Diary
XIII Corps War Diary
XXX Corps War Diary

Special Raiding Squadron

Operational Record Books

45 Squadron
74 Squadron
111 Squadron
249 Squadron
324 Wing

Documents

Alexander, Harold R. A., Papers
British Casualty Figures
JG 77 Operations in the Mediterranean
Kappler, Herbert, Interrogation Reports
Lessons from the Italian Campaign
Luftwaffe Reports, Sicily
Major Capron's Statement

NATAF Report on Operations
Order of Battle, Sicily
Port of Naples
Special Report on Events in Italy
Training Notes from the Sicilian Campaign
Ultra Decrypts, Italy

National Archives and Records Administration, College Park, Maryland

1st Armored Division Operations Reports
3rd Infantry Division in Sicily Report on Operations
15th Infantry Regiment in Sicily
34th Infantry Operations and Reports
36th Infantry Operations and Report
45th Infantry Division Operations and Reports
Training Notes from the Sicilian Campaign
US Wire Monitoring
Weekly Intelligence Summaries

Naval Historical Branch, Portsmouth

Dürchführung Landungsunternehmen
Packer, Bertie, Diary
RN Battle Summary No. 37 Salerno
RN Captured German Documents
RN Morale, Efficiency & Organisation
RN Signals Operation AVALANCHE

Papers of Nigel Nicolson

Interviews, documents, papers relating to Field Marshal the Earl Alexander

Second World War Experience Centre, Otley, Lancashire

Kingstone, J., Diary
Knowles, S. W., 'Soldier On'
Milnes-Coates, R. E. J. C., Papers

Tagebuch Archiv, Emmendingen

Lemperle, Hermann, Diary and Letters

US Army Heritage Center, Carlisle, Pennsylvania

Memoirs, Diaries, Papers and Veterans' Surveys

Beehard, Maurice, Diary, Veterans Survey

Boyer, Robert H., Memoir, Veterans Survey

Brown, Joseph T., Memoir, Veterans Survey

Chafin, Mitchell, Diary, Veterans Survey

Childers, Ernest, 'The Operations of Company C, 180th Infantry (45th Infantry Division) at Oliveto, Italy, Northeast of Salerno, Italy, 21–22 September 1943'

Cloer, Russell W., 'The Road to Rome', Veterans Survey

Francis, William H., Diary, Veterans Survey

Gavin, James M., Diary, Papers

Gay, Hobart, Diary

Griffin, Eugene 'Breezy', Veterans Survey, Memoir

Hall, George, 'Ranger Scout', Veterans Survey

Hannum, Thomas, Memoir, Veterans Survey

Harper, George C., Memoir, Veterans Survey

Hooper, Vincent, 'My Favourite War'

Howze, Hamilton, 'Thirty Years and Then Some', 'Breakout from Anzio'

Kunz, William J., Memoir, Veterans Survey

Lindquist, Harold E., Veterans Survey

Lucas, John P., Diary, Papers

MacDonald, Donald E., Diary, Veterans Survey

Maffei, Norman, Papers and Diary, Veterans Survey

Marsh, Robert M., Memoir, Veterans Survey

Moses, Russell T., Papers

Mueller, Gustav, Memoir, Veterans Survey

Pritchard, James, Diary, Veterans Survey

Ridgway, Matthew B., Diary, Papers

Saidel, Ray, Journals, Veterans Survey

Schunemann, Gustave, Memoir

Smith, Stanley, Memoir

Valenti, Isadore, Veterans Survey, 'Combat Medic'

Williams, Warren, Memories

Wilson, Lloyd, Memories

Foreign Military Studies

B-269, *German Rear Area Organization – Italy*

B-270, Kesselring, Albert, *German Strategy During the Italian Campaign*

B-338, Blumentritt, Günther, *German Soldier (Morale)*

C-013, Kesselring, Albert, *Special Report on the Events in Italy Between 25 July and 8 September 1943*

C-014, Kesselring, Albert, *Concluding Remarks on the Mediterranean Campaign*
C-015, Kesselring, Albert, *Italy as a Military Ally*
C-031, Kesselring, Albert, *Fortifications in Italy*
C-064, Kesselring, Albert, *The Campaign in Italy Part II*
C-95b, Senger und Etterlin, Fridolin von, *War Diary of the Italian Campaign*
D-112, Fries, Walter, *29th Panzer Grenadier Division*
D-168, Glasl, Anton, *Mountain Infantry Regiment 100*
D-301, Klinkowström, Graf Karl-Heinrich, *Italy's Break-Away and the Fighting Around Rome*
D-316, Bernstorff, Graf Douglas, *The Operations of the 26th Panzer Division in Italy*

CONTEMPORARY PAMPHLETS, BOOKLETS AND TRAINING MEMORANDA

Army Life, War Department Pamphlet 21-13, US Government Printing Office, 1944
Basic Field Manual: First Aid for Soldiers, FM 21-11, US War Department, 1943
The Battle of the Atlantic: The Official Account of the Fight Against the U-Boats, 1939–1945, HMSO, London, 1946
By Air to Battle: The Official Account of the British Airborne Divisions, HMSO, 1945
Combat Instruction for the Panzer Grenadier by Helmut von Wehren, 1944, English translation by John Baum, germanmanuals.com
Company Officer's Handbook of the German Army, Military Intelligence Division, US War Department, 1944
Der Dienst-Unterricht im Heer by Dr jur. W. Reibert, E. S. Mittler & Sohn Berlin, 1941
The Development of Artillery Tactics and Equipment, War Office, London, 1951
Field Service Pocket Book, various pamphlets, War Office, 1939–45
German Infantry Weapons, Military Intelligence Service, US War Department, 1943
The German Squad in Combat, Military Intelligence Service, US War Department, 1944
German Tactical Doctrine, Military Intelligence Service, US War Department, 1942
German Tank Maintenance in World War II, Department of the US Army, June 1954
The Gunnery Pocket Book, 1945, Admiralty, London, 1945
Handbook of German Military Forces, TM-E 30-451, US War Department 1945
Handbook on the British Army with Supplements on the Royal Air Force and Civilian Defense Organizations, TM 30-410, US War Department, September 1942
Handbook on the Italian Military Forces, TME-30-240, Military Intelligence Service, US Army, August 1943

Infantry Training, Part VIII – Fieldcraft, Battle Drill, Section and Platoon Tactics, War Office, 1944

Infantry Training: Training and War, HMSO, 1937

Instruction Manual for the Infantry, Vol. II, Field Fortifications of the Infantry, 1940, H.Dv. 130/11, English translation by John Baum, germanmanuals.com

Instruction Manual for the Infantry, Vol. 2a, The Rifle Company, 1942, H.Dv. 103/2a, English translation by John Baum, germanmanuals.com

Instruction Manual for the Infantry, Vol. 3a, The Machinegun Company, 1942, H.Dv. 130/3a, English translation by John Baum, germanmanuals.com

Logistical History of NATOUSA & MTOUSA, US War Department, 1945

Pilot's Notes General, Air Ministry, London, 1943

The Rise and Fall of the German Air Force (1933–1945), Air Ministry, 1948

Shooting to Live by Capt. W. E. Fairbairn and Capt. E. A. Sykes, 1942

Der Schütze hilfsbuch, 1943 by Oberst Hasso von Wedel and Oberleutnant Pfasserott, Richard Schröder Verlag, Berlin, 1943

Statistics Relating to the War Effort of the United Kingdom, HMSO, November 1944

Tactics in the Context of the Reinforced Infantry Battalions by Generalmajor Greiner and Generalmajor Degener, 1941, English translation by John Baum, germanmanuals.com

TEE EMM: Air Ministry Monthly Training Memoranda, Vols I, II, III, Air Ministry, 1939–45

Truppenführung: On the German Art of War, Condell, Bruce and Zabecki, David T. (eds.), Stackpole, 2009

What Britain Has Done 1939–1945, Ministry of Information, London, 1945

OFFICIAL HISTORIES

Aris, George, *The Fifth British Division 1939 to 1945*, The Fifth Division Benevolent Fund, 1959

Behrens, C. B. A., *Merchant Shipping and the Demands of War*, HMSO, 1955

Burdon, R. M., *24 Battalion*, War History Branch, Department of Internal Affairs, New Zealand, 1953

Cody, J. F., *28 (Maori) Battalion*, War History Branch, Department of Internal Affairs, New Zealand, 1956

Cosmas, Graham A. and Cowdrey, Albert E., *United States Army in World War II: Medical Service in the European Theater of Operations*, Historical Division Department of the Army, 1992

Craven, Wesley Frank and Cate, James Lea, *The Army Air Forces in World War II*, Vol. II: *Europe: Torch to Pointblank*, University of Chicago Press, 1947

Delaney, John P., *The Blue Devils in Italy: A History of the 88th Infantry Division in World War II*, The Battery Press, 1988

Duncan Hall, H. and Wrigley, C. C., *Studies of Overseas Supply*, HMSO, 1956

Echternkamp, Jörg (ed.), *Germany and the Second World War*, Vol. IX/I: *German Wartime Society 1939–1945: Politicization, Disintegration, and the Struggle for Survival*, Clarendon Press, 2008

Fairchild, Byron and Grossman, Jonathan, *United States Army in World War II: The Army and Industrial Manpower*, Office of the Chief of Military History, 1959

Fisher, Ernest F. Jr, *United States Army in World War II: Cassino to the Alps*, Center of Military History, United States Army, 1977

Garland, Albert N. and McGaw Smyth, Howard, *Sicily and the Surrender of Italy*, US Army in World War II, Center of Military History, United States Army, 1986

Hancock, W. K. and Gowing, M.M., *British War Economy*, HMSO, 1949

Harris, C. R. S., *Allied Military Administration of Italy, 1943–1945*, HMSO, 1957

Hinsley, F. H., *British Intelligence in the Second World War*, HMSO, 1993

Howard, Michael, *Grand Strategy*, Vol. IV: *August 1942–September 1943*, HMSO, 1972

George F. Howe, *The Battle History of the 1st Armored Division*, Combat Forces Press, 1954

Hurstfield, J., *The Control of Raw Materials*, HMSO, 1953

The Institution of the Royal Army Service Corps, *The Story of the Royal Army Service Corps 1939–1945*, G. Bell and Sons Ltd, 1955

Knickerbocker, H. R. et al., *United States Army in World War II: Danger Forward: The Story of the First Division in World War II*, Society of the First Division, 1947

Leighton, Richard M. and Coakley, Robert W., *United States Army in World War II: Global Logistics and Strategy 1940–1943*, Office of the Chief of Military History Department of the Army, 1955

—*United States Army in World War II: Global Logistics and Strategy 1943–1945*, Office of the Chief of Military History Department of the Army, 1968

Militärgeschichtliches Forschungsamt, *Germany and the Second World War*, Vol. V: *Organization and Mobilization of the German Sphere of Power, Part 1: Wartime Administration, Economy and Manpower Resources, 1939–1941*, Clarendon Press, 2000

—*Germany and the Second World War*, Vol. V: *Organization and Mobilization of the German Sphere of Power, Part 2B: Wartime Administration, Economy and Manpower Resources, 1942–1944/5*, Clarendon Press, 2003

—*Germany and the Second World War*, Vol. VI: *The Global War*, Clarendon Press, 2001

—*Germany and the Second World War*, Vol. VIII: *The Eastern Front 1943–1944: The War in the East and on the Neighbouring Fronts*, Clarendon Press, 2017

Molony, C. J. C., *The Mediterranean and the Middle East*, Vol. V, HMSO, 1973

Morison, Samuel Eliot, *History of the United States Naval Operations in World War II: Sicily-Salerno-Anzio, January 1943–June 1944*, Castle Books, 2001

Naval Historical Branch, *Invasion Europe*, HMSO, 1994

Nicholson, G. W. L., *Official History of the Canadian Army in the Second World War*, Vol. II: *The Canadians in Italy, 1943–1945*, Edmond Cloutier, 1957

Norton, Frazer D., *26 Battalion*, War History Branch, Department of Internal Affairs, New Zealand, 1952

Otway, T. B. H., *Airborne Forces of the Second World War 1939–45*, HMSO, 1951

Palmer, Robert R., Wiley, Bell I. and Keast, William R., *United States Army in World War II: The Procurement and Training of Ground Combat Troops*, Historical Division Department of the Army, 1948

Parker, H. M. D., *Manpower: A Study of War-time Policy and Administration*, HMSO, 1957

Pogue, Forrest, *United States Army in World War II: The Supreme Command*, Historical Division Department of the Army, 1954

Postan, M. M., *British War Production*, HMSO, 1952

Postan, M. M., Hay, D. and Scott, J. D., *Design and Development of Weapons*, HMSO, 1964

Puttick, Edward, *25 Battalion*, War History Branch, Department of Internal Affairs, New Zealand, 1960

Rapport, Leonard and Northwood, Arthur, *Rendezvous with Destiny: A History of the of 101st Airborne Division*, 101st Airborne Association, 1948

Richards, Denis, *Royal Air Force 1939–1945*, Vol. II: *The Fight Avails*, HMSO, 1954

—*Royal Air Force 1939–1945*, Vol. III: *The Fight is Won*, HMSO, 1954

Risch, Erna, *The Technical Services, United States Army in World War II: The Quartermaster Corps: Organization, Supply, and Services*, Vol. I, Historical Division Department of the Army, 1953

Rissik, David, *The D.L.I. at War: The History of the Durham Light Infantry 1939–1945*, The Depot: Durham Light Infantry, no date

Roberts Greenfield, Kent et al., *United States Army in World War II: The Organization of Ground Combat Troops*, Historical Division Department of the Army, 1947

Roy, R. H., *The Seaforth Highlanders of Canada, 1919-1965*, The Seaforth Highlanders of Canada, 1969

Scott, J. D. and Hughes, Richard, *The Administration of War Production*, HMSO, 1955

The Sextant, Eureka and Second Cairo Conferences, jcs.mil

Stevens, G. R., *Fourth Indian Division*, McLaren & Sons, 1948

Trident Conference Papers and Minutes of Meetings, jcs.mil

Wardlow, Chester, *United States Army in World War II: The Transportation Corps: Movements, Training, and Supply*, Office of the Chief of Military History, 1956

Warren, John C., *Airborne Operations in World War II, European Theater*, USAF Historical Division, 1956

—*Airborne Missions in the Mediterranean, 1942-1945*, USAF Historical Division, 1955

EQUIPMENT, WEAPONS AND TECHNICAL BOOKS

Barker, A. J., *British and American Infantry Weapons of World War 2*, Arms and Armour Press, 1969

Bidwell, Shelford and Graham, Dominick, *Fire-Power: British Army Weapons and Theories of War 1904–1945*, George Allen & Unwin, 1982

Bouchery, Jean, *The British Soldier*, Vol. 1: *Uniforms, Insignia, Equipment*, Histoire & Collections, no date

—*The British Soldier*, Vol. 2: *Organisation, Armament, Tanks and Vehicles*, Histoire & Collections, no date

Brayley, Martin, *The British Army 1939–45 (1) North-West Europe*, Osprey, 2001

—*British Web Equipment of the Two World Wars*, Crowood Press, 2005

Bruce, Robert, *German Automatic Weapons of World War II*, Crowood Press, 1996

Bull, Dr Stephen, *World War II Infantry Tactics*, Osprey, 2004

—*World War II Street-Fighting Tactics*, Osprey, 2008

Chamberlain, Peter and Ellis, Chris, *Tanks of the World*, Cassell, 2002

Chesneau, Roger (ed.), *Conway's All the World's Fighting Ships 1922–1946*, Conway Maritime Press, 1980

Dallies-Labourdette, Jean-Philippe, *S-Boote: German E-Boats in Action 1939–1945*, Histoire & Collections, no date

Davies, W. J. K., *German Army Handbook 1939–1945*, Military Book Society, 1973

Davis, Brian L., *German Combat Uniforms of World War II*, Vol. II, Arms & Armour Press, 1985

Doyle, David, *The Complete Guide to German Armored Vehicles*, Skyhorse, 2019

Enjames, Henri-Paul, *Government Issue: US Army European Theater of Operations Collection's Guide*, Histoire & Collections, 2003

Falconer, Jonathan, *D-Day Operations Manual*, Haynes, 2013

Farrar-Hockley, Anthony, *Infantry Tactics 1939–1945*, Almark, 1976

Fleischer, Wolfgang, *The Illustrated Guide to German Panzers*, Schiffer, 2002

Forty, George and Livesey, Jack, *The Complete Guide to Tanks and Armoured Fighting Vehicles*, Southwater, 2012

Gander, Terry and Chamberlain, Peter, *Small Arms, Artillery and Special Weapons of the Third Reich*, Macdonald and Jane's, 1978

Gordon, David B., *Equipment of the WWII Tommy*, Pictorial Histories, 2004

—*Uniforms of the WWII Tommy*, Pictorial Histories, 2005

—*Weapons of the WWII Tommy*, Pictorial Histories, 2004

Grant, Neil, *The Bren Gun*, Osprey, 2013

Griehl, Manfred and Dressel, Joachim, *Luftwaffe Combat Aircraft: Development, Production, Operations, 1935–1945*, Schiffer, 1994

Gunston, Bill, *Fighting Aircraft of World War II*, Salamander, 1988

Hart, S. and Hart, R., *The German Soldier in World War II*, Spellmount, 2000

Hogg, Ian V. (intro.), *The American Arsenal: The World War II Official Standard Ordnance Catalog of Small Arms, Tanks, Armored Cars, Artillery, Antiaircraft Guns, Ammunition, Grenades, Mines, Etcetera*, Greenhill Books, 1996

—*The Guns 1939–1945*, Macdonald, 1969

Jowett, Philip, *The Italian Army 1940–45 (1)*, Osprey, 2000

—*The Italian Army 1940–45 (2)*, Osprey, 2001

—*The Italian Army 1940–45 (3)*, Osprey, 2001

Kay, Antony L. and Smith, J. R., *German Aircraft of the Second World War*, Putnam, 2002

Konstan, Angus, *British Battlecruisers 1939–45*, Osprey, 2003

de Lagarde, Jean, *German Soldiers of World War II*, Histoire & Collections, no date

Lavery, Brian, *Churchill's Navy: The Ships, Men and Organisation 1939–1945*, Conway, 2006

Lee, Cyrus A., *Soldat*, Vol. II: *Equipping the German Army Foot Solider in Europe 1943*, Pictorial Histories, 1988

Lepage, Jean-Denis G. G., *German Military Vehicles*, McFarland & Company, 2007

Lüdeke, Alexander, *Weapons of World War II*, Parragon, 2007

Mason, Chris, *Soldat*, Vol. VIII: *Fallschirmjäger*, Pictorial Histories, 2000

McNab, Chris, *MG 34 and MG 42 Machine Guns*, Osprey, 2012

Ministry of Information, *What Britain Has Done, 1939–45*, HMSO

Mundt, Richard W. and Lee, Cyrus A., *Soldat*, Vol. VI: *Equipping the Waffen-SS Panzer Divisions 1942–1945*, Pictorial Histories, 1997

Musgrave, Daniel D., *German Machineguns*, Greenhill Books, 1992

Myerscough, W., *Air Navigation Simply Explained*, Pitman & Sons, Ltd, 1942

Ruge, Friedrich, *Rommel in Normandy*, Macdonald and Jane's, 1979

Saiz, Augustin, *Deutsche Soldaten*, Casemate, 2008

Spayd, P. A., *Bayerlein: From Afrikakorps to Panzer Lehr*, Schiffer, 2003

Stedmoan, Robert, *Kampfflieger: Bomber Crewman of the Luftwaffe 1939–45*, Osprey, 2005

Suermondt, Jan, *World War II Wehrmacht Vehicles*, Crowood Press, 2003

Sumner, Ian and Vauvillier, Francois, *The French Army 1939–1945* (1), Osprey, 1998

Sutherland, Jonathan, *World War II Tanks and AFVs*, Airlife, 2002

Trye, Rex, *Mussolini's Soldiers*, Airlife, 1995

Vanderveen, Bart, *Historic Military Vehicles Directory*, After the Battle, 1989

Williamson, Gordon, *Gebirgsjäger*, Osprey, 2003

—*German Mountain & Ski Troops 1939–45*, Osprey, 1996

—*U-Boats vs Destroyer Escorts*, Osprey, 2007

Windrow, Richard and Hawkins, Tim, *The World War II GI: US Army Uniforms 1941–45*, Crowood Press, 2003

Zaloga, Steven, *Armored Thunderbolt: The US Army Sherman in World War II*, Stackpole, 2008

—*Sicily 1943: The Debut of Allied Joint Operations*, Osprey, 2013

—*US Anti-Tank Artillery 1941–45*, Osprey, 2005

MEMOIRS, BIOGRAPHIES ETC.

Alanbrooke, Field Marshal Lord, *War Diaries, 1939–1945*, Weidenfeld & Nicolson, 2001

Alexander, Field Marshal Earl, *The Alexander Memoirs 1940–1945*, McGraw-Hill, 1962

Alexander, Mark J. and Sparry, John, *Jump Commander*, Casemate, 2012

Altieri, James, *The Spearheaders*, Popular Library, 1960

Ambrose, Stephen E., *Eisenhower: Soldier & President*, Pocket Books, 2003

—*The Supreme Commander: The War Years of Dwight D. Eisenhower*, University Press of Mississippi, 1999

Ardizzone, Edward, *Diary of a War Artist*, Bodley Head, 1974

Arneson, Paul S., *I Closed Too Many Eyes: A World War II Medic Finally Talks*, self-published, no date

Awatere, Arapeta, *Awatere: A Soldier's Story*, Huia, 2003

Badoglio, Marshal, *Italy in the Second World War*, Oxford University Press, 1948

Balck, Hermann, *Order in Chaos*, University Press of Kentucky, 2015

Ball, Edmund F., *Staff Officer with the Fifth Army*, Exposition Press, 1958

Bentivegna, Rosario, *Achtung Banditen! Roma 1944*, Mursia, 1983

Binder, L. James, *Lemnitzer: A Soldier for His Time*, Brassey's, 1997

Blumenson, Martin, *Mark Clark*, Jonathan Cape, 1985

Booth, T. Michael and Spencer, Duncan, *Paratrooper: The Life of General James M. Gavin*, Casemate, 2013

Bosworth, R. J. B., *Mussolini*, Arnold, 2002

Bradner, Liesl, *Snap Dragon: The World War II Exploits of Darby's Ranger and Combat Photographer Phil Stern*, Osprey, 2018

Bruno, James F., *Beyond Fighter Escort*, Ken Cook Co., 1995

Buchner, Emajean, *Sparks*, Thunderbird Press, 1991

Bull, Peter, *To Sea in a Sieve*, Peter Davies Ltd, 1956

Bulteel, Christopher, *Something About a Soldier*, Airlife, 2000

Burgwyn, H. James, *Mussolini Warlord: Failed Dreams of Empire 1940–1943*, Enigma Books, 2012

Burnes, John Horne, *The Gallery*, New York Review Books, 2004

Butcher, Harry C., *Three Years with Eisenhower*, William Heinemann, 1946

Byers, E. V., *With Turbans to Tuscany*, self-published, 2002

Caddick-Adams, Peter, *Monty and Rommel: Parallel Lives*, Arrow, 2012

Capponi, Carla, *Con cuore di donna*, Il Saggiatore, 2000

Caracciolo, Filippo, *43/44 Diario di Napoli*, Valecchi Editore, 1964

Carboni, Generale Giacomo, *L'Armistizio e la Difesa di Roma*, Donatello de Luigi, 1945

Caruso, Pasqualina, *Vivere per raccontare: diario di uerra, 1940–1945*, Città di Eboli, 2008

Cederberg, Fred, *The Long Road Home*, General Paperbacks, 1989

Chandler, Alfred D. Jr (ed.), *The Papers of Dwight David Eisenhower: The War Years II*, Johns Hopkins Press, 1970

—*The Papers of Dwight David Eisenhower: The War Years III*, Johns Hopkins Press, 1970

Churchill, Winston S., *The Second World War*, Vol. V: *Closing the Ring*, Cassell, 1952

Ciano, Galeazzo, *Ciano's Diary 1937–1943*, Phoenix, 2002

Clark, Mark W., *Calculated Risk*, Harper & Brothers, 1950

Clarke, Rupert, *With Alex at War*, Pen & Sword, 2000

Cole, David, *Rough Road to Rome: A Foot Soldier in Sicily and Italy 1943–44*, William Kimber, 1983

Comfort, Charles Fraser, *Artist at War*, Remembrance Books, 1995

Corrado Teatini, Giuseppe, *Diario Dall'Egeo*, Murso, 1990

Corti, Eugenio, *The Last Soldiers of the King*, University of Missouri Press, 2003

Corvo, Max, *Max Corvo: OSS in Italy, 1942–1945*, Enigma Books, 2005

Cunningham, Admiral of the Fleet Viscount, *A Sailor's Odyssey*, Hutchinson, 1951

Darby, William O. with Baumer, William H., *Darby's Rangers*, Ballantine Books, 2003

Davis, Peter, *SAS: Men in the Making*, Pen & Sword, 2015

Davis, Richard G., *Carl A. Spaatz and the Air War in Europe*, Center for Air Force History, 1992

Deakin, F. W., *The Brutal Friendship: Mussolini, Hitler and the Fall of Italian Fascism*, Pelican, 1966

Defazio, Albert, *The Italian Campaign: One Soldier's Story of a Forgotten War*, Merriam Press, 2020

De Grada, Magda Ceccarelli, *Giornale del tempo di Guerra,* Il Mulino, 2011

De Rosa, Fernando, *L'Ora Tragica di Montecassino*, Editrice SIGRAF, no date

Destefano, Anthony M., *The Deadly Don: Vito Genovese Mafia Boss*, Citadel Press, 2021

De Wyss, M., *Rome Under the Terror*, Robert Hale, 1945

Doolittle, James H. 'Jimmy', *I Could Never Be So Lucky Again*, Bantam, 1992

Doughty, Roswell K., *Invading Hitler's Europe*, Frontline Books, 2020

Dundas, Hugh, *Flying Start*, Penguin, 1990

Durnford-Slater, John, *Commando: Memoirs of a Fighting Commando in World War Two*, Greenhill, 2002

Eisenhower, Dwight D., *Crusade in Europe*, William Heinemann, 1948

Fairbanks, Jr, Douglas, *A Hell of a War*, St Martin's Press, 1993

Farrell, Nicholas, *Mussolini: A New Life*, Phoenix, 2004

Forman, Denis, *To Reason Why*, Pen & Sword, 2008

Gavin, James M., *On to Berlin: Battle of an Airborne Commander, 1943–1946*, Viking, 1978

Gilmour, David, *The Pursuit of Italy*, Penguin, 2012

Gnecchi-Ruscone, Francesco, *When Being Italian Was Difficult*, Milan, 1999

Eusebio Grossetti and Martino Matronola, *Monte Cassino under Fire: War Diaries from the Abbey*, Pubblicazioni Cassinesi, Montecassino, 1988

Guest, John, *Broken Images*, Leo Cooper, 1949

Gunner, Colin, *Front of the Line: Adventures with the Irish Brigade*, Greystone Books, 1991

Gorle, Richmond, *The Quiet Gunner at War: El Alamein to the Rhine with the Scottish Divisions*, Pen & Sword, 2011

Hamilton, Nigel, *Monty: Master of the Battlefield 1942–1944*, Hamish Hamilton, 1983

Hamilton, Stuart, *Armoured Odyssey*, Tom Donovan Publishing, 1995

Hirst, Fred, *A Green Hill Far Away*, Charlesworth, 1998

Horne, Alastair, *Macmillan 1894–1956*, Macmillan, 1988

Horsfall, John, *Fling Our Banner to the Wind*, Roundwood Press, 1978

Howard, Michael, *Captain Professor: A Life in War and Peace*, Continuum UK, 2006

Huebner, Klaus H., *Long Walk Through War*, Texas A&M University Press, 1987

Jackson, W. G. F., *Alexander of Tunis as Military Commander*, Batsford, 1971

Kemp, Nick, *Ever your own, Johnnie – Sicily and Italy, 1943–45*, Nick Kemp Books, 2016

Kennedy, Alex, *The Liberator: One World War II Soldier's 500-Day Odyssey*, Arrow, 2013

Kennedy, I. F., *Black Crosses on My Wingtip*, GSPH, 1995

Kershaw, Ian, *Hitler: 1936–1945 – Nemesis*, Penguin, 2001

Kesselring, Albert, *The Memoirs of Field-Marshal Kesselring*, Greenhill Books, 2007

Klein, Joseph, *Fallschirmjäger*, self-published, 2008

Lewis, Norman, *Naples '44*, Eland, 1983

Macmillan, Harold, *The Blast of War 1939–1945*, Harper & Row, 1967

—*War Diaries: The Mediterranean 1943–1945*, Macmillan, 1984

Masella, Mirella, *Through a Child's Eyes*, New Generation Publishing, 2022

Mauss, Hans-Jörg and de Rijke, Roger, *The War Diary of Dr. Wilhelm Mauss*, Mook Publishing, 2016

McCrum, Tony, *Sunk by Stukas Survived at Salerno*, Pen & Sword, 2010

McIntosh, Charles, *From Cloak to Dagger: An SOE Agent in Italy 1943–1945*, William Kimber, 1992

Meon, Marcia and Heinen, Margo, *Heroes Cry Too*, Meadowlark Publishing, 2002

Miller, Victor, *Nothing Is Impossible*, Pen & Sword, 2015

Millers, Lee G., *The Story of Ernie Pyle*, Viking, 1950

Milligan, Spike, *Mussolini: His Part in My Downfall*, Penguin, 2012

Montanaro, Elena, *Tra le Pieghe della Memoria*, Edizione a cura dell'Amministrazione Comunale di Piedmonte S. Germano, 2004

Montgomery, Field Marshal the Viscount, *El Alamein to the Sangro*, Hutchinson, 1944

—*Memoirs*, Collins, 1958

Moore, Peter, *No Need to Worry*, Wilton 65, 2002

Moorehead, Alan, *Eclispse*, Penguin 2022

Mowat, Farley, *And No Birds Sang*, Douglas & McIntyre, 2012

—*The Regiment*, McClelland & Stewart, 1955

Murphy, Audie, *To Hell and Back*, Picador, 2002

Murphy, Thomas D., *Ambassadors in Arms*, University of Hawaii Press, 2020

Nicolson, Nigel, *Alex: The Life of Field Marshal Earl Alexander of Tunis*, Weidenfeld & Nicolson, 1973

—*Long Life: Memoirs*, Weidenfeld & Nicolson, 1997

O'Brien, Phillips Payson, *The Second Most Powerful Man in the World: The Life of Admiral William D. Leahy, Roosevelt's Chief of Staff*, Caliber, 2020

Orange, Vincent, *Coningham: A Biography of Air Marshal Sir Arthur Coningham*, Center for Air Force History, 1990

Origo, Iris, *War in Val d'Orcia*, Flamingo, 2002

Packer, Joy, *Deep As The Sea*, Corgi, 1977

Pearce, John A., *A Private in the Texas Army*, State House Press, 2021

Peyton, John, *Solly Zuckerman*, John Murray, 2001

Pogue, Forrest C., *George C. Marshall: Interviews and Reminiscences*, Marshall Foundation, 1991

Pöppel, Martin, *Heaven & Hell: The Wartime Diary of a German Paratrooper*, Spellmount, 1988

Pyle, Ernie, *Brave Men*, Henry Holt, 1944

—*Here Is Your War*, Forum Books, 1945

Reed, James E., *The Fighting 33rd Nomads in World War II*, Vol. II, Reed Publishers, 1988

Reynolds, L. C., *Motor Gunboat 658*, Cassell & Co, 2002

Reynolds, Quentin, *The Curtain Rises,* Random House, 1944

Richardson, Robert L., *The Jagged Edge of Duty: A Fighter Pilot's World War II*, Stackpole, 2017

Ridgway, Matthew B., *Soldier: The Memoirs of Matthew B. Ridgway*, Harper & Brothers, 1956

Roberts, William F., *Bonus Time: One Pilot's Story of World War II*, Xlibris Corporation, 2002

Robinson, James A., *Alexander*, Banbridge Chronicle Press, 1946

Robinson, Stephen, *Panzer Commander: Hermann Balck Germany's Master Tactician*, Exisle, 2019

Ross, Hamish, *Paddy Mayne*, History Press, 2004

Samwell, H. P., *Fighting with the Desert Rats: An Infantry Officer's War with the Eighth Army*, Pen & Sword, 2012

Scislowski, Stanley, *Not All of Us Were Brave*, Dundurn Press, 1997

Senger und Etterlin, Frido von, *Neither Fear Nor Hope*, Presidio, 1989

Smith, David A., *The Price of Valor: The Life of Audie Murphy, America's Most Decorated Hero of World War II*, Regnery History, 2015

Smith, Roger, *Up the Blue*, Ngaio Press, 2000

Steinbeck, John, *Once There Was a War*, Penguin, 2000

Stowers, Richard, *Wellingtons Over the Med*, Richard Stowers, 2012

Sullivan, T. Michael, *Life in the Service: Echoes of the Army*, General Advertising Publishers, 2013

Teatini, Giuseppe Corrado, *Diario dell'Egio*, Mursia, 1990

Tedder, Marshal of the Royal Air Force Lord, *With Prejudice*, Cassell, 1966

Tobin, James, *Ernie Pyle's War*, University of Kansas Press, 1997

Tompkins, Peter, *A Spy in Rome*, Simon & Schuster, 1962

Tregaskis, Richard, *Invasion Diary*, Random House, 1944

Truscott, Lucian K., *Command Missions*, Presidio, 1990

Ullrich, Volker, *Hitler: Downfall, 1939–45*, Bodley Head, 2020

Valenzi, Maurizio, *C'è Togliatti!*, Sellerio Editore, 1996

Vrilakas, Robert 'Smoky', *Look Mom – I Can Fly!*, Amethyst Moon Publishing, 2011
Wagner, Bud, *And There Shall Be War: World War II Diaries and Memoirs*, Wilmer Wagner & Lloyd Wagner Press, 2000
Warlimont, Walter, *Inside Hitler's Headquarters 1939–45*, Presidio, 1962
Warner, Oliver, *Cunningham of Hyndehope: Admiral of the Fleet*, John Murray, 1967
Whicker, Alan, *Whicker's War*, HarperCollins, 2005
Winton, John, *Cunningham: The Greatest Admiral Since Nelson*, John Murray, 1998

GENERAL

Allport, Alan, *Browned Off and Bloody-Minded*, Yale University Press, 2017
Alonso, Miguel et al. (eds.), *Fascist Warfare 1922–1945*, Palgrave Macmillan, 2019
Anon., *The Rise and Fall of the German Air Force 1933–1945*, Air Ministry, 1948
Anon., *Italy*, Vol. I, Naval Intelligence Division, 1944
—*Italy*, Vol. II, Naval Intelligence Division, 1945
Arthur, Max, *Men of the Red Beret*, Hutchinson, 1990
Associazione Nazionale Combattenti della Guerra di Liberazione Inquadrati nei Reparti Regolari delle Forze Armate, *La Ricossa dell'Esercito: Il Primo Raggruppamento Motorizzato Monte Lungo*, Cassino, 1993
Atkinson, Rick, *The Day of Battle: The War in Sicily and Italy, 1943–1944*, Abacus, 2007
Baedeker, Karl, *Southern Italy and Sicily*, Karl Baedeker, 1912
Ballantine, Duncan S., *US Naval Logistics in the Second World War*, Princeton University Press, 1949
Battaglia, Roberto, *The Story of the Italian Resistance*, Odhams Press, 1957
Bekker, Cajus, *The Luftwaffe War Diaries*, Corgi, 1972
Black, Robert W., *Rangers in World War II*, Ballantine, 1992
Bosworth, R. J. B., *Mussolini's Italy: Life Under Dictatorship*, Penguin, 2006
Bowlby, Alex, *Countdown to Cassino*, Leo Cooper, 1995
Carafano, James Jay, *GI Ingenuity: Improvisation, Technology and Winning WWII*, Stackpole, 2006
Champagne, Daniel, *Dogface Soldiers: The Story of B Company, 15th Regiment, 3rd Infantry Division*, Merriam Press, 2003
Christensen, Ben, *The 1st Fallschirmjäger Division in World War II*, Vol. II: *Years of Retreat*, Schiffer, 2007
Citino, Robert M., *The German Way of War*, University Press of Kansas, 2005
—*The Wehrmacht Retreats: Fighting a Lost War, 1943*, University Press of Kansas, 2012
Clark, Lloyd, *Anzio: The Friction of War*, Headline, 2006
Cook, Tim, *The Necessary War*, Vol. I: *Canadians Fighting in the Second World War 1939–1943*, Allen Lane, 2014
Dancocks, Daniel G., *The D-Day Dodgers: The Canadians in Italy 1943–1945*, McClelland & Stewart, 1991
Daudy, Philippe, *Naples*, Editions Recontre, 1964

David, Saul, *The Force*, Hachette, 2019

Deakin, F. W., *The Brutal Friendship*, Pelican Books, 1966

De Luna, Giovanni, *Storia del Partito D'Azione,* Feltrinelli, 1982

Dickson, Paul, *The Rise of the G.I. Army, 1940–1941*, Atlantic Monthly Press, 2020

Di Marco, Andrea, *Assolutamente Resistere!*, Abruzzo Edizioni Menabo, 2013

Dinardo, R. L., *Germany and the Axis Powers: From Coalition to Collapse*, University of Kansas Press, 2005

—*Germany's Panzer Arm in WWII*, Stackpole, 1997

Doherty, Richard, *Clear the Way! A History of the 38th (Irish) Brigade, 1941–47*, Irish Academic Press, 1993

Duggan, Christopher, *Fascist Voices: An Intimate History of Mussolini's Italy*, Bodley Head, 2012

Edgerton, David, *Britain's War Machine*, Penguin, 2012

—*Warfare State: Britain 1920–1970*, Cambridge University Press, 2006

Ellwood, David W., *Italy 1943–1945*, Leicester University Press, 1985

Eriksson, Patrick G., *Alarmstart South and Final Defeat*, Amberley, 2019

Faguet, Guy B., *The War on Cancer: An Anatomy of Failure, A Blueprint for the Future*, Springer, 2005

Fennell, Jonathan, *Fighting the People's War*, Cambridge University Press, 2019

Ford, Ken, *Battleaxe Division*, Sutton, 2003

Fraser, David, *And We Shall Shock Them: The British Army in the Second World War*, Cassell, 1999

French, David, *Raising Churchill's Army: The British Army and the War Against Germany 1919–1945*, Oxford University Press, 2000

Gardiner, Wira, *The Story of the Maori Battalion*, Reed, 1995

Gavin, James M. and Lee, William C., *Airborne Warfare*, Infantry Journal Press, 1947

Gooderson, Ian, *Air Power at the Battlefront: Allied Close Air Support in Europe, 1943–45*, Frank Cass, 1998

Gregory, Barry, *British Airborne Troops*, Macdonald & Jane's, 1974

Harrison Place, Timothy, *Military Training in the British Army, 1940–1944*, Frank Cass, 2000

Harris Smith, Richard, *OSS: The Secret of America's First Central Intelligence Agency*, The Lyons Press, 2005

Heaton, Colin D. and Lewis, Anne-Marie, *The German Aces Speak*, Zenith Press, 2011

Holland, James, *Heroes: The Greatest Generation and the Second World War*, Harper Perennial, 2007

—*Italy's Sorrow: A Year of War 1944–45*, Harper Press, 2008

Howard, Michael, *The Mediterranean Strategy in the Second World War*, Greenhill Books, 1993

Hoyt, Edwin P., *The GI's War*, Cooper Square Press, 2000

Irving, David, *The Rise and Fall of the Luftwaffe: The Life of Luftwaffe Marshal Erhard Milch*, Weidenfeld & Nicolson, 1973

Jackson, W. G. F., *The Battle for Italy*, Harper & Row, 1967

Jadecola, Costantino, *Vallerotonda, Da Volturno a Cassino*, no date

Joseph, Frank, *Mussolini's War*, Helion, 2010

Katz, Robert, *Fatal Silence*, Cassell, 2004

Knox, MacGregor, *Hitler's Italian Allies*, Cambridge University Press, 2000

Kogan, Norman, *Italy and the Allies*, Harvard University Press, 1956

Kurowski, Franz, *The History of the Fallschirm Panzerkorps Hermann Göring*, J. J. Fedorowicz Publishing, 1995

Lamb, Richard, *War in Italy 1943–1945: A Brutal Story*, John Murray, 1993

Leccisotti, Tommaso, *Monte Cassino*, Pubblicazioni Cassinesi, Montecassino, 1987

Linklater, Eric, *The Campaign in Italy*, HMSO, 1951

LoFaro, Guy, *The Sword of St. Michael: The 82nd Airborne Division in World War II*, Da Capo, 2011

Lopez, Jean et al., *World War II Infographics*, Thames & Hudson, 2019

Macintyre, Ben, *SAS Rogue Heroes*, Viking, 2016

Malatesta, Saverio, *Orsogna 1943*, Edizioni Menabo, 2016

Mallinson, Jennifer, *From Taranto to Trieste: Following the 2nd NZ Division's Italian Campaign, 1943–45*, Fraser Books, 2019

Marlantes, Karl, *What It Is Like to Go to War*, Atlantic Monthly Press, 2011

McGaw Smyth, Howard, *Secrets of the Fascist Era*, Southern Illinois University Press, 1973

McManus, John C., *American Courage, American Carnage: 7th Infantry Chronicles 1812 Through World War II*, Forge Books, 2009

—*Deadly Sky: The American Combat Airman in World War II*, Presidio Press, 2000

—*Grunts: Inside the American Combat Experience World War II Through Iraq*, Dutton Caliber, 2011

—*The Deadly Brotherhood: The American Combat Soldier in World War II*, Presidio Press, 2003

Mead, Richard, *Churchill's Lions: A Biographical Guide to the Key British Generals of World War II*, Spellmount, 2007

—*The Men Behind Monty*, Pen & Sword, 2015

Midson, Harold John 'Peter', *The Thomas Cook Division*, self-published, 2022

Mortimer, Gavin, *Stirling's Men: The Inside History of the SAS in World War II*, Cassell, 2005

Murray, Al, *Command*, Headline, 2022

O'Brien, Phillips Payson, *How the War Was Won*, Cambridge University Press, 2015

O'Connor, Garry, *The 1st Household Cavalry, 1943–44*, Pen & Sword, 2013

Parker, Matthew, *Monte Cassino*, Headline, 2004

Pond, Hugh, *Salerno*, William Kimber, 1961

Prien, Jochen, *Jagdgeschwader 53: A History of the 'Pik As' Geschwader May 1942–January 1944*, Schiffer, 1998

Quilter, D. C. (ed.), *'No Dishonourable Name'*, William Clowes & Sons Ltd, 1948

Reynolds, Leonard C., *Dog Boats at War*, The History Press, 1998

Roskill, Stephen, *The Navy at War 1939–1945*, Wordsworth Editions, 1998

Saunders, Anne Leslie, *A Travel Guide to the World War II Sites in Italy*, Travel Guide Press, 2016

Schmitz, Günter, *Die 16. Panzer-Division 1938–1945*, Podzun-Pallas-Verlag, no date

Shores, Christopher, Massimello, Giovanni et al., *A History of the Mediterranean Air War 1940–1945*, Vol. IV: *Sicily and Italy to the Fall of Rome, 14 May 1943–5 June 1944*, Grub Street, 2018

Short, Neil, *German Defences in Italy in World War II*, Osprey, 2006

Solly, Major A. E. (ed.), *The 'Faugh-a-Ballagh': The Regimental Gazette of The Royal Irish Fusiliers, 1943–1949*, Combined Services Publications Ltd, 1950

Stargardt, Nicholas, *The German War: A Nation Under Arms, 1939–45*, Bodley Head, 2015

Steinhoff, Johannes, Pechel, Peter and Showalter, Dennis, *Voices From the Third Reich: An Oral History*, Da Capo, 1994

Thompson, Julian, *Ready for Anything: The Parachute Regiment at War 1940–1982*, Weidenfeld & Nicolson, 1989

Todman, Daniel, *Britain's War: Into Battle, 1937–1941*, Allen Lane, 2016

—*Britain's War: A New World, 1942–1947*, Allen Lane, 2020

Tompkins, Peter, *Italy Betrayed*, Simon & Schuster, 1966

Tooze, Adam, *The Wages of Destruction: The Making and Breaking of the Nazi Economy*, Penguin, 2007

Weal, John, *Jagdgeschwader 53 'Piks-As'*, Osprey, 2007

Werthen, Wolfgang, *Geschichte der 16. Panzer-Division*, Podzun-Verlag, 1958

Whiting, Charles, *Hunters From the Sky*, Cooper Square Press, 2001

Zambardi, Maurizio, *Memorie di Guerra*, Edizione Eva, 2003

Zuehlke, Mark, *Ortona*, Douglas & McIntyre, 2003

PERIODICALS, JOURNALS, MAGAZINES AND PAMPHLETS

After the Battle, No. 13, *Cassino Battlefield Tour*

After the Battle, No. 18, *The Battle for San Pietro*

After the Battle, No. 95, *Salerno*

After the Battle, No. 142, Rowe, Perry, *Faking Monte Cassino*

After the Battle, No.183, *The Battle of Ortona*

After the Battle, No.192, *The Battle for Orsogna*

Clift, Pfc Glenn C., *A Letter from Salerno*, New York Public Library, 1943

Varsori, Antonio, 'Italy, Britain and the Problem of a Separate Peace During the Second World War: 1940–1943', *The Journal of Italian History*, Vol. 1, No. 3

A soldier of the 4th Hampshires, armed with a Tommy gun, keeps watch from a farmhouse near Naples on 25 September 1943.

Acknowledgements

Writing a book such as this involves spending a huge amount of time in one's own company. There's research to be done, which, for the most part, is carried out alone. Then there's the phase of marshalling all the information that has been gathered, and getting ducks in a row. Finally, there's the writing, and there's only one person who can do that. None the less, all these phases of the book's genesis and creation can only be fulfilled with the help of an embarrassingly large amount of help and from so many different quarters.

I've been lucky enough to visit a number of archives and at every turn those who look after and work at these places have been unfailingly helpful. My thanks to all the staff at the Imperial War Museum in London, but particularly Jane Rosen, also to the staff of The National Archives at Kew, and the staff at the Liddell Hart Archives for Military History at King's College, London; to Glyn Prysor and the gang at the National Army Museum in Chelsea. In the United States, my thanks to the staff at the National Archives and Records Administration at College Park, Maryland, and to the brilliant team at the United States Army Education and Heritage Center at Carlisle, Pennsylvania – and especially to Tom Buffenbarger, who could not have been more helpful during my time there. Thank you to Tessa Updike and the team at The Citadel in Charleston, South Carolina, for being so helpful and for making me so welcome. The team at the National World War II Museum in New Orleans are now firm friends as well as unfailingly helpful, and special thanks are due to the brilliant Sarah Kirksey, Becky Mackie and Jeremy Collins. In Germany, I'd like to thank the staff of the Bundesarchiv-Militärarchiv at Freiburg and also the staff of the Tagebuch Archiv at Emmendingen.

In Italy, numerous people gave incredible help, and I owe particular thanks to the following: Dr Greta de Angeles Curtis at the CDSC Centro Documentazione e Studi Cassinati; Costantino Jadecola, who helped considerably with researching the Collelungo massacre; Cristina Cangi at the Archivio Diaristico Nazionale at Pieve Santo Stefano; John Simkins of the Monte San Martino Trust; Berniero Barra, the Director of the Centro Culturale Studi Storico; to Giuseppe Caucci of the Associazione Linea Gustav Fronte Garigliano, who gave me a guided tour of his superb museum there in Castelforte; to Alberto Turinetti di Priero and Valentino Rossetti for their help with the Collelungo research; to Anna Balzarro at the IRSIFAR Istituto Romano per la Storia d'Italia dal Fascismo all Resistenza, Roma; Antonella at the Archivio di Stato in Chieti; Mario Renaudi at the Museo Specialistico della Linea Gustav in Castel di Sangro; Don Mariano Dell'Omo at the Archivio di Montecassino; Gaetano Bonelli at the Museo di Napoli Collezione Bonelli; Monica Sperabene at the Sala Collezioni Speciali at the Biblioteca Nazionale Centrale di Roma; and Kate at the Institute of Historical Research at the University of London. My special thanks, however, go to Andrea di Marco in Ortona and to Dr Damiano Parravano, who have become good friends and who have been unfailingly helpful at every turn. Damiano also led me up to the summit of Monte Sammucro, up Monte Camino and Bare Arse Ridge and took me to see the massacre site at Collelungo, while Andrea took me on a memorable tour around Ortona. *Grazie mille*, Damiano and Andrea.

A number of other people have helped along the way. I am hugely grateful to brothers Richard and Eddie O'Sullivan, who do incredible work keeping the flame alive for the 38th Irish Brigade and who helped get permission for me to use the extraordinary wartime letters of Lawrie Franklyn-Vaile. Joe Hudgens has been incredibly kind in compiling and sending me the wartime air graphs of his wife's great-uncle, Leonard Obermeier, who served with the 36th Division. Henry Wilson has very kindly shared with me his great-grandfather's wartime letters. Earl Alexander has, over many years, been incredibly generous in sharing many of his father's papers and letters. Among others who have sent me material, photos and shared details of their various relations who served in Italy are the following: Jake Haywood, Andy de Rosa, Philip Trounsdell, Arturo Bugaon, Athol Forbes, Rod Whitamore, Thomas Bone, Jay Lowrey, Konrad Harandon, Simon Kovach, Richard Willan, Ray Moroney, Patrick Herring, Emma Howard, Charlie Barne, Oliver Davey and Frank Barnard.

Others who have helped in various ways are Alex Garrick in Canberra, Jenny Isted and Lorraine Davidson at Traveller's World in Salisbury, Joanne Muhammad, Jane O'Hara and Hugh Alexander.

There are also a host of fellow historians and friends who have helped along the way with material, advice and lending an ear. Huge thanks are due to Matt Doncaster, a former fighter pilot with the RAF, for reading the manuscript and checking the aerial sequences and generally giving it the once-over with his eagle eye. I'm very grateful to Matthew Parker for sharing his archive with me, and also Saul David, a great friend, who has kindly shared material. Mike Neiberg has been a great help as well as brilliant company along with his wife, Barbara, while in Carlisle, PA. Huge thanks to James Scott and his family for their company and for putting me up in Charleston. Peter Caddick-Adams is another great old chum who has offered a number of incredibly useful pointers, thoughts and suggestions; conversations with Peter are always invaluable and he has, as ever, steered me in various directions and given me much over which to ponder. Thank you, Peter. Stephen Fisher has been very helpful with the naval aspect of the campaign, as has Steve Prince, another great pal and sounding board. My thanks, too, to Kate Brett and Steve's team at the Naval Historical Branch. Thanks also to Jonathan Fennell and John Tregoning.

Huge thanks to the History Hit team: the brilliant Dan Snow, Joe Greenway and Bill Locke and the amazing posse with whom I toured southern Italy and who gave me the chance to have one more look at the battlegrounds before signing off the manuscript – to Mark Edger and Laura McMillen, massive thanks and especially for such brilliant company, enthusiasm and professionalism.

A couple of people have given special help with archival work and translations. Pete Connor in New Zealand has been very generous with sharing his own research into the New Zealanders' experience in Italy and especially his work on the 24th Battalion. Thank you, Pete. Brad St Croix has done a terrific job in Canada – huge thanks, Brad. Dorothee Schneider is an old friend but also a great travelling companion in Freiburg and Emmendingen – Dorothee, thank you, as always. Charlie Mitford has not only been a brilliant and tireless help with translations but has also been a great addition to the History Hit team in Italy – Charlie, I cannot thank you enough for all your immense help. Laura Bailey has helped out at Kew, the IWM, transcribing and generally being incredibly helpful at every turn – Laura, thank you. Thanks, too, to Oli Senior, neighbour and fellow cricketer, who was roped in to help with translations and my ever-growing archive. Merryn Walters has also been brilliant transcribing diaries, offering pointers and extra documents and for coming up with the title for this book. Merryn – you're a pal. Thank you.

I am extremely fortunate to be published by such brilliant teams either side of the Atlantic. At Grove Atlantic in New York, I am enormously grateful to all the team – to Deb Seager, Kait Astrella, Andrew Unger, Ian Dreiblatt, Natalie Church, Emily Burns, the ever-supportive head man, Morgan Entrekin, and most of all to George Gibson, a brilliant editor, friend and a man whose judgement I have come to trust and value immensely. Thank you. In London, huge thanks as always to the brilliant Bantam Press team: to Larry Finlay, Eloisa Clegg, Nicole Witmer, Katrina Whone, Phil Lord for so brilliantly pulling all the maps, pictures and the overall look of the book together, Tony Maddock for the absolutely stunning jacket artwork, Tom Hill for all his hard work on the PR front, and to Melissa Kelly for such a terrific marketing campaign. Especial thanks, as ever, are due to Bill Scott-Kerr, a great friend and colleague and simply a brilliant editor and publisher. I always feel in such incredibly safe hands and know you'll always have my back – I cannot thank you enough. Massive thanks, too, are due to Linden Lawson, who has taken over the extremely challenging task of copy-editing my books and has faced a savage storm of her own licking this into shape. You've done a brilliant job, Linden, and I am enormously grateful to you. Huge thanks, too, to Patrick Walsh, an extraordinary agent, and great friend. I feel very blessed – thank you.

I have also been lucky to have had the opportunity to share the development of this book as it has progressed on the podcast I co-host with Al Murray, *We Have Ways of Making You Talk*, and also, once a week, John McManus. John has been an enormous help – patiently listening to my theories and proving an invaluable sounding board. Huge thanks, John. The team at Goal Hanger who produce the podcast are all owed a *Warspite*-size amount of thanks – so, to Tony Pastor, Joey McCarthy, Jon Gill, Harry Lineker, Izzy Reid and all the team there, good on you. Thank you, too, to all the listeners and especially the Independent Company members, for tuning in and for allowing me to indulge in waffling on about the Italian campaign at such length.

But I cannot write these acknowledgements without a *Yamato*-size nod to a great pal and the co-host of the pod, Al Murray. Thank you, Al, for patiently listening, for sharing thoughts and ideas, for chewing the cud over whether Mark Clark really should be better appreciated and for providing me with such great company as we strive to understand this enormous subject a teeny bit better. And, of course, thank you for reading the book so beautifully.

Finally, thank you to my family, Rachel, Ned and Daisy, for putting up with this sometimes all-consuming job, to Ned for joining the History Hit team in Italy, and to all three of you for always being there for me. And last, but by no means least, *grazie mille* to my old friend David Walsh, great painter and Italophile, to whom this book is dedicated, for accompanying me on a wonderful tour of the battlegrounds in October 2022 and for your friendship, enthusiasm, immense good humour and unswervingly optimistic outlook.

Above: Two Fallschirmjäger pause to light their pipes.

Below: German POWs marched back away from the front lines. They don't look particularly sorry to be out of the war.

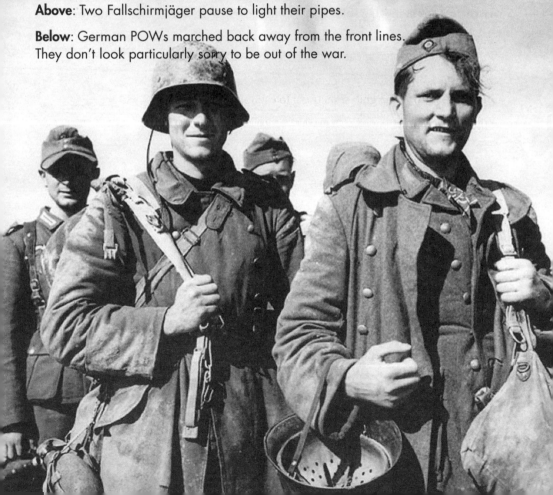

Picture Acknowledgements

Page 1, top left
Bombs over Foggia: Courtesy National Archives and Records Administration, USA (Photo no. A-25149)

Page 1, top right
German column moving southwards: Supplied by the author

Page 1, centre left
Pilots resting between sorties at Cancello: Jochen Prien

Page 1, centre right
Fighter pilots of JG53 grab something to eat: Jochen Prien

Page 1, bottom left
Lockheed P-38 Lightning plane: Supplied by the author

Page 1, bottom right
Photocall after the Italian armistice: In Public Domain

Page 2, top left
A British Tommy looks down at the mass of landing craft: © IWM NA 6283

Page 2, top right
Journalist Alan Moorehead on General Montgomery's assault craft: © IWM NA 6212

Page 2, centre
American DUKWs drive on to the beaches of Calabria: © IWM NA 6636

Page 2, 2nd centre row, left
Carnage in Calabria: © IWM NA 6477

Page 2, 2nd centre row, right
Italian soldiers, prisoners of war: © IWM NA 6270

Page 2, bottom
Even civilians welcomed the Allies as liberators: © IWM NA 6388

Page 3, top left
German engineers laying mines: Lüthge/Bundesarchiv, Bild 101I-303-0598-04

Page 3, top right
Tommies climb steep slopes of southern Italy: © IWM 6495

Page 3, 1st centre row, left
Bombed home with single figure: © IWM NA 6431

Page 3, 1st centre row, right
Bombed home with three figures: © IWM NA 6651

Page 3, 2nd centre row, left
Hungry Italian boy: © IWM NA 7004

Page 3, 2nd centre row, right
Messerschmitt 110s and fuel drums abandoned: © IWM NA 6704

Page 3, bottom
Unloading at Taranto docks: © IWM NA 7017

Page 4, top left
The 36th Texan Division landing at Paestum: Courtesy National Archives and Records Administration, USA (Photo no. A-67068A.C)

Page 4, top right
Troops from the British 56th Division landing: Courtesy National Archives and Records Administration, USA

Page 4, centre left
Texans on the beach: Courtesy National Archives and Records Administration, USA

Page 4, 2nd centre row, left
Tommies of 46th Division move inland: Courtesy National Archives and Records Administration, USA

Page 4, 2nd centre row, right
Packed landing ship approaches the coast: Courtesy National Archives and Records Administration, USA (Photo no. 67067A.C)

Page 4, bottom left
US troops from 36th Division hit the beach as it comes under fire: Courtesy National Archives and Records Administration, USA

Page 4, bottom right
A British heavy machine-gun team firing just inland: © IWM NA 6720

Page 5, top left
A British mortar team amongst the vines: © IWM NA 6814

Page 5, top right
German soldiers loading a gun: Dohm/Bundesarchiv, Bild 101I-304-0628-12A

Page 5, centre left
British infantry moving forward through the vines: © IWM NA 7055

Page 5, centre right
German troops looking down on the bridgehead: Dohm/Bundesarchiv, Bild 101I-304-0619-25A

Page 5, 2nd centre row, left
German occupation of Rome: Supplied by the author

Page 5, 2nd centre row, right
A Nebelwerfer, as operated by Hans Golda's battery, in action: Lüthge/Bundesarchiv, Bild 101I-304-0643-11A

Page 5, bottom left
Italian former troops trudging home through the middle of the Salerno battle: © IWM NA 6851

Page 5, bottom right
B-17 Flying Fortresses take off amid the dust: Courtesy National Archives and Records Administration, USA

Page 6
A British wiring party and their jeep suddenly coming under shellfire: *top left* © IWM NA 6854; *top centre*: © IWM NA 6855; *top right*: © IWM NA 6857

Page 6, centre
US Rangers attacking through a smoke screen in the mountains: © IWM NA 6999

Page 6, 2nd centre row, left
A Panzer III pauses near the bridgehead: Fraß/Bundesarchiv, Bild 101I-308-0799Q-23A

Page 6, 2nd centre row, right
. . . a column of artillery, including this 88mm, heads towards the battle: Biedermann/Bundesarchiv, Bild 101I-568-1542-31A

Page 6, bottom
General Mark Clark addressing men of the 504th PIR: Courtesy National Archives and Records Administration, USA

Page 7, top left
A camouflaged Sherman tank passes by an American heavy machine-gunner: © IWM NA 7417

Page 7, top right
Men of 5th Division clamber up a steep hillside: © IWM NA 8507

Page 7, centre left
A British Sherman rumbles through the damaged edges of Salerno: © IWM NA 6902

Page 7, centre right
. . . a shattered town and a destroyed bridge: © IWM NA 6976

Page 7, bottom left
Men of the 56th Heavy Regiment load a big 7.2-inch howitzer: © IWM NA 7441

Page 7, bottom right
On the road to Naples, a British carrier carrying a mortar team: © IWM NA 7171

Page 8, top left
A four-day popular insurrection rose up in Naples at the end of September: © IWM NA 7409

Page 8, top right
Allied bombing had caused immense devastation in Naples: Courtesy National Archives and Records Administration, USA

Page 8, centre left
Church damaged by Allied bombing: Courtesy National Archives and Records Administration, USA

Page 8, centre right
Italians welcoming liberating Allied troops: Courtesy National Archives and Records Administration, USA

Page 8, bottom left
A bare-foot boy – one of the *scugnizzi* – clambers over the rubble: © IWM NA 7304

Page 8, bottom right
American troops pause on a Naples side street: © IWM NA 7406

Page 9, top left
The first Allied supply ships reach Naples: © IWM NA 7414

Page 9, top right
The ferocious heat of September was suddenly and dramatically replaced by relentless rain: © IWM NA 7526

Page 9, centre left
British tank crew from the Desert Rats: © IWM NA 7782

Page 9, centre right
Wreckage of a Messerschmitt 109: © IWM NA 7751

Page 9, bottom left
Tommies crawling through a sugar beet field: © IWM NA 7869

Page 9, bottom right
Men of the 34th Red Bulls cross the Volturno on a hastily built pontoon bridge: © IWM NA 7740

Page 10, top left
German engineers demolish a road: Supplied by the author

Page 10
Allied engineers repairing roads and bridges, Naples docks: *centre left*: © IWM NA 8151; *centre right*: John P. Lucas Collection, United States Army Heritage and Education Center; *2nd centre row, left*: Mark W. Clark Collection, The Citadel Archives and Museum; *2nd centre row, right*: Mark W. Clark Collection, The Citadel Archives and Museum; *bottom left*: Mark W. Clark Collection, The Citadel Archives and Museum; *bottom right*: Mark W. Clark Collection, The Citadel Archives and Museum

Page 11, top left
British troops advancing across one of the many irrigation ditches: © IWM NA 7908

Page 11, centre left
Infantry hack into the rock: © IWM NA 8239

Page 11, centre right
Bren gun team (5th Division) taking cover behind a pile of stones: © IWM NA 8980

Page 11, 2nd centre row, left
A Fallschirmjäger clips his MG42 on to a stand: Supplied by the author

Page 11, bottom left
Troops from the 34th Red Bulls move through the village of Caiazzo: Courtesy National Archives and Records Administration, USA

Page 11, bottom right
The generals confer at Lucas's OP: John P. Lucas Collection, United States Army Heritage and Education Center

Page 12, top left
An American half-track and gun cross a pontoon bridge over the Upper Volturno: John P. Lucas Collection, United States Army Heritage and Education Center

Page 12, top right
A German Panzer III moves up through another blasted Italian town: Supplied by the author

Page 14, top right
Yet more flooding of the Upper Volturno, vehicles pulled across by wires: Courtesy National Archives and Records Administration, USA

Page 14, centre
Men of the 180th Infantry out of the line: Mark W. Clark Collection, The Citadel Archives and Museum

Page 14, bottom left
American infantrymen wait while an engineer disables a mine: Mark W. Clark Collection, The Citadel Archives and Museum

Page 14, bottom right
An American mule train heading up Monte Sammucro: Mark W. Clark Collection, The Citadel Archives and Museum

Page 15, top left
German dead and battle debris lie scattered on the slopes: Mark W. Clark Collection, The Citadel Archives and Museum

Page 15, top right
Italian troops on the southern end of Monte Lungo: Mark W. Clark Collection, The Citadel Archives and Museum

Page 15, centre left
Misery in the mud and mountains: © IWM NA 9444

Page 15, centre right
Guardsman clambers up the slopes of Monte Camino: © IWM NA 9632

Page 15, bottom left
The 15th Air Force finally began moving to Foggia: Courtesy National Archives and Records Administration, USA

Page 15, bottom right
Orsogna under fire: © IWM NA 10216

Page 16, top left
Guardsmen near the summit of Monte Camino: © IWM NA 9366

Page 16, top right
Major Roy Durnford conducts a burial ceremony: Lieut. Frederick G. Whitcombe / Canada. Dept. of National Defence / Library and Archives Canada / PA-167913

Page 16, centre right
A paratrooper from the 509th PIR passes one of the knocked-out Shermans: Mark W. Clark Collection, The Citadel Archives and Museum

Page 16, 2nd centre row, left
A dead Fallschirmjäger in Ortona: Terry F. Rowe / Canada. Dept. of National Defence / Library and Archives Canada / PA-115188

Page 16, 2nd centre row, right
Rosa Fuoco, killed in the village square: Mark W. Clark Collection, The Citadel Archives and Museum

Page 16, bottom left
The ruins of San Pietro after the battle: Mark W. Clark Collection, The Citadel Archives and Museum

Page 16, bottom right
Canadians run for cover in mud and blasted landscape south of Ortona: Lieut. Frederick G. Whitcombe / Canada. Dept. of National Defence / Library and Archives Canada / PA-166566

Integrated Pictures

Part I, pp. 6/7
Sherman tank moving along the beach after coming ashore: © IWM NA 6661

Part II, pp. 108/9
Infantrymen setting off on patrol: © IWM NA 9326

Part III, pp. 284/5
Soldiers queuing for rations: Mark W. Clark Collection, The Citadel Archives and Museum

Gallery of Principal Personalities

pp. xlv-xlviii
All pictures supplied by the author with the exception of:
Hermann Balck: Bauer 1943/1944 / Bundesarchiv, Bild 101I-732-0118-03
Quent Reynolds: CBS via Getty Images

Index

Abdiel, HMS 215

Acerno 268

Acero, Monte 278, 281

ACHSE (AXIS), Operation 44, 83, 100, 153, 174

Acquapendola Ridge 395

Action Party (Italy) 80, 299, 303–4, 351, 457

Adams, Captain Hersel 119, 137

Advisory Council 378, 379

Agropoli 111, 117, 119, 170, 195

Aked, Major Ted 368

Akinaka, Fukuo ('Isaac') 264–5, 342, 343

Alamein, Battle of (1942) 2, 15, 47

ALARIC, Operation 42, 44

Albanella 116, 205; Station 187, 196, 202, 203, 205

Alburni Mountains 183

Alexander, General Sir Harold: personality 47; army career 47, 414; 'no more retreats' 51; at 15th Army Group HQ, Cassibile 23, 61; discussions with Eisenhower 47; and Clark 50; signs armistice with Castellano 62–3; and planned 82nd Airborne drop 86, 95; further consultation with Eisenhower 103; and battle for Salerno 118, 126, 142, 172, 187, 188, 189, 199, 200, 203, 208; discusses plans for 15th Army Group with Clark 222; is given a tour of Naples 262; at conference with Clark and Coningham 280; agrees with Eisenhower on securing further airfields 288; receives complaint from Montgomery on slowness of mail 308; attends Commanders' Conference in Tunis 325–6; drives Macmillan around Tunisian battlefields 325; visits the front near Mignano Gap 327, 328; from Bari HQ adopts tactic of two-handed punch 335; as Military Commander of the Occupied Territories 336–7, 378; directs Clark to

renew attack 350, 367; and French Corps 373; under shellfire at the front 373, 374; ill with jaundice 374, 422; has gloomy view of Italian campaign 374, 411–12, 413; as Macmillan's choice for Supreme Commander 414–15; joins talks with Brooke and Eisenhower 415; with Brooke in Brindisi 415; accused unfairly of 'lack of grip' 421–2, 425–6, 450, 470; visits front after fall of San Pietro 442–3; and Clark's cancellation of Operation SHINGLE 443, 444

Alexandria, Egypt 217

Algiers: Allied Forces HQ 30, 34, 37, 38, 41, 46, 48, 59, 60, 102, 103, 297; Information Services 103

Alife 406

Allfrey, General Charles 238, 368

Allied Control Commission 378–9

Allied Military Government of the Occupied Territories (AMGOT) 215, 250–51, 297, 301, 303, 336–7, 378

Allied Military Mission 303

Allied Strategic Air Forces 321–2, 326, 335, 348, 354

Altamura 83

Altavilla 183, 195, 197, 208, 224, 225

Alvignano 295, 297

Amalfi/Amalfi coast 116, 117, 121, 122, 195

Amaro, Monte 381

Ambrosio, Generale Vittorio 28–9, 38, 88, 89, 90, 102–3, 104, 107, 115, 128, 129, 141, 215

Amendola 417–18

AMGOT *see* Allied Military Government of the Occupied Territories

Ancon, USS 92, 94, 105, 114, 116–17, 118, 126, 136, 172, 181

Andaman Islands 409, 410

Antonio (US soldier) 270–71, 276–7
ANVIL, Operation 409, 410
Anzio 336, 473
Apulia 83, 100, 134, 149, 215, 237, 249, 417;
    German air bases 134; ports 147, 238
armies *see* British Army; Canadian Army;
    French Army; German Army; Italian
    Army; New Zealand Army; US Army
  15th Army Group 23, 222, 287, 288, 355, 411,
    422, 423
Arnold, General Hap 17, 35, 307, 355, 407, 429
Asa 201
Aspromonte massif 70
Asquith, Captain ('Squithy') 293–4, 331, 365, 366
Augsburg, Germany: Messerschmitt plants 418
Aurora, HMS 209
AVALANCHE, Operation 37, 39, 40, 41, 48, 50,
    51, 52–3, 55, 60, 62, 66, 76, 86, 90–95, 107,
    113–14, 115–26, 131–4, 148, 162, 173, 189,
    212, 307, 349, 425
Avellino 116, 179, 192, 226
Aversa 20, 231
Avezzano 130, 335, 367, 402
Avvocata, Monte dell' 121

Baade, Generalmajor Ernst-Günther 273, 380
Badoglio, Marshal (Maresciallo) Pietro: appointed
    prime minister by the King 27–8; and
    armistice negotiations with the Allies 28–30,
    38, 61, 63, 86, 87, 88, 89, 90, 96–7, 102–3,
    104, 105, 107, 115; escapes from Rome with
    the King 129, 175; and 'OP 44' 141; offers to
    open up ports of Taranto and Brindisi 147;
    in Sicily with the King 193; meets with
    Macmillan in Brindisi for the
    implementation of the armistice agreement
    214, 215; declares war on Germany 301;
    holds press conference 302; and Count Carlo
    Sforza 303; his government is obliged to
    provide labourers for the Allies 378; and the
    King's refusal to abdicate 457
Bagnara 3, 75–9, 81–2, 145
Bagnoli shipyards 233
Bähr, Siegfried (paratrooper) xliii, 446–7, 457,
    458–9, 463–4, 473
Balck, Generalleutnant Hermann 83–4; inspects
    his new corps 83, 84–5; survives air crash
    85; and Kesselring 99; cannot contact von
    Vietinghoff 134, 135; orders defence of
    coast north of Naples 135–6, 174; and
    counter-attack 142, 164; misjudges Allied
    threat 184; thrashes out plans with von
    Vietinghoff 191–2; believes British are
    reinforcing around Salerno 203; and Scholl
    232; and uprisings in Naples and Salerno
    233, 235; and Maus 243; returns to
    Germany 273; after the war 473

Bari 83, 215, 217, 237, 301, 335, 416–17, 421
Barletta 240–41
Barnes, John 361
Battipaglia 111, 142, 178, 184, 185, 186, 187, 192,
    207, 249
BAYTOWN, Operation 37, 39, 40, 50, 53, 58, 66,
    67, 75
Beaverbrook, Max Aitken, 1st Baron 64
Bedell-Smith, General Walter 37–8, 47, 59,
    60–61, 63, 87, 88, 414, 443, 470
BEDLAM, Operation 148
Beecken, Gefreiter 370
Benedict of Nursia, St 314–15
Benedictine monks 235, 314–15
Benevento 265, 268–9, 342
Bentivegna, Rosario ('Paolo') 351, 352, 455–6
Bergamini, Ammiraglio Carlo 152, 153
Bernhard Line 273–4, 288, 310, 320, 324, 327,
    332, 335, 338, 357, 362, 365, 391, 404, 405,
    408, 425, 429, 439, 470; *see also* Winter Line
Bessell, Generalmajor Hans 221–2, 235, 273
Biferno, River/Biferno Valley 253, 288, 292, 387
Bird, Dicky 147
Biscayne, USS 117
Bizerte, Tunisia 19, 100, 103, 189
Blankney, HMS 113
Boise, USS 148, 209
Bologna 43, 44
Bolzano 154, 155, 156, 418
Bône, North Africa 152
Bonin, Oberst Bogislaw von 99, 306, 324
Bornemann, Unteroffizier Heinrich 281
Bourke-White, Margaret 385
Bradley, General Omar 120
Brandon, Corporal 228–9
Brecciarola Ridge 402
Brenner Pass 30, 154, 156, 193
Briatore, Maggiore Albert 90, 159
Brindisi 147, 214, 215, 217, 237, 302, 303, 378, 415
British Army 307
  1st Airborne Division 147, 148, 215, 219, 238
  8th Argyll and Sutherland Highlanders 254–5
  4th Armoured Brigade 384
  1st Armoured Division 189
  7th Armoured Division (Desert Rats) 234,
    262, 279, 339, 373
  Eighth Army 15, 36, 37, 39, 46, 53, 58, 63, 66,
    67, 69, 74, 144, 147, 174, 199, 203, 212, 217,
    218, 222, 238, 239, 248, 267, 289, 296, 308,
    309, 313, 326, 328, 334, 335, 336, 338, 357,
    366, 367–8, 374, 381, 387, 412, 413, 425,
    470; casualties 469
  2nd Cameronians 68
  3rd Coldstream Guards 131–2, 142, 184, 185,
    220, 226–7, 393–6, 397, 423
  Commandos 116, 118, 119, 121, 142, 165, 173,
    239, 245, 247, 260

X Corps 53, 120, 142, 173, 184, 204, 222, 234, 262, 271, 289, 338, 374, 391, 443
XIII Corps 58, 245
XXX Corps (of Eighth Army) 147
3rd County of London Yeomanry 254, 260
6th Grenadier Guards 374, 395, 424
201st Guards Brigade 142, 185, 201, 210, 226, 294–5, 339, 393, 394, 423
Hampshire Regiment 167
56th Heavy Regiment, Royal Artillery 234, 271, 391
51st Highland Division 222
8th Indian Infantry Division 217, 218, 236, 238, 293–4, 313, 331, 336, 337, 365, 366–7, 368, 381, 383, 400, 408, 447, 448
Infantry Brigades: 13th 67, 68, 70, 145, 335; 17th 448; 139th 167
Infantry Divisions: 5th (Yorkshire) 57, 67, 75, 76, 81, 203, 218, 238, 313, 334, 447; 46th 53, 116, 126, 131, 142, 167, 187, 192, 222, 226, 229–30, 233, 279, 339; 50th (Tyne Tees) 222; 56th 53, 116, 126, 131, 142, 168, 173, 187, 222, 233, 279, 339, 349, 350, 423, 425; 78th (Battleaxe) 238–9, 246, 253, 293, 313, 336, 357, 367, 368, 381, 387, 388
2nd Inniskillings 56, 57, 70, 145, 203, 218, 334–5, 448
Intelligence Corps 168–70
38th Irish Brigade 239, 254, 259–60, 313, 379, 384
King's Dragoon Guards 242
2/5th Leicestershire Regiment 167, 168, 186, 198–9, 205–6
London Irish Rifles 380
Parachute Brigades: 1st 148; 4th 148
Royal Engineers 217
1st Royal Irish Fusiliers ('Faughs') 239–40, 313, 314, 317–19, 379–80, 384–5, 387, 388
Royal Scots Greys 131, 242
2nd Scots Guards 185–6, 395
Sherwood Foresters 186–7, 198
Special Air Service 77, 245, 256
Special Raiding Squadron (SRS) 75–9, 81–2, 145, 239, 245, 252–3, 256, 259–60, 262
Brixen 155
Brodrick, Major Michael 185
Brooke, General Sir Alan 189, 414, 415, 421, 422, 425, 426, 442, 443, 470
Brown, Sergeant 293
Bull, Captain Peter 139–40, 223, 472
Bulteel, Lieutenant Christopher 131–2, 142, 184, 185, 186, 203, 220, 226–7, 472
Burma 30, 31, 47, 65, 375; Burma Road 377, 409
Burnford, Lieutenant Alfred 428
Burns, Colonel George 395
BUTTRESS, Operation 37, 50, 51, 52, 53, 75

Caiazzo 280
Caira, Monte 311, 352
Calore, River 196, 197, 268–9, 278
Calvi di Bergolo, Generale Count Giorgio Carlo 140–42, 159, 160, 171, 172, 177
Camino 339, 475, 407
Camino, Monte/Camino massif 243, 325, 339, 340, 344, 349, 374, 391, 393–5, 396, 397, 423, 425, 429, 430, 442–3, 445
Campbell, Major Alex 57–8, 219, 220, 290, 291, 390, 422, 453–4; poetry 459–60, 476
Campbell, Sarah 58
Campinola 121
Campobasso 291, 292, 387
Canadian Army 75, 203, 216, 238, 239, 248, 251, 252, 313, 373, 408, 431, 449, 451, 462, 475–6
  Hastings and Prince Edward Regiment ('Hasty Ps') 57, 70, 146, 218–19, 290–91, 292, 387, 388, 389, 390, 398–400, 419–20, 431, 442, 450, 452, 453, 457–8, 459, 460, 475
  48th Highlanders 291
  Infantry Brigades: 1st 70, 145, 146, 452, see also Hastings and Prince Edward Regiment (above); 2nd 420, 452, see also Seaforth Highlanders (below); 3rd 70, 358, 390, 419, 420
  1st Infantry Division 58, 420
  Loyal Edmontons ('Eddies') 462
  Princess Patricia's Canadian Light Infantry (PPCLI) 390, 398, 400
  Seaforth Highlanders 145–6, 148, 289–90, 389, 390, 398, 420, 462
  Three Rivers Regiment 260, 462
  West Nova Scotia Regiment 358
Cancello airfield 9, 18, 20, 52, 73–4, 265, 275
Canosa 294
Capaccio 125, 142, 172
Capodichino 321; airfield 407
Capponi, Carla ('Elena') 157–9, 175–6, 351–2, 455–6
Caprara, Palazzo 96, 97, 101, 106, 129
Capri 113, 321
Capua 4, 18, 19, 231, 262, 274, 279, 294
Caracciolo, Filippo, Prince of Castagneto 79–80; forges links between Allies and Action Party 80–81; meets Dulles and McCaffrey in Switzerland 85; and the armistice 85, 106–7, 156–7; in Rome 175; shocked by the devastation in Naples 231–2; adapts to lockdown rules 232–3; tries to form Neapolitan Committee of National Liberation 233, 241; and uprising against German Organisation Todt 233; and liberation of Naples 242; meets with Colonel Hume, head of AMGOT 251;

Caracciolo, Filippo, Prince of Castagneto *cont.*
  invited by him to visit Salerno bridgehead
  263; frustrated by lack of political
  movement 299–300; heads Allied Military
  Mission 303; in stand-off over the King
  remaining in power 304; fails in his
  attempts to create a Corpo Volontari della
  Libertà 456–7
Caramanti, Signor 221
Carboni, Generale Giacomo 88; and the drafting
  of 'OP 44' 88–9; and his motor corps'
  inability to take on German divisions 89;
  and Allied invasion 96, 115; takes
  Americans to meet Badoglio 96–7; learns of
  Salerno landings 101–2; summoned to see
  Badoglio 102, 103; and announcement of
  armistice 104, 106; and German attack on
  Rome 128–31; distributes weapons to
  civilians of Rome 157; realizes he has been
  duped 140–41; refuses terms with
  Kesselring 159–60; meets Caviglia in Rome
  171, 172; back in command 172, 174;
  distrusts Germans 177, 350; refuses to sign
  surrender document 176–7; after the war
  473
Cardito 312–13, 427, 464, 466
Carfora, Dom Tommaso 352
Carton de Wiart, General Adrian 38
Caruso, Pasqualina ('Lina') 24–5, 106, 127–8,
  193–4, 207–8, 220–21, 271–2, 350, 457, 473
Casa Berardi 447, 475
Casablanca 322; Conference 14, 31, 33, 34, 37,
  59, 410
Casale, Monte 312, 404, 435
Cascano 4, 5
Caserta 4, 19, 72, 135, 327, 374, 407, 443, 461
Casey, Bombardier 215
Cassibile, Sicily 23, 46, 47, 61, 62
Cassino 221, 244, 274, 311, 315–17, 320, 327,
  339, 352, 443, 467, 473
Cassino, Monte/Monte Cassino massif 221–2,
  315, 316, 445, 461; *see also* Monte Cassino
  Abbey
Castel di Sangro 358, 362, 420, 446, 448
Castelfrentano 381–2
Castellammare 210
Castellano, Generale Giuseppe: meets with Sir
  Samuel Hoare 29–30; talks terms with
  Alexander 23; has further talks at British
  Embassy in Lisbon 37–8, 59; his warnings
  confirmed by Ultra decrypts 39–40; on
  retreat to Pisa–Rimini Line 44, 55, 115; and
  armistice negotiations 59, 61, 62, 63, 88;
  heads Military Mission 86; unable to
  discover Allied invasion plans 86, 87; and
  announcement of armistice 90; helps in
  Americans' secret mission to Rome 95, 96

Castelpizzuto 335
Castelvetrano 407
Castel Volturno 279, 281
Castropignano 387, 388
Catania, Sicily 46
Catanzaro 218, 219
Cava de' Tirreni 121, 178–9, 229, 305
Cava Nocera Valley 226, 229 30, 234
Cavalletto 438
Cavallo, Monte 427, 464
Caviglia, Maresciallo Enrico 171–2, 177
Centuripe 239
Cephalonia, island of 324
Ceppagna 404, 439
Cerasuolo 404
Cercola 234, 271
Cerignola 294
Cervaro 466, 467
Chiang Kai-shek 375, 376, 377, 409, 410
Chiang, Madame 376–7
Chiasso, Switzerland 85, 107
Chieti 402
China/Chinese 375, 376–7, 409, 410
Chiunzi Pass 121, 142, 179, 180, 195
Churchill, Randolph 437
Churchill, Winston: on army commanders
  requesting air support 15; relationship with
  Roosevelt 31; has grandiose plans 32, 36;
  pessimistic 33–4; confident of taking Rome
  35–6, 51; at Quadrant Conference 37;
  relationship with Clark 50; and Macmillan
  59; approves Eisenhower's course of action
  103; puts pressure on Clark 267; his
  operations in the Dodecanese 288, 376; in
  bed 375; at Sextant Conference 376; and
  Operation OVERLORD 376, 410; agrees
  with Roosevelt about Vittorio Emanuele
  378; tired but triumphant 414; wants to
  know Macmillan's views on Generals
  Wilson and Alexander 414, 415; illness 415,
  421, 426, 437–8, 442; and the Italian
  campaign 471
Ciampino airfield 174
Ciano, Count Galeazzo 26, 27, 29
Cicerale, Monte 170–71, 180
Clark, Major Geoffrey 395
Clark, General Mark ('Wayne') 48–9, 181;
  friendship with Eisenhower 49; given
  command of Fifth Army 49–50; and
  Operation AVALANCHE 48, 50–54, 94–5,
  115, 117, 118, 119, 126, 136, 137, 142–3,
  172–3, 187, 188–9; on USS *Ancon* 92, 94,
  105, 115, 116–17, 118, 126, 172; and
  armistice announcement 114; and General
  Walker 120, 136, 172; and German
  counter-attack 196–7, 199, 202–3; visits
  forward troops 204, 205; visited by

Coningham and Alexander 208, 222; has doubts about Dawley 208–9, 227; as commander 212–13, 267–8, 428–9, 470; blamed for destruction of Battipaglia 249; 'gives Naples' to his wife as birthday present 262; and crossing the Volturno 262–3, 265, 276; in discussions with Alexander, Coningham and Montgomery 280; and British X Corps 289; and Lucas's plan for crossing the Volturno 327, 328; disappointed at his Army's failure to break through 348–50; goes to the front with Alexander 373–4; ignores his suggestion to hold fire 374; awarded Distinguished Service Cross 406–7; his views on desertion 408; belittled by Montgomery 321; unfairly blamed 422; recommends Operation SHINGLE be cancelled 443–4; see also US Fifth Army

Clark, Renie 262
Clemm, Baron Werner von 128
CLN see Comitato di Liberazione Nazionale
Coccia Ridge 254, 255, 260, 261
Cole, Captain David 56, 57, 67–8, 70, 145, 203, 218, 334–5, 448, 472
Colle 393
Collelungo 464
Colle Marabella 369
Colle Vecchio 435
Collier's 93
Combined Chiefs of Staff 18, 31, 34, 35, 36, 37, 39–41, 52, 60, 61, 65, 93–4, 103, 107, 287, 303, 326, 349, 375, 411, 413, 414, 421–2, 425–6, 470–71
Comitato di Liberazione Nazionale 175, 177, 303–4, 351; Military Council (Rome) 455, 457
Comité français de Libération nationale 375
Conca Casale 341
Coningham, Air Marshal Sir Arthur ('Mary') 15, 16, 208, 280, 416
Conrath, General Paul 165, 273, 317
Centocelle airfield 102
Corato 294
Corno, Monte 341, 372, 434
Corsica 34, 36, 40, 287, 322, 324, 338, 401
Corti, Achille 301
Corti, Tenente Eugenio 153–4, 194, 235–6, 272–3, 292, 301–2, 456, 473
Cosenza 82, 83, 149
Couch, Sergeant 205
Crast, Major Glenn 200
Crawford, Colonel Joe 137
Croce, Benedetto 80
Croce, Monte 341
Crotone 36, 146, 148, 322
Crowther, Colonel A. B. 91–2, 105

Cunningham, Admiral Sir Andrew Browne 74, 103, 189, 190, 202
Cuozzo, Tanino 193
Curry, Sergeant 395

Daily Express 64
Danneker, Hauptsturmführer Theodor 351
Darby, Colonel William O. ('Bill') 117–18, 120–21, 142, 173, 180, 195, 341–2, 372–3, 404, 434, 471
Davis, Lieutenant Peter 76–9, 81, 245, 246, 252–3, 256, 257, 262, 472
Dawley, General Ernest 'Mike' 119, 120, 192, 196, 202, 208–9, 227
de Courten, Ammiraglio Raffaele 100, 101, 152
Dederichs, Leutnant 179–80, 305
Delhi, HMS 211
De Marinis, Virgilio 236
Dempsey, Lieutenant-General Sir Miles 245
De Nobili, Rino 85, 106–7
DEVON, Operation 245, 253
Diamare, Padre Abate Gregorio 315, 316
Dibble, Lieutenant Jimmy 22, 23
di Mascio, Addolorata 428, 465
di Mascio, Angelina (Pierino's aunt) 313, 428, 465
di Mascio, Angelina (Pierino's sister) 465, 466
di Mascio, Antonietta 465
di Mascio, Antonio 312–13, 465, 466
di Mascio, Domenico (Pierino's uncle) 313, 465
di Mascio, Domenico (Pierino's brother) 465
di Mascio, Pierino 312–13, 437, 465–6
di Mascio, Teresa 312–13, 465, 466
Dodecanese, the 288, 376
Doolittle, General Jimmy 15–16, 355
Doughty, Captain Roswell K. 90–91, 92, 105, 119, 123–6, 136–7, 142, 170–71, 180, 225, 295, 299, 405–6, 471
Douhet, Giulio 54
DUKE (Dominions, UK and Empire) forces 15, 147, 238, 367, 414, 472; 324 Wing 201, 330–31
DUKWs 69
Dulles, Allen 85
Dundas, Wing Commander Hugh 'Cocky' 162–3, 187, 188, 201, 212, 321, 330–31, 472
Dundas, John 162–3
Dunn, Major Dennis 261, 308
Durnford, Captain Roy (padre) 145–6, 219–20, 290, 389, 400, 420–21, 463, 472, 476

Eaker, General Ira 354, 355
Eboli 24–5, 91, 106, 111, 119, 127–8, 192, 193, 194, 195, 207–8, 209, 220, 221, 271–2, 297, 350, 457

Eboli, Monte 184

Eisele, Unteroffizier 281

Eisenhower, General Dwight D.: as Supreme Allied Commander 30, 34; and plans to invade Italy 35, 36–7, 40; meets with Montgomery in Sicily 46–7; visits Alexander 47–8; relationship with General Clark 49, 213, 227, 265; runs through plans for Operation AVALANCHE 48, 50, 51–2, 54; and Italian surrender negotiations 58–9, 60, 62; and Macmillan 59, 214, 303; announces armistice 86, 90, 92, 97, 102, 103, 104, 105, 107; and Operation AVALANCHE 93, 95, 147, 189, 190; realizes the difficulties of reaching Rome 287–8; at Commanders' Conference in Tunis 325; still hopes to reach Rome before Christmas 326; commits heavy bomber forces to Italian air bases 353–4; creates Fifteenth Air Force 354, 355; nominated commander of Operation OVERLORD 410, 414, 469–70; and Alexander 415, 421; and the cancellation of Operation SHINGLE 443–4

Eitt, Captain Herb 170

Elena of Montenegro, Queen of Italy 129, 171

Eleusis airfield, Greece 418

ENCROACH, Operation 366

Engineer Petroleum Distribution Company 353

Etna, Mount 70, 230

Ettore, Salvatore 312

Evans, Lieutenant 444

Faiano 111, 198

'Fairfield Camp', Sicily 61, 62, 86

Farbrother, Sergeant Leslie 364

Ferrazzano 291

Ferri, Angela 432–3

FEUERSBRUNST, Operation 112

Fife, Corporal James 270, 345

Filignano 404, 435

Fingler (driver) 281

Fisher, Sergeant 293, 336

Fiuggi 439

Florence 52, 80, 157, 220

Foggia 34–5, 147, 148, 161, 216, 238, 246, 289, 294, 323, 348, 411; airfields 217, 322, 326, 353, 355, 356, 412, 413, 417, 446, 470

Foiano di Val Fortore 289–90

Foligno 371

Forgan, David (medical officer) 395

Forin, Major Douglas 146

Formella 394

Formidable, HMS 93

Fossacesia 379, 380

Franco, Lieutenant Charles 192

Franklyn-Vaile, Lieutenant Lawrie 239–41; first battle experience 260, 261; has supper with Italians 296–7; correspondence with his wife 308, 309, 313, 317, 379, 384–5; friendship with Glennie 308, 314, 318; and his death 318–19, 363–4, 379; wounded 319, 363; rejoins the Faughs 363, 364–5; suffers from 'desert sores' 365; survives shelling 379–80, 384; *see also* 1st Royal Irish Fusiliers *under* British Army

Franklyn-Vaile, Olive 240, 261, 313, 314, 364, 379, 384

Franklyn-Vaile, Valerie 240, 313

Frascati 84, 98, 101, 128

Fratte 166, 198, 226

Free French 52, 378

French Army 222
    Corps Expéditionnaire Français 36, 373
    2e Division d'Infanterie Marocaine (Moroccans) 373, 374, 403, 406, 461, 466
    Royal 22e Régiment 447

Frömming, Oberleutnant Ernst 216, 247

Frosinone 73, 335–6, 443

Fuoco, Rosa 433, 434, 441

Gaeta 95–6

Gaeta, Bay of 5

Gambara, Generale Gastone 88

Gamberale 362, 448

GAP (Gruppi di Azione Patriottica) 351; Centrale/Gappisti 351, 455–6

Gardiner, Colonel William 95, 96, 101, 102

Gargano hills 417

Garigliano, River 274, 310, 338, 339, 352, 391, 396, 397, 462

Gaulle, Charles de 375

Genoa 14

German Army 135, 268, 305–7, 392–3, 411, 422–3, 424, 425, 471; casualties 73, 155, 156, 273, 445, 466
    6. Armee 154
    10. Armee (Armeeoberkommando (AOK) 10) 44, 55, 84, 100, 134, 174, 191, 221, 305–6, 337, 338, 380, 446, 449; casualties 469
    15. Armee 44
    Armeeoberkommando (AOK) 10 see 10. Armee; 14 337
    Division Hermann Göring (HG) 84, 121, 135, 136, 164–5, 179, 187, 191, 192, 198, 279, 310, 316, 397, 423; Aufklärungs-Abteilung 450
    Division Sizilien 2, 3
    Fallschirmjäger 55, 290–91, 447, 462–3, 475
    1. Fallschirmjäger-Division 82, 147, 148, 149, 191, 216, 238, 248, 310, 338, 362, 382, 423, 446, 448, 449; Maschinengewehr-Bataillon

82, 111, 216, 248, 251; Pionier-Bataillon 150, 248, 260
2. Fallschirmjäger-Division 40, 101, 106, 128, 130, 159
Fallschirmjäger-Gruppen 458, 460
3. Fallschirmjäger-Regiment 149, 247, 249, 358, 362, 420, 449
4. Fallschirmjäger-Regiment 149
Gebirgsjäger 435
5. Gebirgsjäger-Division 461, 464, 465
100. Gebirgsjäger-Regiment 464, 465
Heeresgruppe B 39, 43, 310
Heeresgruppe C 44, 237, 337
44. Hoch- und Deutschmeister-Division 154, 237, 371, 403–4; 3. Bataillon 154, 155
65. Infanterie-Division, 357, 367, 380, 446, 449
94. Infanterie-Division 310, 371, 423
302. Infanterie-Division 135
305. Infanterie-Division 310, 371, 403, 404, 423
Kampfgruppen 82, 167, 192, 196
Kampfgruppe Cosenza 82
1. Panzerarmee 337
Panzer IV 175–6
16. Panzer-Division 44, 84–5, 91, 105, 112, 119, 134, 135, 136, 142, 166, 187, 192, 198, 247, 253, 254, 260, 305,317, 367; 16. Panzer-Aufklärungs-Abteilung 111, 225
17. Panzer-Division 324
Panzergrenadier divisions 55
2. Panzergrenadier-Division 40, 278, 338, 342, 343, 344, 450
3. Panzergrenadier-Division 101, 129, 191, 198, 310–11
15. Panzergrenadier-Division 2, 78, 84, 135–6, 164, 179, 187, 191, 192, 198, 273, 279, 310, 338, 339, 395, 397, 407, 423, 465
29. Panzergrenadier-Division 100, 142, 145, 148, 149, 174, 191, 195, 218, 423, 433, 438, 445
90. Panzergrenadier-Division 338, 367, 384, 401, 420, 446, 449
129. Panzergrenadier-Regiment 445
145. Panzergrenadier-Regiment 381
200. Panzergrenadier-Regiment 401, 419
577. Panzergrenadier-Regiment 403
578. Panzergrenadier-Regiment 403
Panzerkorps 84
XIV Panzerkorps 83, 84, 99, 134, 164, 235, 243, 273, 282, 306, 310, 324, 335, 338, 344, 438
LXXVI Panzerkorps 101, 148, 210, 261, 335, 445, 449
Pionier companies 362
Werfer-Regiment 71 2, 274–5, 325; see also Golda, Leutnant Hans
Giaccone, Tenente-Colonnello Leandro 160, 177
GIANT II, Operation 95, 101, 102
Gilroy, Group commander George 'Sheep' 188
'Giovanni' (Gappisto) 455–6

Giraud, Général Henri 52
Glennie, Lieutenant John 308–9, 314, 318–19, 363–4, 379
GNR see Guardia Nazionale Repubblicana
GOBLET, Operation 51
Goebbels, Joseph 306
Goforth, Captain the Reverend J. F. 388
Golda, Oberleutnant Hans 307; leaves Sicily 1–5, 164; comes under fire 178–80; and Dederichs 179–80, 305; finds some pink pants 229; ordered to pull back 229; enjoys himself in Minturno 274; deployed to Grazzanise on the Volturno 274–5, 279, 281; and deaths of friends 279, 281; not happy at being sent forward to Monte Lungo 324, 340, 344; survives shelling 348; promoted to Oberleutnant 370; comes under attack and Nebelwerfers are submerged 396–7; finds shelter in cave 444–5; given leave in Vienna 445, 460; still at the front in 1944 473
GOMORRAH, Operation 13
Gonzaga, Generale Don Ferrante 153
Goodfellow, Lieutenant John C. 322
Göring, Reichsmarschall Hermann 42, 310
Graham, Major-General Douglas 173
Grassano 216
Grazzanise 279, 281; airfield 275
Griffiths, Lance-Corporal 293
Griffith-Jones, Major Mervyn 132, 226
Grizzana Morandi 417
Grossetti, Dom Eusebio 316, 317, 352, 353, 391, 438, 462, 473
Grottaglie 214, 323
Guagnano 302
Guardia Nazionale Repubblicana (GNR) 304, 305
Guderian, General Heinz 84
Gugelberger, Feldwebel Robert 11, 12–13, 18, 19, 20–21, 72–4, 161–2, 473
Guglionesi 247, 253
Guinness, Alec 140
'Gully, The' 420, 431, 447, 449, 451
Gustav Line 222, 235, 243–4, 273, 282, 288, 316, 320, 324, 328, 335, 338, 439, 440, 442, 445, 447, 461, 466, 469

Hair, Johnny 78
Hall, Admiral John Leslie, Jr 136
Hamburg 13, 416
Hamilton, Lieutenant John 394, 395
Hammond, Lieutenant Franky 420
Hanover 320
Harris, Air Chief Marshal Arthur 354
Harrison, Derrick 78
Hartle, Major-General Russell P. 118
Heales, Corporal 293
Heidorn, Leutnant 458, 463

Heidrich, General Major Richard 148–9, 449
Heilmann, Oberst Ludwig 247, 249, 358, 362, 449
Helme, Lieutenant David 393–5, 396, 397, 472
Herr, General Traugott 101, 210, 261
Hewitt, Admiral H. Kent 92–3, 114, 116, 117
Hilary, HMS 173
Himmler, Heinrich 304
Hitler, Adolf: abandons invasion of Britain 53, refuses to retreat 32; and Italy 41–3, 44–5, 98, 114–15, 148–9, 267, 291, 338, 449, 450; anxious to find Mussolini 38, 43; and Rommel 42, 43, 44, 237; and Kesselring 44, 98, 99, 133, 134, 237, 266, 289, 337–8, 397, 445–6, 471; and Italian armistice 237, 238; and General Hube 273, 310; prevaricates 288–9; refuses to retreat 338, 397, 445–6
Hoare, Sir Samuel 29
Hobday, Corporal 125
Hopkins, Harry 407
Hopkinson, Major-General George ('Hoppy') 148, 215
Horrocks, Lieutenant-General Brian 52, 53
Howe, HMS 148
Hube, General Hans-Valentin 84, 243, 273, 281, 282, 306, 310
Hume, Colonel Edgar E. 250, 251, 263
HUSKY, Operation 33, 39, 93, 413

Illustrious, HMS 93
Imperial War Museum 472
Isernia 313, 335
Italia (battleship) 152
L'Italia Libera (newspaper) 351
Italian Army 113
  2a Armata 89
  4a Armata 87–8
  6a Armata 324
  Fourth Army 43, 44
  Eighth Army 153
  Comando Supremo 29, 41, 89, 129, 130–31, 140, 141, 148, 157, 171, 172, 214
  Corpo d'Armata Motocorazzato 88, 89, 106
  Acqui Division 324
  Ariete Division 106, 129, 130, 141, 159, 171, 174
  Centauro Division 140, 141
  Granatieri Division 128, 129–30, 175
  Granatieri di Sardegna Division 159, 160
  Piacenza Division 128, 129
  Piave Division 130, 141, 159
  61 Raggruppamento di Artiglieria 153
  1. Raggruppamento Motorizzato 373, 405–6, 407
  Montebello Regiment 106
Italy
  Air Force (Regia Aeronautica) 10, 29, 74; Macchi 202s 2
  Communist Party (PCI) 351

Navy (Regia Marina) 147, 148, 153; *Baionetta* 172
Servizio Informazioni Militare (SIM) 88, 101, 106, 130, 171; *see also* Italian Army

James O'Hara, USS 90, 91, 105, 119
Japan/Japanese 30, 31, 32, 33, 55, 65, 144, 375, 377, 409, 410, 473; Japanese-Americans 264, 342; Japanese-Hawaiians 264
Jewell, Major Toby 384
Jodl, General Alfred 44, 105, 337
John Harvey (Liberty ship) 416
Juin, Général Alphonse 373

Kabinger, Feldwebel 254–5
Kalamaki airfield, Greece 418
Kaltenbrunner, Obergruppenführer Ernst 304, 351
Kappler, Obersturmbannführer Herbert 350–51
Kawasaki, Captain Isaac 265, 342, 343
Keitel, Feldmarschall Wilhelm 43, 44, 305
Kenison, Lance-Corporal 293, 366
Kennedy, Major Bert 387, 389, 398–400, 419, 420, 452, 453
Kerrigan (in Murphy's squad) 270, 277, 346
Kersten, Heinz (radio operator) 459
Kesselring, Feldmarschall Albert 98–9; and antipathy from corps staff 99, 324; commands Heeresgruppe C 39, 44, 45; ordered to reinforce Naples-Salerno area 44, 99–100, 154; briefs General Hube 84; survives bombing of Frascati 101, and von Vietinghoff 100, 105–6, 134, 135, 248, 282; and Italian armistice 101, 105–6, 177; and Hitler 98, 99, 133–4, 237, 266, 289, 337–8, 397, 445–6, 471; clashes with Rommel 134; Calvi surrenders Rome to him 141–2, 159, 160, 177, 350; shares a cordial conference with de Courten 152; and Salerno 172, 174, 177, 191–2, 203, 210, 237; orders withdrawal of troops 210, 221, 222; and Bessell 222, 235; and defence of Termoli 248; determined to reclaim Salerno 248; prepares defence south of Rome 266, 282, 287, 289, 324; uses Jews as forced labour 351; orders defences to be strengthened at the front 367; appointed as supremo in Italy and orders divisions south 371; and Allied bombing 380, 416; prevents withdrawal 397, 429; and Monte Cassino Abbey 438; is reckless with troops 445, 446; and Lemelsen 449, 450
Keyes, Lieutenant-General Geoffrey 408, 429, 439
King, Admiral Ernest 32

King George V, HMS 148
Klein, Unteroffizier Jupp 149–50, 307; on
    truck-scouting mission 150–51; in the
    'Battle of the Roadblock' 151–2; ordered to
    detonate stacks of bombs 216–17; captures
    British Tommies 246–7; and mine-laying
    246, 247, 262–3, 446; reaches Termoli 247;
    ordered to abandon town 247; knocks out
    British tanks 254–5; survives battle 260–61;
    appalled at Panzer troops raising white flag
    261, 305; at Gamberale 361, 448; still at the
    front in 1944 473
KONSTANTIN, Operation 42, 44
Krakauer, Charlie (medical officer) 452
Kranefeld, Leutnant 150–51, 152
Kraus, Hauptmann 73
Kursk, Battle of (1943) 45, 144, 375
Kurz, Feldwebel Eugen 10

La Difensa, Monte 374, 391
Lamb, Lieutenant Tom 330
Lane, Private First Class Charlie 136–7
Lanzi, Tenente 130
La Torre 388
'Lattarullo' (informer) 333
Laube, Oberleutnant Martin 73
Leahy, Admiral William D. 407
Leese, General Sir Oliver 470
Lemelsen, General Joachim 338, 380, 381, 397,
    445, 449–50, 465
Levis, Captain (padre) 395
Lewis, Sergeant Norman 168–9, 203, 205,
    249–50, 258–9, 298, 333–4, 472
Limatola 278
Lionetti, Vincenzo 297
Lipton, Tattie 277, 346, 347
Liri, River/Liri Valley 221–2, 235, 325, 339, 352,
    374, 387, 396, 442, 443, 444
Littoria 202
Lucas, General John 227–8, 262, 267, 268–9,
    275–6, 277–8, 279, 280, 327–9, 406,
    407, 408
Lucera 201, 358
Luftflotte II 192, 415, 416
Luftwaffe 10, 14, 16, 33, 74, 91, 101, 161, 202,
    212, 321, 323, 354, 412, 415–16, 417
  Jagdgeschwader 53 161
  2./Jagdgeschwader 53 9, 18, 72
  4./Jagdgeschwader 53 11, 12, 23, 162
  6./Jagdgeschwader 53 11, 20
  8./Jagdgeschwader 53 73
  II. Fliegerkorps 11
  Focke-Wulf 190s 113, 114, 161, 163, 192, 200,
    209, 210, 280
  Heinkel 111 19
  Jagdbomber ('Jabos') 201
  Junkers: JU87 'Stuka' 99; Ju88 416

Messerschmitt: Me 109s 9, 10, 11–12, 21, 22,
    99, 132, 137, 161–2, 163, 184, 192, 280, 323;
    Me 110s 416
Lungo, Monte 243, 274, 311, 325, 340, 344, 345,
    346, 348, 374, 405, 407, 425, 428, 429, 430,
    440, 443, 466

McCaffrey, John 85
McCreery, Lieutenant-General Dick 53, 120, 173,
    187, 203, 204, 223, 225, 262, 338, 349, 442
Macdonald, 'Doc' 292
Macdonald, Squadron Leader Ken 188
Mackensen, Generaloberst Eberhard 337
Macmillan, Harold 59–60; as British Resident
    Minister of State in the Mediterranean 37;
    and signing of the armistice 'Short Terms'
    38, 58–9, 60, 61, 62, 63, 103–4, 107; on
    mission to Badoglio and the King 214–15;
    taken aback by rural life in Italy 220; illness
    302–3; at conference about Italy's future
    303, 304; in praise of Eisenhower 303; at
    Commanders' Conference in Tunis 325;
    driven round battlefields by Alexander 325;
    at Sextant Conference (Cairo) 374–5;
    summoned to see Churchill 375; attends
    meetings at the Kirk Villa 376; meets
    Madame Chiang 376–7; returns to Algiers
    377; flies to Brindisi as member of new
    Advisory Council 378–9; thinks Alexander
    the better choice as new Supreme
    Commander 414–15; and Churchill's illness
    437, 442; in politics 472
McMullen, Captain James 290
McNair, General Lesley 49
McNally, Major John 384
McNinch, Sergeant Bill 81, 256
McSherry, General Frank J. 250
Maddaloni 277
Maggiore, Monte 374
Maiella Mountains 381
Maiori 116, 121
Malaya 409
Malta 42, 74, 75, 96, 99, 102, 113, 148, 152, 211,
    223, 224, 237; Air Command 13
Manduria 301
Mare, Monte 464
Mareth Line, the 131
'Maria' (Gappista) 455–6
Marron, Monte 427
Marshall, General George C. 34, 35, 36, 40, 41,
    49, 118, 353, 355, 414, 470, 475
Masella, Antonia 332–3, 433, 441, 473
Masella, Antonietta 441
Masella, Bernardino 433
Masella, Lucia 433
Masella, Serafino xliv, 332, 433–4, 441, 473
Mason-MacFarlane, General Sir Noel 214, 215

Massico, Monte 338
Mastanuono, Mariantonia 432–3
Matera 149
Matese Mountains 335
Mateur 19, 23
Mauss, Oberstarzt Wilhelm 243–4, 282; feels
    uncomfortable about German mines and
    booby traps 269; and General Hube 243,
    273, 282, 310; attends division
    commanders' meeting 273, 274; his
    musings 278, 306, 343, 404, 475; moves to
    Roccasecca 310–11; worries about his
    family in Hanover 320; and the British
    attack on Monte Camino 391; frustrated by
    lack of Luftwaffe 415; incensed by bombing
    of his field hospital 438–9; has an enjoyable
    Christmas 460–61; reflections on New
    Year's Eve 466; still at the front in 1944 473
Mayne, Lieutenant-Colonel Blair ('Paddy') 76,
    77, 239, 245, 253, 256, 257
Medenine (Tunisia), Battle of (1943) 131
Mediterranean Air Command 13, 14, 16
Mediterranean Allied Air Forces 162, 212
Medjerda Valley, Tunisia 325
Mellors, Lieutenant Freddie 331
Mercer, Corporal Al 420
Messerschmitt Wiener-Neustadt plant 15
Messina, Sicily 46, 58, 63, 67, 68, 150
Messina, Straits of 1, 3, 32, 36, 37, 46, 50, 52, 53,
    56, 58, 63, 66, 67, 70–71, 74, 100, 162, 204,
    209, 224, 334
Middle East Air Command 13
Middleton, Major-General Troy 275–6
Mignano 243, 273, 282, 311, 328, 405
Mignano Gap 273, 325, 327, 328, 338, 339, 340,
    397, 403, 404, 407, 418, 425, 443, 475
Milan 14, 80, 85, 156–7; La Scala 14; Santa Maria
    delle Grazie (The Last Supper) 14
Militello, Sicily 57, 58, 62
mines/minefields 146–7, 203, 269, 292, 327, 329,
    360–61, 362, 363, 444
Minturno 243, 374, 469
Mitchell, Corporal 79, 81
Molise Mountains 272, 290, 293
Monopoli 150, 151
Montagano 292
Monte Cassino, Abbey of 314–17, 353, 391, 438,
    443, 462
Montecorvino airfield 143, 185, 187, 201
Montefalcone 336
Monterosi 101, 129
Monterotondo 105
Montescaglioso 149
Montgomery, General Sir Bernard: with
    Eisenhower in Sicily 46–7; and General
    Clark 50, 51; visits 2nd Inniskillings 56–7;
    and Operation BAYTOWN 37, 64–5, 67,

68–9; cheered at Reggio 69; and landing of
    SRS at Bagnara 75, 76; and pressure from
    above 267; joins conference at Clark's CP
    280; writes to Alexander on slowness of
    mail 308; his plans 313, 357–8, 366, 447,
    449, 450; meeting with Clark put off 407;
    tours the Sangro front with Brooke 421,
    422, 425; unfairly blamed for failure of
    Italian campaign 470; see also Eighth Army
    under British Army
Moore, Lieutenant Peter 167–8, 186, 187, 198–9,
    205–6, 225, 472
Moorehead, Alan 63–4, 68–9, 204, 208, 220, 225,
    302, 304, 473
Moran, Charles Wilson, 1st Baron 375, 415, 437
Mork, Grenadier Werner 400–1, 431–2, 450–51,
    473
Moro, River/Moro Valley 239, 381, 382, 384,
    388, 389, 390, 398–9, 400, 401, 419, 445,
    448, 451, 475
Moroni, Tenente Antonio 153, 154, 194, 235–6,
    272–3, 292, 301–2
Mostaganem, Algeria 48, 51, 53
Mowat, Lieutenant Farley ('Squib'): in Sicily 57;
    at Militello rest camp 57, 58; corrals Italians
    on Aspromonte massif 70; survives mine
    146–7, and Italian anti-tank gun 218–19;
    writes an optimistic letter home 219;
    searches dead German paratroopers
    290–91; survives German submachine-gun
    fire 291–2; greeted by ecstatic villagers in
    Ripalimosani 292; helps with burial party
    292; grumbles at lack of mail 308; takes jeep
    up to Sangro front 287–8, takes over from
    78th Division 388; in the Moro Valley
    388–90, 398–400; nearly deserts 419–20;
    writes to his parents 452; shelled at San
    Leonardo 452–3; gives rum to dying
    German 453; given a poem by Alex
    Campbell 454, 459–60; spends Christmas
    on salient west of Ortona 454, 459; and
    death of friends 460
Mozzagrogna 367, 368, 379, 383
Müller, Oberfeldwebel 432
Murdock, Corporal 420
Murphy, Corporal Audie 228–9, 270, 276–7,
    279, 340, 345–7, 348, 349, 404, 471
Murphy, Robert ('Bob') 59, 61, 62, 63, 214, 307,
    374–5
Mussolini, Benito 24, 25–7, 33, 41, 43, 44, 98,
    153, 154, 158, 171, 193, 215, 235, 236, 294,
    296, 302, 304, 305

Naples 4, 25, 3679; and Allied bombing 26, 231–2;
    amphibious assault planned for 39, 51, 52,
    116; 2/5th Leicestershires advance on 168;
    under German administration 232–3;

popular rising 233, 241; liberation 242; devastation and humanitarian disaster 244, 249, 251, 258, 271, 295, 297, 298, 321; Allies move in 249–51, 258–9, 289, 298–9, 391
Nares, Lieutenant Raymond 227
Neapolitan Committee of National Liberation (CNL) 233, 241, 251
Nelson, Ted 224
Nettuno 153, 154, 194, 235
New Zealand Army 236, 239, 408, 447–8
    4th Armoured Brigade 381–2
    23rd Battalion 448
    6th Brigade 359, 381
    Expeditionary Force (NZEF) 359
    2nd Infantry Division 357, 358, 359, 367, 368, 401–3, 447–8; 24th Battalion 358, 381, 402; 25th Battalion 359, 368; 26th Battalion 359; 28th Battalion (Maori) 359, 402
    prisoners-of-war 236
    Royal New Zealand Navy (RNZAF) 359
Niesen, Unteroffizier Leo 23
Nocera 121, 178, 195, 207, 220, 230
Northwest African Tactical Air Force 15
Northern Attack Force 120, 127
Northwest African Air Forces 13, 16, 18

Oberkommando der Wehrmacht (OKW) 41, 42, 43, 44, 98, 105, 134, 154, 155, 241, 305, 320, 337
O'Dowd, Chris 256, 257
Office of Strategic Services (OSS), US 80, 85, 156
OKW see Oberkommando der Wehrmacht
Oran, Algeria 90, 92, 100, 264
Organisation Todt 233
ORKAN, Operation 112
Orpi (tug) 211
Orr, Lieutenant-Colonel 168
Orsogna 382, 390, 398, 401–2, 446, 448, 450; Pink House 402, 403, 405
Ortì 70
Ortona 235, 382, 384, 389; battle for 390, 398, 401, 402, 403, 419, 431, 442, 446, 447, 449, 450, 451, 452, 453, 454, 457–9, 462–4, 471; Canadian memorial 475–6
OSS see Office of Strategic Services, US
OVERLORD, Operation 33, 34, 35, 40, 287, 288, 354–5, 373, 375, 376, 377, 409–10, 412–13, 414, 415, 469, 470

Packer, Captain Bertie 74–5, 113–14, 209–10, 211, 224, 472
Packer, Joy 209
Padua 418
Paestum 4, 53, 84, 85, 105, 116, 120, 123, 139, 142, 169, 172, 178, 187–8, 192, 199, 200, 202, 204, 208, 330; Tower of 126
Pagano, Antonietta 311–12, 332, 433

Pagano, Benedetto 311–12, 332, 433, 473
Pagano, Enrichetta 311–12, 332–3, 433, 473
Paglieta 365, 366
Palermo 406–7, 409
Palmi 2
Palmoli 336
Park, Lieutenant Al 452–3, 460
Partito d'Azione see Action Party
Patton, General George S. 50, 92, 227
Pavone, Giuseppe 299
Pearce, Private First Class Frank 183–4, 188, 198, 202, 205, 224–5, 249, 259, 298–9, 372, 428, 440, 444, 462, 471
Pegler, Westbrook 472
Penelope, HMS 209
Penta 206
Persano 183, 195
Pescara 239, 326, 335, 367, 387, 388, 402, 442, 450
Petacciato 314
Pétain, Marshal Philippe 27–8
Philadelphia, USS 209
Piccardi, Leopoldo 241
Picentino Valley 198
Pick, Leutnant Ewald 463, 464
Pietravairano 327–8
Pisa–Rimini Line 40, 44, 55, 287, 289
Pius XII, Pope 350
Ploesti oilfields, Romania 14, 35, 238
Poat, Captain Harry 77, 78, 81, 245
POINTBLANK, Operation 14, 17, 33, 35, 238, 353, 354, 355, 412, 418
Polish Corp 222
Pollack, Oberstleutnant 438
Pomigliano 443
Pontecagnano 173, 198
Pöppel, Oberleutnant Martin 82–3, 149, 216, 248–9, 251–2, 473
Portal, Air Chief Marshal Sir Charles 17–18, 355
Potenza 302
Pozzilli 342, 343
Pratica di Mare 128
Pretoro 235–6
Pucara 121
Putignano 151
Pyle, Ernie 385–7, 430–31, 436–7, 473

Quadrant Conference, Quebec 37, 238, 375

RAF (Royal Air Force)
    Bomber Command 10, 13, 14, 17, 320, 354, 415; Lancaster bombers 13; Wellington bombers 207, 208
    Desert Air Force 15, 260, 357, 368
    111 Fighter Squadron 331
    Spitfires 94, 161, 162, 163, 192, 201
    93 Squadron 187–8
    609 Squadron 163

Rahn, Rudolf 304
RAINCOAT, Operation 374, 397, 424
Rapido, River/Rapido Valley 312, 352, 396, 443, 466
Rastenburg, Prussia: Hitler's HQ 41
Reed, Lieutenant Jim E. 163–4, 192, 200–1, 320–21, 230, 471–2
Regensburg 306
Reggio 69, 70
Reichssicherheitshauptamt (RSHA) 304, 351
Repubblica Sociale Italiana (RSI) 304, 378
Reynolds, Quent 93, 94–5, 105, 114, 181–2, 385, 472–3
Rhodes, Greece 376, 410, 411
Rhodes, Lance-Corporal Ginger 384
Richthofen, Feldmarschall Wolfram von 416
Ridgway, General Matthew 95
Rigney, Harry 21
Ripalimosani 272–3, 292, 297
Roatta, Generale Mario 38, 87, 88, 89–90, 100, 101, 102, 104, 105, 115, 128, 129–31, 141, 215
Rocca d'Evandro rail halt 325, 340
Roccamandolfi 335
Roccamonfina 5
Roccasecca 311, 324, 439
Rocholl, Leutnant Herbert 111–13, 114, 122, 132–3, 153, 166, 167, 168, 180–81, 186, 198, 206–7, 225
Roma (ship) 152–3
Rome: and Allied bombing 29; as Allied goal 35, 71, 87; Italian defends against German Army 88, 106, 128–31; Allied operation (GIANT II) 95, 101; meeting of the Crown Council 104; surrendered by Calvi to Kesselring 140–42; popular uprising 157–9; Carboni loses battle against Germans 159–60, 171–2, 174–7; Allied plans to capture 287–8, 326, 327, 328, 348, 376, 391, 410, 411, 469; German round-up of Jews 350–51; Gappisti attacks 455–6
Rommel, Feldmarschall Erwin 39, 42, 44, 45, 134, 237, 266, 289, 304, 310, 324, 337, 445
Roosevelt, President Franklin D. 31, 103, 267, 375–6, 377, 378, 407, 409, 471
Rosario 3
Roseberry, Colonel Cecil 303
Roseto Valfortore 249, 252
Rosso, Tenente Ettore 128
Rotondo, Monte 243, 311, 340, 344, 345, 346, 404, 405, 406. 428, 429
'Rover Davids' 17
Royal Navy 74, 113, 119, 202, 210–11, 212, 215, 302
    2nd Cruiser Squadron 472
    12th Cruiser Squadron 148
    Force V 93, 120, 201

Force K 120
    see also Warspite, HMS
RSHA see Reichssicherheitsamt
RSI see Repubblica Sociale Italiana 304
Ruys, MS Willem 218, 236
Ryan, Paddy 58
Ryder, Major-General Charles 'Doc' 264, 328, 408

Sabludowski, Oberfeldwebel 463
Salerno: Allied landings see AVALANCHE, Operation; Germans disarm Italian forces 153; Allies hold the bridgehead 165, 166–7, 174, 189, 213, 263, 305, 470, and the town 186, 188; and a renewed German attack 198–9; airfields open up 200; and Allied bombing 207; the plight of ordinary Italians 220; German withdrawal 221, 230, 248; mutiny among Allied forces 222–3, 233; Allied casualties 226
Salerno, Bay of 4, 117, 179, 209
Salò 304
Salvi, Colonnello Giorgio 130
Sammucro, Monte 243, 311, 312, 325, 339, 340, 372, 374, 404, 405, 407, 424, 425, 428, 429, 436, 439, 440, 466
San Angelo 444–5
San Bartolomeo in Galdo 251–2
San Donato 220–21
San Felice del Molise 331, 332
San Giacomo 253, 255
San Giacomo Ridge 252, 254, 255, 261
San Leonardo 388–9, 390, 398, 400, 419, 420, 452, 454, 462, 475
San Pietro Infine 311–12, 314, 332–4, 372, 402, 404, 405, 406, 425, 428, 429, 432–4, 435–6, 439–41, 443, 444, 466, 471, 473, 475
San Salvo 364
San Severino 116
San Severo 246
San Stefano 292, 387
San Vito 384, 389, 450, 451–2
San Vittore 466
Sangro, River/Sangro Valley 239, 309, 335, 336, 337, 357, 358, 359, 362, 365, 367, 369, 379, 380, 381, 383, 389, 390, 421
Santa Maria Imbaro 367, 379
Santa Scolastica Monastery 235
Sant'Elia a Pianisi 3, 290, 475
Sapri 3
Sardinia 34, 36, 40, 287, 322, 401, 417
Savannah, USS 181–2
Sawyers, Frank 375
Schiess, Oberleutnant Franz 73
Schlegel, Oberstleutnant Julius 316–17
Schleger, Unteroffizier 151, 152
Schmalz, Oberst Wilhelm 164, 165, 179, 180, 210

Schneider Trophy Air Race (1925) 16
Scholl, Oberst Walter 232, 241, 242, 337
Schulman, Sammy 181–2
Schweinfurt, Germany 355
Scripps-Howard syndicate 385
Seafires 94, 201
Seekings, Reg 256
Selassie, Emperor Haile 96
Sele, Ponte 183, 187
Sele, River 116, 142, 143, 167, 173, 182, 196
Selkirk, Captain 218
Senger und Etterlin, Generalleutnant Fridolin
    von 324–5, 338, 339, 342, 396, 397, 429,
    440, 442, 446, 462
Sessa 5
Sextant Conference, Cairo 374–7, 409, 442
Sforza, Count Carlo 80, 303, 304
Shakespeare, HMS 119
SHINGLE, Operation 443, 444
Shunstrom, Captain 372
Sicily 23, 26, 54, 70, 102, 297, 378; Allied
    invasion 16–17, 26, 31, 33, 39, 55, 56, 57,
    58, 93, 113, 164, 297–8, 321; German forces
    2, 4, 41, 45, 55, 180, 324
Sieckenius, Generalmajor Rudolf 134–5, 184, 260
Sieja, Joe 270, 277, 346, 347
Simonds, Major-General Guy 389
SLAPSTICK, Operation 148, 190, 215
SLEDGEHAMMER, Operation 49
Smith, Lance-Corporal Roger 358–9, 360–62,
    368–9, 381, 382, 402–3, 448, 472
Smuts, General Jan 35
Snuffy (American soldier) 346, 347
SOE see Special Operations Executive
Soltano, Monte 116
Soprano, Monte 116, 123, 125, 142, 170, 172,
    180, 195, 205
Sora, German field hospital 438–9
Soviet Union 30, 42, 44, 135, 144, 165, 263, 324,
    371, 375, 377, 378, 379, 409, 410, 449;
    Red Army 84, 150, 165, 269, 375, 409, 424;
    see also Kursk, Battle of; Stalingrad,
    Battle of
Spaatz, Lieutenant-General Carl 'Tooey' 16, 17,
    18, 35, 93, 190, 207, 307, 353, 354, 355, 407,
    429
Spanish Civil War (1936) 64
Sparanise 295, 297
Special Operations Executive (SOE), British 80
Spiers, Corporal 236, 293–4, 331–2, 448
Spitfires 417
Stalin, Joseph 375, 378, 379, 409, 410
Stalingrad, Battle of (1942–3) 44, 45, 84, 135,
    144, 154, 273, 306, 409, 461
Stars and Stripes (newspaper) 327
Steiner (American soldier) 228, 229
Steiner, Hauptmann 254

Steinmüller, Feldwebel 13, 21
Stirling, David 76
Stockdale, Colin 225
Strong, Brigadier Kenneth 37
Subiaco 235
Sullivan, Lieutenant T. Michael 322–4, 356,
    417–18, 471
Sumatra 409
Swayle, Lieutenant Gerry 291, 292, 387

Takata, Sergeant Joe 265, 342
Taormina, Sicily: Villa Florida 46–7
Taranto 26, 36, 74, 83, 147–8, 149, 152, 159, 203,
    214, 215, 217, 236, 237, 238, 302, 322
Tarvisio 43
Taylor, Brigadier-General Maxwell 95, 96–7,
    101–2, 104, 174, 214
Tedder, Air Chief Marshal Arthur 15, 16, 48, 51,
    52, 103, 189, 190, 207
Tehran: Eureka Conference 375, 376, 377,
    409–10, 442
Terelle 352
Termini, Sicily 113, 164, 200
Termoli 235, 239, 245, 246, 247, 248, 252,
    259–60, 261, 262, 305
Thompson, Sid 420
Tifata, Monte 270
Titerno, River 278
Tivoli 129, 130, 140, 171
Tobin, Charlie 81
Tobruk, Libya 15, 401, 428
Tokyo 16
TORCH, Operation 34, 49, 140, 169, 402
Torre Annunziata 207
Tramonti Mountains 12
Trento 154
Trident Conference, Washington DC 31, 33, 34, 40
Triflisco Gap 262
Trigno, River 239, 313, 314, 317, 331, 335, 336,
    357, 363
Triquet, Captain Paul 447
Trocchio, Monte 325, 352, 443
Truscott, General Lucian 118, 270, 276
Tscheschow, Leutnant 401
Tucker, Colonel Reuben 202
Tunis: Lycée Carnot 417
Tunisia 19, 90, 95, 102; campaign 15, 19, 30, 40,
    42, 49, 76, 131, 164, 165, 321, 411;
    Commanders' Conference 325–6
Tunstall, Ted 81
Turbort, Lieutenant Garth 359–61, 368,
    369, 402
Turin 14, 323
Turkey 32, 77, 376
Turner, Lieutenant-Colonel Farrant L. 264
Tusciano 201
Tweedsmuir, John Buchan, 2nd Baron 387

'Ultra' 39, 40, 55
Umberto, Prince 129
Unicorn (fleet carrier) 93
United States Armies 49, 268, 307, 410
  Fifth Army 36, 37, 39, 48, 49–50, 52, 53, 54,
    92, 103–4,107, 139, 142–3, 144, 167, 168,
    164, 174, 188–90, 196, 197, 205, 212–13,
    222, 223, 241, 249, 265, 268, 271, 279, 280,
    289, 294, 295, 296, 309, 326, 327, 332,
    335–6, 338, 348, 350, 372, 373, 391, 398,
    403, 406, 408, 413, 423, 425, 429, 443, 444,
    470; casualties 469
  Seventh Army 50
  1st Airborne Division 203
  82nd Airborne Division 62, 86–7, 88, 95, 115,
    189, 199, 206, 242, 373, 412
  1st Armored Division 439
  83rd Chemical Mortar Battalion 121,
    341, 434
  II Corps 227, 289, 350, 373, 374, 408, 429,
    439, 443
  V Corps 148, 368
  VI Corps 119, 172, 182–3, 184, 192, 195, 202,
    204–5, 227, 278, 262, 267, 268, 327, 344,
    404, 406
  111th Engineer Combat Battalion 184
  151st Field Artillery Battalion 137, 138, 403
  65th Field Artillery Brigade 210
  3rd Infantry Division 118, 189, 199, 227, 228,
    270, 276, 278, 280, 327, 328, 340, 344, 408,
    443; RCTs 199
  7th Infantry Division 425
  30th Infantry Division 340
  34th Infantry Division ('Red Bulls') 118, 137,
    138, 189, 224, 262, 263, 264, 275, 276, 278,
    280, 295, 327, 328, 342, 374, 403, 406,
    408–8, 461–2; 133rd RTC 263–4
  36th Infantry Division ('Texas') 53, 90–91, 92,
    105, 116, 119, 120, 122, 123, 136–7, 139,
    142, 170, 172, 180, 181, 182–3, 195, 197,
    212, 218, 224, 295, 373, 374, 385, 404, 405,
    429, 439–40, 441, 444
  45th Infantry Division ('Thunderbirds') 53,
    116, 143, 173, 183, 195,196, 199, 202, 218,
    227, 275, 278, 281, 403, 404, 408, 461; 157th
    RCT 173; 179th RCT 167, 187; 180th RCT
    199, 202, 208, 327, 328, 341
  179th Infantry Division 204
  504th Infantry Division 205
  15th Infantry Regiment 228, 270, 340, 404; B
    Company 345
  133rd Infantry Regiment 343
  141st Infantry Regiment 90–91, 120, 122, 123,
    125, 126, 137, 142, 172, 205, 404–5, 429,
    439, 440
  142nd Infantry Regiment 90–91, 120, 122,
    123, 138, 142, 195, 430, 440

  143rd Infantry Regiment 90–91, 142, 184,
    196, 404, 424, 425, 429, 436, 440
  100th 'Nisei' Battalion 263–4, 342–3
  504th Parachute Infantry Regiment 102, 199,
    202, 373, 374, 429
  505th Parachute Infantry Regiment 202, 208
  509th Parachute Infantry Regiment 206, 208,
    341
  Rangers 116, 117–18, 119, 121, 142, 173, 179,
    180, 195, 340–42, 404, 434; Cannon
    Company 341
  531 Shore Engineers 126
  Special Service Brigade 425
  1 Special Service Force 373
  753rd Tank Battalion 429, 439
United States Army Air Force (USAAF) 14, 17,
  353, 355
  Eighth Air Force 415
  Fifteenth Air Force 354, 356, 412, 417, 418
  Twelfth Air Force 16, 323, 354
  2nd Bomb Group 322, 417, 418
  429th Bomb Squadron 322–3, 417
  319th and 320th Bombardment Groups 20
  XII Bomber Command 354
  1st Fighter Group 19
  33rd Fighter Group ('Fighting Nomads') 192,
    200, 320–21
  27th Fighter Squadron 22, 23
  59th Fighter Squadron 163, 192
  71st Fighter Squadron 23
  94th Fighter Squadron 18, 21, 23
  64th Fighter Wing 201
  Tactical Reconnaissance Squadron 225
  aeroplanes
  Boston Bombers 367
  C-47 Dakotas 192
  B-17 Flying Fortresses 101, 207, 214, 322–3,
    417, 418
  P-40 Kittyhawks 94, 161, 163, 192, 201, 337,
    367
  B-24 Liberators 417
  P-38 Lightnings 10, 12–13, 19, 20, 21, 22, 53,
    72, 73, 93, 94, 161, 162, 201, 323, 417
  B-26 Martin Marauders 20, 417
  P-51 Mustangs 201
  P-47 Thunderbolts 417
US Navy 74, 90, 105, 119, 181, 209, 223
  Higgins Boats 65
  landing craft 65–6, 113, 139, 140, 413–14;
    USS *LST-357* 117
  see also Ancon, USS
Ustica, island of 95

Valiant, HMS 209, 210
Vallecupa 404
Vallerotonda 312, 313, 427, 445, 464, 467, 474
Vallo 212

Varna 156
Velletri 141, 194
Venafro 327, 328, 341, 372, 404, 407, 425, 439
Vesuvius, Mount 4, 230, 234, 271
Vibo Valentia 203
Vietinghoff, Generaloberst Heinrich von 44; and
    Allied invasion 100–1; and Kesselring 105,
    134, 174; decides to fight back 135, 142;
    orders 1. Fallschirmjäger to withdraw
    northwards 148, 216; visits Salerno front
    with Kesselring 191; receives faulty
    intelligence 203; opposed to Kesselring's
    plans 210; and Salerno 221, 237; ordered to
    take back Termoli 248; agrees to General
    Hube pulling his corps back 281; illness 338
Vietri 116, 121–2, 178, 179, 192, 198
'Viktor' Line 273
Villa Rogatti 388, 390, 398, 400
Villa San Giovanni 3, 70, 280
Villa Santa Lucia 352
Vittorio Emanuele III 25; and Mussolini 25, 27,
    28, 98, 302; calls Badoglio to take over as
    Prime Minister 27, 28,171; summons
    Badoglio and Ambrosio to a meeting of the
    Crown Council 103, 104; offers to open up
    Taranto and Brindisi ports 147; tells
    Badoglio to announce the armistice 104,
    107; asks Carboni if his troops will defend
    Rome against Germans 128; leaves Rome
    with his Queen 129, 175; and invasion at
    Taranto 148; and General Caviglia 171–2; a
    refugee in Sicily 193; meets Macmillan in
    Brindisi 214, 215; and the CLN 303–4;
    refusal to abdicate causes an impasse
    377–8, 457
Vogel, Lieutenant Henry 418
Vokes, General Chris 389, 390, 400, 420,
    449, 450
Volontari della Libertà 299–300, 456
Volturno, River/Volturno Valley 115, 135, 164,
    189, 221, 231, 262–3, 265, 270, 271, 273,
    274–6, 278–9, 281–2, 288, 294, 295, 327,
    328, 342, 386, 407, 425, 470
Volturno–Biferno Line 288
Vrilakas, Lieutenant Robert 'Smoky' 18–20, 21,
    22–3, 162,   207, 323, 471
Vyshinsky, Andrei 379

Waag, Feldwebel Gerhard 18, 201–2, 473
Wagner, Corporal Bud 137–9, 142, 183, 202,
    205, 224, 263, 280, 295, 296, 372, 386, 403,
    407, 461–2, 471
Wagner, Ray 138
Walker, General Fred L. 92, 119–20, 123, 136,
    172, 429, 435–6, 439
Walshall, Company Sergeant Major 237, 293
Walz, Feldwebel Erwin 458

Ward, Regimental Sergeant-Major Jack 234–5,
    271, 277, 279, 280, 294–5, 296, 308, 338,
    339, 343, 391, 462, 466, 472
Ward, Elsie 234
Warlimont, General Walter 42, 43, 45, 337
Warspite, HMS 74–5, 113–14, 120, 209, 210–11,
    212, 223–4
Waskow, Captain Henry 436–7
weapons
    bazookas 136
    Bofors guns, 40mm 181
    Browning automatic rifle (BAR) 265, 345
    cannons, 20mm 181
    Fritz X bombs 152–3, 182, 211
    Garand rifle 279
    howitzers 138–9, 234
    Maschinengewehre (MGs) 122; MG42s 255,
        276
    mustard gas mortar bombs 416–17
    Nebelwerfers 2, 178, 179, 186, 340, 396–7, 448,
        449
    Oerlikon 20mm cannons 139
    Panzerabwehrkanone (PAK) anti-tank gun 248
    Panzerfaust 458
    quick-firing 2-pounder pom-poms 139
    S- or Schü-Mine 269
    StuGs 125, 136, 164, 254, 255, 402
    'window' 416
Wentzell, Generalmajor Fritz 380
Werner, Colonel Richard J. 125–6, 137
Westphal, General Siegfried 105, 141, 142,
    380–81
Wiener Neustadt, Austria 323, 324
Wilson, D. 400
Wilson, Corporal Harry 217–18, 236–7, 293–4,
    331–2, 336, 337, 365–6, 367, 381, 383,
    448–9, 459, 472
Wilson, General Henry Maitland ('Jumbo')
    414–15
Winter Line 327, 328, 348, 349, 373, 407, 423,
    428, 440, 442
Wiseman, Johnny 256, 257, 262
Wolff, General Karl 304
Wood, Major Richard 384
Wöste, Heinrich 279

Yearbury, Sergeant Ted 359, 360, 361, 368

Zambuks (medics) 361
Zanussi, Generale Giacomo 38, 60–61, 87, 105,
    130
Zellner, Brigette 156
Zellner, Franziska 156
Zellner, Major Georg 154–6, 237, 306, 371–2,
    403–4, 415,   435, 442, 445, 461, 466–7,
    473, 474
Zellner, Gernot 156

A patrol of Tommies walk past an unexploded bomb as they head along a goat track in the mountains north of Salerno.

A Lewis machine-gunner of the Saskatoon Light Infantry near Potenza, 20 September 1943.

The shattered remains of Ortona from the air, taken on 27 December 1943, the day the Germans finally retreated from the town.

ABOUT THE AUTHOR

James Holland is an internationally acclaimed and award-winning historian, writer and broadcaster. The author of a number of bestselling histories, including, most recently, *Brothers In Arms and Normandy '44*, he has also written nine works of fiction and a dozen Ladybird Experts.

He is the co-founder of the annual Chalke Valley History Festival, which is now in its twelfth year, and he has presented – and written – many television programmes and series for the BBC, Channel 4, National Geographic and the History and Discovery channels.

With Al Murray, he has a successful Second World War podcast, *We Have Ways of Making You Talk*, which also has its own festival, and he is a research fellow at St Andrew's University and a Fellow of the Royal Historical Society. He can be found on Twitter as @James1940 and on Instagram as @jamesholland1940.